T0135041

Communications
in Computer and Information Science   **1224**

Commenced Publication in 2007
Founding and Former Series Editors:
Simone Diniz Junqueira Barbosa, Phoebe Chen, Alfredo Cuzzocrea,
Xiaoyong Du, Orhun Kara, Ting Liu, Krishna M. Sivalingam,
Dominik Ślęzak, Takashi Washio, Xiaokang Yang, and Junsong Yuan

More information about this series at http://www.springer.com/series/7899

Constantine Stephanidis ·
Margherita Antona (Eds.)

HCI International 2020 - Posters

22nd International Conference, HCII 2020
Copenhagen, Denmark, July 19–24, 2020
Proceedings, Part I

 Springer

Editors
Constantine Stephanidis
University of Crete
and Foundation for Research
and Technology – Hellas (FORTH)
Heraklion, Crete, Greece

Margherita Antona
Foundation for Research
and Technology – Hellas (FORTH)
Heraklion, Crete, Greece

ISSN 1865-0929   ISSN 1865-0937   (electronic)
Communications in Computer and Information Science
ISBN 978-3-030-50725-1   ISBN 978-3-030-50726-8   (eBook)
https://doi.org/10.1007/978-3-030-50726-8

This Springer imprint is published by the registered company Springer Nature Switzerland AG
The registered company address is: Gewerbestrasse 11, 6330 Cham, Switzerland

Foreword

The 22nd International Conference on Human-Computer Interaction, HCI International 2020 (HCII 2020), was planned to be held at the AC Bella Sky Hotel and Bella Center, Copenhagen, Denmark, during July 19–24, 2020. Due to the COVID-19 coronavirus pandemic and the resolution of the Danish government not to allow events larger than 500 people to be hosted until September 1, 2020, HCII 2020 had to be held virtually. It incorporated the 21 thematic areas and affiliated conferences listed on the following page.

A total of 6,326 individuals from academia, research institutes, industry, and governmental agencies from 97 countries submitted contributions, and 1,439 papers and 238 posters were included in the conference proceedings. These contributions address the latest research and development efforts and highlight the human aspects of design and use of computing systems. The contributions thoroughly cover the entire field of human-computer interaction, addressing major advances in knowledge and effective use of computers in a variety of application areas. The volumes constituting the full set of the conference proceedings are listed in the following pages.

The HCI International (HCII) conference also offers the option of "late-breaking work" which applies both for papers and posters and the corresponding volume(s) of the proceedings will be published just after the conference. Full papers will be included in the "HCII 2020 - Late Breaking Papers" volume of the proceedings to be published in the Springer LNCS series, while poster extended abstracts will be included as short papers in the "HCII 2020 - Late Breaking Posters" volume to be published in the Springer CCIS series.

I would like to thank the program board chairs and the members of the program boards of all thematic areas and affiliated conferences for their contribution to the highest scientific quality and the overall success of the HCI International 2020 conference.

This conference would not have been possible without the continuous and unwavering support and advice of the founder, Conference General Chair Emeritus and Conference Scientific Advisor Prof. Gavriel Salvendy. For his outstanding efforts, I would like to express my appreciation to the communications chair and editor of HCI International News, Dr. Abbas Moallem.

July 2020   Constantine Stephanidis

HCI International 2020 Thematic Areas and Affiliated Conferences

Thematic areas:

- HCI 2020: Human-Computer Interaction
- HIMI 2020: Human Interface and the Management of Information

Affiliated conferences:

- EPCE: 17th International Conference on Engineering Psychology and Cognitive Ergonomics
- UAHCI: 14th International Conference on Universal Access in Human-Computer Interaction
- VAMR: 12th International Conference on Virtual, Augmented and Mixed Reality
- CCD: 12th International Conference on Cross-Cultural Design
- SCSM: 12th International Conference on Social Computing and Social Media
- AC: 14th International Conference on Augmented Cognition
- DHM: 11th International Conference on Digital Human Modeling and Applications in Health, Safety, Ergonomics and Risk Management
- DUXU: 9th International Conference on Design, User Experience and Usability
- DAPI: 8th International Conference on Distributed, Ambient and Pervasive Interactions
- HCIBGO: 7th International Conference on HCI in Business, Government and Organizations
- LCT: 7th International Conference on Learning and Collaboration Technologies
- ITAP: 6th International Conference on Human Aspects of IT for the Aged Population
- HCI-CPT: Second International Conference on HCI for Cybersecurity, Privacy and Trust
- HCI-Games: Second International Conference on HCI in Games
- MobiTAS: Second International Conference on HCI in Mobility, Transport and Automotive Systems
- AIS: Second International Conference on Adaptive Instructional Systems
- C&C: 8th International Conference on Culture and Computing
- MOBILE: First International Conference on Design, Operation and Evaluation of Mobile Communications
- AI-HCI: First International Conference on Artificial Intelligence in HCI

Conference Proceedings Volumes Full List

38. CCIS 1224, HCI International 2020 Posters - Part I, edited by Constantine Stephanidis and Margherita Antona
39. CCIS 1225, HCI International 2020 Posters - Part II, edited by Constantine Stephanidis and Margherita Antona
40. CCIS 1226, HCI International 2020 Posters - Part III, edited by Constantine Stephanidis and Margherita Antona

http://2020.hci.international/proceedings

HCI International 2020 (HCII 2020)

The full list with the Program Board Chairs and the members of the Program Boards of all thematic areas and affiliated conferences is available online at:

http://www.hci.international/board-members-2020.php

HCI International 2021

The 23rd International Conference on Human-Computer Interaction, HCI International 2021 (HCII 2021), will be held jointly with the affiliated conferences in Washington DC, USA, at the Washington Hilton Hotel, July 24–29, 2021. It will cover a broad spectrum of themes related to Human-Computer Interaction (HCI), including theoretical issues, methods, tools, processes, and case studies in HCI design, as well as novel interaction techniques, interfaces, and applications. The proceedings will be published by Springer. More information will be available on the conference website: http://2021.hci.international/.

General Chair
Prof. Constantine Stephanidis
University of Crete and ICS-FORTH
Heraklion, Crete, Greece
Email: general_chair@hcii2021.org

http://2021.hci.international/

Contents – Part I

User Characteristics, Requirements and Preferences

Recognizing Human Psychological States

Human Perception and Cognition

AI in HCI

Contents – Part II

Virtual, Augmented and Mixed Reality

Virtual Humans and Motion Modelling and Tracking

Learning Technology

Contents – Part III

Smartphones, Social Media and Human Behaviour

Interacting with Cultural Heritage

Human-Vehicle Interaction

Transport, Safety and Crisis Management

Security, Privacy and Trust

Design and Evaluation Methods
and Tools

All You Need is Web: Visual Interaction with No Graphic Background

Andrii Bogachenko[1]([⊠]) ⓘ, Igor Tolmachov[1] ⓘ,
Daria Voskoboinikova[1] ⓘ, Inna Bondarenko[1] ⓘ,
Yevhenii Buhera[1] ⓘ, Dongjoo Ko[2] ⓘ, and Svitlana Alkhimova[1] ⓘ

[1] Samsung R&D Institute Ukraine (SRK),
57, Lva Tolstogo Str., Kyiv 01032, Ukraine
{an.bogachenk, i.tolmachev, d.voskoboyni, i.bondarenko,
y.buhera, s.alkhimova}@samsung.com
[2] Samsung Electronics, Seoul R&D Campus,
33 Seongchon-gil, Seocho-gu, Seoul 06765, Korea
dongjoo.ko@samsung.com

Abstract. Effective communications between designers and developers remain a crucial aspect of the software development process. In the current study, we propose the approach of sharing the visual interaction design. The proposed approach is based on the idea that the designer shares animations directly from the designer's application environment with a single click. Developers access design data via the web browser in a convenient form where the visual interaction design represents an interactive video. According to the conducted user study, most designers (69%) and developers (81%) were satisfied with the approach concept in general. Both groups of specialists highly evaluated the user interface of the implementation. Performance measurements revealed that interactive video is about 92% faster than pure graphics on average design complexity. Most survey participants (82%) agreed with the idea that interactive video is good enough to express animation. The results show that application development using the proposed approach improved human-computer interaction. It allows designers to save time on sharing design information and allows developers to effectively adopt comprehensive design for new applications.

Keywords: Visual interaction · Animation design · Motion design · Software development processes · Designer-Developer collaboration

1 Introduction

New trends and technologies dictate continuous design changes. The design techniques' complexity level is growing considerably. In the application development process, communication and collaboration between designers and developers are crucial, especially when the visual interaction (VI) design is considered.

VI design sharing is a time-consuming part in the application development process. Because design can iteratively change depending on requirements and technical capabilities, it is critical to share design quickly, provide updates easily, and share the only required information.

C. Stephanidis and M. Antona (Eds.): HCII 2020, CCIS 1224, pp. 3–10, 2020.
https://doi.org/10.1007/978-3-030-50726-8_1

We provide an approach that allows designers to share and developers to implement animations quickly and easily

2 Background

The global community offers a wide range of approaches to share the design information, and therefore simplify design developer interaction. We've defined the most commonly used approaches into four categories: manually prepared documents, design tools for all, design hand-off tools, and design-to-code tools.

The most common and conservative approach is preparing information as documentation guides manually. Designers often require to share multiple documents to communicate different aspects of their designs for a developer. A designer describes animation in words and numbers as text descriptions and data tables. Usually, it is required to take screenshots or make videos in addition to the prepared guides. This process is time-consuming, bearing risks of mistakes, and could be unclear for developers [1].

Design tools may be available for both: a designer to build, a developer to view and observe the design [2]. Both designer and developer, seeing identically the same picture and the same data. No need to perform any extra resources or documents by a designer. But, usually, it is redundantly inefficient since a developer might use the design applications only a few times a year. Also, a developer should be well-enough acknowledged with design tools, that gives much more information than might be required.

One more approach is to use design hand-off tools for sharing the design inside its own ecosystem. Applications like Zeplin, InVision, Protopie, are widely used for UI/UX prototyping, only a few of them support VI with a limited feature set [3].

Design-to-Code tools allows transforming design to a set of code lines [4]. This highly reduces developer's work, allowing not to implement graphics from scratch, but only to integrate graphics into application code. No doubt, automation is something we'll be facing more often in future. However, current implementations are not yet reliable enough, and have feature set limits. One more, a problem of result verification appears, as far as designer cannot check the intermediate result. Such tools, like Lottie, provide some level of automation but require additional dependencies and match with limitations described above [5].

Apart from commercial solutions, research community is actively studying the issue of collaboration between designers and developers.

Brown et al. [6, 7] in their studies describe main aspects of cooperation between the designer and the developer: collaboration processes and artifacts that are interacted by both cooperation participants.

The research by Leiva et al. [8] identifies recurring types of problems in design developer collaboration: missing critical details, and ignoring edge cases as one of most crucial. As a solution they proposed to create tools that mitigate these problems: provide multiple viewpoints, maintain a single source of truth, reveal the invisible, and support design with the guideline.

The goal of our study is not only to propose the approach to resolve the communication problems between designers and developers, but also to simplify interaction with artifacts they share with each other.

3 Proposed Approach

We consider the approach to extract all the data required for development directly from the VI design tool, including objects properties and rendered video. The design can easily be accessed via the web-application, representing the data in the format suitable for a developer.

According to the proposed approach, the designer works exactly inside the habitual design eco-system, while the developer is guided only with the necessary and required information for implementation.

One of the most powerful tools for motion graphics development is Adobe After Effects (AAE)[1]. It has highly developed API for interaction with the design content and data, which makes it ideal for approach prototyping.

3.1 Implementation

Our product consists of two major components: extension integrated into AAE, and web-application for viewing. Designer develops animation within the AAE and exports the required compositions using extension, which collects and exports necessary and sufficient animated objects properties into a JavaScript Object Notation (JSON) format and renders animation into a video. Developer accesses a web-application, which stands for interactive VI design documentation guide, and presents the exported data through the regular web-browser (see Fig. 1).

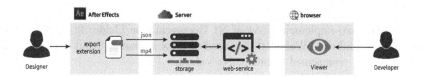

Fig. 1. General approach scheme.

VI Guide contains two major parts: first shows animation itself, second represents the data about animation. The animation area is an interactive and scalable container for displaying generated video and additional information. Object's position, size, selection area, bounding, anchors and moving trajectories are the features that may be shown in the layer drawn above the video (Fig. 2).

---

[1] https://www.adobe.com/products/aftereffects.html.

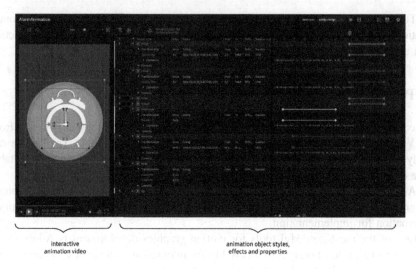

interactive
animation video

animation object styles,
effects and properties

Fig. 2. VI guide web-application user interface.

Data representing area displays animation object styles, effects, and properties. The table shows values for both static and animated object properties. Additional data such as interpolation, duration, value range shows for animated properties. Timeline, on the right, displays animation snippets in the time perspective. Amount of displayed data can be easily customized via filters.

The data is changing in real-time as the video plays, allowing the developer to explore updates on a timeline interactively.

4   Study 1: Solution Performance

We compared two implementations of VI Documentation Guide. In the first, Web-based Graphics Library (WebGL)[2] was used to draw animations, and in the second – animations were represented as interactive videos.

4.1   Apparatus and Procedure

We conducted all measurements on the PC with the following parameters: Intel Core i7-3630QM; 16 GB RAM; NVIDIA GeForce GT 650 M; Windows 10 x64.

Three compositions for experiment were prepared in the AAE with different complexity levels: simple, medium, complex. The complexity of compositions depends on the number of animated objects, composition size, feature set, and hierarchy complexity level. The compositions were exported with both WebGL and interactive video implementations. We recorded runtime performance and measured the resources

---

[2] https://www.khronos.org/webgl/.

required to draw a single frame in the VI Guide. Chrome DevTools[3] were used to make all the measurements.

4.2   Results and Discussion

The following Table 1 gives a summary of all measurements taken for both approaches and all test cases. For the simple complexity composition, the results of performance for both approaches are comparable: 33 ms vs 18 ms per frame. The performance benefits of the video approach becomes more and more noticeable with the complexity growth. For the complex VI Guide case, the performance of the approaches differs in 43 times.

Table 1. WebGL & Interactive Video approaches performance measurements.

Activity	WebGL performance, ms			Interactive video performance, ms		
	Simple	Medium	Complex	Simple	Medium	Complex
Rendering	3.0	4.2	12.8	2.1	1.9	4.7
Painting	2.0	5.7	318.7	1.0	1.8	1.8
Scripting	19.8	27.0	931.0	6.0	7.9	13.1
System	8.8	15.0	12.8	6.0	14.7	10.0
Idle	0.0	0.0	0.0	2.9	0.0	0.0
Total	33.6	51.9	1275.3	18.0	26.3	29.6

In general, the WebGL approach is more flexible, giving opportunity to extend the VI Guide interface with powerful features, like objects editing. Scripting takes the most amount of time for the WebGL approach, and this is probably where some additional optimizations can be performed. However, it might be harder to optimize painting, which also takes pretty much time (319 ms) for the complex case.

5   Study 2: Usability

To evaluate the approach we prepared a survey with questions about the approach idea in general, the usability of application UI, and the key concepts of the approach.

5.1   Participants and Procedure

We involved two groups of specialists: designers and developers to evaluate the usability of the product. The survey responses collected from 22 volunteers (15 designers and 7 developers), 22–54 years old. All the participants were familiar with design sharing process and have appropriate skills.

---

[3] https://developers.google.com/web/tools/chrome-devtools.

All participants filled online questionnaire. We assume that online survey gives more fair results, compared to face-to-face survey. Questions about the product idea and application UI were evaluated from negative to positive with a rating scale from −3 to +3. According to the User Experience Questionnaire (UEQ–S) [9], both subjects included eight paired questions.

5.2   Results and Discussion

The distribution of usability study answers is shown below (Fig. 3).

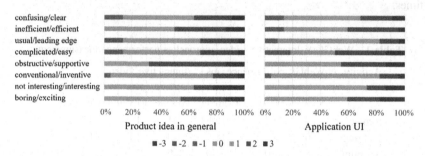

Fig. 3. Distribution of the answers about application UI and the product idea.

Supportive rather than obstructive scored the highest evaluation for both designers and developers which proves that the approach successfully implements it's main idea. From the weakest results, we can determine there's some level of complexity and confusion in the implementation. Another not highly evaluated pair "usual/leading edge" might be explained with the plainness of the proposed approach.

The questionnaire summary separated by the group of specialists is shown in the Table 2. The results demonstrated that developers were more satisfied with the product. This can be explained because developers were acknowledged only with the VI Guide implementation, while designers were evaluating the whole approach.

Table 2. Results of UEQ-S for two groups of users

Group	Evaluated item	Pragmatic	Hedonic	Overall
Designers	Application UI	0.95	0.84	0.89
Developers	Application UI	1.75	1.11	1.43
Designers	Product idea	0.93	0.78	0.86
Developers	Product idea	1.89	1.29	1.59

Survey participants also answered three more questions, each corresponding to one of the main concepts of the approach:

- Are you satisfied with the data obtained in the VI Guide?
- Does VI Guide reduce or simplify communication with the designers/developers?
- Is the interactive video good enough to express the animation?

Answers distribution represented in the Fig. 4.

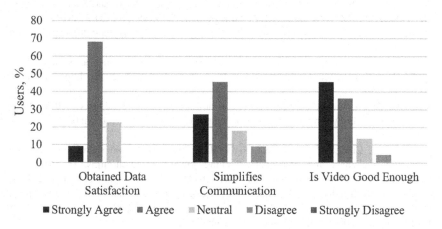

Fig. 4. Distribution of user answers to the additional questions.

The results show that all three conceptual questions got positive feedback from both designers and developers. No negative replies about the data represented in the VI Guide were collected. Only a few persons disagreed that a video is good enough to express and that the approach can simplify the communication.

6   Conclusions

We proposed the approach to extract all information needed for development from the VI design tools into a general web format that is easy to share. The study showed how improvement of design-developer cooperation can be achieved by using the proposed approach in software development process.

The performance results showed how much more effective the interactive video can be, especially with the design complexity level growth. The approach also allows designers not to be limited with the feature set. Results of the usability study proved that the approach gives developer enough data for implementation, while video represents animation design with all design features covered.

From all the results obtained from the study, we can assume that no animation graphics technologies are required to implement the VI design-sharing tool, while the web is required.

References

1. Brown, J.M., Lindgaard, G., Biddle, R.: Joint implicit alignment work of interaction designers and software developers. In: Proceedings of the 7th Nordic Conference on Human-Computer Interaction Making Sense Through Design, pp. 693–702. ACM, New York (2012). https://doi.org/10.1145/2399016.2399121
2. Maudet, N., Leiva, G., Beaudouin-Lafon, M., Mackay, W.: Design breakdowns: designer-developer gaps in representing and interpreting interactive systems. In: Proceedings of the 2017 ACM Conference on Computer Supported Cooperative Work and Social Computing, pp. 630–641. ACM, New York (2017). https://doi.org/10.1145/2998181.2998190
3. Palmer, T.: Design Tools Survey (2019). https://uxtools.co/survey-2019/#prototyping. Accessed Dec 2019
4. D'Souza, C., Deufemia, V., Ginige, A., Polese, G.: Enabling the generation of web applications from mockups. Softw. Pract. Exp. **48**(4), 945–973 (2018). https://doi.org/10.1002/spe.2559
5. Steelkiwi Inc.: Lottie by Airbnb: Innovation or Limitation For Designers? (2019). https://uxplanet.org/lottie-by-airbnb-innovation-or-limitation-for-designers-11cc7666ea2c. Accessed 18 Jan 2019
6. Brown, J.M., Lindgaard, G., Biddle, R.: Collaborative events and shared artefacts: agile interaction designers and developers working toward common aims. In: 2011 Agile Conference, pp. 87–96. IEEE, Salt Lake City (2011). https://doi.org/10.1109/agile.2011.45
7. Brown, J. M., Lindgaard, G., Biddle, R.: Stories, sketches, and lists: developers and interaction designers interacting through artefacts. In: Agile 2008 Conference, pp. 39–50. IEEE, Toronto (2008). https://doi.org/10.1109/agile.2008.54
8. Leiva, G., Maudet, N., Mackay, W., Beaudouin-Lafon, M.: Enact: reducing designer-developer breakdowns when prototyping custom interactions. ACM Trans. Comput. Hum. Interact. **26**(3), 1–48 (2019). https://doi.org/10.1145/3310276
9. Schrepp, M., Hinderks, A., Thomaschewski, J.: Design and evaluation of a short version of the user experience questionnaire (UEQ-S). Int. J. Interact. Multimed. Artif. Intell. **4**(6), 103–108 (2017). https://doi.org/10.9781/ijimai.2017.09.001

Research in User-Centered Design 2009 to 2018: A Systematic Keyword Network Analysis

Yongyeon Cho[1](✉), Hye Jeong Park[2](✉), and Huiwon Lim[3](✉)

[1] Interior Design Department, Iowa State University, Ames, IA 50011, USA
yongyeon@iastate.edu
[2] Human-Computer Interaction Program, Iowa State University,
Ames, IA 50011, USA
hjpark@iastate.edu
[3] Graphic Design Department, Penn State University,
State College, PA 16801, USA
hjl5360@psu.edu

Abstract. User-centered design (UCD) has become an important concept in Human-Computer Interaction (HCI) and other disciplines. While there is abundant UCD research, keyword analysis research has been less studied even though keywords are important for achieving better understanding of UCD. Therefore, this study provides keywords network a visual analysis of UCD articles published between 2009 and 2018 to answer the following questions: (1) What UCD-related keywords have been studied and in which disciplines? and (2) How have keywords been connected to on another? The study analyzed 304 keywords articles from IEEE, ACM, and ScienceDirect that included "UCD" in their titles. It utilized Gephi 0.9.2 to visualize keyword frequencies, relationships, and authors' disciplines. The findings presented that the five most frequently mentioned keywords regarding UCD were "usability," "HCI," "User Experiences," "User-Centered," and "User Interfaces". The top five most identified disciplines in the UCD articles were Computer Science, Design, Engineering, Education, and Psychology. In visualizing this data, we created a keyword hierarchy with various sizes of texts and circles, and we denoted various relationship levels between keywords by different weights of edges. This visualization of the selected 43 keywords shows a clear relationship between keywords in which UCD is strongly related to usability, UX, user-centered, HCI, Persona, prototype, interaction design, interface design, assistive technology, design thinking. The findings can be valuable in understanding the current UCD research mainstream for researchers and designers pursuing interdisciplinary approaches.

Keywords: User-centered design · UCD · Keyword · Content analysis · Network · Gephi · Interdisciplinarity

© Springer Nature Switzerland AG 2020
C. Stephanidis and M. Antona (Eds.): HCII 2020, CCIS 1224, pp. 11–18, 2020.
https://doi.org/10.1007/978-3-030-50726-8_2

1 Introduction

User-centered design (UCD) has become an important concept, philosophy, and method in studies of Human Computer Interaction (HCI) and design [1] since Norman and Draper's publication entitled: *User-Centered System Design: New Perspectives on Human-Computer Interaction* in 1986 [2]. There have been several studies regarding UCD usability and evaluation methods such as user task analysis, expert guidelines-based evaluation, formative user-centered evaluation, comparative evaluation of virtual environments, and the state of user-centered design practice [3, 4].

Keyword analysis has been adopted in diverse disciplines such as business intelligence [5], computer science [6], and education [7], and keyword analysis can also be found in HCI domain. Liu et al. [8] studied co-word analysis published by CHI conference between 1994 and 2013. Liu et al. [8] used co-word analysis to analyze trends and links of Ubicomp in CHI communities [9]. However, although keywords are essential to understanding areas [10] related to UCD, keyword research itself has been less studied, thus the purpose of this study is to reveal the mainstream of UCD research by keyword analysis of UCD publications from 2009 through 2018. We collected 304 articles, including peer-reviewed journals and conference papers from IEEE, ACM, and ScienceDirect databases, and extracted 1234 keywords. We then plotted these keywords using a network analysis and clustering tool called Gephi and proposed three research questions: (1) What keywords have been studied in UCD and in which disciplines? (2) How have keywords been related to one another? The findings would provide meaningful data in understanding the mainstream of UCD research for researchers and designers pursuing interdisciplinary research and design approaches.

2 Keyword Network Analysis and Gephi

Keyword network analysis could be described as investigation of links between items in a given data set displayed by keywords and connectedness between keywords [11], and this characterization of network analysis clearly suggests that important information can be represented by visualization [9]. In particular, keyword analysis provides an explanation of content and reveals links between topics [12]. Since it is assumed that a particular keyword appearing with high frequency may represent a specific research topic [9], keyword network analysis allows us to investigate major patterns and trends of the domain [13–15]. There have been many efforts to present relationships among interdisciplinary research areas through visual network mapping [6]; the first visual map of scientific trends was proposed by Garfield, Sher, and Torpie [16], and the first keyword network map was introduced by Small, Sweeney, and Greenlee in the form of the Science Citation Index (SCI) [17]. Recently, Gephi, an open source software that provides visual representation of data [18], has been applied to discovery of a network. Since Gephi provides real-time data visualization as well as many different types of export [18], it has been used in a variety of disciplines. For example, Ortega et al. [6] used Gephi to seek the most shared labels by creating a keyword map of computer science-related domains. Wan et al. [19] generated a keyword map with Gephi for investigating recommendation method based on e-learning systems.

3   Method and Procedure

This study used a quantitative method to find answers related to keywords that have appeared in UCD research publications and what disciplines have collaborated in conducting UCD research. The study followed the systematic keyword review analysis process shown in Table 1.

Table 1. A systematic keyword review process and screen eligible articles or keywords.

Steps	Review process	Total number of articles or keywords
1. Title search	Search all titles that include "User", "centered" & "design", "User-centered" & "design", and "UCD" in the three main digital libraries of "IEEE", "ACM", and "Science Direct" between 2009 and 2018	347 articles
2. Title-duplication filtering	Remove duplicate titles from the list developed in step 1	338 articles
3. Title-unrelated topic	Remove unrelated topics – inaccurate abbreviations – from the list produced in step 2 result (e.g. UCD: urethral catheterization device)	304 articles
4. Keyword search	Search all author-chosen keywords from the step 3 result	1234 keywords
5. Keyword-merge same meaning	Edit/merge keywords with identical meanings (e.g. User-Centered Design to UCD, User Experience to UX)	1234 keywords
6. Keyword-duplication filtering	Remove duplicate keywords from the step 5 result. Each keyword is designated as a **node** in Gephi	752 nodes
7. Keyword relation connection	For visualization in Gephi, keywords in the same article must each be linked in Excel; each link is designated as an **edge** in Gephi	5582 edges
8. Discipline search	Search authors' fields of studies and disciplines from ResearchGate	619 authors' disciplines in 24 disciplines

We searched peer-reviewed articles published between 2009 and 2018 that included keywords "user," "centered," "design," "user-centered", "design," and "UCD" in their titles via three digital database repositories: IEEE Xplore Digital Library, ACM Digital Library, and ScienceDirect. These three selected digital database repositories are well-known digital libraries describing technical, scientific, and medical research [20]. This title search as a first step found 347 articles from journal articles, conference proceedings excluding videos, magazines, and books. From these 347 titles found during the first step, duplicate titles (9 articles) were removed as a second step. As a third step, we filtered 34 inaccurate abbreviations (e.g., UCD: urethral catheterization device) from the results of the second step. As a fourth step we searched all author-chosen keywords and gathered 1,234 keywords from the 304 articles. To produce a proper keyword network and accurately count keywords, we merged keywords representing identical same meanings, e.g., User Centered Design and User-Centered Design merged to UCD, User Experience merged to UX. This methodology utilized Microsoft Excel and Gephi 0.9.2, a software tool for open-source network analysis and visualization [18], to visualize keyword frequencies, relationships of keywords, and authors' disciplines. In creating a keyword network via Gephi, this study created 752 nodes by removing duplicate keywords and generating 5,582 edges from an article that should be linked to one another. For example, if an article contained three keywords – UCD, UX, and UI, three nodes: UCD, UX, and UI, and six edges: UCD-UX, UCD-UI, UX-UCD, UX-UI, UI-UCD, and UI-UX, were generated. As the last step in the systematic review, we searched for authors' disciplines using the ResearchGate website, a social networking site for sharing papers and looking for collaborators that in 2020 contained names of than 15 million researchers [21]. In ResearchGate a user can self-define his/her disciplines in terms of up to 3 of the 24 discipline names.

4 Results

Through 8 steps of analysis, the researchers found what keywords appearing most frequently in UCD studies, which disciplines have been primarily involved in UCD studies, and how the keywords have been linked to one another. The top five UCD-related keywords other than UCD appearing most frequently were "Usability," "HCI", "UX," "User-Centered" and "UI" as shown Table 2. The percentiles in Table 2 indicate the percentage use of a specific keyword relative to the total number of keywords (e.g., Usability = Frequency/Total = 34/1234 = 2.78%).

Table 2. Frequencies of keywords related to UCD.

Rank	Top 10 UCD-related keywords mentioned in articles	Frequency	Percentile
1	UCD (User-Centered Design)	160	13.09
2	Usability	34	2.78
3	HCI (Human-Computer Interaction)	25	2.05
4	UX (User Experience)	23	1.88
5	User-centered	14	1.15
6	UI (User Interface)	12	0.98
7	Assistive technology	8	0.65
7	Design method	8	0.65
7	Prototype	8	0.65
7	Usability test	8	0.65

Figure 1, Fig. 2, and Fig. 3 are visualizations produced by Gephi. The sizes of letters and circles in these figures reflect the keyword frequencies found through the systematic keyword review. The various relationship levels between the two keywords are represented by different line weights, e.g., the line thicknesses in Fig. 1, Fig. 2, and Fig. 3 represent the number of connections between keywords revealed by the systematic keyword review. Figure 1 is a visualization of the relationships between the total author-chosen keywords (N = 1234) from the filtered articles that include UCD (N = 304). Figure 1 has 752 nodes and 5,582 edges resulting from steps 6 and 7 of the systemic keyword review.

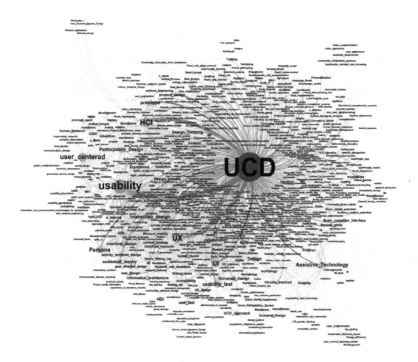

Fig. 1. UCD related keyword network, a total of 752 nodes and 5582 edges.

Figure 1 shows that, using this form keyword visualization, it would be difficult to clearly identify relationships between nodes, thus we filtered the degree range of keywords to visualize it more simply (see Fig. 2). The upper left of Fig. 2 describes connectivity of all 752 nodes, the upper right of Fig. 2 shows the connectivity of 80 nodes, the lower left of Fig. 2 shows the connectivity of 21 nodes, and the lower right of Fig. 2 shows the connectivity of 7 nodes.

Figure 3 describes the associations among the 43 most frequent keywords found in UCD articles. According to the visualization, while UCD has strong connections with keywords usability, UX, user-centered, HCI, Persona, prototype, interaction design, interface design, assistive technology, and design thinking, all keywords do not have

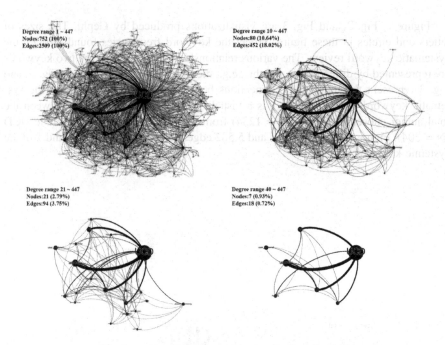

Fig. 2. UCD related keyword network (four levels).

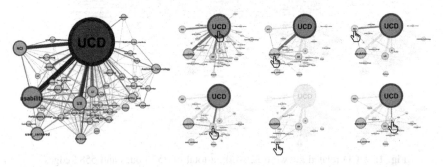

Fig. 3. Visualized results from Gephi of the selected 43 nodes network (on left) and the top six node's network (six images on right): the highlighted nodes and edges show the keywords' association from the selected keyword in red. (Color figure online)

links to one another. For example, while UCD connects to 37 out of the 43 keywords, HCI has connections only with 13 out of the 43 keywords.

From the systematic keyword review of step 8, we found the five disciplines post actively participating in UCD research were Computer Science (N = 194), Design (N = 113), Engineering (N = 72), Education (N = 44), and Psychology (N = 34) (see Table 3), with the percentiles in Table 3 indicating the percentage associated with each specific discipline (e.g. Computer Science, N = 194) relative to the total number of disciplines (N = 619).

Table 3. Frequencies of keywords related to UCD.

Rank	Top 10 fields/disciplines related UCD of authors	Frequency	Percentile
1	Computer science	194	31.34
2	Design	113	18.26
3	Engineering	72	11.63
4	Education	44	7.11
5	Psychology	34	5.49
6	Medicine	31	5.01
7	Economics	29	4.68
8	Social science	27	4.36
9	Entertainment and arts	15	2.42
10	Linguistics	15	2.42

5 Discussion

This study described an attempt at integrated analysis based on the findings from a systematic keyword review. The 7 most frequently mentioned keywords in the 304 articles are Usability, HCI, UX, User-centered, UI, Assistive technology, and Design method. Our finding revealed that these keywords are highly associated with UCD because they are related to the characteristics of UCD, the methods of practicing UCD, a field of the study area in UCD, the philosophical approach of UCD, and disciplines associated with UCD. Regarding the disciplines, the outcome of this study clearly indicates that the disciplines related to UCD are not only in product design and HCI but also in computer science, design, engineering, education, psychology, medicine, economics, and other disciplines. Thus, we could confirm that UCD has been studying actively in various domains and has great potential to collaborate each other.

This study had several limitations. We observed a keyword hierarchy represented by various node sizes, providing at a glance a view of organic connections among keywords using data visualization provided by Gephi. Although this visualization represents clear correlations between keywords by thickness of edge, for future studies the consistency between these visual results and results of consistent statistical analysis results need to be confirmed. Moreover, the visualization complexity makes it difficult to determine how each keyword is derived and connected to the sub-levels of UCD. Therefore, future studies should consider how to efficiently simplify data visualization. Since this study describes the current research mainstream in UCD, our finding would be helpful to researchers, designers, and practitioners through knowledge of UCD keyword research in determining future research topics.

References

1. Abras, C., Maloney-Krichmar, D., Preece, J.: User-centered design. In: Bainbridge, W. (ed.) Encyclopedia of Human-Computer Interaction, vol. 37(4), pp. 445–456. Sage Publications, Thousand Oaks (2004)

2. Norman, D.A., Draper, S.W.: User Centered System Design: New Perspectives on Human-Computer Interaction. CRC Press, Boca Raton (1986)
3. Gabbard, J.L., Hix, D., Swan, J.E.: User-centered design and evaluation of virtual environments. IEEE Comput. Graph. Appl. **19**(6), 51–59 (1999)
4. Mao, J., Vredenburg, K., Smith, P., Carey, T.: The state of user-centered design practice. Commun. ACM **48**(3), 105–109 (2005)
5. Vaughan, L., Yang, R., Tang, J.: Web co-word analysis for business intelligence in the Chinese environment. In: ASLIB Proceedings. Emerald Group Publishing Limited (2012)
6. Ortega, J.L., Aguillo, I.F.: Science is all in the eye of the beholder: keyword maps in google scholar citations. J. Am. Soc. Inf. Sci. Technol. **63**(12), 2370–2377 (2012)
7. Ritzhaupt, A.D., Stewart, M., Smith, P., Barron, A.E.: An investigation of distance education in North American research literature using co-word analysis. Int. Rev. Res. Open Distrib. Learn. **11**(1), 37–60 (2010)
8. Liu, Y., Goncalves, J., Ferreira, D., Hosio, S., Kostakos, V.: Identity crisis of ubicomp? Mapping 15 years of the field's development and paradigm change. In: Proceedings of the 2014 ACM International Joint Conference on Pervasive and Ubiquitous Computing, pp. 75–86 (2014)
9. Liu, Y., Goncalves, J., Ferreira, D., Xiao, B., Hosio, S., Kostakos, V.: CHI 1994–2013: mapping two decades of intellectual progress through co-word analysis. In: Proceedings of the SIGCHI Conference on Human Factors in Computing Systems, pp. 3553–3562 (2014)
10. Börner, K., Chen, C., Boyack, K.W.: Visualizing knowledge domains. Ann. Rev. Inf. Sci. Technol. **37**(1), 179–255 (2003)
11. Calma, A., Davies, M.: Studies in Higher Education 1976–2013: a retrospective using citation network analysis. Stud. High. Educ. **40**(1), 4–21 (2015)
12. Cambrosio, A., Limoges, C., Courtial, J., Laville, F.: Historical scientometrics? Mapping over 70 years of biological safety research with coword analysis. Scientometrics **27**(2), 119–143 (1993)
13. Ding, Y., Chowdhury, G.G., Foo, S.: Bibliometric cartography of information retrieval research by using co-word analysis. Inf. Process. Manag. **37**(6), 817–842 (2001)
14. Hu, C.-P., Hu, J.-M., Deng, S.-L., Liu, Y.: A co-word analysis of library and information science in China. Scientometrics **97**(2), 369–382 (2013)
15. Liu, G.Y., Hu, J.M., Wang, H.L.: A co-word analysis of digital library field in China. Scientometrics **91**(1), 203–217 (2012)
16. Garfield, E., Sher, I.H., Torpie, R.J.: The Use of Citation Data in Writing the History of Science. Institute for Scientific Information, Philadelphia (1964)
17. Small, H., Sweeney, E., Greenlee, E.: Clustering the science citation index using co-citations II. Mapping science. Scientometrics **8**(5–6), 321–340 (1985)
18. Bastian, M., Heymann, S., Jacomy, M.: Gephi: an open source software for exploring and manipulating networks. In: Third international AAAI Conference on Weblogs and Social Media (2009)
19. Wan, X., Rubens, N., Okamoto, T., Feng, Y.: Content filtering based on keyword map. In: 2015 2nd International Conference on Electrical, Computer Engineering and Electronics. Atlantis Press (2015)
20. Turner, M.: Digital libraries and search engines for software engineering research: An overview. Keele University, UK (2010)
21. About ResearchGate. https://www.researchgate.net/about. Accessed 05 Mar 2020

Measuring the Accuracy of Inside-Out Tracking in XR Devices Using a High-Precision Robotic Arm

Daniel Eger Passos$^{(\boxtimes)}$ and Bernhard Jung

Institute of Computer Science,
Technical University Bergakademie Freiberg, Freiberg, Germany
{egerpas,jung}@informatik.tu-freiberg.de

Abstract. We present a method for measuring the accuracy of inside-out tracking capabilities of XR devices. The XR device is attached to an industrial robotic arm that can repeat motions with high precision. A calibration procedure based on point cloud matching is used to determine the relative transformation between the robot arm and the XR device. In tests conducted so far, we experimented with different XR devices, and lighting conditions. For example, under good environmental conditions, tracking accuracies of <1 cm were achieved by the Oculus Quest and <2 cm by the Samsung Galaxy S9. However, under less benevolent environmental conditions, mean error and variance increased significantly. We conclude that the proposed method provides high repeatability of conducted experiments. It also offers diverse opportunities for future investigations regarding the sensitivity of achievable tracking accuracies of XR devices in different environment conditions such as lighting and feature richness.

Keywords: Inside-out tracking · Augmented reality · Virtual reality

1 Introduction

Many state-of-the-art AR/VR devices provide inside-out position tracking based on one or more cameras and other sensors. In contrast to outside-in tracking, no instrumentation of the environment with special beacons ("lighthouses") is required. While inside-out tracking thus enables more mobile XR experiences, its accuracy not only is more dependent on the specific hardware (number, type, quality, spatial arrangement of sensors) and visual odometry software used but is also more susceptible to specific environmental conditions such as lighting and feature-richness. Developers of VR/AR applications may therefore greatly benefit from quantitative evaluations of the tracking accuracies to be expected from various XR devices under different environmental conditions.

There are several methods for measuring the accuracy of tracking algorithms and hardware that are dedicated for specific AR/VR devices and applications: A

© Springer Nature Switzerland AG 2020
C. Stephanidis and M. Antona (Eds.): HCII 2020, CCIS 1224, pp. 19–26, 2020.
https://doi.org/10.1007/978-3-030-50726-8_3

gear head allowing translational movement and angular adjustment provides very accurate ground-truth information, as demonstrated in [12]. In [4], a rotating platform was used to control head (HMD) movements. Several works like [8] and [13] evaluate the tracking precision using optical tracking with retroreflective markers attached to the XR-device. Checkerboard calibration was also used in [2] and GPS information provides ground-truth information for [14]. A different approach was presented in [10], where the use of benchmark datasets allows a fair comparison (with high levels of repeatability) between tracking algorithms.

Despite of this variety, none of these methods can easily be adapted for arbitrary XR-devices and environments: GPS is not very precise and will not work well in indoor or underground environments. Rotating platforms or gear heads have both very limited working and movement ranges. Checkerboard and optical tracking are viable rather for indoor laboratory conditions and both lack of repeatability. Benchmark datasets offer repeatability, but they are produced for a very specific hardware setup.

To the best of our knowledge there are just a few works documenting the use of robotic arms to evaluate the precision of XR-devices. For example, a motorized arm is used in [1] to evaluate latency, and [3] briefly mentions that a robotic arm was used in one of their test cases. In this paper, we describe the first results of using a UR5 robotic arm for measuring the accuracy of inside-out tracking from two different XR-Devices: a Samsung Galaxy S9 (AR) and a Oculus Quest (VR).

Robotic arms can be used for mimicking the way humans move and swing tools, objects or controllers in XR experiences [6,15], with one crucial difference: repeatability. Human movement performance is highly influenced by motor variability [9]. Industrial-strength manipulators such as the UR5 used in our experiments operate with high levels of accuracy and repeatability. Pre-programmed trajectories are repeated by the arm with a positional precision of 0.1 mm, providing the ground-truth information needed for the evaluation. Figure 1 illustrates the difference between tracked trajectories of a hand-held AR-device operated by a human or a robotic arm while executing the task of drawing three times a 30×40 cm square on the air.

2   Methodology

In our setup, the UR5 arm is equipped with a Robotiq 3-finger gripper which allows easy attachment of a variety of AR/VR devices (Fig. 2a). The attached device (we call it D_{XR} from now) sends wireless UDP packages with its tracked pose information to a computer, where a UR5 robotic arm is also connected that is sending the coordinates of its tool center point (TCP). The information from the TCP is our ground-truth information. Before starting to compare its trajectory with the one of D_{XR} two other steps are necessary: alignment of the rotation center and the calculation of a transformation between the UR5 and the D_{XR} reference frames.

Once D_{XR} is attached, a manual calibration process aligns the initial TCP pose (TCP_0) to the rotation center (RC_{XR}) of D_{XR}. If TCP_0 and RC_{XR} do

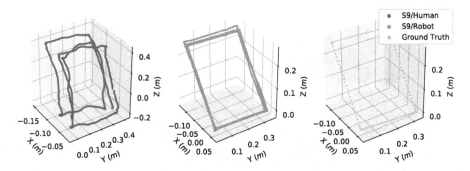

Fig. 1. Tracked trajectories from a Samsung Galaxy S9 while operated by an human (left) or a robotic arm (middle). Our method uses the position of the robot's tool center point (right) as ground-truth information for evaluating tracking accuracy of XR devices.

not coincide, there will be differences in the trajectories registered by the inverse kinematics calculations from the robot and the ones registered by the inside-out tracking from D_{XR}.

There are two situations where the rotation center needs to be determined experimentally: when it is not given via factory specifications or when it is not possible to manually measure its distance to TCP_0. The latter happens e.g. when a HMD is attached to the gripper and it is not possible to visually reach the point between the lenses anymore (where the rotation center is usually located - see Fig. 2b). In these cases, moving and rotating systematically the robot's TCP will reveal where the center is located.

Figure 3 illustrates the process of determining the correct coordinates of the rotation center of an attached HMD. In this case, RC_{XR} is somewhere between 160–180 mm away from TCP_0. Since it is not possible to measure it directly, we experimentally move TCP_0 along the z axis (10 mm steps), rotate the end-effector around the x axis and measure the displacement along the y axis (Δx). The same process can be repeated measuring the displacement (Δy) when rotating around the x axis. The TCP of the robot is moved to the position where Δy and Δx is minimal (we call it now the position TCP_{XR}).

Once D_{XR} is attached and TCP_{XR} is aligned to RC_{XR}, pre-programmed trajectories are executed by the UR5. Both poses of D_{XR} and TCP_{XR} are saved in two point clouds. Then, the two point clouds are aligned first by manually picking point pairs and later by a finer registration method (Iterative Closest Point Algorithm).

The evaluation is based on control points (CPs) located along the pre-programmed trajectory. When reaching a CP the robotic arm stops moving, stays put for 2 s, and then starts moving again to the next CP. Only the information (position of D_{XR} and TCP_{XR}) during the last motionless second of a CP is used in the evaluation. In our experiments each trajectory has five control points, and we have repeated each trajectory five times.

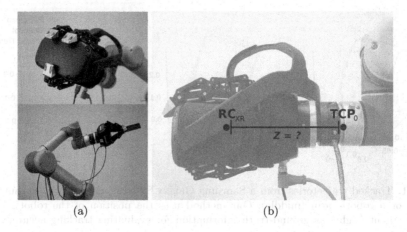

(a)   (b)

Fig. 2. A 3-finger gripper attached to the robotic arm permits easy attachment of diverse AR and VR devices (a). Correct alignment of the XR device is required but not always trivial, due to obstructions caused e.g. by the housing of head mounted displays (b).

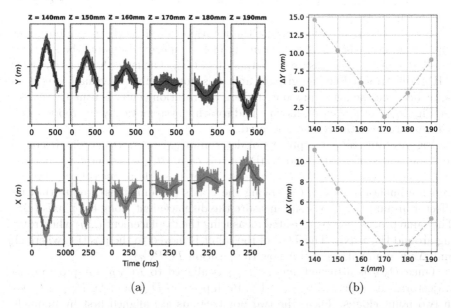

(a)   (b)

Fig. 3. Experimentally aligning the robot's TCP to the rotation center of the XR-Device. a) Rotating the end-effector ($0° \rightarrow 45° \rightarrow 0°$ in slow, $5\,\mathrm{s}$ movements) around the x or y axis and recording displacement along, respectively, the y(red) and x(green) axis, while searching for an optimal z (in $10\,\mathrm{mm}$ steps). b) Δy and Δx should be close to zero if the TCP of the robot is aligned to RC_{XR}. Optimum values are reached around $z = 170\,\mathrm{mm}$ for both axis x and y, where the displacements Δy and Δx are minimal. (Color figure online)

The mean and standard deviation of the euclidean position error between the ground-truth information and XR-device tracked information is calculated for all CPs along the trajectory (and for all repetitions of the trajectory).

Depending on the trajectory taken, sometimes the end-effector is going to strongly vibrate, and unfortunately these vibrations are not registered in the ground-truth information from TCP_{XR}. These vibrations are caused by the robot control and there are several works discussing this topic, e.g. [5,7,11]. In the experiments described here, trajectories were discarded when vibrations exceeded a threshold. We experiment with two different methods for measuring vibrations: *a)* reading the IMU acceleration values from the D_{XR}; *b)* measuring the torque at the end of the robotic arm using a FT-Sensor attached between the gripper and the arm. We prefer using the FT-Sensor variant, since not all XR-devices will allow access to their raw IMU information, at least not without losing performance and/or increasing overhead during data transfer. Figure 4 illustrates the measured vibrations for two similar trajectories using methods a and b.

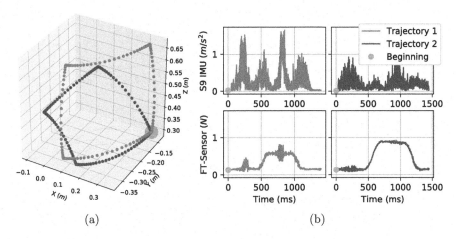

(a)   (b)

Fig. 4. a) Two slightly different trajectories that could be used by the robotic arm for evaluating a XR Device. b) Different methods for measuring vibrations at the end-effector: using XR device internal IMU hardware, or an external FT-Sensor (attached between robotic grip and arm). Trajectory 2 is better than Trajectory 1 for evaluation purposes.

In pre-test trials with different candidate trajectories resembling human motions, we evaluated the degree of vibrations occurring when executed by the robot. Trajectories where stronger vibrations occurred (amplitude higher than $1.5\,\mathrm{m/s}^2$, or $0.5\,\mathrm{N}$) were discarded. In the example from Fig. 4, trajectory 1 is not going to be used for evaluating D_{XR}.

3 Experiments

In tests conducted so far, two different cases where analyzed: *A)* same environmental conditions but different XR-devices; *B)* same XR-device but different environmental conditions.

We selected a Samsung Galaxy S9 and a Oculus Quest for case *A*. Although both devices serve completely different purposes in the XR spectrum, this choice is deliberate in order to demonstrate the flexibility of our setup. As expected, the Oculus Quest – that makes use of four wide-angle cameras among other sensors for its tracking capabilities – provided a better accuracy under same environmental conditions. For the considered trajectory (Fig. 5) the mean Euclidean position error was 6.86 mm for the Quest, against 16.85 mm for the S9. The standard deviation was around 1.5 mm (Quest) against 6.3 mm (S9).

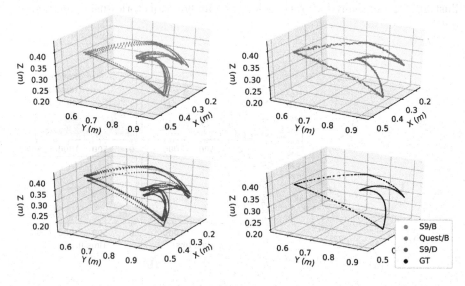

Fig. 5. Motion trajectories of different XR devices under varying lighting conditions. In each subfigure, the point cloud represents the five-fold repetition of the same motion trajectory. Top row: Samsung Galaxy S9 (S9/B), left, v. Oculus Quest (Quest/B), right, under same environmental conditions (bright artificial light, office environment). Accuracies of <2 cm and, respectively, <1 cm were reached. Bottom left: Samsung Galaxy S9 (S9/D) under worse lighting conditions (natural light on a cloudy day) with tracking accuracy of ~3.2 cm. An increased variance between the five motion repetitions as compared to the better lighting conditions top left is clearly noticeable. Bottom left: The motion trajectories reported by the UR5 robotic arm are essentially identical in each repetition of the motion. The robot's motion serves as ground truth (GT) in the experiments.

In case *B* we evaluate the effects of different environmental lighting for the Samsung Galaxy S9. The same trajectory and location from the first experiment were used, but first with artificial environmental lighting and later with only natural daylight (cloudy winter day in Germany, around 11:00 a.m.) coming from the window. The mean positional error and standard deviation were 16.85 mm and 6.3 mm under good lighting conditions (artificial lighting), and degraded to 31.75 mm and 9.5 mm under poorer lighting (cloudy day natural lighting).

4 Conclusion and Future Work

We presented a method for evaluating the tracking accuracy of XR devices using a high-precision robotic arm. After initial XR-device alignment and trajectory validation (exclusion of trajectories exhibiting excessive vibrations when performed by the robot), the proposed experimental setup ensures high repeatability. We showed that the method can be applied to different XR devices and performed initial investigations on the sensitivity of XR tracking to different environmental conditions. A wide range of future work may be considered. For example, by positioning the robot in a CAVE with synthetically generated virtual environments, the influence of varying environmental conditions on inside-out tracking could be examined in a highly controlled manner. Likewise, a mobile robot unit equipped with the UR5 will enable further analysis in specific real environments e.g. industrial laboratories, underground mining districts, surgery rooms and other particular locations of interest where high-precision device tracking is crucial for planning, optimizing and success of XR applications.

References

1. Adelstein, B.D., Johnston, E.R., Ellis, S.R.: Dynamic response of electromagnetic spatial displacement trackers. Presence Teleop. Virt. Environ. **5**(3), 302–318 (1996). https://doi.org/10.1162/pres.1996.5.3.302
2. Agnus, V., Nicolau, S., Soler, L.: Illumination independent marker tracking using cross-ratio invariance. In: Proceedings of the 20th ACM Symposium on Virtual Reality Software and Technology - VRST 2014. ACM Press (2014). https://doi.org/10.1145/2671015.2671119
3. Bleser, G., Stricker, D.: Advanced tracking through efficient image processing and visual-inertial sensor fusion. Comput. Graph. **33**(1), 59–72 (2009). https://doi.org/10.1016/j.cag.2008.11.004
4. Chang, C.M., Hsu, C.H., Hsu, C.F., Chen, K.T.: Performance measurements of virtual reality systems. In: Proceedings of the 2016 ACM on Multimedia Conference - MM 2016. ACM Press (2016). https://doi.org/10.1145/2964284.2967303
5. Dimo, H., Jin, D., Zhang, J., Gruver, W.: Vibration control of a redundant robot for grinding. In: 2001 IEEE International Conference on Systems, Man and Cybernetics, e-Systems and e-Man for Cybernetics in Cyberspace (Cat. No. 01CH37236). IEEE. https://doi.org/10.1109/icsmc.2001.969843
6. El-Gohary, M., McNames, J.: Human joint angle estimation with inertial sensors and validation with a robot arm. IEEE Trans. Biomed. Eng. **62**(7), 1759–1767 (2015). https://doi.org/10.1109/tbme.2015.2403368

7. Furusho, J., Zhang, G., Sakaguchi, M.: Vibration suppression control of robot arms using a homogeneous-type electrorheological fluid. In: Proceedings of International Conference on Robotics and Automation. IEEE. https://doi.org/10.1109/robot.1997.606868

8. Hoff, W., Vincent, T.: Analysis of head pose accuracy in augmented reality. IEEE Trans. Visual Comput. Graphics **6**(4), 319–334 (2000). https://doi.org/10.1109/2945.895877

9. Komar, J., Seifert, L., Thouvarecq, R.: What variability tells us about motor expertise: measurements and perspectives from a complex system approach. Mov. Sport Sci. **89**(3), 65 (2015). https://doi.org/10.3917/sm.089.0065

10. Lieberknecht, S., Benhimane, S., Meier, P., Navab, N.: A dataset and evaluation methodology for template-based tracking algorithms. In: 2009 8th IEEE International Symposium on Mixed and Augmented Reality. IEEE, October 2009. https://doi.org/10.1109/ismar.2009.5336487

11. Meckl, P., Seering, W.: Controlling velocity-limited systems to reduce residual vibration. In: Proceedings of 1988 IEEE International Conference on Robotics and Automation. IEEE Computer Society Press. https://doi.org/10.1109/robot.1988.12267

12. Moser, K.R., Axholt, M., Swan, J.E.: Baseline SPAAM calibration accuracy and precision in the absence of human postural sway error. In: 2014 IEEE Virtual Reality (VR). IEEE, March 2014. https://doi.org/10.1109/vr.2014.6802070

13. Niehorster, D.C., Li, L., Lappe, M.: The accuracy and precision of position and orientation tracking in the HTC Vive virtual reality system for scientific research. i-Perception **8**(3), 204166951770820 (2017). https://doi.org/10.1177/2041669517708205

14. Reitmayr, G., Drummond, T.: Going out: robust model-based tracking for outdoor augmented reality. In: 2006 IEEE/ACM International Symposium on Mixed and Augmented Reality. IEEE, October 2006. https://doi.org/10.1109/ismar.2006.297801

15. Xie, B., Zhao, J., Liu, Y.: Human-like motion planning for robotic arm system. In: 2011 15th International Conference on Advanced Robotics (ICAR). IEEE, June 2011. https://doi.org/10.1109/icar.2011.6088543

Wherein is the Necessity and Importance of Changing Human-Computer Interaction Well-Known Design Methods?

Vera Fink$^{(\boxtimes)}$ and Maximilian Eibl$^{(\boxtimes)}$

Chair of Media Informatics, Technische Universität Chemnitz,
Straße der Nationen 62, 09110 Chemnitz, Germany
{vera.fink, maximilian.eibl}@informatik.tu-chemnitz.de

Abstract. In positive psychology, aspects of everyday human life that extend beyond the zero-state play a central role. Positive user experience (UX) based on positive psychology can potentially offer improvement in the design of user interfaces at a fundamental level. The parallel whereby positive psychology developed from classical psychology has also taken place in human-computer interaction (HCI) research. Software ergonomics in the world of work examines the *how* and the *why* regarding the negative effects on users. Usability has simplified the use of the application. With the increase in complex problem situations approached from a problem-solving perspective, we must move away from the concept of solution. The results and procedures from human-centered methods and models are not sufficient for the design process of fulfilling needs. On the other hand, the findings from positive UX research have not yet incorporated into the human-centric user interface/user experience design. These statements reflect why there are efforts to create new opportunities and possibilities to integrate positive user experience into the design process or introduce a completely different approach to HCI design.

Keywords: HCI · HCI design methods · Psychology and technology · Positive design · Well-being · Positive user experience · Positive UX · Social design · Human needs

1 Introduction

This paper presents the essential aspects that argue for the further development of known or new HCI methods. The first step is to distinguish terms like usability and user experience according to ISO standards from the definition of positive UX. Since all models of positive UX derive from the theory of positive psychology, this plays an important role. For reference to this and would like to outline the roots and definitions of positive psychology briefly. From the historical development of positive psychology, there is a parallel to HCI research. The presented results form the basis for motivation. In assuming that positive UX can make a significant contribution to improving the design of user interfaces at a fundamental level. This potential mainly based on the fact that positive user experience quality characteristics and psychological concepts of dealing with user interfaces can methodically develop. To date, these

C. Stephanidis and M. Antona (Eds.): HCII 2020, CCIS 1224, pp. 27–34, 2020.
https://doi.org/10.1007/978-3-030-50726-8_4

features have been outside the field of vision of classical HCI paradigms or could not adequately address methodologically.

With his inaugural speech to the president, Seligman directed the focus to the examination of health and thus the (re- [16]) birth of positive psychology. As Seligman writes in his books and articles, he spent many years helping those suffering from depression, alcoholism, schizophrenia, and trauma [18]. Like classical psychology, he and his colleagues were concerned with the understanding of human misery and from where it comes. With the commonly-applied psychology of suffering, it was insufficient to make people less depressed, anxious, or angry. With these therapies, the experts only helped people to a zero state in which human suffering alleviated, and debilitating circumstances minimized [27]. However, the ability to experience one's state of happiness is different from the ability to reduce pain. Positive psychology is about increasing general well-being by focusing on the strengths of the individual. According to Seligman, we should experience our forces and then live and communicate in all situations of life. We are supposed to choose things for the sake of the item itself.

In HCI research, scientists have focused on how negative effects occur, and they have developed methods to prevent negative experiences. In the book Software Ergonomics, we are concerned with understanding the human negative effects in the workplace [9]. The book explains the ignorance, violation, and lack of knowledge about laws and regulations of software ergonomic quality as the reason for the development of negative effects. Another reason is the insufficient knowledge of the context of the use of the software.

Positive UX models provide another reason for negative effects. With Hassenzahl et al.'s [6] publication of models on hedonic and pragmatic quality, he stated a statement that proven in studies that there is currently a pragmatic quality. It is a quality that prevents negative experiences and refers to hygiene factors (a term from psychology). Whenever they are present, users have negative experiences. However, when these are absent, users experience neutral experiences.

Donald Norman [15] – a representative of human-centered design methods – claims that his research and principles are designed for usability. The book Design of Everyday Things describes the fundamental principles of good design of things of daily use. Among many other theories, Norman and Jakob Nielsen have simplified the use of products "*that assesses how easy user interfaces are to use*" [14] to reduce frustration. These findings correspond to the zero-state in positive psychology.

Due to the increase in complex problem situations, design processes from human-centered approaches must further develop. "*If design is entering a time of true complexity, we have to radically shift our thinking and move away from design paradigms based on problem-solving to create a new paradigm based on complexity theory and systems thinking. These disciplines demonstrate that in really complex systems, newness comes from the emergence of order, rather than goal-directed creation; change achieved through influencing the system, rather than implementation of a plan to solve the problem; and new state of relative stability achieved by creating resilience, rather than striving for an immutable structure – that so-called solution*" [5]. Accordingly, we can shape technology in terms of how we imagine and desire it.

2 Usability vs. Positive UX

DIN EN ISO 9241-11:2018 [10] describes usability as the extent to which a product can be used by specific users within a particular application context to achieve specific goals effectively, efficiently, and satisfactorily. The term user experience is defined in DIN EN ISO 9241-210:2019 [11] as "*a person's perceptions and responses that result from the use and/or anticipated use of a product, system or service.*" This definition extends usability by aesthetic and emotional factors and – more recently – by goal formation and motivation. Thus, UX is deeply rooted in usability.

The processes of the classical human-centered design models and well-known design approaches alone are, in part, poorly or unsuited to create positive user experiences. It is insufficient to talk to the users and proceed according to methods of standard user interface (UI)/UX methods. Basic questions about positive UX, how positive emotions, and thus positive experiences generated have answered by Hassenzahl and other colleagues, as well as defining user experience [7, 8] "*as a momentary, primarily evaluate feeling (good-bad) while interacting with a product or service*" (Table 1).

Table 1. Differences between usability and (positive) user experience regarding the design process [2]

	Usability	(Positive) user experience
Goal	Effectiveness, efficiency	Fulfillment of needs
Focus	User behavior	User experience
Ideal	Intuitive interaction	"The good life"
Analysis	Goals, tasks	Needs, positive experiences
Design	Build tools	Opportunities for positive experiences
Evaluation	Uncover problems, avoid stress	Understand and enhance positive experiences

In addition to the differences in definition, another difference between human-centered user experience, according to DIN EN ISO standards and positive user experience lies in the methods' respective approaches. The design of positive user experience – a very theory-based approach – concerns which needs are relevant in a particular context [1]. According to Lowson [13], the human-centered design process involves analysis (understanding what the design requirement is), producing design solutions, and evaluation involving some iteration. The study of positive UX looks different: it is not looking for goals and tasks, but instead needs and positive experiences that it can fulfill. In the design phase, no tools are created, but rather possibilities for positive experiences. The evaluation does not reveal any problems to avoid negative emotions but gives positive experiences if better understood and expanded.

3   Results

The following methods and models such as Positive Computing according to Rafael A. Calvo and Dorian Peters [3], Need Satisfaction according to Sheldon et al. [12], Positive Design Theory according to Desmet and Pohlmeyer [4], Experience Design according to Hassenzahl 2010 [6] and Positive Technologies according to Riva et. al 2012 [20] are already working with needs or experiences. A summary of the most frequently mentioned needs is shown in the figure below.

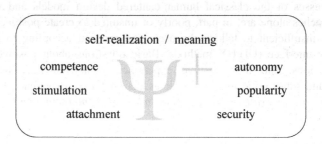

Fig. 1. Needs to be fulfilled in positive UX were related to three models of needs and the result was summarized from [1] (Ryan & Deci [21]; S: Sheldon et al. [12]; Reiss & Haverkamp [19]; Hassenzahl [8]; Hassenzahl et al. [6]; Tuch et al. [23]; Tuch et al. [24] Leisure context; Tuch et al. [24] Working context; Tuch and Hornbæk [22])

HCI research is a problem-solving oriented science [17]. If a classification of the procedure – which is explained in detail below – is to be made, so prefer the third type of problem, namely scientists with their emphasis on theories, concepts, and models, including a light mixture form with empirical research. In the article, the authors launch a call to look beyond design problems and user problems, study interaction purely from a conceptual perspective, develop designs that only serve research, and study empirical phenomena that only help to learn. At the same time, this classification justifies the choice of the following procedure. This way of thinking is a similarity imprinted on arising problems to find solutions. This established chain of processes could help us to gain new insights and solutions.

A1 Systematization. With this insight and the models that take aspects from Fig. 1, and given the open questions from the introduction, a propose the systematic processing of existing positive UX approaches concerning useful quality criteria and analysis methods. With this collection of classifications, it is possible to describe a positive UX design process. The difference compared with human-centered approaches involves highlighting and developing ideas on how to create positive experiences. The example *Quintuple of Usability* [25] provides a suggestion for systematization from the perspective of a problem solution. According to Speicher, usability comprises the following:

usability $\in$ **LEVEL** $\times$ **PRODUCT** $\times$ **USERS** $\times$ **GOALS** $\times$ **CONTENT**

Quintuple can be used to raise awareness of the careful specification of the usability concept. Each element contains a subset of other items. LEVEL comprises internal usability, external usability, and usability in use. With this definition, the author tries to cover all dimensions and characterize the exact kind of usability to ensure its quality. If the results from the primary studies of positive UX described with set theory, then the overall concept of happiness can be systematized with the help of a tuple. This suggestion would be a start to work out the quality characteristics of existing models.

A2 Methodology Performance. The next step is to assess the methodological efficacy of positive UX using current research and existing practice. This priority divides into A2.1 novelty application and A2.2 enforced application.

A2.1 Novelty Application. For the new creation of a software tool, the construction of the improvement process based on selected needs to address is crucial. The most critical points are the development process of the positive UX itself and which needs can meet with the new software. With the help of experience-interviews, it is possible to learn more about the intended use and the context of use. In addition to the standard interview, questions are taken up that lead to positive experiences in a company. For example, the experience interview uses to design concepts with positive user experience for project management software [27]. As a result of specific technologies, the virtual feeling of belonging, the need for connection, or the feeling of identification with the company – the need to have meaning in one's work – was fulfilled.

A2.2 Enforced Application. Complementary to this, the bottom-up method for reconstructing an improvement process uses existing software as the object of investigation and a starting point for iterative improvements. Current applications investigated in terms of positive UX design experiments (workshops). The study by Tuch and Hornbæk presents a practical reference. The examination tests Herzberg's theory of hygiene factors and motivators [22] with the assumption that users experience positive emotions when motivators are present and no negative emotions when they are absent. The results of the study prove this assumption. In the absence of technical quality (hygiene factor), the users were angry, disappointed, frustrated, angry, and dissatisfied. In the presence of usefulness (motivator), the users were happy, satisfied, pleased, and enthusiastic. The shift in the weighting of needs compared with previous studies was interesting. Accordingly, the factors competence, self-esteem, and safety in the context of mobile device use were considered more important than competence, connectedness, and autonomy. From this research, we can observe that the weighting of needs also depends on the context.

4   Discussion

With the experience interviews, not only positive experiences can be ascertained, but also a better understanding of the context of use built up. Moreover, with the positive UX, we go one step further beyond the zero-state. From the statements of the previous chapters and sections, this can deduce that the positive UX approach touches on concepts of user experience that strongly linked to emotional or socio-cultural or temporal-cognitive aspects of the participants' world reference. To date, classical theories have only focused on the elements of immediate work management or eliminating immediate situational negative resonance patterns. Therefore, the current methodological incentives should be systematized in an appropriate reference framework to reflect this relationship.

The developed method can transform into adequate decision support and creative foundations of an actual design process. In the course of the clarification process, it should work out in which sufficient form of expression suitable design aids derived and how their effectiveness evaluated to some extent. At this point, this does not wish to commit itself to the classical design norms or working aids in the creative process.

In the previous chapters, we have dealt with the motivation and challenges of positive UX, whereas subsequently, this will summarize the next steps. When systematizing the positive UX concepts, the difference between the human-centered UX that goes beyond classical paradigms must work out. This system and the suggestions from the current state of research and practical experience can be transferred to an expert setup for analyzing a selected possible case, with the help of a pilot experiment to ensure an adequate experimental setup. Finally, the evaluation and re-assessment of the possibilities of the newly-conceived method in practice should seek.

5   Conclusion

The project is concerned with methodological research in the field of user interface design. It aims to develop approaches from the field of *positive psychology* that complement and supplement the paradigm of usability and human-centered user experience in such a way that they integrated into the design process. The introductory sections highlight the fundamental motivation for this, based on the underlying potential of positive psychology compared with classical psychological approaches to user interface design. Besides, the *positive user experience* paradigm first characterized, and fundamental differences compared with the methods known thus far introduced.

A particular difficulty arises from the fact that concrete software tools or other user interfaces that could serve as suitable candidates for investigation have already developed for a pre-formed purpose. Therefore, it would be necessary to evaluate them in terms of their usefulness or novelty established as the object of investigation. This process, in turn, seems to be inextricably connected with systematization.

References

1. Brohm-Badry, M., Peifer, C., Greve, J.M.: Positiv-Psychologische For-schung im deutschsprachigen Raum-State of the Art. (Tabelle 3: Unter-schiede im Gestaltungsprozess, Seite 164). Pabst Science Publishers, Lengerich (2017). ISBN 978-3-95853-310-3

2. Burmester, M., Laib, M., Schippert, K.: Interaktion als positives Erlebnis – Technolo-giegestaltung neu denken in Mittelstand-Digital, Wissenschaft trifft Praxis. Medien-haus PLUMP GmbH Ausgabe 3, Rheinbreitbach (2014). ISSN (Print) 2198-8544, ISSN (Online) 2198-9362

3. Calvo, R.A., Peters, D.: Positive Computing – Technology for Well-being and Human Potential. The MIT Press, Cambridge (2014). ISBN 978-0-262-53370-6

4. Desmet, P.M.A., Pohlmeyer, A.E.: Positive design: an introduction to design for subjective well-being. Int. J. Des. 7(3), 5–10 (2013). http://www.ijdesign.org/index.php/IJDesign/article/viewFile/1666/587

5. Dorst, K.: Design beyond design. J. Des. Ergon. Innov. 5(2) 2019. https://doi.org/10.1016/j.sheji.2019.05.001. Tongji: Article, she ji

6. Hassenzahl, M., Diefenbach, S., Göritz, A.: Needs, affect, and interactive products – facets of user experience. Interact. Comput. J. 22(5), 353–362 (2010). https://doi.org/10.1016/j.intcom.2010.04.002

7. Hassenzahl, M.: Experience Design: Technology for All the Right Reasons. Synthesis Lectures on Human-Centered Informatics, vol. 3, no. 1, pp. 1–95. Morgan & Claypool, Breinings-ville (2010). https://doi.org/10.2200/S00261ED1V01Y201003HCI008

8. Hassenzahl, M.: User Experience (UX): towards an experimental perspective on product quality. In: IHM 2008: Proceedings of the 20th International Conference of the Association Francophone d'Interaction Homme-Machine, pp. 11–15 (2008). https://doi.org/10.1145/1512714.1512717

9. Herczeg, M.: Software-Ergonomie, Theorien, Modelle und Kriterien für Gebrauchstaugliche interaktive Computersysteme. De Gruyter Studium, 4. Auflage, Oldenburg (2018). ISBN 978-3-11-044685-2

10. DIN EN ISO 9241-11:2018. Ergonomics of human-system interaction – Part 11: Usability: Definitions and concepts. https://www.iso.org/standard/63500.html

11. DIN EN ISO 9241-210:2019. Ergonomics of human-system interaction – Part 210: Human-centred design for interactive systems. https://www.iso.org/standard/77520.html

12. Sheldon, K.M., Elliot, A.J., Kim, Y., Kasser, T.: What is satisfying about satisfying events? Testing 10 candidate psychological needs. J. Pers. Soc. Psychol. 80(2), 325–339 (2001). https://doi.org/10.1037//O022-3514.80.2.325

13. Lowson, B.: How Designers Think, 4th edn. Biddles Ltd., Great Britain (2005). ISBN-13: 978-0-7506-6077-8

14. Nielsen, J.: Usability 101: Introduction to Usability, 2012. World Leaders in research-Based User Experience. https://www.nngroup.com/articles/usability-101-introduction-to-usability/

15. Norman, D.: Emotional Design – Why We Love (or Hate) Everyday Things. Basic Books, New York (2004). ISBN-13: 978-0465051359

16. Maslow, A.: A Philosophy of Psychology. The Need for a Mature Science of Human Nature. McGraw-Hill, New York (1965). F. Severin (Hrsg.), Humanistic viewpoints in psychology

17. Oulasvirta, A., Hornbæk, K.: HCI research as problem-solving. In: chi4good, Computer Human Interaction Conference 4956-4967, CA, USA. San Jose (2016). http://dx.doi.org/10.1145/2858036.2858283

18. Raps, C.S., Reinhard, K.E., Seligman, M.E.P.: Reversal of cognitive and affective deficits associated with depression and learned helplessness by mood elevation in patients. J. Abnorm. Psychol. 89(3), 342–349 (1980). https://doi.org/10.1037//0021-843x.89.3.342

19. Reiss, S., Havercamp, S.M.: Toward a comprehensive assessment of fundamental motivation: factor structure of the reiss profiles. Psychol. Assess. 10(2), 97–106 (1998). https://doi.org/10.1037/1040-3590.10.2.97

34   V. Fink and M. Eibl

20. Riva, G., Baños, R.M., Botella, C., Wiederhold, B.K., Gaggioli, A.: Positive technology: using interactive technologies to promote positive functioning. Cyberpsychol. Behav. Soc. Netw. **15**, 69–77 (2012). https://doi.org/10.1089/cyber.2011.0139
21. Ryan, R.M., Deci, E.L.: Self-determination theory and the facilitation of intrinsic motivation, social development, and well-being. Am. Psychol. **55**(1), 68–78 (2000). https://doi.org/10.1037/0003-066X.55.1.68
22. Tuch, A.N., Hornbæk, K.: Does Herzberg's notion of hygienes and motivators apply to user experience? ACM Trans. Comput. Hum. Interact. **22**(4), 16:1–16:24 (2015). https://doi.org/10.1145/2724710
23. Tuch, A.N., Trusell, R., Hornbæk, K.: Analyzing user's narratives to understand experience with interactive products. In: SIGCHI Conference on Human Computer Interaction, Paris (2013). https://doi.org/10.1145/2470654.2481285, ISBN 978-1-4503-1899-0
24. Tuch, A.N., van Schaik, P., Hornbæk, K.: Leisure and work, good and bad: the role of activity domain and valence in modeling user experience. ACM Trans. Comput. Hum. Interact. **23**(6) (2016). http://doi.org/10.1145/2994147, Article 35
25. Speicher, M.: What is usability? a characterization based on ISO 9241-11 and ISO/IEC 25010. Journal arXiv (2015). https://arxiv.org/pdf/1502.06792.pdf oder https://medium.com/@maxspeicher/what-is-usability-bf578c2a772d
26. Seligman, M.E.P.: Wie wir aufblühen – Die fünf Säulen des persönlichen Wohlbefindens. Goldmann Verlag, München (2015). ISBN 978-3-442-22111-0
27. Zeiner, K.M., Laib, M., Schippert, K., Burmester, M.: Das Erlebnisinterview – Methode zum Verständnis positiver Erlebnisse. In: Hess, V.S., Fischer (Hg.) MuC 2016– Usability Professionals, Gesellschaft für Informatik e. V. und die German UPA, Aachen (2016). http://dx.doi.org/10.18420/muc2016-up-0144

Towards Interaction Design for Mobile Devices in Collocated Mixed-Focus Collaboration

Romina Kühn[1(✉)], Mandy Korzetz[1(✉)], Dominik Grzelak[1(✉)],
Uwe Aßmann[1(✉)], and Thomas Schlegel[2(✉)]

[1] Institute of Software and Multimedia Technology, TU Dresden, Dresden, Germany
{romina.kuehn,mandy.korzetz,dominik.grzelak,uwe.assmann}@tu-dresden.de
[2] Institute for Ubiquitous Mobility Systems, Karlsruhe University
of Applied Science, Karlsruhe, Germany
thomas.schlegel@hs-karlsruhe.de

Abstract. In collocated collaboration, applied methods and technologies to support the collaboration process mainly comprise either analog paper and pen methods, large display applications or the usage of several laptops. Whereas paper and pen are easy to use, they impair the digital documentation and further editing. Large displays are expensive, stationary, and depend on specific environments. Furthermore, laptops build physical barriers between people, which impedes face-to-face communication. This leads to the fact that direct digitization is still not often performed in collocated collaborative scenarios, although it would be useful for further processing or permanent storing of created content. To address advantages of analog media, especially small size and high ubiquity, and eliminate the disadvantages, namely the lack of direct digitization, we aim at applying mobile devices to collocated collaboration. To contribute to the development of future collaboration tools, we derive and propose concrete design goals for applying mobile devices in collocated mixed-focus collaboration.

Keywords: Collocated interaction · Device-based interaction · Design goals · Mixed-focus collaboration · Mobile phone

1 Introduction

To support collocated collaboration, there is a broad variety of approaches and tools. A very common but analog approach is the usage of paper and pen to create and share content in collaboration. This approach is very easy to perform and only needs little preparation, i.e. just paper and pen, which is often a normal part of things people are having and carrying during their work or school day. Since laptops have arrived the consumer market, they started replacing paper and pen approaches. Two advantages of using laptops instead of paper and pen are direct digitization for further editing and storing as well as combining several supportive tools for collaborative tasks, e.g. digital dictionary or reference

© Springer Nature Switzerland AG 2020
C. Stephanidis and M. Antona (Eds.): HCII 2020, CCIS 1224, pp. 35–43, 2020.
https://doi.org/10.1007/978-3-030-50726-8_5

Fig. 1. Collocated mixed-focus collaboration scenario where group members apply mobile devices to create and discuss collaborative tasks.

works. However, due to the form of laptops they build physical barriers between collaborating people that impedes face-to-face communication [21], which is an important aspect of good collaboration [4]. Other approaches comprise the application of large horizontal or vertical displays to present and discuss content (e.g. [9,11,24]). Such systems provide a shared presentation space for all group members but lack space for individual work in terms of mixed-focus collaboration [7] where group members switch between individual and joint tasks. Furthermore, large displays are stationary and depend on specific environments that provide such screens. This impedes spontaneous collaboration. Additionally, such environments are still expensive. Applying mobile devices, especially smartphones or tablets, seems to be beneficial for mixed-focus collaboration. Such devices are already an indispensable part of our everyday life [1]. Furthermore, they have a similar form factor as paper and can therefore eliminate the paper's disadvantage of lacking direct digitization. However, the majority of approaches still uses mobile devices in combination with other technologies, mainly large displays (e.g. [2,16,18,26,28]). Although, this combination is comprehensible in terms of enlarging presentation areas it still needs additional equipment. When applying mobile devices without further equipment in collaboration, such as shown in Fig. 1, one drawback is the interaction with mobile devices, especially the lack of intuitive, easy to perform and seamless integrated interactions in current approaches [5,19]. However, there are also further issues when applying mobile devices in collaboration. We address these issues by investigating current approaches and deriving design goals and recommendations for designers and developers of collaborative technologies. With the design goals we aim at giving a starting point for integrating mobile devices in collaboration as well as important aspects to consider when developing appropriate solutions.

To elaborate general design goals for the usage of mobile devices for different activities [15], we first present related work concerning mobile devices in collocated collaboration. Then, we describe derived design goals and summarize with concrete recommendations of using mobile devices in mixed-focus collaboration.

2   Related Work

We investigated two main areas of related work. First, we examined current approaches that realize the application of mobile devices in collaborative multi-user scenarios. Second, we looked into the literature concerning general challenges in collocated collaboration. We present the results from our investigations below.

2.1   Mobile Devices in Collocated Multi-user Scenarios

As mentioned above, there are several approaches that apply mobile devices in collaborative scenarios. The majority of approaches uses such devices together with large displays to overcome the issue of small display size. This includes, for example, *MobiSurf* by Seifert et al. [28] which uses a combination of mobile devices and a horizontal display to share and present content that was browsed on the mobile device beforehand. Similar approaches were presented by Lucero et al. [18] introducing *MobiComics* for collaborative comic drawing on mobile phones and presentation on a large display, by Buchner et al. [2] with a collaborative TV where mobile devices are used as a remote control, or by Langner et al. [16] describing several ways to transfer data between mobile phone and large display. Although *HuddleLamp* presented by Rädle et al. [26] uses mobile devices solely, they also need additional equipment, i.e. tracking devices. Consequently, these approaches need a concrete and predefined set-up before they can be utilized and are stationary due to the additional devices. However, some approaches also describe the usage of mobile devices without further tracking or presentation devices. Lucero et al. have been doing a lot of work in this field, for example, *Pass-them-around* [17] to collaboratively share photos or an application to curate sources of inspiration [20]. Schwarz et al. [27] as well as Huang et al. [8] both present playful ways to utilize several mobile devices to enlarge the presentation area. Introducing *JuxtaPinch*, Nielsen et al. [22] describe several ways to share photos and simultaneously use several devices to enlarge the presentation area. The *LetsPic* approach of Kim et al. [10] also addresses photography but with focus on collaborative sharing. Overall, the presented approaches describe concrete solutions on either a specific application domain or a specific collaborative activity [15] without taking into account general design challenges or decisions.

2.2   General Challenges in Collocated Collaboration

Whereas the above-mentioned approaches describe concrete applications of mobile devices, we aim at having a closer look into challenges and other important aspects when using mobile devices in collocated collaboration. We identified several works that address these issues. Cole and Stanton [3] derived important considerations for designing and using mobile devices in collaboration by comparing applications for children. They found three general aspects that support collocated collaboration with mobile devices, namely (1) the importance of well-structured information, (2) the possibility to share information between devices using physical gestures, and (3) the presence and usage of the devices while collaborating. Oja's [25] approach comprises the application of Nielsen's usability heuristics [23] to design for collaboration in terms of usable software systems. Although, Oja does not address mobile collaboration explicitly, she found that (1) visibility of information, (2) adaptation, and (3) the intuitiveness of the system and tools are important aspects of designing for collaboration. Fails et al. [6] derive several factors that influence mobile collaboration in learning settings. These factors include the size and number of devices, user arrangement, and the superimposition of display space on input space, i.e. when screen content is overlapped by an input device. One of the most important challenges for using multiple mobile devices that was identified by Dong et al. [5] is the difficulty of designing interactions. Although the work of Kim et al. [12] focused on mobile games, they found some characteristics and challenges for designing for multiple mobile devices. First, they found that the interfaces depend on the direction of the mobile device order. Second, the space between arranged devices is important in terms of a virtual space and the unity of an arrangement. Finally, the interaction that can be performed is important. Additionally, user arrangement as well as ownership of the devices were identified as issues to consider when designing for collocated collaboration. In summary, we found several design challenges but also important aspects from the literature that we use to derive design goals and recommendations for applying mobile devices in collocated collaboration.

3 Design for Mobile Devices in Collocated Collaboration

In the literature, we found several challenges when designing or implementing for collocated collaboration. To facilitate the usage of mobile devices in such scenarios, we condensed the presented approaches to find the essential design needs for collaboration. From the identified challenges, we give some concrete recommendations that designers and developers should consider to create meaningful solutions that apply mobile devices in collocated collaboration.

3.1 Design Goals for Mobile Devices in Collocated Collaboration

We identified and derived the following design goals for applying mobile devices in collocated collaboration. These design goals serve as a basis for further recommendations and describe the impact of mobile devices in collaboration.

Support of Spontaneous Collaboration. We found that many approaches with collaborative mobile devices need additional tools (e.g. [2,26,28]). This need impedes ad-hoc sessions in general because the usage of the mobile devices always depends on the availability of these tools. In contrast, when using mobile devices solely, groups can collaborate independently from specially equipped surroundings. This facilitates planning and organization, for example, in terms of scheduling a room. Therefore, we state that the usage of mobile devices exclusively supports spontaneous and location-independent collocated collaboration.

Supporting Different User (and Device) Arrangements. As stated by Kim et al. [12] and Fails et al. [6], user arrangement as well as ownership of devices are important issues in collocated collaboration. Large displays are stationary and only allow for different user arrangements in front of the display, but without the possibility of changing the device arrangement. Furthermore, such devices are owned by a company or institution and not necessarily by a group member. In contrast, laptops normally belong to one person, but mainly focus on their display while collaborating. Furthermore, such devices build barriers between people and impede collaboration. Focusing on mobile devices, nearly everybody owns such a device, which leads to clear ownership. Furthermore, such devices can be utilized in different user arrangements with varying group sizes because users can easily participate with their personal device. Additionally, due to the size and shape of mobile devices they can be arranged in different ways with different orientation, e.g. as a ring [12]. This offers a wide range of arrangements for both users and devices.

Supporting Different Coupling Styles. Switching from individual to collaborative usage in terms of mixed-focus collaboration [7] enables users to focus on specific topics while working individually and starting discussions in collaboration. This approach can be useful in terms of efficiency. Mixed-focus collaboration on large displays can be performed by dividing the display's space. However, there are several drawbacks, namely the limited space of displays when many users want to interact with the display as well as the close proximity that can impede concentration. Using mobile devices for collaborating in terms of mixed-focus collaboration allows for withdrawing to work individually and coming back to discuss or further working on the content.

Showing Awareness of (Mobile) Devices. Cole and Stanton [3] stated that the presence of the (mobile) devices during the usage is important. However, from our perspective it is important to be aware of devices without focusing to much on the device. Whereas large displays as well as laptops are present all the time due to their form factor and size, smaller mobile devices can be either used very actively, e.g. when browsing information on the device, but also more in an implicit way, e.g. when using a mobile device as tangible device.

Providing Intuitive Interactions. The intuitive usage of devices and tools is one main goal to achieve when applying them in collaboration [19,25]. However, it is also very difficult to design intuitive interactions [5]. Mobile devices use a broad range of built-in sensors and therefore already include various possibilities to implement interactions. In contrast, large displays mainly provide multi-touch technologies and laptops still use the mouse and keyboard paradigm. With the variety of input and output possibilities of mobile devices, they can easily provide intuitive interactions for different collaborative activities [15]. Consequently, interactions need to be easy to learn and to use.

3.2   Recommendations for Using Mobile Devices in Collaboration

The presented design goals show that the application of mobile devices in collocated collaboration can be very useful. However, they do not clearly specify how they can be achieved in detail. Cole and Stanton [3] argued that, for example, sharing information between devices should be possible using physical gestures. Furthermore, both Lucero et al. [19] and Dong et al. [5] stated that unsuitable interactions are one of the main reasons why mobile devices are seldom used in collaboration. To address these issues and the above-mentioned design goals, we recommend applying mobile device-based interactions as proposed by Korzetz et al. [13]. Such interactions base on physical actions, i.e. movements and arrangements of mobile devices. In the following, we describe the main characteristics of such interactions and how they address the design goals.

Usage of Metaphors for Design. Device-based interactions are designed by using metaphors of everyday actions. Metaphors can be beneficial for increasing the intuitiveness of a system in general due to the mapping of a known concept to another device or scenario. Furthermore, applying metaphors in the design process can increase learning and remembering an interaction. Although, the usage of metaphors is not limited to device-based interactions, the degrees of freedom are higher in contrast to screen-based interactions due to the different spatial options. Furthermore, depending on the metaphor, such interactions can support different user or device arrangements, e.g. stacking several devices.

Unobtrusive and Eyes-Free Usage of Mobile Devices. Device-based interactions focus on movements and positions of the devices. Whereas such movements can be explicit and even excessive, e.g. when waving with a device, small movements on the other hand are unobtrusive, e.g. shifting a device [14]. Unobtrusiveness of interactions is twofold. The performance needs to be easy and fast, so that the interaction does not interrupt the collaborative process neither for the interacting user nor the other group members. Additionally, it can be beneficial to the user to interact unobtrusively to enter personal information. In both cases, all group members can be aware of the mobile devices without necessarily need to know how single members interact with them. This addresses both the design goal *awareness* and *different coupling styles*. Eyes-free performance of device-based interactions aims at increasing usability in terms of fast and easy interactions, which addresses *intuitiveness*. Furthermore, eyes-free interactions do not need much user attention which is positive for the collaboration process.

4 Conclusion and Future Work

In this work, we described several challenges coming from the literature and design goals for applying mobile devices in collocated collaboration. With these design goals, we aim at providing designers and developers concrete starting points when designing for collocated collaboration. We have elaborated benefits of using mobile devices in collaboration and recommended to use mobile device-based interactions for the application of such devices. In future work, we aim at validating the design goals and recommendations performing user studies with designers to assess usefulness and with potential users of concrete applications. Finally, we will derive concrete guidelines from the design goals.

Acknowledgements. The European Social Fund (ESF) and the German Federal State of Saxony have funded this work within the project CyPhyMan (100268299). This work is also funded by the German Research Foundation (DFG, Deutsche Forschungs-gemeinschaft) as part of Germany's Excellence Strategy – EXC 2050/1 – Project ID 390696704 – Cluster of Excellence "Centre for Tactile Internet with Human-in-the-Loop" (CeTI) of Technische Universität Dresden.

References

1. Abowd, G.D., Iftode, L., Mitchell, H.: The smart phone: a first platform for per-vasive computing. IEEE Pervasive Comput. **4**(2), 18–19 (2005)
2. Buchner, K., Lissermann, R., Holmquist, L.E.: Interaction techniques for co-located collaborative TV. In: CHI 2014 Extended Abstracts on Human Factors in Computing Systems, CHI EA 2014, pp. 1819–1824. ACM, New York (2014)
3. Cole, H., Stanton, D.: Designing mobile technologies to support co-present collaboration. Pers. Ubiquit. Comput. **7**(6), 365–371 (2003)
4. Diehl, M., Stroebe, W.: Productivity loss in brainstorming groups: toward the solution of a riddle. J. Pers. Soc. Psychol. **53**, 497–509 (1987)
5. Dong, T., Churchill, E.F., Nichols, J.: Understanding the challenges of designing and developing multi-device experiences. In: DIS 2016: Proceedings of the 2016 ACM Conference on Designing Interactive Systems, pp. 62–72 (2016)
6. Fails, J.A., Druin, A., Guha, M.L.: Mobile collaboration: collaboratively reading and creating children's stories on mobile devices. In: Proceedings of the 9th International Conference on Interaction Design and Children, pp. 20–29. ACM (2010)
7. Gutwin, C., Greenberg, S.: Design for individuals, design for groups: tradeoffs between power and workspace awareness. In: Proceedings of the 1998 ACM Conference on Computer Supported Cooperative Work (CSCW 1998), pp. 207–216 (1998)
8. Huang, D.Y., et al.: MagMobile: enhancing social interactions with rapid view-stitching games of mobile devices. In: Proceedings of the 11th International Conference on Mobile and Ubiquitous Multimedia - MUM 2012, p. 4 (2012)
9. Jakobsen, M.R., Hornbæk, K.: Negotiating for space? Collaborative work using a wall display with mouse and touch input. In: Proceedings of the 2016 CHI Conference on Human Factors in Computing Systems, pp. 2050–2061. ACM (2016)
10. Kim, A., Kang, S., Lee, U.: LetsPic: supporting in-situ collaborative photography over a large physical space. In: Proceedings of the 2017 CHI Conference on Human Factors in Computing Systems, pp. 4561–4573 (2017)

11. Kim, H., Snow, S.: Collaboration on a large-scale, multi-touch display: asynchronous interaction and multiple-input use. In: Proceedings of the 2013 Conference on Computer Supported Cooperative Work Companion, pp. 165–168. ACM (2013)
12. Kim, S., Ko, D., Lee, W.: Utilizing smartphones as a multi-device single display groupware to design collaborative games. In: Proceedings of the 2017 ACM Conference on Designing Interactive Systems, pp. 1341–1352. ACM (2017)
13. Korzetz, M., Kühn, R., Schlegel, T.: Turn it, pour it, twist it: a model for designing mobile device-based interactions. In: Proceedings of the 5th International ACM In-Cooperation HCI and UX Conference, pp. 20–23. ACM (2019)
14. Kühn, R., Korzetz, M., Büschel, L., Korger, C., Manja, P., Schlegel, T.: Natural voting interactions for collaborative work with mobile devices. In: Proceedings of the 34th of the International Conference Extended Abstracts on Human Factors in Computing Systems, pp. 2570–2575 (2016)
15. Kühn, R., Schlegel, T.: Mixed-focus collaboration activities for designing mobile interactions. In: Proceedings of the 20th International Conference on Human-Computer Interaction with Mobile Devices and Services, pp. 71–78 (2018)
16. Langner, R., von Zadow, U., Horak, T., Mitschick, A., Dachselt, R.: Content sharing between spatially-aware mobile phones and large vertical displays supporting collaborative work. In: Anslow, C., Campos, P., Jorge, J. (eds.) Collaboration Meets Interactive Spaces, pp. 75–96. Springer, Cham (2016). https://doi.org/10.1007/978-3-319-45853-3_5
17. Lucero, A., Holopainen, J., Jokela, T.: Pass-them-around: collaborative use of mobile phones for photo sharing. In: Proceedings of the 2011 Conference on Human Factors in Computing Systems, pp. 1787–1796 (2011)
18. Lucero, A., Holopainen, J., Jokela, T.: Mobicomics: collaborative use of mobile phones and large displays for public expression. In: Proceedings of the 14th International Conference on HCI with Mobile Devices and Services, pp. 383–392. ACM (2012)
19. Lucero, A., Jones, M., Jokela, T., Robinson, S.: Mobile collocated interactions: taking an offline break together. Interactions 20(2), 26–32 (2013)
20. Lucero, A., Porcheron, M., Fischer, J.E.: Collaborative use of mobile devices to curate sources of inspiration. In: Proceedings of the 18th International Conference on HCI with Mobile Devices and Services Adjunct, pp. 611–616 (2016)
21. Newman, W., Smith, E.L.: Disruption of meetings by laptop use: is there a 10-second solution? In: CHI 2006 Extended Abstracts on Human Factors in Computing Systems, pp. 1145–1150. ACM (2006)
22. Nielsen, H.S., Olsen, M.P., Skov, M.B., Kjeldskov, J.: JuxtaPinch: exploring multi-device interaction in collocated photo sharing. In: Proceedings of the 16th International Conference on HCI with Mobile Devices & Services, pp. 183–192 (2014)
23. Nielsen, J.: Enhancing the explanatory power of usability heuristics. In: Proceedings of the SIGCHI Conference on Human Factors in Computing Systems, pp. 152–158 (1994)
24. Nolte, A., Brown, R., Poppe, E., Anslow, C.: Towards collaborative modelling of business processes on large interactive touch display walls. In: Proceedings of the International Conference on Interactive Tabletops & Surfaces, pp. 379–384. ACM (2015)
25. Oja, M.K.: Designing for collaboration: improving usability of complex software systems. In: CHI 2010 Extended Abstracts on Human Factors in Computing Systems, pp. 3799–3804. ACM (2010)

26. Rädle, R., Jetter, H.C., Marquardt, N., Reiterer, H., Rogers, Y.: HuddleLamp: spatially-aware mobile displays for ad-hoc around-the-table collaboration. In: Proceedings of the International Conference on Interactive Tabletops and Surfaces, pp. 45–54 (2014)
27. Schwarz, J., Klionsky, D., Harrison, C., Dietz, P., Wilson, A.: Phone as a pixel: enabling ad-hoc, large-scale displays using mobile devices. In: Proceedings of the SIGCHI Conference on Human Factors in Computing Systems, pp. 2235–2238 (2012)
28. Seifert, J., et al.: MobiSurf: improving co-located collaboration through integrating mobile devices and interactive surfaces. In: Proceedings of the 2012 ACM International Conference on Interactive Tabletops and Surfaces, pp. 51–60 (2012)

Developing a Presentation Mode for Socio-technical Process Walkthroughs

Jan Lukas Knittel$^{(\boxtimes)}$, Thomas Herrmann, and Markus Jelonek

Ruhr University Bochum, 44801 Bochum, Germany
{jan.knittel,thomas.herrmann,markus.jelonek}@rub.de

Abstract. This poster describes the development of a presentation mode for process models that are created with the sociotechnical modeling method SeeMe. It explains how such a mode can be valuable to guide an audience through a presentation and assist in the discussion of a model. Based on the characteristics of a typical presentation scenario and the analysis of an existing version of a presentation mode in the process editor, arising challenges are identified. These include reliably drawing the attention of different stakeholders to the same information, dynamically integrating feedback into the model during the discussion and guaranteeing intuitive and user-friendly interaction for different input methods. A first iteration of a new presentation mode in a web-based editor is introduced. It aims to meet these challenges by using flexibly enlargeable and movable windows within the editor that can be placed around relevant model elements to highlight them, while greying out the rest of the model. First test results with this version reveal issues with the user interface and the touch interaction but hint at the general benefit of the approach. In the future, a larger-scale evaluation of usability and user experience is planned.

Keywords: Sociotechnical design · Process design · User interface

1 Introduction

In process design, notations like BPMN, UML or others are used to create graphical models that describe and visualize processes. For the design of sociotechnical processes and systems the semi-structured, sociotechnical modeling method SeeMe can be used [3]. Process modeling itself is an iterative process, as feedback of different stakeholders has to be gathered and integrated during the development of a model. In order to achieve this, the different versions of a model must be iteratively discussed with the stakeholders. To support these discussions, the presenting of the process models has to be supported. Ideas and improvements that result from these discussions are then integrated into the model, creating the next iteration. Most process modeling editors do not provide such a presentation mode, which may also be due to the fact that, compared to other areas of process modeling, sociotechnical process modeling integrates different perspectives of multiple stakeholders in the modeling process.

© Springer Nature Switzerland AG 2020
C. Stephanidis and M. Antona (Eds.): HCII 2020, CCIS 1224, pp. 44–51, 2020.
https://doi.org/10.1007/978-3-030-50726-8_6

The presentation of such a process model can result in several challenges. For example, stakeholders might not be familiar with the presented process, the process diagram or with the modeling notation. Moreover, process models can quickly evolve into large and complex diagrams, spanning various topics and relationships. As a result, different stakeholders might focus on very different aspects of the model, depending on their own expertise. A specific mode is required to guide the focus of the audience on the same information under discussion and assist them in understanding the model. Such a mode helps to provide a successful presentation and to facilitate a comprehensive discussion.

An example for a method that integrates the development and presentation of process models is the sociotechnical walkthrough (STWT) [5]. It aims to support the communication during the development of a sociotechnical system and to share knowledge between the different perspectives of the people involved. The STWT uses the modeling notation SeeMe. A characteristic of SeeMe is that it allows vagueness in the process models. For example, if there are parts of a process model where different stakeholders disagree about the details, those details do not need to be explicitly defined. SeeMe allows to explicitly state where potential details are omitted. During the development of the model, more information can be added to these aspects [4].

For the design and development of SeeMe models, an editor for desktop PCs is available. The editor integrates a presentation mode for the STWT that allows focusing the attention of the audience/stakeholders to specific model elements and the relationships between them. However, although this feature of the editor went through several design cycles of improvement, there are a number of issues impairing the full acceptance by the users. As the desktop version will eventually be replaced by a web-based SeeMe editor, design issues of the desktop presentation mode should be resolved in the web-based version. Experiences collected from the development and use of the original presentation mode are used to improve upon the existing implementation.

The following section describes typical scenarios in which the presentation mode is used. It then presents the implementation of this mode in the desktop editor and explains arising difficulties. Then challenges that have to be met by the web version are collected, before we present potential solutions to these challenges as they are implemented in a first iteration of the new presentation mode. Additionally, experiences with this implementation are described and further design challenges are discussed. Finally, an outlook into the further evaluation and development is given.

2 Presenting Models with the SeeMe Desktop Editor

2.1 Characteristics of a Typical Presentation Scenario

In a typical presentation scenario, the presenter stands in front of a screen onto which the model is projected. Their interaction with the modeling software primarily focuses on drawing attention to the parts of the model that are currently relevant, but the presenter might also edit the model in the course of the discussion, implementing feedback given by the audience. The discussion creates a dynamic situation in which for example the presenter may change as different aspects are discussed.

Feedback coming up in discussions is best immediately implemented into the model to prevent misunderstandings that might arise if discussion points are only noted and implemented afterwards. Another advantage of directly changing the model is that it can accelerate the discussion, by providing a visual representation of the discussed changes and serving as an inspiration for further ideas [2]. Therefore, the model dynamically changes during the discussion. In particular the current topic of the conversation and with it the relevant elements of the model can change quickly.

Interaction with the model during a presentation is usually done in two ways: The presenter can remotely control the software using a computer mouse and a keyboard or they can use a smartboard which supports touch commands. It is also possible that both methods are used during one session.

Using touch commands requires more physical movement to perform different actions to different parts of the model than the use of a mouse does. On the other hand, as every action of the presenter is visible to the audience, they have a better chance to follow changes in the model.

2.2   The Presentation Mode of the SeeMe Desktop Editor

In the existing presentation mode for the SeeMe desktop editor, elements can be selected and deselected as part of the presentation by clicking on them. Selected elements are highlighted, giving them their usual colors, while the rest of the

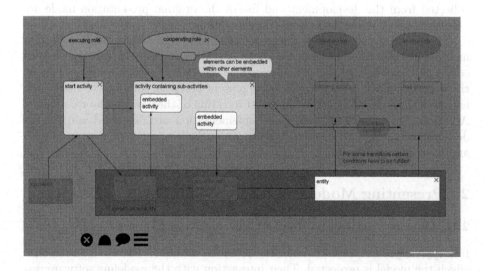

Fig. 1. Presentation mode of the SeeMe desktop editor

model is greyed out (see Fig. 1). At the bottom of the screen there is a zoom slider with which the zoom level of the entire model is controlled (see Fig. 1, bottom right). In addition, there are several buttons (see Fig. 1, bottom left) to suspend the presentation mode, to hide the currently selected element, to add comments to elements or to hide and show an existing comment.

Known Issues with the Existing Mode. The presenter can find themselves in the situation that they are standing at one side of the smartboard but the buttons are located on the other side of the board. On smartboards with a width of several meters, the user has to walk a relatively large distance which delays the presentation.

Editing is not possible during the presentation. Users may add comments to the model, but to change any other content, the presenter has to suspend the presentation mode and continue it after the changes are made. A consequence of this is are interruptions of the discussion.

Shifting the attention from one part of the model to another, one requires deselecting all currently highlighted elements individually and selecting the desired ones. Many clicks are necessary for this shift that takes much time and provides many possibilities for mistakes to be made.

Some of the functions available in this mode are not intuitive enough for inexperienced users. For instance hiding elements is only needed in rare cases and leads to confusion if used by accident. All in all, the presentation mode was not intuitively usable and therefore not used by newcomers for running presentations.

3 Challenges

Based on the characteristics of a typical presentation scenario and the experiences and feedback collected from using the desktop version, it is possible to formulate challenges that have to be met when developing the new presentation mode.

The basic functionality a presentation mode has to provide, is guiding the attention of the audience to those parts of the model that are crucial at that particular moment of the presentation. Relevant information is not necessarily found in close proximity within a diagram but elements at different locations might have to be highlighted simultaneously. Furthermore, the placement of the information – e.g. the representation of an activity – can change over the course of the discussion. The presentation mode should therefore provide ways to dynamically deal with informational elements of various sizes at several disconnected locations within the model.

The discussion of a model is a vital part of a presentation and the resulting feedback should be directly integrated into the model. To perform this integration immediately, the presentation mode must allow editing the model according to the received feedback. Switching between presenting and editing should happen seamlessly in order to avoid delays or disruptions of the discussion.

Using the presentation mode has to be intuitive. If too complex interactions are required this might result in a high cognitive load for the presenting person and the audience who might not be able to follow the presentation and understand what the presenter is doing, especially if they are not familiar with the model or the editor. To achieve this, functions that are important during the presentation have to be made easily and directly accessible to the presenter. They have to be intuitively understood even by users who do not have much experience with using the editor.

Another important functionality is changing the zoom level of a process model. This allows presenters to deal with models of various scales. The possibility to hide comments within the model has also shown to be advantageous to the clarity of the model. Functions of the desktop version that are only used in rare cases should be left out to reduce the complexity.

A satisfying usability has to be guaranteed for both methods of interaction, mouse and keyboard as well as touch interaction on a smartboard. In the latter case, it is important to keep in mind that the presenters most likely cannot concentrate on the audience and the model at the same time. While they are talking to the audience, the important information has to stay highlighted. Moreover, the touch interaction has to be designed in a way that minimizes the required physical movement.

The presenter has to be able to quickly and reliably navigate through the model according to the course of the presentation. This means in particular that they are able to quickly change those parts of the model that are placed within focus of the audience.

4 Designing an Improved Presentation Mode

4.1 First Iteration of the Web Version

The fundamental concept of the presentation mode of the web editor is the use of so-called presentation windows. These are frames that can be placed on the model. Everything inside the frame is visible as usual, while everything outside the frame is greyed out (see Fig. 2). This way, the attention of the audience is supposed to be drawn to the elements within the windows.

An arbitrary number of such presentation windows can be used. Each window can be moved and resized individually on the model. This allows the presenter to quickly adapt as the topic of the presentation or discussion changes. Groups of neighboring elements can be highlighted with a single window.

The usual functions for editing of the web editor are available within the window but cannot be used outside of it. This allows for a seamless editing of the highlighted areas. Since the interaction required for this does not differ from the normal editing mode, users should be able to do it intuitively if they are familiar with the editor. If changes to larger parts of the model are required, the presentation mode can temporarily be suspended, to switch to the editing mode, and later be restored with the windows at the positions where they were left.

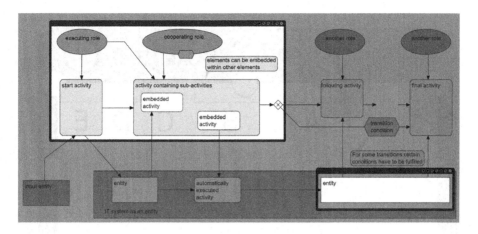

Fig. 2. Presentation mode of the SeeMe web editor

The interaction with the presentation windows is the same for both input methods, mouse and touchscreen. A single window can be moved across the model by dragging its frame. If instead a dragging motion is performed on the grey area outside the windows, all presentation windows will keep their position relative to the browser and instead the whole model moves. Dragging on the empty canvas within a presentation window moves everything, the presentation windows and the entire model, relative to the browser. This allows quickly changing the view without additional commands.

Clicking on a presentation window reveals markers (handles) on the frame (see Fig. 3). By dragging these markers, the size and aspect ratio of that window can be changed. This works the same way as resizing elements does in the default editing mode of the software and in many other editors as well and should feel familiar to most users.

Integrated into the frame of each window are several buttons that provide basic functions (see Fig. 3). This way the buttons are always near the highlighted area and hence in reach of the presenter, limiting the required movement.

4.2   Pre-test of this Iteration

The first iteration of the new presentation mode has been tested with expert users of the system, in order to identify major issues and difficulties. Several issues were mentioned, for example that the design of the presentation window frames with seven buttons draws too much attention and therefore distracts the audience from the actual content of the window that is supposed to be highlighted. As the functions of the buttons are expected to be used only occasionally, users suggested to hide them in a drop-down menu. Moreover, the control of the zoom level with just two buttons found little acceptance and will most likely be replaced with a slider.

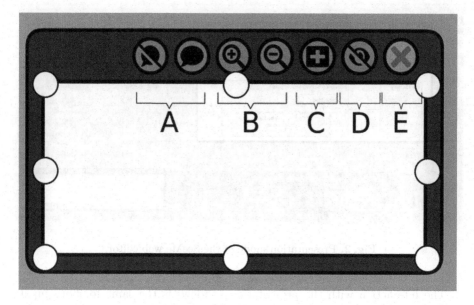

Fig. 3. A presentation window with markers for resizing and several buttons providing the following functions: Hide/Show comments within the window (A); Increase/Decrease the zoom level of the model (B); Create another presentation window (C); Suspend the presentation mode (D); Delete this window (E)

The interaction with the windows was intuitively understood by the experts but it was found that the required touch gestures have to be quite precise to correctly hit the frame and buttons of a presentation window. The presenter had to concentrate on the touch precision and it became difficult to reliably resize or move a window while simultaneously moderating a discussion. A new challenge resulting from that is to make the touch interaction more reliable without increasing the complexity of the required gestures, or without enlarging touchable areas, since such an enlargement would also draw additional attention by their visual appearance.

5   Outlook

When all issues are resolved that were mentioned in the first iteration, a larger evaluation of the presentation mode is planned. In this larger-scale evaluation, the presentation mode is supposed to be used by students in seminars to present projects with corresponding process/system models. After a presentation, the presenter will leave the room and participate in a semi-structured interview, whereas the audience's comments on the presentation mode will be noted. To assess the usability of the system, the System Usability Scale (SUS) [1] will be used, as well as interviews to understand the reasons behind problems and to identify possibilities for improvement. Additionally, video recordings of the presentations can be used for a more detailed analysis of the system use, including for instance an assessment of the movements the presenter performed or the preference for using certain features of the presentation mode.

As the editor is under constant development, upcoming features and updates will lead to changes in the presentation mode. Usage during the course of a seminar phase should offer enough aspects to improve. At the end of the seminar, the usability scores should reflect the software's maturity. Based on the evaluation results, it should be possible to determine which challenges were met and which aspects have to be considered when developing the next iteration. The most prominent challenge under evaluation is that newcomers intuitively understand that they can switch to the presentation mode when they explain a model to others that they have drafted, and that they go on using this mode.

Additionally, the presentation mode of the web editor will most likely be expanded by adding further features. For instance, SeeMe models can contain hyperlinks that point to additional information or important references. These information may help the audience to understand certain aspects of the process. Therefore it could be beneficial to extend the presentation mode by a feature to display linked information as part of the presentation.

References

1. Brooke, J.: SUS-a quick and dirty usability scale. In: Jordan, P.W., Thomas, B., Weerdmeester, B.A., McClelland, I.L. (eds.) Usability Evaluation in Industry, pp. 189–194. Taylor & Francis, London (1996)

2. Herrmann, T.: Systems design with the socio-technical walkthrough. In: Whitworth, B., de Moor, A. (eds.) Handbook of Research on Socio-Technical Design and Social Networking Systems, pp. 336–351. IGI Global, Hershey (2009). https://doi.org/10.4018/978-1-60566-264-0.ch023

3. Herrmann, T., Hoffmann, M., Kunau, G., Loser, K.U.: A modelling method for the development of groupware applications as socio-technical systems. Behav. Inf. Technol. **23**(2), 119–135 (2004). https://doi.org/10.1080/01449290310001644840

4. Herrmann, T., Loser, K.U.: Vagueness in models of socio-technical systems. Behav. Inf. Technol. **18**(5), 313–323 (1999). https://doi.org/10.1080/014492999118904

5. Herrmann, T., Loser, K.U., Jahnke, I.: Sociotechnical walkthrough: a means for knowledge integration. Learn. Organ. Int. J. **14**(5), 450–464 (2007). https://doi.org/10.1108/09696470710762664

A Design Kit for Mobile Device-Based Interaction Techniques

Mandy Korzetz[1(✉)], Romina Kühn[1(✉)], Uwe Aßmann[1], and Thomas Schlegel[2]

[1] Software Technology Group, TU Dresden, Dresden, Germany
{mandy.korzetz,romina.kuehn}@tu-dresden.de
[2] Institute of Ubiquitous Mobility Systems, Karlsruhe University
of Applied Sciences, Karlsruhe, Germany
thomas.schlegel@hs-karlsruhe.de

Abstract. Beside designing the graphical interface of mobile applications, mobile phones and their built-in sensors enable various possibilities to engage with digital content in a physical, device-based manner that move beyond the screen content. So-called mobile device-based interactions are characterized by device movements and positions as well as user actions in real space. So far, there is only little guidance available for novice designers and developers to ideate and design new solutions for specific individual or collaborative use cases. Hence, the potential for designing mobile-based interactions is seldom fully exploited. To address this issue, we propose a design kit for mobile device-based interaction techniques following a morphological approach. Overall, the kit comprises seven dimensions with several elements that can be easily combined with each other to form an interaction technique by selecting at least one entry of each dimension. The design kit can be used to support designers in exploring novel mobile interaction techniques to specific interaction problems in the ideation phase of the design process but also in the analysis of existing device-based interaction solutions.

Keywords: Design kit · Design space · Device-based interaction · Gestures · Mobile phone

1 Introduction

Smartphones have become constant companions of our daily life. They are included in our daily activities and support us on the way, for example, with playing our favorite music or podcast, writing shopping lists, planning trips, or taking and sharing photos with others. Usually these functions can be started using touch interactions of the graphical interface. Beside touch screens, common smartphones are equipped with a variety of sensors that can be used to provide alternative ways to interact with the device in a physical, device-based manner. For example, users can share information with other devices by performing a throw movement [18], expand the working area by juxtaposing multiple devices [16], or rate displayed content by ordering multiple devices on a

C. Stephanidis and M. Antona (Eds.): HCII 2020, CCIS 1224, pp. 52–59, 2020.
https://doi.org/10.1007/978-3-030-50726-8_7

table [10]. Such mobile device-based interactions provide an easy and fast way to access specific smartphone functionality. They harness built-in sensors to estimate device movements and positions or in general user actions in real space [9]. As mobile usage often occurs when user's attention is divided among multiple tasks, such interactions enable an intuitive and seamless integration into daily activities. Moreover, they can enhance collaborative scenarios by enabling physical multi-device interaction and facilitate working digitally face-to-face without media breaks.

Although there is a lot of research that proposes device-based interaction solutions for individual, e.g. [13,19], as well as collaborative use cases, e.g. [5,7,11], only little guidance is available to support designers and developers in ideating and designing novel device-based interaction solutions. This is one of the main reasons why only a few device-based interactions have found their way into commercial applications. Early phases for designing interfaces often are characterized by sketching. Resources like templates and stencils (e.g. UI Stencils[1]) can support paper work, various software tools (e.g. Adobe XD[2], Framer[3]) support digital design of mobile interfaces. Reference guides or gesture cards (e.g. *Touch Reference Guide* by Luke Wroblewski[4]) help designing touch interactions. Such tools focus on the visual aspects of designing interfaces but lack supporting physical interaction and rely on knowledge of the possibilities of the device sensors that go beyond the screen. Hence, the potential for designing mobile interactions is seldom fully exploited. To fill this gap, we propose a design kit to support designers and developers of mobile interfaces that is suited for device-based interaction techniques. Furthermore, the kit enables designers and developers to get a general idea of physical interaction possibilities.

Our design kit follows a morphological approach developed by Zwicky [21] and intends to support especially the early phases of designing interactions. It can be used twofold: for exploring and communicating novel interaction techniques during ideation (bottom-up approach) but also for analyzing existing device-based interaction solutions to learn from them (top-down approach). The kit comprises seven dimensions with different elements that can be easily combined with each other to form an interaction technique. The dimensions span the design space for physical interaction techniques with mobile phones, and help researchers and practitioners to continue working on concepts that enhance mobile interaction.

The paper is organized as follows: First, we give an overview of related work concerning approaches for designing interactions and gestures as well as using morphology for design. Based on this, we describe the details of our design kit for mobile device-based interaction techniques and how it can be applied in interaction design. Finally, we discuss the implications of this work and give an outlook on next steps.

---

[1] https://www.uistencils.com/.

[2] https://www.adobe.com/at/products/xd.html.

[3] https://www.framer.com/.

[4] https://static.lukew.com/TouchGestureGuide.pdf.

2   Related Work

In order to develop a design kit to define novel concepts for mobile device-based interactions, we considered approaches for designing interactions within the related research area of gestural interfaces. Furthermore, we examined related work in terms of using the morphological approach for design.

2.1   Approaches for Gestural Interaction Design

Nielsen et al. proposed a participatory design approach by involving potential end users in the design process [17]. The design process works as follows: given several tasks, study participants were asked to specify gestures that would execute these tasks. Commonly used gestures were collected in a gesture set. Within a last step, the resulting gesture set is checked back by asking participants to guess functions to presented gestures. Designing gestures with user involvement has been applied in different interaction domains, e.g. hand gestures [17], surface gestures for tabletop interaction [20], motion gestures with mobile phones [19], and three-dimensional mobile gestures for smart home control [12]. The participatory approach is intended to reach a high level of intuitiveness and ergonomics in the developed gestures but is also a complex and time consuming process. Additionally, it needs knowledge about user research methods. Because of the high effort it is less appropriate for projects with limited time and budget. Furthermore, mobile-based interactions are still relatively unfamiliar to users, the outcome of novel ideas may be limited. Overall, existing interaction solutions are only taken into consideration to a very limited extent. To meet the requirements of the user's needs as well as technological innovations, interaction designers should start with their ideas from metaphors [6], which we included in our design kit as first inspiration.

2.2   Morphology for Design

Using a morphological box for solving problems can be traced back to Zwicky, who introduced it to the classification of astrophysical objects and the design of jet engines and rocket propulsion systems [21]. It is a methodical framework for structuring and analysing any type of multi-dimensional, non-quantified problem with the aim to explore possible solutions [1]. As a morphological box maps all possible parameters of solutions, it also defines the design space of an abstract construct. The morphological approach has been applied to many diverse domains, from engineering and product design to policy analysis and organisational design. In the fields of visualization and interfaces, the morphological approach was applied, for example, to the graphical design of diagrams, networks, and maps [2] and to timeline design [3]. Mackinlay and Card proposed the morphological approach for describing the design space of input devices [4,14]. To our best knowledge there is no research that applied that morphology to physical interaction with mobile phones. To address this issue, we propose a design kit especially for mobile device-based interaction techniques and define the design space to support producing novel interaction designs.

3   Interaction Design Kit

The development of our design kit bases on a comprehensive analysis of related work from research and practice, which includes a broad range of specific interaction solutions for individual (e.g. [13,18,19]) and collaborative usage scenarios with multiple devices (e.g. [5,7,10,11,16]) as well as the *mobile spaces* model by Korzetz et al. [9]. We extracted relevant elements and aggregated them to dimensions using reverse engineering. The elements were combined with each other to form an interaction technique. Figure 1 shows the design kit with its seven dimensions. In the following, we address these dimensions in more detail.

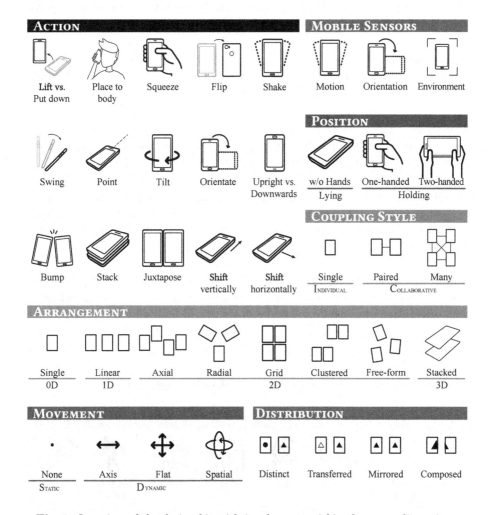

Fig. 1. Overview of the design kit with its elements within the seven dimensions.

Action. This dimension describes the users' possibilities to manipulate their devices physically, e.g. flipping [19] or swinging [18]. The elements of this dimension cover user actions which are simple and lightweight to use and well-known from everyday life.

Position. The position describes the placement of the device in relation to the users' hands. Users can hold the phone with one hand or with both hands. It is also possible to design an interaction where the device is lying on a surface.

Coupling Style. This dimension characterizes the devices' connection within a device group (cp. [15]). Devices can operate independently (*single*), in pairs (*paired*), or each device is connected to all others (*many*).

Arrangement. This dimension refers to the physical arrangement of one or more mobile devices. An arrangement can be static or serve as a starting point for dynamic interactions where devices are replaced.

Movement. The movement dimension maps possible device motions in space that range from a static position (*none*) to dynamic motions in one (*axis*), two (*flat*), or three dimensions (*spatial*).

Distribution. This dimension describes how information is distributed and if it is available for all devices at any time. Information can be *transferred* from one device to another, *mirrored* to other devices, or information among devices is *composed* or *distinct*.

Mobile Sensors. Mobile sensors bridge the gap between design and implementation. This dimension refers to the main sensor classes of motion (e.g. accelerometer), orientation, and environmental sensors (e.g. illumination).

Inspirational Metaphors. An additional set of metaphors (see Fig. 2) that we excerpted from our literature review helps designers to organize design thinking and to identify appropriate elements for their linked system functions.

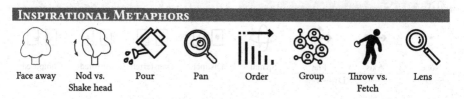

INSPIRATIONAL METAPHORS

Face away   Nod vs.   Pour   Pan   Order   Group   Throw vs.   Lens
             Shake head   Fetch

Fig. 2. Metaphors as additional ideation support (extract).

4   Usage of the Design Kit

Our design kit can be applied bottom-up for creating and exploring novel inter-action solutions (*composing*) but also in a top-down approach for analyzing existing solutions by *decomposing* interaction techniques. For composing new interaction techniques, the elements can be combined by assigning at least one element from each of the seven dimensions. Figure 3 shows *Order to Vote* [10] as an example of a mobile-based interaction technique, where multiple devices are arranged in a row on a table and users are enabled to rate displayed con-tent by rearranging their order. This interaction can be described by combining the elements *juxtapose, lying, many* coupling, *linear* arrangement, *axial* move-ment, *distinct* content distribution, and by using the *motion* sensors. In further steps, designers can complement the resulting combination by describing the connected task (here: voting or rating) and how the connection works (discrete or continuous). The main application of the design kit is exploring new and dif-ferent mobile-based interactions to facilitate brainstorming and communicating interaction ideas. This can be done by using the provided elements. Moreover, it serves as a starting point for capturing interaction knowledge by extending the design kit with new elements if possible.

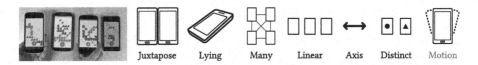

Fig. 3. Description of *Order to Vote* [10] with the design kit.

5   Conclusion and Future Work

We proposed a design kit for mobile device-based interaction techniques, which are characterized by physical manipulations in real space. The design kit aims at supporting designers and developers in the ideation phase of the design process. It follows a morphological approach and therefore provides a structured inventory of possible solutions. The kit comprising of dimensions and elements can be easily applied top-down for analyzing existing interaction solutions and bottom-up for exploring and composing novel interaction techniques. With an example, we presented how users can capture their ideas by combining the elements. To ensure the reuse of proven solutions, we plan to expand the capturing in form of interaction patterns.

Our next steps include a user study with designers and developers of mobile interfaces to assess the structure and elements of the design kit in terms of the usage and completeness. We further plan a digital variant of our current paper-based design kit that enables users to integrate their interactions in existing design tools. To support further processing in terms of creating interactive prototypes, we intend to integrate relevant kit elements in our *MilkyWay* toolbox [8]. As mobile device-based interaction solutions exist in research, we hereby provide an easy to use tool with the aim to gain more visibility of mobile device-based interactions in practice.

Acknowledgements. The European Social Fund (ESF) and the German Federal State of Saxony have funded this work within the project CyPhyMan (100268299). Also funded by the German Research Foundation (DFG, Deutsche Forschungsgemeinschaft) as part of Germany's Excellence Strategy – EXC 2050/1 – Project ID 390696704 – Cluster of Excellence "Centre for Tactile Internet with Human-in-the-Loop" (CeTI) of Technische Universität Dresden. The figures of this work include icons made by Flaticon (https://www.flaticon.com).

References

1. Álvarez, A., Ritchey, T.: Applications of general morphological analysis: from engineering design to policy analysis. Acta Morphologica Generalis (AMG): On-line Res. J. Swed. Morphological Soc. **4**(1) (2015). ISSN 2001-2241
2. Bertin, J.: Semiology of Graphics. University of Wisconsin Press, Madison (1983)
3. Brehmer, M., Lee, B., Bach, B., Riche, N.H., Munzner, T.: Timelines revisited: a design space and considerations for expressive storytelling. IEEE Trans. Visual Comput. Graphics **23**(9), 2151–2164 (2017)
4. Card, S.K., Mackinlay, J.D., Robertson, G.G.: A morphological analysis of the design space of input devices. ACM Trans. Inf. Syst. **9**(2), 99–122 (1991). https://doi.org/10.1145/123078.128726
5. Jokela, T., Lucero, A.: FlexiGroups: binding mobile devices for collaborative interactions in medium-sized groups with device touch. In: Quigley, A., Diamond, S., Irani, P., Subramanian, S. (eds.) Proceedings of the 16th ACM International Conference on Human-Computer Interaction with Mobile Devices and Services, pp. 369–378. ACM (2015). https://doi.org/10.1145/2628363.2628376
6. Keck, M., Lapczyna, E., Groh, R.: Revisiting graspable user interfaces. In: Marcus, A. (ed.) DUXU 2014. LNCS, vol. 8517, pp. 130–141. Springer, Cham (2014). https://doi.org/10.1007/978-3-319-07668-3_14
7. Korzetz, M., Kühn, R., Heisig, P., Schlegel, T.: Natural collocated interactions for merging results with mobile devices. In: Proceedings of the 18th International Conference on Human-Computer Interaction with Mobile Devices and Services Adjunct, MobileHCI 2016, pp. 746–752. ACM (2016). https://doi.org/10.1145/2957265.2961839
8. Korzetz, M., Kühn, R., Kegel, K., Georgi, L., Schumann, F.-W., Schlegel, T.: *MilkyWay*: a toolbox for prototyping collaborative mobile-based interaction techniques. In: Antona, M., Stephanidis, C. (eds.) HCII 2019. LNCS, vol. 11573, pp. 477–490. Springer, Cham (2019). https://doi.org/10.1007/978-3-030-23563-5_38
9. Korzetz, M., Kühn, R., Schlegel, T.: Turn it, pour it, twist it: a model for designing mobile device-based interactions. In: Proceedings of the 5th International Conference on Human-Computer Interaction and User Experience in Indonesia, CHIuXiD 2019, pp. 20–23. ACM (2019). https://doi.org/10.1145/3328243.3328246

10. Kühn, R., Korzetz, M., Büschel, L., Korger, C., Manja, P., Schlegel, T.: Natural voting interactions for collaborative work with mobile devices. In: Proceedings of the CHI Conference Extended Abstracts on Human Factors in Computing Systems, CHI EA 2016, pp. 2570–2575. ACM (2016). https://doi.org/10.1145/2851581.2892300

11. Kühn, R., Korzetz, M., Schumann, F.-W., Büschel, L., Schlegel, T.: Vote-for-it: investigating mobile device-based interaction techniques for collocated anonymous voting and rating. In: Lamas, D., Loizides, F., Nacke, L., Petrie, H., Winckler, M., Zaphiris, P. (eds.) INTERACT 2019. LNCS, vol. 11746, pp. 585–605. Springer, Cham (2019). https://doi.org/10.1007/978-3-030-29381-9_36

12. Kühnel, C., Westermann, T., Hemmert, F., Kratz, S., Müller, A., Möller, S.: I'm home: defining and evaluating a gesture set for smart-home control. Int. J. Hum. Comput. Stud. **69**(11), 693–704 (2011). https://doi.org/10.1016/j.ijhcs.2011.04.005

13. Ljubic, S., Kukec, M., Glavinic, V.: Tilt-based support for multimodal text entry on touchscreen smartphones: using pitch and roll. In: Stephanidis, C., Antona, M. (eds.) UAHCI 2013. LNCS, vol. 8011, pp. 651–660. Springer, Heidelberg (2013). https://doi.org/10.1007/978-3-642-39194-1_75

14. Mackinlay, J., Card, S.K., Robertson, G.G.: A semantic analysis of the design space of input devices. Hum. Comput. Interact. **5**(2–3), 145–190 (1990). https://doi.org/10.1080/07370024.1990.9667153

15. Neumayr, T., Jetter, H.C., Augstein, M., Friedl, J., Luger, T.: Domino: a descriptive framework for hybrid collaboration and coupling styles in partially distributed teams. In: Proceedings of the ACM on Human-Computer Interaction 2(CSCW), pp. 1–24 (2018). https://doi.org/10.1145/3274397

16. Nielsen, H.S., Olsen, M.P., Skov, M.B., Kjeldskov, J.: JuxtaPinch: exploring multi-device interaction in collocated photo sharing. In: Proceedings of the 16th International Conference on Human-Computer Interaction with Mobile Devices & Services, MobileHCI 2014, pp. 183–192. Association for Computing Machinery (2014). https://doi.org/10.1145/2628363.2628369

17. Nielsen, M., Störring, M., Moeslund, T.B., Granum, E.: A procedure for developing intuitive and ergonomic gesture interfaces for HCI. In: Camurri, A., Volpe, G. (eds.) GW 2003. LNCS (LNAI), vol. 2915, pp. 409–420. Springer, Heidelberg (2004). https://doi.org/10.1007/978-3-540-24598-8_38

18. Paay, J., et al.: A comparison of techniques for cross-device interaction from mobile devices to large displays. In: Proceedings of the 14th International Conference on Advances in Mobile Computing and Multi Media, MoMM 2016, pp. 137–146. ACM (2016). https://doi.org/10.1145/3007120.3007140

19. Ruiz, J., Li, Y., Lank, E.: User-defined motion gestures for mobile interaction. In: Tan, D. (ed.) Proceedings of the SIGCHI Conference on Human Factors in Computing Systems (CHI 2011), p. 197. ACM Digital Library, ACM, New York (2011). https://doi.org/10.1145/1978942.1978971

20. Wobbrock, J.O., Morris, M.R., Wilson, A.D.: User-defined gestures for surface computing. In: Proceedings of the SIGCHI Conference on Human Factors in Computing Systems, CHI 2009, pp. 1083–1092. ACM (2009). https://doi.org/10.1145/1518701.1518866

21. Zwicky, F.: The morphological approach to discovery, invention, research and construction. In: Zwicky, F., Wilson, A.G. (eds.) New Methods of Thought and Procedure, pp. 273–297. Springer, Heidelberg (1967). https://doi.org/10.1007/978-3-642-87617-2_14

Conceptual Structure
of the Virtual Environment as a Factor
# of Human-Computer Interaction

Sergey I. Kruzhilov[1,2]([✉])

[1] Financial University under the Government of the Russian Federation,
49 Leningradsky Prospekt, 125993 Moscow, Russian Federation
SKrujilov@fa.ru
[2] National Research University "Moscow Power Engineering Institute",
Krasnokazarmennaya 14, 111250 Moscow, Russian Federation
KruzhilovSI@mpei.ru

Abstract. The study discusses the principles of systematization of the conceptual basis of the user's virtual space. The conceptual unification of the environmental structure allows combining an operating systems environment and the global information environment into a single system, which will simplify the process of user interaction with the system. The conceptual homogeneity of the environment is ensured by the unification of the conceptual basis of space with the categories "personality, domain, site, data object". The spatial category of "domain" is a means of delineating ownership rights and structuring virtual space. Its use allows us to rid the user of concepts such as "computer" and "memory device" and to combine all kinds of areas from local disk space to the cloud services into a single whole. The spatial category "site", a place for interacting with people and working with data, allows abandoning the concept of "program". Using work sites with toolsets and desktops, the user solves their application tasks. Sites with Data partitions and containers become the primary means of organizing data. The data object category associated with user application objects is a means of combining different data into a single structure. The "portal" concept is a means of "transferring" users from one place of virtual space to another. Portals hiding the specifics from the user interaction are a universal means of ensuring methodological homogeneity. The concept of "portal" is an extension of concepts such as "reference" and "shortcut". The requirement of methodological uniformity also implies the use of a single client-server principle for organizing the user interface, with the separation of the user "client" from the executive site server providing services for solving user tasks.

Keywords: Human-Computer interaction · Virtual space · System homogeneity · Conceptual basis

1 Introduction

Currently, user activity in a virtual environment is complicated by the heterogeneity of this environment, which arose due to the weak connection of various processes of its formation. Currently, the principles of virtual operating system environments are

C. Stephanidis and M. Antona (Eds.): HCII 2020, CCIS 1224, pp. 60–67, 2020.
https://doi.org/10.1007/978-3-030-50726-8_8

different from those of a virtual web environment. They differ in both a set of concepts and methods of interaction.

The structures of the operating system environments are built on the "desktop" metaphor [1–3], which is strongly related both to the concepts of computer architecture and to the specific categorical basis of the scientific community that created and developed computer technologies. This conceptual basis, up to the designation of concepts, is used in all widespread operating systems [4–6]. The basic principle of these systems is the "program-data" dichotomy. The "program" category corresponds to such concepts as "application", "task", and "window". The categories "data" correspond to the concepts of "file system": "memory devices", "desktops", "folders", and "files". For references to applications and data, shortcuts are used. For the average user, the concept of a program, like the concept of a memory device, are abstractions. He interacts not with programs, but with intellectual graphic signs on a monitor screen. The same signs represent his data. An ordinary user does not need to know the details of computer architecture, just like he does not need to go into the details of the mechanics of the car to drive it.

The structure of the web space that arose later is based on other principles that are less related to computer architecture [7]. In this space, the user dispenses with the concepts of "computer", "program", or "memory device". The user represents the network environment as a set of "domains" with informational "sites" with data. The site structure is built on the principles of the hypertext book model.

The data is located on the "pages" and consists of text, tables, figures, and links to other pages and sites. Hypertext was later expanded to "hypermedia" by the inclusion of interactive graphics, sound, and video. In the future, sites appeared in their function indistinguishable from software applications. Thus, the concept of a site began to be used for both data and applications.

There have been several attempts to unify the structure of the virtual space. However, unification was carried out due to the almost complete transfer of user space to the web environment, for example, as in Chromebook with Chrom OS [8]. This work aims to unify the conceptual structure of virtual space for combining local and global environments into a single virtual environment based on general system principles.

2   The Conceptual Structure of the Space

Systematization of the virtual space involves both the conceptual and the methodological homogeneity of the user environment. The conceptual homogeneity of the medium implies a unity of conceptual basis for operating system environments and web environments. At the same time, independence of this basis from specific concepts of computer architecture has to be provided [9]. Also, the conceptual structure of the virtual environment should be as close as possible to the structure of the human physical environment, which will allow the user to transfer his personal experience and thus reduce the period of adaptation of the user to the virtual environment. Methodological homogeneity implies the dependence of the methods of user interaction with the objects of the environment only on their conceptual type. The methods of interaction should be the same for both local and remote objects.

The principles of the human cognitive apparatus underlie the object-oriented perception of the world. A person automatically selects entities, limited by the contour, from the general background of the environment. The concept of "object" corresponds to limited entities, and "space" corresponds to the general background of the environment. The most important objects for a person are other people, which requires the inclusion of the concept of "person" in a common conceptual basis. Thus, the basis expands to the triad "person - space – object". In this space, people interact with each other, creating social groups to solve various problems jointly. To solve these problems, people use various objects as means. People divide their spaces into separate areas for effective orientation. To interact with people and work with objects, a person uses specific worksites with tool kits for interaction, work, study, or rest. People create warehouse sites for storing objects. Thus, the general conceptual basis of the human environment expands to the tetrad "person - space - worksite - object".

It is easy to see that the conceptual basis of the person and the basis of the web environment are very close. None of these bases are related to specific concepts of computer architecture. Therefore, when developing the general structure of virtual space, it is natural to take as a basis a modified categorical basis of the web environment. The structure of the virtual space can be described in machine-independent categories "person", "domain", "site", and "data object".

"Person" is the central category basis. Virtual space is an environment for solving problems of people, giving them the ability to coordinate their actions, to use the resources of this environment, and share them. Individuals are owners and users of resources of the virtual space. A person is associated with property rights. As an owner, person defines a policy of access to his resources.

A "domain" is a category used as a means of structuring a virtual space environment and sharing property rights. This category allows providing a conceptual uniformity in the organization structure of the userspace. Virtual space from the user's point of view consists of an ordered group of domains. User data are physically stored on computer memory devices. The concept of "domain" allows hiding from the user the specifics of working with devices. The user must deal not with devices, but with structurally homogeneous regions of the environment. With this approach, domains or subdomains are all sections of memory on permanent and mounted computer memory devices, as well as sections of the web environment, such as "cloud spaces" or web domains. "Desktops" of operating systems are becoming varieties of subdomains.

The concept of a personal computer can be replaced by the concept of a user's domain, which allows the user to be abstract from the specifics of the devices used. From the user's point of view, virtual space does not become a network of computers, but a network of interconnected domains. A personal domain, as a device-independent environment, can be transferred from one device to another. When connected to a global network, this domain becomes its integral part. The user environment becomes scalable due to the ability to connect the domains of other users to the network of personal domains.

Registration of personal domains can be carried out in global domains of a higher level, national and international. Upon registration, the personal domain receives a unique global identifier consisting of the domain identifier and the unique identifier within the domain. Subdomain and site identifiers are generated automatically.

A personal domain name is its additional property, which is necessary for distinguishing domains by a person in a local context.

"Site" is a category related to places intended for interaction between individuals or for working with data objects. The concept of "site" allows you to abandon the use of the concept of "program" and change the principles of structuring data in the environment of operating systems. A site is not a program, but an environment with sets of iconic graphic objects. In essence, the concept of "site" corresponds to the concept of "task window". Sites contain the necessary toolkits and desktops for displaying data object structures. A single virtual environment should provide the ability for the user to work both on their local sites and sites in the global environment, including the sites of other users. At the same time, the user's work methods should not depend on the location of sites. Data sites receive their unique digital identifiers automatically within a personal domain. Personal site names, as a way of common naming for a person, are assigned by the user. For remote access to the site, it needs to know the identifier of the user's domain and the identifier of the site in this domain.

The introduction of the concept of "data site" will make it possible to unify the user data organization system. Traditional web sites, consisting of a set of web pages with data, are nothing more than structured places for storing data. With this approach, the data structure can be described using the concepts of "data site", "section", and "container". Data sites are places to store user data. They become the top of the data structure. Structuring data within the site is carried out using the concepts of "section" and "container". A section is a separate place on the data site as a means of classifying data. Sections play the same role on a data site as domains in a virtual space. Containers, like folders, are a mobile means of storing related data sets. They can be moved along with the data. This method of structuring data is an alternative to the concept of a "file system", where the concept of a "folder" is a universal structuring element. The identification of storage data objects should be carried out inside the data site itself. That is, when moving or copying a data object from one site to another, it changes its identifier. Accordingly, an object identifier consists of a domain identifier, a data site identifier, and an object identifier within the data site.

Worksites are designed to work with data objects. In the general case, the structure of work sites includes a desktop for displaying data structures and corresponding toolkits. Different approaches to organizing the structure of work sites differ in the principle of work organization. In practice, two organizational principles are used: classification and technological. The traditional classification principle is to split the entire set of tools into disjoint subsets. When using this principle, there is no redundancy. Knowing the appropriate class allows reducing the access time to the desired tool. With this approach, the user as a handicraftsman, works at one desktop, using all the tools available to him. The implementation of the classification principle is carried out using the menu and sets of interchangeable toolbars.

The technological principle of the organization of work is based on the division of labor and consists of dividing the technological cycle of work into separate types of work. Each type of work is carried out at its working place with its desktop and a limited set of tools. The set of tools should be sufficient to carry out work at the appropriate technological stage. At the same time, the same tools can be included in different sets at different workstations. Currently, the classification principle dominates in the computer environment, although the technological one dominates in the real production environment. Using the technological principle allows in many cases to make the user interface friendly.

The difference between the described approaches can be illustrated by the example of organizing the environment of a Microsoft Word text editor [15]. The tools there are divided according to the classification principle into disjoint classes according to specific criteria: File, Home, Insert, Design, Layout, References, Mailing, and others. The toolbox on the ribbon changes when the user selects a class.

For a technological approach, it would be more logical to divide the document creation process into stages according to the logic of building the document structure. The number of conceptual element types of any document is limited. To create each of these elements, users need a desktop with a specific set of tools. From this approach, to create a document, a group of specialized workplaces is needed: "Document" - a workplace with tools for working with a document as a whole, "Text" - a workplace with tools for entering and formatting text, "Table" - with tools for creating tables, "Drawing" - with tools for inserting and editing images, "Reference" - for inserting links and others. However, in this case, some of the tools could be repeated at different workplaces.

A site is a local place that provides the user with everything necessary for productive work. The site should ensure the reliability of the user and give him the ability to access all the resources necessary for work. Therefore, the site must-have tools for local management and a database to save the results and context of the user's work. Access to the site is carried out from the site management system. Access to all other resources necessary for work should be carried out inside the site. The user should not lose the results of his work under any circumstances [9]. For the reliability of the work, users can use data sites associated with the work site, which will store both work objects and operation logs to restore the results of failures, containers for deleted objects, the clipboard, and settings for the site environment. When working with data sites, the work context can be stored in one of the service partitions of this site. Examples of sites similar in organization principles include browsers, which include a local line for managing open sites, a download area, job logs, transaction history, and user-customizable directories of selected links [10–12].

The concept of "data object" or "data" as a more general one can completely replace the concept of "file". There are different points of view on the structure of data objects: users can consider an object as a single aggregate or as a structure consisting of a set of related objects. In the first approach, the data object is considered as a single entity, which is stored as a single binary structure. Work with such objects is usually carried out on one desktop using the classification principle of access to tools. In the second case, the data object can be considered as a set of separate interconnected binary objects. For example, a document is a structure of a text, figures, tables, formulas, and links. In the same way, a film is a structure consisting of video sequences, audio tracks, and subtitles. Work with individual parts can be carried out as part of a technological approach at separate workplaces with separate desktop and corresponding sets of tools. Storage of a group of interrelated objects is carried out in a single package. The concept of "packaging" is close to the concept of "container" except that each packaging "has its specific conceptual type. The package has its table of contents indicating the corresponding data structure elements. Packaging can be considered as a development of the concept of a file. Examples of packaging are data storage formats such as AVI [13] or JPEG [14].

3   The Methodological Homogeneity of the Interaction

A user's work in virtual space is interaction with sets of intelligent iconic objects on a monitor screen. The following types of iconic objects can be distinguished: signs of data objects, signs of tools, and signs of portals. The signs of data objects are rigidly associated with specific binary structures of data objects in the computer's memory. Moving a character from one place in space to another leads to a movement of the corresponding binary structure of the object in the computer's memory. Signs of data objects are used to denote both data objects and individuals. The "Avatar" sign of the person in the address book allows you to integrate social information about a person and how to communicate with him. The structure of data objects can only be changed at the corresponding work sites. Signs of tools are a means for influencing other objects. Tools are associated with hidden software agents that implement their functions. Typically, such signs are used to indicate tools on sites.

Portal signs are "vehicles" for moving a user to various places in the virtual space. The concept of "portal" is an extension of such concepts as "link" and "label". Activation of the portal sign causes a software agent that changes the visible structure of the signs on the monitor screen, which is perceived by the user as moving to another area of the virtual space. Thus, portals are a universal way of forming hyper network structures for all basic conceptual types of objects.

Portals are the means of implementing methodological homogeneity in virtual space. Their use makes it possible to ensure both uniform access to the resources of virtual space and uniform methods of interaction with these resources, regardless of their location. Uniformity of access consists in the fact that users can get into any part of the space only by activating the sign of the corresponding portal. Since the portal is the entry point into the space, an exit portal should be provided inside the space that returns the user to the original location.

Using portals allows hiding from the user the specifics of the organization of interaction with local and remote resources of the environment. With this approach, the methods of interaction with environmental resources will be determined only by the conceptual type of the corresponding iconic object and not depend on its location. A particular case of this approach can be seen, for example, in the Android system [6].

The difference between portals and regular links is that portals, in the general case, are not only a means of transition but also a means of integrating programs with data. The portal structure can include not only links to software resource agents and protocols for interacting with them but also links to sets of parameters passed to agents and links to data platforms for storing the context of work on these sites. The transmitted parameters provide the adaptive interaction of software agents. Moreover, maintaining the context of work makes it possible to ensure the reliability and stability of the user in case of possible system failures or errors.

In virtual space, the user should not be burdened with the work of creating portals. The portal structure should be generated automatically. For this, the system has all the necessary information. Signs of portals with the necessary information can be sent to other users as a means of access to their resources. Varieties of portals providing access to personalities can be "visiting cards" of people with the necessary personal information about a person and how to contact him.

The requirement of methodological uniformity implies the use in the local environment of the same network client-server principle of organization of interaction as in the global environment. With this approach, programs consist of two interacting parts: the user interface agent ("client") and the corresponding resource agent ("server"). The "client" function is to display on the screen the iconic structure of space transmitted by the resource agent. The task of the "server" is to adequately respond to user commands. The languages for interaction may be different. The implementation of the graphical interface can be carried out both with the vector graphics metafile and with the hypertext markup languages. For the exchange of information between the "client" and the "server" in the system, a local information transmission channel is needed, integrated with the global network. Server agents can be located on the server-side of both the local and the remote domain. By specifying the necessary information transfer channel in the portal, it is possible to provide both local and remote user access to the sites. With this method of organizing interaction, interface agents are separated from programs and become universal parts of the system.

4 Conclusion

By the basic principle of science, "Occam's Razor", the maximum simplification of the explanatory model without losing its functionality makes it easier to use in practice. The work systematized the structure of space at three levels: conceptual, symbolic and physical.

At the conceptual level, the transition to a single conceptual basis with the categories of "personality, domain, site, data" will allow unifying the structure of local and global space. This basis does not contain concepts related to computer architecture. Besides, the transition to the proposed conceptual basis will provide an opportunity at the conceptual level to bring the virtual environment closer to the familiar social environment of users. Similar environments will allow users to transfer experience from one environment to another.

At the sign level, portals, as a means of accessing virtual space resources, will ensure the methodological uniformity of user interaction with iconic environment objects. When using portals hiding the specifics of interaction from the user, interaction methods become dependent only on the conceptual type of the corresponding sign object.

At the implementation level, the client-server principle of organizing the user interface will ensure uniform access to both local and remote resources of the environment.

The proposed principles of structuring the virtual space will allow the user to create a complete personal environment with resources located both on their personal computer and on remote computers. The thin client environment, in which user resources are located mainly on other servers, becomes a special case of this approach. The results can be used in the design of interfaces of perspective operating systems.

Acknowledgments. The article was prepared based on the results of studies carried out at the expense of budget funds on the state order of the Financial University under the Government of the Russian Federation.

References

1. Desktop metaphor. https://en.wikipedia.org/wiki/Desktop_metaphor. Accessed 20 Feb 2020
2. Desktop environment. https://en.wikipedia.org/wiki/Desktop_environment. Accessed 20 Feb 2020
3. Freedesktop organization. https://www.freedesktop.org/wiki/. Accessed 20 Feb 2020
4. Windows. https://en.wikipedia.org/wiki/Windows_10#User_interface_and_desktop. Accessed 20 Feb 2020
5. MacOS. https://en.wikipedia.org/wiki/MacOS#Aqua_user_interface. Accessed 20 Feb 2020
6. Android, https://en.wikipedia.org/wiki/Android_(operating_system)#Interface. Accessed 20 Feb 2020
7. The World Wide Web. https://en.wikipedia.org/wiki/World_Wide_Web. Accessed 20 Feb 2020
8. The Chrome OS. https://en.wikipedia.org/wiki/Chrome_OS. Accessed 20 Feb 2020
9. Cooper, R., Reimann, R., Cronin, D., Noessel, C.: About Face: The Essentials of Interaction Design, 4th edn. Wiley, Hoboken (2014)
10. Google Chrome. https://en.wikipedia.org/wiki/Google_Chrome. Accessed 20 Feb 2020
11. Safari. https://en.wikipedia.org/wiki/Safari_(web_browser). Accessed 20 Feb 2020
12. Firefox. https://en.wikipedia.org/wiki/Firefox. Accessed 20 Feb 2020
13. Audio Video Interleave. https://en.wikipedia.org/wiki/Audio_Video_Interleave. Accessed 20 Feb 2020
14. JPEG. https://ru.wikipedia.org/wiki/JPEG. Accessed 20 Feb 2020
15. Working with Word 2016 User Interface. https://www.wikigain.com/word-2016-user-interface/. Accessed 20 Feb 2020

Assessing User Behavior
by Mouse Movements

Jennifer Jorina Matthiesen[✉] and Ulf Brefeld

Machine Learning Group, Leuphana University of Lüneburg, Lüneburg, Germany
jennifer.matthiesen@stud.leuphana.de, ulf.brefeld@leuphana.de

Abstract. In this working paper, we study user identification via mouse movement. Instead of treating the problem as a multi-class classification task, we cast user identification as a one-class problem and propose to learn an individual model for every user. Preliminary empirical results show that our approach works for some but not all users. We report on lessons learned.

Keywords: Mouse movement · User identification · User behavior

1 Introduction

User identification is not only key to privacy and security but also offers a way to personalize user experiences, e.g., by displaying user-specific content. Apart from biometric user identification, a non-intrusive alternative is offered by user behavior. In contrast to physical traits, behavioral-based authentication allows for continuous (re-)identification during user sessions. In this context, particularly mouse movements is of interest, as it does not require additional hardware and allows implicit and non-inversive measurements of behavioral biometrics [10,11,16,17].

Similar to gestures in human communication, the dynamics of the pointing device in human-computer interaction are unique and can deliver valuable and deterministic information about the user [2,9,11,16,17]. However, the question raises how such a system could be reasonably build. Traditionally, a multi-class classification approach suggests itself: every user is identified with a class and a classifier chooses the most likely user among the candidates. While such an approach may work for hardly changing environments, dynamic scenarios with many new and deleted users require frequent retraining of the classifier. For a large user base with many sessions per day, this could quickly become infeasible.

By contrast, we treat user identification as an anomaly detection problem [12,13,15] and propose to learn a model of normality for every user. The idea is as follows: As long as the user interacts with the system, the corresponding model correctly identifies the user. If a third user takes over, the identification fails and the model considers the third party as an anomaly and may shut down critical applications and data access points. Maintaining a multitude of these models is simple. Once a user logs in, the right model is retrieved and used until the end of the session.

© Springer Nature Switzerland AG 2020
C. Stephanidis and M. Antona (Eds.): HCII 2020, CCIS 1224, pp. 68–75, 2020.
https://doi.org/10.1007/978-3-030-50726-8_9

Retraining can be trivially parallelized for all users, new user models are integrated by training a single new model, and a deletion of a user simply deletes the corresponding model without any side effects for other models.

Our contributions are as follows: (i) We cast user identification as an anomaly detection problem, where user profiles are learned in a rich (non-linear) feature space spanned by a set of automatically derived features [13, 15] and in a deep neural architecture [12]. (ii) We evaluate the impact of splitting sessions into sequences including pause-based and an equal number of data points splits. (iii) We report on lessons learned that may shed light on future research in this area.

2   Related Work

Mouse movement has been investigated in the context of user authentication [4, 5, 14] and behavioral analyses [2, 3, 10, 16]; a great deal of these publications rely on hand-engineered features [2, 3, 5, 8, 14, 16] though. User identification based on biometrics extracted from mouse behavior has been first introduced by Gamboa & Fred [6]. They proposed a number of features and split the session into single sequences based on mouse clicks. Features are subsequently reduced by greedy search and fed into a sequential classifier. Feher et al. [5] introduce a hierarchical structure of mouse features, proposing in total 66 features. With these features, a random forest classifier is trained using 30 actions for verification. Recently, Chong et al. [4] investigate different architectures for user authentication using mouse data. However, their approach requires to retain the full model with samples of all users, when a new user is added.

3   Algorithms

Perhaps the most prominent one-class-classifier is the **One-Class Support-Vector-Machine** (OC-SVM) [13]. Its objective is to find the max-margin hyperplane that separates the origin from the data, where the latter is mapped by a function ϕ into a (possibly nonlinear) feature space spanned by $\phi : \mathcal{X} \mapsto \mathcal{F}$. Given a training set $\mathcal{D} = \{x_1, ..., x_n\}$ with $x_i \in \mathcal{X}$, the primal problem of the OC-SVM can be written as

$$\min_{\omega, \rho, \xi} \quad \frac{1}{2}\|\omega\|^2 - \rho + \frac{1}{\nu n}\mathbf{1}^\top \xi \quad \text{s.t. } \forall\, i: \; \omega^\top \phi(x_i) \geq \rho - \xi_i \,\wedge\, \xi_i \geq 0$$

where ρ is the distance of the hyperplane to the origin and acts as a threshold such that a new instance x is considered anomalous (not belonging to the class that is represented by data $\mathcal{D}$) if $f(x) = \omega^\top \phi(x) - \rho < 0$.

The **Support Vector Data Description** (SVDD) [15] is similar to the OC-SVM, but uses a hypersphere as a model of normality. The objective of the SVDD is to find the smallest hypersphere, given by radius $R > 0$ and center $c \in \mathcal{F}$, which encloses the majority of the data in feature space. The primal optimization problem is given by

$$\min_{c, R, \xi} \quad R^2 + \frac{1}{\nu n}\mathbf{1}^\top \xi \quad \text{s.t. } \forall\, i: \; \|\phi(x_i) - c\|^2 \leq R^2 + \xi_i \,\wedge\, \xi_i \geq 0.$$

New points are considered anomalous if they lie outside of the hyperball, that is, if $\|\phi(\boldsymbol{x}) - \boldsymbol{c}\|^2 > R^2$.

Recently, [12] presented a deep variant of the SVDD. An autoencoder is used for dimensionality reduction while a second part of the network minimizes the volume of the data-enclosing hypersphere. The objective of the **Deep SVDD** [12] is given by

$$\min_{c,R,\mathcal{W}} \quad R^2 + \frac{1}{\nu n} \sum_{i=1}^{n} \max\{0, \|\phi(\boldsymbol{x}_i; \mathcal{W}) - \boldsymbol{c}\|^2 - R^2\} + \frac{\lambda}{2} \sum_{l=1}^{L} \|\mathcal{W}^l\|^2 \quad \text{s.t. } R > 0$$

The second term penalizes points lying outside the sphere analogously to the traditional SVDD.

4   Empirical Study

We use data from the Balabit Mouse Dynamic Challenge[1] that comprises sessions from ten different users. The training data encompasses five to seven longer sessions for each user while the test set contains multiple smaller sessions. The test set contains also out-of-sample users not present in the training set as well as sessions from anonymous attackers. The latter are simulated by mixing sessions from other users into the test session of a third user. Table 1 summarizes the data.

Table 1. Overview of Balabit Mouse Dynamics Challenge dataset

User	Training			Test				
	files	min_length	max_length	legal	illegal	sessions	min_length	max_length
7	7	43484	**83091**	36	37	73	164	6966
9	7	54418	72732	23	43	66	141	10991
12	7	29722	48244	56	49	105	127	8086
15	6	16971	44015	45	70	115	119	5656
16	6	28428	53816	68	38	106	**114**	3104
20	7	31441	60087	30	20	50	146	**12672**
21	7	15343	21465	37	22	59	154	2170
23	6	17127	28435	38	33	71	157	4706
29	7	**13640**	32601	43	20	63	134	5207
35	5	16901	23107	35	73	108	114	3771
	65			411	405	816		

---

[1] https://github.com/balabit/Mouse-Dynamics-Challenge.

 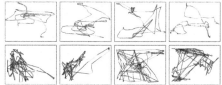

Fig. 1. Sequences produced by the TDS-method, using the 98% quantile of the overall pauses as a splitting criterion. The first row shows legal, while the second row shows illegal sessions of user 7.

Fig. 2. Sequences produced by the EDPS-method, using 200 data points as a splitting criterion. The first row shows legal, while the second row shows illegal sessions of user 7.

4.1 Session Splitting

We split the mouse movement within a session into short sequences. We investigate two different splitting criteria, the first Time Difference Split (TDS) and Equal Number Of Data Points Split (EDPS).

The former splits the session by time differences between two consecutive mouse coordinates. The pauses made by the user during the interaction with the system are an active field of mouse movement research [5,6,16]. Our approach is similar to [4], but instead of setting a hyper-parameter for the time difference splitting criterion, we determine the parameter based on the users' mouse data using quantiles. We study the effect of splitting mouse movements at 95%, 98% and 99% quantiles. This leads to a unique splitting criterion for every user, see Fig. 1.

EDPS splits mouse data into sequences by using a fixed number of data points. We investigating different lengths of sequences ($m \in \{50, 100, 200, 500\}$). Using a fixed number of data points as a splitting criterion ensures that the session is separated and provides sequences of the same length, see Fig. 2.

The splitted sequences are cleaned and the resulting logs contain the following variables: timestamps, (x, y) coordinates, mouse buttons (left, right, scroll) and the action type (move, pressed, released, drag). Since the velocity of a scroll is not given we discard the related actions and ignore scroll operations entirely. We compare the 65 features from [5] with additional 12 features described in the Appendix (Table 2). All features are normalized.

We evaluate area under the curve (AUC) and the equal error rate (EER). The latter is identical to the intersection of the false acceptance rate (FAR) and the false rejection rate (FRR). To not clutter the evaluation part unnecessarily, we report only results for TDS using the 99% quantile and EDPS with length 100 that worked best over all tested parameter settings.

We compare OC-SVM, SVDD, and Deep SVDD and also include a vanilla SVM trained in a one-versus-rest manner, denoted by OvR-SVM for interpretability. The results are shown in Fig. 3 for TDS-99% and Fig. 4 for EDPS-50.

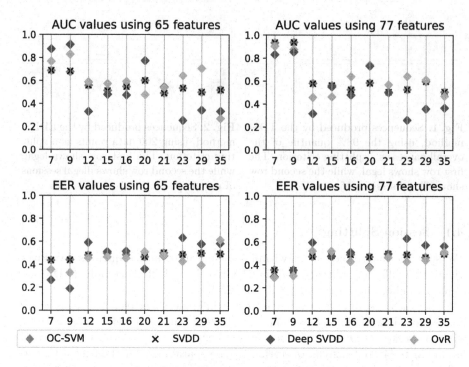

Fig. 3. Results for TDS-99%

Unsurprisingly, the OvR-SVM clearly outperforms the one-class approaches. However, OvR-SVM also uses more information by including unified data from all other users as the negative class in the training process. Thus, OvR-SVM shows that there is room for improvement for the methods of interest, but, by construction, poses a solution that is clearly inappropriate in many practical scenarios. Also unsurprisingly, OC-SVM and SVDD perform equivalent throughout the experiment; for certain normalized feature representation, their objective functions become identical and provide naturally the same solution. The Deep SVDD performs well for user 7, 9 and 20 for sequences derives by the EDPS- as well as the TDS-method on 65 and 77 respectively. This finding gives rise to two conjectures: The first is that some users can, in general, be identified by their mouse movement as was also shown e.g., in [1,4–6,14]. And second, that perhaps the feature representation was simply not the right one for the other users. Thus, it can be hypothesised that the features learned for the authentication process have to be individualized so that the detection performance is maximized (see e.g., [7]).

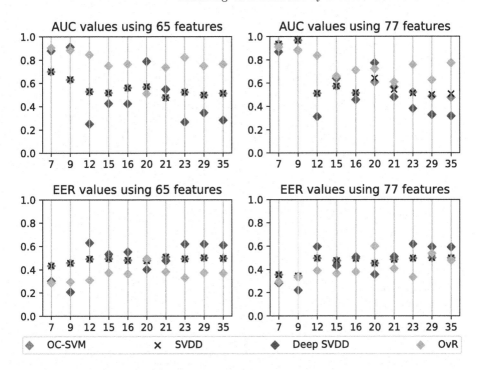

Fig. 4. Results for EDPS-100

5   Conclusions

We studied user identification by mouse movements. Conceptually, we interpreted the problem setting as an anomaly detection problem and evaluated traditional (OC-SVM, SVDD, OvR) and recent (DeepSVDD) methods. Preliminary empirical results showed that some users can actually be identified solely based on their mouse movement. This finding however does not hold for most of the users. Our lessons learned is twofold: (i) We conjecture that mouse behaviour is idiosyncratic, which is in line with other studies [1,4–6,14], and (ii) that we might be able to improve user identification by tailoring (learning) an individual feature representation for every user.

A   Additional Features

Table 2. List of additional features

Feature name	Description	Formal definition
Traveled distance	The sum of the distance between points	$\delta s = \sqrt{\sum_{i=1}^{n}(x_{i+1} - x_i)^2 + (y_{i+1} - y_i)^2}$
Number of data points	Just used in TDS-method	n
Pauses length	$min, max,$ $mean, \sigma$ $(max - min)$	δt
Number of pauses	–	$\sum_{i=1}^{n} p_i \ where \ p_i = \begin{cases} 1, & \delta t_i > threshold \\ 0, & \text{otherwise} \end{cases}$
Number of clicks	–	$\sum_{i=1}^{n} c_i$
Dispersal x	–	$dis_x = \sqrt{(x_{max} - x_{min})^2}$
Dispersal y	–	$dis_y = \sqrt{(y_{max} - y_{min})^2}$
Dispersal	–	$dis = dis_y * dis_x$

References

1. Antal, M., Egyed-Zsigmond, E.: Intrusion detection using mouse dynamics. IET Biometrics **8**, 285–294 (2019)
2. Arapakis, I., Lalmas, M., Valkanas, G.: Understanding within-content engagement through pattern analysis of mouse gestures. In: Proceedings of the 23rd ACM International Conference on Information and Knowledge Management, pp. 1439–1448. ACM (2014)
3. Arapakis, I., Leiva, L.A.: Predicting user engagement with direct displays using mouse cursor information. In: Proceedings of the 39th International ACM SIGIR Conference on Research and Development in Inform. Retrieval, pp. 599–608. ACM (2016)
4. Chong, P., Elovici, Y., Binder, A.: User authentication based on mouse dynamics using deep neural networks: a comprehensive study. IEEE Trans. Inf. Forensics Secur. **15**, 1086–1101 (2020)
5. Feher, C., Elovici, Y., Moskovitch, R., Rokach, L., Schclar, A.: User identity verification via mouse dynamics. Inf. Sci. **201**, 19–36 (2012)
6. Gamboa, H., Fred, A.: A behavioral biometric system based on human-computer interaction. In: Jain, A.K., Ratha, N.K. (eds.) Biometric Technology for Human Identification, vol. 5404, pp. 381–392. SPIE (2004)

7. Kloft, M., Brefeld, U., Sonnenburg, S., Zien, A.: Lp-norm multiple kernel learning. J. Mach. Learn. Res. **12**, 953–997 (2011)
8. Lagun, D., Ageev, M., Guo, Q., Agichtein, E.: Discovering common motifs in cursor movement data for improving web search. In: Proceedings of the 7th ACM International Conference on Web Search and Data Mining, pp. 183–192. ACM (2014)
9. McNeill, D.: Hand and Mind: What Gestures Reveal About Thought. University of Chicago Press, Chicago (1992)
10. Mueller, F., Lockerd, A.: Cheese: tracking mouse movement activity on websites, a tool for user modeling. In: CHI 2001 extended abstracts on Human factors, April 2001
11. Navalpakkam, V., Churchill, E.: Mouse tracking: measuring and predicting users' experience of web-based content. In: Proceedings of the 2012 ACM Annual Conference on Human Factors in Computing Systems - CHI 2012 (2012)
12. Ruff, L., et al.: Deep one-class classification. In: Dy, J., Krause, A. (eds.) Proceedings of the 35th International Conference on Machine Learning. Proceedings of Machine Learning Research, 10–15 July 2018, vol. 80, pp. 4393–4402. PMLR (2018)
13. Schölkopf, B., Platt, J.C., Shawe-Taylor, J.C., Smola, A.J., Williamson, R.C.: Estimating the support of a high-dimensional distribution. In: Neural Computing, vol. 13, p. 1443–1471. MIT Press, Cambridge, MA, USA (Jul 2001)
14. Shen, C., Cai, Z., Guan, X., Du, Y., Maxion, R.A.: User authentication through mouse dynamics. IEEE Trans. Inf. Forensics Secur. **8**, 16–30 (2013)
15. Tax, D., Duin, R.: Support vector data description. Mach. Learn. **54**, 45–66 (2004). https://doi.org/10.1023/B:MACH.0000008084.60811.49
16. Tzafilkou, K., Protogeros, N.: Mouse behavioral patterns and keystroke dynamics in end-user development: what can they tell us about users' behavioral attributes? Comput. Hum. Behav. **83**, 288–305 (2018)
17. Zimmermann, P., Guttormsen, S., Danuser, B., Gomez, P.: Affective computing - measuring mood with mouse and keyboard. Int. J. Occup. Saf. Ergon. **9**, 539–51 (2003)

The Utility of Digitally Supported Manual Interactive Mockups

John Sören Pettersson[(✉)] [ID]

Karlstad University, 65188 Karlstad, Sweden
john_soren.pettersson@kau.se

Abstract. By a longitudinal account of applications of one Wizard-of-Oz supporting tool, Ozlab, this paper highlights the utility of such tools beyond ordinary design evaluation. The Wizard-of-Oz method does not only allow for performing user test evaluation of interaction designs not yet programmed. Rather, the versatility of a digital but manually controlled prototype allows for many combinations of who determines the mocked up system's responses and who acts as the prototypical user. It also supports co-design in that users will be presented interactive substantiations of their suggestions as the co-design sessions proceeds.

Keywords: Interactivity in design · Participatory design · Digital design support

1 Introduction

The Wizard-of-Oz (WOz) method allows researchers and practitioners to conduct prototyping, including interactive evaluations, without programming. The aim of the present account is to display the many ways digital, but manually controlled, interactive mockups can be used. It is based on a longitudinal study of one WOz supporting tool, Ozlab. The discussions here are not made in contrast to any existing general theory of users-in-the-development-loop or Participatory Design. Rather, they demonstrate resemblance with many statements or observations by others, even if the recurrent line of argument in the present paper is that (1) human-machine interaction is a very important part in prototype construction and not only in prototype evaluation – this argument is generally not emphasized by participatory designers – and that (2) plasticity in the defining process of an interactive design is well worth a specific tool.

The plethora of tools addressing designers, allowing them to create mockups and add interactivity, do not offer functions for negotiations in the user interface. That is, such tools are not means for negotiations in the medium of the user interface. They are merely means for assessment of interaction ideas. Surely, they allow for iterative refinements, but they do not allow situational exploration in the same way as WOz does, and they are not as cost-effective as WOz.

Other ways of finding good requirements for interaction design also lack the immediate *substantiation in use* allowing use-based evaluation of new ideas as these ideas take form. For instance, simply parsing user reviews to gather requirements is not

C. Stephanidis and M. Antona (Eds.): HCII 2020, CCIS 1224, pp. 76–84, 2020.
https://doi.org/10.1007/978-3-030-50726-8_10

cost-effective without combination with WOz, as announced by Abad et al. (2017; "Learn more – pay less!"). The essential ingredient in WOz is the possibility to form the interaction design as the interaction with users takes place. Such plasticity is demonstrated when humans are interacting with humans but it is often not in focus in HCI; that is why (1) was highlighted above. This plasticity in the formative phase of an interaction design development is not discussed in three conceptual studies of the notion of 'interactivity' or 'interaction' that all appeared in 2017 after a rising interest in HCI circles for the concept at the very core of the discipline, the 'I' in 'HCI' (Barry and Doherty 2017; Hornbaek and Oulasvirta 2017; Janlert and Stolterman 2017; the same holds for Hornbaek et al. 2019). Thus, it can be in place to have a look at what interaction via the user interface with users means in the process of defining interaction automation.

The account given here of uses of our tool for concept development through concept substantiation (that is, concept realization in interaction), spans 2000–2019 and is chronologically ordered as the extension of the types of use of Ozlab came gradually as did the valuation (2) of it. Historically, WOz was becoming a frequently used method in the '80s for faking Natural Language Processing (NLP). NLP had in the '70s appeared to provide an alternative to the command-line horror. However, by the turn of the century, GUI ruled human-computer interaction which explains the idea behind Ozlab inaugurated in 2001: quick implementation of GUI elements, movable elements, less emphasis on support for generating sentences (e.g. Pettersson and Wik 2015).

An account of the varying employments of wizard-controlled interactive mockups through twenty years reveals a two-pronged conceptual development: **tool functions** and **methods**, respectively. This paper, in all its brevity, will emphasize method, in particular arrangements for user interface interaction between designers and various kinds of users. Of course, the tool features bias the material base that makes possible the negotiation in the GUI. The "material without qualities" (Löwgren and Stolterman 2004) needs machinery to substantiate the interaction designers' design. Thus, the highlights made below are not in any sense unbiased, but this account provides for a rich picture of what it means to be designing by interacting in the very user interfaces of prospective digital artefacts (i.e., of *mockups* of the prospective artefacts – these mockups may range from empty slates to detailed proposals).

2   The Material Bias/Basis of This Study

The Ozlab concept of a general-purpose, mainly GUI Wizard-of-Oz system has had two major implementations; one from 2001 based on the multimedia production tool Director, and one web-based implementation from 2013 which is still developed. In contrast to so many other attempts to make general WOz systems, Ozlab was not an off-spring of any particular project and thus did not have the limited scope of such other systems (Pettersson and Wik 2015). Experiences were drawn from a range of applications, especially where these were guiding new users in introductory sessions (whether for the use of a program or for explaining a subject content; examples included both adult multimedia and preliterate children), that is, when the expressive recourses of the GUI were used to their limits.

This resulted in a detailed list of what a system for Wizard of Oz should be able to support a test leader with, some directed to functions which always should be in place during test sessions, some to be available in preparation of a mockup: GUI widgets and placeholders for texts and images that were inserted into the screens of a prototype if meant to be accessible there during a session with a "user".

The examples following in Sect. 3 will show how different employments developed this setup. "Shell" is our word for the prototypes built in Ozlab as they are empty, i.e. mainly without automatic functionality (but full of widgets, texts, and images). Another note on terminology is TL for Test Leader (wizard) and TP for Test Person (participant, often a prospective "user" of the prototyped system). The abbreviations are easy to use, even if we nowadays in some instances regret the connotation to "test" rather than to "co-design".

3   Examples of Uses

This section highlights insights gained from the ever expanding range of uses of Ozlab. The highlights are numbered *H1*, *H2* etc. From the above-mentioned systematic review of graphical and auditory means of communicating with a PC user, an idea formed, *H1:* Potentially, a general WOz setup would let others than professional interaction designers trial layout and responses with peers or clients.

2001 Development. A low-pace pilot study ran for several months concurrently with the development of Ozlab. Real-life conditions for non-professional designers: the three test wizards from a Department of Special Education had no reduction in their ordinary workload. They were inexperienced in programming and even in simple multimedia tools. *H2:* Great enthusiasms through the whole process. Often noticeable excitement during the test runs. *H3:* A programmer or designer is needed who acts TP to raise awareness of designing computer responses also for aberrant inputs.

2002 Portable Lab. Continued experimentation within special education. A wizard laptop with Ozlab was used for easy installation of TP files on "any" computer at the site of experimentation. This meant also that no dedicated test room could be used, and wizard voice had to be pre-recorded. A similar setup had already been used for discussion among Ozlab users: the "mini-Ozlab" where TL and TP computers are positioned close to each other. *H4:* A portable package and mini-Ozlab emphasized the notion of Ozlab as a computer system rather than as a type of experimental setup.

2002–2003 Multimedia Students in HCI Classes. It took a year before we understood how to teach early user testing to students already familiar with GUI design.

Spring 2002: students did not take advantage of the possibility of testing during the design phase. Spring 2003: more time was spent on explaining Wizard-of-Oz experimenting and Ozlab. Within two weeks, eleven teams produced 22 usability tested proposals. One of the participants later used her team's proposals in a user interface programming course she taught for schoolteachers. *H5:* Students who have learnt multimedia production are not mentally ready to rest implementations until after usability testing. Later this also showed to be the case for programmers in large R&D projects – proposition (1) is very hard to prove to programmers until it is too late.

2002–2003 Student Thesis Projects. Student projects were conducted where Ozlab was used or was the object of study. The portable package was utilized in some cases, so students clearly got the idea that usability work can be conducted outside a lab. On the other hand, students are often new to the idea of Wizard of Oz and to perform usability tests and, consequently, their real-time exploration of real-time exploration of interaction details was limited. *H6:* Students using Ozlab often lack a drive to explore the design space – this does not provide a basis for rich GUI dialogue.

To even out response time in comparison tests and other fidelity differences between existing software and students' improvements, also existing software was sometimes mocked up in Ozlab. *H7:* Comparing existing software with a new design can be facilitated by mockups built on screen captures of the existing software. This evens out response time and other fidelity differences between the comparanda. This made us more aware of the unimportance of instantaneous responses until interaction flow has been settled.

2003–2004 Robot Surgery. Some 60 operations had been made where operators complained about ambiguities in the work sequence and about details of the user interface of the robot arm. To redevelop the touch screen and trackball user interface, an Ozlab shell with archived X-rays was made for the user interface. There was also some smaller development of user interfaces for the nurses who were to pull the robot from storage into the operating theatre and set it up for use. *H8:* Usability tests demonstrate that even if users are participating in re-design sessions they may later stumble on their own design – this shows that users do not always anticipate the problems they will have. *H9:* Ozlab can be used as a training tool before implementation is finished. A supervisor mediating the user-machine interaction allows a gradual withdrawal of the support that comes from outside the user interface (cf. Mavrikis and Gutierrez-Santos 2010).

The flexibility of Ozlab makes tests into co-design sessions: surgeon (TP) "gives some suggestion for improvements [and] is eager to see the results of the suggestion and asks if it will take long to implement. The alteration is made in approximately ten minutes and it is then possible to perform a new test run." (Larsson and Molin 2006, p. 367) *H10:* Immediate feedback can contribute to the willingness to continue to participate in a long development process.

Moreover, as envisioned originally, in one test session one of the surgeons acted as a wizard (TL) with another surgeon as TP. *H11:* If a designer prepares the infrastructure, user dialogues via the user interface is possible even for highly complicated and specialized products.

2004–2006 Daily Use in Larger Project. For a project with complicated concepts about anonymity and pseudonymity, Ozlab prototyping was intensively used in the start-up phase, partly to see how various concepts could be presented to ordinary Internet users, partly to facilitate communication between developers in Germany and usability evaluators in Sweden. Laptop-to-laptop variant of the mini-Ozlab was sometimes used for internal project demos as this European Union project involved much travelling. *H12:* No need to hide wizards: contents walk-throughs with experts and also real usability tests were made by simple mini-Ozlab settings (TPs seem to believe that test leaders simply monitor the trials and make notes).

H13: Re-use of TP input in output (temporary stored in Ozlab's "hidden fields"). Includes labels of checkboxes, radio buttons etc. This facilitates mockups of many kinds of web sites for ordinary testing, but from 2014 it also proved valuable in more co-designed oriented uses as written inputs (also by TL) can appear in various places.

Mockups were exploited for making videos, so-called "user interface animations". Example of employment: in evaluations with larger audiences giving answers on paper questionnaires. But also as introduction to group co-design sessions to show problematic interaction before WOz is used to try out alternatives ways or layouts. *H14:* Video extends WOz demonstration in several directions as "users" can in addition to watch also experiment with new interaction flows in the same prototypes.

2009 Code Quality. This study was based on a post-hoc analysis of a major three-year re-development of a software package. Code quality was assessed when the software "was either programmed based on mock-upped and user-tested designs, initially made from perceived needs by real users, or programmed only according to perceived needs by real users" (Pettersson and Nilsson 2011, p. 502) *H15:* Programmers reported that code was less difficult to maintain if Ozlab tests had preceded the programming.

In one case, the content expert had seen pictures of the new design for her module and approved it but had not interacted with the WOz mockup. Later user tests, after programming was completed, generated 24 new requirements from this expert. We see this as an indication of how essential the interactive demonstration is. It illustrates the factors behind H15 and can be phrased as, *H16:* user interface interaction matters: "late" requirements can be spotted early if all user groups are included in the pre-testing; real users (incl. expert users) are not experts enough to make go/no-go decisions from detailed GUI pictures. This underpins both proposition (1) and (2) in Sect. 1.

2003–2012 Course Assignments. There were always some multimedia students who tried inserting programming code in the Director file that constituted their shell. *H17:* We realized that a little bit of AI was good to make the WOz method stand out: a board game with simple but hard to program rules makes the Wizard necessary. It still is our standard introductory assignment for undergraduates.

The multimedia production tool in which wizards composed their Ozlab shells, Macromedia's Director, became increasingly outdated as the producer was not updating it for new versions of operation systems (Flash took over during this decade). *H18:* Software does not last very long: update, update, update. (Pettersson and Wik 2015).

2013–2015 (−2019) Web-Based Ozlab. Booking lab time or handing out pairwise connected laptops (TL + TP) was now replaced by providing a web address to each student group. For us to be able to examine students and give advice, they had to run one pilot and also the final test sessions in the lab which also allowed us to evaluate Ozlab. *H19:* Acting as wizard can come with heavy cognitive load and stress if wizards have the feeling that they have to produce a response "as fast as a computer". Web lag adds to this, unfortunately. *H20:* On the positive side, the time needed to learn the wizard-role is surprisingly short (at least if the wizards are supported like they are in Ozlab).

2014–2015 Embedded Websites. *H21:* Use of embedded web sites (embedded Ozlab shells) makes it possible for two TLs acting on independent areas in the same shell; also makes possible borrowing from external web sites but TP actions in such areas are not effectible by TL. *H22:* Screen sharing were used for sharing the entire TP screen to TL – this is to go outside Ozlab but even if it is hard to pursue in some environments, it makes sense for co-design (Wik and Pettersson 2019).

2015–2019 Remote Co-design. As accessing Ozlab now was very easy for a TP even if TL did not travel to this TP, we trialed slow-paced long-distance interaction evaluation based on Ozlab and phone (or Skype, GoToMeeting) in EU projects (Italy, German, Norway, but also internally in Sweden. (Pettersson et al. 2018; and with South Africa, see Wik and Khumalo 2020). One noticeable web defect was the following. *H23:* Need to pacify TP in long-distance WOz tests to counteract lag.

However, by further removing TL and TP from a *testing* mindset, an elaboration started of immediate co-designing, that is, acting together in the user interface when designing it. *H24: GUI interactive interviews* (GUI-ii) names a "remote" Participatory Design method combining design and evaluation, both within a session and between sessions. Co-design in this way can be done one-by-one: the repeated confrontations with co-designers provide an opportunity for a designer to cross-trial suggestions to mitigate the risk of inbreeding when contributors test their own design. *H25:* GUI-ii TPs in their own office can add supplementary material from their computers and directly reference paper materials stacked in the book shelves of their offices.

2017 Two-Device TP. In two-factor authentication it is quite common to use a smartphone for verifying a web user. Using assistants to carry out some of the experiments was facilitated by letting one TL run two Ozlab prototypes while TP handled one laptop and one phone (Karegar et al. 2018). *H26:* Serial use of two TP devices is not more demanding for TL than single shell setups.

2017–2018 Measuring Co-design. Student research project on co-designers' verbal productivity when co-designing in four different ways including GUI-ii (Boodaghian-Asl 2020). *H27:* Need to develop measurements for activity and contribution in co-design in order to gauge the impact of the material basis on the design session.

2018–... . Wizard of Oz may be hard when developing designs for mobile apps. Students assignments, student thesis, and research studies on high school students and hospital visitors ran on the topic of way finding. WOz and GUI-ii as methods evaluated. The promise of GUI-ii to overcome distance in co-design is stretched to the limit by engaging ambulant TPs. (Report will follow in 2021).

4 Conclusion: Ways of Interacting Around Digital Sketches

To illustrate (1) and (2) in the Introduction, our Wizard-of-Oz method evolved from a testing method which also users-as-interaction-designers should be able to utilize, to a designers' support for discussions with content experts or with team members, and further via slow-paced walkthroughs and immediate redesign to a digital co-design method for interactive GUI interviews over distances where design activities and user's walkthroughs take turns (Pettersson et al. 2018; Wik and Khumalo 2020). The original thoughts on a system to support wizards' GUI articulation had come to encompass several types of "GUI dialogue" and purposes:

1. Professional developers/designers utilise test subjects (to test/explore)
2. Users test on peers
3. Users test on clients
4. Users test on developer
5. Developers and users test/discuss together
6. Developers and content experts test/discuss together

The first point is exemplified by several project uses although the development of Ozlab was not primarily aimed at this constellation but rather at point 3 (and the students as semi-professional designers). It can be seen that some studies like the initial pilot, the user interface for robot orthopaedic, and the GUI-ii ones, have been more focused on participatory aspects than others even if every study per definition includes prospective users of some mocked up system. Other studies have been trials and evaluations of WOz in HCI courses, but likewise they may also be useful in participatory-design settings. For instance, the tendency among some IT students to strive to insert code in a Wizard-of-Oz mockup may of course also occur in a professional project where developers are let to do the early prototypes. Noteworthy, the web-based Ozlab by remote co-design and testing captures some of the advantages of programmed prototypes, namely that they can be distributed for review. Certainly, some problems might arise with remote modi operandi. The Nielsen Norman Group recently published an article on "Tools for Remote UX Workshops" (Fessenden 2020). Three "major difficulties raised by remote workshops" are mentioned:

- People are not wholly engaged or feel like their input does not matter
- New tools can be intimidating and decrease participation
- People do not have time to do a long workshop or meeting

We all recognise these problems from big projects' meetings and it is reasonable to fear the same for participatory design pursued remotely. However, for the interactive GUI interviews the first and third of Fessenden's difficulties are negligible, while the real problem for the second difficulty can be that company restrictions do not allow access to Ozlab or conferencing software. Then TP can be asked to use her own laptop with mobile access to Internet or join a session before she goes to work (Pettersson et al. 2018). The one-to-one setting makes for trusted relation between TL and TP.

Of course, it has to be admitted that for the roles digital tools play in interaction design work and in workshops with users, there are also other aspects to treat than the ones discussed in this brief paper. The relationship between the prototypes and the final system is affected by the notion of what the prototypes are representing. Even for the single system treated here there are noticeable shifts in how the notion of the tool and the mockups changes over time depending often on small changes in their implementation or on a fortuitous use of the WOz technique. But this has to be treated in other studies.

References

Abad, Z.S.H., Sims, S.D., Cheema, A., Nasir, M.B., Harisinghani, P.: Learn more, pay less! Lessons learned from applying the Wizard-of-Oz technique for exploring mobile app requirements. In: IEEE 25th International Requirements Engineering Conference Workshops, pp. 132–138. IEEE (2017)

Barry, M., Doherty, G.: How we talk about interactivity: modes and meanings in HCI research. Interact. Comput. **29**(5), 697–711 (2017)

Boodaghian-Asl, A., Gokan Khan, M.: Model-based interview method selection approach in participatory design. In: Isaias, P., Blashki, K. (eds.) Interactivity and the Future of the Human-Computer Interface, pp. 206–223. IGI Global, Hershey (2020)

Fessenden, Th.: Tools for Remote UX Workshops. NN/g Nielsen Norman Group (2020). https://www.nngroup.com/articles/tools-remote-ux-workshops/

Hornbaek, K., Oulasvirta, A.: What is interaction? In: CHI 2017. Proceedings of the 2017 CHI Conference on Human Factors in Computing System, pp. 5040–5052. ACM, New York (2017)

Hornbaek, K., Mottleson, A., Knibble, J., Vogel, D.: What do we mean by "interaction"? An analysis of 35 years of HCI. ACM Trans. Comput. Hum. Interact. **26**(4), 30 (2019). Article 27

Janlert, L.-E., Stolterman, E.: The meaning of interactivity—some proposals for definitions and measures. Hum. Comput. Interact. **32**(3), 103–138 (2017)

Karegar, F., Lindegren, D., Pettersson, J.S., Fischer-Hübner, S.: User evaluations of an app interface for cloud-based identity management. In: Paspallis, N., Raspopoulos, M., Barry, C., Lang, M., Linger, H., Schneider, C. (eds.) Advances in Information Systems Development. LNISO, vol. 26, pp. 205–223. Springer, Cham (2018). https://doi.org/10.1007/978-3-319-74817-7_13

Larsson, N., Molin, L.: Rapid prototyping of user interfaces in robot surgery — Wizard of Oz in participatory design. In: Nilsson, A.G., et al. (eds.) Advances in Information Systems Development, vol. 1, pp. 361–371. Springer Science, New York (2006). https://doi.org/10.1007/978-0-387-36402-5_31

Löwgren, J., Stolterman, E.: Thoughtful Interaction Design: A Design Perspective on Information Technology. MIT Press, Cambridge (2004)

Mavrikis, M., Gutierrez-Santos, S.: Not all wizards are from Oz: iterative design of intelligent learning environments by communication capacity tapering. Comput. Educ. **54**(3), 641–651 (2010)

Pettersson, J.S., Nilsson, J.: Effects of early user-testing on software quality – experiences form a case study. In Song, W., et al. (eds.) Proceedings of the 18th International Conference on Information Systems Development: Asian Experiences (ISD 2009), pp. 499–510. Springer (2011). https://doi.org/10.1007/978-1-4419-7355-9_42

Pettersson, J.S., Wik, M.: The longevity of general purpose Wizard-of-Oz tools. In: OzCHI 2015: Proceedings of the Annual Meeting of the Australian Special Interest Group for Computer Human Interaction, pp. 422–26. ACM (2015)

Pettersson, J.S., Wik, M., Andersson, H.: GUI interaction interviews in the evolving map of design research. In: Paspallis, N., Raspopoulos, M., Barry, C., Lang, M., Linger, H., Schneider, C. (eds.) Advances in Information Systems Development. LNISO, vol. 26, pp. 149–167. Springer, Cham (2018). https://doi.org/10.1007/978-3-319-74817-7_10

Ozlab. http://www.kau.se/en/ozlab

Wik, M., Khumalo, A.: Wizardry in Distributed Participatory Design. From design to implementation. In: Presented at HCII 2020. Springer (2020, to appear in proceedings)

Wik, M., Pettersson, J.S.: Lack of multimedia tools in intervention support for running systems. Int. J. Web Sci. 3(2), 148–173 (2019)

How Can We "Visualize" the World? Essential Foundations of Information Design for Best Practices

Cristina Pires dos Santos[1,2(✉)] , Maria João Pereira Neto[1] ,
and Marco Neves[1]

[1] Lisbon School of Architecture, CIAUD – Research Center in Architecture,
Urbanism and Design, University of Lisbon, Lisbon, Portugal
`cristina.santos@ipbeja.pt`,
`{mjoaopneto,mneves}@fa.ulisboa.pt`
[2] Polytechnic Institute of Beja, Beja, Portugal

Abstract. Relations between data can be very complex, and therefore finding unique ways to accurately convey these data in order to detect trends, patterns and outliers is a very valuable opportunity. The purpose of this study is to highlight current challenges facing Information Design (ID), considering the overload of information that is inherent to modern living. How can we "visualize" the world? What are the functional, aesthetic and cognitive principles that interfere with the way we visualize information and prepare that information? What visual variables can we use to produce visual information that aims to build a functional visual message that a particular audience can understand? The main objectives are: a) to clarify some concepts linked to the act of visualizing; b) to present certain factors that influence the perception of visual information; c) to highlight the main advantages of visual information.

The present study is qualitative, and it was supported based on the documentary analysis of several authors.

The role of ID is to transform chaos into order and information into meanings and knowledge, helping people to reach information. In an era where we are constantly surrounded by information and messages, all of which trying to get our attention, the way in which information is organized, written and presented is extremely important, so that we can all understand it. Visualizing the world is the best way to understand it in an efficient way.

Keywords: Information Design · Visualizing information · Visual communication

1 The Need for Information Design (ID)

Spiekermann [1] reports that we are constantly bombarded by messages, all trying to make us look, listen and react. Some of these messages, however, are more important than others – but often the information we need is not provided in a way that we can easily understand. In the modern world there is clearly a need for ID, in the way that data is organized, written and presented so that we can all understand it. When things get too

© Springer Nature Switzerland AG 2020
C. Stephanidis and M. Antona (Eds.): HCII 2020, CCIS 1224, pp. 85–93, 2020.
https://doi.org/10.1007/978-3-030-50726-8_11

complex, when an environment defies common sense, when technical requirements are allowed to prevail over human considerations, then someone has to intervene – and this is where the information designer comes in. Baer and Vacarra [2] highlight the same idea by saying that we are currently loaded with too much information and we often come across navigation problems that make us feel lost. Hansen [3] states that information overload is continuously presented to us, clamoring for our attention. The information around us exceeds what our minds can manage and use in a productive way, reaching us, word by word, in a way that is difficult to synthesize and give meaning to. Words can prevent understanding, as they are often inadequate to deal with information overload, chaos, disorder and randomness. However, the author states that words and phrases that represent concepts and ideas can be displayed and stored graphically in mind maps – somehow, our brains know that there is something of value in what we consciously perceive as randomness and disorder, and this can make phenomena, relationships and ideas visible, allowing patterns to emerge from apparent disorder and become detectable and available to our senses and intellect. Krum [4] quotes George Miller, one of the founders of the field of cognitive psychology, who in 1983 created the term *"informavore"* to describe human behavior when accessing, and consuming, information. According to Miller, *"just as the body survives by ingesting negative entropy, so the mind survives by ingesting information. In a very general sense, all higher organisms are informavores"*. Sless [5] says that it has become a "cliché" to say that we live in an information society, but that it is important to realize the relevance of ID in society, what information means to people as workers, citizens and consumers. Costa [6] states that in an era of communication, the mere increase in the number of channels, means and supports, or the increase in superstructure networks and digital platforms, does not necessarily imply an increase in the quality of information; moreover, it is necessary to reduce the noise that invades the environment and imposes information, allowing individuals to transform it into knowledge. Shedroff [7] says that knowledge is a phenomenon we can build for others, just as we can build information for others from data. According to Costa [6], when we see, we transform chaos into order and information into meanings. We convert a neutral surrounding of signals into a human environment and make it understandable and usable.

2 Visualization of Information – Enlarging the World of the Perceptible

Hansen [3] states that information comes to us through three general sources: *external* – the observable world; what is seen and perceived; printed texts, verbal elements, media presentations, and so forth; *internal* – one's own images, ideas, visualizations and perceptions; *combined external and internal sources* – informing the cognitions and perceptions that give rise to new combinations of knowledge and information. According to Costa [6], the limitations of our ocular system have been intensely fought by props and instruments invented by mankind to overcome this limitation. In this way, we can attest that visual perception is no longer limited exclusively to what the eye sees directly, but to what it can see, thanks to the mediatization of instruments, prostheses and props. However, there is another reality that we cannot see, either directly or indirectly, because it is not a visual reality, but rather a universe of phenomena. Ever since, mankind has been aware that reality is not just what we perceive or see, and the desire to learn invisible phenomena is as strong as the desire to make them communicable. Trying to understand and then explain such phenomena presupposes a work of mind and hand aided by technical means; a work of translation of what is real, through visual means, or more precisely, graphics. In this way, and following Costa's definitions, we can understand more precisely what it is *"to visualize"*. *"To visualize"* is therefore to make visible and understandable to humans, aspects and phenomena of reality that are not accessible to the eye, many of which are not even visual in nature. It is therefore neither an implicit result of the act of seeing, nor a spontaneous product of the individual who reads already visualized information – rather, it results from the work of the viewer (e.g. information designer, graphic designer, illustrator, schematic, visual communicator). Costa [6] concludes that if what we call reality is what we perceive, it is understood that visualizing is a means of enlarging the world of the perceptible. An infographic can therefore represent phenomena of reality, but also phenomena that are not visible. Graphical display can be either figurative or non-figurative. A news infographic on a catastrophic plane crash can be considered figurative, and when a graphic displays abstract phenomena, it is non-figurative. Here there is no mimetic correspondence between what is being represented and its representation – for example, we can represent the unemployment rate through a graph of multicolored rectangles [8].

3 Challenges of ID

3.1 Functional Principles

Costa [9] says that we call ID the part of graphic design that is specifically oriented to spreading useful and usable messages to individuals and society. He emphasizes that the emergence of ID has to do with the current dimension of the diffusion of messages and the reaction that this has provoked in the most committed designers, creating a conscience that is totally opposed to consumerism, saturation and suffocating media banality that spreads many redundant and alienating stimuli, which we may call "junk design". Bonsiepe [10] states that the growth of information has promoted reassessment of the graphic designer's traditional vision. In addition to visualizing concepts, the designer organizes information with the purpose of reducing cognitive entropy. The information designer structures and organizes information and provides guidance so that the user can find his/her way through the information maze. The author points out that this change requires cognitive and organizational skills that are sometimes neglected in design training. This perspective is shared by Sless [5], who reinforces the idea that there is a great difference in objectives between ID and traditional graphic design. According to Horn [11], the values that distinguish ID from other types of design are efficiency and effectiveness in achieving the communicative purpose. Pettersson [12, 13] presented eight functional principles for ID: facilitation learning; providing a clear structure of a message; providing clarity; providing simplicity; providing unity; securing a high-quality message; limiting the total costs; respecting

88   C. Pires dos Santos et al.

copyright. Later, Pettersson [13] added two aesthetic message design principles to the list: information aesthetics and harmony, and proportion.

The goal in ID should always be clarity of communication, and any graphical message should be legible, readable and also well worth reading for the intended audience.

3.2 Benefits of Visual Information and the Use of Images

Hansen [3] notes that the great advantage of using graphics with words and phrases is being able to see structures and relationships in data that are hidden in a text-only presentation. The detection of patterns – which are visual phenomena – in a text field is virtually impossible and requires a powerful memory and the ability to absorb, store, categorize and retrieve information in order to read and analyze every page of text. However, when information is presented graphically and the concepts are given, the relationships between the various elements are easier to notice, long-term memory is triggered and even more information and perceptions can be added, allowing viewers to detect new patterns, processes and other phenomena. Besides improving the ability to perceive patterns in situations of confusion, complexity, disorder or chaos, a graphical approach helps us to think visually. Hansen [3] further states that the need to understand the complexity and apparent disorder is crucial to extending our ability to think visually and systemically, as well as to visualizing (seeing) systems as whole entities. Several studies demonstrate that we have a greater ability to memorize the information we get from images than from text. Krum [4] mentions studies estimating that 50 to 80% of the human brain is dedicated to forms of visual processing, such as vision, visual memory, colors, shapes, movement, patterns, and spatial awareness. This idea is also reinforced by Costa [9] and Serra [14], as we can see in Fig. 1.

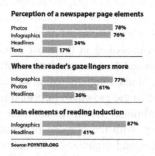

Fig. 1. In 1990, Poynter, an Institute of Journalism Studies of Miami, created *Eyetrack*, a video tool that allows the way our eyes observe the media to be recorded with millimetric precision. Adapted from Serra [14].

4   Understanding the Meanings and Structure of Visual Information

Meirelles [15] states that representing multidimensional information structures in a two-dimensional visual display is not trivial: *"The design process requires both analytical and visual/spatial methods of reasoning. Graphic design in general, and information design in particular, depend upon cognitive processes and visual perception for both its creation (encoding) and its use (decoding). If the decoding process fails, the visualization fails"*. It is therefore extremely important to understand the constraints and capabilities of cognition and visual perception, as they are essential to the way we visualize information. The concept of perception is a collective designation for different processes in which an animal or a person obtains information about the outside world. We have the tendency to organize and analyze information that we pay attention. Colors, illustrations, photographs, lines, images, sounds, symbols, texts and words must be integrated so that they can be meaningfully interpreted as a whole rather than a number of individual elements. Wurman [16] created the acronym *LATCH* for the five finite ways of organizing information: *Location, Alphabet, Time, Category*, and *Hierarchy*. Shedroff [7] also refers to these five ways of organizing everything, but he considers that seven are clear to him: *Alphabets, Locations, Time, Continuums, Numbers, Categories*, and *Randomness*. Meirelles [17] presents several infographic examples based on typologies of structure/organization/relationships, such as: hierarchical structures - trees; relational structures - networks; temporal structures - timelines and flows; spatial structures - maps; spatio-temporal structures; textual structures. These examples turn out to be representative of the various possibilities to organize and relate the visual information, according to the stipulated goals. Previously, Tufte [18] assigned several typologies of graphics according to the organization, relation and type of data they presented: *data maps* (they combine cartography with specific themes, allowing different types of information to be linked with the physical and geographical dimension); *time series* (they refer to a type of information in relation to a time scale, allowing a phenomena to be explored according to predetermined time intervals; *narrative graphics of space and time* (a mean of increasing the informational potential of a time-series is to introduce the representation of space, constructing a narrative structure based on integration between time and space); *relational graphics* (a more abstract form of representation, enabling the comparison between quantitative variables). Meirelles [17] also highlights some factors considered essential to the organization of visual information: *visual hierarchies* - the author emphasizes the importance of the hierarchy of the visual elements, in order to provide emphasis and attention, so that the eyes follow a certain direction or purpose; *spatial encoding* - Meirelles states that we process spatial properties (position and size) separately from object properties (such as shape, color, texture); furthermore, position in space and time has a dominant role in perceptual organization, as well as in memory; in visual representations, the use of space is always schematic, independent of whether depictions of elements are direct or metaphorical and the spatial encoding is central to visualization construction.

4.1 Perceptual and Cognitive Processes in the Visualization Process

Meirelles [17] notes that our extraction of information from visual displays is done separately and over stages, although the information is presented simultaneously – from precognitive and preliminary processes to high-level processing processes, in which the results of the previous stages are combined with previous knowledge and knowledge structures. Ware [19] proposes a three-stage model of perception: *stage 1* - rapid parallel processing to extract basic features; *stage 2* - slow serial processing for the extraction of patterns and structures; *stage 3* - sequential goal-oriented processing with information reduced to a few objects and held in working visual memory to form the basis of visual thinking. To illustrate the relevance of pre-attentive features in visual tasks, we can analyze the four numerical images showing the same sequence of numbers and try to discover the total number of occurrences of the number "7" (Fig. 2).

```
012345678901234567890123456789012    012345678901234567890123456789012
345678901234567890123456789012345    345678901234567890123456789012345
678901234567890123456789012345678    678901234567890123456789012345678
901234567890123456789012345678901    901234567890123456789012345678901


012345678901234567890123456789012    012345678901234567890123456789012
345678901234567890123456789012345    345678901234567890123456789012345
678901234567890123456789012345678    678901234567890123456789012345678
901234567890123456789012345678901    901234567890123456789012345678901
```

Fig. 2. The examples use the same numbers but with different encoding for number 7. We can observe that in some examples it is easier to detect the target "7". Source: adapted from Meirelles [17].

Meirelles [17] also highlights that the visual properties of color hue (red), intensity or color value (gray/black) and line weight (bold) help us to perform the task, because they are pre-attentively processed. Some of these factors that the brain uses effortlessly to discriminate between objects are also pointed out by Cairo [8]. We can also consider form, color, motion and spatial position. There are, however, factors that can impair the detection of pre-attentively designed symbols, such as the number and variety (degree of differentiation) of distractors in the representation and whether they represent targets or non-targets (distractors). It is important to understand that pre-attentive properties are not perceived equally; the hierarchy depends on other features that are present in the visualization, such as color saturation and the degree of distinctness from the surrounding marks, and effective visualizations make intentional use of pre-attentive features in the representation of graphical marks [17]. On *Stage 2*, elements and patterns are detected and ordered through discrimination in early vision. Patterns are central to how visual information is structured and organized, and the *Gestalt laws* propose a series of principles that describe the way we detect patterns and how individual units are integrated into a coherent percept: *proximity, similarity, common fate, good continuation, closure, simplicity, familiarity and segregation between figure and ground* [8, 17]. According to Cairo [8], the word *gestalt* means pattern and the main principle behind Gestalt theory is that brains see patches of color and shapes not as individual entities but as aggregates. The brain follows certain principles of perceptual organization. Wertheimer [20], said that Gestalt principles are effective not only in enhancing perceptual inferences but also in facilitating problems – solving and thinking processes; they facilitate the understanding of structural requirements of problems, allowing problems to be viewed as integrated and coherent wholes.

4.2   Visual Variables

Jacques Bertin [21] defined the basic elements of visual information and the relation between them. Bertin distinguished between place, size, greyness, texture, orientation, color and shape. Mijksenaar [21] developed a practical variant of Bertin's principles to provide designers with a series of useful and intelligible guides. This author divided the variables into two categories: *"Hierarchial variables that indicate a difference in importance, and distinguishing variables that indicate a difference in type"*. The first set of variables can be expressed by size and intensity, and the second by means of color and shape. In addition, there are also visual support elements such as color areas, lines and boxes, whose function is to emphasize and organize. It is also possible to find differences in importance and type. This distinction between visual elements makes it possible to analyze in advance the various elements involved in an instruction manual, leaflet or magazine. According to Meirelles [17], Bertin was the first to have proposed a theory of graphical representation of data for use in maps, diagrams and networks. Although Bertin's system has been widely adopted by cartographers and designers when selecting the appropriate type of marks for encoding data, it has also been expanded to include other variables that were not considered initially. Meirelles refers to the variable of color saturation to the other color variables of hue and value, the inclusion of tactual elements in maps for visually impaired users, and dynamic variables for maps that change over time. According to the author, the basic graphic elements, the primitives of visual represen-tation, and their semantics are: *point* (has no dimension and provides a sense of place); *line* (has one dimension and provides a sense of length and direction); *plane* (has two dimensions and provides a sense of space and scale). Kandinsky [22], previously men-tioned that painting must start with the simplest and most necessary elements: the *point*, from which all other shapes start, and the *line*. Kandinsky considered that the line is the trail of the moving point and represents the leap from static to dynamic, representing the contrast with the point. Meirelles [17] does not consider *volume* here as a basic graphic element, but the author affirms that it could be added to the system depending on the needs of the system (some visualizations make use of simulated volumes in two-dimensional visual displays). Meirelles [23] underlines that *"the visual variables correspond to visual channels and the way features are extracted in our brains"*. The bases of visual repre-sentation are supported by several authors. In the creation of images, Pettersson [13] also highlights the use of certain elements and aspects that influence our perception of form, such as: points, lines, areas, volumes, size, shape, color (tone, value, saturation, color systems), contrast, texture, light, composition, organization, balance, perspective. Wong [24] adds the plan and the space as important factors in the composition of an image. Arnheim [25] adds movement (direction, speed), dynamics and expression as values that can be expressed and perceived through visual representation. Tufte [26] emphasizes that attaching color to information is as basic and direct as the color technique in art. Hansen [3], through her research work, presented a set of six graphic tools (GTs) for graphical displays: 1 - Circle or curvoid; 2 - Square with right-angled corners/Square with round corners; 3 - Triangle; 4 - Line; 5 - Point; 6 - Fuzz; *combinations:* two or more GTs; *the palette:* the surface on which a graphical display is drawn. Dondis [27], Poulin [28], Zelansky and Fisher [29] are also essential references on the topic for understanding the grammar of image and the basic elements of visual language, an issue that is essential in the practice of visual communication.

5 Conclusions

We can get information from external sources – the observable world; from internal sources – one's own images, ideas, visualizations and perceptions; or combined external and internal sources. We can also define the visible world as the whole continuous set of things that are given to our eyes, which are part of the seeing act, and the invisible world as a universe of phenomena of reality that we cannot see, either directly or indirectly. ID helps to explain and understand such phenomena (which are directly incomprehensible), and results in a work of translation of what is real through visual means or, more precisely, graphics (figurative or non-figurative). Through visual information, we detect patterns and relationships, and long-term memory is triggered – we have a greater ability to memorize the information we obtain from images than from text. The design process depends upon cognitive processes and visual perception for both its creation (encoding) and its use (decoding). Information designers have to be aware of these issues so they can organize and structure, emphasize and hierarchize the information. It is important to understand the process of extracting information, to be aware of the pre-attentive features (color hue, intensity or color value, line weight, line orientation, size, and so forth) or the gestalt principles that describe the way we detect patterns and how individual units are integrated into a coherent percept. We must always take into account basic graphical elements and primitives of visual representation, which influence our perception of shapes, as well as taking into account the functional principles of ID. The role of ID is to transform chaos into order and information into meanings and knowledge, helping people to reach information and to understand the world in a better way. With this study we intended to reflect on some issues that we consider fundamental to the good practice of ID.

References

1. Spiekermann, E.: Information Design. AIGA (2002). http://www.aiga.org/content.cfm/information-design_1. Accessed 01 Aug 2009
2. Baer, K., Vacarra, J.: Information Design Workbook: Graphic Approaches, Solutions, and Inspiration + 30 Case Studies. Rockport Publishers, Beverly (2008)
3. Hansen, Y.M.: Visualization for Thinking, Planning, and Problem Solving. In: Jacobson, R. (ed.) Information Design, pp. 193–220. The MIT Press, Massachusetts (2000)
4. Krum, R.: Cool Infographics: Effective Communication with Data Visualization and Design, p. 9. Wiley, Hoboken (2014)
5. Sless, D.: What is information design. In: Proceedings of the Designing Information for People Symposium, pp. 1–16 (1992). https://www.academia.edu/449792/What_is_Information_Design. Accessed Mar 2020

6. Costa, J.: La Esquemática - Visualizar la información [Schematic: Visualize the Information]. Paidós Ibérica, Barcelona (1998)
7. Shedroff, N.: Information Interaction Design: A Unified Field Theory of Design, pp. 267–292. The MIT Press, Massachusetts (2000)
8. Cairo, A.: The Functional Art – An Introduction to Information Graphics and Visualization. New Riders – Voices that Matter, San Francisco (2013)
9. Costa, J.: Design para os olhos – Marca, Cor, Identidade, Sinalética [Design for the eyes - Brand, Color, Identity, Signage]. Dinalivro, Lisbon (2011)
10. Bonsiepe, G.: Interface - An Approach to Design. Jan Van Eyck Akademie, Maastricht (1999)
11. Horn, R.E.: Information design: emergence of a new profession. In: Jacobson, R. (ed.) Information design, pp. 15–33. The MIT Press, Massachusetts (2000)
12. Pettersson, R.: Information Design: An Introduction, vol. 3. John Benjamins Publishing Company, Amsterdam (2002)
13. Pettersson, R.: It Depends: ID – Principles and Guidelines, 4th edn. International Institute for Information Design (IIID), Austria (2012). https://www.iiid.net/PublicLibrary/Pettersson-Rune-ID-It-Depends.pdf. Accessed Mar 2020
14. Serra, J.: Seguiendo los ojos [Following the eyes], p. 38. La Vanguardia, 2 March 2014
15. Meirelles, I.: Design for Information: An Introduction to the Histories, Theories, and Best Practices Behind Effective Information Visualizations, p. 9. Rockport Publishers, Gloucester (2013)
16. Wurman, R. S.: Information Anxiety 2. Que, Indianapolis, Indiana (2001)
17. Meirelles, I.: Design for Information: An Introduction to the Histories, Theories, and Best Practices Behind Effective Information Visualizations. Rockport Publishers, Gloucester (2013)
18. Tufte, E.R.: The Visual Display of Quantitative Information, 2nd edn. Graphics Press, Cheshire (2001)
19. Ware, C.: Information Visualization: Perception for Design, 3rd edn. Morgan Kaufmann, Boston (2012)
20. Wertheimer, M.: Productive Thinking. Harper & Brothers, New York (1959). quoted in Meirelles, I.: Design for Information: An Introduction to the Histories, Theories, and Best Practices Behind Effective Information Visualizations. Rockport Publishers, Gloucester, p. 23 (2013)
21. Mijksenaar, P.: Visual Function: An Introduction to Information Design, p. 39. Princeton Architectural Press, New York (1997)
22. Kandinsky, W.: Point and Line to Plane. Dover Publications, New York (1979)
23. Meirelles, I.: Design for Information: An Introduction to the Histories, Theories, and Best Practices Behind Effective Information Visualizations. Rockport Publishers, Gloucester, p. 126 (2013)
24. Wong, W.: Principles of Form and Design. Willey, New York (1993)
25. Arnheim, R.: Art and Visual Perception: A Psychology of the Creative Eye. Los Angeles (1974)
26. Tufte, E.R.: Envisioning Information. Graphics Press, Cheshire (1990)
27. Dondis, D.: A Primer of Visual Literacy. MIT, Chicago (1974)
28. Poulin, R.: The Language of Graphic Design: An Illustrated Handbook for Understanding Fundamental Design Principles. Rockport Publishers, Gloucester (2012)
29. Zelansky, P., Fisher, M.P.: The Art of Seeing, 8th edn. Pearson Education, New Jersey (2011)

Micro-innovative Design of Internet Products from the Perspective of User Stickiness—Illustrated by the Case of 360 Applets

Ke Sun and Hong Chen[✉]

East China University of Science and Technology, Shanghai, China
hong-engoy2008@163.com

Abstract. The mobile Internet has entered a new period of super applets. Applets occupy the core position of mobile Internet traffic because of its miniaturization, which reduces develop costs and makes the product easier to use. Therefore, the research on applets has become more and more necessary and dynamic, and developers are paying more attention on user stickiness. Qihoo 360, a service website with monthly active user over 400 million, is the specific case studied in this paper. In order to explore user needs, behaviors, psychology, and to analyze how these factors are related to user stickiness, this paper uses research methods including observing, interviewing and other methods which combine big data information from the internet. Furthermore, based on the above, three design methods are proposed from the perspective of micro-innovation. Through practical projects, the effectiveness of improving the 360 applet users' stickiness is verified. These help to further explore the application of micro-innovative design methods in Internet websites and other related scenarios.

Keywords: User stickiness · Micro-innovation · Internet · 360 applet · User analysis

1 Related Theoretical Foundations of Micro Innovation

The originator of micro-innovation is Steve Jobs, who once said: "Small innovations can change the world". Zhou Hongyi, chairman of Qihoo 360, is the first to propose micro-innovation theories in China. In 2010 he claimed: "The innovation of user experience, which is called micro-innovation, is the key to determine whether Internet applications will be popular or not. Micro-innovation has two principles of innovations. The first one is the focus on details and keeping a close eye on user needs. The second one is moving quickly with constant trial and error" [1].

With the rapidly development of the Internet, the amount of user in the Internet has been increased continuously, and user experience has become the leading role during the development of Internet products, and micro-innovation has been increasingly valuable. Today, micro-innovation has become an innovation approach which aims at touching the users from a single perspective. By continuous accumulation, it changes gradually from quantitative to qualitative, and finally becomes a transformative product [2], which is also more suitable for lightweight applet developer companies.

© Springer Nature Switzerland AG 2020
C. Stephanidis and M. Antona (Eds.): HCII 2020, CCIS 1224, pp. 94–99, 2020.
https://doi.org/10.1007/978-3-030-50726-8_12

2   User Stickiness Analysis of Applet Internet Products

User stickiness includes user's length of access time and the ability of social networks to retain users. User stickiness refers to long time usage and frequent access to social media platforms [3]. In the era of the experience economy, user stickiness is an important indicator for evaluating the quality of Internet products. Applets rely on super APP or platform, and provide a ready-to-use and scene-oriented application form. It absorbs the advantages of the original website, which is click-to-use, and use-and-go, and offer user experience of active user interaction of APP meanwhile. The 360 applet is attached to the 360 Safe Browser in which the user's usage scenario is basically an 8-h office scenario. This paper analyzes users' characteristics and studies several factors that affect user stickiness.

The 360 Safe Browser has 400 million monthly users, of which male users (52.2%) are slightly higher than female users (47.8%). The users are younger and the urban coverage is balanced. From the perspective of user demands of the 360 Safe Browser, Search, Q & A, and online tools are all in high-frequency demand; Usage scenarios of shopping, social, news, and videos are relatively infrequently demanded; online education, financial management are the needs of special groups, and different types of demand determine the means to increasing user stickiness. From the perspective of user behaviors, IiMedia Research shows that the browser's feedback speed, the rationality of the information structure, the visual effects of the interface, and the way of prompting information are important factors that influence users to stay or not. In addition, the 360 browser is a highly active product for white-collar who use it more frequently and for a longer period of time. The advantages of the 360 browser provide the services that white-collar users cannot enjoy in mobile, such as the depth and breadth of content, the richness and thoughtfulness of operations, and the intuitiveness of the interface when users are engaged in work and learning activities. The development of the 360 applet should make full use of the advantages of the platform and the user characteristics, and be highly compatible with usage scenarios, and match the usage time to better retain users. As of the end of 2019, there are nearly 1,000 360 applets officially launched, covering more than 30 fields such as education, office, tools, e-commerce, video, life services, games and with 1.5 million daily active users and an average stay of about 7 min.

3   Methods to Improve User Stickiness

3.1   Micro-innovation of Demand Design

Micro-innovation is demand-driven innovation. It aims at meeting user needs better [4]. The KANO model defines user needs as three types: basic demand, expectation demand, and excitement demand. This section mainly explains that applet design can better serve users by inspiring the users' basic needs, as well as continuously innovating the design of expecting and exciting needs.

Basic demand is the core attribute of a product. For example, office tools are more necessary for PC users. Such products are based on expectations demand and their user stickiness can be improved through innovation and excitement. Some products with low-frequency basic demand have to stimulate user needs through tiny designs. For example, shopping is not a necessary high-frequency requirement for users, but some online promotion design will stimulate users' desire to buy, and some gamified functional designs will enhance user stickiness. Products with very low-frequency basic demand, such as moving, renting, and weddings, especially need to use micro-design to create usage scenarios for users.

The basic demand of office and tool products in 360 applets are strong, and the large-screen features of products such as stock and funds, and online education meet users' expectation demand. Micro-innovation in demand design requires different attributes of optimization and development for different types of products, which must be integrated into the iterative update process of the product, and the designer must fully understand users to satisfy, guide and retain them gradually (Fig. 1).

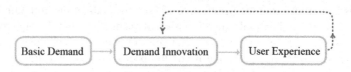

Fig. 1. Micro-innovative process of demand design

3.2   Micro-innovation of Interactive Design

Interactivity is used to explain the communication between people and the emerging media in the Internet age. Many researches have shown that there is a positive correlation between interactive design and user stickiness. Compared with mobile products, PC products have natural large screen as an advantage and are more suitable for interactive design.

Now, interaction design for user and system on internet products is mature, such as loading waiting pages, button special effects, screen switching effects, and so on. The interaction between users and content is mainly reflected in two aspects: content customization and content selection [5]. Personalized content customization improves user self-satisfaction and user experience. Products through algorithm recommendation can provide a better browsing experience for user content selection. Although the time for the user of browsing 360 applet content is limited, the message pop-up window and sidebar of the 360 browser can be designed to remind the user to enhance user stickiness. User-to-user interaction is difficult to implement for the 360 applet because of the difficulty of forming a complete user system. The solution is enabling users to log in via WeChat scan code, computer QQ account, and a 360 browser account. Based on this, office tool products need to strengthen collaboration functions or payment functions, entertainment products need to design malls, sharing and community functions, stocks products and online education products need to maintain consistency with WeChat Mini Program experience.

Micro-innovation of interactive design requires optimization and innovation in terms of product interface design, content design, and functional design. It is necessary to make full use of the unique attributes of the product to design, and the product-related functions to improve product interaction, to better reflect the "strong interactive, highly immersive" product features.

3.3 Micro-innovation of Emotional Design

Micro-innovation focuses on the user experience of the product. As the key to improving the user experience, emotional design is the main area where the product should continue to innovate in the process of development.

Maslow's "Hierarchy of Needs" proposes that human self-emotional needs are the highest-level needs. As people's consumption level increases and market competition becomes more intense, people's emotional psychological needs receive unprecedented attention. The rapid development of Internet products makes people no longer satisfied with the basic functions of Internet products, and people's demand for Internet products is moving in an emotional direction. The product design of applets should retain users for a long time with the characteristics of emotion and humanity. The popular WeChat applet "Little Mochi" (an electronic photo album making tool) that rose to fame in 2019 captures the social needs of the elderly, meets the emotional needs of users who desire to be expressed and understood, and has attracted countless users through simple interface design. At the end of each year, the emotional billing features such as the annual bill introduced by Alipay and the annual song list introduced by the NetEase cloud music have also firmly grasped the hearts of millions of users and enhanced their trust and sense of achievement.

For small program products, emotional design should fully understand user needs, touch user emotions, serve as the basis and starting point for product design, and carry out detailed innovative design based on the integrity of the product (Fig. 2).

Fig. 2. Micro-innovative process of product iteration.

Product design is a gradual process, which requires to meet different needs at different stages [6], and continuous innovation through continuous trial and error. Micro-innovation design is integrated into the product design process through requirements design, interaction design, and emotional design, which can continuously improve the product and achieve good performance.

4 Micro-innovation Design Case of 360 Applets from the Perspective of User Stickiness

This chapter takes the 360 applet design practice project I participated in Qihoo 360 as an example to analyze the micro-innovation of demand design, interaction design and emotional design in the process of product design. The positive correlation between the above three micro-innovation design directions and user stickiness is verified through the analysis of user visit duration, user retention rate, user conversion rate and other data analysis (Table 1).

Table 1. Partial data display of the 360 applet "Good Luck Perpetual Calendar".

Period	Iterative function	DAU	RR	DTP	CVR	DTP of the game	DTP of the robot
1st week	Calendar, Draw lot	1700	8%	–	–	–	–
2–3 week	Horoscope analysis	2000	1.5–3%	3 min	1%	–	–
4–5 week	–	3000	3–4%	4 min	4.2%	–	–
6th week	A tree-growing game	3500	3.9%	4.8 min	4.2%	7.5 min	–
7th week	–	3700	4.7%	3.2 min	3.4%	10 min	–
8th week	AI fortune robot	3500	4.5%	3 min	4.2%	17.5 min	40 min

The 360 applet "Good Luck Perpetual Calendar" was originally an online calendar based on daily fortune analysis, with a single functional interface and less user traffic. Our team designed a series of extended requirements based on the high-frequency needs of users to watch the calendar every day during the applet iteration process, such as daily fortune, daily signing, and tricks, etc., which increased the duration of applet users' stay. When the number of users reached a certain level in the medium-term, our team launched online small game functions (receiving rewards for tasks) by using the gamified operation strategies, and the game rewards cooperated with the 360 Little Vest Charity Program to meet the psychological needs of users to achieve their own value and increased user stickiness. The calendar query and seeking sign functions are the strong interaction points of the good luck perpetual calendar applet. The functional design of the AI fortune robot has enhanced the interaction between the user and the system. During the continuous optimization of the interaction design, the user retention rate has been effectively improved. It is expected that the store and community functions will be launched later in the product to enhance the interaction between users and content and users.

Figure 3 is a data visualization of effects of some product iterations on user sticky growth. The average daily active amount, the retention rate and conversion rate of the user the next day show an upward trend during the update iteration. The length of the user's stay fluctuates greatly in the early period while the data has gradually stabilized with the continuous expansion of the scale of users.

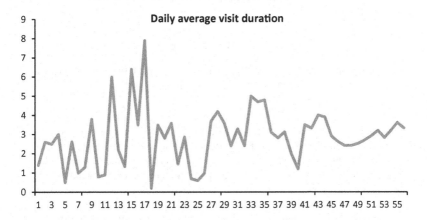

Fig. 3. User visit duration data display.

5   Conclusion

The advent of the applet Internet era has brought many opportunities and challenges for product developers and enterprises and user stickiness has gradually become the focus of creators. This article takes the new 360 applet platform as the research object, and proposes three micro-innovation design methods of demand design, interaction design and emotion design. Based on this, applet products can effectively improve user stickiness through the iterative process of micro-innovation. These three design directions will also provide methods and ideas for micro-innovative design in the era of applet Internet.

References

1. Zhou, H.: Welcome to the era of micro innovation. Chin. Foreign Manag. **11**, 53 (2016)
2. Xi, T., Zheng, X.: Research on iterative innovation design method of Internet products in the era of big data. Packag. Eng. **37**(08), 1–5 (2016)
3. Wang, C., Tala, M.: User stickiness and product life cycle: research based on literature and fuzzy QFD. Shanghai Qual. **08**, 40–48 (2016)
4. Yin, L., Wu, G., Xiong, W.: Research on product design mode of micro-innovation in modern design management. J. Wuxi Commer. Vocat. Coll. **12**(03), 97–101 (2012)
5. Guo, X.: Research on the Impact of the Interaction of Sports Information App on User Stickiness. Hebei University (2018)
6. Lai, H., Chu, Y.: Research on design leading micro-innovation of internet products from the perspective of user experience. Des. Art Res. **8**(05), 83–87 (2018)

Bringing Socio-Technical Design Back to Its Roots: Improving Digitization in the Manufacturing Industry

Felix Thewes[(⊠)] ⓘD

Ruhr-University Bochum, Universitätsstraße 150, 44801 Bochum, Germany
felix.thewes@rub.de

Abstract. The research of socio-technical systems went a long road from its beginning in the London Tavistock Institute in the early 1950s [1]. In recent years a shift in socio-technical research publications from blue to white collar work could be observed. This paper proposes a combination of methods from user experience (UX) design and industrial engineering to improve the socio-technical work environment on industrial shopfloors.

The contribution of this paper is threefold: First, an overview of the state of the art in inspection methods in the fields of HCI and industrial engineering is presented. This is based on a literature review and expert interviews. Secondly, a combination of methods from these areas is proposed. In the final part, a preliminary design for a tool supporting the combined methods is presented.

Keywords: Socio-technical design · Inspection method · Digitization

1 Introduction

The rapid increase in the use of information technology in the manufacturing industry is creating new challenges and opportunities for workers. Factories are replacing existing production lines and machines with highly computerized "cyber-physical systems" (CPS) [2]. Information is gathered and displayed throughout the production process. The generated data is used to inform the management in real-time through shopfloor management systems or enterprise resource planning software [3].

Workers have to interact with displays and computers on their machines. Workflows are controlled by algorithms, which in turn have to be adjusted. These technological advancements risk overburdening workers who are used to working with mechanical machines and conducting information on paper. Additionally to the change in required skillsets, Hirsch-Kreinsen [4] points out that the role of factory workers changes from machine operators to experience guided decision makers.

To address these challenges successfully, it is not advised to examine humans and technology separately. An approach that combines focus on humans, technology and organization examines the "socio-technical system" (STS). In the design or analysis of STS the emphasis lies on the relations and interdependencies between humans, the technology they use and the organization they work in [5]. Principles how to design STS were developed for the manufacturing industry for many decades [6–9]. The speed

© Springer Nature Switzerland AG 2020
C. Stephanidis and M. Antona (Eds.): HCII 2020, CCIS 1224, pp. 100–106, 2020.
https://doi.org/10.1007/978-3-030-50726-8_13

of recent technological advancements not only challenges the application to modern systems but the careful planning and development of STS. Therefore, the need to inspect and evaluate modern agile manufacturing settings arises.

2 Related Work

2.1 Continuous Improvement in Industrial Engineering

In industrial engineering, there are several concepts for improvement of work environments. A key-aspect of these concepts is the inclusion of workers in improvement efforts. Bessant and Caffyn [10] describe "Continuous Improvement" (CI) to enable organizations to react to "uncertain markets, rapidly changing technological threats and opportunities, increasing regulatory pressures, shifting customer and competitive requirements, and a host of other variables". Employees are encouraged to use their experience to suggest improvements in quality and productivity and therefore increase the capabilities in creative problem-solving. This increase in innovation capacity enables small incremental improvements which can be continuously sustained throughout the company [11].

In lean manufacturing the production is viewed from the perspective of the customer. All unnecessary steps and resources that do not increase the value for the customer are eradicated [12]. To achieve this, all involved personnel is encouraged to suggest improvements to the production process.

The Japanese Kaizen philosophy focusses on the workers and facilitates an optimized work environment [13]. By inducing a pride for their work the workers are motivated to improve their environment and optimize their production processes [14].

In modern western adaptations of these improvement concepts regular inspections are used, in addition to spontaneous suggestions, to improve the work environment. Workers and officers inspect the industrial plant with guidelines or checklists. Suggestions and inspection results are often gathered by an innovation department and referred to design teams. In contrast to the aforementioned concepts the implementation of worker participation is often flawed. The design teams often do not include shopfloor workers early or at all [15]. Participation of shopfloor workers in these design efforts would not only harnesses their extensive experience but also raise the acceptance of new methods and workflows.

2.2 Heuristic Evaluation

In HCI, especially in software and web development, inspection methods for usability and user experience are well established. Their goal is to enable domain experts to evaluate interfaces with regard to their needs and workflows. A commonly used inspection method is heuristic evaluation [16]. In heuristic evaluation an interface is evaluated for compliance with a set of guidelines. These guidelines each describe a general design concept. These concepts are not to be viewed as strict rules but as an orientation for the evaluators discretion [17] and are therefore called heuristics. For an evaluation of an interface multiple evaluators inspect the interface with the same set of

8–10 heuristics. Subjective interpretation and application of personal experience cause substantial variance in the evaluation results. This "evaluator effect" inhibits reliable statistical analysis, but can be addresses by a higher number of evaluators [18].

For the evaluation of domain-specific interfaces special sets of heuristics are developed to address the specific issues prevalent in the field of application [19]. These heuristic sets usually resemble established heuristic sets. Revisions range from adjusted wording tailored to the target domain to inclusion of aspects like privacy for interfaces in the health sector or motion sickness in the development of virtual-reality applications [20, 21].

3 Socio-Technical Inspection

A combination of heuristic inspection methods with inspection methods from industrial engineering could broaden the spectrum of considered aspects. Many issues can be spotted when an inspector is looking for them. Heuristics can enable novices to detect potential problems without extensive experience in system design. The familiarity of similar methods already in use can increase acceptance of the workers. Workers who are experienced in inspecting their workplace know the critical processes. They understand the interactions and problems which occur in their workflows. In the combined design, this familiarity with their work domain gets coupled with the guidance from heuristic inspection methods. As usability heuristics are usually designed to inspect interfaces, a challenge is to evaluate entire work environments, which have a much broader spectrum of potential issues. The inspection of socio-technical aspects is supported through a set of socio-technical heuristics developed by Herrmann and Nierhoff [22].

The socio-technical heuristic inspection process consists of four phases (see Fig. 1). In the first phase the heuristic inspection process is introduced and explained. In the second phase, each heuristic is briefly introduced and subsequently used to inspect the work environment. Findings from these iterations are revised in workshops in the third phase. In the final phase, the results from the previous phases are handed over to an innovation department.

3.1 Tool Development

Based on the heuristic inspection, a software tool is being developed to enable workers to conduct inspections on socio-technical criteria. To improve understanding for documented issues by other people during the improvement process, the documentation should be more comprehensive than a short textual description. Additional videos of suboptimal process steps or locations of problematic areas can help to visualize the ideas to people outside the shopfloor team.

Further, necessary requirements and features for a socio-technical inspection tool can be derived through the literature:

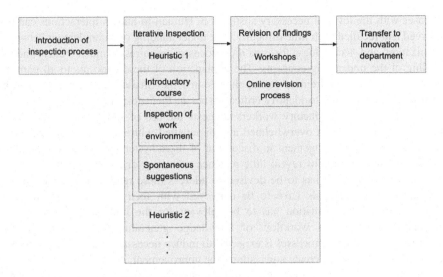

Fig. 1. Socio-technical inspection process

- Simple interface accessible for users with little experience using computer interfaces.
- Guidance through learning and documentation processes.
- Short, introductory curses to expand knowledge and understanding of socio-technical topics.
- Visibility of progress for suggestions in the improvement process.
- Overview of documented issues and collected suggestions.
- Feedback for accepted and rejected proposals.

In interviews with experts in industrial engineering and digitalization in the manufacturing industry, these findings were generally confirmed. An emphasis was put on the need for visibility of progress and feedback for suggestions. All experts noted the lack of tools or methods to identify shortcomings in digitalization efforts and provide guidance how to improve existing systems or organizational structures. These responses show the demand and desire to improve socio-technical systems on the shopfloor.

3.2 Challenges

Socio-technical systems have a strong inter-dependency on connections between humans, technology and organization. Methods for improvement or inspection of STS have to examine these connections and conceptualize reliance of critical aspects. Traditional socio-technical design-principals were developed for experts in system design. Their extensive experience enabled them to apply a meta-design perspective and to observe implicit dependencies.

The integration of shopfloor workers introduces the need to explicitly address hidden or implicit dependencies. The resulting effort in visualizing these interactions increases with the level of necessary abstraction. Human-to-human interactions can be observed and recalled with little difficulty. The understanding of entanglement between organization and technology for specific processes requires a much better understanding of the underlying concepts. The explanation of these concepts to all participants is a critical requirement for applicable results. Shallow annotation of work processes is not suitable to identify critical issues in their design.

The demographic of factory workers suggests the use of simple and precise language. Workers are often overwhelmed and dissatisfied with rapid technological progress. Incentives for engagement in discussion of these systems have to be clear and concise. Preliminary results reveal little patience with long or complex texts.

A didactic approach has to be devised to address these requirements. The socio-technical design principals have to be conveyed with focus on incentives for the workers. Provided information has to be relevant for the immediate focus of the inspection. A combined workflow of knowledge generation and application by examination of relevant processes is expected to induce necessary understanding of the inspected STS to enable create suggestions for improvement.

First attempts indicate promising results by splitting the introductory course (see Fig. 1) in separate core aspects. These aspects are presented easily understandable in form of a checklist for the inspection. Workers can examine the first subsection of their work environment without extensive theoretical preparation or training. When a worker detects a violation of one of the principles, it has to be marked and provisionally documented. This documentation is used to identify the investigated object and initial thought process. After the checklist for the examined subsection is completed a more thorough documentation is required for all identified potential issues. This documentation includes a short questionnaire specific for the aspect that identified the issue. This questionnaire guides the inspector through sub-aspects and collects relevant information on the STS. This inquiry facilitates deeper understanding of the environment and encourages critical, creative and lateral thinking.

4   Conclusion

Traditional methods for continuous improvement enable organizations in the manufacturing industry to improve their work environments and products. Rapid technological advancements cause sudden and significant changes to these environments. These changes are not necessarily organically prompted by innovation from within the company but incited by external manufacturers and opportunities. This requires the application of additional inspection methods to address the new challenges for organization, technology and human interaction. Socio-technical principles and heuristics are especially suited for inspections of manufacturing facilities.

The proposed process for socio-technical inspection is outlined and preliminary observations are discussed. Identified and possible future challenges are addressed. Novel approaches for solutions to these problems are identified and discussed.

Further research is necessary to explore different approaches and identify additional requirements for human-centered inspection and improvement methods for rapid technological advancements in the manufacturing industry.

References

1. Mumford, E.: The story of socio-technical design: reflections on its successes, failures and potential. Inf. Syst. J. **16**, 317–342 (2006). https://doi.org/10.1111/j.1365-2575.2006.00221.x
2. Geisberger, E., Broy, M.: agendaCPS: Integrierte Forschungsagenda Cyber-Physical Systems. Springer, Heidelberg (2012). https://doi.org/10.1007/978-3-642-29099-2
3. Larsson, Ö., Wiktorsson, M., Cedergren, S.: The third wave of automation: critical factors for industrial digitisation (2014). https://doi.org/10.13140/2.1.4636.3203
4. Hirsch-Kreinsen, H.: Digitization of industrial work: development paths and prospects. J. Labour Mark. Res. **49**, 1–14 (2016). https://doi.org/10.1007/s12651-016-0200-6
5. Dregger, J., Niehaus, J., Ittermann, P., Hirsch-Kreinsen, H., ten Hompel, M.: The digitization of manufacturing and its societal challenges: a framework for the future of industrial labor. In: 2016 IEEE International Symposium on Ethics in Engineering, Science and Technology (ETHICS), pp. 1–3 (2016)
6. Cherns, A.: The principles of sociotechnical design. Hum. Relat. **29**, 783–792 (1976)
7. Cherns, A.: Principles of sociotechnical design revisted. Hum. Relat. **40**, 153–161 (1987)
8. Mumford, E.: Designing Human Systems for New Technology: The ETHICS Method. Manchester Business School, Manchester (1983)
9. Mumford, E.: A socio-technical approach to systems design. Requir. Eng. **5**, 125–133 (2000)
10. Bessant, J., Caffyn, S.: High-involvement innovation through continuous improvement. IJTM **14**, 7 (1997). https://doi.org/10.1504/IJTM.1997.001705
11. Boer, H., Gertsen, F.: From continuous improvement to continuous innovation: a (retro)(per) spective. IJTM (2000). https://doi.org/10.1504/IJTM.2003.003391
12. Salah, S., Rahim, A., Carretero, J.A.: The integration of Six Sigma and lean management. Int. J. Lean Six Sigma **1**, 249–274 (2010). https://doi.org/10.1108/20401461011075035
13. Singh, J., Singh, H.: Kaizen philosophy: a review of literature. IUP J. Oper. Manag. **8**, 51 (2009)
14. Berger, A.: Continuous improvement and kaizen: standardization and organizational designs. Integr. Manuf. Syst. **8**, 110–117 (1997). https://doi.org/10.1108/09576069710165792
15. Pfeiffer, S., Held, M., Lee, H.: Digitalisierung „machen" – Ansichten im Engineering zur partizipativen Gestaltung von Industrie 4.0. In: Hofmann, J. (ed.) Arbeit 4.0 – Digitalisierung, IT und Arbeit. EH, pp. 113–129. Springer, Wiesbaden (2018). https://doi.org/10.1007/978-3-658-21359-6_7
16. Nielsen, J.: Heuristic evaluation. In: Usability Inspection Methods, pp. 25–62. Wiley, New York (1994)
17. Nielsen, J., Molich, R.: Heuristic evaluation of user interfaces. In: Proceedings of the SIGCHI Conference on Human Factors in Computing Systems, pp. 249–256. ACM, New York (1990)
18. Hertzum, M., Jacobsen, N.E.: The evaluator effect: a chilling fact about usability evaluation methods. Int. J. Hum. Comput. Interact. **13**, 421–443 (2001). https://doi.org/10.1207/S15327590IJHC1304_05
19. Quiñones, D., Rusu, C., Rusu, V.: A methodology to develop usability/user experience heuristics. Comput. Stand. Interfaces **59**, 109–129 (2018). https://doi.org/10.1016/j.csi.2018.03.002

20. Jiménez, C., Rusu, C., Roncagliolo, S., Inostroza, R., Rusu, V.: Evaluating a methodology to establish usability heuristics. In: 2012 31st International Conference of the Chilean Computer Science Society, pp. 51–59 (2012)
21. Quinones, D., Rusu, C., Roncagliolo, S., Rusu, V., Collazos, C.A.: Developing usability heuristics: a formal or informal process? IEEE Lat. Am. Trans. **14**, 3400–3409 (2016). https://doi.org/10.1109/TLA.2016.7587648
22. Herrmann, T., Nierhoff, J.: Heuristiken zur Evaluation digitalisierter Arbeit bei Industrie-4.0 und KI-basierten Systemen aus soziotechnischer Perspektive. FGW. Digitalisierung von Arbeit 16 (2019)

Sustainable Interactive Design
of Cross-cultural Online Maker Space

Wei Yu[(⊠)] and Baiyang Wang

School of Art Design and Media,
East China University of Science and Technology, Shanghai, China
weiyu@ecust.edu.cn

Abstract. Under the background of knowledge society, Innovation 2.0 mode is formed. As a new innovation mode, mass innovation expands the concept of maker space. With the development of globalization, the concept of community of shared future of human beings appears on the world stage. Based on the theoretical support of cultural commonality and civilization integration, this paper proposes the cross-cultural online maker space, through cultural diversity to stimulate innovation, to achieve a virtuous circle of maker space and social civilization. This paper systematically designs cross-cultural online maker space, and studies the design strategy of cross-cultural system, adopting the method of sustainable interaction design. In addition, this paper explores the impact of 5G, blockchain and other new technologies on the development of maker space, so as to ensure its feasibility and sustainability.

Keywords: Online maker space · Cross-culture · Sustainable interactive design · Open innovation

1 Introduction

In the context of the information age, the advanced information and media technologies have broken the boundaries of time and space, greatly shortened the distance between countries. The globalization of economy, technology, and culture makes each country depend on and promote each other. In addition, driven by information technology, innovation has become the mainstream of the development of the times. The traditional innovation model has gradually transformed into an Innovation 2.0 model centered on mass innovation and open innovation. In the first two backgrounds, the exchanges and collisions of different cultures are becoming more and more intense. Nowadays, how to balance and coordinate this situation, and achieve co-creation and win-win cooperation among different countries has been a hot research direction.

The concept of maker space is constantly expanding, and its interaction space has changed from physical space to regional virtual space, which gives more possibilities for interaction forms and methods. Based on the characteristics of openness and innovation of Makers, we boldly propose a new cross-cultural online maker space, that is, a maker platform for multi-national collaborative innovation, so as to mobilize the vitality of the whole "global village" to realize the sustainable innovation of human civilization.

© Springer Nature Switzerland AG 2020
C. Stephanidis and M. Antona (Eds.): HCII 2020, CCIS 1224, pp. 107–114, 2020.
https://doi.org/10.1007/978-3-030-50726-8_14

2 Concept of Online Maker Space

2.1 Overview of Maker Space

Maker space refers to a kind of socialized innovation platform. It can realize creative sharing and cross-border cooperation by providing service platform for communication, open physical space, equipment and resources needed for creative practice, so as to promote the practice and productization of creative inspiration. In the second half of the 20th century, the emergence of the third scientific and technological revolution brought mankind into the information age. And the wave of globalization, technology and interconnection gave birth to the maker movement. In 1981, "chaos computer club" was born in Berlin, Germany, and became the first maker space recognized in the world. Since then, maker space has sprung up. In addition, the emergence of new technologies such as computing design, 3D printing and open-source hardware also provides effective support for the realization of creativity, thus promoting the development of maker space.

With the development of Internet technology, the main body and mode of innovation are constantly changing. Scientific and technological innovation projects are gradually turning into user centered Innovation 2.0 mode. Therefore, the concept of maker space has changed, from the original small group of maker movement to mass innovation. In addition, maker space breaks through the shackles of physical space, expanding into an online and offline integrated space combined with virtual space.

2.2 Challenges of Maker Space

At this stage, maker space is in the period of transformation and development, and the difficulties and challenges faced by different regions are also different. As far as China is concerned, based on the investigation of the more developed Yangtze River Delta region and the more backward western region in China, the challenges faced by maker space mainly include two aspects.

On the one hand, the field equipment of maker space is not in place, and the capital investment is insufficient. The development of maker space needs to pay a lot of costs, including venue leasing, equipment purchase, operation management, etc. The shortage of funds is mainly due to the lack of effective operation organization mode. Relying on government subsidies and members' financial contributions alone, not only the makers' dreams cannot be realized, but also maker space itself will face the problems of unsustainable profits and scale expansion.

On the other hand, it is the imbalance of regional development and the shortage of human resources. The development of maker space is closely related to the participation of top talents. Compared with the eastern Yangtze River Delta, the economic development of Western China is backward and the environment for innovation and entrepreneurship is poor. So talent flow tends to the East. In addition, from the perspective of overall development, the number and diversity of senior makers, management talents and talents in other fields are also lacking, the public awareness of innovation has not really formed, and the multi-agent interaction mode has not been realized.

In addition, maker space also faces copyright issues, system maintenance issues, etc. How maker space can achieve sustainable development remains to be further explored.

2.3   Cross-cultural Online Maker Space

Based on the development of maker space model and the problems faced, the establishment of online platform becomes the key to realize the sustainable development of maker space. With the development of science and technology, the arrival of big data, cloud computing, 5G, blockchain and other innovative technologies has given a new mode of innovation and entrepreneurship. The mode of maker space dominated by physical space will be transformed into a new mode of regional linkage dominated by virtual space. Due to the existence of online platforms, we can further establish distributed maker space [1], reduce operating costs and optimize resource utilization through the sharing and collaboration of small maker space and central maker space.

As mentioned above, the concept of online maker space referred to in this paper is no longer limited to maker activities, but "mass innovation". Based on the current upsurge of globalization, this paper boldly proposes the cross-cultural online mass innovation space, which can further expand the diversity of the main body of mass innovation, link the vitality of the whole "global village" to achieve innovation projects, and even solve global problems. At the same time, it can promote the interaction between different cultures to the greatest extent, achieve the aesthetic common of psychological space and virtual space, and facilitate the harmonious and stable development of "global village".

3   Overview of Cross-cultural Studies

3.1   Comparative Study of Cultures

On the cultural level, it is particularly important to solve the obstacles of cultural differences for the construction and sustainable development of maker space. The concept of culture is very extensive, so far scholars all over the world do not have a unified concept to define it. Cultural differences can be explained from horizontal and vertical dimensions.

First of all, in the horizontal dimension, the cultural differences between the East and the west not only include the semantic differences, but also the aesthetic, physiological and psychological differences. For example, avoiding uncertainty, the West pays attention to the logic of thinking and rejects ambiguity. The East, however, tends not to speak thoroughly and prefers to leave some room or room for reflection, which may cause cultural misunderstanding and hinder the process of global co-creation.

Secondly, in the vertical dimension, the pace of cultural change and change is faster and faster. As for China, there will be new annual buzzwords on the Internet every year, such as "OMG, buy it" in 2019, reflecting the outbreak of social e-commerce in China. Design has evolved organically with cultural changes. In the era of low human civilization, human beings mainly pay attention to physical or physiological needs and design sickles, houses, etc. With the development of technology and society, human beings begin to pay attention to the design of reason, reason, ethics and other aspects. On this basis, human beings reflect on the relationship between man and nature, and pay attention to the design of the unity of man and nature. Human civilization and discovery and invention promote each other and complement each other. Exploring the change of culture in time provides the basis for social development.

Culture is the best entry point to study different social civilization, while the intersection of time and space is the empathy of human cross-cultural communication, that is, cultural commonality.

3.2   Cross-culture Study

According to the definition of culturology, cross-culture refers to the interaction between two or more cultures, across the national boundaries. This paper holds that the development of human civilization has always been homologous and symbiotic, and cross-culture is a key step in cultural integration. So it is feasible and necessary to integrate cross culture into online mass innovation platform.

From a macro perspective, as a community of shared destiny, all kinds of civilizations have something in common. For example, the natural concept of slow design in northern Europe coincides with that of Zen in China. We can use the development of audio-visual art to simulate the evolution of different social civilizations. After thousands of years of development and evolution, plastic arts and music arts have gradually formed different complex categories, but based on the similarity and primitivism of early human society, they always have the common aesthetic principles, that is, the ecological view of the unity of man and nature.

From a micro perspective, in today's globalization, social mobility makes the collision and integration of culture reach a climax. Therefore, design should not be limited to and centered on the domestic user experience, but should put cross-cultural communication at the front of design, design with international thinking, and interact with different cultures in adaptability and complementarity. Through this method, on the one hand, it can reduce the impact of cultural differences on product audiences, on the other hand, it can reduce the impact of cultural change on product life cycle, and improve the cultural added value of products.

Cross-culture can be embodied in human language, aesthetics, values, ways of thinking and communication. In order to analyze all kinds of culture, many studies have put forward different cultural psychological models. For example, Choong et al. [2] divide culture into four dimensions when designing cross-cultural web pages, including cognitive dimension, emotional dimension, perceptual dimension and functional dimension. The perceptual dimension includes the use of metaphor, and the functional dimension includes uncertainty avoidance. This paper divides culture into two levels. One is the external level, which refers to people's most intuitive feelings of cultural differences, including language, time zone, currency, etc. The other is the internal level, which mainly emphasizes the harmony of human psychological space, including aesthetics, metaphor, logic, communication mode, etc.

4   Design Strategies of Online Maker Space System

In this paper, the method of sustainable interactive design is used to ensure the sustainability of the system. Through the research of cross-cultural system, three community platforms of cross-cultural online maker space system are put forward innovatively:

4.1   Sustainable Interaction Design

Sustainable interactive design ensures the sustainability of the system through interactive design thinking, including the sustainability of environment, society, culture and economy. The significant trend of design development is the improvement of user participation. In the past, the traditional designer monopolized the design, gradually appeared the user customization, and then to the current trend of experience economy, all told us that the future of design must be user-oriented. On the one hand, the cross-cultural online maker space provides new opportunities for product innovation through the cultural diversity of participants, so that the product can be iterated organically. On the other hand, cultural and social sustainability can be achieved through cultural exchanges. How to realize the sustainable system of cultural empowerment design and management of mass innovation platform, and how to gather and coordinate the cross-cultural innovation power are the topics of this paper.

Interactive technology drives the development of open innovation, which lays the foundation for global communication, mass innovation and instant interaction. In order to solve the impact of cultural differences on the operation of online maker space and realize the social sustainability of the system, the international and inclusive goals should be taken in the system development. Mustaquim et al. [3] proposed an inclusive innovation framework (IIF) designed to achieve sustainable development goals. The design mainly improves the overall user satisfaction through simple and flexible use, easy to perceive and understand the system and low physical requirements, so as to achieve sustainability. Through the combination of multi-media and multi-mode, the new interaction technology enhances the system's inclusiveness and facilitates the use of cross-cultural users.

4.2   Cross-cultural System Design

As mentioned above, deep-rooted cultural differences can easily lead to cultural misunderstanding among users, so cross-cultural systems need to design effective mechanisms to alleviate this contradiction. Day [4] divides the consideration of cultural factors in system design into three levels: Globalization (emphasizing the objectivity of culture, ignoring the subjective factors), internationalization (reducing the influence of cultural symbols, improving the internationalization), localization (catering to the needs of different cultural groups). Based on the fact that the cross-cultural online maker space is still in the initial stage of development, this paper proposes to design the cross-cultural system internationally, only considering the external level of culture, so as to improve the universality of the system. During system operation, big data is used to explore the internal characteristics of different cultures, so as to realize localization and improve the adaptability of the system to different cultures.

In the international design of cross-cultural system, the translation of different languages, time zone and currency annotation should be considered in the interface design. In addition, the design should try to maintain cultural neutrality and avoid culturally sensitive factors such as racial discrimination. Localized design is the goal of cross-cultural systems to make products suitable for specific cultural groups. In the process of accumulating the internal characteristics of different cultures, we can adopt the method of identifying "cultural markers". Cultural markers were put forward by Barber and Badre [5] in 1998, which means the most accepted and expected interface design elements of cultural groups in specific regions. In other words, cultural markers are the embodiment of cultural internal characteristics, including color, logic, metaphor, etc. Through the collection and accumulation of big data on cultural markers, we can further iterate the system and integrate specific cultural markers into the system design.

4.3   Design Strategies of Cross-cultural Online Maker Space Ecosystem

The sustainable online maker space needs to build an innovation ecosystem with the characteristics of self-growth, self-profit and self-repair. Therefore, the cross-cultural online maker space can be divided into education community, inspiration community and innovation community.

At the level of educational community, on the one hand, maker education can rely on Colleges and universities to carry out formal curriculum education and research; on the other hand, it needs to pay attention to interdisciplinary, creative practice, experience education, etc., so as to cultivate open and innovative talents. Formal courses can be combined with steam Education (Science, technology, engineering, art, Mathematics) to improve students' interdisciplinary innovation ability. In addition, maker education is inseparable from practice. The establishment of education system can work closely with universities, enterprises and governments to realize the socialization of maker education. While teaching practice, educational community can also promote the development of innovative community. The innovation community can provide projects to the education community in the form of crowdsourcing, and the makers can provide a lot of creativity to the initiators through project practice, so as to realize a virtuous circle.

At the level of inspiration community, it is mainly user-centered to share knowledge and creativity of cross-cultural or interdisciplinary groups. First of all, it is necessary to reduce the threshold of communication, provide a platform for resource sharing, further integrate big data space based on communication data, mix and edit different cultures, and intelligently analyze the different semantic systems, aesthetic concepts, and thinking modes of people from different cultural backgrounds. Through the collection and classification of cultural markers, we can find the common genes of culture on the basis of exploring the cultural differences of different countries. Secondly, we can further design the physiological and psychological level through big data, such as building personalized interaction interface according to different behavior habits, or building symbol semantic database, integrating different cultural meanings, promoting cultural identity, so as to promote cross-cultural communication. Finally, we can explore multisensory experience interaction, from hearing, touch, smell and so on, to promote the maximization of communication mode and experience.

At the level of innovation community, the first thing is to have an open-source platform to provide makers with design tools, software and hardware, project library, etc. Next is the project management system. One is to have good ecological information guidance, realize the rational allocation of information resources, and encourage users to carry out cross-cultural design or join the cross-cultural design team. The second is the project schedule management system, which can track and monitor the project and protect the privacy. Finally, we need to have reflection and evaluation mechanism, online tracking and calculation of design process and problems, and dynamic system design based on the comprehensive feedback of users. The extensible interactive Modular Simulation (SIMS) proposed by Ferrara [6] is a kind of sustainable design model based on sharing. Based on this, users can develop their own design and give full play to their innovation ability. The project community can refer to the Sims model for user guidance. Based on the generation design of SIMS, which is mainly based on the recombination elements, the future research needs to further explore the user independent innovation system and cross-cultural cooperation system.

5 Technical Support of Cross-cultural Online Maker Space

With the development of science and technology, the construction of online maker space ushered in significant opportunities. Based on 5G and blockchain, this paper creatively proposes the following technical support points for cross-cultural mass creation.

First of all, 5G's characteristics of high data transmission rate and low delay level facilitate the real-time transmission of big data, high-definition video and even virtual reality. So it can provide technical support for information exchange and supervision and management of cross-regional projects. In addition, the large network capacity of 5G can meet the real-time connection scenarios of massive equipment, such as telemedicine projects and radio-controlled industrial manufacturing projects. Combined with artificial intelligence, the innovation system can be mobile, data-based, collaborative and intelligent, and then the software and hardware system of maker space will be combined to transition from digital maker space to intelligent maker space. Last but not least, users will generate a lot of data during the use of the platform, which is not only conducive to the system iteration, but also can depict user profiles in different countries according to user data. Therefore, based on the construction of a universal platform, differentiated content services can be provided.

In addition, as a research hotspot at this stage, the characteristics of blockchain, such as decentralization, openness, independence and security, coincide with the concept and demand of online maker space. Through the blockchain's distributed ledger technology, project personnel in different position and regions can jointly complete data recording, greatly improving the efficiency of cooperation. Besides, they can jointly participate in the supervision of the project. In addition, using an appropriate consensus mechanism can allow project partners reach a consensus, identify the reliability and effectiveness of project records, and provide a foundation of trust for cross-cultural stakeholders. Based on these reliable data records, smart contract technology can automatically implement some consensus rules and terms in the process of the project, making the interactive innovation of online maker space efficient and transparent. In addition, using intelligent contract and blockchain technology to realize cross organization RBAC mechanism [7], that is, according to the roles of different users to control their access to certain services, so as to enhance the flexibility and security of the platform.

6 Conclusion

With the academic support of cultural commonality and the technical support of 5G and blockchain, the development of cross-cultural online maker space is necessary and feasible. This paper divides cross-cultural maker space into education community, inspiration community and innovation community, so as to make the system more orderly and sustainable. This system can provide a platform for resource sharing, and promote people's cultural identity in the virtual space and psychological space, based on the mixed editing of different cultures by big data. Furthermore, it can also realize the creation, implementation, management and supervision of transnational design projects, provide new opportunities for global innovation, and ultimately achieve sharing, co-creation and win-win results.

References

1. Shahzad, B., Saleem, K.: Benefits of establishing makerspaces in distributed development environment. In: Latifi, S. (ed.) Information Technology - New Generations. AISC, vol. 738, pp. 621–625. Springer, Cham (2018). https://doi.org/10.1007/978-3-319-77028-4_79
2. Choong, Y.Y., Plocher, T., Rau, P.L.: Cross-cultural web design. In: Proctor, R.W., Vu, K.-P.L. (eds.) Handbook of Human Factors in Web Design. Lawrence Erlbaum Associates, Publishers (2005)
3. Mustaquim, M.M., Nyström, T.: Designing information systems for sustainability – the role of universal design and open innovation. In: Tremblay, M.C., VanderMeer, D., Rothenberger, M., Gupta, A., Yoon, V. (eds.) DESRIST 2014. LNCS, vol. 8463, pp. 1–16. Springer, Cham (2014). https://doi.org/10.1007/978-3-319-06701-8_1
4. Day, D.L.: Cultural bases of interface acceptance: foundations. In: Sasse, M.A., Cunningham, R.J., Winder, R.L. (eds.) People and Computers XI, pp. 35–47. Springer, London (1996). https://doi.org/10.1007/978-1-4471-3588-3_3
5. Barber, W., Badre, A.: Culturability, the merging of culture and usability. In: Proceedings of the 4th Conference on Human Factors and the Web. Basking Ridge, NJ (1998)
6. Ferrara, L., Dadashi, N.: SYSTEMATEKS: scalable interactive modular simulation (SIMS): towards sustainable design. In: Rau, P.-L.P. (ed.) CCD 2016. LNCS, vol. 9741, pp. 173–181. Springer, Cham (2016). https://doi.org/10.1007/978-3-319-40093-8_18
7. Cruz, J.P., Kaji, Y., Yanai, N.: RBAC-SC: role-based access control using smart contract. IEEE Access 6, 12240–12251 (2018)

User Characteristics, Requirements
and Preferences

Investigating Perceived Task Urgency as Justification for Dominant Robot Behaviour

Annika Boos[(✉)] [iD], Michaela Sax[iD], and Jakob Reinhardt[iD]

Chair of Ergonomics, Technical University of Munich,
Boltzmannstrasse 15, 85747 Garching, Germany
annika.boos@tum.de

Abstract. For the ubiquitous application of mobile robots, robots will need strategies to efficiently navigate through spaces shared with humans. To accomplish time-critical tasks, it can be necessary for robots to take precedence over humans. Giving a justification for such dominant robot behaviour, based on the urgency of its task, might mitigate negative effects on trust and acceptance and enhance behavioural compliance by waiting for the robot to pass. This study investigates the perceived urgency of different tasks a robot might perform. Therefore, 129 participants rated and compared ten tasks in an online study. The results reveal differences in perceived task urgency, related to time pressure in accomplishing the task. Differences in task urgency also affected the choice of who should be given priority to precede in a spatial conflict (human or robot). Furthermore, the results indicate a bias around human-robot interactions: Priority was more often granted to the human than the robot, when equally urgent tasks were presented for both entities.

Keywords: Human-robot interaction · Dominant robot behaviour

1 Theoretical Background

A steep increase in the number of mobile service robots is expected in the near future [3]. The number of mobile robots that have applications in public spaces is also likely to increase steeply. For a socio-economically reasonable application, a robot's efficiency in accomplishing a given task is considered to be crucial. Therefore, robots will not only have to consider humans when planning a path, but will in addition have to negotiate spatial conflicts in close proximity to humans. In order to accomplish efficient, safe and economically feasible human-robot coordination, robots will need to have flexible motion and decision strategies available. A lot of attention has been allocated to the incorporation of defensive decision-making when in potential conflict with humans [4,14]. Such approaches limit the amount of possible solutions in spatial conflicts and can thereby diminish system efficiency.

© Springer Nature Switzerland AG 2020
C. Stephanidis and M. Antona (Eds.): HCII 2020, CCIS 1224, pp. 117–124, 2020.
https://doi.org/10.1007/978-3-030-50726-8_15

Therefore, more approaches in system design are being taken into account that allow for more flexible motion and decision-making strategies. For example [7] present an algorithm that enables robots to decide whether or not to obey human orders based on human preferences. This work aims to provide insights into the circumstances that make dominant robot behaviour acceptable.

1.1 Dominance and Taking Precedence

As robots will encounter people with varying levels of robot expertise in public space, it appears sensible to build human-robot-interaction strategies on the basis of interpersonal communication concepts. This is also based on findings related to the *Media Equation Theory* proposing that computers are seen as social actors [9]. Dominance is considered a key strategy in interpersonal interaction that helps to resolve goal conflicts. Generally, dominance can be defined as the degree to which one actor attempts to regulate the behaviour of another [1].

Robot motion is termed "dominant" when the robot continues with its task despite possible interference with a person, causing the person to give priority to the robot, and is otherwise termed "submissive" [11]. Concerning robot motion, [5] found that motion patterns derived from human nonverbal communication can effectively convey the dominance of a robot. Results collected in a hospital show that staff felt disrespected when service robots took precedence in a hallway [8]. It was found that faulty robot behaviour significantly lowered subjective trust and perceived reliability, but did not affect user's willingness to comply with requests made by the robot [13]. Hence, in the context of dominant robot motion behaviour, it is of high relevance to communicate the robot's decision to move first legibly (as defined in [2]) to prevent human observers from attributing the dominant motion (taking precedence) as faulty behaviour.

A recent study compared submissive-only robot behaviour to alternating dominant-submissive robot behaviour at a narrow passage. No significant difference in compliance with variable robot behaviour was found, but trust was lowered in the alternating dominant-submissive motion condition [10]. In dialogues between human and robot, dominant robot behaviour was found to correlate with lower trust in both the robot and its human conversational partner [6]. In line with this, [11] found that submissive robot behaviour enhanced trust compared to dominant behaviour. These results highlight the need to investigate which factors influence the acceptability of a robot taking precedence, and how to preserve trust when applying more complex decision and motion strategies.

1.2 Robot Task as Justification for Dominant Behaviour

Corresponding explanations are considered important in enhancing the user's understanding of system decisions. A better understanding could thus increase trust in and acceptance of the system and the decision [12,15]. Giving an explanation for dominant robot behaviour based on the relevance of its task could therefore help mitigating a decline in trust in and acceptance of the robot's behaviour, and in turn enhance compliance by waiting for the robot to pass if it takes precedence while accomplishing an urgent task.

When enabling more complex robot decisions and motion strategies, it is of high relevance to take human preferences into account. It is therefore crucial to know which tasks are perceived as being more or less important to mediate reactance (acting contrarily to the suggested behaviour) as well as decrements in trust and acceptance in response to the robot taking precedence. In the domain of consumer research, [16] proposed a task categorisation based on importance (big versus small outcome magnitude) and urgency (immediate versus long completion windows). The authors found a tendency to prioritise unimportant, but urgent tasks over important, but not urgent tasks.

This study focuses on perceived task urgency and the influence of differences in task urgency on granted priority to proceed through a narrow passage first. The above-mentioned categorisation [16] is adopted for this study, assuming that task urgency increases with decreasing time budgets for task completion.

2   Method

A two-part online survey was conducted using ten different tasks (listed below). For the robot, tasks can be categorised into the areas of (1) Transport: Tasks one and eight, (2) Information submission: Tasks three, seven and ten and (3) Telepresence: Tasks two, four, five, six and nine.

1. Deliver an allergy-emergency set to a person undergoing an allergic shock.
2. Attend a crisis-management meeting discussing the evacuation of the area due to a reactor incident.
3. Help rescue workers by acquiring information on the situation after an accident.
4. Acquire information for the police after theft (secure means of evidence).
5. De-escalate a conflict between two persons which is threatening to turn violent.
6. Give a conference talk at short notice.
7. Fetch an important guest who is waiting.
8. Deliver documents to a colleague for signing.
9. Attend a lecture that will begin soon.
10. Photograph an object for a colleague.

2.1   Measures

Perceived Task Urgency: Participants rated each task for perceived urgency on a 6-point Likert scale, between "1 - very low urgency" and "6 - highest urgency". The arithmetic mean task urgency was taken as the average.

Priority Decisions: Participants were asked to imagine the situation that human and robot would meet at a narrow passage that requires one party to take precedence over the other. Human and robot were each presented with one of the previously urgency-rated tasks. Participants indicated whether human or robot should be given priority to precede through the narrow passage first (forced choice). As the total of possible combinations out of the ten tasks was too high to present every participant with each possible task combination, each participant was presented with a maximum of 20 randomly chosen task combinations to limit the length of the survey. The differences in task urgency were calculated based on individual task-urgency ratings and not mean urgency ratings per task.

2.2   Sample Description

A total of 192 persons participated in the study. Out of these, 129 participants completed the whole study and were included in data analysis. The sample includes 57% (N = 74) female and 43% (N = 55) male participants with a mean age of 29.53 years (SD = 8.13 years, ranging from 20 to 62 years).

3   Results

3.1   Perceived Task Urgency

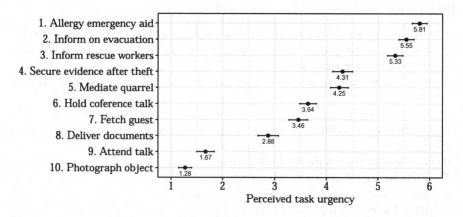

Fig. 1. Mean rated task urgency per task; whiskers indicate lower and upper boundaries of 95% confidence intervals.

Figure 1 shows the mean rated task urgency for the ten tasks. Friedman's test of task urgency indicates a highly significant difference, with $X^2(9) = 883.66$, $p < 0.0001$. Pairwise comparisons using the Wilcoxon signed-rank test (Bonferroni - Holm corrected) indicate that all tasks were rated as having different levels of urgency ($p < 0.05$) except for two pairs: Task four (secure evidence after theft) and task five (de-escalation of a quarrel): $p = 0.54$; as well as task six (hold a conference talk) and task seven (fetch an important guest) $p = 0.08$.

3.2 Priority Decisions

Figure 2 shows the percentage of priority given to the human or robot depending on the difference in task urgency. Task urgency differences indicate whether the human or the robot were allocated tasks that were rated equally urgent (difference of zero) or more urgent than the other party (differences of one to five), using the individual task urgency ratings for each participant. For example, a difference of three in task urgency describes all cases where task pairs were presented for human or robot that were rated 4 vs. 1, 5 vs. 2 and 6 vs. 3 on urgency by the participant making the priority decision. In total, 2,041 priority choices were made by the participants. Table 1 contains total numbers of priority decisions.

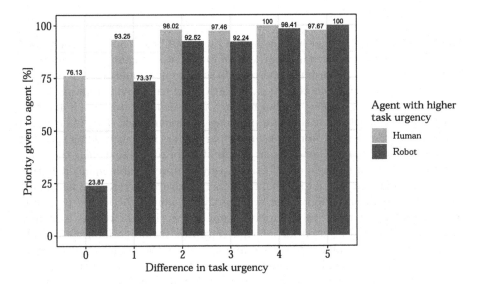

Fig. 2. Percentage of participants who gave precedence to each agent (human or robot) depending on the difference in perceived task urgency.

Table 1. Total numbers of cases of priority being given and denied to the human or the robot, depending on differences in task urgency.

Difference in task urgency	0		1		2		3		4		5	
Agent with higher urgency	H	R	H	R	H	R	H	R	H	R	H	R
N given priority	507	159	235	146	198	136	115	107	37	124	42	135
N denied priority	159	507	17	53	4	11	3	9	0	2	1	0

[a] Human (H) or robot (R) presented with higher rated task urgency.
[b] Number (N) of participants who gave priority to each agent.

The results indicate that the difference in perceived task urgency has a strong influence on who is given priority. Furthermore, a human-robot bias can be observed that is most pronounced for the task urgency differences of zero (equal task urgency) and one. For equal task urgency conditions, a surplus of 52.26% priority given to the human over the robot and for task differences of one, a surplus of 19.88% in favour of the human over the robot, indicate that the human is given priority more often than the robot when both are pursuing equally urgent or a slightly more urgent task than the counterparty. However, this bias cannot be observed in the data for larger differences in task urgency (differences of two or more), indicating that human and robot are both given priority in over 92% of the cases when pursuing a more urgent task than the other agent.

4   Discussion

The results of this study show that the ten presented tasks can be distinguished according to their perceived urgency, except for two task combinations (four and five; six and seven). Accordingly, perceived task urgency could serve as a source of information in spatial coordination. While a robot can provide information on its current task on a display, further research is needed to determine if and how humans communicate that they are pursuing an urgent task. This information could possibly be derived from measurable parameters such as walking speed. It will also be useful to consider different possibilities for robots to display their current task and its urgency in an effective, easily-comprehensible manner. Future research should also take into account whether tasks are perceived to be equally suited for human and robot. This was partly accounted for in the presented study by adapting tasks to the robot's capabilities, in that it was explained that the robot could be used for multiple purposes, including information submission, telepresence and video streaming as well as the transport/delivery of items. Nevertheless, ancillary assumptions as to the robot's performance in some tasks could have influenced the choice of who should precede.

Perceived task urgency influenced whether human or robot was given priority to proceed through a narrow passage first. The agent with the higher task urgency (differences of two to five) was given priority to proceed first in over 92% for all cases. Accordingly, no difference was observed in the priority attributed to human or robot for high differences in task urgency (higher than two). On the contrary, a strong human-robot bias in favour of the human occurred for differences of zero (same task urgency) as well as the lowest urgency difference of one. The robot was denied priority in 76.13% of cases, when both agent's tasks were rated to be equally urgent and, which is more surprising, the robot was denied priority in 26.63% of cases when the robot's task was rated to be more urgent than the human's, opposed to 6.75% of cases in which the human was denied priority despite of higher task urgency (referring to differences of one in task urgency). This suggests that people prefer submissive robot behaviour, such that the human is attributed priority if there is no strong justification for the robot to behave dominantly (when the robot task is not considered to be much more urgent). This finding should therefore be considered in motion-planning and decision hierarchies when implementing variable dominant-submissive robot behaviour. Whether the high task urgency of a pursued task can serve as justification for dominant robot behaviour and effectively mitigate the negative effects on acceptance and trust needs evaluation in real-world applications. In that respect, safety implications when applying dominant motion and decision strategies need to be evaluated critically. Incorporating variable motion behaviour and more flexible decision-making as to whether to move dominantly or submissively may not compromise safety in human-robot interaction. This could be achieved by prioritising safety as the highest possible hierarchy level, and subordinate dominance and other decisions underneath this layer.

4.1   Limitations

The tasks chosen for this study are only examples for tasks that a robot might be given in the future, and were chosen to explore the highest and lowest task urgency boundaries. Some tasks were much less likely and more unusual than others, which could have influenced perceived urgency. A 6-point Likert scale was chosen to rate task urgency. This may have been too narrow a scale for participants to separate the task urgency of different tasks from each other.

Furthermore, task-urgency differences for priority choices were unequally distributed. Task-urgency differences of zero occurred most often (666 times). Accordingly, the human-robot bias observed for the difference of zero in task urgency may be considered sufficiently backed by the data, while the results concerning other differences need further validation.

The results of this study are based on an online survey and need validation in a real-world application. As the priority ratings were given from a third person's perspective, and participants did not experience any costs when deciding in favour of the agent with the less urgent task in this setting, it remains unclear how people would react if they were themselves facing the robot.

5   Conclusions and Future Work

Based on the results, recommendations for trajectory planning can be given. Accordingly, the task each agent has to accomplish may serve as an aid in deciding whether a robot should move dominantly or submissively in the case of a spatial conflict. When the difference in task urgency between human and robot tasks is low, the results of the presented study indicate that robots should behave submissively and yield priority to humans. When task-urgency differences are high, dominant movement strategies could be acceptable and should be considered to enhance system efficiency. A follow-up study building on these results in a real-world setting is planned, with a focus on how justifications for dominant robot motion behaviour affect trust and acceptance.

References

1. Dillard, J.P., Solomon, D.H., Palmer, M.T.: Structuring the concept of relational communication. Commun. Monogr. **66**(1), 49–65 (1999)
2. Dragan, A.D., Lee, K.C., Srinivasa, S.S.: Legibility and predictability of robot motion. In: 2013 8th ACM/IEEE International Conference on Human-Robot Interaction (HRI), pp. 301–308. IEEE (2013)
3. International Federation of Robotics: Executive summary world robotics - service robots (2018)
4. Lam, C.P., Chou, C.T., Chiang, K.H., Fu, L.C.: Human-centered robot navigation—towards a harmoniously human–robot coexisting environment. IEEE Trans. Robot. **27**(1), 99–112 (2010)
5. Li, J., Cuadra, A., Mok, B., Reeves, B., Kaye, J., Ju, W.: Communicating dominance in a nonanthropomorphic robot using locomotion. ACM Trans. Hum. Robot. Interact. (THRI) **8**(1), 1–14 (2019)
6. Li, J., Ju, W., Nass, C.: Observer perception of dominance and mirroring behavior in human-robot relationships. In: 10th ACM/IEEE International Conference on Human-Robot Interaction (HRI), pp. 133–140. IEEE (2015)
7. Milli, S., Hadfield-Menell, D., Dragan, A., Russell, S.: Should robots be obedient? In: Proceedings of the Twenty-Sixth International Joint Conference on Artificial Intelligence (IJCAI-17), pp. 4754–4760 (2017)
8. Mutlu, B., Forlizzi, J.: Robots in organizations: the role of workflow, social, and environmental factors in human-robot interaction. In: 3rd International Conference on Human-Robot Interaction (HRI), pp. 287–294. IEEE (2008)
9. Reeves, B., Nass, C.: The Media Equation: How People Treat Computers, Television, and New Media Like Real People and Places. Cambridge University Press, Cambridge (1996)
10. Reinhardt, J., Boos, A., Bloier, M., Bengler, K.: Effect of variable motion behavior of a mobile robot on human compliance in human-robot spatial interaction. In: 66. Fruehjahrskongress der Gesellschaft fuer Arbeitswissenschaft (GfA). GfA-Press (2020)
11. Reinhardt, J., Pereira, A., Beckert, D., Bengler, K.: Dominance and movement cues of robot motion: a user study on trust and predictability. In: IEEE International Conference on Systems, Man, and Cybernetics (SMC), pp. 1493–1498. IEEE (2017)
12. Rosenfeld, A., Richardson, A.: Explainability in human-agent systems. Auton. Agents Multi Agent Syst. **33**(6), 673–705 (2019)
13. Salem, M., Lakatos, G., Amirabdollahian, F., Dautenhahn, K.: Would you trust a (faulty) robot? Effects of error, task type and personality on human-robot cooperation and trust. In: 10th ACM/IEEE International Conference on Human-Robot Interaction (HRI), pp. 141–148. IEEE (2015)
14. Trinh, T.Q., Schroeter, C., Kessler, J., Gross, H.-M.: "Go ahead, please": recognition and resolution of conflict situations in narrow passages for polite mobile robot navigation. ICSR 2015. LNCS (LNAI), vol. 9388, pp. 643–653. Springer, Cham (2015). https://doi.org/10.1007/978-3-319-25554-5_64
15. Yetim, F.: A framework for organizing justifications for strategic use in adaptive interaction contexts. In: European Conference on Information Systems (ECIS), pp. 815–825 (2008)
16. Zhu, M., Yang, Y., Hsee, C.K.: The mere urgency effect. J. Consum. Res. **45**(3), 673–690 (2018)

A Practical Framework for Enhancing the Effectiveness of Gamification Taking into Account Personality Types in HEIs

Brunella Botte[(✉)] and Carlo Maria Medaglia

Link Campus University, Rome, Italy
{b.botte, c.medaglia}@unilink.it

Abstract. Gamification strategies are often used in contexts where heterogeneous people have to accomplish heterogeneous tasks, in order to foster their motivation and to scaffold their engagement in the long term. In order to improve gamification quality, many scholars investigated the relationship among personality types, game mechanics and enjoyment of the gamified activities. This literature review analyses the main findings in this field, in order to define a starting point for future research about a framework able to enhance the gamification design through the customization of the reward system, according to personality types.

Keywords: Gamification · Personality types · Game mechanics · Games · Motivation

1 Introduction

With the term gamification is met the use of game mechanics in non-ludic contexts, like for instance work tasks [1]. In recent times the use of gamification strategies has become very popular, being applied in very different fields such as healthcare [2], education [3], wellbeing [4], economics and marketing [5] and so on.

In most cases, the decision to adopt a gamified solution can be considered forward-looking, since it meant to take advantage of an innovative tool to achieve preset goals, but, on the other side, the adopted solutions are often of the "one size fit all" kind, and that means low efficacy in a very varied target group [6, 7].

What emerged is the need for a better gamification design, able to better fit users' needs. Taking this into account, many academic studies were devoted to investigate in what way the users' personality types influence the enjoyment and the motivation that should derive from the adoption of gamification strategies [8–10].

Some other studies, by adopting a different approach, tried to presume the users' personality types by observing their behaviors into the digital game world [11, 12].

Systematic literatures reviews about this topic has already been conducted [13], having as objective the quantitative analysis of the results achieved.

This review, on the other hand, aims to reflect on the main findings of the studies that dealt with the customization of gamification, highlighting common points and differences in the approaches adopted.

C. Stephanidis and M. Antona (Eds.): HCII 2020, CCIS 1224, pp. 125–129, 2020.
https://doi.org/10.1007/978-3-030-50726-8_16

The ultimate goal, of which this analysis represents the starting point, is to understand how it is possible to further improve the gamification design process, through the development of an ad hoc framework that takes into account the differences in personality of the users.

The literature review was conducted starting from the search for keywords such as gamification, personality types, games, motivation, reward system, by consulting the main databases: Google Scholar, SpringerLink, IEEEXplore and Research gate. Some of the papers examined were identified through other sources, such as bibliographies of research works.

Among all the results, 16 papers have been taken into consideration for a more in-depth study, as results that are overall more pertinent to the topic and objectives of the research.

From the examination of the papers considered eligible, the following considerations arose.

Considering the final objective of the research, we started to identify the elements that the majority of the studies consider having an impact on the success of the gamified activities. The elements can be summarized as follows: personality types, game/gamification mechanics and motivation, game/gamification environment.

2   Personality Types

In order to establish a relationship between personality types and gamification enjoyment, scholars took into account different personality types models. In some cases [7], a general examination is made, but in general, the models most taken into consideration in the studies are the Five Factors Model [6, 14] and the Meyer-Briggs model [15–17].

Regardless of the Personality Types Model adopted, thought, what has emerged from all the studies is that exist correlations between the personality types and the user's preferences in terms of game mechanics enjoyment (both in the case of gamified activities and games *tout court*) and that all results have significant affinities with each other.

In addition, another feature that almost all the papers examined have in common is that the main focus of each of them is the identification of the relationship between personality types and users' game mechanics preferences [3, 6–10, 13, 14].

3   Game/Gamification Mechanics

The large part of the research works examined, consists in matching personality types and game mechanics and, as result of this matching, in proposing users' classifications.

Studies mainly adopted two different approaches: one, aiming at defining general components, or categories, of the activity [7, 8, 10, 15], the other aiming at associate more specifically the personality types with game mechanics [3, 6, 9, 15, 16].

In both cases, though, no specific mention is made about how to use game mechanics in the design of a gamified activity.

4   Motivation and Reward System

In all the studies examine, no reference is made to how to manage practically game mechanics in gamification: all highlights that different personalities are motivated by different mechanics, but none consider another element that can influence the level of satisfaction in being rewarded, namely the effort required to the users in order to accomplish the task. This would require a customized reward system.

5   The Game/Gamification Environment

None of the examined studies has highlighted how the environment is a crucial element when it comes to players behavior except one [15], that deals specifically with the impact of game environment in in-game behavior.

6   Conclusions and Next Steps

The analysis of previous research work, as stated before, aimed at defining a starting point for the design of an adaptive gamification framework, which should take into account the influence of personality types on the enjoyment and effectiveness of gamified activities.

The first consideration regards the relationship among personality types, game mechanics, especially the reward system, and the effort required to accomplish a task. In gamified activities, is not possible to change the activity according to what the player/user likes most, but can be possible to design a reward strategy customized for different personality types both in terms of reward type and amount.

A deeper study about how personality types impact on the perceived effort required to accomplish usual tasks in HEIs educational activity should be performed, in order to design an effective gamification reward system. The design of an adaptive reward system though, could lead to a further issue. In the specific case of HEIs education, students in the same class, performing the same tasks could consider unfair a reward strategy that adapts itself *ad personam*.

In order to motivate the adaptive method and to make it understandable, it could be necessary to adopt a strategy borrowed from Role Playing Games: the gamification framework should be designed as RPGs are. Personality types should be the equivalent of the game characters, each one with different characteristics which impact on the difficulty encountered in completing a task. Rewards should be assigned according to the coefficient of difficulty identified in the previous phase devoted to design the reward system, function of the personality type analysis.

The second consideration is referred to the gamification context. Differently from games' digital environment, that can be far different from our everyday life, it can be observed that in class the learning context, is the usual context in which people act, so maybe, to have an impact on the player behavior is not the environment but the gamified layer we add when gamifying learning activities. What should be considered in this case is the impact of the game mechanics on the environment and, consequently, the users' perception of them deriving from their personality types.

References

1. Deterding, S., Dixon, D., Khaled, R., Nacke, L.: From game design elements to gamefulness: defining "gamification". In: Proceedings of the 15th International Academic MindTrek Conference: Envisioning Future Media Environments, pp. 9–15 (2011)
2. Lister, C., West, J.H., Cannon, B., Sax, T., Brodegard, D.: Just a fad? Gamification in health and fitness apps. JMIR Serious Games 2(2), e9 (2014)
3. Codish, D., Ravid, G.: Personality based gamification-educational gamification for extroverts and introverts. In: Proceedings of the 9th CHAIS Conference for the Study of Innovation and Learning Technologies: Learning in the Technological Era, vol. 1, pp. 36–44 (2014)
4. Johnson, D., et al.: Gamification for health and wellbeing: a systematic review of the literature. Internet Interv. 6, 89–106 (2016)
5. Hamari, J.: Transforming homo economicus into homo ludens: a field experiment on gamification in a utilitarian peer-to-peer trading service. Electron. Commer. Res. Appl. 12 (4), 236–245 (2013)
6. Jia, Y., Xu, B., Karanam, Y., Voida, S.: Personality-targeted gamification: a survey study on personality traits and motivational affordances. In: Proceedings of the 2016 CHI Conference on Human Factors in Computing Systems, pp. 2001–2013 (2016)
7. Ferro, L., Steffen, S., Walz, P., Greuter, S.: Towards personalised, gamified systems: an investigation into game design, personality and player typologies. In: Proceedings of The 9th Australasian Conference on Interactive Entertainment: Matters of Life and Death, pp. 1–6 (2013)
8. Ghaban, W., Hendley, R.: How different personalities benefit from gamification. Interact. Comput. 31(2), 138–153 (2019)
9. Codish, D., Ravid, G.: Personality based gamification: how different personalities perceive gamification (2014)
10. Tondello, G.F., Mora, A., Nacke, L.E.: Elements of gameful design emerging from user preferences. In: Proceedings of the Annual Symposium on Computer-Human Interaction in Play, pp. 129–142 (2017)
11. Van Lankveld, G., Schreurs, S., Spronck, P.: Psychologically verified player modelling. In: GAMEON, pp. 12–19 (2009)
12. Tekofsky, S., Van Den Herik, J., Spronck, P., Plaat, A.: PsyOps: personality assessment through gaming behavior. In: Proceedings of the International Conference on the Foundations of Digital Games (2013)
13. Hamari, J., Koivisto, J., Sarsa, H.: Does gamification work?–a literature review of empirical studies on gamification. In: 2014 47th Hawaii International Conference on System Sciences, pp. 3025–3034. IEEE (2014)
14. Canossa, A., Badler, J.B., Seif El-Nasr, M., Tignor, S., Colvin, R.C.: In your face (t) impact of personality and context on gameplay behavior. In: FDG (2015)
15. Cowley, B., Charles, D.: Behavlets: a method for practical player modelling using psychology-based player traits and domain specific features. User Model. User Adapt. Interact. 26(2–3), 257–306 (2016)

16. Butler, C.: A framework for evaluating the effectiveness of gamification techniques by personality type. In: Nah, F.F.-H. (ed.) HCIB 2014. LNCS, vol. 8527, pp. 381–389. Springer, Cham (2014). https://doi.org/10.1007/978-3-319-07293-7_37

17. Shabihi, N., Taghiyareh, F., Hossein Abdoli, M.: Enhancement of educational games based on personality type indicators. Int. J. Inf. Commun. Technol. Res. 9(3), 37–45 (2017)

Peer-to-Peer Traded Energy: Prosumer and Consumer Focus Groups about a Self-consumption Community Scenario

Susen Döbelt[(⊠)] and Maria Kreußlein

Research Group Cognitive and Engineering Psychology,
Chemnitz University of Technology, Chemnitz, Germany
susen.doebelt@psychologie.tu-chemnitz.de

Abstract. Renewable energy cooperatives were found to facilitate the uptake of renewable and distributed energy resources and require the willingness of participants to trade energy within their local community. To gather user requirements for the design of such scenarios, we conducted two focus groups with potential participants. Prosumers ($n = 7$) and consumers ($n = 9$) worry about regulatory conditions and potential taxes applied on energy trading. We found that in particular consumers demanded for secure energy supply, while prosumers wanted to keep control of their energy production. Prosumers expressed their interest in detailed consumption and sales information, while consumers were interested in the legal matters of the contract and the energy source. Furthermore, the concept of connectedness was valued as the most important gamification approach for self-consumption communities, followed by the development of competence, in particular important for consumers.

Keywords: User-centered design · Smart Grid · Gamification · Blockchain

1 Introduction

The combustion of fossil resources accounts for two third of carbon emissions worldwide [3] and therefore progressively contribute to climate change [4]. In order to face ecological challenges, a changeover from the traditional, centralized power grid to an integration of renewable and distributed energy resources (DER) is needed [1]. DERs enable demand response, grid stabilization and reduce the transmission costs. Consequently, the integration of DERs applies for being more energy-efficient [2]. Different technical solutions are suggested to realize reliable trading of distributed produced energy, for instance the use of blockchain technology seems to be promising [6, 7].

Besides the technical design, user research can contribute to a usable implementation of solutions for locally produced energy and its trading. On a social level, renewable energy cooperatives were found to facilitate the uptake of DERs [5] in general. But the question remains: Which requirements need to be fulfilled to encourage people to participate in a local energy community in short- and long-term? Therefore, we conducted two focus groups with pro- and consumers.

C. Stephanidis and M. Antona (Eds.): HCII 2020, CCIS 1224, pp. 130–140, 2020.
https://doi.org/10.1007/978-3-030-50726-8_17

2 Related Work

2.1 User Research for Smart Grids

The involvement of active con- and prosumers in terms of optimal production and consumption of energy provides many opportunities for new, smart energy models facilitating the integration of DERs. The willingness of people to participate is one main contributor to the adoption [8] and success [11] of these models, as the development and transition to energy communities based on renewables in Denmark [16], Austria [18] and Norway [17] already have shown. Hence, the integration of user requirements, preferences and barriers is of fundamental importance in the design process [8, 9]. One of our previous studies [10] showed that pro- and consumer differ in their acceptance of energy scenarios involving DERs. Especially with regard to a self-consumption community scenario, consumers criticized the complexity and the uncertainty of costs, whereas prosumers favored the innovativeness of a Peer-to-Peer approach.

A field trial in Austria – the HiT Housing Project [18, 19] – showed that users were disappointed especially about the benefit-cost ratio. Eight residential buildings (129 apartments) were equipped with a heating system consisting of a biogas-based unit, a heat pump, and an energy storage. Residents perceived their effort to adjust their behavior as high, but the financial benefit was rather low. With regard to informational demand, they mentioned an interest in what kind of energy source was used, in order to adjust their consumption to locally produced solar power [19]. A promising suggestion for a possible user interface indicating availability of green power was made by Schrammel et al. [20]. Research shows that the implementation of energy communities, which are enabled with local production and supply, need the integration of user-oriented and social approaches to start and continue the transition to DER integration.

2.2 Gamification for Motivating Active Participation

Most concepts, which promote sustainable energy behavior, incorporate people as individuals motivated by self-interest [11]. As local energy approaches of production and consumption involve small communities, group-based approaches addressing motivational aspects of participation are interesting as well. In the field of human-computer-interaction, there is one motivational design strategy covering a range of individual and community interests, called gamification. It is defined as *"the use of video game elements, to improve user experience and user engagement"* [21]. Gamification uses elements that target the basic pillars of intrinsic human motivation. Namely autonomy, competency and relatedness. Within our two focus groups, we want to identify if and what kind of gamification strategy would be suitable for a user interface in a local energy community. The focus groups aimed at contributing to the user-centered design of a self-consumption community scenario. Therefore, we investigated *which requirements do pro- and consumers have for a self-consumption community scenario in terms of energy?*

3   Method

We decided to conduct two separate focus groups, one for pro- and one for consumers as a homogenous group composition is known to facilitate a common basis in the discussion [12]. A focus group is a qualitative survey instrument [12] and a moderated process in which a small group of 6 to 9 users [13] is stimulated to discuss a specific topic [12]. This informal technique helps to assess users' needs and feelings [13].

3.1   Sample

The consumer focus group was conducted with 9 consumers (4 female), who were on average 50 years old ($M = 50.33$; $SD = 16.60$). The majority (5) indicated to have a university degree as their highest level of education, followed by a PhD (2). In the mean ($Mdn = 5.00$) they lived in a city with "*100.000 to 500.000*" inhabitants. We had 7 participants in the prosumer focus group (one female) with a mean age of $M = 48.00$ years ($SD = 12.22$). Again, the majority held a university degree (6), here followed by one participant, who indicated an apprenticeship. On average also the prosumers' place of residence has "*100.000 to 500.000*" ($Mdn = 5.00$) inhabitants. The consumers "slightly" and prosumers "largely" agreed being affine to technology ($Mcon = 4.29$; $SDcon = 0.49$; $Mpro = 4.65$; $SDpro = 0.73$), least lies above the standard value [14].

3.2   Procedure and Materials

The focus group notifications were sent out via email to the participant panel of our research group. The two groups of interest were described as follows: 1. Prosumers: "*people, who produce electricity themselves, e.g. with a photovoltaic plant*"; 2. Consumers: "*people, who purchase electricity*". The final invitation included an introduction to the topic and a description of the self-consumption scenario (Annex 1). First of all, the participants were asked to sign the consent form and a demographic questionnaire was handed (including age, gender, level of education, size of the city or place of residence, affinity for technology interaction [14]). Additionally, prosumers were asked to indicate the age and a description of their energy plant. Participants then received a briefing on the *NEMoGrid* research project [15] and the scenario. We then questioned openly about the potential advantages and disadvantages of the scenario and the desired information of the pro- and consumers in such a scenario. Keywords from the participants' statements were noted and placed on a table. Afterward, participants rated the importance of the collected information individually (Fig. 1). Therefore, they had to allocate max. 9 colored dots (red = "*I personally do not need this information.*", yellow = "*That's good to know, but I'm sure I just check it every once in a while.*", green = "*Very important, I always want to have quick access to this information.*").

Subsequently, we focused on the development of gamification concepts. Therefore, the pro- and consumers should complement three different sentences individually: 1. "*In order to strengthen my **competence** in dealing with energy, I would like, within the framework of my self-consumption energy community, that…*"; 2. "*To strengthen my*

Fig. 1. Focus group participants during assessment of information needs.

*sense of **autonomy** within my self-consumption energy community, I would...*"; and 3. "*In order to strengthen my sense of **connection** with other energy producers and consumers in my self-consumption community, I would...*". Eventually, participants briefly presented their best idea to the group. Every participant received a remuneration of 50 € (approx. 55 $). The maximum duration was 2 hours.

3.3 Data Collection and Analysis

Qualitative Data. One research assistant took notes to document the group discussions. Additionally, we used a dictaphone to gather original quotations. We classified notes into positive feedback and concerns. For the qualitative data collected on an individual level (completions of phrases on gamification strategies), the written answers of each participant were split up into single statements. In a first step, the assignment to the available gamification approaches was reviewed. After that, a category system was built bottom-up. Descriptive frequencies per approach and category are reported to indicate major tendencies.

Quantitative Data. Firstly, we summated the number of dots indicating the importance of information needs and determined a weighted value per information requirement. Therefore, we took the colors of the dots into account (3 for one green dot, 2 for yellow, 1 for red). Secondly, we relativized this weighted value per information to the weighted total value of all requirements mentioned. Third, we generated a ranking of the requirements named in each focus group.

4 Results

4.1 Scenario Evaluation

Consumer Concerns and Positive Feedback. The warm-up discussion revolved mainly around ensuring the security of supply and the regulatory framework. The participants doubted storage capacities and volatile energy sources to be sufficient for a continuous supply. Consumers rated the applicability of this scenario as more likely to be in rural areas, due to the installation of space-consuming infrastructure. In their opinion, the high taxes on energy would certainly be passed on to the energy community. Participants in the scenario were expected to face bureaucratic hurdles for trading electricity. Furthermore, costs and effort were addressed critically. Some consumers feared that people with less affinity for technology would be excluded. In addition, they worried about the time required and had doubts as to whether the scenario is more cost-effective because new costs will emerge, e.g. for the algorithm, infrastructure, and maintenance.

On the positive side, the consumers stated that the scenario is innovative and can be combined with new technologies such as electric vehicles. Furthermore, one participant mentioned the environmental benefits. But one participant replied that the integrated blockchain technology is very energy-intensive and should be taken into account.

Prosumer Concerns and Positive Feedback. The main topics of the discussion were the installation costs and again expected regulatory difficulties. The prosumers considered the concept, it's infrastructure and administration as too demanding for communities of smaller producers and consumers. They additionally mentioned bureaucratic difficulties, with regard to the billing in apartment buildings and the separation of the own consumption. They worried about intensive maintenance costs that possibly would exceed profits. The principle of independence of the community was evaluated as a positive aspect by the prosumers.

4.2 Information Needs in a Self-consumption Community

Consumers Information Needs and its Importance. The consumers mentioned nine different aspects they would like to be informed about: 1. Security of supply (relativized weighted importance: 15.65); 2. Exit/Termination option (14.97); 3. Drafting of contracts (14.92); 4. Assessment of producers (11.56); 5. Power source (11.56); 6. Installation effort (10.88); 7. Definition of locality (8.84); 8. Information about grid stability (6.12); 9. Electricity mix (6.12). Table 1 illustrates the three most important needs with an exemplary quotation from both focus groups.

Prosumer Information Needs and its Importance. We gathered 14 different information needs: 1. Priority for self-consumption (13.04); 2. Consumer related information (12.07); 3. Definition of thresholds (10.43); 4. Power composition (7.83); 5. Taxation (6.96); 6. Temporal consumption information (6.96); 7. Sales overview (6.96); 8. Variable prices (6.96); 9. Price information (6.96), 10. Information about grid stability (6.09); 11. Data protection (5.22); 12. Comparative prices (4.35); 13. Weather forecast (3.48); 14. Sunshine duration (1.74).

4.3 Gamification and Motivating Extensions

Consumer Individual Ideas. Most of the overall 22 consumer statements (9) can be assigned to the approach *connectedness with others*, followed by the *competence* (8) and at least to the *autonomy* (5) approach. We formed categories for ideas mentioned more than once. The connectedness approach subsumed ideas on *"physical community activities"* (mentioned 4 times) and *"enabling exchange with others"* (2). The competence approach triggered the ideas *"offering topic-related learning"* (3); *"making expert knowledge accessible"* (2) and *"recommendations for behavior"* (2). Under the autonomy approach only *"ensuring security of supply"* (3) was mentioned more than once.

Creating or maintaining a sense of community was considered the central core of the concept. This could be achieved, for example, by information that creates a positive image of the community. At the same time, the formation of a community and the organization of coordination processes, e.g. with joint investments, was seen as the biggest hurdle. In the discussion on competence-promoting measures, the participants underlined a need for accessible, empirical knowledge. In addition, action-relevant information (times for favorable electricity prices) was desired. Autonomy related objections were mentioned as a kind of counter-argument to ideas on the topic of connectedness and had been discussed less in the group.

Prosumer Individual Ideas. The overall 21 individually written statements equally (7) distributed along the three gamification approaches. The built categories for connectedness again entailed *"physical community activities"* (3). Additionally, prosumers considered *"formulating common objectives"* (2) as interesting. The competence approach subsumed ideas dealing with *"making electricity information accessible"* (3) and *"making expert knowledge accessible"* (2). For autonomy, we formed two categories: *"reduce bureaucratic hurdles"* (2) and *"create individual control/influence possibilities"* (2). Example quotes for the most frequently named categories are illustrated in Table 2.

Table 1. Three most important information needs, illustrated by an example quotation and its relativized weighted importance (RWI).

Information need	Example quotation	RWI
Consumer		
Security of supply	*"My question is about the security of supply. How does this relatively small system guarantees that nothing can happen? Neither what can happen because our storage is empty, nor that the person who sells says: 'Well, I'm not selling at these prices today. I will wait half a year."*	15.65
Exit/Termination option	*"If I have to make investments at the beginning, for example, another meter or something else. What options do I then have for getting out of the investment? [...] if I participate [...] and it does not correspond with my ideas, I would like to have the possibility to get out of such a concept and without great effort."*	14.97

(continued)

Table 1. (*continued*)

Information need	Example quotation	RWI
Drafting of contracts	*"Let's put it this way: For me it shouldn't be any different from the current provider situation... that at the end of the year I see what I have to pay and in the best case that's cheaper than what I pay now."*	14.29
Prosumer		
Priority for self-consumption	*"How much I sell and when; I'd like to be able to influence that by myself. Not that I would then sell more than I consume and then have to buy electricity. That should be realized in a way that I don't have to do anything."*	13.04
Consumer related information	*"I lie in my hospital bed and I see when my wife turns on the dishwasher. That's interesting."*	12.17
Definition of thresholds	*"I'd like to be able to set the thresholds* [from the automated selling system] *myself."*	10.43

Table 2. Exemplary quotations for the categories formed from the sentence completions of the three gamification approaches.

Approach	Category	Example quotation
Consumer		
Connectedness	Physical community activities	*"[...] we meet at least one time per month."*
Competence	Topic related learning	*"All participants are trained that all have the same level of knowledge."*
Autonomy	Security of supply	*"Attach importance to functioning delivery!"*
Prosumer		
Connectedness	Physical community activities	*"Meet with the others."*
Competence	Accessible electricity information	*"[...] clearly show what's happening. Production, withdrawals, various producers displayed, various consumers and their consumption behavior in the community; also external reference and its parameters."*
Autonomy	Create individual control/influence possibilities	*"Interactive intervention options with regard to the variables."*

In the subsequent discussion, ideas on the topic of connectedness were in the foreground. Here, social activities that reduce anonymity in the community were mentioned. The participants considered it as interesting getting to know the other consumers and producers personally and promoting the exchange among them. During the discussion, it was emphasized that fairness within the community should be ensured.

During the discussion of autonomy-based approaches, the participants emphasized that they highly appreciate the self-determination of energy supply. Competence-based approaches had hardly been discussed.

5   Conclusion and Discussion

Initially, the discussions in both focus groups naturally concentrated on hurdles, especially with regard to the functional and organizational implementation of a self-consumption community. Positive feedback was on a more general level. These results are in line with our previous research [10]. Here the innovativeness of the community-based approach was appreciated in contrast to the suspected increased effort and the diminished security of supply. The least concerns were especially mentioned from the consumers, as they are more depending on a secure supply. Indicated information needs underlined consumers' interest in the basic security of supply. Consequently, confidence-building information about producers in their community are considered important.

Furthermore, we conclude that local, community-based energy supply should be offered to consumers as an additional (and not exclusive) option to the "normal" grid-based supply. Accordingly, prosumers mentioned interest in functionalities that ensure control. This underlines their avoidance of the feeling of being overruled [10]. As prosumers showed a strong interest in detailed consumption and sales information, we recommend implementing user interfaces that entail information and control options.

Gamification approaches that promote connectedness with other community members have been considered as central by pro- and consumers. Social activities have been discussed in particular. Jans, Boumann and Fielding [11] underlined in this context already the importance of social identity theory. It promotes that interactions contribute to group forming and the definition of group identity. Further, the emphasis on similarities and differences to other groups will foster group definition. In addition, our results revealed that for consumers, building competence, e.g. by access to expert knowledge, is demanded. Therefore, we conclude that a combination of: 1.) Information about community members enabling to identify similarities and 2.) Possibilities to exchange competence, knowledge and therefore form a group identity can contribute to the motivation to share energy within a self-consumption community.

Our results contribute to requirements collection from the pro- and consumer perspective so that future work could build interface design for local energy communities upon it. Furthermore, future work can enhance requirements forming by the aggregation of individual and/or quantitative research.

Acknowledgements.   The current research is part of the *NEMoGrid* project and has received funding in the framework of the joint programming initiative ERA-Net SES focus initiative Smart Grids Plus, with support from the EU's Horizon 2020 research and innovation program under grant agreement No. 646039. The content and views expressed in this study are those of the authors and do not necessarily reflect the views or opinions of the ERA-Net SG+ initiative. Any reference given does not necessarily imply the endorsement by ERA-Net SG+.

Annex 1: Description of the Self-consumption Community Scenario for the Pro- and Consumer Group

Imagine…

… You draw your electricity mainly from your local grid/your own photovoltaic (PV) system at home and you form a self-consumption energy community together with your neighbors. The energy supplier and distribution system operator considers this community to be a single entity. Within the community, you can trade energy with your neighbors at prices that are cheaper than those of the energy supplier. You have paid for the PV system installed in your household and the grid connection. In addition, a smart meter is installed in your home and you are connected to a storage facility that is also used by other people from the neighborhood. Furthermore, there is a storage facility that is used by you and your neighbors. Users can rent the storage from the energy supplier and charge it with the energy surplus from their PV system.

The essential part of this scenario is the trade of your surplus energy with your neighbors. Trading is automated by an algorithm that is realized via a double auction mechanism. This means by buying energy, the buyer is making an offer for the energy that a prosumer wants to sell. At the same time, the seller/prosumer also makes an offer for the price at which he wants to sell his energy. This means by selling energy, you submit your desired price for the energy as a prosumer, while the buyer makes a bid simultaneously. Trading is carried out using blockchain technology. A blockchain is a distributed database that manages an ever-growing list of transactions. The database is expanded chronologically linear, similar to a chain. In the end, new elements are constantly added (hence the term "block chain" = "blockchain"). When one block is complete, the next one is created. Each block contains a checksum of the previous block. Energy prices in your community (at the local market) are lower than real-time prices in the grid. However, you can still get energy from the grid. The price you get for the PV surplus you produce in your community is higher than the real-time prices in the grid and the feed-in tariff. Furthermore, the additional PV price is more attractive than self-consumption. The difference between the selling price and the levelized cost of electricity (LCOE) is your revenue. The LCOE is the average minimum cost at which your electricity must be sold to reach the breakeven threshold.

Costs for the construction and operation of a power plant during an assumed financial cycle of life and use. The energy supplier takes care of the P2P market's management. There is a monthly invoice consisting of five components: You pay…

1. … the share for the use of network services (transmission and distribution of electricity). However, there is a discounted rate for your share of use.
2. … the price you offered in the auctions for the electricity you used. The money you pay is lower than a real-time price for electricity from the grid./… the amount of electricity you have drawn.

   - If you use your own PV generated electricity, you pay a levelized cost of electricity (LCOE).

- If you trade the PV surplus, the earnings depend on the auction. However, the money you receive is higher than a feed-in tariff or the real-time price of electricity on the grid.

Costs for transmission and distribution of P2P trading electricity are excluded. You can draw energy from the grid at any time, which is more expensive.

3. … the power storage facility. This storage battery can either be rented or purchased. Monthly rental rates or one-off purchase costs, therefore, do incur.
4. … the algorithm that fixes local (energy) bottlenecks and offers the ability to obtain cheap energy via auctions.
5. … the share for the P2P management carried out and set up by the energy supplier and distribution system operator.

By trading (locally) in your community, the energy transmission fees are lower. Although there are costs for the P2P (management) algorithm, these costs are less than the total profits. The advantage for consumers/prosumers are that, as a flexible consumer, he or she can obtain energy from a prosumer at a lower price than the network price/they sell their surplus energy to a flexible consumer at a higher price compared to the distribution system operator. You can reduce the payback time of your PV system and thus lower the levelized cost of electricity (LCOE).

In short, you pay your energy bill, including additional shares for storage and the algorithm.

References

1. Döbelt, S., Jung, M., Busch, M., Tscheligi, M.: Consumers' privacy concerns and implications for a privacy preserving Smart Grid architecture—results of an Austrian study. Energy Res. Soc. Sci. **9**, 137–145 (2015). https://doi.org/10.1016/j.erss.2015.08.022
2. Akorede, M.F., Hizam, H., Pouresmaeil, E.: Distributed energy resources and benefits to the environment. Renew. Sustain. Energy Rev. **14**(2), 724–734 (2010). https://doi.org/10.1016/j.rser.2009.10.025
3. Loesche, D.: Die Geschichte des Kohldendioxidausstoßes [The history of carbon dioxide emissions] (2018). Downloaded at 27th of January 2020. https://de.statista.com/infografik/13569/weltweite-kohlendioxidemissionen/
4. Nelles, D., Serrer, C.: Kleine Gase, große Wirkung [Small gases, big effect]. KlimaWandel GbR (2018)
5. Viardot, E.: The role of cooperatives in overcoming the barriers to adoption of renewable energy. Energy Policy **63**, 756–764 (2013). https://doi.org/10.1016/j.enpol.2013.08.034
6. Musleh, A.S., Yao, G., Muyeen, S.M.: Blockchain applications in smart grid-review and frameworks. IEEE Access **7**, 86746–86757 (2019). https://doi.org/10.1109/ACCESS.2019.2920682
7. Mylrea, M., Gourisetti Gupta, S.N.: Blockchain for smart grid resilience: exchanging distributed energy at speed, scale and security. In: 2017 Resilience Week (RWS). IEEE (2017). https://doi.org/10.1109/rweek.2017.8088642
8. Wolsink, M.: The research agenda on social acceptance of distributed generation in smart grids: renewable as common pool resources. Renew. Sustain. Energy Rev. **16**(1), 822–835 (2012). https://doi.org/10.1016/j.rser.2011.09.006

9. Kubli, M., Loock, M., Wüstenhagen, R.: The flexible prosumer: measuring the willingness to co-create distributed flexibility. Energy Policy **114**, 540–548 (2018). https://doi.org/10.1016/j.enpol.2017.12.044

10. Döbelt, S., Kreußlein, M.: Imagine 2025: prosumer and consumer requirements for distributed energy resource systems business models. In: Ahram, T. (ed.) AHFE 2019. AISC, vol. 965, pp. 631–643. Springer, Cham (2020). https://doi.org/10.1007/978-3-030-20454-9_62

11. Jans, L., Bouman, T., Fielding, K.: A part of the energy \"in crowd\": changing people's energy behavior via group-based approaches. IEEE Power Energy Mag. **16**(1), 35–41 (2018). https://doi.org/10.1109/MPE.2017.2759883

12. Schulz, M., Mack, B., Renn, O.: Fokusgruppen in der empirischen Sozialwissenschaft: Von der Konzeption bis zur Auswertung [Focus groups in empirical social science: from conception to evaluation]. Springer, Wiesbaden (2012). https://doi.org/10.1007/978-3-531-19397-7

13. Nielsen, J.: The use and misuse of focus groups. IEEE Softw. **14**(1), 94–95 (1997). https://doi.org/10.1109/52.566434

14. Franke, T., Attig, C., Wessel, D.: A personal resource for technology interaction: development and validation of the affinity for technology interaction (ATI) scale. Int. J. Hum. Comput. Interact. **35**(6), 456–467 (2019). https://doi.org/10.1080/10447318.2018.1456150

15. Project website: https://nemogrid.eu/. Accessed 13 Feb 2020

16. Jantzen, J., Kristensen, M., Christensen, T.H.: Sociotechnical transition to smart energy: the case of Samso 1997–2030. Energy **162**, 20–34 (2018). https://doi.org/10.1016/j.energy.2018.07.174

17. Throndsen, W., Skjølsvold, T.M., Ryghaug, M., Christensen, T.H.: From consumer to prosumer. Enrolling users into a Norwegian PV pilot (2017). https://ntnuopen.ntnu.no/ntnu-xmlui/handle/11250/2457629. Accessed 7 Mar 2020

18. AIT, CURE, Siemens AG Österreich, Salzburg AG, Salzburg Netz GmbH, Salzburg Wohnbau GmbH, Vienna University of Technology: Results and Findings from the Smart Grids Model Region Salzburg (2013). http://www.smartgridssalzburg.at/content/dam/websites/smartgrids/Downloads/SGMS_Results_2013.pdf. Accessed 5 Feb 2020

19. Ornetzeder, M., Sinozic, T., Gutting, A., Bettin, S.: Deliverable D2.1.: Case study report Austria - Findings from case studies of Model Village Köstendorf, HiT Housing Project and VLOTTE. Institute of Technology Assessment, Austrian Academy of Sciences (2017)

20. Schrammel, J., Gerdenitsch, C., Weiss, A., Kluckner, P.M., Tscheligi, M.: FORE-watch – the clock that tells you when to use: persuading users to align their energy consumption with green power availability. In: Keyson, D.V., et al. (eds.) AmI 2011. LNCS, vol. 7040, pp. 157–166. Springer, Heidelberg (2011). https://doi.org/10.1007/978-3-642-25167-2_19

21. Deterding, S., Dixon, D., Khaled, R., Nacke, L.: From game design elements to gamefulness: defining "gamification". In: Proceedings of the 15th International Academic MindTrek Conference: Envisioning Future Media Environments, pp. 9–15, September 2011. https://doi.org/10.1007/978-3-642-25167-2_19

Do User Requirements of mHealth Devices Have Differences for Gender and Age?

Vivian Emily Gunser(✉), Emma Dischinger, Nina Fischer,
Paula Pons, Janis Rösser, and Verena Wagner-Hartl

Faculty Industrial Technologies, Furtwangen University, Campus Tuttlingen,
Kronenstraße 16, 78532 Tuttlingen, Germany
vivian.gunser@hs-furtwangen.de

Abstract. The present article focuses on how mHealth tools for medical devices like hearing aids or blood glucose meters for diabetics should be designed. Overall, 125 participants aged between 18 and 79 years participated in an online survey. The results of the study show that on average the participants were partly willing to have the use of a medical device explained exclusively by a mHealth app instead of medical professionals. Interestingly, older participants were significantly more positive regarding mHealth tools than younger participants. The findings of the presented exploratory study can help to understand customers' needs. These findings have the potential to support the design and development of more user-friendly apps and other digital products.

Keywords: Medical devices · mHealth · Product development

1 Introduction

For a few years now, smartphones and apps have been a part of our everyday life. Why don't we use them to handle medical health devices? Due to the ongoing digitalization process it is expected that the health care system will become more digital in the future. Therefore, it can be assumed that this development will affect our private lives [1]. The initial idea of mobile health apps (mHealth) is the use of mobile devices in order to promote health. Often, these devices are combined with sensors on the body. Commonly known mHealth tools are for example fitness apps or blood sugar trackers. They are used to visualize health data of any kind and to track its progress [2].

In an American study [3] in 2015 with 3677 participants, the use of health apps for health promotion has been associated with intentions to change diet and physical activity. The main users of health apps were younger, more educated people with higher income and with good health.

The use of avatars as digital representations of the patient or health professionals might also have a positive impact on the user's healthy lifestyle habits [4]. Several avatar-based apps have shown an improvement in self-care, knowledge and motivation of patients with chronic diseases such as diabetes or depression [5, 6].

Johnson et al. [5] discovered in 2014 that diabetes-patients, acting as an avatar in a virtual environment for therapy purpose, have shown a significant improvement in their self-efficacy and perceived social support. Both self-efficacy and social support are

© Springer Nature Switzerland AG 2020
C. Stephanidis and M. Antona (Eds.): HCII 2020, CCIS 1224, pp. 141–146, 2020.
https://doi.org/10.1007/978-3-030-50726-8_18

related to self-care behaviors and therefore better self-management [5, 7]. Asides from interaction, the appearance of the avatar seems to play an important role [8].

Mobile health tools might be an advantage in coping with the challenges of demographic change. The use of medical health apps could counteract social problems such as the increasing number of care-dependent people and a lack of doctors, as well as the rising costs of healthcare. Additionally, people are more flexible with an app due to the fact of having permanent insight into their health data and disease information [9].

According to a review of Martínez-Pérez, de la Torre-Díez and López-Coronado [10], there is a lack for some health apps, for example with focus on anemia, hearing loss, or low vision.

It is still uncertain, whether people will accept apps for medical health devices in their daily lives. Therefore, the aim of the exploratory study was to survey the acceptance level of the participants. Further aspects were if they would trust a mHealth app or prefer a medical professional for explaining the use of health devices as well as, how avatars should be used and designed in mHealth apps. Thereby, it is especially worth knowing whether elderly people would like to use mHealth apps. Furthermore, the factor gender might influence acceptance and requirements of mHealth devices.

2   Materials and Methods

2.1   Participants

In this sample of 125 participants, 71.20% were female, and 28.80% were male. Participants were between 18 and 79 years old ($M = 36.30$, $SD = 17.70$). Following the definition of WHO [11] which defines "aging workers" or "older workers" as workers who are aged 45 years and older, the participants were grouped into two age groups. According to that, 75 participants (60.00%) belong to the younger and 50 participants (40.00%) belong to the older group. All participants had a smartphone. Participants were invited to participate in an online study via e-mails and the link was posted in social networks. All participants provided their informed consent at the beginning of the online study.

2.2   Materials and Procedure

The exploratory study was examined with an online survey. On average it took the participants about 18 min to complete the questionnaire. The questionnaire examined different aspects of the participants' opinions about mHealth apps: The experience level with apps in general as well as with mHealth apps, the acceptance of mHealth apps, questions concerning the use and design of an avatar, as well as questions about two exemplary apps for different medical devices. These examples were apps for the use of hearing aids and blood glucose meters for diabetics but are not part of the presented paper and are therefore not described in detail.

Another question was whether people would trust a mHealth app more regarding the explanation of the use of the corresponding health device, than a medical professional. Their attitude for the usage of an avatar was examined with the same response format and if participants would trust the advices of the mHealth app. Participants had to rate those aspects using a 5-point scale: very unlikely (1) - rather unlikely (2) - neutral (3) - rather likely (4) - very likely (5). In case people would like to have a mHealth app to interpret their health values and giving based on these values health advices, participants could rate this with a 5-point scale that ranges from I don't like it at all (1) - to I like it very much (5). Further gender and age differences for mHealth apps were examined.

2.3   Statistical Analyses

For the statistical analyses, the software IBM SPSS for Windows was used. The analyses were based on a significance level of 5%.

3   Results

3.1   Trust in mHealth Instruction

To examine whether people would trust a mHealth app more regarding the explanation of the use of health devices instead of medical professionals an ANOVA was conducted. Overall, participants are partly to less willing to use the app for an explanation ($M = 2.05$, $SD = .98$). The results of the ANOVA showed a significant age-effect, $F(1, 21) = 7.40$, $p = .007$, $\eta^2_{part.} = .058$, but no significant effects of gender, $F(1, 121) = .40$, $p = .531$, $\eta^2_{part.} = .003$, or the interaction age x gender, $F(1, 121) = .54$, $p = .463$, $\eta^2_{part.} = .004$. Elderly people would trust the mHealth tool instruction significantly more than younger ones.

When the 125 participants were asked, how they would like to learn the instruction of a mHealth app (multiple answers possible), 54.40% would prefer explanation texts for each function in the mHealth app, half of the participants (52.80%) would also like to have a conversation with a medical professional and only 12 of 125 participants (9.60%) would like to have a written, printed manual.

3.2   Interpretation of Health Values and Advices of a mHealth App

Another research question was whether people would like a mHealth app to interpret their health values and giving, based on these values, health advices. The results show that on average, participants would like partly to rather have those advices ($M = 3.40$, $SD = 1.02$). The results of an analysis of variance show that age or gender differences did not reach the level of significance [gender: $F(1, 121) = .15$, $p = .704$, $\eta^2_{part.} = .001$; age: $F(1, 121) = 1.17$, $p = .281$, $\eta^2_{part} = .010$; age x gender: $F(1, 121) = 1.17$, $p = .281$, $\eta^2_{part} = .010$].

Furthermore, participants would partly trust advices of a mHealth app ($M = 3.04$, $SD = 1.0$). Following the results of an analysis of variance, a tendency towards interaction is shown for the interaction age x gender, $F(1, 121) = 2.81$, $p = .096$,

$\eta^2_{part.}$ = .023. No significant effects can be shown for age, $F(1, 121) = 1.23$, $p = .269$, $\eta^2_{part.}$ = .010, and gender, $F(1, 121) = .46$, $p = .499$, $\eta^2_{part.}$ = .004. Post-hoc analyses (Sidak) show that younger women assessed their trust in advices of a mHealth app significantly poorer than elderly women did ($p = .013$).

3.3   Avatar

First, participants were asked if they would like to use an avatar, which will guide them through the app. This avatar could answer to questions and problems, immediately. The results show that overall people are rather neutral regarding the use of an avatar ($M = 3.20$, $SD = 1.30$). Following the results of an analysis of variance, there was a significant effect of gender, $F(1, 121) = 3.85$, $p = .052$, $\eta^2_{part.}$ = .031, but not for age, F $(1, 121) = 1.27$, $p = .261$, $\eta^2_{part.}$ = .010, or the interaction of both, $F(1, 121) = .48$, $p = .488$, $\eta^2_{part.}$ = .004. Women are more interested in using an avatar than men.

Second, all participants that would (rather) like or were neutral regarding the use of an avatar ($n = 83$) were asked how the avatar should be designed (multiple answers possible). 77.11% of them prefer an avatar that looks like a human being. Furthermore, 27.71% would like to have an avatar that looks like an imaginary creature and only 12.05% would like to have an animal as avatar, interestingly all of them were women. In addition, 10.84% of the participants that would use an avatar had different ideas about the avatar design. For example, three persons suggested that app users should be able to design the avatar on their own.

4   Discussion

The results of the study show that participants were partly to less willing to have the use of a medical device explained exclusively by a mHealth app instead of medical professionals. Interestingly, elderly participants were significantly more positive about this form of introduction than younger participants were. There was no significant gender effect or an interaction of both. For the medium of introduction (multiple answers possible), half of the participants preferred explanatory texts for each function in the mHealth app. Almost as many participants further liked to have a personal introduction by a medical professional and only ten percent of the participants liked to have a written printed manual.

Another result was that participants partly to rather chose the app to interpret their health data and to give them health advices based on these values. Furthermore, participants chose that they would partly trust these medical advices. The results show a tendency towards significance for the interaction of age and gender, according to which younger women, assessed it poorer than elderly women did.

The participants' overall attitude towards the application of avatars as guidance through the app was rather neutral. Hereby it was shown that women were significantly more interested in using avatars than men. A majority of the participants who evaluated their willingness to use an avatar as neutral or higher voted for a humanoid appearance of the avatar. This tendency of users towards human avatars has been reported in a prior study by Nowak and Rauh [12]. The attributes users associate with a certain avatar appearance seem to depend on more factors than the level of anthropomorphism of the avatar. Therefore, assumptions about why human avatars were chosen more frequently in this context cannot be made. Nevertheless, the result that humanoid avatars were preferred for these mHealth applications should be noted for the future design of such apps. This study shows there are some gender or age differences regarding avatar appearance, however a growing body of literature is still needed [13]. Regarding the ongoing demographic change, this research topic might hold potential for the further improvement of virtual avatars.

Also, personal customization of the avatar could be crucial in order to increase its effectiveness. The present study did not ask about this, but three people indicated in the comment section that they would like to design the avatar by themselves. The findings of Kim [14] have shown that a personal adjustment of the avatar appearance promoted the emotional bond between user and avatar, which might encourage the user to change behaviour intentions and be more active against a disease. In further studies, it would be interesting to see how users design their own avatar and whether this would improve their medical compliance.

The presented study has some limitations. Since the sample in this study consisted of more than two-thirds women, the representativeness for the overall population is questionable. Future research should avoid unbalances in gender distribution. This is especially important for avatar-related issues, because a significant gender effect was found in this study regarding this topic. Another fact was that participants were only asked about their opinion as part of an online study but did not get to use a mHealth app for mHealth devices. Future studies could provide patients with a mobile device and a corresponding mHealth app. In addition, it would be interesting to observe how upcoming, unexperienced users receive a medical device and learn its functions through the mHealth app. Therefore, in future studies it could be also interesting to examine whether novices and experts in using mHealth apps have a different attitude regarding the acceptance of mHealth apps.

In conclusion, the results of the presented exploratory study can help to understand customers' needs regarding mHealth apps. Gender and age differences were also identified. These findings have the potential to support the design and development of more user-friendly apps and other digital products.

Acknowledgements.   The authors would like to thank all participants.

References

1. Tresp, V., Overhage, J.M., Bundschus, M., Rabizadeh, S., Fasching, P.A., Yu, S.: Going digital: a survey on digitalization and large scale data analytics in healthcare. Proc. IEEE **104** (11), 2180–2206 (2016)
2. Al Issawi, J.: mHealth Apps: Die Zukunft der Medizin? In: Forschungsbeiträge der eresult GmbH [mHealth apps: The Future of medicine? in research contributions of the eresult GmbH] (2014). https://www.eresult.de/ux-wissen/forschungsbeitraege/einzelansicht/news/mhealth-apps-die-zukunft-der-medizin/. Accessed 18 Mar 2020

3. Carroll, J.K., Moorhead, A., Bond, R., LeBlanc, W.G., Petrella, R.J., Fiscella, K.: Who uses mobile phone health apps and does use matter? A secondary data analytics approach. J. Med. Internet Res. **19**(4), e125, 1–9 (2017)
4. Lin, J.J., Mamykina, L., Lindtner, S., Delajoux, G., Strub, H.B.: Fish 'n' steps: encouraging physical activity with an interactive computer game. In: Dourish, P., Friday, A. (eds.) UbiComp 2006. LNCS, vol. 4206, pp. 261–278. Springer, Heidelberg (2006). https://doi.org/10.1007/11853565_16
5. Johnson, C., et al.: Feasibility and preliminary effects of a virtual environment for adults with type 2 diabetes: pilot study. JMIR Res. Protoc. **3**(2), e23, 1–19 (2014)
6. Pinto, M.D., Hickman, R.L., Clochesy, J., Buchner, M.: Avatar-based depression self-management technology: promising approach to improve depressive symptoms among young adults. Appl. Nurs. Res. **26**(1), 45–48 (2013)
7. Tang, T.S., Brown, M.B., Funnell, M.M., Anderson, R.M.: Social support, quality of life, and self-care behaviors among African Americans with type 2 diabetes. Diabetes Educ. **34** (2), 266–276 (2008)
8. Fox, J., Bailenson, J.N.: Virtual self-modeling: the effects of vicarious reinforcement and identification on exercise behaviors. Media Psychol. **12**, 1–25 (2009)
9. Boulos, M.N.K., Brewer, A.C., Karimkhani, C., Buller, D.B., Dellavalle, R.P.: Mobile medical and health apps: state of the art, concerns, regulatory control and certification. Online J. Public Health Inform. **5**(3), 229 (2014)
10. Martínez-Pérez, B., de la Torre-Díez, I., López-Coronado, M.: Mobile health applications for the most prevalent conditions by the world health organization: review and analysis. J. Med. Internet Res. **15**(6), e120, 1–19 (2013)
11. World Health Organization (WHO): Aging and Working Capacity. WHO, Geneva (1993)
12. Nowak, K.L., Rauh, C.: The influence of the avatar on online perceptions of anthropomorphism, androgyny, credibility, homophily, and attraction. J. Comput. Mediat. Commun. **11** (1), 153–178 (2006)
13. Straßmann, C., Krämer, N.C.: A categorization of virtual agent appearances and a qualitative study on age-related user preferences. In: Beskow, J., Peters, C., Castellano, G., O'Sullivan, C., Leite, I., Kopp, S. (eds.) IVA 2017. LNCS (LNAI), vol. 10498, pp. 413–422. Springer, Cham (2017). https://doi.org/10.1007/978-3-319-67401-8_51
14. Kim, H.: Emotional bond between the creator and the avatar: Changes in behavioral intentions to engage in alcohol-related traffic risk behaviors. Doctoral dissertation (2014). https://scholarcommons.sc.edu/etd/2574

MEMO: Designing for the Bereaved

Karine Harridsleff[(⊠)], Maren-Elise Saarenpää Øien[(⊠)],
and Klaudia Çarçani[(⊠)]

Faculty of Computer Science, Østfold University College, Halden, Norway
{karine.harridsleff,maren.e.oien,
klaudia.carcani}@hiof.no

Abstract. In this paper, we present a design study of people's mourning experience after the loss of a loved one. We took a design thinking approach for studying people's needs and further designing and prototyping a digital solution. MEMO, a wooden box designated to keep both physical and digital objects from the deceased, was developed. The digital memories are presented in an organized way in a touchscreen monitor installed in the frontal part of the box. Moreover, MEMO supports sharing the digital memories with other boxes being a part of the same family package of boxes. Finally, MEMO gives the possibility to attach digital content to physical objects through NFC tags and display its digital content in the touch screen just by laying the objects on top of the box lid. We contribute to HCI with our prototype and a better understanding of people's needs during grief. Our aim is to continue exploring other design alternatives for facilitating grief for the bereaved.

Keywords: Design thinking · Bereaved · Mourning · Memory box · Tangible

1 Introduction

The HCI community has turned the focus toward the *End of Life* (EOL) [1–7]. However, mostly concerning the management of digital presence after death [1, 5, 7]. Less research has been focused on how people experience bereavement and how technology can support people to cope with loss. This is very relevant, considering that the loss of a loved one and how people go through grief can influence their life. In this paper, we focus on the bereaved and their needs on going through grief and how technology can support this process that we all go through sooner or later in life.

To conduct our study, we took a design thinking process [8]. Through literature review, interviews, and cultural probes with people that had gone through loss, we found that people want to talk and remember the dear bereaved, the beautiful moments, the special objects that relate to that person, and the situated use of those objects. However, they want to share these memories exclusively with people that appreciate the memories the same as them. Together they enter a collaborative remembrance process that alleviates the grief.

Thus, we developed MEMO, the memory box, which incorporates the idea of a shared digital memorial with a tangible interface for material elements, physically positioned in the box. In Sect. 2, we will describe what constitutes the design thinking

© Springer Nature Switzerland AG 2020
C. Stephanidis and M. Antona (Eds.): HCII 2020, CCIS 1224, pp. 147–154, 2020.
https://doi.org/10.1007/978-3-030-50726-8_19

process and how we applied it in our specific context. Further, we will conclude the paper in Sect. 3 by highlighting some of the main findings and contributions of the paper.

2 Design Thinking Process

As a methodology for investigating our case, we chose the design thinking process, a five-stage design process proposed by Hasso Plattner Institute of Design at Stanford [8]. Design Thinking is defined as "a *methodology that provides a solution-based approach to solving problems. It's extremely useful in tackling complex problems that are ill-defined or unknown, by understanding the human needs involved, by re-framing the problem in human-centric ways, by creating many ideas in brainstorming sessions, and by adopting a hands-on approach in prototyping and testing.*" [8]. The definition shows the compatibility of this methodology with our interest in exploring how people go through a loss, what the needs are, and how technology can contribute. The problem we study is unknown or ill-defined, and what we researched were the needs of people gone through a loss and framed the problem on their terms. As stated, the design thinking process is compounded by five stages:

1. Empathy – this stage contributes to creating an empathic understanding of the problem the researcher is trying to solve or getting to know better the needs of the user groups studied [8].
2. Define – in this stage, the researchers or designers synthesize and analyze the information gathered during the empathy stage. This stage is useful in narrowing down the scope of the research and focusing on a specific problem or issue generated from a close look at people's real needs. Thus, a statement of a problem in a human-centric way is articulated [8].
3. Ideate – in this stage, the researchers or designers ideate new digital solutions to the problem stated in the define stage. The aim is to generate as many ideas as possible. These diverging thinking would then converge once the people involved in the ideation phase should choose what idea to develop further [8].
4. Prototype – in this stage, the ideas of the previous phase are used to iteratively generate artifacts that can help in better solving the problem defined [8]. Different categories of prototypes can be built [9].
5. Test – in this stage, feedback for the solution is solicited. The aim of this stage is to learn more about the solution and also learn more about the user group needs [8].

How we applied each stage of the design thinking process will be described in detail below.

2.1 Empathy

Our aim in the empathy phase, as also stated above, was to get a deeper understanding of the needs people have during grief, what could help in healing the pain, how, and if technology could contribute. In order to empathize with the user group, we chose to apply three methods: Literature Search, Interviews, and Cultural probes.

Literature Search. It was relevant for us to understand what other researchers had found out as elements of supporting mourning [1–7]. We followed recommendations from Timmins and McCabe [10] on how to conduct a literature search. We focused on HCI literature regarding the EOL. Among the literature, we have interpreted to be divided mostly into two categories [1]: how to handle the digital presence of people after death [5, 7] and building digital memorials [1–3, 6]. Our focus was the same as in [1], "A death in the family and designing technology for the bereaved". A relevant work that received our attention was the "Penseive Box" by Chaudhari, et al. [4]. They have developed a physical wooden box with a digital screen (tablet) fitted inside, which would present photos, videos, timeline, and so on. The box also had thin LED panels on its edges, which would produce an ambient glow on special occasions. This was a speculative design, so they used it as a provocation to have interviews with users and understand their view, and it was not based on previous research. They found that people appreciate automated memorialization. Moreover, they found out people were not willing to share this kind of box with others. The design thinking process has a different approach on studying a specific phenomenon. The users' needs and perspectives are explored prior to the solution which can make the prototype closer to what people need.

Knowledge acquired through the literature helped us plan our interviews and cultural probes better by approaching people to involve in the research in a more considerate way and always respect their feelings. Our research was based in Halden, a small town in southeast Norway.

Semi-structured Interviews. We conducted two semi-structured interviews [11]—the first, with a deacon giving grief counseling in the role of an expert. The second interview was with a twenty-seven years old woman who lost her father when she was ten years old. The interviews' aim was to gain an insight into how people working with grief looked at it and how people experiencing it were taken care of. Both interviews were audio-recorded, and consent was granted from the interviewees beforehand. The interviews were initially analyzed through content analysis [12].

Interesting insight flourished during the interviews. As we found out from the expert, during grief, people tend to close themselves and have difficulties in sharing their pain with others. Even though help is offered, people hesitate. This was confirmed from our end-user interview, who stated she wouldn't have preferred to talk to any strangers about her feelings. However, she emphasized that her mother was the main support saying, "my mom has pretty much forced me to talk about it (..) I'm still struggling with a lot today, stuff I think could have been easier if I had resolved certain feelings/issues earlier (..) we have become very close. Now I'm talking to my mom about everything". Thus, the mother, the closest person to her dad, was the best comfort and help through the grief. They could relieve the pain together. Moreover, in the quote, a call for help was raised. The need to find ways to help people through grief was reinstated.

Cultural Probes. Were used to get a deeper understanding of the user's thoughts, feelings, and needs. Cultural probes are a user research method used to inspire ideas in the design process [13]. Probes are "simple objects or prototypes of a design, which are placed in person's environment to find out about their habits, patterns of communication, and so forth, and hopefully, return with interesting data". A cultural probe is a kit made up with a variety of artifacts and tasks intended to provide a unique glimpse in people's lives, values, and thoughts. The aim of our probes was to find out "how to facilitate people's grief".

We made a kit of five tasks and artifacts which were given to five participants of both genders in the age of twenty-seven to thirty-five years old where the participants had lost someone to cancer, sudden illness or death by suicide. We used a white and floral theme for all the probes to create a sense of serenity. A summary of the findings from the cultural probes is shown in a probe collage in Fig. 1. The probes involved the following tasks:

Probe 1: Take pictures of (places, situations, objects, or people) something reminding you of the good memories with the person you've lost.
Probe 2: Whom did you feel comfortable talking to after your experience with loss?
Probe 3: Write a letter to yourself that you would have liked to receive in that difficult period.
Probe 4: From 1–5, rate the most important to less important things that would have helped you after losing someone you love.
Probe 5: Write a postcard for the person you've lost. Please write about your relation to the person and when it happened.

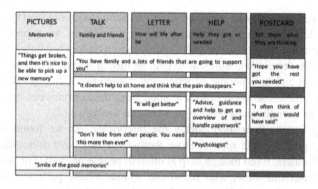

Fig. 1. Cultural probes summary collage

2.2 Define

To analyze our data, we used the Empathy Map (EM) method [14] as suitable for data collected during the empathy phase. EM is a method that assists in designing business models according to customer perspectives. It goes beyond demographic characteristics and develops a better understanding of the customer's environment, behavior, aspirations, and concerns. The EM's goal is to create a degree of empathy for a specific person or user group by analyzing the data and categorizing them into what people *Say*, *Think*, *Do*, and *Feel*. The discussion of differences and similarities among these four categories lead to the creation of a set of *Needs* of the user group and further *Insights* about the specific problem at hand.

In our empathy map, different needs were highlighted. What was defined as most important was that people need to be more open about their situation and appreciate the good memories because it can make them feel better during the process and in their everyday life. The findings exhibited the importance of taking care of the memories, talking with family and friends, as well as being open about the life situation as the aid to precede the anguish of grief and being able to move on. The relevance of memories and memorials as a way of helping people against the terror of forgetting after the loss of a loved one has been discussed in the literature [15, 16]. Thus, the problem we decided to work further on was "designing a digital tool which can support people to enhance their memories during grief and having the possibility to share these memories with other close people that are part of the family and share the same memories and pain for the bereaved".

2.3   Ideate

In the ideate phase, we started with brainstorming about possible digital solutions that could satisfy the defined needs of people in the grieving process and alleviate the pain after the loss. After three rounds of brainstorming and sketching and inspired from the work of Chaudhari, et al. [4], we landed on the idea of a memory box we decided to call MEMO, a box which can be the personal and a family companion in the time of a loss and after.

To refine our ideas, we created personas [17], fictional characters representing the users the solution is designed for. Personas are very useful in ideating how the digital solution will be used and integrated into the user's life. In our case, we created four personas, the husband, mother, daughter, and son of Mary - our persona who had recently passed away. All the personas were going through grief due to Mary's passing. In order to ideate the usage of our MEMO box, we created scenarios for each persona [18] on how they interacted with possible functionalities of the box. These scenarios were further visualized through storyboards [19], another technique used in ideating or prototyping.

The ideating phase started with divergent thinking, where a set of ideas were discussed and ended by converging the idea of the MEMO box more towards the needs of the people experiencing grief highlighted during our empathy study.

2.4   Prototype

Prototyping was an iterative process. We experimented with different ideas and materials. Moreover, different prototype categories were created [9]. Several experiments with the materiality of the box were conducted. Different materials and digital tools, such as a box made with cardboard to a box made of wood using a laser cutter, were made. Our final prototype is a wooden box that incorporates the idea of a shared digital memorial with a tangible interface for material objects, physically positioned in the box. The box is made of woodcuts in fine lines with a laser cutter. On the front side of the box, a detachable touchscreen is integrated. The box lid is supposed to have an integrated NFC tag reader. However, due to time constraints for prototyping, we used a microcontroller. Each of the box parts has specific functionalities.

- The box itself is in analogy with boxes used to save things from lost ones after their loss, highlighting memorialization.
- The touchscreen has an integrated application developed exclusively for the box. The application was designed in ADOBE XD in order to simulate the possible functionalities. The application serves as a repository of digital traces of memories such as pictures, videos, details regarding events related to the deceased person. The user owning the box has a possibility to log into a website from the computer and populate the repository. The box owner as well has the possibility to control the display of the material. For instance, wedding pictures can be set to be displayed on the wedding day. Another, very relevant functionality is the possibility to share digital content with other family members. The box can be configured into a family package with other boxes, and digital content can be shared from one box to another.
- The lid is related to another functionality in which NFC tags can be populated with digital content and attached to a specific object in the box. When this object with the NFC tag attached is put on top of the box, led lights to signalize the object are being read from the NFC tag reader, and the content is displayed in the touchscreen on the front side of the box as a slideshow.

2.5   Testing

In design thinking, testing is not considered the end. Testing is considered as an opportunity to get feedback from the user about the prototype and get the chance to gain learn more about the users' needs, the problem, and potential solutions [8]. Thus, we conducted testing in two rounds.

In the first round, we invited three participants, woman (35), man (55), and woman (73), where all of them have experienced the loss of a loved one. The prototype was then still in the form of a card box, as shown in Fig. 2.a. Testing was task-oriented and was conducted in a specific room allowing participants to engage fully in the task without any distractions. The tests were conducted with the thinking aloud-technique and separately. Two of the authors participated in the testing by adapting to the roles of host and observer. Written notes were taken during the test. The data from the testing were analyzed through content analysis [12].

Fig. 2. MEMO box changes - Left (a) – cardboard box, Middle (b) – showing the NFC tags functionality and Right (c) showing the sharing function

In the second round, the prototype had been improved further as shown in Fig. 2.b and c, and the testing was conducted by sharing with the potential users a video prototype (look here) and asking for their feedback on the usability of the solution and the concept the solution represents "a shared digital memorial". We tested with eight participants from the age of six to seventy-four years old. Written notes were kept from the testing and analyzed through content analysis [12]. Kids involved in the study were asked if they liked the prototype and if they wanted to use it. The influence in the grief process was not discussed with them. However, we found their involvement relevant because kids also can lose people they are very attached to, and they also need even more careful support that a grown-up one.

From the testing, it shows MEMO was appreciated by the users in terms of usability. This because the material (fine Norwegian wood) and the shape (adaptable to shelves) could easily be integrated into people's homes. Moreover, they told us the box was convenient for being positioned in visible places at home, creating a special place for the person they've lost integrated into their everyday life. This can help with the fight and fear of forgetting. However, suggestions for improving user-friendliness were noted and will be taken into consideration further.

Moreover, similar to Chaudhari et al. [4] Penseive box, we found out people prefer having a personalized box because they have individual memories and might not live in the same place. However, in contrast to Chaudhari et al. [4], our participants said they appreciated the sharing functionality. They said sharing memories with the closest family members were extremely relevant while experiencing grief as the family members share the same pain for the person passed. Talking together about the deceased can create a positive feeling helping through the healing process. Hence, we concluded that our MEMO prototype and the idea of a shared digital memorial can accompany people during grief. Our testing participants suggested even if some people during the initial grieving process might not be able to integrate MEMO in their life, they would eventually in time find it interesting and important.

3 Conclusion

In this paper, we presented the design of MEMO, a wooden box designated to hold both physical and digital objects of the deceased explained in detail in Subsect. 2.4.

The contribution of the paper is in the development of a prototype that serves as a shared digital memorial in times of grieving. These times are usually associated with loneliness and pain. As one of our testing participants stated, our user group involves all the people of the world at any time. Hence, even if only a few people are reached, it will still make a considerable contribution.

Furthermore, we contribute to more knowledge in empathizing and a better understanding of the grieving process and people's needs in that very dark period of life. Our design process resulted in MEMO, however, our findings can contribute to inspiring other researchers or designers in investigating other options of digital solutions. In the future, we want to experiment with more design alternatives.

Finally, the paper contributes to the HCI community through a detailed description of the design thinking process as an approach that contributes not only to the development of useful prototypes but as well expanding knowledge of specific user groups and their needs and using design as the basis for conducting the research.

References

1. Massimi, M., Baecker, R.M.: A death in the family: opportunities for designing technologies for the bereaved. In: Proceedings of the SIGCHI Conference on Human Factors in Computing Systems 2010
2. Massimi, M., Odom, W., Kirk, D., Banks, R.: HCI at the end of life: understanding death, dying, and the digital. In: CHI'10 Extended Abstracts on Human Factors in Computing Systems, pp. 4477–4480 (2010)
3. Massimi, M., Moncur, W., Odom, W., Banks, R., Kirk, D.: Memento mori: technology design for the end of life. In: CHI'12 Extended Abstracts on Human Factors in Computing Systems, pp. 2759–2762 (2012)
4. Chaudhari, C., Prakash, A., Tsaasan, A.M., Brubaker, J.R., Tanenbaum, J.: Penseive Box: themes for digital memorialization practices. In: Proceedings of the TEI '16: Tenth International Conference on Tangible, Embedded, and Embodied Interaction, Eindhoven, Netherlands, pp. 398–403. Association for Computing Machinery (2016)
5. Moncur, W.: 13. Digital ownership across lifespans. In: Aging and the Digital Life Course, vol. 3, p. 257 (2015)
6. Moncur, W., Kirk, D.: An emergent framework for digital memorials. In: Proceedings of the 2014 Conference on Designing Interactive Systems, Vancouver, BC, Canada, pp. 965–974. Association for Computing Machinery (2014)
7. Moncur, W., Bikker, J., Kasket, E., Troyer, J.: From death to final disposition: roles of technology in the post-mortem interval. In: Proceedings of the SIGCHI Conference on Human Factors in Computing Systems (2012)
8. Brown, T., Katz, B.: Change by design. J. Prod. Innov. Manag. **28**(3), 381–383 (2011)
9. Houde, S., Hill, C.: What do prototypes prototype? In: Handbook of Human-Computer Interaction, pp. 367–381. Elsevier (1997)
10. Timmins, F., McCabe, C.: How to conduct an effective literature search. Nurs. Stand. **20**(11), 41–47 (2005)
11. Longhurst, R.: Semi-structured interviews and focus groups. Key Methods Geogr. **3**(2), 143–156 (2003)
12. Lazar, J., Feng, J.H., Hochheiser, H.: Research Methods in Human-Computer Interaction. Morgan Kaufmann, Burlington (2017)
13. Gaver, B., Dunne, T., Pacenti, E.: Design: cultural probes. Interactions **6**(1), 21–29 (1999)
14. Ferreira, B., Silva, W., Oliveira Jr, E.A., Conte, T.: Designing personas with empathy map. In: SEKE (2015)
15. Kirk, D.S., Sellen, A.: On human remains: Values and practice in the home archiving of cherished objects. ACM Trans. Comput. Hum. Interact. (TOCHI) **17**(3), 1–43 (2010)
16. Hallam, E., Hockey, J.: Death, Memory and Material Culture. Unknown Publisher (2001)
17. Pruitt, J., Grudin, J.: Personas: practice and theory. In: Proceedings of the 2003 Conference on Designing for User Experiences (2003)
18. Carroll, J.M.: Scenarios and design cognition. In: Proceedings IEEE Joint International Conference on Requirements Engineering, p. 3–5. IEEE (2002)
19. Andriole, S.J.: Storyboard Prototyping: A New Approach to User Requirements Analysis. QED Information Sciences Inc., Wellesley (1989)

User Experience Principles for Systems with Artificial Intelligence

Ronald Hartwig[1]([✉]) and Lukas Rein[2]

[1] FOM Hochschule gGmbH, Leimkugelstraße 6, 45141 Essen, Germany
research@rhaug.de
[2] RHaug GmbH, Burgstr. 17, 59192 Bergkamen, Germany

Abstract. The user experience (UX) of typical B2B and B2C software is aimed at being user friendly and thereby hiding as much information from the internal part of the software as possible. Users shall not be confused by database-details, decision trees that are "below the waterline". That has been common sense for decades and lead to systems which look clean and users like the idea of the things underneath to be "automatic".

But now we are confronted with a different challenge: Systems with artificial intelligence inside no longer work as an intelligent assistant but are starting to take control over decision processes which were once in the domain of the user. The ethical question could be if this is wanted at all. But practice already answered it with a clear "yes, because it makes processes faster, more reliable and in the end cheaper". The following question must be: How will human users and machines interact? And from the user experience perspective: What and how do we tell the users that they are maybe not in control alone anymore?

Keywords: Ethics · Artificial intelligence · User experience

1 Introduction

The rise of Artificial Intelligence (AI) is inevitable. In the last decade we have had a tremendous increase of Software or Machines that use AI or AI-like processes. This trend will continue with smarter and more intelligent systems with no end in sight. Self-driving cars, now more than ever, seem to be right around the corner (although it might still take longer than we assume). AI will dramatically change the way we work and interact with machines. Digitalization is probably a big chance, but at the same time a big risk for humans. Humans and Machines get more and more connected, but sometimes it feels like they drift apart.

The authors expect that the use artificial intelligence will soon be an integral party of everyday live. We don't want to warn anyone from the dangers of AI. On the contrary, we very much support it. It should assist humans whenever usable. AI-Systems will bring many new creative possibilities, but also a risk for abuse (both intentional and by accident).

The role of a UX-Designer will face new Challenges, as they are the intersection between humans and autonomous systems; someone who assist the collaboration of these two.

© Springer Nature Switzerland AG 2020
C. Stephanidis and M. Antona (Eds.): HCII 2020, CCIS 1224, pp. 155–160, 2020.
https://doi.org/10.1007/978-3-030-50726-8_20

We formulated four theses of how we think the field of user experience might change:

1. UX must change, if it still wants to be relevant. With the rise of AI, the classical interface and graphic designer won't be enough anymore.
2. Digitalization and artificial intelligence will give UX a chance, to create holistic personal experiences that exceed typical visual user interfaces.
3. UX will take a central position in finding solutions to complex problems and will be a strategic factor when digitalizing intelligently.
4. Now, more than ever, it will be important to approach systems with a human, and not technical aspects. Artificial intelligence will have to understand humans as a part of a holistic system between humans and machines to generate good results.

Design responsibilities cannot be left to its own devices. That why it's not enough to simply create new conceptual principles in dealing with AI, but we also must integrate ethical principles. Therefore, we formulated ethical principles that serve as thought-provoking impulses when creating new design principles.

2 Theoretical Background

2.1 Ethics of Algorithms

When we delegate decision making tasks to machines, we always must ask ourselves what the resulting consequences are. In the case of self-driving cars, this can be a matter of life and death.

The goal of having software and machines assist us is to lower the (cognitive) load. Lowering that load helps to free resources to focus on different parts of a process. This can reach from simply assisting a user at a crucial step to make a decision [1]. But ethical problems can arise through this, for example the evaluation of whom to blame for an accident. Mittelstedt et al. propose six types of ethical concerns raised by algorithms [1]: Inconclusive evidence, inscrutable evidence and misguided evidence in software raise epistemic concerns, while unfair outcomes, transformative effect raise normative concerns. Traceability is important to be able to follow the decision chain.

Failures in the design can lead to severe information gaps. Therefore, it is crucial for UX-Designer to consider the ethical problems that might arise and try to minimize them through good design by designing the right degree of decision transparency into the user interfaces (UI).

2.2 Anthropomorphism

Anthropomorphism is the practice of assigning human-like properties to objects [2]. Smart Assistants like Amazon Alexa or Google Home are trying to make their smart home devices as human like as possible. Movies and art have for a long-time depicted Robots of the future as human-looking.

Anthropomorphism can help to elevate trust in Autonomous machines which can help to make users feel save in a self-driving car [3]. But there's also risks.

Anthropomorphized products or software can lead to lowered inhibitions towards that product. On the one hand this can be helpful because users will trust it and built an emotional connection to a product. On the other hand, this can lead to user not questioning the advice or decision that software might make [4]. Emotions are a strong tool to help and involve users, but they should be used responsibly in every way, to avoid misguidance.

2.3 Overruling

Especially with the debate around self-driving cars the question where the autonomy of humans ends and where the autonomy of artificial intelligence starts. Shouldn't we give up our autonomy if increases safety? [5].

Overruling is concerned to assess when humans should be able to overrule the decision of a system. Even if they are suboptimal decisions. Decreasing safety risks and restricting personal freedom must be assessed on a case by case basis. There is no ethical rule that puts safety above freedom [5]. Therefore, it must be defined and visible at every point, who's in control when interacting with an autonomous system [5].

3 Methodology

On an annual basis the authors host a "Future of User Experience" (FUX) symposium as a use case of their new work approach "Work in Paradise" in Can Picafort (Mallorca). A group of UX experts from different backgrounds and different roles and software companies like IBM, SAP, GAD, Google, DB, EON and groups like bitkom or german UPA gather to explore visions of upcoming User Experience roles and methods (Fig. 1).

Goal of the 2018 retreat was to evaluate current challenges that the field of user experience faces in regards which role user experience might have to take when working with artificial intelligence [6].

The methodology was a grouped version of brainwriting and expert interviews. After some impulse lectures groups were set up to find and discuss key theses. Then the groups had to swap their ideas and had to work on the ideas of the other group. Then a first draft was created and later we compared the principles that were compiled to the current scientific standard to justify their validity. We have had great experiences with the format of having people work in a collaborative format for a limited, but focused and result driven, amount of time. The results are always interesting and discussion worthy. The "work in paradise" approach which located the experts in a beautiful surrounding on a beach helped to unlock creativity and allowed some more open-minded discussions due to 3 days of this intense single theme workshop.

Fig. 1. Members of the "Future (of) UX" Retreat 2018 in Can Picafort (Mallorca, ES)

4 Results

In order to make the principles easier to reproduce we set up the acronym "ETHICA" which shall resemble the "ethics" approach even though one might doubt if this is a real ethical or more a pragmatic approach though.

4.1 ETHICA-Principles

Emotions
An AI-based System should consider the emotions of its users and take in regard that humans tend to form relationships even with dehumanized machines. While we claim that an emotional connection would be great, it should never be used to misguide or mislead the user.

Transparency
When interacting with an AI system, users should be aware of it. Transparency can lead to trust, and especially if a system, that seems to be human (e.g. a chatbot where it's not clear if one is talking to a bot or an employee) and leads the user on, will lose trust when it does not fulfill a task or reveals itself to be an autonomous system later on. For example, humans may feel bad being unnecessarily polite to machine. We claim that transparency can lead to trust.

Humanity

While we say that computer systems should be identifiable as such, they should also consider the possibilities and limits of human cognitive abilities and act according to it. Human computer interaction in the past has strived to implement ergonomic principles into our everyday lives, be it work or leisure activities. The increase of autonomous processes must consider the cognitive and emotional boundaries that humans have. An AI that assist at the wrong time, or assists with the wrong things, can limit our own intelligence or even compromise our health. We may feel uncomfortable being underchallenged or confronted with overload.

"Intelligence Frugality"[1]

Analog to data minimization, we should be frugal about our use of AI. User needs come first. Only because we could use AI might not mean we actually should. AI should always bring additional value to a process and if this isn't a given, we should consider not using it at all. Especially with impactful moral decisions this is of immense importance.

Control

Users should be able to overrule AI. We are aware of the harshness of the claim, but for the current state of AI we think it still holds true. Giving users the possibility of control ensures trust in the system in general, even if it increases the risk in some situations. One main reason is that AI systems lack a holistic understanding of complex situations that are totally new or unexpected. This is when humans still may perform better because their trained "world knowledge". For example, a human may handle the extremely rare event of an aeroplane hitting the highway right in front of a car. It is very unlikely that an AI would be trained for that while a human may guess correct that a very low flying plane may go down. If a system absolutely can't give control to the user, users should be made aware of the resulting consequences.

Attention

It will be a challenge for UX-experts, to keep the attention of users over time in systems with a high automation factor. They will have to plan the integration of user's attention and keep it up according to expectable Workflows. In general, the more classical interfaces take a backseat, the more important it will be to design the whole system and experience. This is the well-known effect of "Vigilance" that UI designers struggle from beginning of monotone control jobs. But with AI in place a lot more work and processed may end up running smoothly without user interaction but then have to do an immediate handover in case of unexpected incidents.

5 Conclusion and Discussion

We are aware that our results are just a set of theses to be discussed. The authors did not come across a comparable list yet. The of course arbitrarily picked list of experts is in no way representative or a scientifically valid approach for an in-depth study. But on

---

[1] We are aware that this is not an existing term but found it helpful to define it new.

the other hand, it comes from consultants which have to deal with these systems now and in future and we are sure it is helpful to consider their opinions and findings in future (academic) work.

We take the theses now as a basis for some more academic research and are optimistic to develop them into more and more helpful guidelines and principles.

References

1. Mittelstadt, B.D., Allo, P., Taddeo, M., Wachter, S., Floridi, L.: The ethics of algorithms: mapping the debate. Big Data Society **3**(2), 2053951716679679 (2016)
2. Oxford English Dictionary, 1st edn. "anthropomorphism, n". Oxford University Press, Oxford (1885)
3. Lee, J.G., Kim, K.J., Lee, S., Shin, D.H.: Can autonomous vehicles be safe and trustworthy? Effects of appearance and autonomy of unmanned driving systems. Int. J. Hum. Comput. Interact. **31**(10), 682–691 (2015)
4. Hur, J.D., Koo, M., Hofmann, W.: When temptations come alive: how anthropomorphism undermines self-control. J. Consum. Res. **42**(2), 340–358 (2015)
5. Bundesminister für Verkehr und digitale Infrastruktur (BMVI): Bericht der Ethik-Kommission Automatisiertes und Vernetztes Fahren, Berlin (2017)
6. Hartwig, R., Rein, L.: Die ETHIKA Prinzipien - Ethik für die User eXperience (UX) von KI-Systemen, Blogpost (2018). https://www.benutzerfreundlichkeit.de/2018/12/die-ethika-prinzipien-ethik-fur-die.html

Detecting Themes Related to Public Concerns and Consumer Issues Regarding Personal Mobility

Xu Li, Harim Yeo, and Hyesun Hwang$^{(\boxtimes)}$

Department of Consumer Sciences, Sungkyunkwan University, Seoul, Korea
h.hwang@skku.edu

Abstract. This study is conducted to explore the problems that are being discussed in society and investigate consumers' feelings or experiences regarding personal mobility which have been started to receive attention, by conducting both news and social data analysis.

Using the R 3.5.3 and Trendup 4.0 programs, this study gathered 1163 news reports and 10332 twitter reviews regarding personal mobility dating to the period between January 1, 2019 and December 31, 2019. Topics were extracted from the selected news reports through Latent Dirichlet Allocation (LDA) topic-modeling; the news and twitter reviews were analyzed using the bigram network analysis.

The results of topic modeling show that issues related to personal mobility in news data included safety issues related to operation and for the product itself, growth issues for companies, and service issues such as sharing services. The results of the network analysis showed that the news data contained content on sharing services, service releases, and safety issues. Twitter data showed both consumers' desire to use personal mobility in their lives and concerns about the safety of it. It is recommended to continually identify and improve the problems consumers feel and reflect them in relevant regulations.

Keywords: Personal mobility · Consumer issue · Twitter

1 Introduction

Developed in America in 2001, the "Segway" is the most widely known personal mobility device in the market. The Segway appears to be the first personal mobility device that is used as a personal transportation vehicle and has a maximum speed of 20 km per hour. The market size of personal mobility devices in America has risen from 8.4 billion dollars in 2013 to 10.8 billion dollars in 2018 [1]. In Korea, 60,000 personal mobility devices were sold in 2016, and it is estimated that the number will reach 200,000 in 2020 [2].

Personal mobility is a transportation method powered by electricity that is used by one or two people, and includes electric wheelchairs, bicycles, and scooters [3]. In previous research, the concept of personal mobility appears to be used interchangeably with the concept of smart mobility. Generally, smart mobility focuses more on smart functions, such as autonomous driving. In addition, electric wheelchairs used as a

© Springer Nature Switzerland AG 2020
C. Stephanidis and M. Antona (Eds.): HCII 2020, CCIS 1224, pp. 161–166, 2020.
https://doi.org/10.1007/978-3-030-50726-8_21

means for individuals to move themselves are not classified as personal mobility devices because they are classified as medical appliances [4]. In this study, we focus on personal mobility devices used as a means for individuals to move themselves.

Previous research mainly focuses on the improvement and development of the design and function of personal mobility vehicles as well as security and regulation issues [3, 5–7]. As personal mobility devices have recently been accepted as a personalized means of transportation and a part of leisure life, consumers' perceptions and experiences of the products with this new technology need to be closely investigated. However, previous research has mainly dealt with personal mobility in terms of regulatory issues regarding new technologies and product development, and there is a lack of substantive investigation of consumer experiences and perceptions. Therefore, it is necessary to explore how consumers feel and experience personal mobility products.

2   Method

2.1   Text Mining

The current research uses the latent Dirichlet allocation (LDA) technique for topic modeling. Based on the algorithm, LDA is a method that uses the procedural probability distribution model, which first appears in the research of Blei, Ng, and Jordan [8]. As a generative model, the LDA algorithm is used to search the related topics in data. It can be used to identify the appropriate topics and words with respect to every topic in the data [9]. In other words, LDA is a method in which a computer automatically binds the words and extracts the topics instead of containing a certain classification standard [10].

2.2   Data Collection and Refinement

Using the R 3.5.3 and Trendup 4.0 programs, this study gathered 1162 news reports and 10,332 Twitter reviews pertaining to personal mobility for the period between January 1 and December 31, 2019. The data were refined by deleting unnecessary words and punctuation, and similar expressions were transformed into standard expressions.

2.3   Data Analysis

Using the Simplepos22 function from the Klnop package in the R 3.5.3 package, nouns and adjectives were extracted from the refined news and Twitter data. Five topics were extracted from news reports through LDA topic modeling. Bigram network analysis was used to explore the keywords on how consumers respond and experience personal mobility.

3   Results

3.1   Issues Extracted from News Data

The results of the topic modeling of news data are shown in Table 1. The results reveal that there is a lot of discussion in Korean society regarding the safety of personal mobility devices. Topic 3 shows safety issues related to driving personal mobility, such as "safety," "driving," and "driving license." Topics 1 and 5 represent topics related to the safety of the product itself, such as "fire," "battery," and "charging."

Table 1. Topic modeling of news data

	Topic 1	Topic 2	Topic 3	Topic 4	Topic 5
1	Service	Mobility	Bicycle	Service	Product
2	Gas station	Enterprise	Driving license	Mobility	Battery
3	Charging	Business	Transportation	Sharing	Fire
4	GS Caltex	Industry	User	Market	Charging
5	Apartment	Service	Use	Korea	Investigation
6	Mobility	Smart	Personal	Sharing service	Occurrence
7	Police officer	Plan	Driving	Use	Use
8	Fire	Establish	Safety	Offer	Electronic
9	Lime	Technology	Drive	Area	Sale
10	Offer	Push ahead	Big	Platform	Electromagnetic waves

In Topic 2, words such as "enterprise," "industry," "establish," "technology," and "push ahead" are listed, with the theme of growth of many personal mobility companies and their efforts resulting from the development of technology. In Topic 4, along with words such as "service," "sharing," and "market," a theme emerged on the provision of various services such as personal mobility sharing services.

3.2   Comparative Analysis of News Data and Twitter Data

The results of network analysis of news data and Twitter data on personal mobility are shown in Fig. 1 and Fig. 2. The network analysis of news data has identified the public opinion that is forming within the entire society. Twitter networks reveal how consumers perceive and experience personal mobility.

Looking at Fig. 1, which represents the results of news data analysis, "Personal mobility" represents a strong connection with "service," along with connections to words such as "platform," "sharing," and "sharing service." This shows that there is active discussion about the platform-based services related to personal mobility. The word "service" is linked to "start," "launch," and "extension," indicating that there are many discussions about service launches. The results also has revealed that battery-related safety issues are being addressed, as "charging," which is connected to "service," is linked to words such as "battery" and "safety."

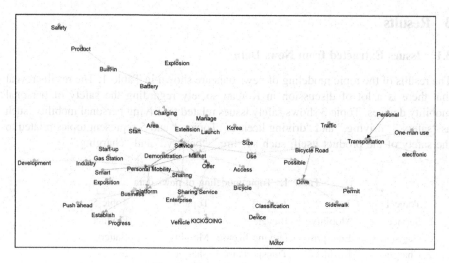

Fig. 1. Network of news data

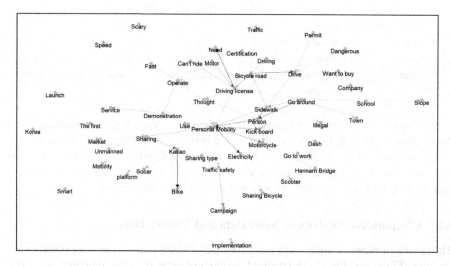

Fig. 2. Network of twitter data

"Personal mobility" is linked to the term "market," along with connections with words such as "industry," "business," and "startup" and "market" are connected to words such as "size," and "extension." This shows that companies providing personal mobility products and services are forming a new market and discussions on this are therefore increasing.

Looking at Fig. 2, which shows the results of Twitter data analysis, "go around" is located at the center and connected to "person," "sidewalk," "company," "school," "town," and "want to buy." These results suggest that consumers are familiar with personal mobility devices and those who use such technology, and also want to use it in their own daily lives.

However, safety-related issues have also been discovered along with the connections between "drive" and "dangerous," and "fast," "speed," and "scary." This shows that consumers are aware of the risks of using personal mobility devices and have a sense of fear. People also mentioned the "need" for a "driving license" to such devices and "traffic safety" "campaign" related to personal mobility.

"Sharing" had a connection with words such as "platform" and "service", and with the words related to car and bicycle sharing service companies "Socar" and "Kakao." This result indicates that consumers have an interest in the shared service itself, which is the main route of use for personal mobility products, and the companies that provide it.

4 Conclusion

This study is meaningful in that it explores the problems and direction of development that are being discussed in society and has investigated the feelings or experiences that consumers have regarding personal mobility by conducting both news and social data analysis, and conducting a comparative analysis of these.

The analysis results are as follows. First, it was shown that issues related to personal mobility in news data included safety issues related to operation, safety issues for the product itself, growth issues for companies related to personal mobility within Korean society, and service issues related to personal mobility, such as sharing services. Second, the results of the analysis comparing news and Twitter data showed that the news data contained content on sharing services, service releases, and safety issues associated with the personal mobility services. Third, Twitter data showed consumers' desire to use it in their lives, along with the perception that personal mobility devices and services are readily available. However, concerns about the safety of personal mobility devices has also emerged. Interest in shared services and related businesses could also be found.

Personal Mobility is a new transport that has recently emerged, bringing many changes to consumers' lives. As it is at the beginning of the change, it is necessary to keep track of changes in the personal mobility market and explore the experiences of consumers. In particular, it is important that safety-related discussions take place to establish itself as a new means of transportation. It will be necessary to continually identify and improve the problems consumers feel, including safety issues, and reflect them in relevant regulations.

References

1. KB Financial Holding Management Research Institute Report
2. Korea Transport Institute: Smart Mobility Brief, **1**(3), 1–115 (2017)
3. Sang-il, K.: The use of personal mobilities and the duty to notify the alteration and increase of risk. Insur. Law Res. **12**, 103–139 (2018)
4. Sa-ri, K., Hee-chul, S.: Personal mobility awareness survey: focusing on the corporate position. Transp. Technol. Policy **14**, 9–17 (2017)
5. Liu, Y., Woo, J.: A study on the safety regulation of personal mobility. In: AIK Spring Conference, p. 1346 (2019)
6. Jeon, D., Kim, J.: Development of smart personal mobility platform. In: Korea Society of Automotive Engineers Conference and Exhibition, pp. 1289–1290 (2015)
7. Park, S.M.: Development of personal mobility charging technology and direction of infrastructure establishment. KIPE Mag. **24**(1), 30–34 (2019)
8. Blei, D.M., Ng, A.Y., Jordan, M.I.: Latent dirichlet allocation. J. Mach. Learn. Res. **3**, 993–1022 (2003)
9. Park, J.H., Song, M.: A study on the research trends in library & information science in Korea using topic modeling. J. Korean Soc. Inf. Manag. **30**(1), 7–32 (2013)
10. Blei, D.M.: Probabilistic topic models. Commun. ACM **55**(4), 77–84 (2012)

Preference Similarity Analysis of User Preference Rules Using a Character Coordination System

Yuka Nishimura[1]([⊠]), Hiroshi Takenouchi[1]([⊠]),
and Masataka Tokumaru[2]

[1] Fukuoka Institute of Technology,
3-30-1 Wajiro-Higashi, Higashi-ku, Fukuoka 811-0295, Japan
yuuka.246.madotuki@gmail.com, h-takenouchi@fit.ac.jp
[2] Kansai University, 3-3-35 Yamate-cho, Suita-Shi, Osaka 564-8680, Japan

Abstract. In this study, we analyzed user preference rules obtained from a character coordination system using the *Kansei* retrieval agent (*Ka*RA) model with fuzzy inference for the acquisition of user rules related to user preferences. The preference rules of the character coordination system were expressed by *if-then* rules. Previous studies have demonstrated that the character coordination system was effective in terms of acquiring preference rules that were the evaluation criteria of users. In this study, we measured the similarity of preference rules by calculating the distance between preference rules. As a result, the proposed system generated fuzzy rules that matched with more than 60% of the users' preferences. The similarity with antecedent labels (*if* part) of each was high when the consequent labels (*then* part) were the same.

Keywords: Fuzzy reasoning · Interactive genetic algorithm · Rule extraction

1 Introduction

Web-search technologies dynamically search and retrieve expressed user interest items. In addition to the searching technologies, we propose a *Kansei* retrieval agent (*Ka*RA) model that uses fuzzy reasoning. Instead of the user, an agent searches for what the user wants [1]. *Kansei* has a variety of connotations, including feelings, emotions, intuitions, senses, etc. The *Ka*RA learns user preferences by evaluating search data and comparing it with user ratings. In previous studies, a character coordination system incorporating the *Ka*RA model was developed, and its effectiveness for real users was verified [1]. *Ka*RA's fuzzy rules are optimized using a genetic algorithm (GA). A previous system was shown to be effective in presenting user preference coordination plans and learning the fuzzy rules that were highly suitable for their preference rules [1]. Fuzzy rules comprise multiple *if-then* forms, and verbal information can express the user's subjective evaluation scale. In this study, we analyze the similarity of a user's preference rules by calculating the distance between the fuzzy rules generated by the character adjustment system. The distance between these rules is calculated using the differences in the features of the rule. We aim to develop a system that, by acquiring and analyzing preference rules for real users, provide useful information to product developers.

C. Stephanidis and M. Antona (Eds.): HCII 2020, CCIS 1224, pp. 167–172, 2020.
https://doi.org/10.1007/978-3-030-50726-8_22

2 Character Coordination System

2.1 Schematic of the Proposed System

Figure 1 shows the outline of the proposed system. First, Elite *Ka*RA, which evaluates the agent closest to the user, gives an evaluation of the data to be searched in the database by selecting *n* data items having high evaluation and by also presenting data p_1 - p_n. The user associates the evaluation values, $u(p_1)$ - $u(p_n)$, with the presentation data, p_1 - p_n. Furthermore, each *Ka*RA associates an evaluation value with the presentation data, p_1 to p_n. The evaluation values from *Ka*RA 1 are represented by $a_1(p_1)$ - $a_1(p_n)$. Generally, the evaluation values given by *Ka*RA *i* are denoted as $a_i(p_1)$ - $a_i(p_n)$. Furthermore, the evaluation error of the user and *Ka*RA can be obtained from the evaluation values, $u(p_j)$ and $a_i(p_j)$, of the user and agent, respectively. The *Ka*RA parameters can be optimized using the GA with an evaluation error. By repeating the operations, *Ka*RA evolves to fit the user's sensitivity.

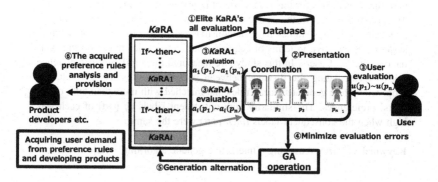

Fig. 1. Outline of the proposed system

2.2 *Ka*RA Evaluation

The *Ka*RA system optimizes itself using the error between the evaluation value given by the user and that provided by the *Ka*RA for the data presented in the database. The evaluation error, $e(i)$, of *Ka*RA *i* is obtained by the following equation:

$$e(i) = \frac{\sum_{j=1}^{n} |a_i(p_j) - u(p_j)|}{n}, \tag{1}$$

where *n* is the number of presentation data elements. When the evaluation error $e(i)$ of the *Ka*RA is small, the difference between the user and the *Ka*RA's sensitivity is also small. Therefore, the agent having the smallest evaluation error among the *Ka*RAs is an elite individual of GA.

Presentation data by *Ka*RAs were evaluated using membership functions and fuzzy rules. Each *Ka*RA performs fuzzy inference on the presented data and gives a real-valued estimate between 0 and 1. *Ka*RA i outputs an evaluation value, $a_i(p_j)$, for one presentation data item, p_j.

2.3 Structure of the Database

In the proposed system, the elite *Ka*RA evaluates the coordination of all patterns stored in the database and presents the coordination plan. Then, the user and *Ka*RA add evaluation values to the presented data to allow the *Ka*RA to learn the user's evaluation tendency. Figure 2 shows the design of the character used in the proposed system. The character coordination design has four features: hair, eyes, shoes, and clothes. Each part of the character coordination has a setting of four bits of hair parts (16 types), three bits of eye parts (eight types), three bits of shoe parts (eight types), and four bits of clothes parts (16 types). The database of the proposed system contains 16,384 patterns of coordination plans generated by combining the four design parts.

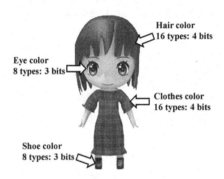

Fig. 2. Bit pattern of design parts

2.4 Fuzzy Rules and Membership Functions

The fuzzy rules of the *Ka*RA model have labeled information corresponding to the features used in the antecedent part and that used in the consequent part as genetic information. Among the features handled by the proposed system, there were five antecedent labels for hair and clothes and three for eyes and shoes. Figure 3 shows the membership function for clothes. The feature values of each part of the character design were set based on the answers of a questionnaire conducted in advance.

2.5 Evaluation Interface

Figure 4 shows the evaluation interface of the proposed system, which uses manual or gaze evaluations to rate the presented coordination. In the case of manual evaluation, the user evaluated each of the 12 proposed coordination plans using 1–5 radio buttons. In the case of evaluation using the gaze information, the evaluation interface was

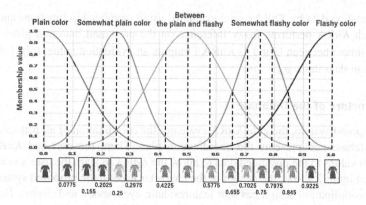

Fig. 3. Membership function of the feature "Clothing"

divided into 12 areas. For each area, it measured which areas were viewed and to what extent. The proposed system used the normalized value of the measurement result as the evaluation value. When user finishes evaluating all coordinations, the user clicks the right-arrow button to proceed to the next generation.

Fig. 4. Evaluation interface of the proposed system

2.6 Similarity of Preference Rules

In this study, the preference rule is a fuzzy rule of the elite *Ka*RA generated by the last generation obtained by the character coordination system. The calculation of the similarity of the preference rule uses the genetic information of the label corresponding to the feature used in the antecedent part of the fuzzy rule. The distance is obtained by calculating the difference between the feature of the base rule and the preference rule. The similarity, *S*, of the base rule and the preference rule is obtained using the following equation:

$$S = \sum\nolimits_{i=1}^{n} |br_i - r_i|, \tag{2}$$

where br_i is the ith antecedent label of the base rule, r_i is the ith antecedent label of the preference rule, and n is the number of features used in the antecedent part of the rule. Then, the rules closest to the distance obtained in Eq. (2) imply a high degree of similarity.

3   The Evaluation Experiment

To verify the effectiveness of the acquisition of the user preference rule in the proposed system, we conducted evaluation experiments with real users. Here, the burden of user evaluation was considered in the experiments targeting the real users. It was reported in a previous study [2] that the evaluation load on the user was reduced when performing an evaluation based on gaze information. We therefore conducted our experiments using two evaluation methods: manual and gaze.

In our experiment, the subjects using the proposed system were 10 university students (five females) in their 20 s. Two types of systems were included: five-stage evaluation via manual evaluation and gaze evaluation via gaze information. Based on the fitness of the fuzzy rules presented by the elite *Ka*RA generated in the final generation, we verified the effectiveness of the subject's preference rule acquisition.

4   Evaluation Result

Figure 5 shows the percentage of subjects who answered, "a little fit" and "fit" for the fuzzy rules having each consequent label. The rate at which the subject answered "a little fit" and "fit" to the fuzzy rules held by *Ka*RA was defined as the fit rate in this experiment. In Fig. 5, the fit rate of the rule in each consequent label exceeded 60%. The proposed system can generate fuzzy rules that matched the user to some extent.

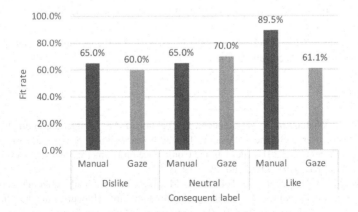

Fig. 5. Fit rate for fuzzy rule with each consequent label

Figure 6 shows the similarity results of the subject's preference rules. In Fig. 6, as a reference rule of the horizontal axis, to calculate the distance to the rule of the vertical axis, the distance between the obtained rules was normalized between 0 to 1. Additionally, the color of the cell closest to 1 was black, and the color of the cell closest to 0 was white. From Fig. 6, we confirmed that the distance was small for preference rules in the consequent part. From this result, we also confirmed that the same preference rules having the same consequent labels had similar features and large similarity. Additionally, when the consequent part is the same, the distance between fuzzy rules tended to decrease in other subjects. However, no clear trend was confirmed. Therefore, we need to further validate the distance between fuzzy rules.

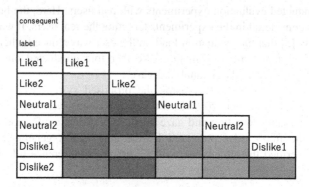

Fig. 6. Similarity of the subject's preference rules

5   Conclusion

In this study, we verified the effectiveness of preference rule acquisition in a character coordination system based on the *Ka*RA model using fuzzy inference. From the experimental results, the *Ka*RA of the proposed system demonstrated effectiveness in learning the fuzzy rules that were highly suitable for the user's preference rules. Additionally, the similarity of antecedent labels to each rule was high when the consequent labels were the same. In future work, we plan to improve the system by optimizing membership functions in addition to *Ka*RA's fuzzy rules, so that the system can respond to finer user sensitivities.

References

1. Shiraishi, R., Nishimura, Y., Takenouchi, H., Tokumaru, M.: Character coordination system for acquiring user preference rules. In: The 20th International Symposium on Advanced Intelligent Systems and 2019 International Conference on Biometrics and Kansei Engineering (ISIS & ICBAKE2019), T10-5, pp. 261-268 (2019)
2. Fujisaki, M., Takenouchi, H., Tokumaru, M.: Developing female clothing coordination generation system using eye tracking information. In: Human-Computer Interaction. Interaction Technologies Volume 10903 of the series Information Systems and Applications, incl. Internet/Web, and HCI (the proceedings of HCI International 2018), pp. 247–257 (2018)

Looking into the Personality Traits to Enhance Empathy Ability: A Review of Literature

Hye Jeong Park[✉] and Jae Hwa Lee

Iowa State University, Ames, IA, USA
{hjpark, jaehwa}@iastate.edu

Abstract. Empathy is an innate capacity that can improve the potential to be creative and innovative in HCI education. The purpose of this study was to explore the relationship between empathy and personality traits through the review of empirical studies. Using the Five Factor Model, the study found that Agreeableness was strongly related to empathy. The rest four traits (Openness, Conscientiousness, Neuroticism, and Extraversion) showed moderate or inconsistent associations with empathy. This study also reviewed educational strategies to enhance students' empathy ability for five personality traits. Academic achievement toward deep and achieving learning approaches was positively related to the most personality traits, except Neuroticism which is interrelated to the surface learning approach. The study suggested individualized learning experiences based on personality traits to enhance empathy ability in HCI education.

Keywords: Empathy · Creativity · FFM · HCI education

1 Introduction

The empathic approach supports building a rich understanding of others' experiences, motivation, and life contexts. Empathy is a significant facet in Human-Computer Interaction practice (HCI), as it allows us to understand human-centered analysis and to creatively solve complex problems across disciplines [12, 24]. These attributes of empathy would encompass broad and diverse interconnections of technologies, perspectives, and people in the field of HCI. Interactive technologies have been developed toward the empathic design approach [23], and strategies and techniques of empathic design have taken designers into the user's life [24]. As Suri [34] stated, empathy would support professionals in the HCI domain to meet future challenges beyond the boundaries and take interdisciplinary opportunities.

Moreover, empathy makes a substantial contribution to improve our potential to be creative and innovative and to collaborate with people from diverse backgrounds. In the HCI domain, several studies have investigated how empathy boosts one's creative problem-solving skills using various approaches and tools, such as persona, scenario, experience prototyping, Empathic Experience Design (EED), and design thinking strategies [20, 21]. Paying more attention to empathy in HCI education would nurture the students to be prepared as creative professionals to better solve complex real-world problems [27].

© Springer Nature Switzerland AG 2020
C. Stephanidis and M. Antona (Eds.): HCII 2020, CCIS 1224, pp. 173–180, 2020.
https://doi.org/10.1007/978-3-030-50726-8_23

As empathy ability is an individual ability to intellectually and emotionally connect with the experience of another, it would be beneficial to develop more personality-focused educational strategies for building empathy ability. The Five Factor Model (FFM) is the major framework in personality research, which could associate with our cognitive and affective experiences across the lifespan and cultures. The FFM is organized in the five personality traits: Openness (to experience), Neuroticism, Extraversion, Agreeableness, and Conscientiousness [4, 15]. Although personality has been studied in HCI discipline to explore better interactive technologies with positive user experience [2], the studies have not provided a holistic perspective of the relationships between personality and empathy.

To promote empathy ability of HCI students, we reviewed empirical studies to identify how empathy and personality traits have related to each other. This study also suggested appropriate teaching strategies for different personality traits to enhance empathy ability within HCI education. By providing personality-focused educational strategies, this study has potential implications for HCI education to promote students' creativity through empathy ability.

2 Empathy, the Five Factor Model, and Learning Approaches

2.1 Empathy

Empathy is related to 'feeling' and 'knowing' process that individual feels, shares the emotional experiences (affective component), and understands experiences (cognitive component) of others [1]. Davis [16] proposed four empathy scales in the Interpersonal Reactivity Index (IRI), using these two components, affective and cognitive. In cognitive component, perspective taking and fantasy scales are associated: perspective taking scale is an ability to understand the perspectives or situations of others; fantasy scale is an imagination of other's feelings within a situation, which is to become a character in an imaginary situation including movie or fiction. In affective component, empathic concern and personal distress are involved: empathic concern scale indicates feelings of compassion and sympathy toward others' experiences; personal distress scale is related to recognizing others' negative experiences and feelings including anxiety and discomfort.

These scales are considered significant skills common to creative thinkers in a variety of disciplines from the arts and humanities to science and business [10]. For example, Webster [37] investigated nursing students' empathy using the IRI and creative reflective assignment. The result indicated that empathy and the creative assignment had a positive relationship to improve students' empathy ability as well as creativity. Genco, Johnson, and Seepersad [21] compared two control groups with learning the EED and without learning EED to examine the levels of originality. The finding revealed that students with experience in EED scored higher originality in idea generation. Other studies also demonstrated that empathy significantly promoted group creativity [38] and students' creative confidence and behaviors [33] using design thinking strategies. For its complex technical issues and new goals of design, HCI may address it beneficial to help students be more creative from empathetic approaches that focus on experiences, emotions, connectedness with user-centered perspectives [11, 24].

2.2 The Five Factor Model

This study explored personality traits as structured variables to understand individual differences in cognitive thinking patterns or emotional tendencies. The FFM, proposed by Costa and McCare [15], is one of the most representative models of personality concept [29].

The FFM is consists of Openness, Extraversion, Conscientiousness, Agreeableness, and Neuroticism. The definition of Openness is 'open' to all experiences indicating the characteristics as curious, interested in diverse contents, and sensitive [28]. Individuals with Openness are associated with strong intrinsic motivation, engagement of creative activities [35]. A person with Extraversion is described as active, passionate, energetic, self-efficient or self-confident, and willing to take risks [5]. Sociality and enjoyment of interacting with others are significant facets of Extraversion [31]. According to Moondarian, Davis, and Matzler (2011) [30], Agreeableness has defined as a prosocial with trust and altruism, and it can be explained as cooperative, tender-minded, and considerate. The representative adjectives for Conscientiousness are achievement-striving, order, efficient, and organized. Neuroticism is the opposite meaning of emotional stability, and it indicates negative emotions, such as fears and anxiety, self-consciousness, depression, and moody [30].

2.3 Learning Approaches and Motivation

An approach to learning indicates how students motivate to achieve and gain knowledge [18]. According to Biggs [8], three approaches to learning have been identified: "surface," "deep," and "achieving" approaches.

A surface approach to learning is considered as appropriate for students who focus on minimum requirements to pass the exam or assignments rather than the whole content. Therefore, students who adopt a surface approach to learning tend to memorize facts for reproduction and follow given procedures to solve problems without questioning [6, 8]. These students are more encouraged by extrinsic motivation, in both positive (e.g., gaining credentials) and negative (e.g., test anxiety) ways. In contrast, students who take a deep approach to learning are influenced by an intrinsic motivation or internal curiosity and exhibit a desire to understand and deeply engage in the given topic. They seek to describe the nature of issues and interact critically with the learning materials [6, 8]. These students can apply ideas to their experiences and to build a coherent body of knowledge, which may relate to their personally meaningful contexts. In addition, an achieving approach to learning links to a high level of effort when students maximize their academic achievement such as grades based on own goals [8]. Students who reflect an achieving approach to learning are motivated by organized behaviors toward competitions or characteristics of role models associated with obtaining high grades. Therefore, unlike deep and surface learning approaches, an achieving approach would closely relate to activities and skills to plan and organize tasks [9].

3   Relationship Between Empathy and the Five Factor Model

To explore the relationship between empathy and the FFM, we reviewed peer-reviewed journal publications, conference articles, and book chapters studied personality traits with the FFM in relation to empathy and learning methods/approaches across disciplines and cultures. The search terms were "empathy," "empathy and personality/FFM," "personality/FFM and teaching/learning methods/approaches," and "personality/FFM and learning motivation." A total of 19 empirical studies were finally selected to recognize the relationship between personality traits and empathy attributes. These studies employed self-reported questionnaires and statistical analysis to examine the samples' level of empathy and personality traits. The most frequently used measurement of empathy was IRI. The subjects of the selected studies varied in their age (i.e., adolescents and adults), disciplines (i.e., medicine, counseling, psychology, etc.), and cultures (i.e., American, Japanese, Spanish, Portuguese, etc.).

Among the five personality traits, Agreeableness was the most closely involved in empathy ability [4, 14, 26, 29, 31]. The result was consistent across cultures. In particular, studies discovered that Agreeableness is the strongest factor in explaining the empathic concern scale and is moderately correlated to the perspective taking and personal distress scales [29, 30]. Individuals with high Agreeableness tend to communicate with others and take 'person-oriented' perspectives easily [26]. That is, attributes of Agreeableness, such as compassionate, good-natured, eager to cooperate and avoid trouble, were closely related to empathy [14].

The results also confirmed positive associations between Openness and empathy from the previous studies [4, 26, 29, 30, 35]. As more empathetic people with the necessary sensitivity and insightfulness could better understand others based on their tendency to meet and communicate with other people, Openness is closely related to the perspective taking scale of empathy [30, 35]. Moreover, the fantasy scale of empathy was only linked to Openness among the five personality traits [26, 29], as highly Open to Experience embodies the ability to generate fictional environments through books or movies.

Extraversion seemed indeterminately related to empathy. Extraversion in the previous studies showed a moderate correlation with empathy [4, 29, 31], in the case of the perspective taking scale [30]. Extraversion implies sociality and enjoyment for social interactions [15, 31]. Therefore, it is expected that energies go to the outer world would promote cognitive empathetic ability. However, Wakabayashi and Kawashima [36] indicated that Extraversion showed no correlation with empathy when the measurement of personality traits was NEO-FFI. The reason was not clearly revealed, but the researchers assumed that this measurement might examine less cognitive aspects [36].

Regarding the relationship between Neuroticism and empathy, studies showed contradictory results. Some studies found that the personal distress scale was associated with Neuroticism, as both constructs indicate relatively negative emotions in our experiences through social interactions [29, 30]. Another affective component of empathy, empathic concern, was also related to Neuroticism in the previous study [30]. This association reflects the role of emotion in empathy and FFM. However, others reported the absence of a relationship between Neuroticism and empathy [4, 26].

Conscientiousness also showed inconsistent correlation to empathy. Several studies identified Conscientiousness as an important predictor of empathy [4, 29]. However, Magalhães and colleagues [26] concluded that the Conscientiousness' degree to explain any empathy scales was negligible.

4 Educational Strategies to Promote Empathy Ability Depending on Students' Personality Traits

This study also reviewed the previous studies that investigated learning approaches depending on students' personality traits. Based on the understanding of the relationships between empathy and personality traits, this study suggested educational strategies to promote HCI students' empathy ability.

Agreeableness was found to link with the most diverse educational opportunities for building empathy ability. A broad range of learning approaches, from the surface to deep and achieving, was associated with Agreeableness. Students higher in Agreeableness preferred lab classes and small group tutorials [13]. Although students with higher Agreeableness generally showed a low correlation with academic performance [13], their academic performance was improved with more extrinsic and achievement motivation [12]. Therefore, diverse learning strategies and tools to encourage more participatory design with an emphasis on small group settings are recommended. In particular, persona and design thinking strategies would be the best examples to nurture empathy ability for the people scoring high on the trait of Agreeableness, as they would provide group-work opportunities to think about others with an ethnographical perspective [11].

Students higher in Openness could have great possibilities to develop empathy ability in educational settings, based on its positive correlation to academic achievement. Representative facets of Openness are intellectually curious, imaginative, and novel [15], which led students with high Openness to positive attitudes toward deep and complex learning experiences [3, 13] with more intrinsic and achievement motivation [12]. Therefore, in response to their novel and intellectual interests, creative activities such as reading books and watching movies in different languages, having diverse cultural experiences as free-time activities, and role-playing would effectively enhance their empathy level [17]. These learning experiences are recommended for people highly Openness to be more aware of different perspectives and challenge any stereotypical or prejudiced ideas [32].

Extraversion is also positively correlated to academic performance [12, 19]. Extraverted students tend to prefer interacting with teachers [19]. Therefore, interactive teaching strategies, including group discussion, participatory design, interview, role-playing, and field study, are great to encourage empathy ability. On the contrary, since persona and scenario are more non-interactive methods, these approaches would be revised into more sociable settings to promote their empathy for the students higher in Extraversion.

Unlike other personality traits, Neuroticism is associated with a surface learning approach rather than a deep learning approach. The characteristics of Neurotic students are worrying about the grade of exams and low in confidence. Consequently, it could cause academic failure [13]. Therefore, for Neurotic students, traditional teaching (i.e., lecture-based) would be recommended with particular design processes or methodologies in guiding them to meet the final outcome with the less challenging learning environment. In contrast, students with emotional stability (low Neuroticism) are associated with a deep learning approach and academic success [13]. Therefore, interaction-based strategies and tools (i.e., interview, participatory design) would positively impact on enhancing their empathy [13].

Conscientiousness is closely associated with academic performance toward deep and achieving learning approaches. [22]. Students with high Conscientiousness are perceived motivated to succeed, organized, making plans, hard-working for success (i.e., study goals), and self-controlled [7, 12, 13, 25]. Therefore, analytical thinking would be a good learning experience for Conscientiousness students with training and discussion opportunities in groups [13, 25]. Educational strategies that are more practical and rational including interview methods are suggested to improve their empathy ability.

5 Conclusion

Understanding of empathy in HCI is critical as it can be a core aspect to improve students' creative potential and performance. This study focused on how empathy is associated with personality traits to promote students' creativity in educational settings through the review of the literature. For educational strategies to enhance empathy ability, a broad range of learning approaches was suggested for Agreeableness, and more creative activities with imagination were recommended for Openness. Students higher in Extraversion would better fit with interactive learning strategies, but Neurotic students could benefit from traditional learning methods. More practical and rational learning approaches would provide more opportunities for students with higher Conscientiousness. These suggestions would be considered to develop personality-focused learning strategies for building empathy ability and creative potential in HCI education. For the next step, additional research may include how HCI students actually build their empathy ability with regards to their academic and professional activities. The study also calls more empirical studies on the relationship between personal factors and empathy-building strategies over time.

References

1. Andres, T., Juanita, G.: Empathic design as a framework for creating meaningful experiences. In: Conference Proceedings of the Academy for Design Innovation Management, vol. 2, no. 1, pp. 908–918 (2019)
2. Arazy, O., Nov, O., Kumar, N.: Personalityzation: UI personalization, theoretical grounding in HCI and design research. AIS Trans. Hum.-Comput. Interaction 7(2), 43–69 (2015)

3. Barrick, M.R., Mount, M.K.: The big five personality dimensions and job performance: a meta-analysis. Pers. Psychol. **44**(1), 1–26 (1991)
4. Barrio, V.D., Aluja, A., García, L.F.: Relationship between empathy and the Big Five personality traits in a sample of Spanish adolescents. Soc. Behav. Personal. Int. J. **32**(7), 677–681 (2004)
5. Barron, F., Harrington, D.M.: Creativity, intelligence, and personality. Annu. Rev. Psychol. **32**(1), 439–476 (1981)
6. Beattie, V., Collines, W., McInnes, W.: Deep and surface learning: simple or simplistic dichotomy? Acc. Educ. **6**(1), 1–12 (1997)
7. Bidjerano, T., Dai, D.Y.: The relationship between the big-five model of personality and self-regulated learning strategies. Learn. Individ. Differ. **17**(1), 69–81 (2007)
8. Biggs, J.B.: Study Process Questionnaire Manual. Australian Council for Educational Research, Hawthorn (1987)
9. Biggs, J.B.: Assessing student approaches to learning. Australian Psychol. **23**(2), 197–206 (1988)
10. Boltz, L.O., Henriksen, D., Mishra, P.: Deep-Play Research Group: rethinking technology & creativity in the 21st century: Empathy through gaming-perspective taking in a complex world. TechTrends **59**(6), 3–8 (2015)
11. Brown, T.: Change by design: how design thinking creates new alternatives for business and society. Collins Business (2009)
12. Busato, V.V., Prins, F.J., Elshout, J.J., Hamaker, C.: Intellectual ability, learning style, personality, achievement motivation and academic success of psychology students in higher education. Personality Individ. Differ. **29**(6), 1057–1068 (2000)
13. Chamorro-Premuzic, T., Furnham, A., Lewis, M.: Personality and approaches to learning predict preference for different teaching methods. Learn. Individ. Differ. **17**(3), 241–250 (2007)
14. Costa, P.T., McCrae, R.: The revised NEO personality inventory (NEO-PI-R). In: The SAGE Handbook of Personality Theory and Assessment, Vol. 2. Personality measurement and testing, pp. 179–198. Sage Publications, Inc. (2008)
15. Costa, P.T., McCrae, R.R.: Revised NEO Personality Inventory (NEO PI-R) and NEO Five-Factor Inventory (NEO-FFI) Professional Manual. Psychological Assessment Resources, Odessa (1992)
16. Davis, M.H.: Measuring individual differences in empathy: evidence for a multidimensional approach. J. Pers. Soc. Psychol. **44**(1), 113 (1983)
17. De Fruyt, F., Mervielde, I.: Personality and interests as predictors of educational streaming and achievement. Eur. J. Pers. **10**, 405–425 (1996)
18. Duff, A.: Quality of learning on an MBA programme: the impact of approaches to learning on academic performance. Educ. Psychol. **23**, 123–139 (2003)
19. Eysenck, H.J., Cookson, D.: Personality in primary school children: 1.—Ability and achievement. Br. J. Educ. Psychol. **39**, 109–122 (1969)
20. Gagnon, C., Côté, V.: Learning from others: a five years experience on teaching empathic design. In: Proceedings of Design Research Society Biennial International Conference (DRS), pp. 16–19 (2014)
21. Genco, N., Johnson, D., Seepersad, C.C.: A study of the effectiveness of empathic experience design as a creativity technique. In: ASME 2011 International Design Engineering Technical Conferences and Computers and Information in Engineering Conference, pp. 131–139. American Society of Mechanical Engineers Digital Collection (2011)
22. Ivcevic, Z., Brackett, M.: Predicting school success: comparing conscientiousness, grit, and emotion regulation ability. J. Res. Pers. **52**, 29–36 (2014)

23. Koskinen, I., Mattelmäki, T., Battarbee, K.: Empathic Design: User Experience in Product Design. IT-Press, Helsinki (2003)
24. Kouprie, M., Visser, F.S.: A framework for empathy in design: stepping into and out of the user's life. J. Eng. Des. 20(5), 437–448 (2009)
25. MacCann, C., Duckworth, A.L., Roberts, R.D.: Empirical identification of the major facets of conscientiousness. Learn. Individ. Differ. 19(4), 451–458 (2009)
26. Magalhães, E., Costa, P., Costa, M.J.: Empathy of medical students and personality: evidence from the Five-Factor Model. Med. Teach. 34(10), 807–812 (2012)
27. Mattelmäki, T., Vaajakallio, K., Koskinen, I.: What Happened to Empathic Design? Des. Issues 30(1), 67–77 (2013)
28. McCrae, R.R.: Creativity, divergent thinking, and openness to experience. J. Pers. Soc. Psychol. 52, 1258–1265 (1987)
29. Melchers, M.C., Li, M., Haas, B.W., Reuter, M., Bischoff, L., Montag, C.: Similar personality patterns are associated with empathy in four different countries. Front. Psychol. 7, 290 (2016)
30. Mooradian, T.A., Davis, M., Matzler, K.: Dispositional empathy and the hierarchical structure of personality. Am. J. Psychol. 124(1), 99–109 (2011)
31. Nettle, D.: Psychological profiles of professional actors. Personality Individ. Differ. 40, 375–383 (2006)
32. Poorman, P.B.: Biography and role playing: fostering empathy in abnormal psychology. Teach. Psychol. 29(1), 32–36 (2002)
33. Rauth, I., Köppen, E., Jobst, B., Meinel, C.: Design thinking: an educational model towards creative confidence. In: DS 66–2: Proceedings of the 1st International Conference on Design Creativity (ICDC) (2010)
34. Suri, J.F.: The next 50 years: future challenges and opportunities for empathy in our science. Ergonomics 44(14), 1278–1289 (2001)
35. Tan, C.S., Lau, X.S., Kung, Y.T., Kailsan, R.A.L.: Openness to experience enhances creativity: The mediating role of intrinsic motivation and the creative process engagement. J. Creative Behav. 53(1), 109–119 (2019)
36. Wakabayashi, A., Kawashima, H.: Is empathizing in the E-S theory similar to agreeableness? The relationship between the EQ and SQ and major personality domains. Personality Individ. Differ. 76, 88–93 (2015)
37. Webster, D.: Promoting empathy through a creative reflective teaching strategy: a mixed-method study. J. Nurs. Educ. 49(2), 87–94 (2010)
38. Woo, Y., Yoon, J., Kang, S.J.: Empathy as an element of promoting the manifestation of group creativity and survey on empathic ability of Korean elementary school students. Eurasia J. Math. Sci. Technol. Educ. 13(7), 3849–3867 (2017)

Estimation of Degree of Interest in Comics Using a Stabilometer and an Acceleration Sensor

Yanzi Sun[1]([✉]), Yu Matsumoto[1], Kazuyuki Mito[1], Tota Mizuno[1],
Naoaki Itakura[1], Takeshi Hanada[2], and Taiyo Nakashima[2]

[1] The University of Electro-Communications,
1-5-1 Chofugaoka, Chofu, Tokyo 1828585, Japan
sun596053467@gmail.com
[2] Coamix Inc., 1-9-9 Kichijoji Zizo Building,
Kichijoji, Musashino, Tokyo 1800003, Japan

Abstract. The current widespread usage of the Internet has made it possible to easily browse through various types of web content. However, owing to the large amount of available web content, it is difficult to recommend items that match the viewer's preferences. Although existing recommendation systems can recommend content based on the viewer's browsing history and previous purchases, there is still a lack of content relevance. Hence, a system is required that can quantitatively evaluate the viewer's degree of interest by incorporating biometric information and thereby recommend the appropriate content. In previous studies, the viewer's concentration was measured by employing an acceleration sensor on the back surface of a chair. However, the viewer's posture cannot be estimated when the viewer does not lean against the backrest. Hence, in this study, we propose a method for estimating the degree of interest by employing a chair equipped with a body stabilometer on the seat and an acceleration sensor on the back. In this study, when the subject was leaning against the backrest, we determined the position of the center of gravity by employing a body stabilometer, and we acquired acceleration data by employing an acceleration sensor. Furthermore, we analyzed the movement vectors of the position of the center of gravity and the acceleration. Consequently, the vector angle was divided after every 15°, and the analysis was conducted by examining the vector magnitude in the angle. The obtained results indicate a positive correlation between the interest in each story and the vector magnitude. Therefore, it can be concluded that the degree of interest can be evaluated by incorporating the vector magnitude of the position of the center of gravity and the acceleration.

Keywords: Body stabilometer · Acceleration sensor · Movement vector · Vector magnitude

© Springer Nature Switzerland AG 2020
C. Stephanidis and M. Antona (Eds.): HCII 2020, CCIS 1224, pp. 181–187, 2020.
https://doi.org/10.1007/978-3-030-50726-8_24

1 Introduction

The current widespread usage of the Internet and smartphones has made it is possible to easily browse through numerous types of web content. However, owing to the large amount of available web content, it is difficult to recommend items that match the viewer's preferences. Although conventional recommendation systems can recommend content based on the viewer's browsing history and previous purchases, there is still a lack of content relevance. Hence, a system is required that can quantitatively evaluate the viewer's degree of interest by incorporating biometric information and thus recommend the appropriate content.

In a previous study, Peter Bull [1] stated that the motion associated with "a body leaning forward" indicates the viewer's high level of interest, and the motion associated with "a body leaning backward" indicates the viewer's lack of interest. Based on this observation, Iwai et al. [2] studied the feature that an object of interest attracts the viewer's neck to the front, and they estimated the degree of interest on the basis of gaze behavior and body movements. By mounting a distance sensor on the object, they estimated the degree of interest by measuring the distance between the subject and the object and measuring the duration of staring at the object with a camera. However, in such a case, the external device must be attached to the object. In another study, Sakamoto et al. [3] estimated the degree of concentration while browsing through comics by employing two body sway meters, but they did not consider cases involving a backrest because they used a chair without a backrest. Furthermore, Okubo et al. [4] measured the viewer's concentration by employing a chair equipped with an acceleration sensor. However, posture estimation was not performed when the subjects were not leaning on the backrest.

Therefore, the objective of this study is to analyze the viewer's behavior when presented with comics and to thereby evaluate the viewer's degree of interest. In this study, we propose a method for estimating the degree of interest by using a chair equipped with a stabilometer on the seat and an acceleration sensor on the backrest.

2 Methodology

The experimental equipment is depicted in Fig. 1. A body stabilometer (with sampling frequency of 100 Hz) was placed on the subject's chair. In addition, a cushion was placed on the chair to ensure that the subject did not feel uncomfortable. A Wii remote control was placed on the chair's backrest as an acceleration sensor. The subjects rested briefly for approximately five minutes after sitting and were subsequently asked to read comics on the computer in a free posture. The subjects randomly read seven types of comics on 150–190 pages. After reading, they were asked to rate their interest in the comics on a scale of 1–10. The participating subjects were two healthy adults.

Fig. 1. Experimental equipment

3   Analysis Indices

In this study, the outer peripheral area of movement and the maximum average size of vector (ASV) were incorporated as analysis indices during sway measurement of the center of gravity.

3.1   Peripheral Area

We determined the central position for the center of gravity sway in the sampling section. The moving outer circumference was thereby divided into $120 \times 3°$, and the area connecting the farthest points in each division was defined as the outer peripheral area. The detailed method is described below with the corresponding equations.

Let $A_1(x_1, y_1)$, $A_2(x_2, y_2)$, ..., and $A_n(x_n, y_n)$ represent the coordinate points. The point at the center of the section can be corrected as a temporary origin by obtaining the average of x and y values in the section and subtracting it from the corresponding coordinate values. Let $tA_1(tx_1, ty_1)$, $tA_2(tx_2, ty_2)$, ..., and $tA_m(tx_m, ty_m)$ represent the corrected coordinates. Then, tx_m can be expressed as follows:

$$tx_m = x_m - \frac{\sum_{k=1}^{n} x_k}{n}$$

The angle θ and distance d from the temporary origin can be calculated as follows:

$$\theta_m = \frac{180}{\pi} \times \tan^{-1}(ty_m/tx_m)$$

$$d_m = \sqrt{tx_m^2 + ty_m^2}$$

Here, θ denotes the frequency, which is in the range of $-180°$ to $180°$. We determined the position in the section where θ was divided into $3°$ units and thereby determined the farthest point among them. Let $G_1(mx_1, my_1)$, $G_2(mx_2, my_2)$, ..., and $G_{120}(mx_{120}, my_{120})$ denote the determined coordinates. Then, the outer peripheral area s can be expressed as follows:

$$s = \sum_{n=1}^{120} \frac{1}{2} |mx_n \times my_{n+1} - my_n \times mx_{n+1}| + \frac{1}{2} |mx_{120} \times my_1 - my_{120} \times mx_1|$$

3.2   Maximum ASV

We examined the vector for each sampling time (start point = coordinates of 0.01 s ago, end point = coordinates of time point of sampling). The vectors were divided into 15° units, and the characteristics of the vectors included in that direction were analyzed. Two features, namely the maximum ASV included in each 15° unit and the number of vectors, were examined.

Let $A_1(x_1, y_1)$, $A_2(x_2, y_2)$, ..., and $A_n(x_n, y_n)$ represent the coordinate points. Furthermore, let n denote the number of samples in the target section. Then, ASV can be expressed as follows:

$$ASV = \frac{\sum_{k=1}^{n-1} \sqrt{(x_{k+1} - x_k)^2 + (y_{k+1} - y_k)^2}}{n}$$

4   Results and Conclusion

In this study, the maximum ASV was calculated for each comic that the subjects read. The correlation coefficient between the maximum ASV and the degree of interest was calculated by evaluating the degree of interest after browsing, and analysis was conducted for each subject.

Firstly, the time spent leaning on the backrest while reading was extracted from the data of the acceleration sensor. The time spent leaning on the backrest was short in each experiment because the subjects browsed through the comics on the computer. Hence, the analysis was performed without discriminating whether the subjects leaned on the backrest or not.

After calculating the peripheral area and the maximum ASV for each comic, the correlation coefficient between the maximum ASV and the degree of interest was estimated. In addition, the correlation coefficient between the peripheral area and the degree of interest was also calculated. The results corresponding to the maximum ASV are illustrated in Fig. 2 and Fig. 3. It can be observed that the maximum ASV of the subjects and the degree of interest indicate a high correlation, which suggests that the maximum ASV of the center of gravity increases as the subject becomes more interested while reading the comics. The results corresponding to the outer peripheral area are illustrated in Fig. 4 and Fig. 5. It can be observed that the correlation coefficient of subject-1 in Fig. 4 is positive but less than or equal to 0.5. Furthermore, in Fig. 5, it can be observed that that the correlation with degree of interest is quite low for subject-2. Therefore, it is can be concluded that it is not sufficient to estimate the degree of interest solely on the basis of the peripheral area. It can also be concluded that irrespective of whether the subject leans on the backrest or not, the degree of interest can be estimated by incorporating the maximum ASV of the center of gravity sway.

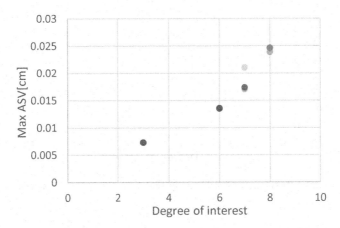

Fig. 2. Correlation between subject-1's maximum ASV and degree of interest (R = 0.94)

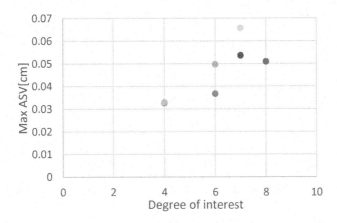

Fig. 3. Correlation between subject-2's maximum ASV and degree of interest (R = 0.79)

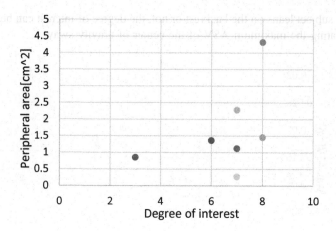

Fig. 4. Correlation between subject-1's peripheral area and degree of interest (R = 0.44)

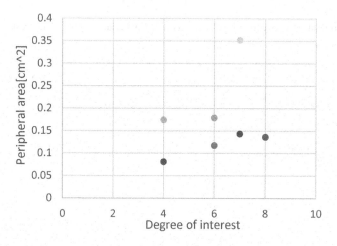

Fig. 5. Correlation between subject-2's peripheral area and degree of interest (R = 0.32)

5 Future Work

In this study, we attempted to analyze the viewer's behavior upon being presented with comics. Hence, we developed a method for estimating the viewer's degree of interest by incorporating the changes in the viewer's posture, and the viewer's body sway was analyzed by employing a stabilometer and an acceleration sensor.

Dividing the object according to the presence or absence of the backrest may affect the calculation of the correlation coefficient because the time spent leaning on the backrest was very short in this study. Therefore, the correlation between the maximum ASV and the degree of interest was calculated irrespective of the presence or absence of the backrest. Furthermore, it can be concluded that the degree of interest can be estimated by incorporating the maximum ASV of the center of gravity sway.

In this study, we did not analyze the presence or absence of the backrest. Hence, as future work, we would like to examine the possibility of estimating the degree of interest by asking the subjects to browse through a paper manga and categorizing the subjects into cases wherein subjects lean on the backrest or not.

References

1. Bull, P.: Posture and Gesture. Pergamon Press, UK (1987)
2. Iwai, Y., Sumi, K., Matsuyama, T.: Estimating the degree of interest in human selection using images. In: Workshop on the Actual Application of Vision Technology, Japan Society for Precision Engineering, pp. 32–37 (2005)
3. Sakamoto, S., Akehi, K., Itakura, N., Mizuno, T.: Evaluation of psychosomatic condition using center of gravity fluctuation in sitting position. In: International Conference on Engineering and Technology (2019)
4. Okubo, M., Fujimura, Y.: Proposal of concentration estimation system using acceleration sensor, WISS Japan Society for Software Science and Technology (2008)

A Recommender System that Considers Contradictory Impression in Fashion

Hiroshi Takamiya[1(✉)], Naoki Takahashi[1], Takashi Sakamoto[2], and Toshikazu Kato[1]

[1] Chuo University, 1-13-27 Kasuga, Bunkyo-ku, Tokyo 112-8551, Japan
a15.5bhj@g.chuo-u.ac.jp,
{naoki,t-kato}@kc.chuo-u.ac.jp
[2] National Institute of Advanced Industrial Science and Technology (AIST),
Tsukuba, Ibaraki 305-8568, Japan
takashi-sakamoto@aist.go.jp

Abstract. We aim to develop a recommender system, that is often used in e-commerce sites, to help users choose and do mix-and-match clothing. A series of users' behavior to choose clothes and accessories according to their liking, and do mix-and-match them is called "fashion coordination" in this paper. The proposed recommender system has a new mechanism that proposes an alternative fashion coordination to boost the user's self-image. This mechanism implemented by utilizing the semantic dimension of impression judgments in the fashion coordination, based on a semantic differential method and a factor analysis. Through this mechanism, the users will be able to consider contradictory impression in the fashion coordination: not only those that they believe will suit them, but also those that they desire but may not suit them. The system provides a comprehensive evaluation of the contradictory impression in the fashion coordination, and a person can be persuaded to buy or wear clothing that they previously believed would not suit them. In this study, as a preliminary stage to construct the recommender system, we conducted a psychological experiment that participants evaluated photo-images of varied outfits. We also constructed 24 evaluation scales based on the experimental results, and examined the semantic differential method and the factor analysis to model user's contradictory impression in the fashion coordination.

Keywords: Fashion coordination · Psychological experiment · Evaluation scale · Self-image · Factor analysis · Semantic differential method

1 Introduction

"Impression" has a great influence on the selection of outfit, in which people think the clothing combination of a day with the impression given by the outfit. A series of users' behavior to choose clothes and accessories according to their liking, and do mix-and-match them is called "fashion coordination" in this paper. People tend to infer the personalities of others based on their clothes as a first impression [2], in addition, people need to synchronize the behavior of others and adjust to society, and this tendency is also seen in fashion adoption [3]. Accordingly, we consider that the

© Springer Nature Switzerland AG 2020
C. Stephanidis and M. Antona (Eds.): HCII 2020, CCIS 1224, pp. 188–195, 2020.
https://doi.org/10.1007/978-3-030-50726-8_25

relation-ship between the impression of fashion coordination and self-image and the selection according to the coordination preference should be considered. Even if people are given favorable fashion coordination impressions, such as "You look good!" and "It looks nice!," they may still avoid wearing or purchasing the clothes if they think that the impression they receive is unsuitable for them. By contrast, they may wear or purchase the clothes if they receive a favorable and suitable impression or feel admired for doing so. However, a system that can provide recommendations and consider the latent desires of users has not been proposed until now.

Accordingly, in this study, we aim to develop a recommender system that can suggest clothing combinations to users and, help users choose and do mix-and-match clothing by considering the impressions on fashion coordination used in EC sites. We perceive fashion coordination by considering the impressions of clothing combinations that the user thinks suit him/her and the user desires (but the user does not think they suit him/her). Our proposed system can encourage the user to pay attention to the coordination category, which is not the object of wearing or purchasing because of the fear that it is unsuitable for oneself and that the impression of others greatly change.

In this study, we created a scale for the SD method and factor analysis to model fashion coordination impressions. By making the evaluation scale through an examinee experiment, we considered the user viewpoint through a discussion rather than the subjective viewpoints of the authors.

2   Related Study

Many existing recommender systems determine items to recommend to users based on their search and browsing history. Therefore, users can receive item recommendations through their purchase desire, browsing experience, and relation of some items to them. However, items that users have not searched or browsed and those that the users think do not suit them cannot be recommended. In addition, even if they searched or viewed some items because they have favorable impressions, they still may not purchase or wear the items unless they think they match their self-image. To date, no system can estimate such latent needs and recommend items that users did not pay attention to. Thus, we adopted a technique that considers clothing coordination that the user thinks suits his self-image and the coordination that the user desires but the user thinks does not suit his self-image.

In a previous study [1], the authors proposed a fashion recommender system using the sensitivities of the user and others. In the proposed method in this research, the sensitivities of the user and others were modeled using colors as a feature quantity and image on a website called WEAR, and the clothing coordination considering both sensitivities was recommended. They used the average of colors of each top and bottom as the feature quantity. The combination of multiple colors and the average of multiple colors do not have the same impression, and whether they surely express the sensitivity is hard to tell. For example, when a white T-shirt and a black jacket are combined with a top, the average color is gray. Then, the impression of the former combination of black and white clothes is different from that of the later average gray color. In addition, when people provide impressions on clothes, a criterion of multiple viewpoints is used behind it, and in addition to colors, shapes and designs are included in the physical features.

Therefore, in our research, we aim to propose a recommender system suitable for human intuitive coordination selection by using impressions instead of physical features, such as colors.

3 Modeling Coordination Impressions

We constructed a mechanism to quantify fashion coordination impressions in order to recommend clothing combinations. First, we framed an evaluation scale from adjective pairs used for evaluating the fashion coordination. We will utilize a questionnaire through the SD method. Using the results of the questionnaire evaluation, the type of semantic dimension impression and the position of evaluation objects on the space with those semantic dimensions using the factor analysis will be clarified. We term the constructed factor score space as "the impression space" [4] and plot the fashion coordination as a point in this space to quantify the impression. Moreover, we assume that there is no large individual difference in the impression of fashion coordination, as people recognize the same categories of fashion, and the data on fashion coordination that users evaluated are shared on the impression space.

4 Experiment

4.1 Evaluation Scale Creation

First, we distributed the questionnaire to create the evaluation scale for the SD method. The patients were women aged 20 to 25 years. They individually examined 16 fashion coordination images and evaluated each image on a five-point scale using 48 adjective pairs. We extracted the sample images taken from 2017 to 2019 and from fashion coordination data of evaluation objects with temperatures of 10 °C to 20 °C from a fashion information site [5], which has a theme "street fashion in Tokyo." By considering the subjective view of the author and discussions with several people, including experienced people from the garment industry, we selected 16 images and processed to cover recent fashion lines (Fig. 1). We hid the faces in the images for privacy and blurred the backgrounds to emphasize the fashion. As for the evaluation items, we selected words used to evaluate fashion coordination impressions by referring to studies on fashion [6–9] and websites [10, 11] and combined adjectives with their opposite meanings, formulating 48 adjective pairs (Table 1). We used five methods to assess the degree of fit on a five-point scale, which includes "hold true," "be somewhat of a fit" on either side and "neither" on the center.

4.2 Creating an Evaluation Score

Among the 48 adjective pairs, we selected adjective pairs with a small individual difference in the evaluation value of each sample image and a large variance in the average value in the evaluation of each sample image as an evaluation scale for the SD method.

Fig. 1. 16 sample images

Point 1: We adopted items with small differences in evaluation between each respondent for each sample image. Because we assume that the fashion coordination impressions given do not differ greatly between users and others, we did not use items that had a large difference in the evaluation between individuals for each sample image, that is, items with a large difference for recognition. In this study, we excluded the items whose difference between the maximum evaluation value and minimum evaluation value was larger than 2.

Point 2: We adopted the evaluation with different values for each sample image. Hence, we also excluded the items whose answers did not change in evaluating the impression of different fashion coordination. In this study, referring to the average score of the evaluation values of the evaluated items for each image as evaluation scores for each image, we excluded the items whose evaluation score variance was 1 or less.

4.3   Results

The results of the experiment are shown in Table 1. The individual difference scores obtained from point 1 are presented in Table 1. The score was the average value of the difference between the maximum and minimum evaluation values for each evaluation item for the image and item (green cell). This score exceeded 2 in 22 items. The results from point 2 are the two numbers on the left in Table 1. No large dispersion was found the evaluation score, implying a comparative unification. Table 1 shows two items with variance values lower than 1: In English, "traditional – fashionable" and "rough – dressy" and in Japanese, "dentotekina – ryukono" and "mutonchakuna – yubina." Similarly, most of the responses were "neither" in the five-point scale because the absolute value of the mean value was less than 1.

Table 1. Evaluation items

japanese	average	variance of each images	indivisual difference score	english
伝統的な—流行の	0.75	0.67	1.63	taraditional - fashionable
無頓着な—優美な	0.29	0.76	1.56	rough - dressy
格式ある—現代的な	1.11	1.01	2.2	classic - modern
野暮ったい—洗練された	0.14	1.03	2.25	unrefined - refined
重々しい—軽快な	0.70	1.07	1.9	
軽薄な—理知的な	0.18	1.08	1.9	frivolous - intellectual
遅れている—流行の	0.25	1.13	2.25	unfashionable - fashionable
下品な—上品な	0.39	1.15	1.38	vulgar - elegant
お手頃そうな—高級感のある	-0.93	1.16	2.3	affordable - hiquality
安価な—高価な	-0.68	1.18	2.44	cheep - expensive
清楚な—セクシーな	-0.60	1.33	1.56	neat - sexy
日常的な—特別な	-1.14	1.34	2.0	everyday, ordinary - special (extraordinary)
気楽な—格式高い	-1.10	1.36	2.00	casual - formal
デザイン性の高い—機能性の高い	-0.60	1.36	1.8	high designability - high fanctionality
無骨な—ふんわりとした	0.23	1.37	1.81	manlike - romantic
気取らない—粋な	-0.28	1.39	2.3	unassuming - nice
気取った—自然体な	0.61	1.51	2.3	genteel - natural
田舎の雰囲気—都会的	0.56	1.57	2.69	country - sophisticate
昔懐かしい—現代的な	0.58	1.59	2.5	old-fashioned - modern
保守的な—進歩的な	0.00	1.59	2.06	conservative - advanced
流行に左右されない—流行を意識した	-0.15	1.60	2.69	not influenced by the fashion - considering the fashion
親しみにくい—親しみやすい	0.65	1.60	2.1	unfavorable - favorable
暗い—明るい	0.89	1.62	1.6	gloomy, (dark) - bright
くつろいだ格好—上品な格好	-0.39	1.66	2.00	casual - elegant
違和感のある—調和の取れた	0.83	1.67	2.5	unharmonious - harmonious
色味の多い—色味の少ない	0.54	1.67	1.81	colorful - colorless
ぴったりとした—ゆったりとした	0.45	1.72	2.13	fit - wide
地味な—派手な	0.24	1.75	1.8	plain - garish
少年らしい—女の子らしい	0.84	1.81	1.2	boyish - girlish
ありふれた—個性的な	-0.10	1.84	2.00	common - unique(original)
嫌い—好き	-0.03	1.85	2.5	dislike - like
一般的な—斬新な	-0.53	1.87	2.44	general, (typical) - novel
引き締まった—柔らかな	0.53	1.90	1.9	tight - soft(mild)
男性らしい—女性らしい	1.04	1.91	0.9	mannish - feminin
簡素な—華やかな	-0.10	1.91	2.3	simple - gorgeous
好感を持てない—好感を持てる	0.40	1.94	2.56	not good - good
露出度の低い—露出度の高い	-1.20	1.98	0.8	not exposing the skin - exposing the skin
すっきりした—ふんわりした	-0.33	2.02	1.8	
着たくない—着たい	-0.70	2.04	3.0	not wanna wear - wanna wear
無難—奇抜	-0.30	2.06	2.00	safe, acceptable - novel, original
きれいめな—かわいらしい	0.29	2.11	1.8	beautiful - cute
子供っぽい—大人っぽい	0.04	2.16	1.81	childish - mature
かっこいい—かわいい	0.28	2.20	2.00	cool - cute
おとなしい—大胆な	-0.40	2.27	1.75	modesty - bold, daring
若々しい—大人らしい	-0.45	2.28	2.1	young - adult
安定感のある—わくわく感のある	-0.33	2.30	1.88	stable - exciting
シンプルな—デザイン性の高い	-0.11	2.30	2.25	simple - gorgeous
落ち着いた—活動的な	0.06	2.62	2.3	calm - cheerful

4.4   Discussion

The items evaluated according to individual preferences with the largest variance were excluded from point 1, for example, "want to wear it – not want to," "like it – not like it," and "like it – hate it." This finding indicates that the fashion preference differs from person to person, and the preference difference appear every 16 images, covering different categories. Moreover, the items evaluated on the knowledge and recognition of fashion trends, such as "It's not about fashion – It's about fashion" and "the atmosphere of the countryside – the urban atmosphere," were excluded. In addition to popular knowledge, the categories considered popular for oneself differ among individuals.

In point 2, only two items rated as "neither" in most cases of the image–respondent combination were excluded due to two factors. First, a neutral evaluation was chosen because it was difficult to evaluate and the pair combination felt unusual. As these pairs were made by combining single words, they were difficult to sense as relative combinations. Second, the word is not suitable for evaluating the impression of fashion as these words are translated from English, Japanese English, and katakana related to fashion. From a lexicographical perspective, there is a sense of incongruity due to the conversion of words to Japanese. For example, we lexically rewrote "indifferent" and "graceful" from "rough" and "dressy," respectively.

Based on points 1 and 2, we adopted 24 items as evaluation scale pairs (Table 2), excluding a total of 24 items that are difficult to evaluate and items with large individual differences in the evaluation.

Table 2. Evaluation scale

The scale for evaluating	
dignified – light	boyish – girlish
frivolous – intellectual	common – unique
vulgar – elegant	tight – soft
neat – sexy	mannish – feminin
ordinary – special	not exposing the skin – exposing the skin
casual – formal	smart – mild
high designability – high fanctionality	acceptable – original
manlike – romantic	beautiful – cute
gloomy – bright	childish – mature
casual – elegant	cool – cute
colorful – colorless	modesty – bold,
plain – garish	stable – exciting

5   Recommendations

Our approach calculates recommendations from two groups of fashion coordination images. First, the user selects the image that is close to the clothing coordination he/she usually wears and the image of the clothing coordination that the user has received praises, such as "It looks good!" and "It looks nice." Based on the selected images, our system creates clusters using the impression space constructed in Sect. 3 and the coordination belonging to the cluster closest to the center of each cluster is the subject of the proposal (Fig. 1). We verified the effectiveness of the impression space in evaluating whether the recommendation contents include both of the above impressions and whether the user wants to wear it.

Furthermore, by conducting an individual difference analysis of the space and analysis of commonality, recommendations considering impressions received by others became possible (Fig. 2).

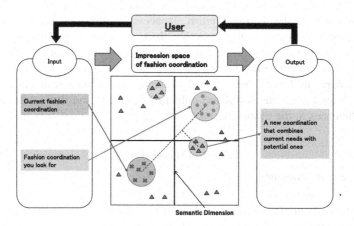

Fig. 2. System overview. Axes are semantic dimensions, lots (dots, crosses, triangles) are the evaluated images.

6   Conclusion

In this study, we aim to propose a new recommender system by considering the self-image and impression of a desired fashion coordination. This method can predict the latent possibility of purchasing and wearing items that users believe do not suit them. Moreover, it can recommend new fashion coordination for users. In this experiment, we made a scale for evaluating impressions. Furthermore, the space with the semantic dimension as an axis was constructed, and after clarifying its effectiveness, the system was developed. In a future study, we will clarify the semantic dimension of impression judgments in fashion coordination through the SD method and factor analysis using our evaluation scale.

References

1. Kajigaya, T.: Fashion recommendation using user and others' sensitivity model (2016)
2. Sakai, N.: Do people judge others by their clothes?: Use TEG-II to measure preconception
3. Yukimura, M., Imaoka, H.: Influence of the desire to synchronize and differentiate on fashion adoption. Textile Products Consum. Sci. **43**(11), 707–713 (2002)
4. Kastura, K., kato, M., Shirakawa, H.: Recommendation of Fashion Coordinates Considering TPO and Impression. IJCCIE **3**(2), 408–411 (2016)
5. Style-Areana.jp, Fashion Association. https://www.style-arena.jp/
6. Yanagida, Y.: Consideration on the suitability of fashion image terms for fashion styles. Nihon Kansei Kogaku Gakkai **16**(1), 9–18 (2017)
7. Reiko, N., Yukiko, H.: Analysis of individual differences in fashion image space structure (1986)
8. Kawamoto, N.: Influence of silhouette on fashion coordination impression. Nihon Kansei Kogaku Gakkai (2017)
9. Oeda, C., Sato, E., Takaoka, T.: Survey on young people's attitudes toward fast fashion. Nihon Kasei Gakkai **64**(10), 645–653 (2013)
10. Mine. A thorough explanation of the fashion system! [ladies' latest edition]. https://www.mine-3m.com/mine/
11. Fashion Work Media. List of fashion genres (ladies and men). https://www.esmodjapon.co.jp/column/

Who Would Let a Robot Take Care of Them? - Gender and Age Differences

Verena Wagner-Hartl[✉], Tobias Gehring, Joshua Kopp,
Ramona Link, Annika Machill, Denise Pottin, Anika Zitz,
and Vivian Emily Gunser

Faculty Industrial Technologies, Campus Tuttlingen, Furtwangen University,
Kronenstraße 16, 78532 Tuttlingen, Germany
verena.wagner-hartl@hs-furtwangen.de

Abstract. It is expected that human-robot collaboration will increase in the future. This also applies to the care sector. Some people are still skeptical about the use of robots in the care sector, others see it as a solution to counteract the care crisis. Therefore, an exploratory study was conducted to get more insight in this important future field. Overall, 194 participants aged between 18 and 85 years participated in an online survey. The results of the study show that the participants' attitudes towards robots in the care sector were rather neutral to negative. In addition, the results show significant differences regarding the need and acceptance of the help of a robot for different care relevant tasks. Regarding gender differences, younger women seem to be a special group. The results of the presented exploratory study can help to understand how human-robot collaboration in the care sector is seen today and shall help to get more insight in this important future field.

Keywords: Human-robot collaboration · Human factors · Care sector

1   Introduction

An increase of human-robot collaboration is expected in the future [1]. This also applies to the care sector [2]. Some people are still skeptical about the use of robots in the care sector, others see it as a solution to counteract the care crisis [2, 3]. According to Vallor [4] robots in the care sector "(…) intended to assist or replace human caregivers in the practice of caring for vulnerable persons such as the elderly, young, sick or disabled." (ibid., p. 194). Following the World Health Organization (WHO) [5], a strong increase of the world's population over 60 years is expected in the next years. Due to an aging population, more and more people need care. This means that the demand for nursing staff is constantly increasing [6]. At the same time, due to the difficult working conditions, there are fewer and fewer skilled workers in this profession [7]. The use of robots can help to solve this problem [2]. The study "Was die Deutschen über Technik denken" ("What Germans think of technology") [8] has investigated the acceptance of robots in the care sector. More than half of the participants stated that robots should take over routine tasks in nursing in order to relieve nurses. About 25% of the respondents rejected robots in nursing completely [8].

© Springer Nature Switzerland AG 2020
C. Stephanidis and M. Antona (Eds.): HCII 2020, CCIS 1224, pp. 196–202, 2020.
https://doi.org/10.1007/978-3-030-50726-8_26

However, the increasing demand is clear [9]. For example, there is the entertainment robot "Pepper", which provides social contact and entertainment for older people. The robot can also perform minor care tasks, such as advising people with dementia that they should for example go back to their room [10, 11]. Other applications are found in the care robot "Lio", which is, for example, able to bring drinks or clear plates [9]. Another example is "RIBA", a care assistant robot that was developed to help the nursing staff by lifting bedridden people [12]. In general, it should be mentioned that research is currently developing a large number of care robots that can also perform lifting and transport tasks [9]. In most cases, developers are focusing on an appearance that is close to the human body, but want to prevent the robots face from looking too much like a human being. In this case the differences to the real human being could then become even more pronounced and possibly have a repulsive effect on the person being cared for. This phenomenon, described by Mori [13], is called uncanny valley effect.

Interestingly, results of age and gender effects related to the acceptance of robots as well as differences in the interaction with robots are not consistent [14, 15]. Following Nomura [15] other factors like tasks should also be considered. Therefore, this should be addressed in the presented study.

The results of a first exploratory study of Wagner-Hartl, Gleichauf and Schmid [16] pointed in the direction that participants' attitude regarding robots in the care sector was rather neutral to negative. This was in line with the results of a special Eurobarometer survey conducted in 2012, in which participants reported mixed feelings about the use of robots in the care sector [3]. The study presented within this paper partly replicates this previous study of Wagner-Hartl et al. [16], which addresses different aspects of participants' opinions about human-robot collaboration at the working place, every day live and in the care sector. In the previous study, questions concerning the care sector were underrepresented, which is why this study focusses more on them. Therefore, the aim of the exploratory study was to survey attitudes towards robots in care. It was of interest if participants' attitude towards robots in the care sector differs if a robot should take care of themselves or on their relatives. Furthermore, different care relevant tasks that can be supported by a robot should be evaluated regarding their acceptance of human-robot collaboration. In addition, differences regarding age and gender were examined.

2   Materials and Method

2.1   Participants

Overall, 203 participants participated in the online study. Nine participants were not included in the final sample because they did not pass the quality check (e.g., completion of the whole questionnaire). Therefore, the final sample consists of 194 participants, 73 men and 121 women aged between 18 and 85 years ($M = 31.97$, $SD = 14.98$). Using a median split, the participants were grouped into two age groups (younger: 25 years and younger, elderly: 26 years and older).

The highest completed level of education of 10.82% of the participants was a (general) certificate of secondary education, 12.89% completed an apprenticeship, 49.48% had an advanced technical college entrance qualification or a general qualification for university entrance, 22.16% of the participants had an academic degree and 4.65% had other completed levels of education like a state examination or examination for the master craftsman's certificate. All participants provided their informed consent at the beginning of the online study.

2.2   Materials

The exploratory study was examined with an online survey. Overall, the participants needed about eight minutes to complete the online questionnaire. As mentioned before, the study partly replicates the study of Wagner-Hartl, Gleichauf and Schmid [16]. Because of the underrepresentation of questions concerning the care sector in the previous study, the study presented within this paper focusses more on them. For this reason, only this (new or rather additional) part of the online study will be examined in the following results section.

Participants' attitudes towards robots in the care sector in terms of let a robot take care on oneself or on relatives were rated using a 5-point scale: no (1) - rather no (2) – maybe (3) - rather yes (4) – yes (5). The different care related tasks support with body care, assistance with feeding, relocation, transport as well as entertainment were assessed with a 5-point scale that ranges from very poor (1) to very good (5) [cf. 16 concerning tasks in the working environment and in everyday live/household].

2.3   Analyses

The statistical analyses of the data were conducted using the software IBM SPSS Statistics. The analyses were based on a significance level of 5%.

3   Results

3.1   Participants' Attitudes Towards Robots

Let a Robot Take Care on Oneself. The results of the study show that the participants' attitudes towards let a robot take care of themselves are rather neutral to negative ($M = 2.66$, $SD = 1.09$). Following the results of an analysis of variance a significant interaction age x gender, $F(1, 190) = 11.32$, $p = .001$, $\eta^2_{part.} = .056$, and a tendency towards significance for gender, $F(1, 190) = 3.49$, $p = .063$, $\eta^2_{part.} = .018$, is shown. No significant effects can be shown for age, $F(1, 190) = 2.07$, $p = .151$, $\eta^2_{part.} = .011$. Therefore, younger women assessed it poorer than younger men (Sidak, $p \leq .0001$) and elderly women do ($p \leq .0001$).

Let a Robot Take Care on Relatives. Following the results of the study the participants' attitudes towards let a robot take care on their relatives are also rather neutral to negative ($M = 2.54$, $SD = 1.04$). The results of an analysis of variance show a significant interaction age x gender, $F(1, 190) = 8.54, p = .004, \eta^2_{part.} = .043$, and a significant effect of age, $F(1, 190) = 6.80, p = .010, \eta^2_{part.} = .035$. Gender differences did not reach the level of significance, $F(1, 190) = 1.90, p = .170, \eta^2_{part.} = .010$. Again, younger women assessed it poorer than younger men (Sidak, $p = .002$) and elderly women do ($p \leq .0001$).

3.2 Need and Acceptance of the Help of a Robot for Different Care Relevant Tasks

Following the results of an analysis of variance with repeated measures, significant differences regarding different care relevant tasks and the need and acceptance of the help of a robot can be shown, $F_{HF}(3.56, 677.07) = 82.25, p \leq .0001, \eta^2_{part.} = .302$ (see Fig. 1). Furthermore, post-hoc analyses show that transportation and relocation tasks were assessed significant better regarding the need and acceptance of the help of a robot than all other tasks (Sidak, for all significant differences: $p \leq .0001$).

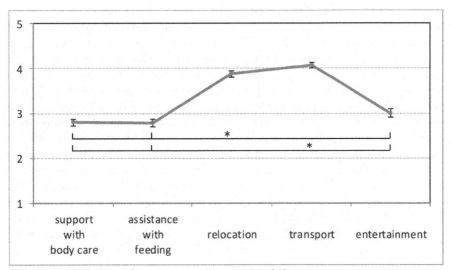

Note: 5-point scale ranges from very poor (1) to very good (5);
     * ... $p \leq .0001$, Sidak; I ... Standard error of mean

Fig. 1. Different care relevant tasks: Need and acceptance of the help of a robot.

Furthermore, the results showed an significant interaction age x gender, $F(1, 190) = 4.34, p = .039, \eta^2_{part.} = .022$, and a significant effect of gender, $F(1, 190) = 6.21, p = .014, \eta^2_{part.} = .032$. Age differences did not reach the level of significance, $F(1, 190) = .83, p = .364 \eta^2_{part.} = .004$. Younger women asses the help of a robot for different care relevant tasks poorer than younger men (Sidak, $p = .001$) as well as elderly women ($p = .016$).

4 Discussion

The results of the study show that the participants' attitudes towards robots in the care sector were rather neutral to negative. This is in line with previous studies [c.f. 3, 16] and was valid for both aspects, to let a robot take care on oneself as well as to let a robot take care on relatives. Interestingly, younger women assessed both aspects poorer than younger men and elderly women do.

In addition, the results show significant differences regarding the need and acceptance of the help of a robot for the different care relevant tasks support with body care, assistance with feeding, relocation, transport, and entertainment. Transportation and relocation tasks were assessed significant better regarding the need and acceptance of the help of a robot than all other tasks. The results indicate that both tasks transportation and relocation were tasks where the support of care robots will be well accepted by the participants. This seems to be different for the other three tasks body care, assistance with feeding and entertainment, which were only partly accepted as tasks where a robot is needed. The results confirm the suggestion of Nomura [15] that beneath sociodemographic variables other aspects like dissimilarities of the acceptance of different tasks should be addressed in studies regarding the need and acceptance of human-robot collaboration. Furthermore, the results of the presented study are in line with previous research [17] in which elderly people (65 years and older) assessed the help of a robot for tasks like bathing and body washing or companionship as not useful. Interestingly, in the same study care givers themselves descriptively rated the help of robots regarding washing tasks as more useful. One reason why tasks that are more emotional and closer to the body are more unaccepted for human-robot collaboration can be that the participants may fear that they will be seen more as objects than as human beings. Following Sharkey and Sharkey [18] this is one ethical issue of the use of care robots because it might reduce the amount of human contact and at the same time give persons in need of care a feeling of being an object and not a human being.

Once again, younger women seem to be a special group. They asses the help of a robot for different care relevant tasks poorer than younger men as well as elderly women. Interestingly, the previous study [16] showed no age and gender effect for the care sector. However, this sector was really underrepresented in the previous study. Therefore, the more differentiated consideration of the care sector in the present study allows to identify younger women as a special group. One explanation could be, that young women in particular maybe attach great importance to personal hygiene and cosmetics and are therefore reluctant to pass these topics on to other people or robots. Overall, to address gender and age effects and especially the interaction of age and gender in this important field, more research is needed in the future. From our point of view, future studies should also address the development of programs and interventions to support people that need care as well as their relatives to get used to interact with robots to improve their acceptance for care relevant tasks.

By using the method of an online survey, this study has some limitations as to the fact that the participants did not interact with a robot for the different care relevant tasks, or experienced how it feels when a robot is used to take care of them or interacts with them. Therefore, further studies should address this. For example, it would be interesting whether the attitude towards human-robot collaboration in the care sector can be improved by providing real examples of collaborative robots for the different analyzed care relevant tasks that can be tested and experienced by the participants.

To sum it up, the results of the presented exploratory study can help to understand how human-robot collaboration in the care sector is seen today. Furthermore, the results demonstrate how important it is to take into account sociodemographic factors like age or gender when developing robots in the care sector.

Acknowledgements. The authors would like to thank all participants who participated.

References

1. Ajoudani, A., Zanchettin, A.M., Ivaldi, S., Albu-Schäffer, A., Kosuge, K., Khatib, O.: Progress and prospects of the human–robot collaboration. Auton. Robot. **42**, 957–975 (2018)
2. Olaronke, I., Oluwaseun, O., Rhoda, I.: State of the art: a study of human-robot interaction in healthcare. Int. J. Inform. Eng. Electron. Bus. **3**, 43–55 (2017)
3. European Commission: Public attitudes towards robots. Special Eurobarometer 382, report, 97 pp. (2012)
4. Vallor, S.: Carebots and caregivers. Robotics and the Ethical Ideal of Care. In: Proceedings IACAP 2011, First International Conference of IACAP. The Computational Turn: Past, Presents, Futures?, pp. 193–196. Verlagshaus Monsenstein und Vannerdat OHG, Münster (2011)
5. World Health Organization (WHO): Ageing and health. Fact sheet. WHO, Geneva (2018)
6. Vereinigung der Bayrischen Wirtschaft e.v. (vbw), Prognos AG: Studie Pflegelandschaft 2030. [Study care landscape 2030], vbw, München (2012)
7. Federal Ministry of Health, Germany (2018). https://www.bundesgesundheitsministerium. de/themen/pflege/pflegekraefte/beschaeftigte.html. Accessed 16 Mar 2020
8. acatech - Deutsche Akademie der Technikwissenschaften, Körber Stiftung: TechnikRadar 2018. Was die Deutschen über Technik denken. Schwerpunkt: Digitalisierung [TechnikRadar 2018: What Germans think about technology. Focus: Digitalization]. Körber-Stiftung, Hamburg (2018)
9. Früh, M., Gasser, A.: Erfahrungen aus dem Einsatz von Pflegerobotern für Menschen im Alter [Experience from the use of care robots for elderly people]. In: Bendel, O. (ed.) Pflegeroboter [care robots], pp. 37–62. Springer, Wiesbaden (2018). https://doi.org/10.1007/978-3-658-22698-5_3
10. Futurezone. Technology news. Roboter "Pepper" hilft Demenzkranken in Österreich [Robot "Pepper" helps dementia patients in Austria]. https://futurezone.at/science/roboter-pepper-hilft-demenzkranken-in-oesterreich/400458436. Accessed 19 March 2020
11. Softbank robotics: Pepper. https://www.softbankrobotics.com/emea/en/pepper. Accessed 19 March 2020
12. Mukai, T., et al.: Development of a nursing-care assistant robot RIBA that can lift a human in its arms. In: The 2010 IEEE/RSJ International Conference on Intelligent Robots and Systems, pp. 5996–6001 (2010)
13. Mori, M.: The uncanny valley. IEEE Robot. Autom. Mag. **19**, 98–100 (2012)
14. Flandorfer, P.: Population ageing and socially assistive robots for elderly persons: the importance of sociodemographic factors for user acceptance. Int. J. Population Res. **2012**, 1–13 (2012)
15. Nomura, T.: Robots and Gender. Gender Genome **1**, 18–25 (2017)

16. Wagner-Hartl, V., Gleichauf, K., Schmid, R.: Are we ready for human-robot collaboration at work and in our everyday lives? - An exploratory approach. In: Ahram, T., Karwowski, W., Pickl, S., Taiar, R. (eds.) IHSED 2019. AISC, vol. 1026, pp. 135–141. Springer, Cham (2020). https://doi.org/10.1007/978-3-030-27928-8_21

17. Mast, M., et al.: User-centered design of a dynamic-autonomy remote interaction concept for manipulation-capable robots to assist elderly people in the home. J. Hum.-Robot Interaction **1**(1), 96–118 (2012)

18. Sharkey, A., Sharkey, N.: Granny and the robots: ethical issues in robot care for the elderly. Ethics Inf. Technol. **14**, 27–40 (2012)

Multimodal and Natural Interaction

Recognition and Localisation of Pointing Gestures Using a RGB-D Camera

Naina Dhingra$^{(\boxtimes)}$ ⓘ, Eugenio Valli, and Andreas Kunz ⓘ

Innovation Center Virtual Reality, ETH Zurich, Zurich, Switzerland
{ndhingra,kunz}@iwf.mavt.ethz.ch,
https://www.icvr.ethz.ch

Abstract. Non-verbal communication is part of our regular conversation, and multiple gestures are used to exchange information. Among those gestures, pointing is the most important one. If such gestures cannot be perceived by other team members, e.g. by blind and visually impaired people (BVIP), they lack important information and can hardly participate in a lively workflow. Thus, this paper describes a system for detecting such pointing gestures to provide input for suitable output modalities to BVIP. Our system employs an RGB-D camera to recognize the pointing gestures performed by the users. The system also locates the target of pointing e.g. on a common workspace. We evaluated the system by conducting a user study with 26 users. The results show that the system has a success rate of 89.59 and 79.92 % for a 2×3 matrix using the left and right arm respectively, and 73.57 and 68.99% for 3×4 matrix using the left and right arm respectively.

Keywords: Pointing gesture · Robot Operating System · Kinect sensor · Openptrack · Localization · Recognition · Non verbal communication

1 Introduction

In a meeting environments, when sighted people and BVIP are working together, sighted people tend to do some habitual gestures, from which the most common ones are: facial expressions, hand gestures, pointing gestures, eye gaze, etc. There are in total 136 gestures [1] which are termed as part of non-verbal communication (NVC). They need to be understood together with the verbal communication to understand the complete meaning of the conversation. However, for BVIP, the information from visual gestures are missing [4]. To understand the meaning of pointing gestures, it is crucial to know where a person is pointing at. Pointing gestures are the most common ones in nonverbal communication, and they become important in meetings where the speakers point towards objects in the room, or at artefacts on a whiteboard, as a reference to their speech. However, these pointing gestures are not accessible for BVIP and thus they lack important information during a conversation within a team meeting. To address

© Springer Nature Switzerland AG 2020
C. Stephanidis and M. Antona (Eds.): HCII 2020, CCIS 1224, pp. 205–212, 2020.
https://doi.org/10.1007/978-3-030-50726-8_27

this issue, we developed a system that automatically detects pointing gestures and determines the position where a person is pointing at. However, although NVC is easily understood by the humans, it is difficult for machines to recognize and interpret it reliably [3] and to avoid false alerts to the BVIP.

The main contributions of this paper are as follows: (1) We developed an autonomous system using OpenPTrack and ROS (Robot Operating System) to detect and localise the position of a pointing gesture. (2) We designed our system to work in real time and performed experiments using 2×3 and 3×4 grids. (3) We conducted a user study with 26 users to evaluate our system. We expect that our work will help the researchers to integrate BVIP in team meetings.

This paper is organized as follows: Sect. 2 describes the state of the art in OpenPtrack software, pointing and related gestures. Section 3 describes the methods and techniques used in our system, while Sect. 4 gives an overview of the user study conducted and the setup of the built system. Finally, Sect. 5 discusses the results obtained from the user study as well as the accuracies obtained by our system in detecting and localizing pointing gestures.

2   State of the Art

2.1   OpenPtrack

OpenPTrack is an open source software for tracking people and calibrating a multi- RGB-D camera setup [7]. It can track multiple people at a frame rate of the sensor. It can also employ heterogeneous 3D sensors group. OpenPTrack uses a calibration procedure which depends on ROS communication networking capabilities and communication. In the past, detection and tracking systems exploited the color and depth information of a user, since cheap RGB-D sensors are available. Further, previous software were limited to single camera usage tracking system. These systems did not use multiple cameras and could not be implemented in distributed settings. Four our system, we use OpenPtrack since it allows expanding our pointing gesture system to multiple camera setup.

2.2   Pointing Gesture Recognition

Pointing gestures can be measured in different ways. Glove based techniques were used initially to sense the gesture being performed by the hand [10]. Nowadays, computer vision based techniques [3,11] or Hidden Markov Models (HMMs) [12] are used for detection. In particular, for pointing gesture detection, cascaded HMMs along with a particle filter was used for pointing gesture detection in [9]. The HMM in their first stage takes estimation of the hand position. It maps the estimated position to a precise position by modeling the kinematic features of the pointing finger. The output 3D coordinates are fed into their HMM in a second stage that differentiates the pointing gestures from other types of gesture. This technique requires a long processing time and a large training dataset.

Deep learning [6] has been successfully used in various applications of computer vision, which has inspired its use for gesture and body pose estimations as well [8]. Deep learning approaches also solved pointing gesture recognition in [5]. However, it requires large training dataset and only works with the specific data type on which it was trained on.

Our problem statement is to solve the pointing gesture recognition for BVIP more robustly. Using deep learning approaches would have required a large training dataset to make them applicable on different setups, such as a variety of meeting room layouts with a different number of people interacting at the same time. Thus, we chose a traditional way by using mathematical geometry and feature localisation. At first, a Kinect sensor along with OpenPtrack is used to locate the body joints. Next a mathematical geometry transformation is applied to achieve the spatial position of the pointing gesture's target. This position is classified into 6 fields (for 2×3 matrix), and into 12 fields (for 3×4 matrix).

3   Methodology

The implementation of our pointing gesture recognizer and localizing system is based on OpenPTrack [2]. Using Kinect v2 as sensor, this software allows person tracking in real time over large areas. However, since this framework is not capable of directly detecting pointing gestures or other behavioral features of a user, we also forward the data to ROS[1]. By doing so, we can obtain the joints' coordinates in space for human gestures such as pointing. The main idea is that different packages of ROS could be implemented that contain so-called nodes, which are units that perform logic and computation for different parts of a robot, i.e. control of actuators, transform or change resolution of images provided by a sensor, etc. The different nodes of ROS can communicate with each other in order to share useful information or the functioning of the whole system, which is done by the *topics*. Every node implementation of a pointing gesture recognizer for blind users can subscribe to such a topic to receive information or publish on a topic to share its content. OpenPtrack thus uses ROS to allow the information provided by Kinect to be further processed. The joints x, y and z coordinates are published under a repository which also contains different IDs for the different joints. The coordinate transformation from the sensor's reference frames to the world reference frame are performed using a ROS package called/TF, which rotates and translates the reference frames to the desired positions.

A deictic (or pointing) gesture consists of the movement of an arm to point at a target in space and to highlight it by this gestures for other people without necessarily having to verbally describe its position exactly. The joint's coordinates that have to be obtained are thus from elbow and hand, since these represent the human forearm and hence the major components for pointing. In order to define a pointing action, the link connecting the two aforementioned joints was measured, and named pointing vector as shown in the Fig. 1.

---

[1] https://www.ros.org/.

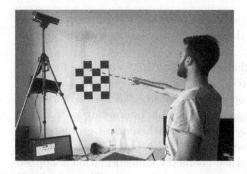
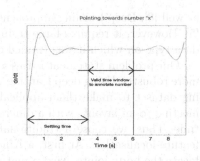

Fig. 1. Left: Pointing gesture with pointing vector. Right: Stabilization time of a pointing gesture where dr/dt is the change in the circle's diameter.

Equation 1 is used to locate the position of the target on a vertical plane (e.g. a whiteboard) the user is pointing at.

$$P_p = H + \frac{(H - P_f) \cdot N_f}{EH \cdot N_f} \cdot EH, \tag{1}$$

where P_f is a point predefined on the ground plane, N_f is the normal vector to the plane and H, E are the positions of hand and elbow joints, respectively.

OpenPtrack defines all measurements in a world reference frame. To understand the definition of the world reference frame in OpenPtrack, the TF package of ROS is used, which is a predefined package for coordinate transformation using rotation matrices and quaternions. The next step is to define a whiteboard/matrix plane coordinate frame in order to obtain the measured target point on it. This plane coordinate frame is achieved by applying the rotation matrix in relation world coordinate frame. The output values from OpenPtrack are converted in whiteboard/matrix plane coordinate frames. These converted values analysed by putting hard limits for each box in the matrix along both x and y direction. All of these values are evaluated on run time.

Before getting the information from the system, on which target a user is pointing at, it is required to wait about 3–3.5 s for the pointing gestures to get stabilized. This waiting time is for a user to reach the stable pointing gesture without moving or vibrating his/her arm. The stability output from the system is achieved after the setting time as shown in Fig. 1. It also has to be noted that the pointing gesture will become unstable again after certain time period.

4   Experimental Setup

The setup resembles an environment in which sighted users have to perform pointing gestures, which are automatically recognized by our system. The pointing gesture's target will then be determined to be provided to a suitable output device for BVIP. The experiments consist of four parts: two studies using the left arm and two using the right arm for pointing. The pointing gestures have to be performed on two different grid sizes in order to evaluate the accuracy of our system, i.e., at each 2×3 and 3×4 grid printed on the board.

The setup is shown in Fig. 2. The board has the dimensions $1290\,mm \times 1910\,mm$ and was $1000\,mm$ above the ground. The Kinect sensor was placed at a height of $1300\,mm$ above the top edge of the board and centered. Each box in the grid was numbered. The setup is shown in 2. The user had to stand at a constant distance of $1.5\,m$ and centered in front of the board. Then he was asked to point towards the numbers following a given sequence told by the experimenter, and point for a few seconds to achieve a stable gesture before moving to the next number in the sequence. The stability time procedure is illustrated in Fig. 1. After the user was prompted to point at a certain box and the wait-time from Fig. 1 was exceeded, the measured target number was recorded.

Fig. 2. Left: Measurement setup; Right: Experimental setup of the system. The Kinect is placed above the board having the matrix of numbers for the user to point at.

5   User Study and Results

The system was evaluated in a user study with 26 participants. Different parameters such as handedness, user's height, and arm length were measured. Since a user's pointing is significantly influenced by the pointing stability, this also impacts the accuracy of our system, resulting in noticeable differences for the 2×3 and the 3×4 grids. The error increases with decreasing box sizes, i.e. it is larger for the 3×4 grid. The confusion matrix in Fig. 3 left gives an overview on the percentage of the correct pointing at a target number in the 2×3 matrix using the left arm. Similarly, Fig. 3 (right) describes the quantitative values for right arm corresponding to 2×3 matrix, Fig. 4 for the left arm pointing at 3×4 matrix and Fig. 5 for the right arm pointing at 3×4 matrix.

2x3 L	N.A.	1	2	3	4	5	6
1	16 12.30%	110 84.60%	3 2.30%	0 0.00%	1 0.80%	0 0.00%	0 0.00%
2	2 1.50%	4 3.20%	113 86.90%	2 1.50%	2 1.50%	6 4.60%	1 0.80%
3	4 3.80%	0 0.00%	4 3.80%	83 79.80%	0 0.00%	6 5.80%	7 6.80%
4	5 3.00%	0 0.00%	0 0.00%	1 0.60%	150 96.40%	0 0.00%	0 0.00%
5	1 0.80%	0 0.00%	0 0.00%	0 0.00%	2 1.50%	125 96.20%	2 1.50%
6	7 5.40%	0 0.00%	0 0.00%	2 1.50%	0 0.00%	0 0.00%	121 93.10%

2x3 R	N.A.	1	2	3	4	5	6
1	10 7.70%	118 90.70%	1 0.80%	0 0.00%	1 0.80%	0 0.00%	0 0.00%
2	8 6.20%	12 9.20%	103 79.20%	1 0.80%	3 2.30%	3 2.30%	0 0.00%
3	7 5.40%	0 0.00%	7 5.40%	114 87.70%	0 0.00%	0 0.00%	2 1.50%
4	22 16.90%	8 6.20%	0 0.00%	0 0.00%	99 76.10%	0 0.00%	1 0.80%
5	4 3.10%	0 0.00%	2 1.50%	0 0.00%	30 23.10%	94 72.30%	0 0.00%
6	1 0.80%	0 0.00%	3 2.30%	16 12.30%	0 0.00%	0 0.00%	110 84.60%

Fig. 3. Pointing accuracy for the left/right arm using a 2 × 3 grid.

3x4 L	N.A.	1	2	3	4	5	6	7	8	9	10	11	12
1	10 19.30%	42 80.70%	0 0.00%	0 0.00%	0 0.00%	0 0.00%	0 0.00%	0 0.00%	0 0.00%	0 0.00%	0 0.00%	0 0.00%	0 0.00%
2	3 5.70%	3 5.70%	37 71.40%	3 5.70%	0 0.00%	3 5.70%	0 0.00%	2 3.90%	0 0.00%	0 0.00%	1 1.90%	0 0.00%	0 0.00%
3	4 7.70%	0 0.00%	4 7.70%	36 69.20%	3 5.70%	0 0.00%	4 7.70%	1 1.90%	0 0.00%	0 0.00%	0 0.00%	0 0.00%	0 0.00%
4	8 15.40%	2 3.80%	2 3.80%	2 3.80%	37 71.40%	0 0.00%	0 0.00%	1 1.90%	0 0.00%	0 0.00%	0 0.00%	0 0.00%	0 0.00%
5	9 17.30%	0 0.00%	0 0.00%	0 0.00%	0 0.00%	43 82.70%	0 0.00%	0 0.00%	0 0.00%	0 0.00%	0 0.00%	0 0.00%	0 0.00%
6	2 3.90%	0 0.00%	2 3.90%	0 0.00%	0 0.00%	4 7.70%	30 57.40%	0 0.00%	0 0.00%	2 3.90%	10 19.30%	2 3.90%	0 0.00%
7	0 0.00%	0 0.00%	0 0.00%	2 3.90%	0 0.00%	1 1.90%	2 3.90%	39 75.00%	0 0.00%	0 0.00%	3 5.70%	3 5.70%	2 3.90%
8	0 0.00%	0 0.00%	0 0.00%	4 7.70%	5 9.60%	0 0.00%	0 0.00%	1 1.90%	33 63.50%	0 0.00%	0 0.00%	6 11.60%	3 5.70%
9	21 40.40%	0 0.00%	0 0.00%	0 0.00%	0 0.00%	0 0.00%	0 0.00%	0 0.00%	0 0.00%	31 59.60%	0 0.00%	0 0.00%	0 0.00%
10	1 1.90%	0 0.00%	0 0.00%	0 0.00%	0 0.00%	0 0.00%	0 0.00%	0 0.00%	0 0.00%	1 1.90%	48 92.30%	2 3.90%	0 0.00%
11	1 1.90%	0 0.00%	0 0.00%	0 0.00%	0 0.00%	0 0.00%	3 5.70%	1 1.90%	0 0.00%	0 0.00%	9 17.30%	38 73.20%	0 0.00%
12	3 5.70%	0 0.00%	0 0.00%	0 0.00%	0 0.00%	0 0.00%	2 3.90%	0 0.00%	0 0.00%	0 0.00%	0 0.00%	1 1.90%	46 88.50%

Fig. 4. Pointing accuracy for the left arm using a 3 × 4 grid.

Table 1 shows the accuracy values achieved in the four experiments, i.e., (1) Left arm using 2 × 3 matrix, (2) Right arm using 3 × 4 matrix, (3) Left arm for 3 × 4 matrix and (4) Right arm for 3 × 4 matrix. This accuracy is calculated by converting the output from the system to binary output, i.e., 1, if the output from the system was correct, otherwise it is 0. Then the total number of correct results is divided by the total of trials in the experiment multiplied by 100 to get the percentage of the accuracy.

Each of the four tests resulted in a higher accuracy when using the left arm for pointing. This could be caused by the inherent asymmetry within Kinect v2. The IR emitter is centered in the Kinect box, while the IR receiver is off-centered. This leads to a camera's perspective that sees the left arm slightly better than the right one, i.e. the left arm is measured slightly longer than the right one.

6   Conclusion

We worked on automatic pointing gesture detection and pointing target localization in a meeting environment. A prototype of the automatic system was built

3x4 R	N.A.	1	2	3	4	5	6	7	8	9	10	11	12
1	6 11.60%	42 80.80%	3 5.70%	0 0.00%	0 0.00%	1 1.90%	0 0.00%	0 0.00%	0 0.00%	0 0.00%	0 0.00%	0 0.00%	0 0.00%
2	16 30.70%	2 3.90%	32 61.50%	0 0.00%	0 0.00%	0 0.00%	2 3.90%	0 0.00%	0 0.00%	0 0.00%	0 0.00%	0 0.00%	0 0.00%
3	12 23.10%	0 0.00%	4 7.70%	31 59.60%	3 5.70%	0 0.00%	0 0.00%	0 0.00%	2 3.90%	0 0.00%	0 0.00%	0 0.00%	0 0.00%
4	9 17.30%	0 0.00%	0 0.00%	0 0.00%	43 82.70%	0 0.00%	0 0.00%	0 0.00%	0 0.00%	0 0.00%	0 0.00%	0 0.00%	0 0.00%
5	7 13.60%	1 1.90%	0 0.00%	0 0.00%	0 0.00%	40 76.90%	0 0.00%	0 0.00%	0 0.00%	3 5.70%	1 1.90%	0 0.00%	0 0.00%
6	0 0.00%	4 7.70%	5 9.60%	2 3.90%	0 0.00%	8 15.40%	28 53.80%	0 0.00%	0 0.00%	4 7.70%	0 0.00%	0 0.00%	1 1.90%
7	0 0.00%	1 1.90%	6 11.60%	0 0.00%	3 5.70%	2 3.90%	1 1.90%	33 63.50%	0 0.00%	0 0.00%	1 1.90%	3 5.70%	2 3.90%
8	2 3.90%	0 0.00%	0 0.00%	2 3.90%	21 40.40%	0 0.00%	0 0.00%	1 1.90%	23 44.20%	0 0.00%	0 0.00%	0 0.00%	3 5.70%
9	9 17.30%	0 0.00%	0 0.00%	0 0.00%	0 0.00%	4 7.70%	0 0.00%	0 0.00%	0 0.00%	36 69.20%	2 3.90%	0 0.00%	1 1.90%
10	2 3.90%	0 0.00%	0 0.00%	0 0.00%	0 0.00%	0 0.00%	0 0.00%	0 0.00%	0 0.00%	14 26.90%	36 69.20%	0 0.00%	0 0.00%
11	0 0.00%	0 0.00%	0 0.00%	0 0.00%	0 0.00%	0 0.00%	2 3.90%	0 0.00%	0 0.00%	0 0.00%	8 15.40%	42 80.70%	0 0.00%
12	0 0.00%	0 0.00%	0 0.00%	0 0.00%	0 0.00%	0 0.00%	0 0.00%	0 0.00%	4 7.70%	0 0.00%	0 0.00%	0 0.00%	48 92.30%

Fig. 5. Pointing accuracy for the right arm using a 3×4 grid.

Table 1. Accuracy for the experiments performed in the user study by using 2×3 and 3×4 matrix and by using left and the right arm.

	Left arm	Right arm
2×3	89.59%	79.92%
3×4	73.57%	68.99%

and tested by conducting a user study. The output of this system will be converted to suitable modality which will help BVIP to get the extra information. Although for our application it is required to have its good performance for 2×3 but it proves to have high precision for small areas for localizer function and performs good for both 2×3 and 3×4 grids in all the four the experiments. We also found out that the stable time for getting the value of localizer is achieved after around 3 s and the hand of the user starts to vibrate after an interval again. Our user study also showed that the height of the user did not effect much on the performance. The arm size which is either very small or very large has a small decrease in the accuracy.

In future, the output of our system will be converted by a suitable haptic interface helping BVIP to access these pointing gestures. Moreover, we will expand our system with multiple cameras, and we will have several users pointing simultaneously. Also, we will improve the system to a have more symmetrical output, i.e., the same performance for pointing using the left and the right arm.

Acknowledgements. This work has been supported by the Swiss National Science Foundation (SNF) under the grant no. 200021E 177542/1. It is part of a joint project between TU Darmstadt, ETH Zurich, and JKU Linz with the respective funding organizations DFG (German Research Foundation), SNF (Swiss National Science Foundation) and FWF (Austrian Science Fund).

References

1. Brannigan, C.R., Humphries, D.A.: Human non-verbal behavior, a means of communication. Etholog. Stud. Child Behav., 37–64 (1972)
2. Carraro, M., Munaro, M., Burke, J., Menegatti, E.: Real-time marker-less multi-person 3D pose estimation in rgb-depth camera networks. In: Strand, M., Dillmann, R., Menegatti, E., Ghidoni, S. (eds.) IAS 2018. AISC, vol. 867, pp. 534–545. Springer, Cham (2019). https://doi.org/10.1007/978-3-030-01370-7_42
3. Dhingra, N., Kunz, A.: Res3atn-deep 3D residual attention network for hand gesture recognition in videos. In: International Conference on 3D Vision (3DV 2019), pp. 491–501. IEEE (2019)
4. Günther, S., et al.: Mapvi: meeting accessibility for persons with visual impairments. In: Proceedings of the 12th ACM International Conference on PErvasive Technologies Related to Assistive Environments, pp. 343–352. ACM (2019)
5. Huang, Y., Liu, X., Zhang, X., Jin, L.: A pointing gesture based egocentric interaction system: dataset, approach and application. In: Proceedings of the IEEE Conference on Computer Vision and Pattern Recognition Workshops, pp. 16–23 (2016)
6. LeCun, Y., Bengio, Y., Hinton, G.: Deep learning. Nature **521**(7553), 436 (2015)
7. Munaro, M., Basso, F., Menegatti, E.: Openptrack: open source multi-camera calibration and people tracking for RGB-D camera networks. Robot. Auton. Syst. **75**, 525–538 (2016)
8. Neverova, N., Wolf, C., Taylor, G.W., Nebout, F.: Multi-scale deep learning for gesture detection and localization. In: Agapito, L., Bronstein, M.M., Rother, C. (eds.) ECCV 2014. LNCS, vol. 8925, pp. 474–490. Springer, Cham (2015). https://doi.org/10.1007/978-3-319-16178-5_33
9. Park, C.B., Lee, S.W.: Real-time 3D pointing gesture recognition for mobile robots with cascade HMM and particle filter. Image Vis. Comput. **29**(1), 51–63 (2011)
10. Quam, D.L.: Gesture recognition with a dataglove. In: IEEE Conference on Aerospace and Electronics, pp. 755–760. IEEE (1990)
11. Rautaray, S.S., Agrawal, A.: Vision based hand gesture recognition for human computer interaction: a survey. Artif. Intell. Rev. **43**(1), 1–54 (2012). https://doi.org/10.1007/s10462-012-9356-9
12. Wilson, A.D., Bobick, A.F.: Parametric hidden markov models for gesture recognition. IEEE Trans. Pattern Anal. Mach. Intell. **21**(9), 884–900 (1999)

Haptic Pattern Exploration
in an Arm-Mounted Solenoid Array

Dean Dijour[(⊠)], Aadya Krishnaprasad, Ian Shei, and Eric Wong

Carnegie Mellon University, Pittsburgh, PA 15213, USA
dijour@cmu.edu

Abstract. A haptic device with a row of 4 solenoids was used to present 7 kinds of pattern stimuli to the forearm. Patterns were uniquely named (e.g. "choppy-motor"), with 3 variants per pattern, designed to be "bad", "moderate", and "good" representations of the verbally-announced sensation. Participants were asked to rank each pattern on a 5-point Likert scale, ranking how well a sensation corresponded to its name. Each participant completed two trials, separated by a 5-min break, ranking the 21 randomized pattern variants twice. The results show general likability for most of the "good" variants of the patterns. Pattern likability increased between trials, indicating that increased exposure to this modality may increase believability of patterns. Data shows a positive, near linear relationship between pattern variant quality and participant's rankings, indicating that participants can distinguish accurate patterns from inaccurate ones.

Keywords: Haptic actuation · Feel effect · Haptic feedback · Haptics media · Human factors · Solenoid actuation · Human-centered computing · Human computer interaction (HCI) · HCI design and evaluation methods · User studies

1 Introduction

With the rise of smartphones and smartwatches, vibrotactile feedback has become the de-facto haptic modality for silently transmitting information to wearers. While this technology is able to effectively convey numeric information and summon a wearer's attention, it lacks an emotional vocabulary and the rich expressiveness of pressure-based human touch. We wanted to investigate whether pressure stimulation can be an effective and more expressive alternative to vibrotactile stimulation.

Prior research has already been conducted on developing a haptic pattern vocabulary for wearable devices, but this vocabulary has not yet been expanded to technologies that apply direct pressure to the skin, such as a solenoid actuator. We apply this prior haptic vocabulary research as a launchpad to explore the effectiveness and believability of haptic patterns in a 1 × 4 solenoid array. Solenoids employ electromagnetics to create a uniform magnetic field around a wound coil, at the center of which houses a magnet. When the coil is charged, the magnet enables linear motion. Utilizing solenoids as a haptic medium is a novel approach to the process of identifying a haptic vocabulary, as most other studies are vibrotactile in nature. If effective and believable, this technology could serve multiple purposes – transmitting information

© Springer Nature Switzerland AG 2020
C. Stephanidis and M. Antona (Eds.): HCII 2020, CCIS 1224, pp. 213–222, 2020.
https://doi.org/10.1007/978-3-030-50726-8_28

from internet connected devices, providing emotional context to conveyed information, and even enhancing audio-visual sensory experiences.

2   Background and Related Work

Haptic feedback as a means of conveying information is not novel. Extensive research has already been conducted on both actuation mechanisms as well as haptic vocabularies. To find guidelines for haptic patterns, we sought out research from Israr et al. on "feel effects" – vibrotactile haptic patterns which, when coupled with non-haptic events, can enhance an experience [2].

The underlying principle behind this enhancement lies in the integratory effects between vibrotactile and auditory/visual stimuli. Integration effects between these modalities can provide more accurate and faster feedback to the wearers of these kinds of devices [4]. Recent work by the University of British Columbia's SPIN lab provides an interactive tool for filtering vibrotactile haptic effects based on sensation, emotion, metaphor, and usage facets [3]. This existing body of work created a large set of patterns and .wav files to sample, varying in perceived urgency and perceived pleasantness, which we could attempt to replicate in the pressure modality with a solenoidal device.

In the present research, we describe efforts to convey pattern information on a 1×4 solenoid array. Our experiment modulates pattern believability by varying the Stimulus Onset Asynchrony (SOA) between actuators, the On Time of each actuator, and the Off Time of each actuator. With just these three variable parameters, our simple device is capable of producing thousands of unique patterns.

3   Method

3.1   Participants

Five Carnegie Mellon University undergraduate students (N = 5, 2 female, 3 male), ages 19 to 21 (M = 20.4 years, SD = 0.8 years), having no prior experience with pressure-based haptic wearable devices participated in $12/hour paid studies. All gave informed consent under a protocol approved by the Carnegie Mellon Institutional Review Board. All subjects were right- handed, and were asked to use their right arm for the study (Figs. 1, 2).

3.2   Device

We developed a simple Arduino controllable device, consisting of 4 neodymium magnets (0.107″ height, 0.589″ diameter), a fused filament fabrication (FFF) 3D-printed polylactic acid (PLA) base plate (7.25″ length, 1.7″ width, 0.44″ height), enameled copper wire, and FFF 3D-printed PLA spacer discs (same dimensions as magnets), along with solenoid control circuitry. Each cell in the 1×4 array of solenoids is individually addressable, and can be actuated at a maximum frequency of once

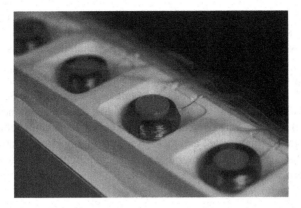

Fig. 1. Each cell wall is wound in enameled copper wire. The cell houses a neodymium magnet, with a spacer on top of it. The protruding piece, 2nd from the right in this picture, shows what an activated cell looks like.

```
void heavyRain(int dwellDuration, int lowRange, int highRange) {
    int target1 = random(3, 7);
    digitalWrite(target1, HIGH);
    delay(dwellDuration);

    int target2 = random(3, 7);
    digitalWrite(target2, HIGH);
    delay(dwellDuration);

    int target3 = random(3,7);
    digitalWrite(target3, HIGH);
    delay(dwellDuration);

    int target4 = random(3,7);
    digitalWrite(target4, HIGH);
    delay(dwellDuration);

    turnOff(target1, random(lowRange, highRange));
    turnOff(target2, random(lowRange, highRange));
    turnOff(target3, random(lowRange, highRange));
    turnOff(target4, random(lowRange, highRange));
}

//utility function to turn off a given pin after a set duration
void turnOff(int pin, int duration) {
    delay(duration);
    digitalWrite(pin, LOW);
}
```

Fig. 2. The Arduino code for the "heavy rain" pattern. This function takes three parameters, and generates random patterns.

every 10 ms (100 Hz). At 100 Hz, the magnet is effectively suspended in mid-air, but due to its high power, the device outputs both vibrotactile as well as standard pressure sensations. At lower activation frequencies, the device produces tapping sensations on the surface of the skin. We mounted this solenoid enclosure to a box constructed of foam core, to elevate the surface and align it with the armrest of the participant's chair. This allowed the device to function as a forearm rest for participants, enabling them to lay their arm down flat, directly on top of the actuators.

3.3 Stimuli

We identified 7 distinct patterns, through a combination of informal prior user testing, consulting with Professor Roberta Klatzky, and from the research insights in the VibViz and Feel Effects studies [Klatzky, personal communication] [2, 3]. Patterns like "light rain" and "racing heart beat" were chosen due to the likelihood that participants had felt the real sensations before, and would be able to give ecologically valid ratings. Other patterns were chosen to see if more unusual and interesting sensations could be simulated.

We initially created "good" variants of each pattern, using samples from the aforementioned research, and mimicking cadences of reference sensations, such as those created by heartbeats and motors. We modulated the three parameters (SOA, On Time, Off Time) until we were content that the quality of the patterns reflected the word descriptors. Creating "moderate" and "bad" variants involved modulating the parameters from the "good" variants in ways that made them progressively more dissimilar to the initial pattern we created (Figs. 3, 4) (Table 1).

Fig. 3. Participants (one of the researchers, in this picture) were instructed to sit upright and comfortable in a chair, while resting their forearm on the device. Participants were first given a test pattern to ensure they were correctly positioned to feel all 4 actuators.

Fig. 4. Close up of participant resting their arm on the device.

Table 1. Each of the 7 patterns, along with the parameters modulated for each of the three variants, can be seen in the table above. All parameters are in milliseconds. The first, second, and third numbers in parentheses next to each parameter correspond to the "bad," "moderate," and "good" variants of each pattern.

Pattern	Description	Parameters (ms)
Frog jumping	All cells turn on sequentially	On Time (500, 700, 100), Off Time (500, 100, 500)
Light rain	Random short sequential pulses in random locations	On Time (20, 240, 140)
Heavy rain	Random short simultaneous pulses in random locations, with random delay	On Time (15, 100, 50), decay Low (100, 50, 10), decay High (150, 100, 50)
Calm heart beat	One cell turns on and off, repeatedly	On Time (200, 500, 500), Off Time (300, 500, 900)
Racing heart beat	One cell turns on and off, quickly, repeatedly	On Time (100, 125, 167), Off Time (180, 225, 300)
Smooth motor	All calls turn on and off *very* quickly, repeatedly	On Time (25, 20, 10) – off time is same
Choppy motor	All cells turn on and off quickly, repeatedly	On Time (200, 100, 50) – off time is same

3.4 Ranking Task

Participants were briefed on the experiment, how to use the Likert scale, and were encouraged to use the full range of the scale. The scale ranged from "Unacceptable," "Acceptable," "Good," "Very Good," to "That's it!". "Unacceptable" implies the pattern feels nothing like its name, and "That's it!" implies a perfect real-world match. This scale was adapted from the work of Israr et al., since the task of ranking believability was quite similar to portions of their study [2]. Each participant was fitted with both ear plugs and noise-cancelling headphones, to ensure they could not hear the device. They were also instructed not to look at the device while the trials were in progress. Participants were first shown a sample pattern, entitled "Wave," before they began the experiment.

When they were seated comfortably and could feel all four actuators, the first half of the experiment began. Each of the 7 pattern groups, split by their 3 variants, was presented in a randomized order, for a total of 21 rankings. Before each pattern was initialized, participants were verbally told the name of the pattern they were going to rate. Participants had up to 30 s to feel the pattern and rate it, but in practice, most only took 5–10 s to provide a rating. At the end of the first half of the experiment, participants were given a five-minute break. After the break was over, Trial 2 began, and participants were asked to rank the same 21 pattern variants they had felt in the Trial 1, in a re-randomized order. The participants were not told that both trials used the same pattern set, but it is possible that they concluded this fact by the end of the second trial.

4 Results

4.1 Variant Preference and Pattern Believability

Across both trials, mean pattern scores indicate that participants were generally in agreement with our intended believability of variants. Pattern variants we designed to be "bad" were rated, on average, as less believable than ones designed to be "good". As can be seen in Fig. 5, every pattern's mean scores, in both trials, exhibit a positive slope from the "bad" to "good" variants. This confirms that, within the set of our designed patterns, participants were able to sense the authenticity of a pattern, and agreed with our design decisions. It should be noted that this positive slope only explains participants' relative preference for patterns, within a small set of possible choices – it does not yet explain the quality or utility of the patterns tested.

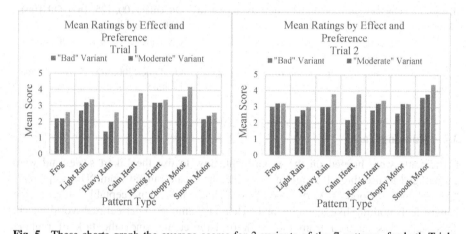

Fig. 5. These charts graph the average scores for 3 variants of the 7 patterns, for both Trials. Trial 1 favorites were the "good" variants of choppy motor, calm heartbeat, and light rain. Trial 2 favorites were the "good" variants of the smooth motor, heavy rain, and calm heartbeat.

In terms of absolute believability, only the "choppy motor" in Trial 1, and the "smooth motor" in Trial 2, achieved average scores above a 4 (meaning "Very good"). These patterns are nearly identical, wherein all 4 cells turn on and off at a regular interval. The "good" variants of these patterns also have activation frequencies nearly 10–50 times greater than those of other patterns. This could indicate a preference for strong (more simultaneously active cells) and frequent (rate of actuation) stimulation. Overall though, the "good" variants of every pattern saw ratings around a 3, which shows that the majority of these patterns are "good" and should be viable for further exploration.

4.2   Inter-trial Sensitivity and Variability

Trial 1's mean rating for all patterns was 2.814, while Trial 2's mean was 3.171 – a 12.689% increase in believability between trials. In Trial 1, participants scored 9/21 (42.86%) of the patterns at an average of 3 or above. This was in line with our expectations, since 7 of the pattern variants were purposely "bad," and another 7 were "moderate". In Trial 2, participants scored 16/21 (76.19%) of the patterns at an average of 3 or above. This is a significant, 77.76% increase in average "good" ratings, despite any change in the pattern stimuli.

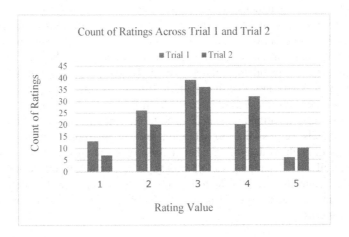

Fig. 6. This chart visualizes the count of individual scores in both trials. Trial 1 appeared more scrutinous, with almost double the "unacceptable" (1) ratings as Trial 2. Trial 2 markedly increased the count of "very good" (4) ratings.

One might wonder if participants were simply more lenient with their ratings, and shifted over their prior scores from Trial 1. As can be seen in Fig. 6, the largest change between trials was in the "very good" category, with Trial 2 increasing by a count of 12.

However, the average 4+ scores for specific variants is identical between trials, and it seems that participants are still hesitant to rate most patterns as "very good" or "that's it!". Both Trial 1 and Trial 2 saw only 1 pattern variant achieve an average score of 4 or above ("choppy motor" and "smooth motor", respectively). Regardless, participants did feel that fewer patterns were "unacceptable" or "acceptable" in Trial 2. Additionally, every participant decreased their usage of the "unacceptable" and "acceptable" ranking, and increased their usage of "good".

5 Discussion

5.1 Data

The significant individual score differences between Trial 1 and Trial 2 are interesting. One could speculate that the duration of exposure to this haptic device may be positively correlated with believability of pattern stimuli. Alternatively, participants may not have initially been sensitized to the stimulus in Trial 1, and as such, stimulus sensitivity may vary as a function of exposure time, rather than believability. Perhaps Trial 1's initial ratings were lower because participants needed device adjustment time, or may not have fully understood the experiment. For this reason, we will not be discussing much data from Trial 1, and we will treat it as an acclimation period.

The positive slope between "bad" and "good" variant ratings seen in Trial 2 is a strong indication that participants, at the very minimum, have the ability to discriminate between authentic and inauthentic pattern stimuli. Further, the average rating for all 21 variants of 3.171 indicates that the pattern stimuli in this study are "good" and believable to a degree – these could benefit from further exploration.

Participants also identified a clear favorite in the smooth motor, which operates at 100 Hz, and feels very similar to vibration emitted by mobile phones and smart watches. It is difficult to determine what makes some patterns more believable than others, since all of our patterns varied widely in cell actuation count and actuation frequency. It would be ideal to do follow-up studies to measure the impact of cell actuation count and actuation frequency, to build a guide for designing the most believable patterns.

5.2 Limitations

As shown in Figs. 7 and 8, the ideal form factor for this technology is a wearable, wrist mounted device. Unlike the prototype used in this study, this device would have 3×12 solenoids, allowing for multi-row stimulation. Such a device could encompass the arm and provide human like stimulation. The present prototype contained only 1 row of solenoids, so complex effects like "rain" had to be abstracted into a single row form. Naturally, with multiple rows and far more cells, a device could produce significantly more convincing patterns.

Fig. 7. Idealized form factor as a wrist-mounted wearable. The device would have 360 degrees of actuation, as well as 2 dimensions of actuation (more than just one row, unlike the prototype in this study).

When activated, the solenoids in our prototype were clearly perceptible and distinct, but due to the nature of the mode of actuation, they only had a maximum displacement of half of the solenoid length. Using a more advanced method of linear movement, the ability to push harder and higher would give this device the power to truly grab a user's attention. At present, the device is more subtle, and requires the wearer to focus on feeling the patterns. In order to be useful in the real world, the device must have sufficient power to be effortlessly noticeable.

Fig. 8. Unrolled version of the idealized form factor. The device would be made up of 3×12 solenoids, enabling the use of a richer haptic vocabulary.

5.3   Further Applications

The study results show that participants can be made to believe they are feeling a sensation that is actually not happening to them. This is not a novel phenomenon, and many haptic technologies can accomplish this with verbal priming. The key distinction for our device will be the ability to "tap," "poke," and "grab".

Vibrotactile actuators cannot authentically simulate these kinds of feelings, and prior research shows that skin becomes overly sensitized to vibrotactile stimulation as time goes on [1]. Vibrotactile stimulation inherently introduces a great deal of noise and interference when multiple actuators are activated simultaneously - creating sensations with more than 2 active actuators becomes noisy and unclear [1]. With pressure-based stimulation, this noise and interference is minimized, and it could be possible to construct wearable devices that evoke clear sensations of grabbing, stroking, poking, etc. – opening a new communication frontier based on rich emotive information. Such a device could calm its wearer down with gentle pulsing, or perhaps, command attention with a strong grab by pulsing a circular array of actuators. The possibilities for this kind of communication are virtually endless, but this study demonstrates the potential for these devices.

6 Conclusion

Although our test device was simple, the implications of our results are clear – pressure-based haptic stimulation has the potential to integrate multi-modal experiences, contextualize information, and create a more emotive future. Further testing, with more subjects, more patterns, and a more powerful device could yield even more insights into the world of haptic language design, and pave a way forward to introduce these insights into the real world.

Acknowledgements.   The authors of this paper would like to thank Carnegie Mellon University Professor Roberta Klatzky and her lab for providing research funding, guiding our experiment design, and assisting in selecting haptic patterns to test. The authors would also like to thank Carnegie Mellon University Professor Lining Yao for providing a fantastic introduction to the world of morphing matter, and for greenlighting the development of this prototype.

References

1. Hong, J., Pradhan, A., Froehlich, J.E., Findlater, L.: Evaluating wrist-based haptic feedback for non-visual target finding and path tracing on a 2D surface. In: Proceedings of the 19th International ACM SIGACCESS Conference on Computers and Accessibility (ASSETS 2017), pp. 210–219. Association for Computing Machinery, New York (2017). https://doi.org/10.1145/3132525.3132538
2. Israr, A., Zhao, S., Schwalje, K., Klatzky, R., Lehman, J.: Feel effects: enriching storytelling with haptic feedback. ACM Trans. Appl. Percept. **11**(3), 17 (2014). Article 11
3. Hasti, S., Zhang, K., MacLean, K.E.: VibViz: Organizing, visualizing and navigating vibration libraries. World Haptics Conference (WHC), 2015 IEEE. IEEE (2015)
4. Courtenay Wilson, E., Reed, C.M., Braida, L.D.: Integration of auditory and vibrotactile stimuli: effects of phase and stimulus- onset asynchrony. J. Acoust. Soc. Am. **126**, 1960–1974 (2009)

Enhancing Bodily Engagements
with Manipulatives for Tangible Programming

Lenard George Swamy[(✉)]

Malmö University, 211 19 Malmö, Sweden
enardgeorge92@gmail.com

Abstract. Tangible User Interfaces are attributed to have a more 'human-like' interaction styles that resembles the experience of interacting with real world objects. Digital manipulatives are the TUIs in Tangible programming Environments. The tangibility of the manipulatives is what gives their characteristic appeal of making programming more interactive by engaging the fine motor skills. However, none of the existing tangible programming languages employ the gross motor skills that engages the entire body. This design project is a 10-week explorative study that seeks to envision a programming environment that is based on whole body movements. This generative and evaluative study is guided by the design philosophies of Movement Based interactions [7], Kinaesthetic Interactions [3] & Child Computer Interaction [4]. The design process is guided by the methodologies primarily influenced by the Design by movement approach [7]. Progressive cycles of conceptual design, supported by prototyping and testing resulted in adding richness to the interactions with the manipulatives of the tangible programming environment. The new interaction style involves the manipulatives to be moved using the entire body in order to build algorithmic structures.

Keywords: Digital manipulatives · Movement based technologies · Tangible programming

1 Introduction

Manipulative materials of various shapes and sizes are found in almost any Kindergarten or Elementary Classrooms today. The physicality of these materials allows kids to move, organise and build things to understand simple scientific and mathematical concepts. This characteristic learning approach rather engages their senses, thereby immersing them into a learning experience that brings them closer to the concepts.

Digital Manipulatives are manipulative materials embedded with computational capabilities. They are designed to expand the range of concepts that children can explore through direct manipulation, enabling them to learn concepts that were previously considered "too advanced" [12]. In Tangible Programming, digital manipulatives are physical blocks that represent Feedback, Control and flow-of-control concepts. The tangibility of these manipulatives allow the construction and execution of physical algorithmic structures that gets compiled in the real world. This rather tangible representation of programs is what gives Tangible Programming Environments its edge over other Visual Programming Environments in-terms of learning

© Springer Nature Switzerland AG 2020
C. Stephanidis and M. Antona (Eds.): HCII 2020, CCIS 1224, pp. 223–230, 2020.
https://doi.org/10.1007/978-3-030-50726-8_29

experience [5]. Children learn better when their interactions with the learning tools are natural.

1.1 The Interaction Blueprint of the Programming Environment

The digital manipulatives act as the Tangible User Interfaces (TUIs) in any Tangible programming environment. TUIs offer a natural way of interacting with digital products by moving interfaces into the physical world [6]. This makes TUIs especially beneficial for children in the classroom as their understanding of materials are found in almost any Kindergarten or Elementary Classrooms today. The design of these TUIs are based on notion of reality-based interaction. Reality-Based Interactions styles are designed to take advantage of users' well-entrenched skills and experience of interacting with the real non- digital world to a greater extent [8].

Interaction with TUI's or relies on the sense of touch and hand movements. In a Tangible Programming Environment, the primary modality of interaction with the digital manipulative is rather tactile as it involves only the hands than the body. Even though the tangibility aspect is said to add richness to the interaction by addressing the body awareness and skills [6], it can still be limiting when the interactions are compared to the involvement of the entire body.

This paper addresses this limitation by taking closer look at how kids interact with these manipulatives and describes how whole body movements would contribute to a richer experience. The motivation behind this design research was driven by the goal to enhance the bodily engagement with the digital manipulatives that would contribute to more natural learning experience.

2 The Design Philosophy

To enhance the bodily engagement with the Digital Manipulative in a Tangible Programming Environment, we have to fundamentally change the way we design these manipulatives. This motive was supported by a design philosophy and methodologies with body movement at its core.

2.1 Discovering Layers of Meaning Through Movement

Shusterman (2012) considers the body to be a central entity that is necessary for all our human perception, action and even thought. It this central entity that mediates the experience with the real physical world. According to Hummels et al. [7], It is through this body, we interact with the world around us to access the different layers of the meaning. Based on this notion, they propose movement based interactions as way to capitalised on all human skills, including emotional and perceptual motor skills.

Movement based interactions is in response to a wide occurrences of interface designs that places a heavy burden on human intellect. In response to the cognitive-oriented uniformity of digital appliances, many designer-researchers advocate for embodiment and for capitalising on all human skills, including emotional and perceptual motor skills that shows respect for a person as whole (with a mind, heart and body) and exploits all his skills [7]. This form of embodiment can help to shape people's engagement with reality by providing us with the information about the world around us and ourselves.

In this era of experience, it is important to design interfaces that addresses the different dimensions of the human body. This means that we need to move away from interface designs that places a heavy burden on human intellect [7]. Body movement plays an important role in not just the physical displacement of the body in space but also constructing and expressing knowledge about the world.

2.2   Addressing the Experiential Aspects from a Kinaesthetic Perspective

Kinesthetic Interaction as a unifying concept for describing the body in motion as a foundation for designing interactive systems [5]. Based on the conceptual framework by Fogtman et al., this study extends kinesthetic interactions to study the experiential aspects of tangible programming environments. The framework identifies design themes and parameters that contributes to what's called a Kinesthetic experience.

As a design theme, Kinesthetic Means describes a process where Kinesthetic Interactions used to provide playful experiences to learning activities [5]. Here The goal of the interaction is something other than improving bodily skills [5]. The conceptual framework also describes 7 design parameters that can be used to both inform and evaluate the design concepts that are centred around Kinesthetic Interactions. Out of the The 7 design parameters, the 5 most relevant ones are *Engagement, Sociality, Explicit Motivation, Movability and Kinesthetic Empathy* [5].

The framework can be used to redesign existing interactive systems. This is achieved through exploring the way in which the system can cut across themes, or incorporate new parameters into the design [5]. By sparking new design ideas through addressing the unused parameters, this framework takes the design concepts into directions that would have otherwise remained untouched. Existing tangible programming projects where studied using these frameworks and design params to reveal what it covered and what it didn't.

3   Methodology and Methods

3.1   Children as Informants

Designing interaction styles with digital manipulatives for children is determined by the level of involvement of children during the design process. *Children's Roles* by Druin [2], looks into the various roles that children take in the design of technologies and the different influences of these roles on the design of the experience.

Building on the notion of *informant design* (Scaifeetal 1997) Druin illustrates how children share ideas and opinions with the designer by acting as consultants or *informants* at key points in the development and design process. As informants it is best to involve them right from the beginning, in the ideation and prototyping phases of the design process. They design directions may not necessarily be expressed directly by children, but may be implied by their actions [2].

Children can also give ideas and share opinions after testing a certain technology that can affect the design process [2]. Being transparent about my motivations and making them aware of how their actions and opinions affected the outcome was critical for them to make a well- informed decision. This role provides a compromise that enables children to contribute their ideas to the design and at the same time is flexible enough that it works for short-term projects.

3.2 Design by Moving

The approach used to address various aspects of kinaesthetic experience is influenced by Hummels & Overbeeke's [7] *Design-by-Moving* approach. They suggest that if one likes to design for movement-based interaction, one has to be or become an expert in movement, not just theoretically, by imagination or on paper, but by doing and experiencing while designing.

Márquez et al's (2016) [10], *Embodied Ideation* methods such as *Bodystorming* and *Embodied Sketching* helped in sketching the experiential aspects. By Bodystorming the designer brainstorms on the different movements possible with an artefact or a physical space [11]. This was mostly used by the designer in an early ideation phase, much before the creation of hi fi prototypes. On the other hand, Embodied sketching can be considered as an activity that happens in a situation that closely resembles the design context thats been addressed. Embodied Sketching was frequently used with children during the user study workshops to validate the prototypes.

For the development of the hi fi prototypes. Buxton [1] talks about sketching as exercising the imagination and understanding through the materials used. By materials he means any physical forms such as 3D or sculpture and suggest that they can take on even more extended forms such as technologies that will be used. Combining Buxton's (2010) notion of Sketching with Márquez et al's methods one can develop hifi prototypes based on body movements.

4   The Design Process

Identifying a design process for creating concepts that could provide as a launch pad for further explorations is a wicked problem in itself. Research-through-Design (RtD) [15] was the most a suitable approach to address this kind wicked problem as it employs design philosophies, methods and processes from design practice as a legitimate form of enquiry. Movement was the heart of each stage of this design process.

4.1   Evaluating the Existing Tangible Programming Environments

Various Design parameters of digital manipulatives of certain tangible programming environments such as AlgoBocks, Mr Wagon and Project Blocks were analysed at the very beginning. This evaluation was about comparing the existing concepts against the KI framework of the user with the manipulatives and identify the underlying functional traits. This analysis helped me establish a underlying skeleton of the programming environment that cannot be altered in any case for this particular research.

Every Tangible Programming environment consisted of an *input space* and *output space*. The input space consists of blocks whose arrangements determines the behaviour of a certain object in the output space. The object in the output space takes various forms, mainly tangible like (Project Blocks) and virtual (Algoblocks). Borrowing the functional characteristics helped me focus solely on the interactions and not on the functional aspects of the environment.

4.2   A Basic Model of a Programming Environment

from the existing on the existing Tangible Programming environments, I developed a similar environment that consisted of a *Start*, *Move* and *Repeat* blocks. The Move blocks will allows a certain character to move or jump in a certain direction by a unit. The *Repeat* blocks will repeat a set of Move blocks placed between *Start Repeat* and *End Repeat* for n times. The *Start* block compiles all the instructions and starts to run the program once they have all been arranged.

Establishing this structure had its own set of important constraints for both the designer and kids that helped me ground the interactions within context and feel the constraints in the existing product.

4.3   Ideation and Lo Fi Prototyping

Based on the evaluating existing digital. What kind of tangible objects would be required as input blocks. The nature of output in output space. Objects from two online games such as the yellow block from Temple Trouble and Pacman world served as characters to be manipulated in the output space. The lo-fi prototypes consisted of random objects of various shapes - cylinders, cubes, ropes and bendables; and materials - styrofoam and cardboards. While I chose these objects I also ensured that they engaged the gross motor skills through a quick body storming session in relation to the programming environment.

4.4   User Study Workshop 1

The kids were asked to enact movements to represent certain. This bodystorming activity was done using movement cards and the lo fi prototypes. Specific movements were studied during the programming stage, they wrote programs using the lo-fi prototypes and the paper-blocks to manipulate the objects in Temple run and Pacman. The wizard of Oz technique was used here to decode the program they have written and move the objects in the output space. The kids not only played the role of users but they also shared their opinion on the lo fi prototypes. They used circular motion for repeat, directional movements to changed based on the orientation.

4.5   Ideation and Hi Fi Prototyping

The output space has a close resemblance to Pacman due its nature to provoke spatial movement. The directional movement of the virtual character could be controlled using a *Move* block. To repeat a set of instruction, the repeat block was used. The Move and Repeat blocks were sketched through bodystorming and rapid development of technologies like Arduino along with Accelerometers. The movement patterns of the *Move & Repeat* action was taken into consideration as the Hifi prototype of these blocks were developed.

4.6   User Study Workshop 2

The interaction with the move block was intuitive as the embodied metaphor was directly translated into the interaction model. Even though the repeat block was the least intuitive block, it didn't mean that the kids didn't like the interaction. As the size of the programs where small, the kids had enough space to arrange themselves and perform the movements freely without any space limitations. Difficulty levels matter a lot when it comes to keeping kids engaged throughout the programming session. Kids can get easily distracted if the digital manipulatives have too many features built on to them. For example, the LEDs in the repeat block were made to blink constantly when they were moved from the placeholder these limits the movements.

4.7   First Concept of a Kinesthetic Programming Environment

The programming environment consists of a 2D virtual output space (Fig. 1 (A)) and some *Move*, *Repeat* and *Start* blocks to manipulate the character in the virtual space. The *Move* instructions are written by moving the digital manipulatives in a certain direction. The *Repeat* instructions are written by moving the *Repeat* block between the *Start* and *End* repeat blocks (Fig. 1 (c)). Kids arrange themselves in a logical order to write a complete program. Once they have finished 'writing' they use the *Start* block to compile the instructions and run the program.

Fig. 1. Components of the programming environment; A (Top left) - The output space; B (Top Right) - the *Move*, *Repeat* and *Start* blocks of the input space; C (Bottom) Illustrations showing a set of kids writing code in a kinesthetic programming environment.

The digital manipulatives in this programming environment engages the gross motor skills of the children for the manipulative to be functional. This puts the kids into a novel learning experience where they have to move to think and solve computational problems. The design parameters by Fogtman et al. [3] used to evaluate the design ideas at different stages also contributed as elements that became a part of the experience. This first concept serves as a glimpse into how a kinesthetic experience of a programming environment based in movement based interactions will look like.

5 Moving Forward

User Experience in education is an emerging field for design researchers. A learning experience is combination of knowledge and the interaction with digital manipulatives used for computational thinking. To better prepare learners from a young age, an increasing number of school leaders and technologists are looking towards incorporating interactive ways build and develop programming knowledge.

This proof of concept is a gateway into a new design space of interactive tools that leverages the gross motor skills of children to learn programming. I firmly believe that this research serves as a starting point for further development of tools and technologies that uses body movement as a modality of interaction.

References

1. Buxton, B.: Sketching User Experiences: Getting the Design Right and the Right Design. Morgan Kaufmann, San Francisco (2007)
2. Druin, A.: The role of children in the design of new technology. Behav. Inf. Technol. **21**(1), 1–25 (2002)
3. Fogtmann, M.H., Fritsch, J., Kortbek, K.J.: Kinesthetics interaction: revealing the bodily potential in interaction design. In: Proceedings of the 20th Australasian Conference on Computer-Human Interaction: Designing for Habitus and Habitat, pp. 89–96. ACM (2008)
4. Hourcade, J.P.: Child-computer interaction (2015)
5. Horn, M.S., Jacob, R.J.: Designing tangible programming languages for classroom use. In: Proceedings of the 1st International Conference on Tangible and Embedded Interaction, pp. 159–162. ACM, February 2007
6. Horn, M.S., Solovey, E.T., Crouser, R.J., Jacob, R.J.: Comparing the use of tangible and graphical programming languages for informal science education. In: Proceedings of the SIGCHI Conference on Human Factors in Computing Systems, pp. 975–984. ACM (2009)
7. Hummels, C., Overbeeke, K.C., Klooster, S.: Move to get moved: a search for methods, tools and knowledge to design for expressive and rich movement-based interaction. Pers. Ubiquit. Comput. **11**(8), 677–690 (2007)
8. Jacob, R.J., et al.: Reality-based interaction: a framework for post-WIMP interfaces. In: Proceedings of the SIGCHI Conference on Human Factors in Computing Systems, pp. 201–210, April 2008
9. Maeng, S., Lim, Y.K., Lee, K.: Interaction-driven design: a new approach for interactive product development. In: Proceedings of the Designing Interactive Systems Conference pp. 448–457. ACM (2012)

10. Márquez Segura, E., Turmo Vidal, L., Rostami, A., Waern, A.: Embodied sketching. In: Proceedings of the 2016 CHI Conference on Human Factors in Computing Systems, pp. 6014–6027. ACM (2016)
11. Márquez Segura, E., Turmo Vidal, L., Rostami, A.: Bodystorming for movement-based interaction design. Hum. Technol. **12** (2016)
12. Resnick, M.: Technologies for lifelong kindergarten. Education Tech. Research Dev. **46**(4), 43–55 (1998)
13. Suzuki, H., Kato, H.: AlgoBlock: a tangible programming language, a tool for collaborative learning. In: Proceedings of 4th European Logo Conference, pp. 297–303, August 1993
14. Shusterman, R.: Thinking Through the Body: Essays in Somaesthetics. Cambridge University Press, Cambridge (2012)
15. Zimmerman, J., Forlizzi, J., Evenson, S.: Research through design as a method for interaction design research in HCI. In: Proceedings of the SIGCHI Conference on Human Factors in Computing Systems, pp. 493–502. ACM (2007)

Online Classification of Motor Imagery Using EEG and fNIRS: A Hybrid Approach with Real Time Human-Computer Interaction

Gerald Hirsch[1,3]([✉]), Matilde Dirodi[1], Ren Xu[2], Patrick Reitner[1], and Christoph Guger[1,2]

[1] g.tec Medical Engineering GmbH, Sierningstraße 14, 4521 Schiedlberg, Austria
e11771143@student.tuwien.ac.at
[2] Guger Technologies OG, Herbersteinstraße 60, 8020 Graz, Austria
[3] TU Wien, Wien, Austria

Abstract. *Introduction:* Brain-computer interfaces have become an important tool in human computer interactions. The area of applications ranges from simple research to profound stroke therapy. In this paper, a novel approach to motor imagery is proposed. We analyzed left and right hand grasping using electroencephalography (EEG) and functional near-infrared spectroscopy (fNIRS). *Material, Methods and Results:* We used the wireless *g.Nautilus fNIRS (g.tec)* with 16 channels of EEG, combined with 8 channels of fNIRS, acquiring optical densities and their corresponding oxygenated (HBO) and deoxygenated (HBR) hemoglobin concentrations. We recorded data from 5 healthy subjects and evaluated the algorithms performance. Real- time positive feedback via functional electrical stimulation and a 3D avatar was provided. Each method: EEG and fNIRS (HBO and HBR) were evaluated separately. The final hybrid prediction was performed by a meta classifier utilizing the scores of the individual linear discriminant analysis classifiers. *Discussion and Conclusion:* The results indicate that fNIRS is applicable for online MI classification. The classification accuracies using fNIRS appear to be equivalent and in some cases superior to those using EEG. However, taking advantage of all modalities appears to improve the robustness. We therefore consider fNIRS as a simple, powerful and affordable amendment in such applications.

Keywords: BCI · EEG · fNIRS · Hybrid · Online · Feedback

1 Introduction

Brain-computer interfaces (BCIs) have become an essential tool in human computer interactions, where applications range from simple research to profound

European Commission project RHUMBO – H2020-MSCA-ITN-2018-813234.

© Springer Nature Switzerland AG 2020
C. Stephanidis and M. Antona (Eds.): HCII 2020, CCIS 1224, pp. 231–238, 2020.
https://doi.org/10.1007/978-3-030-50726-8_30

stroke therapy [15]. BCIs require to asses the brain activity. Electroencephalography (EEG) and functional near-infrared spectroscopy (fNIRS) have been exploited for that goal [3,8,17]. EEG is the most popular brain signal for BCIs [15] and provides information about the brain activity by measuring the resulting voltage on the skull, which originates from the firing of underlying neurons. The resulting potential on the scalp is the summed up activity of billions of such cells [6], consequently EEG provides relatively good temporal, but limited spatial resolution. Such cell activities occur permanently but can also be provoked. Provoked activities are called event-related potentials and are the foundation of countless BCI, including motor imagery (MI) [12].

fNIRS on the other hand, assesses the hemodynamic activity of the observed area, with the aim to measure the oxygenated (HBO) and deoxygenated (HBR) hemoglobin concentrations changes. These hemodynamic responses are associated with neural activity. The device used in this publication uses the continuous wave spectroscopy technique [16]. Light with constant amplitude and wavelength is introduced into the region of interest. The ratio between incoming and reflected light intensity provides information about the underlying relative hemoglobin concentration. The measured optical densities (ODs) can then be converted into relative concentrations by applying modified Lambert's law [4].

Neurovascular coupling is the relation between the activity assessed by EEG and fNIRS. Having the ability to exploit both methods proofed to enhance the robustness and accuracy of several BCIs [3,8,10,17]. We therefore propose a real- time hybrid BCI for MI, combining EEG and fNIRS. Since this scheme has real-time capacity, direct positive feedback is provided for the subjects to facilitate the imagination of the movements.

2   Materials and Methods

2.1   Data Acquisition

For data acquisition the *g.NAUTILUS FNIRS* from *g.tec* was used - a hybrid system combining a 16 channel EEG, sampling at 250 Hz, and an 8 channel fNIRS, sampling at 10 Hz. The concentration changes of HBO and HBR are calculated from the measured OD (at 760 nm and 850 nm) [4]. Overall 5 healthy male subjects, without known pre-conditions participated. The 16 EEG electrodes were placed at *Fz, FFC1h, FFC2h, FC2, Cz, C1, C5, FC3, CP3, C2, C6, FC4, CP4, CPz, CPP1h, CPP2h* and *AFz* (ground). The 8 fNIRS transmitters were placed at: *FCC6h, FCC4h, CCP4h, CCP6h, CCP5h, FCC5h, FCC3h* and *CCP3h*. The two fNIRS receivers at *C3* and *C4*.

2.2   Overview and Paradigm

The proposed paradigm utilizes EEG and fNIRS, each signal is evaluated separately (Fig. 2). The resulting scores from the *individual* linear discriminant analysis (LDA) are utilized by a meta-classifier to perform a final prediction. Based

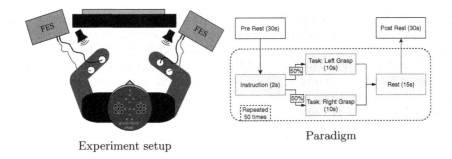

Experiment setup   Paradigm

Fig. 1. Overview of the general experimental setup and paradigm.

on the final prediction the positive feedback is provided. The paradigm itself was split into two phases: calibration (classifier training) and evaluation. For both phases the setup (Fig. 1a), general paradigm(Fig. 1b) and performed number of trials (25 *left grasp*, 25 *right grasp*) was identical. The tasks of left and right grasps were stratified and their sequence was randomized. The instructions were displayed on the screen and an acoustic signal occurred at the onset of the *task* window. During the calibration phase, the *task* period was accompanied by a 3D avatar animation and functional electric stimulation (FES) on both arms(Fig. 1a). For the second phase, the animation and FES were only active when correct classifications were generated (neuronal feedback [18]).

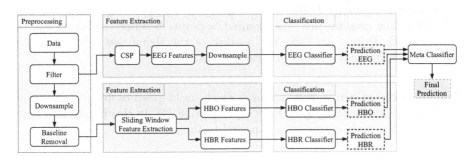

Fig. 2. Overview: The data is preprocessed before EEG and fNIRS based features are extracted. These features are then forwarded to the respective classifiers and the scores are calculated, which are then exploited by the meta classifier.

2.3   EEG Processing

Pre-processing: The raw recorded EEG signal was band pass filtered with a 6th order Butterworth filter($f_{low} = 8\,Hz$, $f_{up} = 30\,Hz$) to limit the bandwidth to the α/μ and β band. Additionally, a 2nd order notch filter at 50 Hz was applied to remove power line interference.

Common Spatial Pattern (CSP): Following, spatial filtering was performed. The overall goal is to maximize the weight of channels which contain relevant information while attenuating the others. Our algorithm facilitates the CSP for this channel weighting. Simplified, CSP filters aim to maximize a signals variance in respect to a first condition, while minimizing it in respect to a second [2]. In the proposed algorithm, the two first and last filters, $\mathbf{Z} = [\mathbf{w}_1, \mathbf{w}_2, \mathbf{w}_{15}, \mathbf{w}_{16}]$, were applied to the BP filtered discrete EEG signal $\mathbf{x}[k] \in \mathbb{R}^N$:

$$\mathbf{x'}[k] = \mathbf{Z}^T \mathbf{x}[k], \ \mathbf{x'}[k] \in \mathbb{R}^4. \tag{1}$$

Feature Extraction: From the four resulting surrogate channels, the logarithmic variance was calculated and normalized over all channels:

$$\mathbf{y}[k] = log \left(\frac{var(\mathbf{x'}_i[k])}{\sum_{i=1}^{4} var(\mathbf{x'}_i[k])} \right). \tag{2}$$

2.4 FNIRS Processing

Preprocessing: The acquired ODs were transformed into the relative concentration changes HBO and HBR [4], resulting in overall 16 signals. The signals were low pass filtered with a 4th Butterworth filter ($f_{up} = 0.3\,Hz$), additionally a 2nd order notch filter was applied.

Baseline Correction: fNIRS signals are prone to significant baseline drifts. Since an online classification was required, a proper baseline correction had to be developed. Prior each task, the average of the signal was calculated and subtracted from the subsequent concentrations.

Feature Extraction: Several features which could grasp usable features from the hemodynamic activity have been reported [7,8,17]. In this publication only *mean* and *slope* were extracted and passed to the classifier.

2.5 Classification

Single Modality Classification: EEG and fNIRS based features were classified using LDA with Fischer's criteria [1]:

$$y[k] = \mathbf{w} \cdot (\mathbf{x}[k] - \frac{1}{2}\mathbf{m}). \tag{3}$$

$y[k]$ being the resulting score value, $\mathbf{w}$ being the trained weight vector at $6.5s$ after the task onset, $\mathbf{x}[k]$ the calculated feature vector and $\mathbf{m}$ the mean feature vector of both classes (C_1, C_2). $y[k] > 0$ and $y[k] \leqslant 0$ correspond to C_1 and C_2 respectively.

Meta Classification: For the final classification the immanent score vector of all three classifiers was taken, $\mathbf{y}[k]$, and the maximum found. $z[k] > 0$ and $z[k] \leqslant 0$ correspond to C_1 and C_2 respectively:

$$z[k] = \arg \max(\mathbf{y}[k]). \tag{4}$$

2.6 Analysis

To evaluate the algorithms performance, the correct classified samples for each time point (trial wise) were accumulated and then averaged. This was performed for *EEG-*, *HBO-* and *HBR-* based classification, as well as for the combination of all three methods.

3 Results

Table 1 is a brief summary of the achieved accuracies. For more detailed results see Fig. 3. In general, all 5 subjects showed accuracies above the chance level for at least one of the three modalities (EEG, HBO and HBR). The maximum HBO and HBR based accuracies are set between 5 and 8 seconds after the task onset, which is the expected temporal response of the hemodynamic activity [9]. HBO proofed to be suitable for all 5 subjects, while HBR based classification struggled with two subjects. The EEG based classification proofed to be suitable for three subjects, particularly *S5* showed satisfying results. Exploiting all modalities lead to the best performance, the lowest achieved accuracy was approximately 70%. Furthermore, the higher temporal resolution of EEG can be seen, as the onset/offset strongly matches the *task* frame.

4 Discussion

The main challenge was to develop an algorithm which has online-capability while still being able to cope with the non-stationarity of both EEG and fNIRS.

Table 1. Overview of the achieved maximum classification accuracies with their relative position within the *task* window. Only the maximum within the *task* window was considered.

Subject no.	Maximum accuracy at timepoint						
	HBO		HBR		EEG		All	
1	72.00%	8.00 s	76.00%	7.50 s	50.00%	–	72.00%	6.50 s
2	86.00%	6.00 s	50.00%	–	75.00%	4.00 s	85.00%	6.00 s
3	72.00%	7.00 s	50.00%	–	70.00%	4.00 s	74.00%	6.00 s
4	70.00%	9.00 s	84.00%	6.00 s	50.00%	–	80.00%	6.00 s
5	86.00%	7.50 s	92.00%	8.00 s	92.00%	6.00 s	92.00%	6.50 s

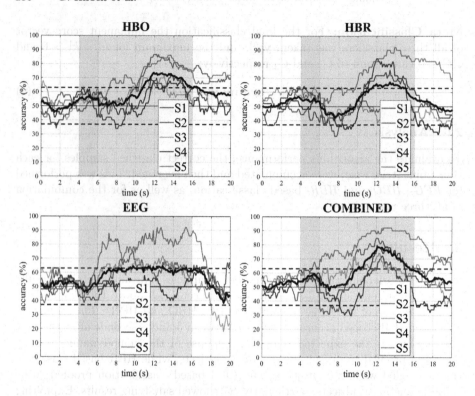

Fig. 3. Time variant accuracy, averaged over all 50 trials for each subject. The blue (4 s–6 s) and red (6 s–16 s) areas represent the *instruction* and *task* window, respectively. Additionally, the mean accuracy (thick line) over all subjects and the real chance level (dashed line) at $\alpha = 0.5$ is plotted. (Color figure online)

To compensate for the overall drift of HBO and HBR, the proposed online baseline correction proofed to be sufficient.

Especially subjects with dense and dark hair tend to complicate proper optode- skin coupling [13]. Evaluating the signal quality can be subjective and a standardized signal quality parameter would make the device application faster and easier, like proposed by Pollonini [14]. Additionally, all modalities would benefit from an online artefact rejection, especially the EEG based classification (limitations of CSP). Further focus should also be put on the *meta* classifier: especially when one of the modalities was not able to correctly classify beyond chance level, the hybrid classification showed unsatisfying results. A simple solution would be to manually exclude modalities which do not perform above chance level during the 10×10 *fold cross-validation* (calibration phase).

Since fNIRS relays on the hemodynamic response of the observed cortex area, the maximum temporal resolution is limited and a delay compared to the actual neural activity is present. A rest time of 15 s after each *task* window was proposed, as a trade off between overall paradigm time and minimum time to reach a certain baseline value for HBO and HBR, respectively [9].

To ensure a relative robust estimate of the real online accuracy, 50 trials were performed during the evaluation phase, which leads to real chance level of 63% ($\alpha = 0.5$) [11]. The average accuracy for all 5 subjects was approximately 79% for the hybrid scheme, showing the suitability of this approach for real-time online classification with feedback. However, EEG showed significantly worse results in 4 out of 5 subjects, compared to the other modalities. One should note that no artefact rejection was performed in this experiment. It is known that the used CSP analysis is sensitive to outliers as it depends on the sample variance [5]. Therefore we will not conclude that fNIRS is superior to EEG in our case. Furthermore, all subjects were healthy males with no known pre- condition. The overall performance of the proposed algorithm has yet to be assesed for people with cognitive restrictions.

5   Conclusion

In this study, we proposed a hybrid paradigm for real-time classification of MI using EEG and fNIRS. The study proofed that the proposed scheme is capable of real online MI classification. The hybrid classifier showed satisfying accuracies above 79% and was able to utilize information from both EEG and fNIRS. Considering the low cost and now shown effectiveness of fNIRS, we consider it a simple, affordable and powerful amendment for MI.

References

1. Bishop, C.M.: Pattern recognition and machine learning. Information science and statistics. Springer, New York, NY (2006). Softcover published in 2016
2. Blankertz, B., Tomioka, R., Lemm, S., Kawanabe, M., Muller, K.: Optimizing spatial filters for robust eeg single-trial analysis. IEEE Signal Process. Mag. **25**(1), 41–56 (2008). https://doi.org/10.1109/MSP.2008.4408441
3. Chiarelli, A.M., Croce, P., Merla, A., Zappasodi, F.: Deep learning for hybrid EEG-fNIRS brain-computer interface: application to motor imagery classification. J. Neural Eng. **15**(3), 036028 (2018). https://doi.org/10.1088/1741-2552/aaaf82
4. Delpy, D.T., Cope, M., van der Zee, P., Arridge, S., Wray, S., Wyatt, J.: Estimation of optical pathlength through tissue from direct time of flight measurement. Phys. Med. Biol. **33**(12), 1433–1442 (1988). https://doi.org/10.1088/0031-9155/33/12/008
5. Guger, C., Ramoser, H., Pfurtscheller, G.: Real-time eeg analysis with subject-specific spatial patterns for a brain-computer interface (BCI). IEEE Trans. Rehabil. Eng. **8**(4), 447–456 (2000). https://doi.org/10.1109/86.895947
6. Herculano-Houzel, S.: The human brain in numbers: a linearly scaled-up primate brain. Front. Hum. Neurosci. **3**, 31 (2009). https://doi.org/10.3389/neuro.09.031.2009
7. Hong, K.S., Khan, M.J., Hong, M.J.: Feature extraction and classification methods for hybrid fNIRS-EEG brain-computer interfaces. Front. Hum. Neurosci. **12**, 246 (2018). https://doi.org/10.3389/fnhum.2018.00246

8. Hong, K.S., Naseer, N., Kim, Y.H.: Classification of prefrontal and motor cortex signals for three-class fNIRS-BCI. Neurosci. Lett. **587**, 87–92 (2015). https://doi.org/10.1016/j.neulet.2014.12.029

9. Huppert, T.J., Hoge, R.D., Diamond, S.G., Franceschini, M.A., Boas, D.A.: A temporal comparison of bold, ASL, and NIRS hemodynamic responses to motor stimuli in adult humans. Neuroimage **29**(2), 368–382 (2006)

10. Khalaf, A., Sejdic, E., Akcakaya, M.: A novel motor imagery hybrid brain computer interface using EEG and functional transcranial doppler ultrasound. J. Neurosci. Methods **313**, 44–53 (2019). https://doi.org/10.1016/j.jneumeth.2018.11.017

11. Müller-Putz, G., Scherer, R., Brunner, C., Leeb, R., Pfurtscheller, G.: Better than random? a closer look on BCI results. Int. J. Bioelectromag. **10**(1), 52–55 (2008)

12. Neuper, C., Wörtz, M., Pfurtscheller, G.: Erd/ERS patterns reflecting sensorimotor activation and deactivation. In: Neuper, C., Klimesch, W. (eds.) Event-Related Dynamics of Brain Oscillations, Progress in Brain Research, vol. 159, pp. 211–222. Elsevier (2006). https://doi.org/10.1016/S0079-6123(06)59014-4

13. Orihuela-Espina, F., Leff, D.R., James, D.R.C., Darzi, A.W., Yang, G.Z.: Quality control and assurance in functional near infrared spectroscopy (fNIRS) experimentation. Phys. Med. Biol. **55**(13), 3701–3724 (2010). https://doi.org/10.1088/0031-9155/55/13/009

14. Pollonini, L., Bortfeld, H., Oghalai, J.S.: Phoebe: a method for real time mapping of optodes-scalp coupling in functional near-infrared spectroscopy. Biomed. Opt. Express **7**(12), 5104–5119 (2016)

15. Ramadan, R.A., Vasilakos, A.V.: Brain computer interface: control signals review. Neurocomputing **223**, 26–44 (2017). https://doi.org/10.1016/j.neucom.2016.10.024

16. Scholkmann, F., et al.: A review on continuous wave functional near-infrared spectroscopy and imaging instrumentation and methodology. NeuroImage **85**, 6–27 (2014). https://doi.org/10.1016/j.neuroimage.2013.05.004. Celebrating 20 Years of Functional Near Infrared Spectroscopy (fNIRS)

17. Verma, P., Heilinger, A., Reitner, P., Grünwald, J., Guger, C., Franklin, D.: Performance investigation of brain-computer interfaces that combine EEG and fNIRS for motor imagery tasks. In: 2019 IEEE International Conference on Systems, Man and Cybernetics (SMC). pp. 259–263, October 2019. https://doi.org/10.1109/SMC.2019.8914083

18. Zich, C., Debener, S., Thoene, A.K., Chen, L.C., Kranczioch, C.: Simultaneous eeg-fnirs reveals how age and feedback affect motor imagery signatures. Neurobiol. Aging **49**, 183–197 (2017). https://doi.org/10.1016/j.neurobiolaging.2016.10.011

Haptic Feedback in Everyday Conversation Situations

Anna Kushnir[✉] and Nicholas H. Müller

University of Applied Sciences Würzburg-Schweinfurt, Würzburg, Germany
info@anna-kushnir.de, nicholas.mueller@fhws.de

Abstract. Everyday face-to-face communication situations use a variety of communication channels. In addition to the verbalized information, several non-verbal cues are communicated, which have to be interpreted by the communication partners. Blind and visually impaired people are limited in interpretation as they are not able to process the visual non-verbal information. The idea behind this work is to design a prototype for a Sensory Substitution Device that aims to support communication. The purpose of the prototype is to remap visual stimuli into tactile information, by utilizing the Facial Action Coding System. For this reason, this work investigates which tactile feedback is particularly suitable for supporting a conversation situation. The feedback types compared here are vibration feedback and temperature feedback such as heat and cold. For the comparison, a within-subject-design experiment was carried out, in which the speech act of a blind person was simulated.

Keywords: Haptic interface · Non-verbal communication · Tactile stimuli

1 Introduction

People with a visual impairment are limited in many everyday activities. For this reason, there are a number of substitution solutions which help to cope with everyday life by compensating the missing or impaired sense of sight. Most solutions support blind people with navigation, reading texts and with object or face recognition. Examples of this are presented in [1–3]. However, less attention has been paid to the development of solutions that deal with social interactions.

A survey carried out with focus groups of blind people and disability experts proves that there are several key needs of non-verbal information, that blind people may need to access during social encounters [4]. These include, but are not limited to, the facial expressions of a person standing in front of a blind communication partner. One of the reasons for this need is that people with a visual impairment aren't able to fully analyze everyday conversation situations because they can't perceive facial expressions of their interlocutor. In order to meet this need, a substitution solution would also be conceivable to support communication. For example, the facial emotions of an interlocutor can be communicated to a blind person during the conversation using tactile stimuli.

© Springer Nature Switzerland AG 2020
C. Stephanidis and M. Antona (Eds.): HCII 2020, CCIS 1224, pp. 239–244, 2020.
https://doi.org/10.1007/978-3-030-50726-8_31

2 Objective

The aim is to investigate which types of tactile stimuli are most suitable to support an everyday conversation situation. For this purpose, the detection rates of heat, cold and vibration feedback are collected and the reaction time to the various stimuli is measured. In addition, information about the degree of distraction by the stimuli is also collected.

3 Related Work

Even though not much attention has been paid to the development of assistive solutions for communication, there are still some solutions that deal with social interactions and are available on the market. For example, the Orcam MyEye [5] has a feature that recognizes people by saving their names and notifying the user. The Microsoft SeeingAI [6] goes even further and offers a feature that describes scenes, people and their emotions. An important shortcoming of SeeingAI and Orcam MyEye is that the solutions provide only aural outputs. If audio signals are played by an assistance system during a conversation, this could be disruptive, since the signal would overlap with the user's voice or that of his interlocutor.

A common alternative to audio-vision substitution is to use vibrotactile feedback, which was already used to support navigation of blind people. Lykawka et al. for instance presented a tactile belt that allows users to navigate in environments including obstacles and to detect the movements of people and objects. The system converts visual information into tactile feedback and conveys it through a vibrotactile belt [1].

McDaniel et al. [4] also presented a haptic belt to assist in communication situations. The work focuses on communicating non-verbal cues, like the number of people in the visual field, the relative direction and distance of the individuals with respect to the user. Experiments with the developed prototype have shown that non-verbal communication can be successfully conveyed trough vibrotactile cues.

In addition to vibro-tactile interfaces, temperature feedback can also be used to convey emotions. So far, temperature feedback has not been used for substitution solutions, but for the direct heating or cooling of the human body [7, 8]. The authors rely on Peltier elements for the temperature feedback supply.

After extensive research, it was determined that there is still no suitable substitution solution to support everyday conversations that communicates emotions.

4 Approach

A quantitative study was carried out to compare the different stimuli. The study consists of a laboratory experiment in which the speech act of a blind person is simulated as well as a survey. The subjects' blindness was simulated by not being able to see when the stimuli were sent. During the experiment, the response times and recognition rates of the stimuli sent were measured. The study has a within-subject design in which all three stimuli are tested on each test subject. After the experiment, demographic data and information about the degree of distraction from the speech act were collected using a questionnaire. In the following the experimental sequence is described in greater detail.

4.1   Experimental Setup

Experiment Procedure. The task of the test subjects in the experiment was to read a text aloud and to react to various stimuli. Depending on the stimulus, the volume should be adjusted when reading. The vibration stimulus signals to continue reading at a normal volume, the heat stimulus calls to read out loud and the cold stimulus is the signal to read on in a whisper.

The study was carried out in a lecture room at the University of Applied Sciences Würzburg-Schweinfurt in December 2019. It was always ensured that the room temperature was kept at 20 °C. At the beginning of the experiment, heat, cold and vibration actuators were attached with Velcro rings to the fingers of the subject's non-dominant hand. After a brief introduction, there was a short training session in which the subjects were asked to read the headline of the text at different volumes depending on the stimulus sent. This was also the first opportunity for the test subjects to feel how the stimuli felt on the skin. Once all questions had been answered, the experiment was started with one of the stimuli. During the reading process, the stimuli were always sent at the same text passages by the experimenter and lasted about two seconds. Each stimulus was sent four times per experiment. Twice at the beginning of a paragraph and twice in the body text. During the experiment, the subject sat with his back to the experimenter who sent the stimuli. In order to eliminate order dependencies, one third of the test subjects received the stimuli in different order variants.

Equipment. Various software and hardware were used to measure and evaluate the response times and detection rates, which are described below. For haptic feedback a vibration motor and two Peltier elements were used, of each only one side was used. The elements were controlled via an Arduino Nano Board V3.3. For the cold feedback a minimum temperature of 10 °C has been set. The temperature was chosen ten degrees lower than in related works that use Peltier elements for cooling [7, 8]. Pretests have shown that a reduction in temperature is necessary. A possible reason for this is that the stimuli only last for 2 s each. A temperature of 40 °C was chosen for the heat signal, since this has already been applied in related works [7, 8] and is below the 45 °C limit, which is the temperature that could lead to first degree burns [9]. An application was programmed to control the Arduino Nano Board and actuators via Bluetooth. Thus, the signals could be sent via the notebook, whereby each signal sent created a logbook entry with a time stamp. Each experiment was recorded with OBS. The recording paired with the logbook entries made it possible to measure the response times and detection rates. Since the test subjects also read in a whisper during the experiment, a Rode microphone was used, though which even low volumes could be heard well in recording.

5 Evaluation

5.1 Descriptive Statistics

The average age of the subjects was 24.34 with the youngest person being 17 and the oldest 40 years old. Of the 55 subjects tested, 36.21% were female, and 64.79% were male.

During the entire study, a total of 220 interventions of each stimulus were sent to the test subjects. Each stimulus was sent four times per person, but the signals were not always recognized correctly (see Table 1). It has also happened that the subjects did not notice or ignored the stimuli. Vibration was most often correctly identified with 217 recognized stimuli, resulting in a recognition rate of 98.63%. All people tested reacted correctly to the vibration signal at least once.

Table 1. Stimuli Recognition.

Stimuli	Recognition rate	Number of recognized stimuli/Number of interventions	Number of test subjects, who recognized stimuli
Vibration	98.63%	217/220	55
Cold	91.36%	201/220	54
Heat	80.45%	177/220	49

The cold stimulus does a little worse, with a recognition rate of 91.36%. Only one person out of 55 did not recognize any of the cold signals sent.

The recognition rate for the heat stimulus was the lowest at 80.45%. A total of 49 out of 55 people reacted to the heat stimulus at least once. The remaining 6 people didn't adjust their volume when reading.

This could be due to the fact that 58.63% classified the intensity of the vibration stimulus as too strong. In contrast, the other two stimuli were more often classified as too weak. 58,62% classified the heat stimulus as too weak and 39% felt that the cold stimulus was also too weak.

The degree of distraction was queried using the questionnaire in which the test subjects were asked to sort the stimuli according to the degree of distraction. Vibration received a rank of 1.6 and was on average the least distracting during the reading. Heat was ranked 2.1 and was on average more distracting than the vibration signal. The cold stimulus has distracted the most on average and therefore has an average rank of 2.7.

5.2 Dependent *t*-Test on Reaction Times

When considering the dependent t-test for the reaction times to the stimuli, the difference becomes clear (see Table 2). On average, the response time to the vibration stimulus was significantly shorter than to the cold ($t = 9.386$, $p = .000$, $n = 52$). The effect size is $r = .80$ and thus corresponds to a large effect.

Table 2. Results of the dependent t-test.

Groups for t-test	Cold/Vibration	Warm/Cold	Warm/Vibration
Number of pairs	52	46	49
Reaction time mean values	2.097/1.376	3.059/2.059	3.091/1.1372
t-statistic	9.386	9.356	17.173
p-value	.000	.000	.000
Effect size r	.80	.81	.93

The situation is similar for the couple warm and cold, where the reaction time to the cold stimulus is significantly shorter than to the warm stimulus ($t = 9.356$, $p = .000$, $n = 46$). The effect size is $r = .81$ and thus corresponds to a large effect.

The mean values of the reaction times to heat and vibration stimuli differ the most. The response time to the vibration stimulus is also significantly shorter compared to the warm stimulus ($t = 17.173$, $p = .000$, $n = 49$). There is also a large effect size with $r = .93$.

5.3 Correlations

A similar result like in the t-test can also be seen if the *reaction times* are correlated with the *intervention type* (see Table 3). This leads to strong, highly significant positive correlations between the intervention type warm and reaction time in all 12 interventions. There are strong, highly significant negative correlations between the intervention type vibration and the reaction time. Detailed values can be found in Table 2. There are no significant correlations for the correlation with the cold intervention type ($p < 0.05$).

Table 3. Pearson correlations of the Variables reaction time and intervention type.

Interventions	Intervention type warm	Intervention type vibration
1. Intervention ($n = 54$)	$r = .474^{**}$; $p = .000$	$r = -.570^{**}$; $p = .000$
2. Intervention ($n = 53$)	$r = .656^{**}$; $p = .000$	$r = -.500^{**}$; $p = .000$
3. Intervention ($n = 45$)	$r = .555^{**}$; $p = .000$	$r = -.585^{**}$; $p = .000$
...	...	...
12. Intervention ($n = 45$)	$r = .471^{**}$; $p = .000$	$r = -.613^{**}$; $p = .000$

6 Conclusion and Outlook

In summary, of the three stimuli examined, vibration is best suited to convey a signal. The reasons for this are shorter reaction times and a high recognition rate in the experiment. In addition, vibration was classified as the least distracting of the three signals examined in the survey, which is significant for supporting communication. The short reaction times in particular are very advantageous as well. This is because, according to the facial action coding system, some emotions only last a few seconds and should therefore be conveyed and recognized as quickly as possible [10].

Temperature feedback is also a way to send signals that should be followed by a reaction. However, the response times here are higher and the recognition rates are lower than when using vibration feedback. Overall, the heat stimulus did the worst, which may be due to the weakly perceived intensity. The maximum temperature has already been selected very close to the limit of a possible burn trauma. Nevertheless, temperature feedback can be useful to support communication. Non-verbal signals with a higher latency, such as mood, would be conceivable. Here, however, it is still necessary to investigate whether the temperature feedback is better recognized if the signal is sent for a longer period.

References

1. Lykawka, C., Stahl, B.K., Campos, M.D.B., Sanchez, J., Pinho, M.S.: Tactile interface design for helping mobility of people with visual disabilities. In: 2017 IEEE 41st Annual Computer Software and Applications Conference (COMPSAC), vol. 1, pp. 851–860 (2017). https://doi.org/10.1109/COMPSAC.2017.227

2. Bhat, P.G., Rout, D. K., Subudhi, B.N., Veerakumar, T.: Vision sensory substitution to aid the blind in reading and object recognition. In: 2017 Fourth International Conference on Image Information Processing (ICIIP), pp. 1–6 (2017). https://doi.org/10.1109/ICIIP.2017.8313754

3. Krishna, S., Little, G., Black, J., Panchanathan, S.: A wearable face recognition system for individuals with visual impairments. In: Proceedings of the 7th International ACM SIGACCESS Conference on Computers and Accessibility, New York, NY, USA, pp. 106–113 (2005). https://doi.org/10.1145/1090785.1090806

4. McDaniel, T., Krishna, S., Balasubramanian, V., Colbry, D., Panchanathan, S.: Using a haptic belt to convey non-verbal communication cues during social interactions to individuals who are blind. In: 2008 IEEE International Workshop on Haptic Audio visual Environments and Games, pp. 13–18 (2008). https://doi.org/10.1109/HAVE.2008.4685291

5. OrCam MyEye. https://www.orcam.com/de/myeye2/. Accessed 20 Mar 2020

6. Seeing AI. https://www.microsoft.com/en-us/ai/seeing-ai. Accessed 20 Mar 2020

7. Lopez, G., Takahashi, K., Nkurikiyeyezu, K., Yokokubo, A.: Development of a wearable thermo-conditioning device controlled by human factors based thermal comfort estimation. In: 2018 12th France-Japan and 10th Europe-Asia Congress on Mechatronics, pp. 255–259 (2018). https://doi.org/10.1109/MECATRONICS.2018.8495727

8. Lopez, G., Tokuda, T., Isoyama, N., Hosaka, H., Itao, K.: Development of a wrist-band type device for low-energy consumption and personalized thermal comfort. In: 2016 11th France-Japan 9th Europe-Asia Congress on Mechatronics (MECATRONICS)/17th International Conference on Research and Education in Mechatronics (REM), pp. 209–212 (2016). https://doi.org/10.1109/MECATRONICS.2016.7547143

9. Trupkovic, T., Giessler, G.: Das Verbrennungstrauma – Teil 1. Anaesthesist **57**(9), 898 (2008). https://doi.org/10.1007/s00101-008-1428-5

10. Ekman, P.: Gefühle lesen [In English: Emotions Revealed], 2nd edn. Spektrum Akad. Verl, Heidelberg (2010)

Active Stylus Input Latency Compensation on Touch Screen Mobile Devices

Roman Kushnirenko$^{(\boxtimes)}$ [iD], Svitlana Alkhimova [iD],
Dmytro Sydorenko [iD], and Igor Tolmachov [iD]

Samsung R&D Institute Ukraine (SRK), Kiev, Ukraine
{r.kushnirenk, s.alkhimova, dm.sidorenko,
i.tolmachev}@samsung.com

Abstract. Input latency adversely affects users experience when they interact with touchscreen devices, especially, when they perform such pointing tasks as writing or drawing with a stylus. To cope with this problem, we capitalize on the deep-learning latency compensation approach, which is considered effective for now, and propose GRU-CNN architecture that enables more accurate prediction of stylus nib future position based on the sequence of the latest input events. To improve prediction accuracy, we minimize the value of custom loss estimating not only distance but direction proximity of actual touches to predicted stylus positions. Additional usage of real-pen specific features generated with an active stylus (tilt, orientation, and pressure values) is also aimed at accuracy improvement. Experiments reveal that the models with proposed GRU-CNN architecture give 0.07, 0.24, and 0.47 mm of prediction error, which are 9.4, 5.3, and 3.8 times lower than the state-of-the-art LSTM-based ones have in cases of prediction in ~ 16.6, ~ 33.3, and 50 ms. The proposed solution provides low-latency interaction in real-time (about 4 ms on Galaxy Note 9) with no cost of hardware complexity.

Keywords: Touch screen · Touch input · Latency · Prediction · Neural network

1 Introduction

Nowadays, touch input is the primary interaction mechanism for a variety of devices, such as interactive displays, smartphones, tablets, and entertainment systems. All of these devices more or less suffer from input latency, i.e. delays between user's actions and corresponding system responses. The studies dedicated to this question revealed that latency degrades user productivity during pointing tasks with touch input and makes the whole system less responsive and interactive [1, 2].

Input latency on touch screen devices is caused by different factors having hardware and/or software nature [3]. The low responsiveness of input and visualization components cause hardware latency. Coping with it is possible within a fixed range, increases the complexity and cost of touchscreen technology, and usually leads to higher power consumption. The reason behind software latency is a long sequence of steps needed to handle user input, which is mainly performed by operating system

© Springer Nature Switzerland AG 2020
C. Stephanidis and M. Antona (Eds.): HCII 2020, CCIS 1224, pp. 245–253, 2020.
https://doi.org/10.1007/978-3-030-50726-8_32

(OS). In particular, until shown on a screen, any user input goes from sensors through an event manager, application, and a buffer manager. Most of the modern mobile OSs control all these steps (except the application one) in the same way for all kinds of interactions [4]. This provides consistent frame rate and absence of frame drops or tearing effect for all the applications. Approaches coping with software latency are categorized into reduction and compensation. Latency reduction implies system-level solutions that aim to optimize intervals between requesting of touch screen state, synchronize sensor driver events, and screen refreshing. Latency compensation is related to the prediction of future touch events. Although both of them offer a possibility to increase system performance, latency compensation can be applied to a specific application or service without influencing the whole system. Of these, latency compensation is especially *preferred due to* its ease of integration into off-the-shelf touch screen devices. Despite the attractiveness, latency compensation approaches still require to be improved to decrease latency to levels perceived by users as low with acceptable quality.

2 Related Work

The effect of touch input latency was widely explored [1, 2] and, as a result, a lot of approaches for input latency compensation on touch screen devices were proposed.

Cattan et al. [5] found that on the system with a lag of 25 ms, latency's negative influence could be compensated effectively by a linear extrapolation, whereas, this approach did not work for lags of 42 ms and above. Nancel et al. [6] examined more complicated prediction models for latency compensation like the Taylor series, curve fitting, and a heuristic approach based on pointer speed and acceleration. They found that side effects brought by these methods disturbed users even more than latency. Instead, they proposed the predictor behaving according to the current pointer velocity and showed that it performed better than compared approaches [7]. However, this predictor was not tested with stylus input, and its efficiency was not compared to neural network approaches. As an alternative to the mathematical methods mentioned above, Henze et al. [8, 9] used neural networks to predict the future position of the finger based on the movement trajectory. The results proved that using neural networks for latency compensation is more precise, but latency compensation obtained with deep-learning approach can still be improved.

It can be found that most researchers were oriented to finger input only or made no difference in input specification while designing latency compensation approaches. However, the stylus input case is believed to be significantly different from the finger one. Using a stylus, a user can perform such pointing tasks as drawing and writing with easy and intuitive interactions because it is similar to a real pen. Moreover, while inputting with a stylus, a user can observe its nib, whereas, during finger input, a point of contact is partly covered. Although these benefits make input more natural, user performance undergoes a more noticeable latency on latency-prone systems.

Therefore, the current study explicitly focuses on latency compensation improvement to keep responsive behavior for users when they perform such pointing tasks as writing or drawing with an active stylus on touch screen mobile devices. We aim to increase the accuracy of the prediction of stylus nib future position based solely on the raw data from touch events and deep learning.

3 GRU-CNN Architecture for Latency Compensation

In order to improve deep learning-based latency compensation, in the current study, we focus *on Android OS only due to its open-source availability and popularity on the mobile device market. In spite of that, many of the concepts could probably be useful in other platforms where active stylus interactions are supported.*

Hardware capabilities of modern mobile devices powered by Android OS are typically locked in at 60 Hz of screen refresh rate. This means that it takes ~ 16.6 ms to have an event-polling loop to be synchronized with screen updates. At the same time, similar to most other mobile OSs, Android uses triple buffering rendering to stabilize the frame rate and avoid tearing effect. This technique implies the usage of three buffers: two buffers (backbuffers) are filled with data while the third one (screenbuffer) is being placed on the screen. The described three-buffer swap chain can result in input latency with duration of three frames. However, when a system is loaded, latency can be more durable, but three frames duration is the minimum amount to be decreased on such devices. In view of this, the current study investigated how to cope with input latency with duration up to three frames. In order to keep frame rate consistent, the results of the prediction of stylus nib future position should appear on the screen in equal intervals of time. In the case of Android OS, this is achieved by using a vsync signal, which is emitted when a screen should be refreshed. Moreover, new input data needed for further prediction is provided by this signal. That is why the current study is directed toward the three cases only: prediction of stylus nib future position in a period of one, two, and three frames duration (on devices that have screen refresh rate equal to 60 Hz, this is equivalent to the positions in ~ 16.6, ~ 33.3, and 50 ms, respectively).

As sampling rate is typically higher that screen refresh rate, Android OS consolidates multiple samples data into the single event. This event is synchronized with screen refresh rate and reflects the most recent samples data. However, to provide fine-grained capture of stylus movements, Android caches all changes reported by sensors (so-called historical values of movement changes in Android OS). In view of this fact, data collected in the current study includes all changes reported by sensors. From now on, for simplicity, each collected changes reported by sensors will be referred as touches.

In contrast to currently available approaches for latency compensation, e.g. [5–9], we propose to utilize not only the previous trajectory of input touch events but also other real-pen specific features (tilt, orientation, and pressure value), which can be generated with an active stylus. We rely on the assumption that these features can provide the predictor with fuller information about input behavior, and as a result, increase its accuracy.

3.1 Dataset and Learning Samples Construction

The representative dataset was collected from 40 participants (30 male, 10 female), 23–51 years old (avg. 32.8), 7 left-handed. All of the participants were frequent mobile device users, and all of them used touch input at least one hour per day. The application that provides the possibility to record touch events was developed in-house to simplify the data collection process. All the data was collected on Galaxy Note 9 devices with screen refresh rate at 60 Hz and input sampling rate at 360 Hz. In total, the collected data contains 20.8 million touch events from 264.3 thousand strokes of writing and drawing inputs with a stylus.

We had a 64%–16%–20% ratio for training, validation and testing datasets respectively. This ratio was obtained with two-stage splitting procedure. Firstly, data was split into 80%–20% parts. 20% formed test dataset and 80% was split into 80%–20% parts again to form training and validation datasets respectively.

Learning samples were obtained as described below. Initially, all events with no changes in x/y coordinates and events obtained not with a stylus were filtered away. After that, we calculated differences in x/y, tilt, orientation, pressure, and timestamp values for each pair of neighboring touch events. Spatial differences were converted to millimeters to prevent dependency on screen resolution. All differences were normalized within the range from 0 to 1 using the min-max normalization method. Every learning sample had the form of two vectors – input and output. An input vector contained information about consecutive differences, where each difference was represented with 6 values (x/y coordinates, timestamp, tilt, orientation, and pressure). An output vector described a spatial shift between the last event used to form the input vector and the timestamp-closest event corresponded to the stylus nib future position in a given time. This vector was represented with 2 values (x/y coordinates). To make a sample rotation-invariant, we calculated a vector between the last two touch events used to form the input vector and rotated the learning sample to align this vector with the line $y = -x$. A similar approach was used by Henze et al. [9].

3.2 Model Architecture

Our study was targeted to capitalize on the recent state-of-the-art approach of LSTM by Henze [9]. However, experiments with GRU, which is another type of RNN architecture [10], revealed that it takes approximately 2.2 times smaller training time, while its accuracy is 16% better compared to LSTM.

Recent studies showed that hybrid RNN and CNN architectures were adopted in works across various domains and showed good results in many tasks. It was hypothesized that combining GRU and CNN can be more effective in solving prediction problems, as CNN can extract higher-level features that are invariant to spatial and temporal shifts. The experiments showed that the GRU-CNN combination is 7% more accurate than architecture solely based on GRU. Proposed GRU-CNN architecture has parallel GRU and CNN branches that obtain the same input event sequence (Fig. 1). Hidden state vector dimensionality of the GRU layer, kernel numbers and kernel sizes of CNN layers were determined by a grid search. Bigger values gave better results but we were restricted with a constraint to have real-time inference on Galaxy

Note 9 (a target device in our study). We found that inference periods up to 4 ms did not cause frame drops and, consequently, did not degrade the user experience.

The GRU branch consists of GRU layer with batch normalization to stabilize the learning process and reduce training time. The CNN branch should be considered in more detail. To make obtained features more and more abstract, we used a sequence of CNN layers as was proposed by Wang et al. [11]. Each CNN layer output is activated with a parametric rectified linear unit (PReLU) that gave 3% accuracy enhancement comparing to the originally proposed architecture. To increase solution convergence, we concatenated features from different abstraction levels according to the proposed by Rumetshofer et al. [12]. CNN branch was divided into two sub-branches after the third convolutional block. The first sub-branch contains only a global average pooling (GAP) layer to adjust the dimension of the convolutional block output. The second sub-branch begins with max pooling layer to be able to extract the important information during position invariance maintaining [13]. GAP layer was used at the end of the second sub-branch for the same reason as in the first sub-branch.

3.3   Implementation Details

We used high-level Keras API from TensorFlow[1] 2.0 library to build models according to the proposed GRU-CNN architecture (Fig. 1).

We applied a grid search to find the best combination of the hyperparameters. If we do not specify some values below, it means that such hyperparameters were left at their respective default values as they are set in TensorFlow library.

We used Glorot uniform initialization to initialize the weights of the network.

The network parameters were optimized using custom loss function with Adam stochastic optimizer. The value of the custom loss function was defined as a weighted linear combination of two quantitative metrics. The first one was a sum of Euclidean distances between corresponding real and predicted touches; the second one was a sum of deviation angles from the target direction. The initial learning rate was set as 0.001 and it was divided by 5 when validation loss value was not improving at least for 5 epochs. To prevent overfitting, early stopping was used to monitor the validation loss. If the validation loss did not improve for 20 epochs, training was stopped.

We used mini-batch gradient descent learning with a batch size of 128 samples shuffled randomly at the beginning of each epoch.

According to the above, we trained three models for prediction of stylus nib future position in ~ 16.6, ~ 33.3, and 50 ms. To choose the optimal length of the touch sequence needed to form an input vector, we analyzed lengths varying from 6 to 25. We obtained less than 0.1% improvement when made this length more than 11, 13, and 20 for prediction of stylus nib future position in ~ 16.6, ~ 33.3, and 50 ms, respectively. Thus, these lengths of touch sequences were used to reduce memory usage and not to slow down inference time on our target device.

---

[1] https://www.tensorflow.org/.

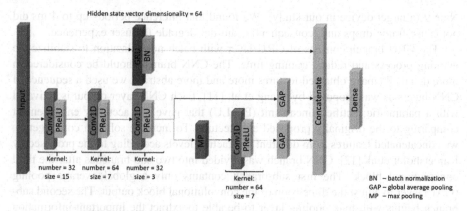

Fig. 1. The overall architecture of the proposed GRU-CNN neural network for prediction of stylus nib future position based on the sequence of the latest input events.

4   Results and Discussion

To assess the prediction accuracy of the proposed solution and compare it to a representative one, we chose LSTM-based neural network architecture[2] described by Henze et al. in [9]. Accordingly, we used a set of metrics that estimated distance and direction proximity of actual touches to predicted stylus positions.

In order to estimate distance proximity, we calculated prediction error as the Euclidean distance between actual touches and predicted stylus positions (Fig. 2a). The prediction error was compared to a baseline value that represented a real gap appearing in the case of inputting without latency compensation. The baseline value was calculated as the Euclidean distance between the stylus nib position and the line head. Experiments revealed that usage of both neural network architectures led to decreasing input latency in each of the analyzed cases. At the same time, the models with proposed GRU-CNN architecture gave 9.4, 5.3, and 3.8 times lower average prediction error than the LSTM-based ones in cases of prediction in $\sim$16.6, $\sim$33.3, and 50 ms, respectively. It should be mentioned that the error of 1.79 mm for prediction in 50 ms with the LSTM-based model is very close to the baseline value (1.81 mm) making this solution unacceptable in most cases.

In order to estimate direction proximity, we analyzed the distribution of deviation angle from the target direction (Fig. 2b). The deviation angle from the target direction is an angle between the stylus direction and the direction from the last visualized real point to the predicted one (it is equal to zero when both directions coincide). Collected data was obtained with horizontal shifts being smaller than vertical ones due to the form factor of devices being used. This disproportion persistently led to greater y-coordinate of output vector comparing to its x-coordinate with providing rotation-invariance for learning samples according to the procedure mentioned above. Consequently, a shift in the distribution of deviation angle can be caused because of

---

[2] https://github.com/interactionlab/MobileHCI17-Touch-Extrapolation.

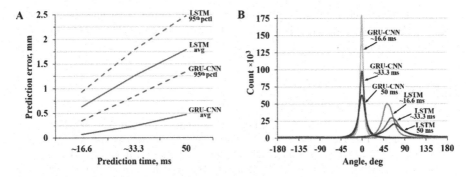

Fig. 2. GRU-CNN vs LSTM comparison. **a** Comparison based on distance proximity. **b** Comparison based on direction proximity.

minimizing the loss neglecting these angles (in our case, it is incidental to LSTM-based models).

Additionally, we used the state-of-the-art root-mean-square-error (RMSE) metric [14]. The models with proposed GRU-CNN architecture had 2.27, 5.88, and 10.02 px errors, which were 3.8, 2.9, and 2.4 times lower than the LSTM-based models had for prediction of stylus nib future position in ~ 16.6, ~ 33.3, and 50 ms, respectively.

The average inference time on CPU of our GRU-CNN architecture is about 4 ms on Galaxy Note 9, which is fast enough for real-time applications.

5 Conclusion and Future Work

Combined neural network architecture with GRU and CNN branches was proposed as an improvement to state-of-the-art deep learning-based latency compensation. It is a software-based solution that provides the ability to cope with latency in real-time (about 4 ms on Galaxy Note 9) with no cost of hardware complexity.

Obtained results showed that the proposed solution can provide the users with responsive behavior while they write or draw with an active stylus on touch screen mobile devices. Models with proposed GRU-CNN architecture gave 0.07 ± 0.05, 0.24 ± 0.13, and 0.47 ± 0.22 mm prediction error and 0.27 ± 15.29, -0.18 ± 23.69, and 0.38 ± 30.26 deg deviation angle in cases of prediction in ~ 16.6, ~ 33.3, and 50 ms, respectively.

Although the prediction accuracy obtained in the current study can be acceptable, new experiments can help to achieve even more decrease in input latency without loss of quality. These experiments will be more important for prediction in longer periods because of less accurate prediction results. Experiments on simultaneous usage of prediction in different periods of a preset number of frames can be conducted to achieve more natural stroke construction. Besides, it is important to investigate different visual side-effects perceived by users when they perform pointing tasks with compensated latency. This investigation can be the aim of another large-scale research with more resources being involved.

References

1. Annett, M., Ng, A., Dietz, P., Bischof, W.F., Gupta. A.: How low should we go?: understanding the perception of latency while inking. In: Proceedings of Graphics Interface 2014, pp. 167–174. Canadian Information Processing Society, Toronto (2014)
2. Deber, J., Jota, R., Forlines, C., Wigdor, D.: How much faster is fast enough?: user perception of latency & latency improvements in direct and indirect touch. In: Proceedings of the 33rd Annual ACM Conference on Human Factors in Computing Systems, pp. 1827–1836. ACM, New York (2015). https://doi.org/10.1145/2702123.2702300
3. Ng, A., Lepinski, J., Wigdor, D., Sanders, S., Dietz, P.: Designing for low-latency direct-touch input. In: Proceedings of the 25th annual ACM symposium on User Interface Software and Technology, pp. 453–464. ACM, New York (2012). https://doi.org/10.1145/2380116.2380174
4. Yun, M.H., He, S., Zhong, L.: POLYPATH: supporting multiple tradeoffs for interaction latency (2016). https://arxiv.org/pdf/1608.05654.pdf. Accessed 11 Mar 2020
5. Cattan, E., Rochet-Capellan, A., Bérard, F.: A predictive approach for an end-to-end touch-latency measurement. In: Proceedings of the 2015 International Conference on Interactive Tabletops and Surfaces, pp. 215–218. ACM, New York (2015). doi: https://doi.org/10.1145/2817721.2817747
6. Nancel, M., Vogel, D., Araujo, B., Jota, R., Casiez, G.: Next-point prediction metrics for perceived spatial errors. In: Proceedings of the 29th Annual Symposium on User Interface Software and Technology, pp. 271–285. ACM, New York (2016). doi: https://doi.org/10.1145/2984511.2984590
7. Nancel, M., et al.: Next-point prediction for direct touch using finite-time derivative estimation. In: Proceedings of the 31st Annual ACM Symposium on User Interface Software and Technology, pp. 793–807. ACM, New York (2018). doi: https://doi.org/10.1145/3242587.3242646
8. Henze, N., Funk, M., Shirazi, A.S.: Software-reduced touchscreen latency. In: Proceedings of the 18th International Conference on Human-Computer Interaction with Mobile Devices and Services, pp. 434–441. ACM, New York (2016). https://doi.org/10.1145/2935334.2935381
9. Henze, N., Mayer, S., Le, H.V., Schwind, V.: Improving software-reduced touchscreen latency. In: Proceedings of the 19th International Conference on Human-Computer Interaction with Mobile Devices and Services, vol. 107. ACM, New York (2017). https://doi.org/10.1145/3098279.3122150
10. Cho, K., Merrienboer, B., Bahdanau, D., Bengio Y.: On the properties of neural machine translation: encoder–decoder approaches. In: Proceedings of SSST-8, Eighth Workshop on Syntax, Semantics and Structure in Statistical Translation, pp. 103–111. Association for Computational Linguistics, Stroudsburg (2014). https://doi.org/10.3115/v1/w14-4012

11. Wang, Z., Yan, W., Oates, T.: Time series classification from scratch with deep neural networks: a strong baseline. In: 2017 International Joint Conference on Neural Networks, pp. 1578–1585. IEEE, Anchorage (2017). https://doi.org/10.1109/ijcnn.2017.7966039

12. Rumetshofer, E., Hofmarcher, M., Röhrl, C., Hochreiter, S., Klambauer, G.: Human-level protein localization with convolutional neural networks (2019). https://openreview.net/forum?id=ryl5khRcKm. Accessed 11 Mar 2020

13. Scherer, D., Müller, A., Behnke, S.: Evaluation of pooling operations in convolutional architectures for object recognition. In: Diamantaras, K., Duch, W., Iliadis, L.S. (eds.) ICANN 2010. LNCS, vol. 6354, pp. 92–101. Springer, Heidelberg (2010). https://doi.org/10.1007/978-3-642-15825-4_10

14. LaViola, J.J.: Double exponential smoothing: an alternative to Kalman filter-based predictive tracking. In: Proceedings of the workshop on Virtual environments 2003, pp. 199–206. Association for Computing Machinery, New York (2003). https://doi.org/10.1145/769953.769976

Machine Translation from Japanese to Robot Language for Human-Friendly Communication

Nobuhito Manome[1,2]($\boxtimes$), Shuji Shinohara[2], Kouta Suzuki[1,2], and Shunji Mitsuyoshi[2]

[1] SoftBank Robotics Group Corp., Tokyo, Japan
manome@bioeng.t.u-tokyo.ac.jp
[2] The University of Tokyo, Tokyo, Japan

Abstract. Humanoid robots should be capable of communicating naturally with humans to act as good partners to humans. However, there are several challenges associated with ensuring that humanoid robots are able to speak human languages. For example, to enable the humanoid robot NAO/Pepper of SoftBank Robotics Corp. to speak human-friendly Japanese, sentences in Japanese must first be translated into robot language. The target language is manually converted to the robot language to ensure that humanoid robots can communicate appropriately using human languages. Two facets ought to be incorporated into such translations: a dictionary for correct pronunciation must be created and another dictionary for expressing emotions must be created. This paper describes an approach that enables the humanoid robot NAO/Pepper to execute human-friendly communication. We manually prepared 32,293 pairs of sentences in Japanese and robot language as training data. Further, we created dictionaries to associate the correct pronunciations and emotional expressions with each pair of sentences using the morphemic analyzer MeCab. Finally, we developed a machine translation system by incorporating these dictionaries to translate Japanese to robot language. The performance of the machine translation system was verified using test sentences, and the results demonstrate the effectiveness of the proposed machine translation system, although some challenges still remain.

Keywords: Humanoid robot · Machine translation · Natural language processing

1 Introduction

Following the advancements in artificial intelligence technology, robots are used in fields such as industrial, households, and entertainment [1, 2]. Therefore, humans interact with robots, especially humanoid robots, in several ways [3]. An emotional expression is an important component in human communication. Consequently, emotional expressions of robots have attracted the attention of scholars [4]. Several studies have investigated the emotional expressions of robots, considering human facial expressions [5–7]. However, humanoid robots, such as NAO/Pepper of SoftBank

© Springer Nature Switzerland AG 2020
C. Stephanidis and M. Antona (Eds.): HCII 2020, CCIS 1224, pp. 254–260, 2020.
https://doi.org/10.1007/978-3-030-50726-8_33

Robotics Corp., have few moving parts on their faces; thus, most investigations have focused on expressing emotions using speech [2] and gestures [4, 8, 9].

Humanoid robots require natural communication with humans to form good partnerships. However, there are several challenges in enabling humanoid robots to communicate in human languages. For example, for NAO/Pepper to speak Japanese with emotions similar to that of humans, it is necessary to first translate Japanese into a robot language, as shown in Table 1.

Table 1. Example of a sentence in Japanese and robot language. "\rspd=value\" indicates the communication speed, and "\vct=value\" indicates the voice pitch. This sentence means "I hope tomorrow will be a good day".

Sentence in Japanese language	明日はいい日になるといいてﾞすね
Sentence in robot language	\rspd=100\\vct=150\明日はイィ火になるといー てﾞす寝ｚｯ?

This translation is based on two approaches. The first is a sentence conversion for the robot to be able to pronounce properly. The second is the adjustment of voice pitch and communication speed for the robot to speak with emotion. We aim to reduce development costs and ensure humanoid robots closely mimic humans by developing machine translation systems to automate these tasks. This paper introduces these approaches for NAO/Pepper to enable human-friendly communication.

The remainder of this paper is structured as follows. First, the collected data is described. Next, two created dictionaries are discussed. Subsequently, a machine translation system incorporating these dictionaries is explained. Finally, we examine the performance of this machine translation system using test sentences and describe the results.

2   Materials and Methods

2.1   Dataset Collection

First, we manually prepared 32,293 sets of Japanese and robot language sentences as training data. Because listening to monotonous speech is boring, all sentences in the robot language were given an appropriate voice pitch and speaking speed. Table 1 shows an example of the training data. "\rspd=value\" indicates the speaking speed, and "\vct=value\" indicates the voice pitch for the robot language sentences.

2.2   Dictionary Creation for Correct Pronunciation

We created a dictionary for humanoid robots to pronounce Japanese words correctly using the dataset. The dictionary was created using the following procedure: First, all Japanese sentences were analyzed using the morphemic analyzer MeCab [10] and the dictionaries "Hatena Keyword" and "Japanese Wikipedia". Table 2 shows an example of the analysis result.

Table 2. Example of the analysis result of the Japanese sentence using the morphemic analyzer MeCab. The label is an identifier corresponding to each morpheme. The analyzed sentence is the same as the Japanese sentence in Table 1.

Morpheme	明日	は	いい	日	に	なる	と	いい	です	ね
Label	A_1	B_1	C_1	D_1	E_1	F_1	G_1	H_1	I_1	J_1

Next, a label is assigned to each morpheme. Subsequently, the dictionary is created by appropriately linking the character strings in the robot language sentence corresponding to each label. Table 3 shows an example wherein a character string in a robot language sentence is linked to each label in Table 2.

Table 3. Example of the result of linking the character strings in the robot language sentence to labels corresponding to each morpheme in Table 2.

Morpheme	明日	は	イィ	火	に	なる	と	いー	です	寝ェッ?
Label	A_2	B_2	C_2	D_2	E_2	F_2	G_2	H_2	I_2	J_2

2.3   Dictionary Creation for Expressing Emotions

The dataset was assigned a voice pitch and speaking speed according to the meaning of the sentence and emotions of the robot. Here, the emotions of the humanoid robot are determined by humans according to emotions associated with speaking the sentences.

We created a dictionary for humanoid robots to express their emotions using this dataset. The dictionary was created using the following procedure: First, all Japanese sentences were analyzed using the morphemic analyzer MeCab, and 340,730 morphemes were output. Next, the morphemes were weighted by term frequency–inverse document frequency (tf–idf) [11]. tf–idf is a term weighting scheme frequently used in current information retrieval systems [12]. The weight is calculated from the following factors:

- Term Frequency

The terms often included in a document are keywords that accurately characterize the document. The term frequency is defined by the following equation:

$$tf(t, d) = freq(t, d) \tag{1}$$

where $freq(t, d)$ is the frequency of occurrence of term t in document d.

- Inverse Document Frequency

The terms that appear less frequently in documents are keywords that characterize the document where they appear. The inverse document frequency is defined by the following equation:

$$idf(t) = 1 + \log\left(\frac{D}{freq(t, D)}\right) \tag{2}$$

where D is the total number of documents.

By using the term frequency and inverse document frequency, the weight of term t in document d can be calculated as:

$$weight(t, d) = tf(t, d) \times idf(t) \tag{3}$$

The dictionary for emotional expression stores the weights of the analyzed morphemes, voice pitch, and speaking speed of each sentence. It operates as follows in the machine translation system. First, the input sentence is decomposed into morphemes by MeCab. Next, a document vector is created from the weights of each morpheme, and the similarity between the sentences is calculated using the cosine similarity method. Finally, the voice pitch and speaking speed of the sentence similar to the input sentence are added to the input sentence.

The doc2vec model [13], which is an extension of the word2vec model [14, 15], effectively performs tasks such as finding similar documents and clustering documents [16]. However, a document vector generated from the doc2vec model cannot provide an intuitive interpretation because its value indicates the weight of the neural network used to train doc2vec. Therefore, the developed machine translation system does not use the doc2vec model.

2.4 Machine Translation System

The machine translation system was developed to convert Japanese language sentences into robot language sentences by incorporating the two dictionaries mentioned above. Figure 1 shows an overview of the developed machine translation system.

The machine translation system converts input Japanese language sentences into robot language sentences using the following procedure. First, the input sentence is decomposed into morphemes via MeCab. Next, each morpheme is converted using the first dictionary so that the robot can speak Japanese correctly. Subsequently, a voice pitch, a speaking speed, and an emotional expression are added to the sentence by the second dictionary. Finally, the converted sentence is output from the machine translation system.

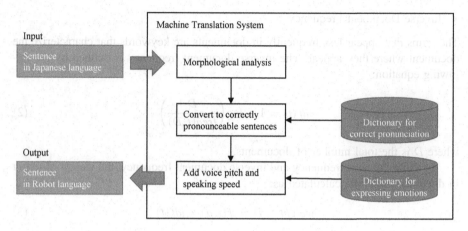

Fig. 1. Overview of the developed machine translation system

3 Experimental Verification

We examined the performance of the machine translation system using test sentences. Table 4 shows the six test sentences and output results. The test sentences include Japanese Kanji, which is difficult to pronounce for humanoid robots, and content, which express strong emotions when communicating.

Table 4. Output result of the test sentences from the machine translation system. The meaning of sentence 1 is "I will tell you important information!" The meaning of sentence 2 is "It is better to bring a folding umbrella when you leave home". The meaning of sentence 3 is "It will be rainy in some areas tomorrow". The meaning of sentence 4 is "It may be rainy in some areas tomorrow". The meaning of sentence 5 is "Yeah! I'm looking forward to it!" The meaning of sentence 6 is "You are often angry, aren't you?"

Sentence	Sentence in Japanese language	Sentence in robot language
Sentence 1	大切な情報なのでお伝えしますね!	\rspd=108\\vct=130\大切な情報なので、お伝えします寝ェッッ、
Sentence 2	家を出る際は、折り畳み傘を持って行った方がいいかもしれませんよ!	\rspd=102\\vct=138\家を出る際は、折りたたみ蛾差を持って行った方がいいかもしれません予ぉ??
Sentence 3	明日は一部地域で雨ですよ	\rspd=98\\vct=130\明日は一部チーキで、雨です予ぉ???
Sentence 4	明日は一部地域で雨らいいてすよ	\rspd=98\\vct=130\明日は一部チーキで、雨らいいてす予ぉ???
Sentence 5	わー!楽しみだなー!	\rspd=120\\vct=180\ファーぁ、\rspd=105\\vct=165\楽しみだナァーー!
Sentence 6	よく怒ってますよね?	\rspd=100\\vct=145\よく怒ってます根ぇ???

In addition, we examined the speech by inputting the text output from the machine translation system into the humanoid robot NAO/Pepper. Consequently, we observed that the output speech of sentences 1 and 2 were accurate in both Japanese pronunciation and emotional expression. Although in the output speech of sentences 3 and 4, the Japanese pronunciation was accurate, there was no significant difference in voice pitch and speaking speed despite the differences in the meaning of the sentences. Although in the output speech of sentences 5 and 6, the Japanese pronunciation was accurate, the meaning of the sentences changed depending on the context. Thus, it was impossible to judge the accuracy of the emotional expression.

4 Discussion and Conclusions

The results show that the machine translation system enables the humanoid robot NAO/Pepper to accurately speak Japanese. However, two main issues exist with humanoid robots when expressing emotions in speech. First, because the meaning of Japanese text changes significantly with minimal changes in characters, it is difficult to provide appropriate voice pitch and speaking speed with a simple similarity method using document vectors. Second, the appropriate emotional expression cannot often be determined from only one sentence.

The problems can addressed by considering the context of the conversation. However, these are "statistically appropriate emotional expressions". "Statistically appropriate emotional expression" refers to the voice pitch and speaking speed appropriately experienced as emotional expressions by a receiver, alternate to the speaker. We believe that humanoid robots can achieve natural communication with humans without incorporating statistically appropriate emotional expressions by incorporating consistent emotions like humans.

This study introduced a machine translation system that converts Japanese to robot language to enable humanoid robots to perform human-friendly communication. Furthermore, the usefulness and limitations of the machine translation system were described from experiments using test sentences. In the future, we will challenge the development of natural language processing technology that considers the context of the conversation and emotions of the robot, rather than single sentences.

References

1. Ma, X.N., Yang, X., Zhao, S.D., Fu, C.W., Lan, Z.Q., Pu, Y.M.: Using social media platforms for human-robot interaction in domestic environment. Int. J. Hum.-Comput. Interact. **30**(8), 627–642 (2014)
2. Yilmazyildiz, S., Read, R., Belpeame, T., Verhelst, W.: Review of semantic-free utterances in social human-robot interaction. Int. J. Hum.-Comput. Interact. **32**(1), 63–85 (2016)
3. Tung, F.W.: Child perception of humanoid robot appearance and behavior. Int. J. Hum.-Comput. Interact. **32**(6), 493–502 (2016)
4. Bretan, M., Hoffman, G., Weinberg, G.: Emotionally expressive dynamic physical behaviors in robots. Int. J. Hum.-Comput. Stud. **78**, 1–16 (2015)
5. Breazeal, C.: Designing Social Robots. The MIT Press, Cambridge (2002)

6. Grammer, K., Oberzaucher, E.: The reconstruction of facial expressions in embodied systems: new approaches to an old problem. ZiF Mitteilungen **2**, 14–31 (2006)
7. Kühnlenz, K., Sosnowski, S., Buss, M.: Impact of animal-like features on emotion expression of robot head EDDIE. Adv. Robot. **24**(8–9), 1239–1255 (2010)
8. Gelder, B.D.: Why bodies? Twelve reasons for including bodily expressions in affective neuroscience. Philos. Trans. R. Soc. B: Biol. Sci. **364**(1535), 3475–3484 (2009)
9. Beck, A., Cañamero, L., Bard, KA.: Towards an affect space for robots to display emotional body language. In: Proceedings of 19th International Symposium in Robot and Human Interactive Communication (2010)
10. Kudo, T., Yamamoto, K., Matsumoto, Y.: Applying conditional random fields to Japanese morphological analysis. In: Proceedings of the Conference on Empirical Methods in Natural Language Processing, pp. 230–237 (2004)
11. Robertson, S.: Understanding inverse document frequency: on theoretical arguments for idf. J. Doc. **60**(5), 503–520 (2004)
12. Beel, J., Gipp, B., Langer, S., Breitinger, C.: Research-paper recommender systems: a literature survey. Int. J. Digit. Libr. **17**(4), 305–338 (2016)
13. Le, Q., Mikolov, T.: Distributed representations of sentences and documents. In Proceedings of the 31st International Conference on Machine Learning, pp. 1188–1196 (2014)
14. Mikolov, T., Chen, K., Corrado, G., Dean, J.: Efficient estimation of word representations in vector space. In: Proceedings of the Workshop at International Conference on Learning Representations, pp. 1–12 (2013)
15. Mikolov, T., Sutskever, I., Chen, K., Corrado, G., Dean, J.: Distributed representations of words and phrases and their compositionality. In: Proceedings of the Advances in Neural Information Processing Systems, vol. 26, pp. 3111–3119 (2013)
16. Dai, A.M., Olah, C., Le, Q.V.: Document embedding with paragraph vectors. arXiv preprint arXiv:1507.07998 (2015)

The Effect of Visual and Vibro-Tactile Feedback During Floor Cleaning Task on Motion and Task Performance

Tsubasa Maruyama[1]([⊠]) [iD], Kodai Ito[2] [iD], Mitsunori Tada[2] [iD],
and Takuro Higuchi[3]

[1] Human Augmentation Research Center, National Institute of Advanced
Industrial Science and Technology (AIST), Kashiwa, Japan
tbs-maruyama@aist.go.jp
[2] Artificial Intelligence Research Center, AIST, Koto City, Tokyo, Japan
{kodai.ito,m.tada}@aist.go.jp
[3] Kao Corporation, Chuo City, Tokyo, Japan
higuchi.takuro@kao.com

Abstract. In this study, we developed a real-time measurement and feedback system for floor cleaning using a sheet-type mop. In this system, the full-body motion of the cleaner and the motion of the mop are measured. The swept area by the mop is estimated from the motion of the mop. During the cleaning, the vibro-tactile, and visual feedback is provided to the cleaner for improving the efficiency of the cleaning. In particular, the vibro-tactile stimulation according to the number of sweeping on the current area (SF: swept-count feedback), the visual information just by showing the swept area to the cleaner through a display (VF: visual feedback), and the vibro-tactile feedback according to the flexion angle of the torso (MF: motion feedback) are implemented. The purpose of this study is to analyze the effect of feedback on the efficiency of the cleaning and motion of both full-body and floor mop. The floor cleaning experiment is conducted with eight males and eight females. For each participant, the cleaning tasks with the three feedback (SF, VF, or MF) are measured. Also, two trials without the feedback are measured before (NFF) and after (NFL) the three trials with feedback. Our results indicated the potential of real-time feedback for improving the efficiency of the cleaning and body posture.

Keywords: Floor cleaning · Digital human · Motion measurement · Feedback

1 Introduction

Floor cleaning using a sheet-type mop is one of the ordinary daily household work. It is performed by full-body motions, including walking, arm swinging, and torso flexing. It also requires the planning of the cleaning path. Measurement and analysis of the individual cleaning motion and strategy are essential for realizing better floor cleaning experience since they are different among individuals depending on the complexity of the task, which finally leads to different efficiency and physical load during task execution. For this reason, several studies have been conducted to evaluate the cleaning

© Springer Nature Switzerland AG 2020
C. Stephanidis and M. Antona (Eds.): HCII 2020, CCIS 1224, pp. 261–269, 2020.
https://doi.org/10.1007/978-3-030-50726-8_34

task from the biomechanical point of view. Higuchi et al. [1] evaluated the physical load during the floor cleaning task by measuring the full-body motion and reaction force between the mop and the floor using force plates in the laboratory environments. Lim et al. [2] evaluated the physical load during the sweeping based on the musculoskeletal simulation. Wallius et al. [3] evaluated the shoulder muscle activity during floor mopping with different handle height. These studies mainly focused on the evaluation of the physical load. However, individual differences in the efficiency of the cleaning and the full-body motion under real living environments remain unstudied in these researches [1–3].

On the other hand, in our previous study [4], we tried to enhance the floor cleaning experience through gamification. In this system, vibro-tactile feedback or 3D surround sound was provided to the cleaners for letting them know the unswept area or for navigating them to the unswept area. Our preliminary results indicated the potential of these feedback on the fun and effectiveness of the cleaning. However, the effect of the feedback on the full-body motion have not been evaluated, since this study focused on gamification of the cleaning task.

The purpose of this study is to analyze the effect of the feedback on the efficiency of the cleaning, and motion of both full-body and floor mop. For this purpose, a real-time measurement and feedback system is developed. In this system, the full-body motion of the cleaner, and the motion of a sheet-type mop are measured. Also, the swept area by the mop is estimated from the mop motion. During the cleaning, vibro-tactile and visual feedback is provided to the cleaner. In particular, the vibro-tactile stimulation according to the number of sweeping on the current position (*SF: swept-count feedback*), the visual information just by showing the cleaned area to the cleaner through a display (*VF: visual feedback*), and the vibro-tactile feedback according to the flexion angle of the torso (*MF: motion feedback*) are implemented. The effect of feedback was evaluated through the floor cleaning experiment in our living laboratory.

2   Measurement and Feedback System for Floor Cleaning

2.1   Overview

The proposed motion measurement and feedback system are overviewed in Fig. 1. The motion of the cleaner and the mop were measured by optical motion capture (MoCap) and inertial measurement units (IMUs). The measured data is then used for reproducing the cleaning motion with computer models consisting of the digital human model (DHM), the floor mop model, and the environment model, including the floors, walls, and furniture. In this system, the measured motions of the cleaner and the mop are transferred to the DHM and the mop model immediately. The swept area on the floor is estimated by computing the proximity between the mop and floor, while the torso flexion angles are obtained from the link structure inside the DHM. In the feedback of SF and MF, the swept area and the torso flexion angles are converted into the vibro-tactile signals. In the feedback of VF, the swept area is visualized and shown to the cleaner through a display in the living laboratory. The details of the measurement and feedback system are described in the following subsections.

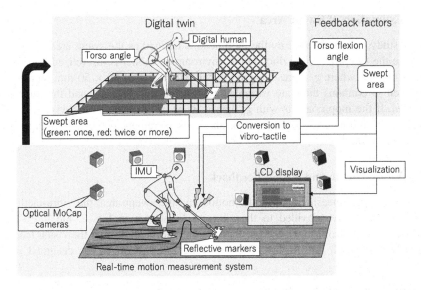

Fig. 1. Overview of the floor cleaning measurement and feedback system

2.2   Full-Body and Mop Motion Measurement

Before the experiment, an individual digital human model is created from the body height and weight of the cleaner, referring to the Japanese body size database [5]. At the beginning of the experiment, 15 IMUs are attached to the pelvis, back, head, and both sides of upper arms, lower arms, hands, upper legs, lower legs, and feet. During the cleaning task, the full-body motion of the cleaner is measured by our IMU-based MoCap system [6], where all joint angles are computed in real-time from the orientation data and the individual DHM.

As shown in Fig. 2, the motion of the mop is measured by combing the optical MoCap with IMUs attached to the mop. The position and orientation of the mop head are determined from the three reflective markers attached to the head using the optical MoCap. The orientation of the mop handle is obtained from the orientation data of the IMU attached to the handle. The position of the handle is determined from the head position since the handle is connected to the head in the middle.

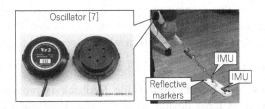

Fig. 2. Sensors and oscillator attached on the sheet-type mop

2.3   Estimation of Swept Area

In this study, the area swept by the mop head is defined as the swept area. In order to estimate the swept area, the floor in the environment model is discretized into the 2D grid $G = \{g_i\}$, where g_i represents the i th cell with a size of 50×50 mm on the floor. Each cell g_i contains the state variable $s_i \in \{$"Contact", "Free"$\}$ and the number of swept n_i. If the mop contacts with g_i then s_i is set to "Contact", otherwise s_i is set to "Free". The initial value of n_i is zero, and n_i is incremented when s_i changes from "Free" to "Contact".

2.4   Vibro-Tactile and Visual Feedback

According to the measured full-body motion and the swept area, the vibro-tactile and visual feedback are provided to the cleaner. As shown in Fig. 2, the vibro-tactile feedback is provided through the oscillator on the mop handle, and the visual feedback is provided through the display. The following three feedback are designed in this study.

(a) *Swept-count feedback (SF).*

In the feedback of SF, the vibro-tactile feedback is provided to the cleaner according to the number of sweeping n_i at the current mop position. In particular, the degree of the oscillation $d_o \in [0, 100]$ decreases logarithmically, 100, 10, and 0 with the increase of the number of sweeping n_i as formulated below.

$$s = \min_{i \in C} n_i, \tag{1}$$

$$d_o = \begin{cases} 10^{2-s} & (s < 2) \\ 0 & (otherwise) \end{cases}, \tag{2}$$

where C represents the indices of the cell in which $s_i =$ "Contact". If the current sweeping area has not been swept, the feedback with the maximum oscillation is provided to the cleaner. In contrast, no vibro-tactile feedback is provided when the current area has been swept more than twice.

(b) *Visual feedback (VF).*

In the feedback of VF, the swept area is visualized on the display, as shown in Fig. 1. On this display, the cleaning environment model is rendered with G from the top. According to n_i, each cell g_i is colorized on the floor model. The color of g_i was set to transparent (no color) when $n_i = 0$, green when $n_i = 1$, and red when $n_i \geq 2$.

(c) *Motion feedback (MF).*

In the feedback of MF, the vibro-tactile feedback is provided to the cleaner according to the current torso flexion angle θ_t. The degree of the oscillation $d_o \in [0, 100]$ increases logarithmically, continuously from 0 to 100, with the increase of the torso flexion angle as formulated below.

$$d_o = \begin{cases} 10^{2(\theta_t-\theta_{min})/(\theta_{max}-\theta_{min})} & (\theta_{min} \leq \theta_t \leq \theta_{max}) \\ 0 & (\theta_t < \theta_{min}) \\ 100 & (\theta_t > \theta_{max}) \end{cases}, \tag{3}$$

where θ_{min} and θ_{max} represent the predefined range of motion. We set θ_{min} and θ_{max} to 10 and 50 degrees, respectively. This feedback is designed to prevent the cleaner from the high physical load on the torso during the cleaning,

3 Experiment

We conducted the floor cleaning experiment in our living laboratory with eight males (age: 40.3 ± 10.6) and eight females (age: 38.4 ± 11.3). Figure 3 shows the experimental environment and the target area of the cleaning. In order to measure the mop motion, 16 MoCap cameras (OptiTrack, Prime 13 [8]) were arranged in the environment. Adhesive tape surrounding the target area was used to indicate the area to be cleaned. The participants were asked to clean the target area using a sheet-type mop from the given starting point. They were also asked to stop the cleaning when they thought they completed the task based on their judgment. Note that the order of the cleaning area and the number of sweeping were not restricted.

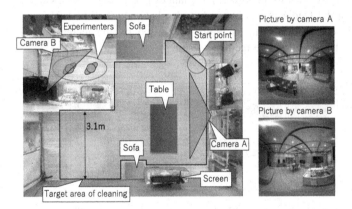

Fig. 3. Experimental environment and the target area of cleaning

Three trials were measured for each participant. In each trial, the participant performed the cleaning task with one of the three feedback (SF, VF, or MF) in random order. Also, two trials without the feedback were measured before (NFF: No feedback at first) and after (NFL: No feedback at last) measuring three feedback conditions. At the beginning of each trial, 16 IMUs (Xsens, MTw [9]) were attached to the participant using elastic belts [6]. Figure 4 shows the results of the cleaning task measurement. As shown in the figure, the full-body motion, the motion of the mop, and the swept area were estimated during the cleaning task. The completion time of the cleaning task T_C

was 108 s on average, with the shortest and longest time of 56 s and 174 s, respectively. The experiment was approved by the ethical review board of our institute.

Fig. 4. Results of the cleaning task measurement

4 Results and Discussions

4.1 Effect on Mop Movement

Figure 5 shows an example of the measured mop motions during different feedback conditions. As shown in the figure, the changes in the mop motions were observed not only among the feedback conditions but also between the two trials without feedback (NFF and NFL). Such changes might be caused by the increase in cleaning skills through trials as well as the feedback itself.

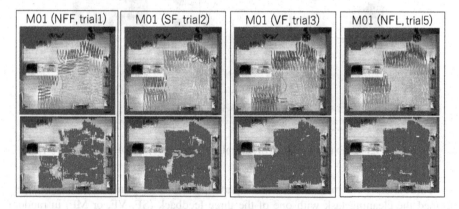

Fig. 5. Example of the changes in the mop motions during different feedback

4.2 Effect on Cleaning Task

Figure 6 shows the average and standard deviation of the swept areas A_1 and A_2 whose number of swept was once and twice, respectively, and the task completion speed $S_2 = A_2/T_C$ in each feedback condition. A_1 and A_2 were calculated as follows.

$$A_1 = 100 \frac{|\{g_i | g_i \in G \wedge n_i = 1\}|}{N_T}, \tag{4}$$

$$A_2 = 100 \frac{|\{g_i | g_i \in G \wedge n_i \geq 2\}|}{N_T}, \tag{5}$$

where N_T represents the number of cells in the cleaning target area.

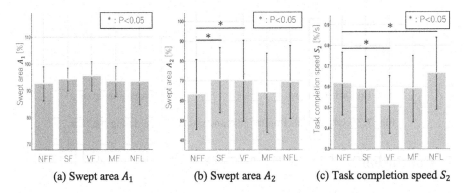

(a) Swept area A_1 (b) Swept area A_2 (c) Task completion speed S_2

Fig. 6. Feedback effect on the cleaning task

In Fig. 6, significant differences between the NFF and each of other conditions (SF, VF, MF, and NFL) were calculated. As shown in Fig. 6(a), there were no significant differences in A_1. This is because A_1 was sufficiently high ($A_1 > 90\%$) even without the feedback. In contrast, as shown in Fig. 6(b), the significant differences in A_2 were confirmed for the SF and the VF. This indicates that the feedback according to the swept area increased the completeness of the cleaning task. On the other hand, the task completion speed S_2 significantly increased in the NFL while it decreased in the VF. The increase in the NFL might be affected by the increase in cleaning skills and familiarity with the environment. In the VF, the task completion speed S_2 decreased since the cleaner looked at the display to check the progress of the cleaning during the task. Thus, it is concluded that the VF has a positive effect on the cleaning completeness, while it has the opposite effect on the task completion speed.

4.3 Effect on Human Motion

Figure 7 shows the maximum torso flexion angle during the cleaning. We divided the participants into two groups, *flexion* (six males and six females) and *extension* (two males and two females), whose torso flexion angle increases or decreases in the MF from the NFF, respectively. In the flexion group, a significant difference was observed between the NFF and MF. However, the increase in the torso flexion angle was not large (approximately 5 degrees on average). In contrast, in the extension group, we observed a considerable decrease (approximately 16 degrees) between the NFF and MF. No significant difference was observed in the extension group due to the small number of participants in this group. Although the tendency of the feedback effect was differed among individuals, our results indicated that the MF facilitates the change in the body posture of the cleaner.

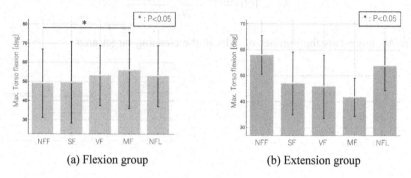

(a) Flexion group   (b) Extension group

Fig. 7. Feedback effect on the maximum torso angle during the task

5   Conclusion

In this study, we developed a real-time measurement and feedback system for floor cleaning using a sheet-type mop. The cleaning experiment was conducted for analyzing the effect of feedback on the efficiency of the cleaning and motion of both full-body and floor mop. As a result, the feedback according to the number of sweeping (SF and VF) changed the efficiency of the cleaning and motion of the mop. In addition, the tendency of the feedback effect of the MF was differed among individuals. However, it facilitated the change in the body posture of the cleaner. Our results indicated the potential of the real-time feedback for improving the efficiency of the cleaning and the body posture of the cleaner.

The developed measurement system required the optical MoCap and 16 IMUs, which make it impossible to apply this system to a real daily-living environment. Our future work will be addressed to develop the measurement and feedback systems using a small number of sensors attached to the mop.

References

1. Higuchi, T., Enomoto, T., Tada, M.: Study of physical load for a floor cleaning motion. In: Proceedings of JSME Annual Conference on Robotics and Mechatronics (Robomec), #1P1-P09 (2017). [In Japanese]. https://doi.org/10.1299/jsmermd.2017.1p1-p09
2. Lim, D., Cho, Y.K., Choi, H.H., et al.: Evaluation of loads imposed on muscles and joints by repeated vacuum cleaning works for estimation of a potentiality of musculo-skeletal disorder occurrence. J. Precis. Eng. Manuf. **13**, 429–438 (2012). https://doi.org/10.1007/s12541-012-0055-x

3. Wallius, M.A., Rissanen, S.M., Bragge, T., et al.: Effects of mop handle height on shoulder muscle activity and perceived exertion during floor mopping using a figure eight method. J. Ind. Health **54**(1), 58–67 (2015). https://doi.org/10.2486/indhealth.2015-0108
4. Makabe, R., Ito, K., Maruyama, T., Miyata, N., Tada, M., Ohkura, M.: Development and evaluation of gamified multimodal system to improve experience value of floor wiping. In: Stephanidis, C. (ed.) HCII 2019. CCIS, vol. 1032, pp. 371–377. Springer, Cham (2019). https://doi.org/10.1007/978-3-030-23522-2_48
5. Endo, Y., Tada, M., Mochimaru, M.: Dhaiba: development of virtual ergonomic assessment system with human models. In: Proceedings of Digital Human Modeling 2014, #58 (2014)
6. Maruyama, T., Tada, M., Toda, H.: Riding motion capture system using inertial measurement units with contact constraints. J. Autom. Technol. **13**(5), 506–516 (2019). https://doi.org/10.20965/ijat.2019.p0506
7. VIBRO TRANSDUCERS Vp2. https://www.acouve-lab.com/products. Accessed 03 Apr 2020
8. OptiTrack Prime X13. https://optitrack.com/products/primex-13/. Accessed 03 Apr 2020
9. Xsens MTw Awinda. https://www.xsens.com/products/mtw-awinda. Accessed 03 Apr 2020

Analysis of Conducting Waves Using Multi-channel Surface EMG Based on Difference in the Electrode Shape

Kohei Okura[✉], Marzieh Aliabadi Farahani, Yu Matsumoto,
Kazuyuki Mito, Tota Mizuno, and Naoaki Itakura

The University of Electro-Communications,
1-5-1 Chofugaoka, Chofu, Tokyo, Japan
italab2019ok@gmail.com

Abstract. Surface electromyography (EMG) is the recording of the interference of action potentials produced by some of the motor units of a muscle. If the composition of the interference wave can be analyzed, a more detailed mechanism of muscle contraction may be elucidated. Therefore, we proposed a multi-channel method, extracted all the conducting waves that existed in the surface EMG, and examined the characteristics of each conducting wave. Consequently, we can consider the detailed mechanism of muscle contraction. In previously conducted research, two types of array electrodes with different sizes were used, and different characteristics of conduction waves were obtained. This can be attributed to the following three factors: size of electrode, time of measurement, and location of attachment. In this study, we proposed a new array electrode and used it in the experiment to consider the difference in the characteristics of the conducting wave obtained. Accordingly, the maximal voluntary contraction (100% MVC) of muscle was measured. Thereafter, the myoelectric potential data were acquired while maintaining the load at 10% MVC and 40% MVC for 30 s. The analysis was performed using the multi-channel method. The experimental results showed that when increasing the electrode size, the number of conducting waves also increased. Although the number of conducting waves was small with a small electrode, it was observed that conducting waves of various patterns could be obtained and more details regarding the muscle contraction could be considered.

Keywords: Surface electromyogram (EMG) · Interference wave · Multi-channel method

1 Introduction

The action potential of the muscle fibers that constitute a skeletal muscle is generated via chemical action at the neuromuscular junction, and it propagates along the muscle fiber from the neuromuscular junction to the tendons at both ends. The conduction velocity of the action potential is called the muscle fiber conduction velocity. It is derived via surface electromyography (EMG) by using methods such as cross-correlation method. Notably, the waveform obtained from the surface EMG is not the

C. Stephanidis and M. Antona (Eds.): HCII 2020, CCIS 1224, pp. 270–276, 2020.
https://doi.org/10.1007/978-3-030-50726-8_35

action potential of a single motor unit but the interference potential of multiple motor units. Therefore, if we pay attention to the waveform shape propagating over multiple channels, a new index different from the propagation velocity will be derived.

Kosuge et al. [1] studied a method of quantitatively determining the conduction wave obtained from a multi-channel surface electromyogram (hereinafter, the method is referred to as the m-channel method) and a method of calculating the conditions and conduction velocity. All the propagating waves were extracted from the surface EMG waveforms using the array electrodes by the m-channel method, and the characteristics of each propagating wave, such as propagation velocity, amplitude, wavelength, etc., were examined. From the results, it became possible to consider a more detailed muscle contraction mechanism.

In a previously conducted study by Kawagoe et al. [2], experiments were performed using an array electrode with large ground area and a cross electrode with small area, and the relative frequency distributions of the amplitude and velocity of the conducting waves differed along the same direction. From these results, the aforementioned difference might be attributed to the following three factors: the difference in the electrode area, difference in the measurement time, and difference in the position of the paste. Therefore, a new electrode, as depicted in Fig. 1, was proposed. The feature of the proposed electrode is that pure silver wire with a diameter of 1 mm and length of 10 mm and circular pure silver wire with a diameter of 1 mm are alternately arranged in a line at 8 mm intervals at 5 mm intervals. By using this electrode, three causes can be investigated.

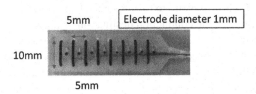

Fig. 1. Proposed electrode

In this study, we aim to perform measurements using both the m-channel method and proposed electrode. We also consider the differences in the characteristics of the conducting waves obtained because of the differences in the electrode shape and muscle contraction state.

2 Methods

2.1 Experimental Method

The test subjects comprised six healthy adult males and one female, and the test muscles were the biceps of the dominant arm, which was self-reported by the test subjects. Each subjects held the elbow joint angle at 90° in the sitting position, following which we measured the maximum exertion muscle strength (100% MVC).

Subsequently, the same posture was maintained for 30 s with a load of 10% MVC and 40% MVC, respectively, and the surface EMG data were acquired. In addition, considering the muscle fatigue between trials, we took sufficient breaks and performed the measurements multiple times.

The proposed electrode was used to derive the surface EMG data. The sampling frequency in the experiment was 5 kHz. In addition, the amplifier settings were as follows: High Cut of 1 kHz, Low Cut of 5 Hz, and amplification factor of 80 dB (Fig. 2).

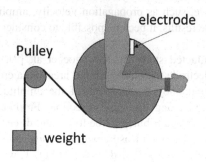

Fig. 2. Experimental protocol

2.2   Analysis Method

The m-channel method was used to perform the analysis. In the method, one of the two adjacent electrodes, both of which are of the same shape, is defined as the conduction source and the other one as the conduction destination. The section where zero crossing occurs twice from the source is extracted as one waveform. We then determined whether the signal had propagated over multiple channels and then calculate the conduction speed. While performing the conduction judgment, one waveform obtained from the conduction source is used as the conduction-wave candidate, and the conduction wave candidate of the conduction destination existing 10 ms before and after the start point of the conduction wave candidate of the conduction source is extracted. Subsequently, to calculate even the waveforms with different wavelengths, the conduction-wave candidates were resampled using the sampling theorem, and the similarity ratio, amplitude ratio, and wavelength ratio were calculated.

While identifying a conduction wave over multiple channels, thresholds are decided for the similarity ratio, amplitude ratio, and wavelength ratio based on the idea that if the waveform shapes between adjacent channels are similar, then the action potential must have propagated between both the channels. Subsequently, when the conduction-wave candidate is equal to or greater than the threshold, it is determined as a conduction wave. The conduction speed is defined as the time difference Δt between channels, and it is obtained by dividing the distance between channels (5 mm) by Δt. In addition, the conduction-velocity-variation coefficient (hereinafter, referred to as CV) is used as a conduction-determination condition to consider the velocity variable of the waveform for which conduction is determined. In this study, the conduction judgment conditions were as follows: the similarity ratio and the wavelength ratio of 0.9 or higher, the amplitude ratio of 0.7 or higher, and CV was 30% or less. Only the conduction waves over three channels were extracted and used for analysis.

3 Result

3.1 Relative Frequency Distribution and the Number of Conducting Waves

To compare the conduction wave obtained using the analysis method with the relative frequency distribution of the amplitude and conduction velocity for each electrode, the total number of conduction waves was set to 100%, and the ratio of the amplitude to conduction velocity was calculated. The results for subject A are depicted in Fig. 3.

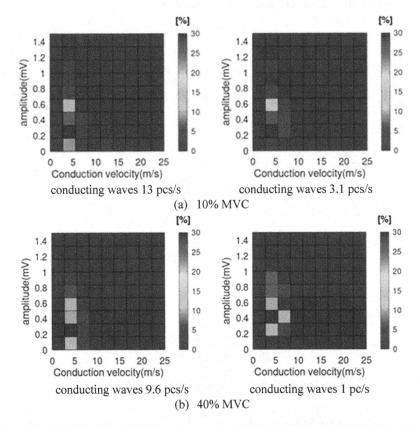

Fig. 3. Relative frequency distribution for Subject A (left column: results for a rectangular electrode; right: results for a circular electrode)

The figure shows that the number of conduction waves obtained using the rectangular electrode is greater than those obtained using the circular electrode, for both the loads. A similar distribution was observed when the load was 10% MVC. In addition, when the load was 40% MVC, more conduction waves with the conduction velocity of 5–7.5 m/s were extracted with a circular electrode, compared with a rectangular electrode, and the amplitude of the conduction wave with the conduction velocity of 2.5–7.5 m/s was observed.

3.2   EMG Data

The myoelectric data obtained for Subject A are depicted in Fig. 4. A comparison of the propagation waves obtained simultaneously using both the types of electrodes showed that the values of amplitude, muscle fiber conduction velocity, and wavelength were almost the same. However, comparing the propagation waveforms, a smooth waveform was observed in each channel with the rectangular electrode, whereas a non-smooth waveform was observed with the circular electrode.

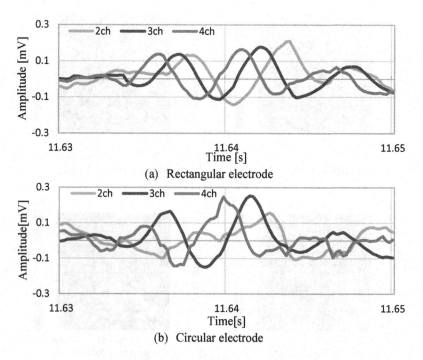

(a) Rectangular electrode

(b) Circular electrode

Fig. 4. Raw data for Subject A (10% MVC)

The EMG data for Subject D obtained with the circular electrode are depicted in Fig. 5. The muscle fiber conduction velocity of the conducting waves obtained from the EMG data was 1 m/s, and this phenomenon was also observed in each of the cases of Subjects E, F, and G.

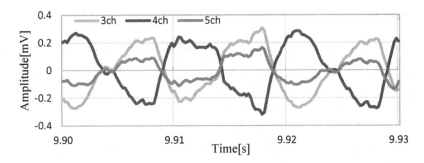

Fig. 5. Raw data obtained with the circular electrode (10% MVC, Subject D)

4 Discussion

4.1 Relative Frequency Distribution and the Number of Conducting Waves

It is considered that the extraction of the propagating wave was easier in the case of the rectangular electrode because more muscle fibers interfered and averaged when compared to the circular electrode. In addition, the muscle activity can be considered in more detail because the circular electrode extracted propagation waves with various propagation speeds compared with the rectangular one.

4.2 EMG Data

In Fig. 4, the interference potential might be attributed a large number of muscle fibers in the case of the rectangular electrode. However, in the case of the circular electrode, the interference potential is attributed to the small number of muscle fibers.

In Fig. 5, the conduction wave obtained from the EMG data cannot consider the muscle activity, and the reason for this is the AC noise (hum).

5 Conclusion

In this study, we examined the differences in the characteristics of the conducting waves obtained based on the difference in the electrode shape and muscle contraction state. Consequently, it became clear that the extraction of the conducting waves was easy because the number of conducting waves obtained with the rectangular electrode was large. However, it also became clear that a more detailed muscle activity could be considered with the circular electrode. In the future, measurements will be continued, and the shape of electrodes will be studied.

References

1. Kosuge, T., Itakura, N., Mito, K.: Conducting waves using multi-channel surface EMG. IEEJ Trans. **C134**(3), 390–397 (2014)
2. Kawagoe, K., Akehi, K., Farahani, M.A., Itakura, N., Mizuno, T., Mito, K.: Estimation of muscle fiber direction from conducting waves pattern using multi-channel surface EMG. In: IEEE 2nd Student Research Conference 2018 (2018)

In-Air Gesture Interaction
Using Ultra Wide Camera

Vyacheslav Olshevsky$^{(\boxtimes)}$ (iD), Ivan Bondarets (iD),
Oleksandr Trunov (iD), Artem Shcherbina (iD),
and Svitlana Alkhimova (iD)

Samsung R&D Institute Ukraine (SRK),
57, Lva Tolstogo Str., Kyiv 01032, Ukraine
{v.olshevskyi, i.bondarets, o.trunov,
a.shcherbina, s.alkhimova}@samsung.com

Abstract. We investigate whether the region of hand gesture interaction with AR glasses can be expanded using a regular camera. We measure the accuracy of gesture recognition in the images obtained by two conventional cameras: wide-angle and ultra-wide angle. For both of them, gestures, typically used in AR scenarios such as pinch, palm, pointer, and grab, are recognized with >90% accuracy. The accuracy improves on the periphery of the ultra-wide camera field of view. A usability study confirms that performing gestures in the periphery of the ultra-wide camera view is as convenient, as in its center. Two gestures, zoom and swipe, are distinctively more convenient when made in the peripheral zone. Our findings pave the way for expanding the region of hand gesture interaction with AR glasses using purely computer vision-based techniques.

Keywords: Hand gesture recognition · Machine learning · Augmented reality

1 Introduction

Augmented (AR) applications are ubiquitous in various fields of human activity, from gaming and entertainment to professional training and industrial work support. AR consists in immersing computer-generated content into the objective footage of the real world shown to the user. Head-mounted wearables such as AR glasses (smart glasses) are especially practical for technical and industrial workers, as they can provide user assistance while leaving both hands free for real-world tasks [1]. Since conventional touch/keyboard user interaction is unavailable in AR glasses, vendors have adopted other input methods. Popular wearables, Microsoft HoloLens 2 and Magic Leap One provide hand gesture (HG) interaction using depth cameras and motion sensors [2, 3]. They employ a variety of gestures, including static gestures, also known as hand poses, and dynamic gestures. The region of space where these wearables are sensitive to gestures, the so called gesture frame, is limited. Gesture frame of Microsoft HoloLens 2 spans from nose to waist and between user's shoulders [4], restricting user interaction capabilities on the sides. User's hands may also obscure the content shown in the AR display, therefore expanding the gesture frame is useful for extending AR glasses applications area.

© Springer Nature Switzerland AG 2020
C. Stephanidis and M. Antona (Eds.): HCII 2020, CCIS 1224, pp. 277–284, 2020.
https://doi.org/10.1007/978-3-030-50726-8_36

We investigate whether the gesture frame can be expanded by using just a regular camera with a wide field of view (FOV). Figure 1 illustrates the difference between FOVs of two conventional cameras used in mobile devices, the ultra-wide angle (UWA) camera (left) and a wide-angle (WA) camera. The FOV of the latter, depicted with a red rectangle in the UWA camera picture, is slightly wider than the FOV of modern AR glasses. Notably, the HGs captured in a broad area on the sides of the UWA camera image would not obscure the content in the AR display.

Fig. 1. a) Example image obtained from the UWA camera. Red rectangle denotes the respective FOV of the WA camera. b) Example image obtained from the WA camera. (Color figure online)

Previous studies have found that information from AR glasses cameras can be used for hazard warning [5] and navigation [6]. The feasibility of camera-based gesture control on a mobile device was demonstrated already five years ago [7]. Since then, versatility and accuracy of computer vision-based HG recognition algorithms have substantially improved. Modern HG recognition methods achieve 90% and better precision in recognizing hand gestures used for human-computer interaction [8]. In the first part of our study we measure the recognition accuracy for gestures typically used in AR scenarios for navigation and manipulation. We compare the accuracy measured in two zones of the WA and UWA camera FOVs, central and peripheral. Finally, we study whether HGs made in the peripheral zones of the UWA camera are convenient for users.

2 Methodology

Typical AR tasks consist in manipulation of virtual objects: grabbing, zooming, rotating, etc., and interaction with user interface (UI): pointing, selecting, swapping, etc. [1, 9, 10]. We investigate whether these gestures can be comfortably performed and accurately recognized in the center of UWA and WA camera FOVs, as well as on their periphery. Therefore, our study is twofold: to estimate the precision of HG recognition and to find out whether gestures performed on the periphery of the UWA camera FOV are convenient for users. In our experiments, the WA and UWA cameras are represented by the Samsung Wide-angle Camera and Ultra Wide Camera of the Galaxy S10

5G smartphone, correspondingly. Their properties are listed in Table 1. As the FOV of the UWA camera is almost twice wider, user's hand appears about twice smaller in size in the UWA camera as compared to the WA camera (Fig. 1).

Table 1. Camera characteristics.

Camera name	Abbreviation	Horizontal FOV	Pixel Size (μm)	Aperture
12MP Wide-angle Camera	WA	64°	1.4	F1.5
16MP Ultra Wide Camera	UWA	105°	1.0	F2.2

2.1 Gesture Recognition Solution

In the current study we use our in-house HG recognition solution which can effectively detect, track, and recover hand skeleton and segmentation of two hands in real time on off-the-shelf smartphones. The detection is performed by a deep convolutional neural network (CNN) resembling the single-shot detector architecture [11]. The locations of 21 hand joints in the 2D frame, predicted using a modified convolutional pose machines algorithm [12], are used to reconstruct 3D hand skeleton as proposed in [13]. A dedicated CNN with upsampling layers derives a hand segmentation map. Hand pose recognition is made through a set of empirically detected rules applied to the relative positions and orientations of the hand joints. Such implementation, potentially, allows to define any custom hand pose or dynamic gesture.

2.2 Gesture Recognition Accuracy Measurements

As we focus on practical usage of HGs, we ask users to perform gestures in front of the camera and measure how accurately each hand pose is recognized in the pictures. Each dynamic gesture is essentially a continuous sequence of hand poses, therefore in this experiment we consider the following hand poses, commonly used by AR devices:

1. 'Pinch' formed by the thumb and the index finger as employed by HoloLens.
2. 'Grab' – essentially a pinch formed by the thumb and any other finger(s).
3. 'Palm Front' – palm facing the user, resembling the HoloLens Start gesture.
4. 'Palm Back' – palm directed away from the user, resembling the HoloLens 'hand ray'.
5. 'Pointer' – the index finger pointed up and into the scene, corresponding to Magic Leap One's Point gesture.

We asked 15 volunteers (3 females) aged 24–51 years (32 on average) to perform these five gestures in front of the smartphone cameras. The smartphone was mounted on a tripod so that participants saw its screen and were able to comfortably position their hands in the camera FOV. Users showed gestures in the center of the camera FOV and moved their hands to the side until the edge of the FOV. To exclude possible dependence of HG recognition accuracy on the distance to the camera, each user did the above procedure first with his/her hand closer to the camera, and then farther from the camera. Images were recorded and processed one-by-one using our HG recognition solution. The examples of images captured by two cameras are shown in Fig. 1. For generality, gestures were filmed on different backgrounds, such as street views, painted walls, office equipment, etc.

2.3 Usability Study

It is natural to assume that showing gestures in front of the camera is more intuitive, thus more convenient for users. Hands shown in the center of the camera FOV, however, might obscure visual content in the AR display. Certain operations, like page flipping or panning, do not necessarily require seeing the hands, and can be triggered by HGs made in the periphery of the camera FOV. We conduct a dedicated usability study to find out which gestures are convenient for the users when performed in the peripheral zones of the FOV.

Miscellaneous factors, including user's habits, skills and physique, define the degree of convenience of gestures shown in different regions with respect to the head-mounted camera. Some users gesticulate with elevated arms, while others are more comfortable with keeping them low. Some prefer showing HGs in the center of the gesture frame, while some make broad hand waives. The latter, horizontal, expansion of the gesture frame is especially important, as continuous raising or lowering hands is exhausting in the work assistance scenarios. Therefore, we address the dependence of gesture convenience on the horizontal distance to the center of the FOV.

Seventeen volunteers (4 females) aged 23–40 years (30 on average) took part in the usability study. The experiment is set up with the smartphone mounted at the height of user's forehead mimicking the location of the AR glasses camera (Fig. 2). The smartphone is installed in front of the whiteboard which has a special markup to control the hand position in the camera FOV. As most interaction with virtual objects in AR happens at the reach of user's hand, the distance to the whiteboard is adjusted to the participant's total arm length. It allows free gesticulation in front of the whiteboard and offers more accurate hand position control.

Fig. 2. Schematic depiction of the usability study setup. (Color figure online)

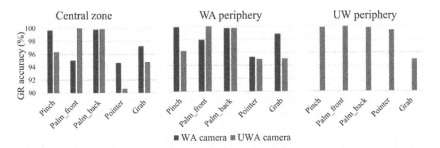

Fig. 3. HG recognition accuracy averaged over three zones.

Participants were asked to show 5 hand poses and 5 dynamic gestures. In addition to the five hand poses described above, we include the following dynamic gestures:

1. 'Finger Push' – resembles a button push made with the index finger.
2. 'Palm Push' – a button push made with the whole palm.
3. 'Zoom' – performed with two hands in the 'Pinch' poses.
4. 'Palm Zoom' – the palm moves back and front to imitate zooming in/out.
5. 'Swipe' – a conventional page swipe made with the whole hand.

In this study the central zone was bound by the horizontal FOV of the WA camera, while the peripheral zones on both sides were only visible to the UWA camera. Two pairs of lines on the whiteboard marked the FOVs of the WA camera (green) and the UWA camera (blue). The central zone, thus, was bound by the green lines, and the periphery was on either side of the center, bound between the adjacent pairs of green and blue lines. Assistants used the whiteboard markup to guide participants, as, by design, they were unable to see the smartphone screen (Fig. 2). Participants were asked to perform the requested gestures in the most convenient way and evaluate which zone, central or peripheral, was more comfortable to perform each gesture.

3 Results

3.1 Gesture Recognition Accuracy Measurements

The HG recognition accuracy is computed as the fraction of the number of correct predictions of the hand pose to the total number of frames with this pose. During the experiment, 7000 images of each of the five hand poses were collected by each camera. Recognition accuracy averaged over hands detected in three zones: center, WA periphery and UWA periphery is summarized in Fig. 3. Zone extents are defined with respect to the average hand width W, computed over all collected images from 2 cameras. We have found $W_{WA} = 200$ and $W_{UWA} = 128$ pixels for the WA and UWA cameras, respectively. The central zone spans for $1.5W_{\{WA;UW\}}$ on both sides of the FOV center; the WA and UWA peripheries are $1.5W_{\{WA;UW\}}$ wide bands adjacent to the edges of the corresponding camera FOV.

Pinch is correctly predicted in 99.5% cases in the WA camera images. Recognition accuracy of Pinch in the UWA periphery is as good, but degrades to 95% in two inner zones. Several hand joints appear obscured in the Pinch pose which makes it harder to reconstruct the hand skeleton. However, as the hand moves towards UWA periphery, more joints are revealed, and it gets easier for the HG recognition algorithm to predict the pose. Perfect recognition by the WA camera is attributed to a larger hand image, which provides more information to the HG recognition algorithm and makes hand skeleton reconstruction easier even in the FOV center.

Both Palm Front and Palm Back are detected with >98% accuracy in all zones with one exception. The accuracy of Palm Front recognition in the center of WA images is slightly worse, 95%. Examination of the collected images from WA suggests that Palm Front misdetections happen in the pictures where the hand is too large and does not fit in the picture. Apparently, for many users it has been more comfortable to show this pose rather close to the camera. Notably, UWA camera does not suffer from this problem and the recognition of both Palm poses is superb in all zones.

Although Pointer is the worst recognized hand pose in our experiment, its recognition accuracy is still very good, 94–95% and 90–95% for the WA and UWA cameras, respectively. In the Pointer pose, as well as in Pinch and Grab, multiple hand joints are obscured, making hand skeleton reconstruction more difficult. Pinch recognition accuracy in the UWA images is better in the peripheral zones, where more hand joints are visible.

The Grab hand pose is defined less strictly than Pinch and Pointer. For instance, we allow it to be shown with two or more fingers. Therefore, its recognition accuracy does not suffer as much from obscured joints as much as Pinch and Pointer. Grab is correctly predicted in 95% of images from the UWA camera, and in 97–99% of WA images.

To summarize, the recognition accuracy of the five considered hand poses is better than 90% in all parts of the WA and UWA camera FOV. The accuracy is better on the periphery where more hand joints are visible to the camera. In the UWA camera periphery Grab is recognized in the 95% of images, while four gestures (Pinch, Palm Front, Palm Back, Pointer) exhibit an excellent 99% accuracy.

3.2 Usability Study

Users assessed the level of convenience of each gesture on the scale from −3 (more comfortable in the central zone) to +3 (more comfortable on the periphery). The scores spread broadly (Fig. 4), confirming that gesticulation preferences are very individual and depend on many factors. For some gestures, however, the median score was negative. Users showed more inclination to perform 4 out of 10 gestures in the central zone: Palm Front, Pinch, Palm Back, and Finger Push. The periphery is slightly more preferred for Palm Push, Palm Zoom, Grab and Point. However, for all these 8 gestures the median is rather close to zero, which allows to conclude that expanding the gesture frame to the periphery would not cause much discomfort.

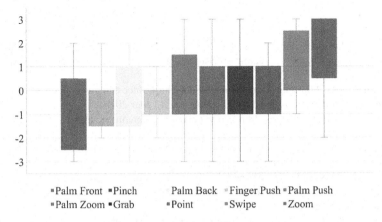

Fig. 4. Results of the usability study.

For two gestures, Zoom and Swipe, users showed a clear preference towards the peripheral zone of the UWA camera FOV. Both gestures are quite intuitive and span a wide body angle, hence gesture frame expansion is beneficial for them. Besides, expanded gesture frame allows for a smoother and more precise Zoom and allows Swipe to be shown solely in the periphery where it is non-obscuring.

4   Conclusions

Five hand poses, typically used for gesture interaction with AR glasses, are correctly recognized in the 90% of frames obtained from conventional WA and UWA cameras. Recognition is harder for the poses in which multiple hand joints are obscured, such as Pointer and Grab. However, when these gestures are shown on the periphery of the UWA camera, the accuracy improves because more joints are revealed. In the periphery of the UWA camera FOV, the recognition precision is 99% for four out of five hand poses. Therefore, the gesture frame can be effectively expanded using the UWA camera.

The usability study addressed five hand poses accompanied by five dynamic gestures, commonly used in AR glasses. For eight out of ten gestures, no strong preference was found towards the central or peripheral zone of the UWA camera FOV. The periphery, however, was more convenient for making Zoom and Swipe gestures.

Our findings show that expansion of the gesture frame using a UW camera is beneficial for the precision and convenience of user interaction with AR glasses.

References

1. Kim, M., Choi, S.H., Park, K.-B., Lee, J.Y.: User interactions for augmented reality smart glasses: a comparative evaluation of visual contexts and interaction gestures. Appl. Sci. **9**(15), 3171 (2019)
2. Microsoft Docs: Multimodal interaction models. https://docs.microsoft.com/en-us/windows/mixed-reality/interaction-fundamentals. Accessed 13 Mar 2020
3. Magic Leap: Magic Leap 1. https://www.magicleap.com/magic-leap-1. Accessed 13 Mar 2020
4. Microsoft Docs. Gaze and Commit. https://docs.microsoft.com/en-us/windows/mixed-reality/gaze-and-commit#composite-gestures. Accessed 13 Mar 2020
5. Younis, O., Al-Nuaimy, W., Alomari, M., Rowe, F.: A hazard detection and tracking system for people with peripheral vision loss using smart glasses and augmented reality. Int. J. Adv. Comput. Sci. Appl. **10**, 1–9 (2019)
6. Chaturvedi, I., Bijarbooneh, F.H., Braud, T., Hui, P.: Peripheral vision: a new killer app for smart glasses. In: Proceedings of the 24th International Conference on Intelligent User Interfaces, pp. 625–636, March 2019
7. Song, J., et al.: In-air gestures around unmodified mobile devices. In: Proceedings of the 27th Annual ACM Symposium on User Interface Software and Technology, pp. 319–329. Association for Computing Machinery (2014)
8. Mohammed, A.A.Q., Lv, J., Islam, M.S.: A deep learning-based end-to-end composite system for hand detection and gesture recognition. Sensors **19**(23), 5282 (2019)
9. Goh, E.S., Sunar, M.S., Ismail, A.W.: 3D object manipulation techniques in handheld mobile augmented reality interface: a review. IEEE Access **7**, 40581–40601 (2019)
10. Vuletic, T., Duffy, A., Hay, L., McTeague, C., Campbell, G., Grealy, M.: Systematic literature review of hand gestures used in human computer interaction interfaces. Int. J. Hum.-Comput. Stud. **129**, 74–94 (2019)
11. Liu, W., et al.: SSD: single shot multibox detector. In: Leibe, B., Matas, J., Sebe, N., Welling, M. (eds.) ECCV 2016. LNCS, vol. 9905, pp. 21–37. Springer, Cham (2016). https://doi.org/10.1007/978-3-319-46448-0_2
12. Wei, S.E., Ramakrishna, V., Kanade, T., Sheikh, Y.: Convolutional pose machines. In: Proceedings of the IEEE conference on Computer Vision and Pattern Recognition, pp. 4724–4732. IEEE (2016)
13. Panteleris, P., Oikonomidis, I., Argyros, A.: Using a single RGB frame for real time 3D hand pose estimation in the wild. In: 2018 IEEE Winter Conference on Applications of Computer Vision (WACV), pp. 436–445. IEEE (2016)

Review on Methods in Touch Tracking for Tabletop Projections

Severin Pereto[(✉)] and Doris Agotai[(✉)]

Institute for Interactive Technologies,
University of Applied Sciences and Arts Northwestern, Brugg-Windisch, Switzerland
{severin.pereto,doris.agotai}@fhnw.ch
https://www.fhnw.ch/iit

Abstract. Interactive tabletop projections overlay an interface into the spatial environment and enable new and frameless fields of interaction. The continually evolving technology has potential in several application areas. In contrast to traditional invasive technology setups such as displays, capacitive foils, or infrared grids, projected systems do not require any construction of the interaction surface. This overview intends to present the current state of the art in touch tracking methods for tabletop projections and identify the potential of such environments as a new generation of interfaces for current and future research in this emerging field. It reviews selected novel methods for touch input, using sensors, on a flat surface projection, including a timeline of selected recent work, and a summary showing the characteristics, primary strengths, and drawbacks. Methods using machine learning are promising and linked to research in mid-air fingertip recognition, as implementations using depth and infrared sensors are more sophisticated in terms of fingertip recognition and accuracy.

Keywords: Touch tracking · Tabletop projections · Human-computer interaction · Fingertip detection

1 Introduction

Unlike traditional invasive technologies, such as displays, foils, or infrared (IR) grids that are limited in detecting interactions based on an assembly, in tabletop interactions, an existing environment integrates into the field of interaction. This integration allows a high degree of freedom to incorporate elements into the environment and provides new interaction possibilities that can fundamentally change traditional user interfaces. Projections liberate us from the thought of an image format, as the physical environment offers the natural boundaries of interaction possibilities, and enables the fusion of the physical world with possibilities of interaction and projection, without invasive assemblies in the environment.

This review is on methods in multi-touch tracking with an image projection on a flat surface (e.g., table or wall) using a projection device (e.g., beamer) and

C. Stephanidis and M. Antona (Eds.): HCII 2020, CCIS 1224, pp. 285–293, 2020.
https://doi.org/10.1007/978-3-030-50726-8_37

sensors (e.g., depth sensor). One of the research topics of the Institute for Interactive Technologies at the University of Applied Sciences and Arts Northwestern lies within the scope of interactive blended projections. They have introduced "Live Paper" [5], an interactive tabletop projection-based environment based on the findings of Xiao et al. [18], to enhance user interaction scenarios. The field of tabletop projections continuously develops in terms of interaction and interface design with potential in multiple areas of application. So far, we have been limited by the lack of possibilities of existing sensors and projection technologies. We are now at a point where there is potential for further development, as new sensors and methods have been introduced.

This review intends to find out the current state of touch tracking for tabletop projections to use in future projects and tries to identify state of the art and the potential of such environments as a new generation of interfaces for current and future research in the institute. It will examine which methods are relevant to the next development steps and identify trends for future research. The main research question, "What is the current state and where lies the potential for current research?" should cover emerging trends and identify further research areas for this application. The following criteria must be fulfilled by a published paper to be included in this review:

- published between 2015–2019
- projection-based on a non-moving surface (e.g., wall and table)
- no assembly of surface needed
- multiple fingertip detection independent of the sensor angle (i.e., a fingertip behind another fingertip should be recognized if in the detection area)

It is not intended to cover the history of projection-based touch tracking. Where required, papers published before 2015 or not meeting the selection criteria can be mentioned. It emerged from a systematic overview of different methods in tabletop projections. As the selected paper do not distribute sufficient statistical data and are difficult to compare, this review excludes statistical comparisons and approaches a narrative review.

2   Overview of Interactive Tabletop Projection Methods

Table 1 shows an overview of milestones in touch tracking for tabletop projections meeting the criteria. For a more detailed summary of the history of projected interfaces, see Xiao et al. [16].

Comparability. Unfortunately, not all methods and measurements can be compared to each other, as they use different sensors, platforms, or not all results are published. For example, Chai et al. [2] state that they could not compare their results to Xiao et al. [18], because of the limitations of the environment and sensors. Figure 1 shows the citation graph of the chosen papers revealing that Lee et al. [10] did not refer to any of the other selected papers, which makes it difficult to compare. To give an overview, Table 2 shows the primary subjective

Table 1. Timeline of selected papers meeting the selection criteria in touch tracking for tabletop projections. Above the dashed line, papers with the most references in the citation graph (see Figure 1) are listed.

2010	Wilson [14]: Using a depth camera as a touch sensor
2012	Murugappan et al. [12]: Extended Wilson [14] by connected components analysis and discarding blobs on area constraints, and introduced a method for touch-gesture detection
2016	Xiao et al. [18]: Introduces sensor fusion with a depth and infrared sensor to improve touchpoint detection
	Cadena et al. [1]: Combines infrared and depth to improve touchpoint detection. [18]
	Zhang et al. [19]: Presents a touch interface using a time-of-flight camera and a mobile projector
2017	Gregor et al. [8]: Presents a wall projected animation game using LIDAR
	Son et al. [13]: Introduces a complementary fingertip model for fingertip detection using a depth sensor
	Matsubara et al. [11]: Two infrared cameras measuring the shape of the finger shadow
2018	Chai et al. [2]: Uses a convolutional neural network to estimate the hand pose
2019	Choi et al. [4]: Introduces cascaded random forests to classify fingertips
	Gao et al. [7]: Programming a robot on an augmented surface
	Lee et al. [10]: Virtual Touch sensor with a depth camera only, using a block pattern for touchpoint detection
	Laput et al. [9]: Reintroduces LIDAR sensor technology in an IoT device to allow ubiquitous sensing
	Wu et al. [15]: Using kraft paper to interact with a projection
	Fujinawa et al. [6]: Uses a convolutional neural network to estimate the hand pose and select interaction modes

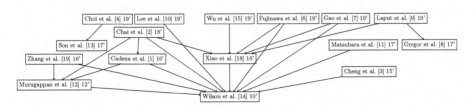

Fig. 1. Citation graph of selected papers published after 2015

Table 2. Strength and drawbacks of tabletop projection systems

Author	Characteristics	Primary strengths	Primary drawbacks
Xiao et al. [18]	– time-of-flight and infrared sensors	– high accuracy on touch-point detection [18, p. 26] – flood-fill segmentation of arm and hand [18, pp. 4–5]	– no fingertip or hand classification
Cadena et al. [1]	– depth and infrared sensors	– high accuracy in fingertip detection [1, p. 1] – fingers are not needed to be stretched to get fingertip [1, p. 2] – real-time multi-user interactions [1, p. 1]	– issues when occlusion of fingers occur [1, p. 6] – no fingertip or hand classification
Zhang et al. [19]	– time-of-flight sensor	– working distance 30 cm and over [19, p. 760] – no background calibration needed and can be moved around freely [19, p. 765]	– no results with higher working distance and top-down view
Son et al. [13]	– depth sensor – fingertip model with a cost function for fingertip detection	– effective when fingers are spread [13, p. 4]	– depends on an initial hand pose [13, p. 4] – no detection where fingers are not spread [13, p. 4]
Matsubara et al. [11]	– an infrared camera and two infrared lights processing the shadow of a finger	– detect a touch on flat and non-flat surface [11, p. 1]	– displacing if the posture of the finger is tilted [11, p. 5] – erroneous detection with higher camera distance [11, p. 5] – effect on recognition due to lens distortion [11, p. 5]
Chai et al. [2]	– structured-light sensor – deep convolutional neural network (CNN) based hand pose estimation – requires GPU	– multi-touch capable [2, p. 7] – outperforms Wilson et al. [14] "in terms of average accuracy" [2, p. 4] – estimate touchpoints based on the "hand skeleton model that is more robust to noise" [2, p. 8]	– occlusion remains a problem in hand pose estimation (hardware limitation) [2, p. 8] – hand pose estimation still needs improvement [2, p. 8]
Choi et al. [4]	– depth sensor – cascaded random forests for detection and classification of thumb and index fingertips – score function to classify or reject fingertips	– random forests are "adequate for real-time applications with limited hardware resources" [4, p. 1497] – outperforms conventional random forest and CNN classifiers [4, p. 1487] – "... method allows the user to freely spread or fold the thumb and distinguishes fingertips of the left and right hands without relying on heuristic assumptions" [4, p. 1489]	– only index and thumb fingertip are classified [4, p. 1494] – "fail to detect candidate fingertips from a non-planar or dynamic background" [4, p. 1496] – if two hands contact each other, then not all fingertips detected [4, p. 1496] – assumes background is planar and static [4, p. 1496]
Lee et al. [10]	– depth sensor – filter with weight parameter and touch path correction	– can be used on curved surface [10, p. 12]	– no dynamic background modeling [10, p. 3] – touchpoint accuracy depends on angle [10, p. 9]

(*continued*)

Table 2. (*continued*)

Author	Characteristics	Primary Strengths	Primary Drawbacks
Laput et al. [9]	– LIDAR sensor integrated into a device – object classification (including touch input) based on contour using nearest neighbor and random forest classifier	– works best on level surfaces [9, p. 9] – recognizes ten static hand poses [9, p. 4] – recognizes six touch gestures [9, p. 4] – tracks body position [9, p. 10]	– decreasing single finger input recognition at longer distances [9, p. 7] – unable to detect objects that do not reflect infrared [9, p. 10]
Fujinawa et al. [6]	– depth sensor – CNN-based hand pose estimation to select interaction modes	– five touch and in-air interactions [6, p. 113]	

strengths and drawbacks of selected papers with their characteristics. Fujinawa et al. [6], Gao et al. [7], Gregor et al. [8], and Wu et al. [15] published to little technical information to be included.

2.1 Review of Selected Methodical Approaches

As there are different approaches on a conceptual level (e.g., depth segmentation or hand pose estimation) but also using separate, or combining, sensors, we identify tasks in touch recognition, which also structures the following sections. Each section contains the approaches of selected papers that made notable public contributions to that topic. Touch needs to be detected (see Sect. 2.2). Such a detected touch can be associated using an approximate region (see Sect. 2.3) and reduced into a touchpoint with an accuracy, measuring the distance from the intended target point to the estimated point (see Sect. 2.4). The detected touchpoint can be associated with the left or right hand (see Sect. 2.5), or further classified with a fingertip such as a thumb, index finger, middle finger, ring finger, and little finger (see Sect. 2.6).

2.2 Touch Detection

The challenge of touch detection is sensing when a finger has physically contacted a surface [18, p. 1]. Cadena et al. [1] compare the average of the assumed touchpoint and neighboring depth values (due to noise) to a threshold above the learned background. Both Cadena et al. [1] and Xiao et al. [18] apply the hysteresis process to avoid rapid changes in the touch state. Xiao et al. [18] distinguish hovering and contact by including the neighborhood around the estimated touchpoint before comparing it to the threshold. In Lee et al. [10], the touch region is determined by comparing the average of depth values of several measurements to the initially calibrated background to reduce the noise of the touch panel and comparing them to a threshold [10, p. 4]. Lee et al. [10] apply 3x3 block patterns on the depth image values on non-background neighboring pixels, which are below a threshold, of a touch region to detect the touchpoint.

Zhang et al. [19] propose a method to determine if a fingertip contacts the surface based on a finger-modeling approach (see Sect. 2.3), comparing the depth values to the part around the fingertip.

2.3   Touch Region Detection

Touch region detection describes how the region of interest (ROI), such as hands and fingers, are extracted omitting the background. Xiao et al. [16,18] divide touch tracking systems into background and finger modeling approaches. A background modeling approach detects contact with the surface by comparing current depth values with a background map [18, pp. 2–3]. In contrast, finger modeling does not require background data because they segment fingers based on their characteristics [18, pp. 2–3].

Wilson [14] suggested a static background model, comparing the surface depth value using a minimal and maximal threshold. Also, Choi et al. [4], Son et al. [13], and Lee et al. [10] capture a static background depth image once. Such methods have been extended by Cadena et al. [1] using the arithmetic mean for each depth pixel, to calibrate the background model initially. Chai et al. [2] use the 30 first frames to build the background model and calculate a per-pixel depth-difference background histogram. Lee et al. [10] enable us to choose the method to obtain the depth values of the background between average, which is faster but could be incorrect if not enough depth values are available, and mode, which is slower because a sort is needed. Xiao et al. [18] introduced a statistical model of the background inspired by "WorldKit" [17], to enable dynamic updating, allowing changes on the projection surface. Son et al. [13] detect the ROI using thresholds and extracts the three largest connected components. Zhang et al. [19] remove static objects from the background to extract the hand blobs on the foreground image.

2.4   Touchpoint Estimation

Xiao et al. [18] and also Cadena et al. [1] are extending the depth sensor, due to its noise, with IR information to detect edge contours better. Cadena et al. [1] extracts the farthest point concerning the center of the hand, but additionally use a k-curvature algorithm to support closed fists or joined fingers and corrects the touchpoint towards the edges extracted from the IR image. Xiao et al. [18] extract the farthest point concerning the center of each finger. If this fails, forward projection using arm and hand position is used. Son et al. [13] compute the skeleton of the connected components using morphological operations, calculate the centroid, and 20 corresponding extremal points using Dijkstra's algorithm to test with an introduced complementary fingertip model and a cost function. Lee et al. [10] determine the touchpoint using a bounding box and 3×3 block patterns. The touch path is corrected using a predicted position, the measured position, and a weight parameter to solve the disadvantage of a slow response in case of a sudden change of touchpoint movement. Fujinawa et al. [6] introduce interaction modes for different hand poses. A convolutional neural network

(CNN) detects positions on the hand (e.g., fingertips, finger joints, center of palm) and obtains the position by comparing the depth value of each fingertip to the background depth, and selects an interaction mode (such as index posture) to reduce false fingertip detection. Matsubara et al. [11] propose a detection method to detect touch by the shape of the finger's shadow using two IR lights.

2.5   Arm, Hand, and Fingertip Detection

Cadena et al. [1] extracts the arm-hand contours from ROI and uses the K-means algorithm to create two clusters, to classify the area with more points inside as hand region. Xiao et al. [18] use a flood fill segmentation to form a hierarchy containing arm, hand, finger, and fingertip and reject finger-like objects. Xiao et al. [18] use only the IR edge to fill fingertips, as the fingers merge with noise, but have built a fallback to depth-only touch tracking if the IR image is unusable (e.g., holes in the edge image). Fujinawa et al. [6] distinguish hands from objects and detect positions of hand fingertips, finger joints, and the center of palm using their CNN. Zhang et al. [19] extracts the hand region using the IR and depth image and applies a modified convex hull algorithm to detect candidate fingertips on the hand contour.

2.6   Fingertip Classification

Knowing which finger triggered the touch can bring extended functionality to a user (e.g., using the thumb as an eraser). As Choi et al. [4] stated, "determining the identity of a fingertip is more difficult than detecting fingertips" [4, p. 1488]. Choi et al. [4] noted that "index fingers and thumbs are the most frequently used fingers for human-computer interaction" and classify fingertips into the (left and right) index and thumb fingertips using cascaded random forests and a score function [4, p. 1487]. Chai et al. [2] developed a deep CNN-based hand pose estimation to identify fingertips.

3   Conclusion

Concerning the main research question, "What is the current state and where lies the potential for current research?" touch tracking on tabletop projections using different sensors and methods have been reviewed. The analysis of the selected papers suggests that there is an increasing trend to use machine learning to estimate the hand posture, which looks very promising. They are closely related to mid-air recognition, an emerging area in current research, which will also provide results for touch tracking in interactive table projections. Nevertheless, implementations using background modeling are more refined in terms of fingertip recognition and accuracy. Different sensors (e.g., depth sensor, IR sensor) are used or even combined to make surfaces touchable. Since it is a challenge to select a specific method for an applied solution, a testing framework would ensure the comparability of a method in the domain of interactive tabletop projections. It would be interesting to use low-power computing devices to enable further implementations in the emerging area of the Internet of Things (IoT). New technological possibilities, such as solid-state LIDAR or radar technology, could also provide new opportunities for the application of interactive table projections. The classification of fingers and hands, but also touch gestures, can improve touch recognition and offer new functionality for touch input (e.g., use the little finger as an eraser). The combination of the mature results of sensor processing with new insights from anatomy and machine learning or even new sensors (e.g., radar) would create more accurate and functional input systems.

References

1. Cadena, A., Carvajal, R., Guaman, B., Granda, R., Pelaez, E., Chiluiza, K.: Fingertip detection approach on depth image sequences for interactive projection system. In: 2016 IEEE Ecuador Technical Chapters Meeting, ETCM 2016. pp. 1–6. Institute of Electrical and Electronics Engineers Inc. (10 2016). https://doi.org/10.1109/ETCM.2016.7750827. http://ieeexplore.ieee.org/document/7750827/

2. Chai, Z., Shilkrot, R.: Enhanced touchable projector-depth system with deep hand pose estimation. CoRR abs/1812.11090 (2018). http://arxiv.org/abs/1812.11090

3. Cheng, J., Wang, Q., Song, R., Wu, X.: Fingertip-based interactive projector-camera system. Sig. Process. **110**, 54–66 (2015). https://doi.org/10.1016/j.sigpro.2014.08.043

4. Choi, O., Son, Y.J., Lim, H., Ahn, S.C.: Co-recognition of multiple fingertips for tabletop human-projector interaction. IEEE Trans. Multimed. **21**(6), 1487–1498 (2019). https://doi.org/10.1109/TMM.2018.2880608. https://ieeexplore.ieee.org/document/8528493/

5. Dolata, M., et al.: Welcome, computer! How do participants introduce a collaborative application during face-to-face interaction? In: Lamas, D., Loizides, F., Nacke, L., Petrie, H., Winckler, M., Zaphiris, P. (eds.) INTERACT 2019. LNCS, vol. 11748, pp. 600–621. Springer, Cham (2019). https://doi.org/10.1007/978-3-030-29387-1_35

6. Fujinawa, E., Goto, K., Irie, A., Wu, S., Xu, K.: Occlusion-aware hand posture based interaction on tabletop projector. In: UIST 2019 Adjunct - Adjunct Publication of the 32nd Annual ACM Symposium on User Interface Software and Technology, pp. 113–115. Association for Computing Machinery, Inc. (10 2019). https://doi.org/10.1145/3332167.3356890

7. Gao, Y., Huang, C.M.: PATI: A projection-based augmented table-top interface for robot programming. In: International Conference on Intelligent User Interfaces, Proceedings IUI, vol. Part F1476, pp. 345–355. Association for Computing Machinery (2019). https://doi.org/10.1145/3301275.3302326

8. Gregor, D., Prucha, O., Rocek, J., Kortan, J.: Digital playgroundz ACM reference format. ACM SIGGRAPH 2017 VR Village on - SIGGRAPH 2017, pp. 1–2 (2017). https://doi.org/10.1145/3089269.3089288. http://dl.acm.org/citation.cfm?doid=3089269.3089288

9. Laput, G., Harrison, C.: SurfaceSight: a new spin on touch, user, and object sensing for IoT experiences. In: Conference on Human Factors in Computing Systems - Proceedings. Association for Computing Machinery, May 2019. https://doi.org/10.1145/3290605.3300559

10. Lee, D.S., Kwon, S.K.: Virtual touch sensor using a depth camera. Sensors (Switzerland) **19**(4) (2019). https://doi.org/10.3390/s19040885
11. Matsubara, T., Mori, N., Niikura, T., Tano, S.: Touch detection method for non-display surface using multiple shadows of finger. In: 2017 IEEE 6th Global Conference on Consumer Electronics, GCCE 2017, vol. 2017-January, pp. 1–5. Institute of Electrical and Electronics Engineers Inc., December 2017. https://doi.org/10.1109/GCCE.2017.8229364
12. Murugappan, S., Vinayak, Elmqvist, N., Ramani, K.: Extended multitouch: recovering touch posture and differentiating users using a depth camera. In: UIST 2012 - Proceedings of the 25th Annual ACM Symposium on User Interface Software and Technology, pp. 487–496 (2012). https://doi.org/10.1145/2380116.2380177
13. Son, Y.J., Choi, O., Lim, H., Ahn, S.C.: Depth-based fingertip detection for human-projector interaction on tabletop surfaces. In: 2016 IEEE International Conference on Consumer Electronics-Asia, ICCE-Asia 2016. Institute of Electrical and Electronics Engineers Inc., January 2017. https://doi.org/10.1109/ICCE-Asia.2016.7804809
14. Wilson, A.D.: Using a depth camera as a touch sensor. In: ACM International Conference on Interactive Tabletops and Surfaces, ITS 2010, pp. 69–72 (2010). https://doi.org/10.1145/1936652.1936665
15. Wu, Q., Wang, J., Wang, S., Su, T., Yu, C.: MagicPAPER. In: ACM SIGGRAPH 2019 Posters on - SIGGRAPH 2019, pp. 1–2. ACM Press, New York (2019). https://doi.org/10.1145/3306214.3338575. https://dl.acm.org/citation.cfm?doid=3306214.3338575
16. Xiao, R.: SIGCHI outstanding dissertation award: on-world computing. In: Conference on Human Factors in Computing Systems - Proceedings, pp. 1–4. ACM Press, New York (2019). https://doi.org/10.1145/3290607.3313774. http://dl.acm.org/citation.cfm?doid=3290607.3313774
17. Xiao, R., Harrison, C., Hudson, S.E.: WorldKit: rapid and easy creation of ad-hoc interactive applications on everyday surfaces. In: Conference on Human Factors in Computing Systems - Proceedings, pp. 879–888 (2013). https://doi.org/10.1145/2470654.2466113
18. Xiao, R., Hudson, S., Harrison, C.: DIRECT: making touch tracking on ordinary surfaces practical with hybrid depth-infrared sensing. In: Proceedings of the 2016 ACM International Conference on Interactive Surfaces and Spaces: Nature Meets Interactive Surfaces, ISS 2016, pp. 85–94. Association for Computing Machinery, Inc., November 2016. https://doi.org/10.1145/2992154.2992173
19. Zhang, L., Matsumaru, T.: Near-field touch interface using time-of-flight camera. J. Robot. Mechatron. **28**(5), 759–775 (2016). https://doi.org/10.20965/jrm.2016.p0759. https://www.fujipress.jp/jrm/rb/robot002800050759

A Proposal of Eye Glance Input Interface Using Smartphone Built-in Camera

Yu Saiga[(⊠)], Yu Matsumoto, Kazuyuki Mito, Tota Mizuno, and Naoaki Itakura

The University of Electro-Communications,
1-5-1 Chofugaoka, Chofu, Tokyo, Japan
yusaiga@uec.ac.jp

Abstract. For character input in smart devices with small screens, there exist problems such as erroneous input due to the small size of each button or even though the input screen is large, the information presentation screen is small. To solve these problems, in a previous research, the eye-gaze input interface was studied as an input method that did not depend on the touchscreen area.

The purpose of this study is to develop an eye-gaze input interface using the eye-glance input method, which uses a glance eye movement and method of estimating the eye-gaze movement by analyzing the image of the area near the eyeball. The motion was discriminated by taking an image using the built-in camera of a smartphone to rapidly look at the four corners of the smartphone and calculate the moving distance of the eyeball, which was divided into horizontal and vertical components using the optical flow function in Open CV library. In the experiment, we obtained data by asking the subjects to look at the reciprocate of quick gaze movements at each of the four corners and the center of the screen. As a result of data analysis, characteristics of waveforms were obtained for the movements looking at the four corners, and we could determine which of the four corners the users were looking at. Furthermore, it was suggested that an operation with eight degrees of freedom can be performed using only one input by dividing the input into two types according to the length of the time required for the input operation.

Keywords: Line-of-sight input system · Eye-gaze input · Input interface

1 Introduction

With the development of technology in recent years, information terminals carried by individuals are changing from being bulky in size, such as laptops, to small ones such as smartphones and tablets. Input to a small-screen device, such as a smartphone, is generally provided using a touch panel. However, when many options such as character input are required, the input target displayed on the small screen becomes considerably small. Therefore, an erroneous input might occur [1]. However, when the size of the input target is increased to reduce the erroneous input, the number of options that can be presented decreases. To solve these problems, various input methods and screen

© Springer Nature Switzerland AG 2020
C. Stephanidis and M. Antona (Eds.): HCII 2020, CCIS 1224, pp. 294–299, 2020.
https://doi.org/10.1007/978-3-030-50726-8_38

designs for smart devices have been studied. In this study, we focus on line-of-sight-based input methods that do not depend on the touch area.

The line-of-sight input is generally used as a gaze position input method [2]. Although the input accuracy has been improved because of the development of research, it is still difficult to distinguish between input intentions during a gaze, and it is also difficult to implement the method on small devices such as smartphones.

However, a method that uses the eyeball movement as an input has been proposed. Ito et al. [3] proposed the eye-glance input interface that used a quick reciprocation of the eye movement as an input action. In this method, the input operation is the reciprocation of the line-of-sight movement along the oblique direction that occurs when returning after looking at any of the four corners of the screen. Therefore, using this method, it becomes easy to measure even small screens, such as smartphones, without requiring high measurement accuracy.

Akehi et al. [4] proposed a method to acquire input images in a non-contact manner by acquiring the face image of a user by employing a web camera and measuring eye movement using Open CV, which is an open source library. This suggests that gaze movement can even be measured using only a smartphone without using external devices such as electrodes.

The purpose of this study is to implement an eye-glance input interface for acquiring facial images and analyzing them using a smartphone.

2 Eye-Movement-Measurement Method

2.1 Optical Flow

Similar to a previous study, we used Open CV's optical flow calculation library for performing the eye-movement measurement. Optical flow is a method that compares two images that are temporally continuous, and it expresses the motion of the object in the image as a vector. Figure 1 shows the measurement range. Based on the coordinates and radius of the face obtained via face detection, a rectangular area near the eyeball was used as the measurement area, and the eye movement was measured by equally disposing 225 measurement points (15 × 15) in the measurement area. The vector obtained using the difference in the movement speed between the eyeball and other parts was divided into horizontal and vertical components, and those vectors with the largest 10% were averaged to obtain one evaluation value.

2.2 Discrimination Algorithm

Figure 2 shows an example of the waveform obtained by the method shown by Akehi et al. [4] the part enclosed by the rectangle corresponds to the eye movement. Along the horizontal direction, the right is positive, and along the vertical direction, the top is positive. The waveform obtained by the eye-glance input has the characteristic that two opposite waveforms are generated along each of the horizontal and vertical directions, and a short dwell time is observed between round trips. In addition, the number of

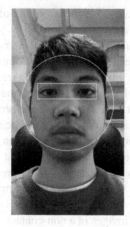

Fig. 1. Measurement area

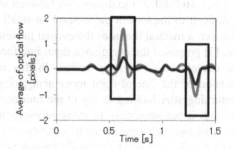

Fig. 2. Example of the upper right input waveform

options to be displayed at once can be increased to eight by dividing the input into two types according to the length of the time required for one eye-glance operation. [5]

3   Experiment

For the experiment, we used an application that performed many tasks ranging from the display of the experiment screen, acquisition of images, to the calculation of the optical flow. The smartphone used an inbuilt-camera with a time-resolution function of 30 fps; however, it was approximately 11 fps when the application was running. After the experiment, the optical-flow data calculated using the smartphone were analyzed on a PC.

3.1   Measurement Conditions

The orientation of the smartphone was set to "vertical", and installation method was "fixed" and "gripped". The subject was in a sitting posture, and the position of the smartphone was adjusted in advance such that the subject could easily observe the screen.

The subject performed eye-glance input operations once at each of the four corners at intervals of 2–3 s under the two conditions of fixed and gripped respectively.

3.2   Analysis Method

Based on the algorithm by Akehi et al. [4], we performed face detection for each acquired image and calculated the optical flow in the rectangular area around the eyeball. The measurement points of the optical flow were distributed as 15 points along the length and 15 along the width of the measurement area, and the gaze movement was measured by averaging the top 10% of the obtained vectors.

4 Results and Discussion

4.1 Impact on Grip Information and Solutions

Figure 3 shows an example of the optical-flow waveform during the input operation. In the fixed state, a characteristic waveform that was considered as eye movement was obtained; however, noise occurred in the gripped state. The noise might be attributed to camera shake and could hinder the eye-movement measurement.

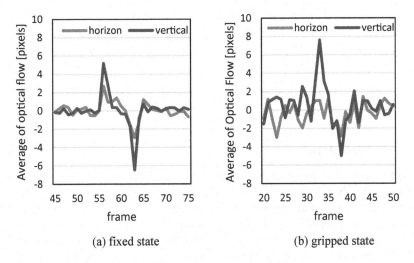

(a) fixed state   (b) gripped state

Fig. 3. Example of optical-flow waveform

Therefore, we calculated the variance by considering that only the eyeball moved. Notably, the variance becomes large when the eye moves, while the entire screen moves when the camera shakes. Figure 4 shows the variance values for the same conditions and same section. Therefore, the characteristic value of the variance along the vertical direction was observed during the movement of the line-of-sight, even in the grasping state. This suggests that eye movement can be estimated by calculating the variance value even in the grasping state.

4.2 Gaze-Movement Discrimination

The variance along the vertical direction during eye movement was greater than that during the case of non-eye movement. Therefore, the eye movement can be identified by setting a threshold along the vertical direction. However, in Fig. 4, no large waveform was observed along both the horizontal and vertical directions. Such examples are often seen during other eye movements. This might be because the smartphone had a long shape along the vertical direction, and the four corners could be seen without horizontally moving the eye. Therefore, the eye movement might be determined by setting a threshold along the vertical direction and then making a positive or negative judgment along the horizontal direction.

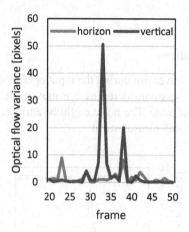

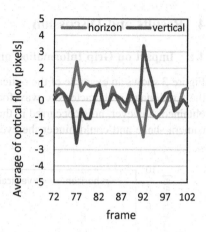

Fig. 4. Optical-flow variance

Fig. 5. Optical flow for extended eye movement

4.3 Long/Short Input

Figure 5 shows an example of the optical-flow waveform when the eye gaze is input for a long time. In Fig. 3(a), there is a difference of 7 frames in the peak value of the line-of-sight movement during reciprocation, whereas in Fig. 5, there is a difference of 15 frames. Consequently, as observed in a previous study [5], the input could be divided into two types according to the length of the time required for gaze movement, and by performing this method at the four corners, we could operate with one input and eight degrees of freedom.

5 Conclusion and Future Work

In this study, we analyzed the obtained waveforms to develop an eye-glance input interface that performed image acquisition and analysis on a smartphone. In the past, images acquired using a smartphone were analyzed on a PC; however, we showed that the eye movement could be determined using only a smartphone by calculating the optical flow within the smartphone. In future, we will conduct real-time discrimination experiments on smartphones and aim at practical applications of the line-of-sight input.

References

1. Siek, K.A., Rogers, Y., Connelly, K.H.: Fat finger worries: how older and younger users physically interact with PDAs. In: Costabile, M.F., Paternò, F. (eds.) INTERACT 2005. LNCS, vol. 3585, pp. 267–280. Springer, Heidelberg (2005). https://doi.org/10.1007/11555261_24
2. Abe, K., Nakayama, Y., Ohi, S., Ohyama, M.: A support system for mouse operations using eye-gaze input. IEEJ Trans. Electron. Inf. Syst. **129**(9), 11–1713 (2009)
3. Ito, Y., Kazama, Y., Itakura, N., Mizuno, T., Mito, K.: Research of eye glance input interface. IEICE Tech. Rep. **112**(483), 17–20 (2013)
4. Akehi, K., Matsuno, S., Itakura, N., Mizuno, T., Mito, K.: Non-contact eye-glance input interface using video camera. J. Signal Process. **21**(4), 207–210 (2017)
5. Matsuno, S., Ito, Y., Akehi, K., Itakura, N., Mizuno, T., Mito, K.: A multiple-choice input interface using slanting eye glance. IEEJ Trans. Electron. Inf. Syst. **137**(4), 621–627 (2017)

Proposal of Character Input Method for Smartphone Using Hand Movement

Kohei Wajima$^{(\boxtimes)}$, Yu Matsumoto, Kazuyuki Mito, Tota Mizuno, and Naoaki Itakura

The University of Electro-Communications,
1-5-1 Chofugaoka, Chofu, Tokyo, Japan
k.wajima0525@gamil.com

Abstract. Character input in smartphones, such as erroneous input due to the small size of each button or the small size of the information presentation screen due to the large size of the input screen, has been considered a problem. To solve these issues, in our previous research, a multi-choice input method with a low degree of freedom was designed, which could input up to sixty-four characters by flicking four buttons in two directions: up and down and repeating it twice. In addition, it was possible to input not only by touch but also by gaze and gestures, thereby proposing four alternatives and a method of dividing these alternatives into two and inputting twice. In this research, the aim is to develop a multi-choice input interface with a low degree of freedom, in which four actions are taken by moving the two corners of the device closer and far from the user's body, and eight actions are performed by tapping the back of the device before performing these actions. The three-axis acceleration sensor of the smartphone was used to determine the movement. Based on the analysis of the four movements, it was suggested that it was possible to determine whether the movement was approaching or moving away by the acceleration sensor's z-axis or y-axis and whether to tilt right or left from the camera depending on the phase of the x-axis and y-axis. Accordingly, we could determine with 100% accuracy for the three movements and 95% accuracy for the remaining movement.

Keywords: Interface · Smartphone · Gesture · Character input

1 Introduction

1.1 Background

At present, smartphone penetration is higher than that of landline phones [1]; smartphones have become indispensable in our daily lives. In addition, opportunities to use SNS, social-networking-service, and internet searches with smartphones are increasing [2]. As a result, the need for character input has also increased. However, operability, such as erroneous input due to small input buttons, has been regarded a problem. However, when the operability is prioritized and the input button size is increased, the amount of information presented decreases. In addition, if the input screen is made smaller to increase the area of the information presentation screen, the input buttons will become smaller. In such a case, there is a possibility of causing the fat-finger

© Springer Nature Switzerland AG 2020
C. Stephanidis and M. Antona (Eds.): HCII 2020, CCIS 1224, pp. 300–305, 2020.
https://doi.org/10.1007/978-3-030-50726-8_39

problem [3] in which a button different from the intended input is selected. Therefore, there is a need for an input method that achieves both operability and screen occupancy.

1.2   A Multi-choice Input Method with a Low Degree of Freedom

In our previous study [4], we proposed a multi-choice input method with degrees of freedom using four buttons. After tapping the button, the user flicks up and down to execute eight operations. By repeating the eight operations twice, 64 characters can be entered. A touch input interface that does not reduce the operability and amount of information presented was developed.

Similarly, if we can propose four options and a method to divide them into two sets, this input method can be used not only for touch but also for input using gaze and gestures. In previous studies [5], we investigated the development of an input interface using eye movements.

In a previous study [6], we investigated the development of an input interface based on wrist motion using a three-axis acceleration sensor. However, the accuracy of motion discrimination was not sufficient, and improvements were required.

The purpose of this study is to improve the accuracy and to develop a multi-choice input with a low degree of freedom interface with a small degree of freedom by gestures.

2   Character Input Interface by Gesture

The previous study [6] considered the following wrist actions:
Action ①: Tilt the upper left corner away from the body (left-far)
Action ②: Tilt the upper right corner away from the body (right-far)
Action ③: Tilt the upper right corner near the body (right-near)
Action ④: Tilt the upper left corner near the body (left-near)
In a previous study [6], the speed (fast and slow) of performing the four actions was divided into eight operations. However, there were significant differences among the individuals performing the fast and slow actions, making it difficult to distinguish between them. Therefore, it is necessary to propose a new method for dividing the operation into two stages. As for the new two-stage method, it is desirable that the user can input easily and in a short time. Therefore, the action of tapping the back of the smartphone was used for input. Eight operations are performed depending on whether or not this back tap is performed before the four wrist actions.

Figure 1 shows the actions and input screen design. Buttons ① to ④, and ①' to ④' present at the bottom of the screen in Fig. 1 each store eight characters. Figure 2 shows the actual input method. By performing an action once, the button corresponding to the action is selected. Next, the eight characters stored in the selected button are expanded to fill the input screen. By repeating this, one of the eight characters is selected and the character input is completed. In addition, to make it easier for the user to understand, we visualized whether the outside, buttons ① to ④, or inside, buttons ①' to ④', is selected by the back tap. It can switch between the outside and inside by tapping the back.

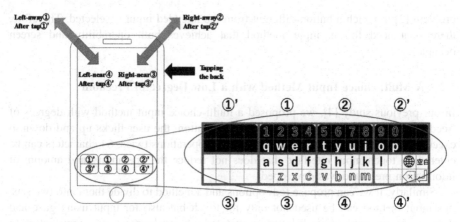

Fig. 1. Proposal actions and input screen

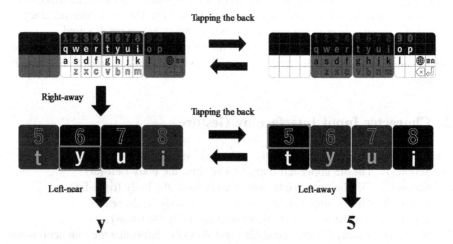

Fig. 2. Input example

3 Acceleration Analysis

Characteristic waveforms can be obtained for the three-axis acceleration data by performing the actions ① to ④. In most cases, the four actions show three peaks on the z-axis and two peaks each on the x-axis and y-axis. Table 1 shows the characteristics of this peak for each action. In a previous study [6], discrimination was performed using two specified axes of the three axes of the acceleration sensor. Using the z-axis, it was determined whether to move near or away from the body. In addition, whether the operation was tilting left or right depending on the x-axis or y-axis was determined. However, there were cases in which erroneous determination was made with respect to the waveforms that cause disturbances, such as the x-axis and y-axis in Fig. 3(a) and the z-axis in Fig. 3(b). Therefore, the action discrimination rate, which was 70–90%, was not sufficient.

In this study, we focused on the phase rather than the peak of the waveform. When tilting to the right, the x-axis and y-axis are in the same phase, and when tilting to the left, they are in opposite phases. In addition, from Table 1, the characteristics of the z-axis and the y-axis are reversed by the actions toward and away from the body, so if the z-axis is disturbed, it is determined by using the y-axis. Based on such an algorithm, there is a possibility that discrimination can be made regardless of waveform disturbance. Table 2 shows the new waveform features for the four actions.

In addition, tapping the back causes a positive to negative waveform characteristic on the z-axis regardless of where the tap is made. Therefore, it can be considered that it can be determined using the z-axis. Since the amplitude is smaller than the tilting motion, it can be expected that the discrimination can be made by setting the threshold to a lower value.

Table 1. Four actions waveform characteristics (conventional method)

Action		① Left-away	② Right-away	③ Right-near	④ Left-near
Wave characteristic	X	Plus → Minus	Minus → Plus	Plus → Minus	Minus → Plus
	Y	Minus → Plus	Minus → Plus	Plus → Minus	Plus → Minus
	Z	Minus → Plus → Minus	Minus → Plus → Minus	Plus → Minus → Plus	Plus → Minus → Plus

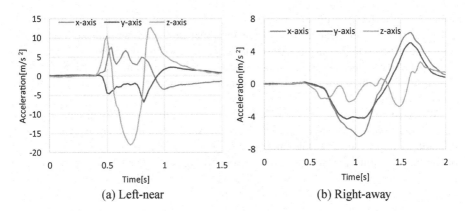

(a) Left-near   (b) Right-away

Fig. 3. Waveform example

Table 2. Four actions waveform characteristics (proposed method)

Action		① Left-away	② Right-away	③ Right-near	④ Left-near
Wave characteristic	X and Y	Opposite phase	Same phase	Same phase	Opposite phase
	Y	Minus → Plus → Minus	Minus → Plus → Minus	Plus → Minus → Plus	Plus → Minus → Plus
	Z	Minus → Plus	Minus → Plus	Plus → Minus	Plus → Minus

4 Four-Motion Real-Time Discrimination Experiment

4.1 Experimental Method

The subjects were six males and females aged 22 to 24 years. The experiment was performed while holding a smartphone (HUAWEI P20) and sitting on a chair. Subjects were asked to perform the specified actions 10 times each. In addition, they used the hands that they normally use to operate smartphones. Subject F operated the smartphone with both hands, so we performed five experiments with each hand. The sampling frequency was 50 Hz. In addition, the data obtained from the acceleration sensor include noise due to camera shaking and gravity. To remove these, band-pass filtering was used to extract the frequency band from 0.5 Hz to 3 Hz. In order to confirm whether the discrimination can be performed using the features in Table 2, an experiment was performed using the following algorithm.

1. A threshold is set on the z-axis to determine whether to move away from or close to the body.
2. Based on the phases of the x-axis and y-axis, it is determined whether the operation is tilting left or right.

4.2 Results and Discussion

Table 3 shows the experimental results. It can be seen that the average discrimination rate was 95% for left-near and 100% for the other three actions with high accuracy. This result shows higher accuracy for all the actions when compared to the previous study [6]. Among the 240 trials, three false detections and no non-detection rate were found. In all the three false detections, left-near was judged to be right-near when held right-handed.

We consider the cause for the observation made. In the case of right hand holding, the left near moves the wrist inward from the state of holding the device, so it is difficult to tilt it. As a result, an operation that was different from the instructed operation of pulling the device more without tilting was sometimes performed. This resulted in a waveform with almost no features on the x-axis or y-axis, resulting in misclassification. However, it is assumed to be possible for the user to learn and adapt from the accuracy of the average classification rate of 95% and the subject with the lowest accuracy of 80%.

Table 3. Four actions discrimination rate

Subject (handle)	Action			
	① Left-away	② Right-away	③ Right-away	④ Left-away
A (right)	100	100	100	100
B (right)	100	100	100	90
C (right)	100	100	100	100
D (right)	100	100	100	100
E (left)	100	100	100	100
F (right, left)	100	100	100	80
Average	100	100	100	95.0

5   Conclusion

The purpose of this study was to develop a multi-choice input interface with a low degree of freedom using gestures. The average discrimination rate of the four actions was higher than that of the previous study [6] for all actions. However, some subjects may not be able to tilt well, so it is necessary to examine the learning effect. Future prospects include enhancing the usability by inputting characters.

References

1. Ministry of Finance Homepage. https://www.soumu.go.jp/johotsusintokei/whitepaper/ja/h30/html/nd252110.html. Accessed 11 Feb 2020
2. Mobile Marketing Data Lab Homepage. https://mmdlabo.jp/investigation/detail_1760.html. Accessed 09 Mar 2020
3. Siek, K.A., Rogers, Y., Connelly, K.H.: Fat finger worries: how older and younger users physically interact with PDAs. In: Costabile, M.F., Paternò, F. (eds.) INTERACT 2005. LNCS, vol. 3585, pp. 267–280. Springer, Heidelberg (2005). https://doi.org/10.1007/11555261_24
4. Matsuno, S., Chida, S., Itakura, N., Mizuno, T., Mito, K.: A method of character input for the user interface with a low degree of freedom. Artif. Life Robot. **24**(2), 250–256 (2019)
5. Akehi, K., Matsuno, S., Itakura, N., Mizuno, T., Mito, K.: Non-contact eye-glance input interface using video camera. J. Signal Process. **21**(4), 207–210 (2017)
6. Matsuura, H., Mizuno, T., Kota, A., Farahani, M.A., Mito, K., Itakura, N.: Study of gesture input interface for smart device by wrist movement. IEEJ Trans. Fundam. Mater. **139**(11), 579–584 (2019)

Designing an Interactive Eco-Feedback Environment

Divya Yendapally$^{(\boxtimes)}$ and Delaram Yazdansepas

Department of Computer Science, University of Georgia, Athens, GA 30602, USA
{dyendapally,delaram}@uga.edu

Abstract. The purpose of this research project is to study the current designs of eco-feedback technologies, assess how effective they are, and propose viable solutions to increase the performance of these technologies, and in turn reduce the cumulative environmental impact. While there are currently many technologies in the works of being created, with similar intent, they all seem to share one common problem; Eco-Feedback technologies are costly to produce with a low net gain, when it comes to user satisfaction and hence future investment. Design expands further than visual appeal, and this project dives into all components of proper design. From the depths of environmental psychology, all the way to visualization design, this paper proposes a future for a more sustainable environment.

Keywords: Eco feedback technology · Environmental HCI · Design methods and evaluation · Visualization design · Human centered computing · Empirical studies in interaction design

1 Introduction

Eco-feedback technologies have recently been introduced; They are technologies that provide users with feedback on the impact of their actions towards the environment. An example of this includes a smart thermostat, that displays information to users on how their usage of the device is impacting the environment around them. Many different feedback technologies have been created, but not many of them are effective enough to make a difference. Persuasive technologies were created with the same purpose of reducing environmental impact. However, their focus is more on using a technique to encourage a certain human behavior [3]. An example of this would be a digital trashcan, that makes a unique sound every time it processes material. This sound was meant to incentivize users to continue to use the device. Unfortunately, both feedback and persuasive technologies have not had high success rates in maintaining users. Learning what works and does not is an essential part in creating a sustainable and efficient design, that can help preserve the environment.

© Springer Nature Switzerland AG 2020
C. Stephanidis and M. Antona (Eds.): HCII 2020, CCIS 1224, pp. 306–313, 2020.
https://doi.org/10.1007/978-3-030-50726-8_40

1.1   Motivation

As we continue to advance in societal growth, many industries have been thriving, thus leaving a negative impact on the environment. Over the years, the public has educated people broadly on many different ways to start making an attempt to reduce environmental impact. Of these, recycling has been the most frequently taught. While we can appreciate that today most public buildings and many homes do have recycling bins, we have to understand that due to a lack of proper education, that certain recycling is actually causing more harm than good. We are at a point in our ecosystem, where so much damage has been done to our planet, that only drastic actions can help save the environment [1]. In other words, we cannot afford to recycle the wrong items, or on a broader spectrum, we need to be as educated as possible in taking the right steps to prevent any further damage. Many Environmental Psychologists, along with Computer Scientists have contributed to research on best practices in educating the public on these issues, and both have revealed that eco-feedback technology has a lot of potential in properly educating users, especially because of how ubiquitous technology is becoming [2]. However, not all studies published on users and their interactions with eco-feedback technologies have shown the results that are wanted. People are still reverting back to their usual habits, when it comes to preserving the environment, despite there being smart technologies such as a thermostat, informing users of the environmental impact that they are having [5].

2   Background and Related Work

Previous works on these topics have focused primarily on Environmental Psychology; Research was conducted on the users of the Eco-Feedback technology more than the technology itself [2], Something gained from these studies are that incentive is a huge motivator for action. One study's participants felt that the feedback technologies did not motivate them to continue using their device, because there was no impact on the price of their monthly bills [5]. To summarize takeaways from these studies, it is clear that dual-income families, though may contribute the most to the negative impact on the environment, may not be the best initial target to influence change. Secondly, feedback technologies alone are ineffective because of their lack of actionability. Lastly, incentive drives users a lot further than any other method of persuasion. These studies have introduced many of the dynamics within households and users of eco-feedback technology, and this has led to a desire in further explore the design of today's technology [3]. Other factors of persuasion include goal setting, incentives, along with disincentives and penalties, feedback, and comparisons. A common theme amongst these potential methods of inclusion are that they are interactive, allowing for the users to be active participants in their own journey towards creating a more sustainable lifestyle. Something controversial discussed are regarding "disincentives and penalties", as not all studies came to this same conclusion. It needs to be determined if these are effective methods in imposing behavioral change, or if in fact it may do the opposite, discouraging users entirely. Most of the studies on these topics were neutral to the users, not offering a positive or a negative impact on the users [2]. However, there is a lot less at stake with a positive impact than a negative one; A positive one may not bring a change, but it will not make users develop a disdain for the technology. A technology with potential penalty to the users can be both discouraging as well as make the users not want to ever use it in the future. That is why it is essential to make these technologies have a dual purpose: helping the environment and helping the user with an issue relevant to them.

3   Methodology

Many studies on Eco-Feedback technologies have stated that users were asked to use a specific prototype for an observable period of time and were then interviewed on their experiences [4]. In this study, users were asked to interact with the newly created prototype as a part of their interview. That being said, this study has a more accurate display of the user response and interaction, since the interviewer actively observed the entirety. The interview, unlike other studies, was not exclusively focused on their experience interacting with the prototype and their motivations, but also allowed the user to analyze the design by doing a think aloud evaluation. The final display of the study includes not just a description of the elements of design, but also visuals of the prototype. This paints a similar experience on paper, to that of what the users experienced, while interacting with the prototype in the study. From previous studies, it has been clear that users have not been very responsive to technologies that exclusively provide feedback, because the feedback shows the impact without giving users a proper plan of action to reduce the impact that they are having. This study is unique in that it is a persuasive technology that also provides feedback, making it extremely clear of what and what not to recycle; It also has a huge focus on the design aspects and principles used in creating this product.

3.1   Datasets

Prior to implementing a design, most effective in reducing environmental impact, we collected data from a random sample within Athens, Georgia. A survey was administered through the University of Georgia (UGA)'s online Qualtrics system. The survey is comprised of questions ranging from the participants' demographics to their recycling habits. It also includes a section, testing participants on their current recycling knowledge. The purpose of this methodology, is to gauge how many users, on average, need to be further educated on proper practices. After collecting this data, we were able to see similar demographic influenced recycling patterns as previous studies have noted. However, a few of the huge takeaways are the users' ideas of proper incentives as well as their current knowledge on proper recycling. Many similar studies have long contemplated incentives which would encourage users to increase their usage of eco-feedback technologies. We took a direct approach, by asking individuals what they considered to be most compelling. Most said they were willing to invest in a technology that offered a financial reward and showed the effects that the individual user is having on the community. The individuals surveyed also stated that they did not want any sort of penalty; they said that even if it temporarily required them to be more engaged, it would push them away from using the product in the future. Many recent papers have discussed the potential of including negative incentives in future designs, but these results indicate that may not be the most effective course of action in the long run. It also became clear that many users are not properly educated on what items can or cannot be recycled. In fact, seventy-six percent of the surveyed sample, were not aware that recycling rules differ between varying locations. Based on these results, we can conclude that the design of these technologies need to be elucidate in instructing users on what to recycle, as well as provide an interactive way for users to be engaged within their respective recycling community, and in turn encouraging them to continue to help preserve the planet.

3.2   Approach

After analyzing the collected data, we decided to create a prototype for a smart recycling bin, which behaves as a persuasive and feedback technology. This urges users to be more environmentally conscious, while simultaneously educating users to recycle the proper items, based on their respective location. This recycling bin will ultimately be able to use sensors to detect which items are being recycled into the bin, while comparing them to the items that can be recycled, according to their local recycling center. For instance, if a user were to recycle a plastic bottle, and the user's local center does not accept this, then the UI (user interface), of the smart recycling bin, would display an error message and sound, notifying the user that they are recycling the wrong item. Likewise, if the user were to recycle the proper item, their behavior would be positively reinforced with a message and sound indicating them of doing so. The local recycling center rules are currently detected depending on the user's location, which can either be detected automatically, or by entering their residential zip code. Another important feature that is included in the design is the users' recycling statistics, which is stored on a separate page and keeps record of the total amount that the user is recycling. It promotes user activity by displaying the cumulative positive environmental impact that each user is having on their community. That being said, the smart recycling bin also includes a feature that compares the user's progress to the progress made by others within their local community; It is a great way to stay keep motivated and encourage one another to get involved within the community. The final feature included is the Rewards page. Concluded from a number of Environmental Psychology papers [5], as well as the surveys conducted within this particular study, we know that the majority of users are primarily motivated by short term results that benefit them. They are more likely to take immediate actions for results that they will see now, not ten years from now. Therefore, it makes sense that a user may not be ready to financially invest in a more expensive recycling bin, solely to reduce their environmental impact. However, if recycling centers were to partner with local businesses, and generate some sort of earnable discounts for users, depending on their recycling habits, then users are likely to be significantly more active in their willingness to participate. Similarly, local businesses may thrive by receiving more recognition, and most importantly, the recycling centers would be saving a lot of time and money. Studies have shown the negative impacts that result from wrong recycling habits, and the fact is that the majority of items recycled end up going to waste or jamming machinery, which does a lot more harm than good. These incentives can lead to an overall growth in environmental sustainability (Fig. 1).

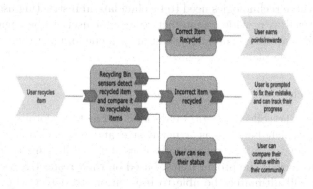

Fig. 1. This UML diagram shows the step by step process of the interaction with the smart recycle device

4   Design

The visual aspects of the UI are a huge part of the design of eco-feedback technology but are not the only factors that should be considered. Design is inclusive of not just the aesthetic of the product, but how simply the users are able to interact with it; We proposed the idea of displaying a screen on the surface of the recycle bin, and it will serve as a familiar platform for users to be able to track their progress. This product has a minimalistic design and keeps the users' jobs as simple as possible. The goal to require little effort is met, especially since the primary task required of the user does not require them to physically interact with the screen at all; They just have to go about recycling items as they normally would. The screen displays a message according to their action, and the only reason that the user would have to physically interact with the device is if they are interested in tracking their progress or claiming their rewards. This makes the experience nearly effortless for users. All of the screens have limited words accompanied with clear visuals, in order reduce the probability of user error. Voice UI is another feature that has been included in the design.

Firstly, it makes the product more accessible to someone who may struggle with their sight. Secondly, the sounds can emphasize and reinforce the importance of a certain recycling behavior. All of these features are optional, to give the user customized control over their experience. The final part of the design is about making sure that the product itself is cost effective. It would be financially draining to invest in a separate screen for four different recycling bins, all for one user. The reason so many bins are considered the proper way to recycle, are because recyclable items do need to be separated. That being said, the recycling bin can have four different sections all contained in one bin, with one screen keep track of what goes into each section (Fig. 2).

Fig. 2. This is the design of the eco-feedback technology prototype for "smart recycle".

5   Evaluation

The evaluation portion of the study has two separate components. The first part of the evaluation revolved specifically around the design of the prototype, whereas the second evaluation focused on the users' combined interactions with it. To produce as little error as possible, these two separate evaluations took place for each interview that was conducted. The first evaluation conducted was a Heuristic Evaluation, such as a cognitive walk through. The purpose of this type of evaluation is to study the usability of the design. Some factors that were considered when doing this evaluation include: visibility of system status, match between the system and real world, simplicity in design, error Prevention, recognition rather than recall, and flexibility and efficiency of use. The second type of evaluation that we performed was on a more theoretical level. We used the GOMS (Goal, Operators, Method, Section Rules). Here the structure in which the user interacted with the device mattered, along with their methodology. For instance, the time it took for a user to navigate from one part to the next part was a vital key in this evaluating method. As we followed through with this evaluation, we made sure that half of the users were experienced in Human Computer Interaction Style interviews, in order to receive an accurate understanding on the usability of our product.

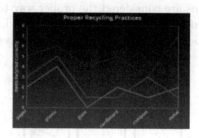

Fig. 3. Graph represents the results seen by users interacting with the prototype.

6   Conclusion and Future Work

The potential impact of this product is to be able to expand awareness on environmental issues and decrease the impact that we have on it. Although this study primarily focuses on a design for a Smart Recycling Bin, the larger objective was to create a formula that can be reused for other technologies in the near future. Once this design is implemented, it is a matter of time before other technologies begin to reproduce similar designs. The study was conducted to create a revolution in design for eco feedback and persuasive technologies, in combining them. The reality is, each of these technologies individually are not strong enough to cause change, but together they have shown a positive impact. When evaluating our prototype, we found that users were significantly more precise with their recycling while using this prototype, as opposed to using a regular recycling bin as it can be seen in Fig. 3. The long-term goal of this study is creating an Interactive Eco-Feedback environment. One recycling bin, will make a huge difference in eliminating waste, but to apply this principle into every technology we use, will change the meaning of what we know as sustainability today. When so much of a user's daily interaction today is dependent upon technology, it could be so beneficial to the environment to incorporate eco-feedback and persuasion into all of these technologies, eventually resulting in every decision that a user makes to be dependent upon that. It may seem a long-term goal that will not be implemented anytime soon, but it is an essential step to take, in order to maintain the current state of the planet. It may be too late to reverse the environmental damage that has already been done, but if immediate action is taken, we can help to sustain this planet for generations to come.

References

1. Environmental psychology. Int. J. Psychol. **51**(S1), 559–568 (2016). https://doi.org/10.1002/ijop.12315. https://onlinelibrary.wiley.com/doi/abs/10.1002/ijop.12315
2. Barreto, M., Karapanos, E., Nunes, N.: Why don't families get along with eco-feedback technologies? A longitudinal inquiry. In: Proceedings of the Biannual Conference of the Italian Chapter of SIGCHI, CHItaly 2013. Association for Computing Machinery, New York (2013). https://doi.org/10.1145/2499149.2499164
3. Froehlich, J., Findlater, L., Landay, J.: The design of eco-feedback technology. In: Proceedings of the SIGCHI Conference on Human Factors in Computing Systems, CHI 2010, pp. 1999–2008. Association for Computing Machinery, New York (2010). https://doi.org/10.1145/1753326.1753629
4. Lavery, D., Cockton, G., Atkinson, M.P.: Comparison of evaluation methods using structured usability problem reports. Behav. Inf. Technol. **16**(4–5), 246–266 (1997). https://doi.org/10.1080/014492997119824
5. Nisi, V., Nicoletti, D., Nisi, R., Nunes, N.J.: Beyond eco-feedback: using art and emotional attachment to express energy consumption. In: Proceedings of the 8th ACM Conference on Creativity and Cognition, C&C 2011, pp. 381–382. Association for Computing Machinery, New York (2011). https://doi.org/10.1145/2069618.2069706

Recognizing Human Psychological States

Accelerometer-Based Evaluation of the Human Psychological State While Viewing Content on Smartphones

Chisato Amada[1]($\boxtimes$), Yu Matsumoto[1], Kazuyuki Mito[1], Tota Mizuno[1], Naoaki Itakura[1], Taiyo Nakashima[2], and Takeshi Hanada[2]

[1] The University of Electro-Communications, 1-5-1, Chofu-gaoka Chofu-shi, Tokyo, Japan
a2030008@edu.cc.uec.ac.jp
[2] Coamix Inc., Kichijoji Jizo Building, 1-9-9, Kichijoji-Minamimachi, Musashino-shi, Tokyo, Japan

Abstract. In recent years, with the abundant availability of digital content, smartphone users have often faced difficulty finding what they prefer. Several recommendation systems have been developed, but conventional ones do not reflect user evaluation. This study focuses on invisible and feeble physiological tremors to reflect user evaluation. The acceleration data of three subjects while reading comic books on a smartphone were collected by using the 3D accelerometer of a smartphone and a smartwatch. Then, the acceleration data in front of the wrist were obtained from the difference values of the two devices. In this method, the measurement was not affected by posture. As a result of performing fast Fourier transforms, the amplitude peak was observed between 2–4 Hz in each data item. In general, the main frequency of a physiological hand tremor is 6 Hz and it is said to decrease as the mass increases. For this reason, it was suggested that the acquisition data included physiological tremors in front of the wrist. Moreover, there was a negative correlation between the user interest in each story and the integral value of amplitude. In particular, the difference value shows a strong correlation. Accordingly, using the difference values of the two devices enables a more accurate evaluation of the psychological state.

Keywords: Evaluation of psychological state · Physiological tremor · 3D accelerometer · Recommendation system

1 Introduction

In recent times, digital devices have become popular, and they allow people to access a large quantity of digital content. However, this abundance of content often makes it difficult for people to find what they prefer. Conventional recommendation systems are primarily based on purchase and browsing history, which do not reflect user evaluation. Therefore, the need for novel recommendation systems that can effectively reflect user evaluation has increased.

Bio-signals are one of the parameters that reflect user evaluation. Matsui et al. estimated user interest by means of an eye-tracking system [1], and Yukawa et al. used

C. Stephanidis and M. Antona (Eds.): HCII 2020, CCIS 1224, pp. 317–322, 2020.
https://doi.org/10.1007/978-3-030-50726-8_41

a web camera and image processing technology [2]. However, such devices are expensive, and it is not easy to apply these technologies on a large scale. On the other hand, a significant number of people use smart devices such as smartphones. These devices have built-in sensors such as accelerometers or gyroscopes. Using these sensors to evaluate user interest leads to the design of a new system that can be widely utilized.

Yan [3] estimated user interest using the 3D accelerometer of a smartphone. He performed fast Fourier transform (FFT) on the acceleration data while subjects viewed Tweets and compared the results with self-evaluations of their interest. He found that the distribution of frequency components tended to spread for the less interesting Tweets. Therefore, it was suggested that the smartphone acceleration data could effectively estimate user interest. However, Yan did not consider the subjects' posture. Because the acceleration data changes as a result of holding a smartphone, it is necessary to obtain an approach to measure the acceleration that is unaffected by posture.

Invisible and feeble physiological tremors are bio-signals, and one factor affecting these tremors is said to be psychological change [4]. However, as physiological tremors are generally measured by fixing joints and wearing a light accelerometer, it is difficult to measure only them while holding a device.

In this research, we attempted to acquire acceleration data including physiological tremors without being affected by posture and extract features reflecting the influence of psychological changes.

2 Methodology

The 3D accelerometers of a smartphone and a smartwatch were used to acquire the acceleration data while subjects viewed content on a smartphone. Moreover, the acceleration data in front of the wrist is obtained from the difference between the measurements of a smartphone and a smartwatch. Taking the difference value negates the necessity to consider the angle of the arm or contact between the elbow and desk. This enables measurement that is unaffected by posture. The psychological state was evaluated by comparing the acceleration data and psychological parameters.

Each accelerometer measures three values, from the x-axis, y-axis and z-axis, respectively. As the axis directions are not the same in the smartphone and smartwatch, it is necessary to re-arrange the values of the two devices in order to obtain the difference value. To do this, the vertical component of "dynamic" acceleration which is caused by motion is focused on. Because the acceleration data of both devices include the gravitational ("static") component, the dynamic component is extracted by dividing the instantaneous values of acceleration (see Fig. 1) into static and dynamic components (see Fig. 2). The difference value is obtained from the sum of each dynamic component of the axis.

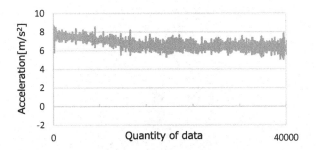

Fig. 1. Instantaneous values of z-axis acceleration

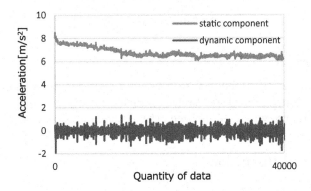

Fig. 2. Static and dynamic component

3 Experiment

Three subjects participated in this experiment. Each subject read three different types of comic books on a comic reading application for smartphones, and the acceleration data were collected as they did so.

3.1 Procedure

The manner in which the experiment was conducted is shown in Fig. 3. First, subjects sat on a chair and wore a smartwatch on the same arm with which they held the smartphone. They remained in the position for about three minutes and evaluated the present five psychological state (comfortable, sleepy, surprised, sad and angry). Then, they began to read the comic books. They were instructed to keep the hand holding the smartphone off the desk or their own body while reading each comic book. After reading, they self-evaluated their psychological state at that time and the story they had just read.

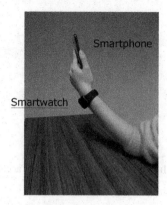

Fig. 3. Subjects' reading posture

3.2   Measurement

An application was developed here to measure acceleration and collect acceleration data from the smartphone and smartwatch; to simultaneously acquire both acceleration data, the two devices were synchronized. The sampling frequency was set to 50 Hz.

4   Results and Discussion

4.1   Frequency Analysis

The result of performing FFT is shown in Fig. 4. The amplitude peak was observed between 2–4 Hz. This tendency was observed in almost all the data.

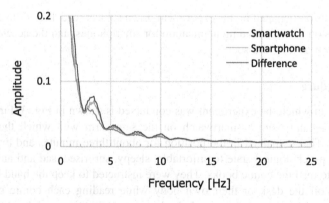

Fig. 4. Result of performing FFT

In general, the main frequency of the physiological finger tremor is 25 Hz, that of the hand is 6 Hz, and that of the forearms is 5 Hz [4]. Based on this, it is presumed that the main frequency of the physiological tremor in front of the wrist could be observed at approximately 5 Hz. In addition, it is said that the main frequency decreases as mass increases [4]. As the subjects held the smartphone, the amplitude peak is likely to be observed below 5 Hz. Therefore, it was suggested that the acquisition data included physiological tremors in front of the wrist.

4.2   Correlations Between Interest in Story and Physiological Tremors

Table 1 shows the average and variance of the correlation coefficient between the interest in each story and the integral value of amplitude in three subjects. The correlation coefficient of four different frequency bands was obtained.

Table 1. Average and variance of correlation coefficient between the interest in each story and the integral value of amplitude

Frequency band [Hz]	Smartwatch		Smartphone		Difference	
	Average	Variance	Average	Variance	Average	Variance
1–2	−0.532	0.021	−0.704	0.036	−0.835	0.002
2–3	−0.453	0.056	−0.675	0.051	**−0.850**	**0.002**
3–4	−0.498	0.028	**−0.812**	**0.027**	−0.795	0.003
4–5	−0.510	0.031	−0.697	0.048	−0.824	0.001

Although there were some differences in the three parts, the interest and integral values had a negative correlation. This indicates that the more interesting a story becomes, the less people move. In particular, the difference value showed a strong correlation on average, and its variance was small. Clearly, using the difference value of smartphone and smartwatch measurements enables a more accurate evaluation of the subject's psychological state.

5   Conclusions

The data that includes physiological tremors in front of the wrist could be acquired using the 3D accelerometer of a smartphone and smartwatch. Moreover, based on the correlation result, it can be concluded that taking the difference value of two devices enables a more accurate evaluation of the psychological state.

In this research, subjects were seated and a limit was set on their posture while reading comic books. However, as individuals may read in any position, it is essential to have no such limits. Therefore, in future work, an approach to evaluating the psychological state with no limit on posture must be explored.

Acknowledgements. We would like to thank Editage (www.editage.com) for English language editing.

References

1. Matusi, K., Suganuma, M., Sriprasertsuk, P., Kameyama, W.: Preliminary analysis on correlation of comic reading time and comic components. In: 2013 International Workshop on Smart Info-Media Systems in Asia (2013)
2. Yukawa, K., Moriyama, M., Imaki, K., Ueno, K., Kaneda, S.: An approach to provide services to estimate degree of interest. J. Inf. Process. Soc. Jpn. 1, 12–21 (2011)
3. Yan, H.: Yuza no Furumai ni Motoduku Kyomi Suitei ni Yoru Kontentsu Etsuran Shien Shuhou ni Kansuru Kenkyu (A Study of Support Methods for Watching Content Based on User Behavior). Kyushu University Institutional Repository, Fukuoka (2016)
4. Sakamoto, K., Shimizu, Y., Mito, K., Takanokura, M.: Seitai no Furue to Shindo Chikaku. Mechanical Vibration no Kino Hyouka (Physiological Tremors and Vibration Perception. Function Evaluation of Mechanical Vibration). Tokyo Denki University Press, Tokyo (2009)

System of Emotion Estimation Support by Shape Identification of Facial Areas for the Elderly

Shuji Fukami[1], Yui Sasaoka[1], and Takumi Yamaguchi[2(✉)]

[1] Advanced Course in Mechanical and Electrical Engineering,
National Institute of Technology, Kochi College,
200-1 Monobe-Otsu, Nankoku, Kochi 783-8508, Japan
s1905@gm.kochi-ct.jp
[2] National Institute of Technology, Kochi College, 200-1 Monobe-Otsu,
Nankoku, Kochi 783-8508, Japan
yama@ee.kochi-ct.ac.jp

Abstract. Humans change not only words but also facial expressions to express various emotions, which are factors that promote rich communication. However, it is difficult for users, such as the elderly or visually impaired, who have difficulty obtaining non-verbal information from others or who have difficulty communicating their feelings to others (i.e., those who have difficulty reading feelings) to use expressions to communicate with them. Therefore, in the communication of the user who has difficulty in recognizing the expression of the other party, the support to estimate the emotion of the other party is very useful. In addition, humans change the shape of the face part in one emotion and form various facial expressions. In this paper, we describe the effectiveness of the emotion estimation support system using the recognition of the facial part shape.

Keywords: Emotional estimation · Validation for the elderly · CNN

1 Introduction

Humans develop interpersonal communication by altering facial expressions and expressing various emotions in addition to words. The Melabian's law suggests that nonverbal information, such as facial expressions and handicrafts, has a high impact on communication, at 55%. Expression of various facial expressions is a factor that promotes smooth and prosperous communication, such as language supplementation and reduction of communication discrepancies.

However, it is difficult for users who have difficulty obtaining non-verbal information from persons with visual disabilities or other interactions to communicate with each other using facial expressions. Hence, it is considered very useful to assist in estimating the emotions of the other party in communicating with users who have difficulty recognizing the other party's expression. Humans can alter the shape of a facial area and form a variety of expressions in one of their emotions. These changes in expression allow a person to read the quality and the size of the other person's emotions. Accordingly, if the support system is able to recognize facial sites and transmit the information, it is possible to infer the emotions of the other party even if the user has difficulty recognizing facial expressions. We implemented an emotional estimation support system using the identification of facial site geometry and confirmed its usefulness through the use of the system.

Figure 1 shows the status of emotional estimation support. By taking pictures of the face of the person with whom the conversation takes place, the user transmits the emotional information of the person and the shape information of the eyebrows, eyes, and mouth, which are the three main parts of the face, in an audio manner. Humans, even with the same emotions, alter the shape of their face parts to form a variety of expressions. Conventional assistive systems [1] only communicate six types of emotional information from the face to the user, and in our proposed systems, we can estimate more diverse patterns of facial expression by combining the shape information of the face with the emotional information. Thus, communicating these estimations allows users to more closely estimate the emotions of the other party of the dialogue.

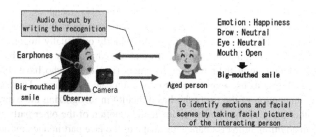

Fig. 1. Basic system configuration

After acquiring the image of the interacting partner, the face is extracted and six different emotions are identified from the extracted facial image. Three facial regions are then extracted to identify the shape of each facial region. As shown in Fig. 1, the emotional discrimination results (e.g., smiling face) are textured by combining the three facial identification results (e.g., open mouth) as modifiers and transmitted to the user by speech conversion.

2 Prototype System for Emotional Estimation Support

2.1 Detector of Face Parts

In this system, the face image of the other party of the interaction is used as the input. However, since there are many unnecessary areas for facial image identification, it is necessary to extract each facial area. Various detectors for extracting facial and facial sites were generated by the Tensorflow Object Detection API, a cascade classifier and object detection framework. To detect the "face" portion and the "eye" portion, we used the published learned cascade classifier "hacarcas-cade_frontalface_alt.xml" and "hacarcascade_mcs_eyepair_big.xml". The Tensorflow Object Detection API was used to create a cascade file with sufficient accuracy to detect the eyebrows and mouths.

The annotation tool "Label Img" was used to annotate the training data. By enclosing the area to be detected in a rectangle, the coordinate data of the detection point and the information of the training data are output as an xml file. Detector construction is accomplished using this XML file and the corresponding training data. The mouth was labeled separately for "closure" and "opening" because of the great change in appearance compared to the eyebrows. Fine-tuning was performed using a pre-learned model to construct a detection model. The pre-learned model used for Fine-tuning was selected as "sd-mobile-v1-co," which is expected to be used on mobile devices and is faster in processing and has a relatively high detection accuracy. In order to shorten the processing time for detecting the eyebrows and mouths, Neural Compute Stick2 (NCS2), an accelerator for deep planning inferences, was used. In addition, OpneVINO was used to convert to a detector executable at NCS2. The training data used to generate were images obtained by the authors and images of the published data set, Flickr-Faces-HQ [2], extracted from the face with a "face" detector.

2.2 Shape Identification Model

Convolutional Neural Network (CNN), a type of hierarchical neural network, is particularly utilized in the field of image recognition for the creation of shape identification models. The shape of each facial site to be identified was selected based on the Facial Action Cording System (FACS) [3] frequently used in facial analysis studies. This system implements to use FACSs in the four emotional expressions [4] of happiness, surprise, anger, and sadness shown in Table 1. Similar AUs were treated as one operation to stabilize the discrimination accuracy.

Table 1. FACS in each facial expression and example description of AU

Facial expression	FACS in each facial expression	No	Action	No	Action
Anger	AU4 + AU5 +AU25	1	Inner Brow Raiser	12	Lip Corner Puller
Happiness	AU6 + AU12 + AU26	2	Outer Brow Raiser	15	Lip Corner Depressor
Sadness	AU1 + AU4 + AU15	4	Brow Lowerer	25	Lips part
Surprise	AU1 + AU2 + AU5 + AU27	5	Upper Lid Raiser	26	Jaw Drop
		6	Cheek Raiser	27	Mouth Stretch

The construction of identifiers is described. The eyebrow discrimination model treats AU1 and AU2 as similar AUs and as one action of "eyebrows up". Classes to be identified are classified into three classes: "no change," "raised eyebrows," and "lowered eyebrows," based on facial expression. The Eye Identification Model treated AU5 as "Open eyes" and defined AU5 as "No change" and "Open eyes" in two classes. The mouth identification model treats AU25, AU26, and AU27 as similar AUs and as one action of "opening the mouth". The four classes to be identified are "No change," "Increase the angle of mouth," "Lower the angle of mouth," and "Open mouth".

The training data were based on images taken by the patient or on images generated by the Flickr-Faces-HQ and the Asia Face DB [5].

2.3 System Implementation

An emotional estimation support system was constructed using the generated detectors and identifiers. This system was constructed using a small portable device (Raspberry Pi3 Model B+) for supportive situations. The 1.3 Megapixel Webcam was used for the camera for shooting the other party of the dialogue. Figure 2 shows the processing times of each part of the recording of the other party of the dialogue to the speech conversion of the emotional estimation results. In the emotional discrimination process from the acquired facial image, the Face API outputs a score indicating the degree of emotional discrimination (anger, disgust, fear, joy, sadness, surprise, and apathy) and selects the highest score. If the emotional discrimination result of the apathy is obtained, the other party is considered not to be expressing the expression, and the subsequent processing is not performed, and the image is returned to the imaging process. In the facial region detection process, when an aperture opened as a detection class "aperture" is detected, the identification result of the aperture portion is used, and the shape identification process of the later aperture portion is omitted, thereby reducing the necessary processing and reducing the processing time and improving the identification accuracy. In the speech conversion process using OpenJTalk, the default acoustic model "nitech_j-p_atr503_m001.htsvoice" was used for the sound quality to be played.

Process	Time[s]
Take picture	1.16
Emotion estimation	1.15
Face parts detection	0.32
Identification of facial parts shape	3.47
Voice conversion	1.25
Total	7.35

Fig. 2. System processing time and snapshot of usability test

3 Evaluation

Detection and identification model performance evaluations were performed using test data not used for training and verification data. In addition, as a usability evaluation, five subjects with healthy hearing and no cognitive impairment were compared with the evaluation of the accuracy of listening to the estimated results output by the system and the estimation support of emotional discrimination alone by using test data with audio video as the interactive partner. The usability evaluation was performed by connecting the system body with the laptop PC for log management so that the log output of the system can be managed. The cognitive evaluation of the output results was performed by having the subjects use the system to answer the interviewed emotional estimation results verbally and compare them to the output logs. Comparative experiments included similar use of the system with a conventional emotional discrimination-only specification, comparing the conventional system with the system's emotional esti- mation support system with facial site information, and conducting a five-step category evaluation questionnaire (1: strongly disagree, 2: disagree, 3: neutral, 4: agree, 5: strongly agree).

Of the six basic emotions, four are "happiness," "anger," "sadness," and "surprise," and a total of eight videos were prepared by taking two videos each. The audio content in the test data was prepared based on the National Language Institute's Modern Japanese Writing Language Equilibrium Corpus [6]. Because the five-point rating questionnaire is classified into ordinal scales, the significance test was performed using the Wilcoxon signed-rank test, a nonparametric test. Figure 2 shows an experiment to evaluate usability. The system body was placed in a waist pouch and placed on the subject. The earphone was used as the output device for the estimation result. Assuming a typical interpersonal communication scene, the distance between the monitor and the subject reflecting the test data was approximately 70 cm, referring to the distance between individuals [7], which is considered to be sufficiently distant to recognize the facial expression of the other person in the dialogue. Subjects were allowed to wear an eye mask to recreate blindness.

3.1 Detection and Identification Model Performance

The accuracy performance of each part is shown in Table 2. Detection accuracy is 85% or more accurate in each facial region and can be recognized with stable accuracy. The reason why the detection accuracy of the eyebrows is slightly smaller than that of other facial sites is that the eyebrows have a greater individual difference in scenery than eyes and mouth. Since there are differences between individuals such as "shape," "size between eyebrows," "thickness," and "alignment," various eyebrows are created and training data are expanded to improve. In addition, the accuracy of shape is 80% or more accurate in each region, and our system can be recognized with stable accuracy.

3.2 Usability Survey

In the cognitive evaluation of the system's output, all subjects were able to recognize the output correctly and to confirm that the estimated results could be heard correctly. The results of comparative experiments are shown in Table 2. "*" indicates the question in which a significant difference was confirmed with a p value of 5% or less. Questions Q1, 2, and 3, "Did you understand your feelings well?" "Did you feel that the system is effective for non-verbal communication in blind situations?" confirmed the effectiveness of the system for non-verbal communication in blind situations. Questions in Q4 and Q5, "Did the use of the system interfere with the recognition of the conversation content?" and "Was the playback rate and voice quality adequate during synthesized speech playback?" did not show any significant differences between

Table 2. Detection and identification accuracy and usability and user experience surveys

Face parts	Brow	Eye	Mouth	
Detection accuracy	87.5	92.5	95	[%]
Identification accuracy	95	90	86	

Item	Emotion only	This system
Q1.Emotional understanding	3.4	4.6 *
Q2.Understanding facial expressions	3.6	4.2 *
Q3.Effective for blind communication	3.2	4.6 *
Q4.The use of the system did not hinder the recognition of the conversation	4.2	4.4
Q5.Playback speed and volume	4.2	4.2
Q6.Effect of adding facial parts shape		4.8
Q7.The number of shape patterns of the face parts		3.2

the two systems, and there was no particular effect on the cognition of the conversation content by adding information on the facial region shape. The question "Is it effective to add facial site geometry information" in Q6 yielded a high evaluation result of 4.8, confirming the contribution to emotional cognition through the transmission of facial site geometry. The Q7 question, "Are the number of face-site-shaped patterns appropriate?" yielded a relatively low evaluation result of 3.2, suggesting that the number of shapes identified in free descriptions is better, and that the recognition rate is faster. These problems are expected to be improved with implementations such as increasing the number of patterns and local emotional discrimination processing.

4 Conclusion

An interpersonal communication support system was implemented and evaluated using the shape identification of facial parts for the elderly or visually impaired persons. As a result, the recognition accuracy of the facial region detector and shape identification model was approximately 80% overall, and the effectiveness of the support system was confirmed by the usability evaluation. In the future, by improving the system, such as increasing the number of patterns for shape identification and improving the recognition speed, the system aims to achieve more natural non-linguistic communication by estimating more diverse expressions.

References

1. Buimer, H.P., Bittner, M.: Conveying facial expressions to blind and visually impaired persons through a wearable vibrotactile device. PLoS ONE **13**(3), e0195737 (2018)
2. Karras, T., Laine, S., Aila, T.: A style-based generator architecture for generative adversarial networks. In: CVPR 2019 (2019). https://arxiv.org/abs/1812.04948
3. Ekman, P., Friesen, W.V.: Unmasking the Face: A Guide to Recognizing Emotions from Facial Clues, pp. 262–266. Prentice-Hall, Englewood Cliffs (1975)
4. Yamaguchi, T., Oda, R., Koutaki, G., et al.: Face recognition by facial expression transformation. ITE Tech. Rep. **35**(52), 1–4 (2011)
5. Asian Face DB. https://sites.google.com/site/asianfacedb/
6. KOTONOHA: Modern Japanese Language Equilibrium Corpus, National Language Research Institute "Japanese Corpus" Project. http://www.kotonoha.gr.jp/shonagon/
7. Hall, E.T.: The Hidden Dimension, pp. 168–169. Peter Smith Pub Inc; Reprint (1992)

Speech Emotion Recognition from Social Media Voice Messages Recorded in the Wild

Lucía Gómez-Zaragozá[✉], Javier Marín-Morales[✉], Elena Parra[✉],
Jaime Guixeres[✉], and Mariano Alcañiz[✉]

Instituto de Investigación e Innovación en Bioingeniería,
Universitat Politècnica de València, Valencia, Spain
{lugoza,jamarmo,elparvar,jaiguipr,
malcaniz}@i3b.upv.es

Abstract. Speech is the most natural way for human communication, carrying the emotional state of the speaker that plays an important role in social interaction. Currently, many instant messaging apps offer the possibility of exchanging voice audios with other users. As a result, a great amount of voice data is generated every day, representing a new challenging approach for speech emotion recognition in real environments. In this study, we investigated emotion recognition from voice messages recorded in the wild using machine-learning algorithms. Unlike most research in this field, which use databases based on emotions evoked in lab environments, simulated by actors or subjectively selected from radio or TV talks, we created an ecological speech dataset with audios from real WhatsApp conversations of 30 Spanish speakers. Four external evaluators labelled each audio in terms of arousal and valence using the Self-Assessment Manikin (SAM) procedure. Pre-processing techniques were applied to the audios and different time and frequency domain features were extracted. Supervised machine learning classifiers were computed using feature reduction and hyper-parameter tuning in order to recognize the affective state of each voice message. The best recognition rate was obtained with Support Vector Machines, achieving 71.37% along the arousal dimension and 70.73% along the valence dimension. These results support the use of emotion recognition models on daily communication apps, helping to understand social human behavior and their interactions with devices in the real world.

Keywords: Speech emotion recognition · Speech database · Vocal social media

1 Introduction

Speech is the most natural and efficient way of communication for humans. It conveys not only linguistic information but also the emotional state of the speaker, which is a key factor for daily human interactions, as it is interpreted and used by the listener to adapt the behavior in response. Currently, speech emotion recognition (SER) is a growing research area that aims to recognize the emotional state of a speaker from the speech signal. It has potential applications both for the study of human-human communication and human-computer interaction (HCI) [1].

C. Stephanidis and M. Antona (Eds.): HCII 2020, CCIS 1224, pp. 330–336, 2020.
https://doi.org/10.1007/978-3-030-50726-8_43

In today's social media era, instant messaging tools such as WhatsApp or Facebook Messenger have spread worldwide, allowing the users to exchange text, voice, image and video messages. These applications do not only facilitate the communication with relatives and acquaintances but also are trending to compete with face-to-face inter-actions, especially among younger generations [2]. The communication in instant messaging tools is mainly performed via text or audio. To date, there has been extensive research in the study of emotions in text-based interactions [3], where the lack of non-verbal emotional cues is compensated by using emoticons, letter repetition or typed laughter, among others [4]. However, speech emotion recognition in mobile environment, and particularly in the context of instant messaging tools, is still at an early stage. One likely reason is that the task of recognizing emotions in real-world conditions is still a challenge.

Currently, the main approach for emotion recognition is based on supervised machine learning techniques, in which the database selection is a primary issue. The vast majority of SER research use databases that can be classified in three categories: acted, induced and natural/spontaneous [5]. The first include speeches that are por-trayed by professional or semi-professional actors who simulate emotions while pro-nouncing pre-determined isolated utterances. Induced datasets contain speeches produced in controlled situations designed to elicit a certain emotional state, for example watching a video, listening a story or conducting a guided discussion. The least frequent category are natural speech emotion databases, in which audios are recorded in real-world situations (such as real psychologist interviews) or they are obtained from movies and radio or TV programs (for instance reality shows or talk shows).

The databases described above have several limitations for its application in the recognition of real-life emotions, as described in diverse studies [5–7]. Acted databases are a popular method, as they are easier to create. However, acted emotions differ from natural emotions, tending to be more exaggerated and stereotypical. Induced databases include speeches that are more similar to real expression of emotions, but the methodology used to obtain them has some limits: each subject may react different to the same stimuli and a further subjective evaluation is needed in order to determine the sample's emotion, in addition to the ethical implications of inducing emotion. Regarding spontaneous databases, the recordings usually have conditions such as background noise and overlapping voices that are typical in natural environments, known as in-the-wild settings. Nevertheless, the emotions may not be spontaneous if the subject is aware of being recorded, as an interview or a radio show. In the case of hidden-recording, due to the artificial situation (lab or studio settings), the subject may subconsciously keep their expressions under control or express them in an unnatural way. It also important to note that recordings that are not produced in a conversational context lack some naturalness due to emotions are produced as a response to various situations. Furthermore, similar to induced databases, the samples showing emotional states are subjectively selected by evaluators and the databases involve legal issues and ethical problems that make public distribution difficult.

Therefore, there is a lack of research using databases that include audios that be-long to historical private communications, showing the underdevelopment of SER models that can be applied to human-human audio messaging. To our knowledge,

Dai et al. (2015) presented the first suitable speech dataset for emotion recognition on voice instant messaging, consisting of vocal messages from the popular Chinese application WeChat [8]. Since their goal was to study the emotion propagation in a particular group, they collected voice historical data from nine familiar members in the same WeChat group in order to extract personalized features and use them for training a machine learning model. However, it is still a challenge to evaluate datasets with a larger number of audios, subjects and languages.

In this work-in-progress research, we investigated emotion recognition from voice messages using acoustic features and machine-learning algorithms. We collected the audio data from real conversations of 30 Spanish speakers conducted in the popular mobile app WhatsApp, in which the expression of emotions is considered to be more suitable than on other social media platforms [9]. We obtained 12 audios for each of the subjects, with an equal number of positive, neutral and negative valence recordings. Four external evaluators labelled each of the audios in terms of arousal and valence. Thus, we obtained an ecological dataset with audios recorded in the wild, on which we applied speech emotion recognition techniques.

2   Materials and Methods

2.1   Participants

The present study initially included 30 Spanish speakers between the ages of 18 and 55 years old. However, as explained in *Data Collection*, six participants were excluded for the analysis, leaving a total of 24 subjects (62.5% females) of ages (Mean ± SD) 31.7 ± 11.1 with no self-reported speech disorder. All methods and experimental protocols were performed in accordance with the guidelines and regulations of the local ethics committee of the Universitat Politècnica de València.

2.2   Data Collection

The data was collected using an online platform designed ad-hoc. The participants completed the study with their computer, following the instructions given in the platform. Once they accepted the informed consent, the participants answered a sociodemographic questionnaire. Then, they were requested to upload 12 voice messages according to two criteria: the audios should have been sent to other contacts prior to the study and one-third of them should have positive, neutral and negative valence, respectively.

Firstly, an expert manually identified the audios recorded in critical background noise conditions, rejecting from the study 6 participants whose majority of audios presented these states. To avoid any possible bias derived of the self-assessment, the audios were assessed adopting the Self-Assessment Manikin (SAM) procedure [10], which consists of a non-verbal scale based on pictures that measures the valence, arousal and dominance related with an emotional response to a stimuli. Four evaluators used the 5-point SAM scale to rate each audio in terms of positive/high (>0), neutral (=0) and negative/low (<0) valence and arousal respectively. Only those samples in which three out of four of the labels were in consensus were chosen for the study. To perform valence classification, 188 samples (49.5% positive valence) were considered, excluding neutral audios as an initial simplification. With regard to arousal classification, the data was unbalanced due to the fact that participants chose the audios on the basis of their valence. For this reason, we considered low and neutral arousal recordings as pertaining to the same group, resulting in 234 samples (59.4% high arousal).

2.3   Data Processing

The audio files, collected in .ogg format with sample rates of 41 kHz and 48 kHz, were processed following the pipeline in Fig. 1 in order to obtain two machine learning models for predicting valence and arousal independently. Each step is detailed below.

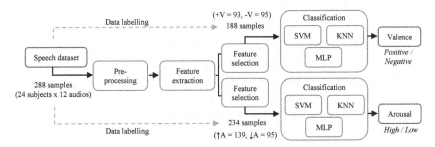

Fig. 1. Pipeline of the proposed speech emotion recognition procedure.

Pre-processing. The audio signals were normalized to range $[-1, 1]$ using the standardisation method and then resampled to 48 kHz.

Feature Extraction. Long-term acoustic features were computed in two stages using the pyAudioAnalysis open source Python library [11]. First, the audio signal was divided into frames of 50 ms with 50% overlap. For each of them, the following features were computed: time domain cues (zero crossing rate, energy and entropy of energy) and frequency domain cues (spectral centroid, spectral spread, spectral entropy, spectral flux, spectral roll-off, 13 Mel-Frequency Cepstral Coefficients (MFCCs), 12-element chroma vector and the standard deviation of the 12 chroma coefficients). Long-term features were finally computed as the statistics (mean and standard deviation) of the frame-based features extracted for the whole audio, assuming that their temporal variations carry the emotional content of the recordings.

Feature Selection. Due to the high-dimensional feature space resulting after data processing, random forest-based feature selection was applied in order to avoid overfitting. The algorithm rank the features according to the importance weights extracted from an artificial classification task and one feature is dropped in each iteration. The process continues until only one feature is considered, thus selecting the vocal cues that contain the most relevant emotion information from speech signals.

Classification. The following machine learning algorithms were applied for recognizing the affective state of voice data based on the extracted acoustic features: K-Nearest Neighbours (KNN), Support Vector Machines (SVM) and Multilayer Perceptron (MLP). We adopted cross-validation procedure for hyper-parameter tuning and feature selection. Specifically, we applied group k-fold cross-validation (k = 6) so that audios from the same subject were not included both in training and validation set.

3   Results

Table 1 and Table 2 show the performance of the three machine learning models that achieved best results after feature selection and hyper-parameter tuning, in terms of valence and arousal respectively. It includes the accuracy of each model, the true positive rate (TPR), the true negative rate (TNR) and the number of features included in the model (N-features).

Table 1. Best accuracy results for each model in terms of valence.

Model	Accuracy (%)	TPR	TNR	N-features
KNN	68.06	63.02	72.43	57
SVM	70.73	70.34	70.35	5
MLP	62.85	63.74	59.03	39

Table 2. Best accuracy results for each model in terms of arousal.

Model	Accuracy (%)	TPR	TNR	N-features
KNN	67.95	86.33	41.78	23
SVM	71.37	79.59	59.28	6
MLP	65.81	75.87	54.30	78

4   Discussion

One of the most critical factors to create an automatic speech emotion recognition system is database selection. Most previous studies performed SER using speech corpus whose application for real-life emotion recognition is rather limited. Here, we collected the speech dataset from voice messages from real conversations, where the participants were not aware that their audios were going to be part of a study and thus, samples can be considered as natural expressions of emotions. In addition, voice data was originally recorded in the wild so the audios presented background noise and only those subjects whose majority of audios had critical noise conditions were dropped from the study. We performed a comparison of different classification models for valence and arousal recognition from acoustic features extracted from the voice messages.

Different classification algorithms are used in the literature for recognizing the affective state of voice data based on the extracted acoustic features. Particularly, SVM is one of the most widely used methods [6, 7], as the results obtained here seem to support.

The results in Table 1 show that SVM obtained the best recognition rate, achieving 70.73% accuracy in predicting positive or negative valence from the voice messages. Since it uses only five features, it avoids the possibility of overfitting, suggesting a promising result. KNN reached close accuracy, 68.06%, but including a large number of features needed.

Regarding arousal results in Table 2, the 71.37% SVM accuracy also outperformed the other two classification models, using also only six features. However, TNR are in general low, which may be caused by the annotation approach that consider both neutral and low arousal as pertaining to the same group.

However, some limitations need to be considered in this work-in-progress. Firstly, six participants were not included in the analysis due to critical noise conditions, which limited the number of speakers in the dataset. The unbalanced distribution of the audio data in terms of arousal led to a reassignment in the labels that may influenced the results. Another critical factor is the annotation method, which is in general a challenging task, as there are several approaches with respect to various factors: the classification of emotions (categories or dimensions), the emotion unit to label (phonemes, single words, sentences or complete utterances) and the evaluator (familiar members, experts or non-experts subjects).

The results highlight many point that need to be addressed in future research. The number of speakers should be increased, and the influence of the gender need to be considered since it could affect many features. In addition, the implementation of noise reduction techniques is also considered as part of ongoing research to deal with the challenge of recognizing emotions in real-world environments.

5   Conclusion

In this work-in-progress research, we collected our speech database using real voice messages from WhatsApp conversation of Spanish speakers. We emotionally labelled the audio samples in terms of valence and arousal. Global acoustic features were computed for each recording and a comparison of several classification models was performed for both valence and arousal prediction.

Preliminary results support the feasibility of using emotion recognition models on daily communication apps. It may help to understand social human behavior and their interactions with devices in the real world, improving personalization and adaptive interfaces in social networks.

Acknowledgments. This work was funded by the European Commission (H2020-825585 HELIOS).

References

1. Khanna, P., Sasikumar, M.: Recognizing emotions from human speech. In: Pise, S.J. (ed.) Thinkquest 2010, pp. 219–223. Springer, New Delhi (2010). https://doi.org/10.1007/978-81-8489-989-4_40
2. Venter, E.: Challenges for meaningful interpersonal communication in a digital era. HTS Teol. Stud. **75**, 1–6 (2019). https://doi.org/10.4102/hts.v75i1.5339
3. Zucco, C., Calabrese, B., Agapito, G., Guzzi, P., Cannataro, M.: Sentiment analysis for mining texts and social networks data: methods and tools. Wiley Interdiscip. Rev. Data Min. Knowl. Discov. **10**, e1333 (2019). https://doi.org/10.1002/widm.1333
4. Sherman, L., Michikyan, M., Greenfield, P.: The effects of text, audio, video, and in-person communication on bonding between friends. Cyberpsychology J. Psychosoc. Res. Cybersp. **7**, Article 1 (2013). https://doi.org/10.5817/cp2013-2-3
5. Swain, M., Routray, A., Kabisatpathy, P.: Databases, features and classifiers for speech emotion recognition: a review. Int. J. Speech Technol. **21**, 93–120 (2018). https://doi.org/10.1007/s10772-018-9491-z
6. Akçay, M.B., Oğuz, K.: Speech emotion recognition: emotional models, databases, features, preprocessing methods, supporting modalities, and classifiers. Speech Commun. **116**, 56–76 (2020). https://doi.org/10.1016/j.specom.2019.12.001
7. El Ayadi, M., Kamel, M.S., Karray, F.: Survey on speech emotion recognition: features, classification schemes, and databases. Pattern Recognit. **44**(3), 572–587 (2011). https://doi.org/10.1016/j.patcog.2010.09.020
8. Dai, W., Han, D., Dai, Y., Xu, D.: Emotion recognition and affective computing on vocal social media. Inf. Manag. **52**, 777–788 (2015). https://doi.org/10.1016/j.im.2015.02.003
9. Waterloo, S.F., Baumgartner, S.E., Peter, J., Valkenburg, P.M.: Norms of online expressions of emotion: comparing Facebook, Twitter, Instagram, and WhatsApp. New Media Soc. **20**(5), 1813–1831 (2017). https://doi.org/10.1177/1461444817707349
10. Bradley, M.M., Lang, P.J.: Measuring emotion: the self-assessment manikin and the semantic differential. J. Behav. Ther. Exp. Psychiatry **25**(1), 49–59 (1994). https://doi.org/10.1016/0005-7916(94)90063-9
11. Giannakopoulos, T.: pyAudioAnalysis: an open-source python library for audio signal analysis. PLoS One **10**(12), e0144610 (2015). https://doi.org/10.1371/journal.pone.0144610

Estimating Immersed User States from Eye Movements: A Survey

Jutta Hild[✉], Michael Voit, and Elisabeth Peinsipp-Byma

Fraunhofer IOSB, 76131 Karlsruhe, Germany
{jutta.hild,michael.voit,
elisabeth.peinsipp-byma}@iosb.fraunhofer.de

Abstract. The cognitive state of a person affects their task performance and learning success. This holds particularly for immersed states like flow and immersion. Hence, estimating immersed user states appears useful for adapting computer systems in order to maintain or achieve user flow or immersion. For practical use, the estimation method must provide continuously quantitative measurements in real-time in order to allow capturing short-term user state changes. In addition, the method should work as unobtrusive as possible in order to impose as less additional load on the user as possible. Tracking eye movement behavior using a remote eye-tracking device meets both requirements. Eye movement parameters are related to various cognitive processes and might therefore be useful for the estimation of immersed user states. This contribution gives an overview on the potential of the eye movement parameters fixation duration, pupil dilation, and spontaneous eye blink rate. As immersed states are complex cognitive states and as the three parameters provide complementary information it appears appropriate to capture all three parameters for the estimation. However, all three parameters are affected by multiple other factors besides the characteristics of the task. Hence, even the estimation using the combination appears to be a challenging issue.

Keywords: Cognitive user states · Flow · Immersion · Eye movement behavior

1 Introduction

Task performance as well as learning success are affected by the cognitive state of a person. Hence, estimating the cognitive state of a system user is of interest in many HCI applications. Of interest are for example user attention, cognitive load, fatigue, emotional state or the general level of activation (a.k.a arousal), but also more complex states like the immersive states flow and immersion. Besides getting insight into the user's mind – which is the primary interest of neuroscience and cognitive psychology – such information can be used in order to adapt systems in HCI. In this contribution, the focus is on software applications with rich dynamic visual input like serious games or video surveillance and the estimation of the user states flow or immersion. For example, considering serious games, a flow detector might be useful as a basis for short-term adaptation of the difficulty level.

© Springer Nature Switzerland AG 2020
C. Stephanidis and M. Antona (Eds.): HCII 2020, CCIS 1224, pp. 337–342, 2020.
https://doi.org/10.1007/978-3-030-50726-8_44

The research literature proposes three types of methods for estimating cognitive user states: performance measures like error rates, subjective measures like questionnaires, and physiological measures like skin resistance, heart rate or eye movement behavior. Their usefulness differs, on the one hand, with the cognitive state of interest but also with the application. For adaptive HCI systems, two issues are important. First, the measure must be able to provide continuously quantitative measurements in order to allow capturing short-term changes in the user state. This is the case for physiological measures that record data in real-time. Second, the measure should work as unobtrusive as possible in order to impose as less additional load on the user as possible. Considering the physiological measures, this is the case for remote eye tracking devices as no technical equipment applied to the body encumbers the user like for skin resistance or heart rate measurement. Today, there are low-cost gaming eye-trackers like the Tobii 4C available that operate at a sampling rate of 90 Hz [1]. The Tobii 4C is easily to set up by simply putting it on the bottom edge of a monitor and connect it to the computer via USB like a computer mouse or a keyboard. Moreover, there are gaming laptops with built-in eye-tracking devices as well [2]. Hence, remote eye-trackers are much closer to typical computer input devices than to other physiological measurement devices that are of great use in lab environments, but inconceivable in practical everyday use. Klingner et al. (2008) were among the first to show that measuring eye movement behavior was possible using a remote eye-tracking device [3].

There are many contributions investigating how to estimate user states like mental load or attention from eye movement behavior, but only few consider immersive states like flow and immersion. Section 2 describes the concepts of flow and immersion; Sect. 3 gives a survey about eye movement parameters that have been proposed or appear to be promising in order to derive flow and immersion. Section 4 provides a short conclusion.

2   Flow and Immersion

Flow and immersion are cognitive states with complex concepts. Csikszentmihalyi (1990) defines flow as "(…) the state in which individuals are so involved in an activity that nothing else seems to matter" [4]. Flow appears to be defined by multiple characteristics: intense and focused concentration on the present task, clear goals, balance between challenge and capabilities, sense of being able to control ones actions, continuous processing of feedback about progress, loss of reflective self-consciousness, distortion of temporal experience, and experience of the activity as intrinsically rewarding [5].

Flow is associated with positive feelings and, hence, a state of low stress. As a result, flow make people accomplish tasks well and nurtures learning processes. Sport psychology defines it as an intrinsic motivated optimal mental state in which persons achieve optimal performance [6]. The cognitive mechanisms behind flow are still a topic of research. A central hypothesis proposes that flow is associated with efficient attention control. Recently, Ulrich et al. (2014, 2015) [7, 8] were able to derive neural correlates of flow looking at brain activity. For example, they report increased activity in brain areas related to subsystems concerned with the flow characteristics defined by Csikszentmihalyi.

Immersion has been investigated mainly in the context of computer gaming. A typical characteristic is the feeling of being drawn into the application or game. Brown and Cairns (2004) identified three levels building on one another: engagement, engrossment, and total immersion [9]. Total immersion and flow overlap in three characteristics: involvement in a challenging task, distortion of time experience, and loosing reality and instead being drawn into the world of the task. In contrast to flow, immersion is not necessarily associated with positive feelings, and furthermore it occurs during passive experiences like watching TV, while flow requires active engagement in a task [2].

3   Eye Movement Parameters for Estimation of Immersive States

Central for the three overlapping characteristics of flow and immersion is the aspect of deep attention that in turn is closely associated with the eye gaze parameter of *fixation duration*. Fixations duration mirrors the linking of attention to a location as well as the time that is required to process the visual stimulus at this location. A higher average fixation duration means that the observer takes more time for the interpretation or processing of a fixated target object [10]. Some authors utilize the inverse measure of number of fixations. For example, Jennett et al. (2008) [11] found a smaller number of fixations per minute with higher immersion in computer games, as attention was now more focused. However, they state that there could also be tasks comprising less fixations even if users feel less immersed. Therefore, it is not appropriate to use fixation duration/number of fixations as the only measure.

Evaluating fixation duration for applications with rich dynamic visual input like in serious games or video surveillance, gaze data analysis has to consider that in such situations besides fixations and saccades there are smooth pursuit eye movements present, too. In order to get correct results for fixation duration, the standard algorithms used for gaze data recorded from static display content are not suitable [12]. Instead, recent contributions propose the use of machine learning to solve this problem [13, 14].

Another important aspect of flow is the balance between capabilities of the person and challenge of the task. Hence, it appears appropriate to derive the mental load of the system user, e.g., to provide adaptively the optimal task difficulty [15]. Mental load is defined as the ratio of cognitive demands imposed by the task and a person's cognitive resources [16]. A prominent gaze parameter for mental load is *pupil dilation*. Pupil dilation is modulated by brain regions that control physiological arousal and attention [17–20]. The higher the fire rate of specific neurons in the brain stem (Locus coerulus), the more dilated the pupil as those neurons inhibit the parasympathic sphinctor eye muscle and activate the sympathic dilator eye muscle. The involved neurotransmitter norepinephrine (NE) supports awakeness in large parts of the cerebral cortex, and at the same time, structures supporting sleep are inhibited. Optimal task engagement can be seen for a medium NE-level [20].

Several contributions showed that pupil dilation gets larger if mental activity and pleasure are higher, and that it gets smaller for displeasure [21–23]. It correlates furthermore with the effort the person spends for the task. Moreover, there is an anticipatory effect: if persons are warned that there will be a difficult task, the pupils dilate slightly [24]. This phenomenon is called the task-evoked pupillary response [17], where the pupil dilates with the task and reduces its size a few seconds after the task has be completed. This reaction occurs involuntarily and for several cognitive processes which can be characterized by increased cognitive load: access to short- and long-term memory, mental arithmetics, sentence completion, vigilance, visual and auditive perception tasks [18].

One big challenge for deriving mental load from the pupil dilation is the fact that besides the task difficultly also the lighting conditions influence the physiological changes in the eye. The primary purpose of the pupil is to regulate the amount of light falling into the eye, thus avoiding that too much light will damage the retina. Authors report a ten-fold larger effect of the light compared to cognitive load. Therefore, contributions try to keep the lighting conditions stable, in order to eliminate the light pupillary effect. For software applications with changing dynamic content, however, this is not easy to accomplish. Unfortunately, both effects are not additive [3]. However, recently Pfleging et al. (2016) [25] proposed a model to derive the pupil dilation individually by applying an individual calibration process. The model requires three informations: the person's typical individual pupil dilation for a certain lighting condition, the current lighting condition and the average pupil dilation of the person for this lighting condition. Furthermore, it has to be considered that issues like negative emotions, subjective preferences, and pharmacological substances also affect pupil dilation.

Another parameter differing in cognitive processes like visual attention and mental load is the *spontaneous eye blink rate*, but also the duration of eye closure. The spontaneous eye blink rate correlates with the dopamine level of the central nervous system that reveals processes of learning and goal-directed behavior [20]. Similar to the relationship between pupil dilation and the norepinephrine level, a medium dopamine level is optimal for task execution.

Spontaneous eye blink rate is inhibited if information is expected, presented and processed [26]. Moreover, several contributions in several application domains showed reduced spontaneous eye blink rate and shorter eye closure durations with increasing mental load. Examples are a military identification game [27] or laparoscopic training of surgeons [28].

Spontaneous eye blink rate is influenced by several issues which have to be controlled [20, 29], for example the humidity of the eye, fatigue, time of the day, or several illnesses. Similar to pupil dilation, the characteristics of spontaneous eye blink rate vary individually. Hence, it is necessary – as for pupil dilation – to determine an individual baseline [28].

4   Conclusion

Estimating immersive states from eye movement parameters appears promising as various authors investigated how to derive different aspects of flow and immersion like attention or mental load using different eye movement parameters. Three parameters occur most frequently: fixation duration, pupil dilation and spontaneous eye blink rate. Eckstein et al. (2017) [20] propose to choose a combination all as they all deliver complementary information. Pupil dilation and spontaneous eye blink rate deliver partly overlapping information, because their underlying systems in the brain (mediated by the neurotransmitters norepinephrine and dopamine) partly overlap functionally concerning their impact on cognition. However, studies show that the information they deliver is not redundant [30, 31].

For all three parameters, it is important to control the various factors that affect them besides the task characteristics. As this will be difficult, even the estimation using the combination appears to be a challenging issue. Considering the rich dynamic visual input with varying lighting conditions of serious games and video surveillance applications, it appears most challenging to apply pupil dilation for flow estimation.

References

1. Tobii. https://gaming.tobii.com/tobii-eye-tracker-4c/. Accessed 19 Mar 2020
2. Windowsreport. https://windowsreport.com/eye-tracking-laptops/. Accessed 19 Mar 2020
3. Klingner, J., Kumar, R., Hanrahan, P.: Measuring the task-evoked pupillary response with a remote eye tracker. In: Proceedings of the 2008 Symposium on Eye Tracking Research & Applications, pp. 69–72. ACM (2008)
4. Csikszentmihalyi, M.: Flow: The Psychology of Optimal Experience. Harper & Row, New York (1990)
5. Nakamura, J., Csikszentmihalyi, M.: The concept of flow. In: Csikszentmihalyi, M. (ed.) Flow and the Foundations of Positive Psychology, pp. 239–263. Springer, Dordrecht (2014). https://doi.org/10.1007/978-94-017-9088-8_16
6. Harris, D.J., Vine, S.J., Wilson, M.R.: Flow and quiet eye: the role of attentional control in flow experience. Cogn. Process. **18**(3), 343–347 (2017)
7. Ulrich, M., Keller, J., Hoenig, K., Waller, C., Grön, G.: Neural correlates of experimentally induced flow experiences. Neuroimage **86**, 194–202 (2014)
8. Ulrich, M., Keller, J., Grön, G.: Neural signatures of experimentally induced flow experiences identified in a typical fMRI block design with BOLD imaging. Soc. Cogn. Affect. Neurosci. **11**(3), 496–507 (2015)
9. Brown, E., Cairns, P.: A grounded investigation of game immersion. In: CHI'04 Extended Abstracts on Human Factors in Computing Systems, pp. 1297–1300. ACM (2004)
10. Toet, A.: Gaze directed displays as an enabling technology for attention aware systems. Comput. Hum. Behav. **22**(4), 615–647 (2006)
11. Jennett, C., et al.: Measuring and defining the experience of immersion in games. Int. J. Hum. Comput. Stud. **66**(9), 641–661 (2008)
12. Andersson, R., Larsson, L., Holmqvist, K., Stridh, M., Nyström, M.: One algorithm to rule them all? An evaluation and discussion of ten eye movement event-detection algorithms. Behav. Res. Methods **49**(2), 616–637 (2017)

13. Zemblys, R., Niehorster, D.C., Komogortsev, O., Holmqvist, K.: Using machine learning to detect events in eye-tracking data. Behav. Res. Methods **50**(1), 160–181 (2018)

14. Startsev, M., Agtzidis, I., Dorr, M.: 1D CNN with BLSTM for automated classification of fixations, saccades, and smooth pursuits. Behav. Res. Methods **51**(2), 556–572 (2019)

15. Palinko, O., Kun, A.: Exploring the influence of light and cognitive load on pupil diameter in driving simulator studies (2011)

16. Wickens, C.D.: Multiple resources and performance prediction. Theor. Issues Ergon. Sci. **3**(2), 159–177 (2002)

17. Beatty, J.: Task-evoked pupillary responses, processing load, and the structure of processing resources. Psychol. Bull. **91**(2), 276 (1982)

18. Beatty, J., Lucero-Wagoner, B.: The pupillary system. In: Handbook of Psychophysiology, vol. 2, pp. 142–162 (2000)

19. Sirois, S., Brisson, J.: Pupillometry. Wiley Interdisc. Rev. Cogn. Sci. **5**(6), 679–692 (2014)

20. Eckstein, M.K., Guerra-Carrillo, B., Singley, A.T.M., Bunge, S.A.: Beyond eye gaze: what else can eyetracking reveal about cognition and cognitive development? Dev. Cogn. Neurosci. **25**, 69–91 (2017)

21. Hess, E.H., Polt, J.M.: Pupil size as related to interest value of visual stimuli. Science **132**(3423), 349–350 (1960)

22. Hess, E.H., Polt, J.M.: Pupil size in relation to mental activity during simple problem-solving. Science **143**(3611), 1190–1192 (1964)

23. Hess, E.H.: Attitude and pupil size. Sci. Am. **212**(4), 46–55 (1965)

24. Kahneman, D., Beatty, J.: Pupil diameter and load on memory. Science **154**(3756), 1583–1585 (1966)

25. Pfleging, B., Fekety, D.K., Schmidt, A., Kun, A.L.: A model relating pupil diameter to mental workload and lighting conditions. In: Proceedings of the 2016 CHI Conference on Human Factors in Computing Systems, pp. 5776–5788. ACM (2016)

26. Fukuda, K., Stern, J.A., Brown, T.B., Russo, M.B.: Cognition, blinks, eye-movements, and pupillary movements during performance of a running memory task. Aviat. Space Environ. Med. **76**(7), C75–C85 (2005)

27. Van Orden, K.F., Limbert, W., Makeig, S., Jung, T.P.: Eye activity correlates of workload during a visuospatial memory task. Hum. Factors **43**(1), 111–121 (2001)

28. Zheng, B., Jiang, X., Tien, G., Meneghetti, A., Panton, O.N.M., Atkins, M.S.: Workload assessment of surgeons: correlation between NASA TLX and blinks. Surg. Endosc. **26**(10), 2746–2750 (2012)

29. Barbato, G., Ficca, G., Muscettola, G., Fichele, M., Beatrice, M., Rinaldi, F.: Diurnal variation in spontaneous eye-blink rate. Psychiatry Res. **93**(2), 145–151 (2000)

30. Siegle, G.J., Ichikawa, N., Steinhauer, S.: Blink before and after you think: Blinks occur prior to and following cognitive load indexed by pupillary responses. Psychophysiology **45**(5), 679–687 (2008)

31. Tharp, J.A., Wendelken, C., Mathews, C.A., Marco, E.J., Schreier, H., Bunge, S.A.: Tourette syndrome: complementary insights from measures of cognitive control, eyeblink rate, and pupil diameter. Front. Psychiatry **6**, 95 (2015)

Classification of Emotions Indicated by Walking Using Motion Capture

Yusuke Ishida and Hisaya Tanaka[✉]

Kogakuin University,
2665-1 Nakanomachi, Hachioji-shi, Tokyo 192-0015, Japan
yusuke1210kk@gmail.com, hisaya@cc.kogakuin.ac.jp

Abstract. Research on the classification of emotions includes research using brain waves and heartbeats. However, in each case, the requirement to wear devices to take measurements is burdensome for subjects. Therefore, the purpose of this study is to classify emotions by analyzing walking. We propose an emotional analysis method that can analyze emotions numerically. The proposed linear model is composed of three matrices: an emotional matrix, A; an emotional vector, Z; and a biological vector, C. The emotion vector represents a subjective value of emotion, and the biological vector represents measured biological data. The emotion matrix converts the biological vector into an emotional vector. Therefore, the linear model is represented by $Z = AC$. Ten sets of walking episodes were measured per person. The first five sets are data for learning, and the second five sets are data for classification. The subjects listened to classical music and quantified their emotions using questionnaires. Five gaits were used for classification: stride length, arm amplitude, speed, foot height, and hand height. The highest accuracy rate in the classification of emotions under the emotional analysis method was 80%. Analysis of data from the walking experiments revealed that subjects with a high classification accuracy rate showed emotions while walking. On the other hand, subjects with a low classification accuracy rate did not show emotions while walking. Since the maximum difference was as large as 60%, it is considered that the ease of expressing emotions greatly affects the classification accuracy rate. It was suggested that the classification of emotions using the emotional analysis method is effective for people who tend to express emotions in their walking style. Future tasks include proposing new analytical methods, examining more suitable gaits, and classifying emotions into more categories.

Keywords: Emotions · Walking · Motion capture

1 Introduction

In modern Japan, the development of a strong economy and technological progress have allowed most people to live comfortably. On the other hand, the number of people who experience stress in their daily lives is increasing to the extent that Japan has been labeled "a high-stress society." In 2013, the Ministry of Health, Labor, and Welfare conducted a national workforce survey on "stress related to work and occupational life" and found that 52.3% of the respondents experienced strong feelings of stress. In 2018,

C. Stephanidis and M. Antona (Eds.): HCII 2020, CCIS 1224, pp. 343–351, 2020.
https://doi.org/10.1007/978-3-030-50726-8_45

the same survey revealed that the proportion of respondents experiencing feelings of stress had increased to 58% [1]. Research on emotions is important to support people who are suffering in this stressful society. There have been many studies on the classification of emotions. Emotions are said to have various effects on the human body, and research has mainly been conducted using biological information. There have been many studies based on biological information, such as Electroencephalogram (EEG), heart rate variability, and respiration [2, 3]. However, many of these measurements were taken while the subjects were resting; there have been few studies in which these measurements were taken while the subjects were in motion. In addition, research in which biological devices are used to collect information can be problematic as subjects find it burdensome to wear these devices.

Venture et al. concluded that "walking can identify human emotions" [4]. Their investigation used a human-like model to simulate five different emotions while walking. When specific parameters, such as speed and posture, were changed, the emotions perceived by observers changed accordingly. The observers' average accuracy rate in recognizing the four different emotions from the gait of the model was 78%. This suggests the possibility of extracting individual characteristics from walking styles and numerically predicting human emotions. Toshimitsu Musha proposed an emotional spectrum analysis method (ESAM) as a method for numerically analyzing and measuring the human mind [5]. This is a method that quantifies emotional states using three determinants and classifies them into four distinct emotions. He showed the effect of music therapy on the psychological states of subjects numerically by measuring their brain waves. Utsunomiya et al. and Takeuchi et al. have used similar approaches in their studies [6, 7].

Walking refers to the relatively slow movement of an animal's legs and is distinguished from "running," which denotes the movement of legs at high speed. Although it is said that emotions can be discerned in people's facial expressions and the quality of their voice, the studies described above show that emotions are also manifested by walking. To our knowledge, there has been no research on the classification of emotions through analysis of walking movements, so it can be said that the classification of emotions according to walking styles is novel and useful.

Gait refers to the state of a person walking, and typical examples include stride length and speed. The gaits used in this study and their definitions are presented in Table 1.

The purpose of this study was to classify walking motions into two emotions (positive and negative) by linear analysis with reference to ESAM. Table 2 presents a comparison with previous studies.

Table 1. Gaits and their definitions

Gait	Definition
Stride	Maximum distance between both heels
Arm swing	Maximum distance between both wrists
Speed	Walking speed
Heel height	The maximum distance between the ground and the heel
Wrist height	The maximum distance between the ground and the wrist

Table 2. Comparison with previous research

Researcher	Emotion	Biological information
Toshimitsu Musha	4 emotions	EEG
Naoko Utsunomiya	Pleasant or unpleasant	EEG
Toshifumi Takeuchi	Pleasant or unpleasant	EEG
Yusuke Ishida	Positive or negative	Walking

2 Method of Analysis

2.1 Emotional Spectrum Analysis Method

The ESAM is a method of numerically analyzing emotions by using the linear models in Eqs. 1 and 2. A is defined as a "sensitivity matrix" for classifying emotions; Z is defined as a "sensitivity vector," representing subjective emotional values; and C is defined as an "input vector," representing measured data. The sensitivity matrix converts the input vector into the sensitivity vector.

$$Z = AC \tag{1}$$

$$\begin{pmatrix} z_{11} & \cdots & z_{1n} \\ \vdots & \ddots & \vdots \\ z_{l1} & \cdots & z_{ln} \end{pmatrix} = \begin{pmatrix} a_{11} & \cdots & a_{1m} \\ \vdots & \ddots & \vdots \\ a_{l1} & \cdots & a_{lm} \end{pmatrix} \begin{pmatrix} c_{11} & \cdots & c_{1n} \\ \vdots & \ddots & \vdots \\ c_{m1} & \cdots & c_{mn} \end{pmatrix} \tag{2}$$

2.2 Emotion Analysis Method (This Study)

Emotion Vector: Z. The emotion vector evaluates the subjective value of the subject numerically and uses it for the determinant. Therefore, in this study, the input value of the emotion vector was determined using a questionnaire.

Biological Vector: C. The biological vector determines the input value based on walking measurement data. In this study, we used five gaits: stride, arm swing, speed, heel height, and wrist height. The reason for choosing these gaits is that the values are generally expected to be large for positive emotions and small for negative emotions.

Emotion Matrix: A. The emotion matrix is a matrix calculated from Eq. 3 transformed from Eq. 1. This matrix was calculated using the emotion vector and the inverse matrix of the biological vector.

$$A = ZC^{-1} \tag{3}$$

Estimated Emotion Vector: $\widehat{Z}$. The matrix used for emotion classification was defined as the "estimated emotion vector" and is represented by $\widehat{Z}$. This matrix represents the subject's estimated subjective value. As with the emotion vector, it was calculated using Eq. 4.

$$\widehat{Z} = AC \tag{4}$$

Classification Method. The emotion classification was performed by comparing the emotion vector with the estimated emotion vector. If z_i in Eq. 5 was the same as $\widehat{z}_i$ in Eq. 6, the classification was correct, but if the signs were different, the classification was incorrect.

$$Z = (z_1 \quad z_2 \quad z_3 \quad z_4 \quad z_5) \tag{5}$$

$$\widehat{Z} = (\widehat{z}_1 \quad \widehat{z}_2 \quad \widehat{z}_3 \quad \widehat{z}_4 \quad \widehat{z}_5) \tag{6}$$

3 Experiment

3.1 Overview

Emotion Matrix Creation Experiment. We performed an emotion matrix creation experiment as a preliminary experiment for this study. In this experiment, an emotion matrix was created from an emotion vector whose input value was determined from the questionnaire results and a biological vector whose input value was determined by data on walking.

Estimated Emotion Vector Creation Experiment. We conducted an estimated emotion vector creation experiment as the main experiment in this research. The estimated emotion vector was created from the emotion matrix created in Sect. 3.2.1 and the biological vector whose input value was determined by the newly measured data from the walking experiments. Emotion classification was performed by comparing the results with the emotion vector determined from the actual questionnaire results.

3.2   Emotion Analysis Method

Input Value of the Emotion Vector. In this study, the input value was determined by a questionnaire. Subjects were stimulated by classical music during the experiment. There were two types of questionnaire, one with a 7-point rating and another with a 100-point rating. These questionnaires were intended to make it easier for the subjects to make more accurate evaluations and were not used directly in data processing. The subject answered with a 7-point scale and then answered with a 100-point scale. This questionnaire allowed responses with a value between -100 and $+100$, providing a more detailed evaluation of the subject's emotions. A value closer to -100 indicated a negative tendency, and a value closer to $+100$ indicated a positive tendency. The emotion vector was converted from -1 to $+1$.

Input Value of the Biological Vector. The biological vector represents the data from the measurements of walking. In this study, we used five gaits: stride, arm swing, speed, heel height, and wrist height. The stride is the maximum value of the distance between the two heels, the arm amplitude is the maximum value of the distance between the two wrists, the speed is the speed when walking at 5 m, and the foot height is the maximum value of the height of the heels from the ground. The wrist height is the maximum value of the height of both wrists from the ground. The stride, arm swing, foot height, and wrist height are the average of all local maxima measured multiple times in a single walk. Therefore, the definition of each element is as presented in Eq. 7–Eq. 11.

$$stride[i] = \frac{1}{n} \sum_{k=1}^{n} stride\_peak(k) \tag{7}$$

$$arm\ swing[i] = \frac{1}{n} \sum_{k=1}^{n} arm\ swing\_peak(k) \tag{8}$$

$$speed[i] = 5/t(i) \tag{9}$$

$$foot\ height[i] = \frac{1}{n} \sum_{k=1}^{n} foot\ height\_peak(k) \tag{10}$$

$$hand\ height[i] = \frac{1}{n} \sum_{k=1}^{n} hand\ height\_peak(k) \tag{11}$$

Equation 7 is the definition of the stride. *stride[i]* is the stride of the *i-th* set, and *stride_peak(n)* is the *n-th* maximum. Equation 8 is the definition of the arm swing. *arm swing[i]* is the arm swing of the *i-th* set, and *arm swing_peak(n)* is the *n-th* maximum. Equation 9 is the definition of speed. *speed[i]* is the speed of the *i-th* set, and *t (i)* is the time taken for the *i-th* set walking. Equation 10 is the definition of heel height. *foot height [i]* is the heel height of the *i-th* set, and *heel height_peak (n)* is the *n-th* maximum. Equation 11 is the definition of wrist height. *wrist height [i]* is the height of the wrist in the i-th set, and *wrist height_peak (n)* is the n-th maximum. In order to equalize the effect of each gait, normalization was performed for each gait so that the maximum value was 1 and the minimum value was 0.

Calculation of Emotion Analysis Method. The determinant in this study was the number of rows and columns presented in Fig. 1. In the biological vector, c_{1n} is the stride of the n-th set, c_{2n} is the arm swing of the n-th set, c_{3n} is the speed of the n-th set, n_{4n} is the foot height of the n-th set, and c_{5n} is the wrist height of the n-th set. In the emotion vector, Z_n indicates the n-th set of the questionnaire results.

$$(z_1 \ z_2 \ z_3 \ z_4 \ z_5) = (a_1 \ a_2 \ a_3 \ a_4 \ a_5) \begin{pmatrix} c_{11} & c_{12} & c_{13} & c_{14} & c_{15} \\ c_{21} & c_{22} & c_{23} & c_{24} & c_{25} \\ c_{31} & c_{32} & c_{33} & c_{34} & c_{35} \\ c_{41} & c_{42} & c_{43} & c_{44} & c_{45} \\ c_{51} & c_{52} & c_{53} & c_{45} & c_{55} \end{pmatrix}$$

Fig. 1. Calculation of the emotion analysis method

3.3   Subject

The subjects were five healthy men in their 20 s. The subjects were anonymized and referred to as Subs. 1–5. Subjects wore bodysuits with trackers as shown in Fig. 2.

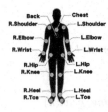

Fig. 2. Bodysuits

3.4   Stimulation Method

We chose classical music to stimulate the subjects' emotions. This is because listening to music has been shown to change emotions [8]. In addition, stimulation of other senses (sight, taste, and touch) was difficult to achieve in walking subjects, and using the sense of smell was not appropriate from the viewpoint of handling in an experimental studio.

3.5   Experiment Flow

First, the subject put on a bodysuit and waited with headphones on at the designated starting point. After that, he listened to classical music through the headphones for 10 s. Then, we walked along the marked-out 7-m-long section (with a 5-m-long section in the center), and finally, we let the subjects answer the questionnaire. Taking the above process as one set, five sets each of the emotion matrix creation experiment and estimated emotion vector creation experiment were undertaken, each for a total of 10 sets.

4   Results of the Analysis and Classification

Table 3 presents a comparison between the estimated emotion vector created in the emotion matrix creation experiment and the biological vector representing the newly measured data from the walking experiments and the emotion vector representing the actual questionnaire result. The emotion classification accuracy was 20% for Sub. 1, 40% for Sub. 2, 20% for Sub. 3, 20% for Sub. 4, and 80% for Sub. 5.

Table 3. Comparison of Z and $\hat{Z}$ (Gray matches)

Sub		6th set	7th set	8th set	9th set	10th set
Sub.1	$\hat{Z}$	−9.91	−2.45	−9.50	3.13	0.22
	Z	0.15	0.60	0.90	0.20	−0.30
Sub.2	$\hat{Z}$	−1.85	−4.33	3.44	−0.90	0.00
	Z	0.30	0.85	0.85	0.50	0.00
Sub.3	$\hat{Z}$	−10.39	−1.14	−1.04	−3.88	−10.95
	Z	0.20	0.70	0.90	0.40	−0.70
Sub.4	$\hat{Z}$	5.10	−3.08	−0.90	4.46	5.31
	Z	0.05	0.40	0.85	−0.20	−0.90
Sub.5	$\hat{Z}$	0.74	1.13	−2.26	−0.17	−4.04
	Z	0.20	0.20	0.45	−0.20	−0.40

5   Discussion

5.1   Discussion of the Rate of Correct Classification

The emotion classification accuracy rate of Sub. 5 was 80%. This rate was higher than the other four subjects. Figure 3 presents the walking data. The vertical axis represents the data from the walking experiments after normalization. The horizontal axis represents the number of sets and recalled emotions.

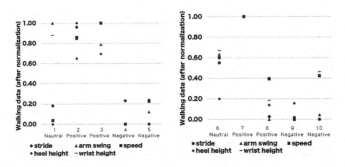

Fig. 3. Walking data (Sub. 5)

In the emotion matrix creation experiment, in the second set that reminded the subject of positive, the stride was 0.96, the arm swing was 0.65, the speed was 0.86, the heel height was 1.00, and the wrist height was 0.84. Similarly, in the third set that reminded the subject of positive, the stride was 1.00, the arm swing was 0.79, the speed was 1.00, the heel height was 0.69, and the wrist height was 1.00. On the other hand, in the fourth set that reminded the subject of negative, the stride was 0.23, the arm swing was 0.00, the speed was 0.00, the heel height was 0.23, and the wrist height was 0.23. Similarly, in the fifth set that reminded the subject of negative, the stride was 0.00, the arm swing was 0.12, the speed was 0.22, the heel height was 0.24, and the wrist height was 0.00. From the above, for Sub. 5, the values from the walking experiments were large if the recalled emotion was positive and small if the emotion was negative. In other words, the data from the walking experiments from Sub. 5 were expressing emotion.

In the estimated emotion vector creation experiment, the same tendency was observed, except in the eighth set. The 6th, 7th, 9th, and 10th sets in which emotions were expressed in the data from the walking experiments were correctly classified. On the other hand, the eighth set, where emotions were not expressed in the data from the walking experiments, was not correctly classified.

From the above, we consider that Sub. 5 recorded a high classification accuracy rate because the emotion tended to be expressed in the data from the walking experiments.

5.2 Discussion for Misclassification

The emotion classification accuracy rate for Sub. 1, Sub. 3, and Sub. 4 was 20%, and for Sub. 2, it was 40%. All rates were lower than for Sub. 5. Due to space limitations, only the results for Sub. 3 are presented in Fig. 4.

In both the emotion vector creation experiment and the estimated emotion vector creation experiment, the data from the walking experiments were scattered regardless of the recalled emotion. From the above, we consider that Sub. 3 recorded a low accuracy rate in the classification of emotions because emotion was not expressed in the data from the walking experiments. Subs. 1, 2, and 4 also had the same tendency as Sub. 5.

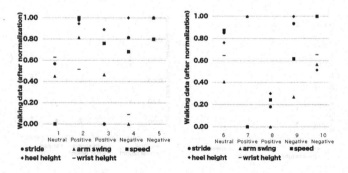

Fig. 4. Walking data (Sub. 3)

The emotion classification accuracy rate for Sub. 1, Sub. 3, and Sub. 4 was 20%, and for Sub. 2, it was 40%. All rates were lower than for Sub. 5. Due to space limitations, only the results for Sub. 3 are presented in Fig. 4.

In both the emotion vector creation experiment and the estimated emotion vector creation experiment, the data from the walking experiments were scattered regardless of the recalled emotion. From the above, we consider that Sub. 3 recorded a low accuracy rate in the classification of emotions because emotion was not expressed in the data from the walking experiments. Subs. 1, 2, and 4 also had the same tendency as Sub. 5.

6 Conclusion

In this study, we conducted two experiments with the purpose of numerically analyzing the act of walking and classifying emotions: an emotion matrix creation experiment and an estimated emotion vector creation experiment. There were large differences of up to 60% between the subjects in their emotion classification accuracy rates. On analyzing the data, it was found that subjects whose emotions were easily expressed in the data from the walking experiments had a high emotion classification accuracy rate, but those who did not easily express emotions had a low emotion classification accuracy rate.

For the future, it is necessary to propose a new method of analysis and improve it by taking into account gait characteristics for different subjects. In addition, we classified emotions into two categories, positive and negative, but it is also necessary to classify emotions in more subtle ways (surprise, fear, etc.), which would be useful for further research. In this study, we focused on five gaits: stride, arm swing, speed, heel height, and wrist height.

References

1. Ministry of Health, Labor and Welfare, 2018 Summary of the results of the occupational safety and health survey (actual survey). https://www.mhlw.go.jp/toukei/list/h30-46-50b.html. Accessed 14 Jan 2020
2. Takeuchi, T., Nozawa, A., Tanaka, H., Ide, H.: Emotion imaging system by EEG. In: FIT 2002, vol. 3, pp. 461–462 (2003)
3. Natsuhara, K., Miura, M.: Use of machine learning to estimate emotional response for musical audio based on listener's electrocardiogram. Nihon Onkyō Gakkai, MA2016-42, pp. 111–116 (2016)
4. Venture, G., Kadone, H., Zhang, T., Grèzes, J., Berthoz, A., Hicheur, H.: Recognizing emotions conveyed by human gait. Int. J. Soc. Robot. 6(4), 621–632 (2014)
5. Musha, T.: Measure "heart". Nikkei Sci. 26(4), 20–29 (1996)
6. Utsunomiya, N., Tanaka, H., Ide, H.: Construction of pleasantness estimation matrix by the correlation coefficients of EEG. IEEJ 122(2), 309–310 (2002)
7. Takeuchi, T., Nozawa, A., Tanaka, H., Ide, H.: The method of visualizing feeling of pleasantness and arousal. IEEJ 123(8), 1512–1513 (2003)
8. Kurino, R., Ito, Y.: A psychological study of emotional change which music listening brings. AIC 14, 75–88 (2001)

Comparison of Stress Reduction Effects Among Heartbeat Feedback Modalities

Kodai Ito[1(✉)] ⓘ, Hiroshi Suga[2], Ryota Horie[2], and Mitsunori Tada[1] ⓘ

[1] Artificial Intelligence Research Center, National Institute of Advanced Industrial Science and Technology (AIST), Tokyo, Japan
{kodai.ito,m.tada}@aist.go.jp
[2] College of Engineering, Shibaura Institute of Technology, Tokyo, Japan
{horie,afl6055}@shibaura-it.ac.jp

Abstract. False heartbeat feedback is a method to provide a modified heartbeat to the participant. It is known to be effective for relieving stress even without instructions. In this study, we compared the effects of false heartbeat feedback on stress reduction among three different modalities, audio, visual, and audio-visual. For this purpose, we developed a feedback system using mixed reality (MR) head-mounted display (HMD) and a wrist band heart rate sensor. Using this system, we performed the experiment where the participants were asked to move small beans from one dish to the other by chopsticks as a stress task. At the same time, they were provided with a false heartbeat in a different modality. The results of the questionnaire showed a stress-reducing effect in audio feedback. In contrast, the results of the heart rate variability (HRV) analysis suggested a stress-reducing effect in visual feedback. In both analyses, audio-visual feedback did not show a stress-reducing effect, suggesting that the combination of multiple modalities has a negative effect on stress reduction.

Keywords: Heart rate · Heartbeat · False feedback · Stress reduction

1 Introduction

Heartbeat feedback is useful for stress reduction. There are two methods in this feedback, true and false. In true heartbeat feedback, heartbeat with the same tempo as the heart rate of the participants is provided through different modalities such as audio, visual, and tactile. Michael et al. provided heartbeat feedback to nonclinical students showing marked claustrophobic fear. They found that heartbeat feedback can relieve the fear of these participants [1]. On the other hand, Kenneth et al. developed a mobile system for controlling feedback of heart rate during outdoor running. They suggested that the participants could exercise more efficiently when the heartbeat feedback was provided [2].

False heartbeat feedback is another variant to provide the modified heartbeat to the participant. It is known to be useful for relieving stress even without instructions, such as asking the participants to take deep breaths during the feedback. Jean et al. designed

© Springer Nature Switzerland AG 2020
C. Stephanidis and M. Antona (Eds.): HCII 2020, CCIS 1224, pp. 352–358, 2020.
https://doi.org/10.1007/978-3-030-50726-8_46

a wearable device to regulate the anxiety of the users by providing false feedback with a slower tempo than the actual heart rate [3].

Recently, occupational stress in the working environment is becoming a serious problem. At the same time, mixed reality (MR) technology has made remarkable progress, and some companies already introduced it for training and working support in the real working environment.

Our purpose is to reduce the stress of the participants during working unconsciously without instructions. Therefore, in this study, we employed false heartbeat feedback. Although there are several modalities, such as audio, visual, and tactile, for providing the heartbeat feedback, the most effective one is yet to be clarified. In this study, we developed a feedback system using an MR head-mounted display (HMD) and a wrist band heart rate sensor. We also evaluate the effects of false heartbeat feedback on stress reduction among three different feedback modalities, audio, visual, and audio-visual.

2   Measurement and Feedback System

We developed a feedback system using an MR HMD (Microsoft HoloLens [4]) and a wrist band heart rate sensor (Polar OH1 [5]). Figure 1 shows the system setup. In our system, we used a fixed heartbeat, 66 beats per minute, as false feedback through the following different feedback modalities during the stress task to make the participants relieved.

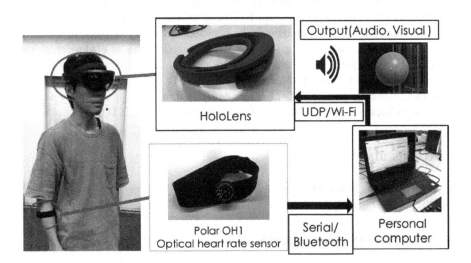

Fig. 1. System setup

- Audio feedback: heartbeats sounds at the 66 bpm was provided
- Visual feedback: animation of spherical shape changes at the 66 bpm as shown in Fig. 2 was provided
- Audio-visual feedback: audio and visual feedbacks were simultaneously provided

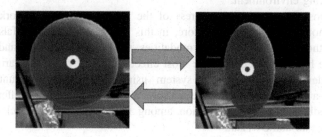

Fig. 2. Shape change of sphere in the visual feedback

3   Experiment

We performed experiment for 11 participants. In this experiment, we asked them to move small beans from one dish to the other with chopsticks as a stress task assuming manual labor in the factory. Participants wore an MR HMD and performed the task under four different conditions, no feedback provided, and one of the three feedbacks provided (audio, visual or audio-visual feedback) in random order.

We evaluated the effects of feedbacks by questionnaire using the card-sort task load index (CSTLX), salivary amylase test, and HRV analysis using an electrocardiogram (ECG). For this purpose, we measured salivary amylase and ECG at the resting state before the task and ECG of the participants at 256 Hz with a wireless ECG sensor (ZMP ECG2) during the task. After the task completed, we measured salivary amylase again and collected subjective workload assessments with the CSTLX.

4   Results and Discussion

The data from one participant who felt sleepy during the experiment were excluded from the following analysis in this section since he could not concentrate on the task.

4.1   Task Score (Number of Beans)

Figure 3 shows the average number of beans that the participants could move in each condition. There were no significant differences among the condition.

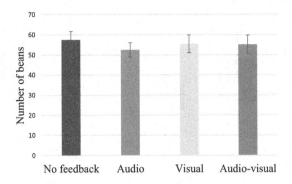

Fig. 3. Task score (number of beans) in each condition.

4.2 Results of the CSTLX

Figure 4 shows the results of the CSTLX. We separated the participants into two groups based on the weighted workload (WWL) score under no-feedback condition, high-stress group (WWL > 50), and low-stress group (WWL < 50). This figure demonstrates that all of the three feedback modalities could reduce WWL for the participants in the high-stress group, and single feedback is more effective for reducing WWL than audio-visual feedback. On the other hand, there is no stress reduction by the feedback for the participants in the low-stress group.

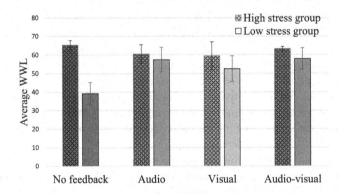

Fig. 4. Results of the CSTLX in each condition for high and low stress group.

4.3 Results of the Salivary Amylase Test

We measured salivary amylase within 1 min before the task started and after the task completed, and calculated the ratio of the salivary amylase change. Figure 5 shows the results of the salivary amylase test. It is known that the salivary amylase increases as the stress increases. We could not find significant differences in the salivary amylase

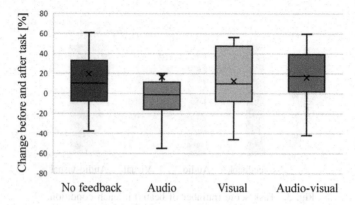

Fig. 5. Results of the salivary amylase test in each condition.

among task conditions. However, we could speculate that the audio feedback is a better way to provide heartbeat feedback since it has a lower score than the control (no feedback) condition and the other two conditions with visual and audio-visual feedback.

4.4 Results of the HRV Analysis

In our system, we employed a photoplethysmogram (PPG) based wrist band heart rate sensor. Since ECG is more reliable than PPG, we also measured ECG before the task and during the task for computing HRV indexes, such as standard deviation of R-R interval (SDNN) and the ratio of low-frequency to high-frequency power (LF/HF).

Figure 6 shows the averages of the heart rate before and during the task for each task condition. There is no significant difference among conditions. Also, the average of the heart rate did not change between before and during the task. This is because the task required low physical activities, the participants performed the task in sitting posture, and only their upper limbs were moving. Figure 7 shows SDNNs of the heart rate before and during the task for each task condition. Same as the average of the heart rate, there is no significant difference among conditions.

Figure 8 shows LF/HFs before and during the task for each task condition. There is no significant difference among conditions. Only the LF/HF in visual feedback was at a low level. It was also clearly low compared to the resting state. A decrease in LF/HF indicates parasympathetic dominance and is often used as an index of stress reduction. Therefore, our results suggest that visual feedback reduced participants' stress. However, these results that visual feedback only has a stress-reducing effect are not consistent with the results of CSTLX and salivary amylase test. We might have detected emotional changes that cannot be detected by the salivary amylase test and CSTLX by LF/HF. This may be because only HRV analysis is a real-time measurement. In this HRV analysis, we set the entire task as target sections. For other tasks from the visual feedback task, it may be necessary to examine and set analysis time section carefully for calculating HRV indexes.

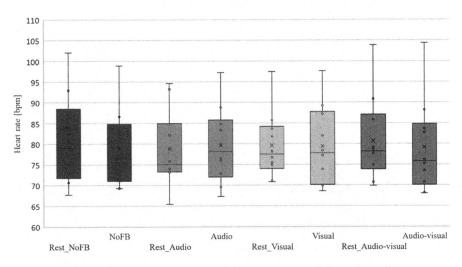

Fig. 6. Averages of heart rate before and during the task in each condition.

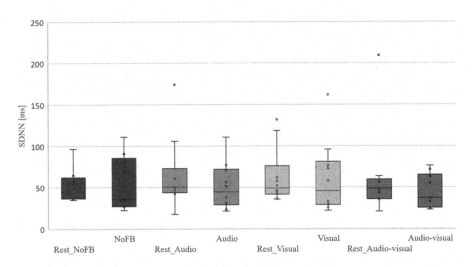

Fig. 7. SDNNs of heart rate before and during the task in each condition.

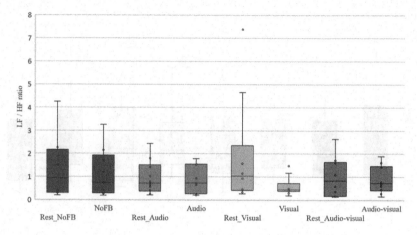

Fig. 8. LF/HFs of heart rate before and during the task in each condition.

5 Conclusion

In this study, we developed a heartbeat feedback system using an MR HMD and a wrist band heart rate sensor. Using this system, we performed an experiment and evaluated the stress-reducing effect by the feedback in different modalities, audio, visual, and audio-visual. In this experiment, the participants were asked to move small beans from one dish to the other by chopsticks as a stress task, while at the same time, they were provided with a fixed heart rate (66 bpm) as false heartbeat feedback.

The results of the questionnaire showed a stress-reducing effect in audio feedback, while the results of the HRV analysis suggested a stress-reducing effect in visual feedback. In both analyses, audio-visual feedback did not show a stress-reducing effect, suggesting that the combination of multiple modalities has a negative effect on stress reduction.

References

1. Telch, M.J., Valentiner, D.P., Ilai, D., Petruzzi, D., Hehmsoth, M.: The facilitative effects of heart-rate feedback in the emotional processing of claustrophobic fear. Behav. Res. Therapy **38**(4), 373–387 (2000)
2. Hunt, K.J., Hunt, A.J.R.: Feedback control of heart rate during outdoor running: a smartphone implementation. Biomed. Signal Process. Control **26**, 90–97 (2016)
3. Costa, J., Adams, A.T., Jung, M.F., Guimbretiere, F., Choudhury, T.: EmotionCheck: leveraging bodily signals and false feedback to regulate our emotions. In: Proceedings of the 2016 ACM International Joint Conference on Pervasive and Ubiquitous Computing, pp. 758–769 (2016)
4. Microsoft HoloLens. https://www.microsoft.com/en-us/hololens/. Accessed 20 Mar 2020
5. POLAR OH1. https://www.polar.com/us-en/products/accessories/oh1-optical-heart-rate-sensor/. Accessed 20 Mar 2020

Physiological Responses Induced by Mental Workload Simulating Daily Work

Chi'e Kurosaka[1]($\boxtimes$), Hiroyuki Kuraoka[1], Hiroto Sakamoto[2],
and Shinji Miyake[1]

[1] University of Occupational and Environmental Health, Japan,
Kitakyushu, Japan
chie-k@health.uoeh-u.ac.jp
[2] Maeda Corporation, Toride, Japan

Abstract. This study investigated the psychological effects of a mental task which is similar to daily work such as detecting a typo in an attempt to provide pathways to improve workers' mental health. Twenty healthy male undergraduate students participated in this study. ECG and SCL were recorded during resting periods and mental task performance alike. NASA-TLX, Japanese UWIST mood adjective checklist, and Subjective feelings of fatigue were employed after the task as the subjective assessments. All participants repeated this task twice under three different visual conditions: against a monochromatic wall, a picture of a forest, and a video of a forest. Mean RR intervals, SD1, SD2, CSI, and CVI were calculated from ECG. Participants' average SCL values were obtained in each block. All indexes were analyzed by repeated measures two-way ANOVA with condition (i.e., control, picture, and video) and block (i.e., REST, TASK1, and TASK2) as factors. In results, the main effects of condition and block in CSI and the main effects of block were found in SD2, CSI, CVI, and SCL. There were significant differences between REST and TASK in all indexes. No condition x block interaction was observed in any indexes. The post hoc test revealed that CSI in the picture condition was significantly longer than it was in other conditions.

Keywords: Mental workload · Daily work · Autonomic nervous system activity

1 Introduction

Several studies have reported relationships between physiological responses and mental stress induced by mental workload such as mental arithmetic task [1, 2] and puzzle game [2]. However, these mental tasks are completely different from actual daily work. Therefore, it is doubtful that these results transferrable to actual office workplace by researchers hoping to evaluate the effects of mental workloads on workers. In addition, other studies have reported that greening an office space by adding plants improves employee satisfaction and quality of life [3]. In this paper, we attempted to extend and combine both of these branches of research by investigating workers' physiological responses during mental tasks which are similar to daily work

© Springer Nature Switzerland AG 2020
C. Stephanidis and M. Antona (Eds.): HCII 2020, CCIS 1224, pp. 359–365, 2020.
https://doi.org/10.1007/978-3-030-50726-8_47

under three different conditions –, accompanied by a picture of a forest, a video of a forest, and with no accompanying visual stimuli – in order to assess the effects of these tasks and office environments on workers' mental health.

2 Methods

2.1 Participants

Twenty healthy male undergraduate students aged between 20–27 years old. (mean 22.8 ± 1.73 years) participated in this study. All participants provided written informed consent. This study was approved by the Ethics Committee of the University of Occupational and Environmental Health, Japan (R1-023).

2.2 Physiological Measurement

Electrocardiograph (ECG) signals from CM_5 lead and skin conductance level (SCL) from the left second and the third fingers were recorded throughout the experiment by 1 kHz sampling. Mean RR intervals (RRI) and mean SCL were also calculated.

2.3 Mental Workload

The work desk employed in this study was surrounded by three partitions. Under the forest video condition, a forest video was shown on a 49 inch LED display which was hung on the front partition (Fig. 1). Two 17-inch computer displays were set on the desk for the typo task. Participants were presented with a report of the Fukushima nuclear power plant accident [4] on the monitor to the participant's left. This report contained typographical errors, added by the experimenter. The monitor scrolled upward automatically at a speed of three pages per five minutes. Each page contained about 1,000 letters and 10 typographical errors, but participants were not informed of how many errors in the report. The monitor to the participant's right showed, the same reference report with no typographical errors. This monitor also displayed participant's task performance as a percentage of their progress (Fig. 2). The right-hand side screen did not scroll, participants had to click the NEXT button on the bottom of the screen in order to see the next page. Participants were required to identify the differences between the two reports and to click the target letter on the right monitor as many as possible.

2.4 Subjective Assessment

The National Aeronautics and Space Administration Task Load Index (NASA-TLX), a widely used subjective workload assessment technique, was used. It consists of six subscales: Mental Demand (MD), Physical Demand (PD), Temporal Demand (TD), Own Performance (OP), Effort (EF), and Frustration Level (FR). The weighted workload (WWL) is calculated from the individual subscale scores and their respective weights obtained from the paired comparisons [5].

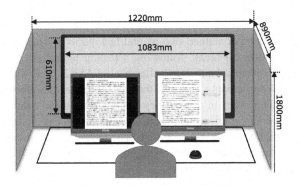

Fig. 1. Experimental setup.

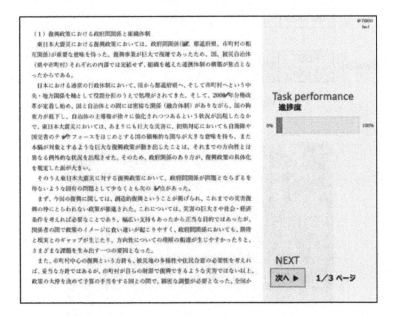

Fig. 2. A screen shot of the task. Four target letters were clicked.

Japanese UWIST mood adjective checklist (JUMACL) was adapted to assess the current mood and emotions of participants. It consists of 20 items, which are used to obtain energetic arousal (EA) and tense arousal (TA).

This study also evaluated participants' subjective feelings of fatigue (SFF) via a five-point Likert scale (ranging from 1–"disagree completely", to 5–"agree strongly") including 25 items. One of the following five factors– feeling of drowsiness (Factor I), feeling of instability (Factor II), feeling of uneasiness (Factor III), feeling of local pain or dullness (Factor IV), and feeling of eyestrains (Factor V), is the total score of the corresponding five items out of the 25 items.

2.5   Procedure

The experimental session contained two mental task periods. These tasks which were separated by a 30-s interval break, following a resting period (REST). SFF, NASA-TLX, and JUMACL were administered after each TASK2. SFF was also conducted before TASK1. All participants repeated the session under the aforementioned three visual conditions. The order in which they encountered these conditions was counterbalanced. The overall experimental procedure is shown in Fig. 3, and the photograph for the picture condition is shown in Fig. 4. The video for the video condition was recorded at the same location as the photograph by a fixed-point camera and was presented to participants without audio.

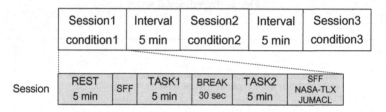

Fig. 3.   Experimental procedure.

Fig. 4.   Forest scene in the picture and the video conditions.

2.6   Statistical Analysis

Two participants were excluded from the analysis due to incomplete data sets. We calculated participants' RRI averages and four Poincaré plot parameters – the length of the transverse axis (SD1), length of the longitudinal axis (SD2), cardiac sympathetic index (CSI), and cardiac vagal index (CVI) [7] from ECG. Furthermore, we obtained the average SCL values for each participant. All indexes were calculated in nine periods, in which participants were presented with a combination of three conditions and three blocks. All indexes were standardized within each participant.

The results were analyzed by two-way repeated measures analysis of variance (ANOVA) with condition and block as factors (SPSS statistics 19). The degree of freedom was adjusted using the Greenhouse-Geisser correction. A Ryan-Einot-Gabriel-Welsch F (REGW-F) test was used as the post-hoc analysis.

3   Results

Table 1 shows the results of ANOVA in each index. Results of the post-hoc test are shown in Table 2. The ANOVA in CSI revealed main effects in both block and condition. The results of SD2, CVI, and SCL showed the main effect of block, there were significant differences between REST and TASK in all these three indexes ($p < .001$). Poincaré indexes decreased (see Fig. 5 and Fig. 6(a)) and SCL increased during task periods. No condition x block interaction was observed in any indexes. REGW-F test revealed that CSI was longer in the picture condition than in the other conditions (Fig. 6(b)).

Table 1. Result of two-way repeated measures ANOVA.

		df	F value	ε	β	η^2	p value	
RRI	BLOCK	1.26	2.04	0.63	0.30	0.11	0.167	
	CONDITION	1.69	0.20	0.85	0.08	0.01	0.783	
	BLK × CON	3.20	0.28	0.80	0.10	0.02	0.852	
SD1	BLOCK	1.48	1.24	0.74	0.22	0.07	0.295	
	CONDITION	1.99	0.65	1.00	0.15	0.04	0.526	
	BLK × CON	2.79	1.57	0.70	0.37	0.08	0.211	
SD2	BLOCK	1.36	32.54	0.68	1.00	0.67	0.000	***
	CONDITION	1.93	0.67	0.97	0.15	0.04	0.516	
	BLK × CON	2.97	1.49	0.74	0.37	0.09	0.229	
CSI	BLOCK	1.67	25.91	0.84	1.00	0.62	0.000	***
	CONDITION	1.94	2.65	0.97	0.48	0.14	0.088	†
	BLK × CON	2.57	0.54	0.64	0.14	0.03	0.632	
CVI	BLOCK	1.39	17.81	0.69	1.00	0.53	0.000	***
	CONDITION	1.95	0.02	0.97	0.05	0.00	0.974	
	BLK × CON	3.14	1.64	0.78	0.41	0.09	0.190	
SCL	BLOCK	1.60	12.66	0.80	0.98	0.41	0.000	***
	CONDITION	1.48	0.67	0.74	0.14	0.04	0.477	
	BLK × CON	3.62	1.74	0.91	0.48	0.09	0.158	

4   Discussion

It is widely known that RRI is a physiological index which is sensitive to mental stress. The sensory intake/rejection hypothesis proposes that the physiological responses induced by tasks depend on the task characteristics [6]. Sensory rejection tasks such as

Table 2. Result of R-E-G-W F test.

		df	F value	β	η²	p value	
SD2	BLOCK	2	31.92	1.00	0.30	0.000	***
CSI	BLOCK	2	23.24	1.00	0.23	0.000	***
CSI	CONDITION	2	6.15	0.88	0.07	0.003	**
CVI	BLOCK	2	21.12	1.00	0.22	0.000	***
SCL	BLOCK	2	16.09	1.00	0.17	0.000	***

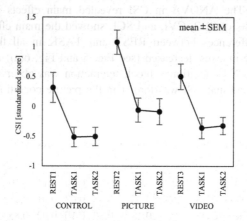

Fig. 5. Standardized Score of CSI in all blocks. Bars indicate the standard errors of mean.

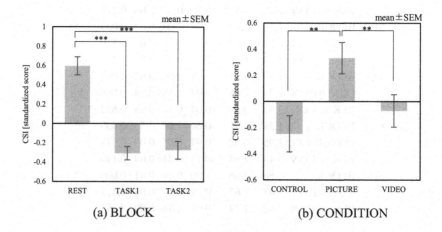

(a) BLOCK   (b) CONDITION

Fig. 6. Post-hoc test (REGW-F test) results of CSI.

mental arithmetic affect cardiac activity resulting in heart rate (HR) and blood pressure increase (Pattern I response). In contrast, sensory intake tasks such as mirror tracing tasks, induce peripheral vascular contraction and decreases in HR (Pattern II response) [7, 8]. Twenty-one blocks out of 54 blocks (18 participants and three conditions) showed HR decreases during TASK1 compared to the resting periods, so the mental task in this study may have a characteristic which induces both Pattern I response and Pattern II response. It is extremely difficult to evaluate mental stress by RRI alone when the task characteristic is uncertain.

Even in such a case, Poincaré indexes and SCL might be able to distinguish between resting periods and task periods. The lengths of SD2 were shorter in the task block than the resting period, because the RR fluctuation width decreased. Changes in CSI and CVI are almost identical because they are strongly affected by the change of SD2 by definition. Previous findings that CSI indicates sympathetic nervous system activity and CVI is cardiac vagal index are doubtful.

This study observed that nature scenes had a slight effect on physiological responses. We will investigate relationships between physiological responses and subjective assessment under each condition to clarify the physiological meaning of these findings in the near future.

References

1. Brian, M.H., Siobhán, H., Jack, E.J., Niamh, M.H.: Individual differences in adaptation of cardiovascular responses to stress. Biol. Psychol. **86**, 129–136 (2011)
2. Trotman, G.P., Veldhuijzen van Zanten, J.J., Davies, J., Möller, C., Ginty, A.T., Williams, S. E.: Associations between heart rate, perceived heart rate, and anxiety during acute psychological stress. Anxiety Stress Coping **32**(6), 711–727 (2019)
3. Nieuwenhuis, M., Knight, C., Postmes, T., Haslam, S.A.: The relative benefits of green versus lean office space: three field experiments. J. Exp. Psychol. Appl. **20**(3), 199–214 (2014)
4. Reconstruction Agency Website. https://www.reconstruction.go.jp/topics/main-cat1/sub-cat1-1/20170718_houkokusyo.pdf. Accessed 17 Feb 2020
5. Hart, S.H., Staveland, L.E.: Development of NASA-TLX (task load index): result of empirical and theoretical research. In: Hancock, P.A., Meshkati, N. (eds.) Human Mental Workload. North Holland, New York (1988)
6. Toichi, M., Sugiura, T., Murai, T., Sengoku, A.: A new method of assessing cardiac autonomic function and its comparison with spectral analysis and coefficient of variation of R-R interval. J. Auton. Nerv. Syst. **62**(1–2), 79–84 (1997)
7. Lacey, J.I.: Psychophysiological approaches to the evaluation of psychotherapeutic process and outcome. In: Rubinstein, E.A., Parloff, M.B. (eds.) Research in Psychotherapy, pp. 160–208. American Psychological Association, Washington, DC (1959)
8. Schneiderman, N., McCabe, P.M.: Psychophysiologic strategies in laboratory research. In: Schneiderman, N., Weiss, S.M., Kaufmann, P.G. (eds.) Handbook of Research Methods in Cardiovascular Behavioral Medicine, pp. 349–364. Plenum Press, New York (1989)

A Proposal for a Correction Method to Obtain Photoplethysmographic Amplitude from a Smartwatch

Yu Matsumoto[✉], Tota Mizuno, Kazuyuki Mito, and Naoaki Itakura

The University of Electro-Communications,
1-5-1 Chofugaoka, Chofu, Tokyo, Japan
yule.vi02@gmail.com

Abstract. In recent years, the number of patients with mental illness due to mental stress has been increasing. Therefore, the evaluation of mental stress in daily life is necessary to prevent a mental illness. Conventional evaluation of mental stress uses biological information such as respiration, heart rate, saliva, and photoplethysmography (PPG). Among them, PPG is measurable by a daily smartwatch. Therefore, we examined the possibility of evaluating mental stress using PPG obtained from a smartwatch. In the mental stress evaluation, we focused on the photoplethysmographic amplitude (PPGA), which is the characteristic point of PPG. PPGA can be used to evaluate mental stress even with intermittent data. This is suitable for mental stress evaluation when the data from smartwatches may not be procured due to body movements. In contrast, the accuracy of acquiring PPGA from a smartwatch might be low owing to various factors such as changes in blood flow or skin temperature. Hence, in this research, we proposed a correction method to obtain a stable and accurate PPGA. In our experiment, the effectiveness of this method was examined by comparing the photoplethysmograph data and corrected data of the smartwatch after measuring with the photoplethysmograph and smartwatch simultaneously. Our results confirmed that the proposed method procures the PPGA with high accuracy.

Keywords: Photoplethysmography · Photoplethysmographic amplitude · Mental stress evaluation

1 Introduction

In recent years, the number of patients suffering from mental illness due to stress has been increasing. Therefore, it is necessary to evaluate mental stress in daily life to prevent mental illness. Conventionally, mental stress is evaluated using a method that employs biological information such as respiration, heart rate, saliva, and photoplethysmography (PPG). Among these biological parameters, PPG can be measured with a smartwatch and can be monitored on a daily basis.

Heartbeat R-wave interval (RRI) is a feature point that can be used to obtain an index of autonomic nervous activity for metal stress evaluation [1]. The RRI is highly correlated with the time interval between the maximum and minimum points of the

C. Stephanidis and M. Antona (Eds.): HCII 2020, CCIS 1224, pp. 366–371, 2020.
https://doi.org/10.1007/978-3-030-50726-8_48

PPG. Thus, this interval is used for general mental stress evaluation by PPG. However, this evaluation method may be affected by respiration, and its accuracy may decrease [2]. Hence, we focused on the photoplethysmographic amplitude (PPGA), which is another feature point. PPGA is the amplitude from the minimum to maximum points of the PPG, and reflects the blood pressure and state of blood vessels [3, 4].

However, there are three problems in obtaining the PPGA from a smartwatch.

1. The minimum and maximum points of the PPG waveform change greatly owing to the fluctuation of the baseline.
2. There is a possibility that the minimum and maximum points cannot be obtained accurately because of the low sampling frequency.
3. Depending on the position of the arm, the gravity of the blood flow path and the state of the blood vessels change and an accurate PPGA may not be obtained.

Addressing these problems, in this study, we propose a correction method to obtain the PPGA.

2 Proposed Method

The proposed method deals with the aforementioned problems of the PPGA using the following three processes.

1. Exclusion of outliers, such as body motion
2. Processing to reduce the influence on PPG due to baseline changes
3. Correction of errors caused by lower arm positions and fewer samples

The first process excludes values that are greater than three times the standard deviation of PPGA considering them as outliers.

Second, the influence on PPGA due to baseline changes is reduced by extracting PPGA, where the baseline does not change significantly. The extraction method first standardizes the PPG data before filtering. Then, after procuring the moving average, the slope of PPG is obtained using linear regression. The regression graph is plotted using the number of data against the width of one cycle of the PPG. Further, the section where the slope is close to 0 is extracted. This method can extract the section where the slope of the PPG waveform is horizontal and suppress the influence of the change in the baseline. In this experiment, we iterated 11-point of moving average and 20-point of linear regression.

The PPGA error between the smartwatch and photoplethysmograph is corrected using multiple regression analysis. The slopes $X_1, X_2, X_3...X_n$ after $t, 2t, 3t,...nt$ s from the minimum point of the PPGA were used as n explanatory variables in the multiple regression analysis. The following equations are obtained.

$$Correction = b_0 + b_1 X_1 + b_2 X_2 + b_3 X_3... \tag{1}$$

$$Corrected\ Amp = Amp + Correction. \tag{2}$$

where, b_0, b_1, b_2, b_3...b_n are the regression coefficients, *Correction* represents the correction value, *Amp* is the PPGA before correction, and *Corrected Amp* is the PPGA after correction.

In this experiment, the maximum time interval between the minimum and maximum points of the PPG of the smartwatch was 0.45 s. Hence, nine slopes were treated as explanatory variables in steps from a sampling frequency of 20 Hz for 0.05 s.

In this study, we measured the PPGA of a smartwatch and photoplethysmograph. The smartwatch was used as a general medical device concurrently. Further, we verified the effectiveness of our measurement technique when there was a change in the vertical distance between the arm, wearing the smartwatch, and the heart.

3   Experimental Method

The experiment was performed to verify if the proposed method could correct the difference between the vertical distance from the heart and the smartwatch.

A photoplethysmograph (NIHON KOHDEN, MPP-3U) was used to accurately measure the PPG. The data were measured through a 0.5–100 Hz analog filter at a sampling frequency of 1 kHz. The PPG measurement position was the earlobe. The smartwatch was measured at a sampling frequency of 20 Hz using a Galaxy watch Gear S2. The subjects were 6 healthy adults in their 20's. The experiment was performed with the elbows bent at the same height as the heart and at a distance of approximately 20 cm above and below the heart. Each pattern was performed three times for 90 s, as illustrated in Fig. 1. The data of the smartwatch and photoplethysmograph were analyzed after the application of the FIR filter at 0.8–4.0 Hz. In the learning of the multiple regression analysis, the correction was performed for each pattern using one trial of an individual subject.

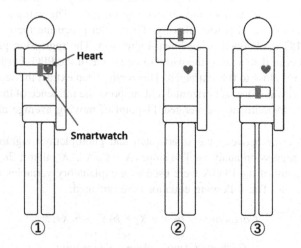

Fig. 1. Experimental procedure

4   Experimental Result

4.1   Raw Data from Smartwatch

The PPG data obtained from the smartwatch has certain noise with respect to the fluctuation of the baseline, as shown in Fig. 2. It is considered that the change in the baseline may affect the minimum and maximum points of the PPGA. Therefore, it was confirmed that it was necessary to extract the PPG part in the section where the change in the baseline was small, as stated in the proposed method.

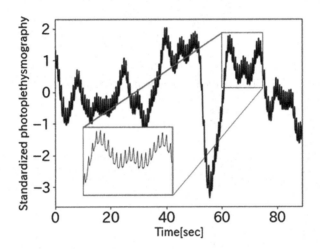

Fig. 2. Raw PPG data from a smartwatch

4.2   PPGA Obtained by the Proposed Method

We compared the pulse wave amplitude values corrected by the proposed method. The change in the pulse wave amplitude value of the smart watch and photoplethysmograph is shown in Fig. 3. This amplitude value is the standardized data after obtaining a moving average at 11 points.

From the correlation before and after employing the proposed method in Fig. 3, it is observed that a strong correlation is obtained by the proposed method. In addition, because the pulse wave amplitude value is evaluated based on the tendency of the relative change, the number of data has been reduced. This makes the evaluation easier. Contrarily, small changes can no longer be obtained, but it is considered that this method is effective because it is not necessary to evaluate stress in a short time.

4.3   Comparison Between the Smartwatch and Photoplethysmograph

The average correlation coefficient for each pattern of the fixed position of the arm is shown in Table 1. In the table, the correlation before and after employing the proposed method and the correlation coefficient of the proposed method are divided into positive

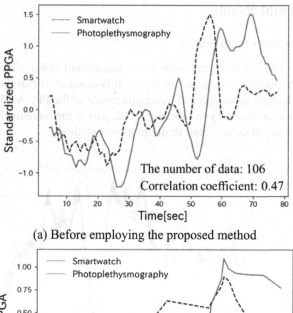

(a) Before employing the proposed method

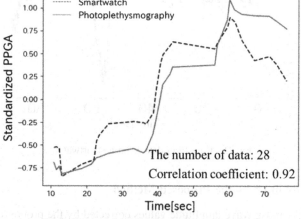

(b) After employing the proposed method

Fig. 3. Correction of PPGA using the proposed method

and negative correlations. The coefficient of the determination of the multiple regression analysis model used for each correction was 0.5 or more.

According to the proposed method, the correlation coefficient was slightly more than 0.50 in the patterns of ① and ②. In contrast, when the correlation was grouped into positive and negative groups, the positive group had a strong correlation of 0.55 or more on an average for all patterns. In addition, it was observed that it was possible to obtain a PPGA with a correlation of 0.50 or more by this method because most data showed a strong correlation with the number of data.

However, it was also found that there was a negative correlation. The interval between the minimum and maximum points of the amplitude value was approximately 0.2 s and the sampling frequency was as low as 20 Hz for the smartwatch. Therefore, it

Table 1. Comparison of PPGA between smartwatch and photoplethysmograph

Pattern	Correlation coefficient		Correlation coefficient of the proposed method	
	No correction	Proposed method	Positive correlation	Negative correlation
①	0.31 ± 0.38	0.55 ± 0.46	0.76 ± 0.12 [14]	−0.41 ± 0.06 [3]
②	0.23 ± 0.33	0.52 ± 0.46	0.66 ± 0.27 [15]	−0.50 ± 0.18 [2]
③	0.13 ± 0.37	0.19 ± 0.45	0.55 ± 0.14 [10]	−0.32 ± 0.20 [7]

*[n]: The number of data

was considered that a negative correlation was obtained because a high-speed component of frequency required for the amplitude value was not obtained.

5 Conclusion

As a result, it was suggested that the proposed method could correct the PPGA obtained from the smartwatch with high accuracy even if the position of the arm was different in the height direction from the heart.

The scope for our future work is to study a method to obtain a stable and accurate PPGA regardless of the arm position.

References

1. Hayano, J., Okada, A., Yasuma, F.: Biological significance of heart rate variability. Jpn. Soc. Artif. Organs **25**(5), 870–880 (1996)
2. Mukai, S., Hayano, J.: Toward standardization of heart rate variability analysis. Jpn. J. Electrocardiol. **16**(3), 217–224 (1996)
3. Yoshida, N., Asarawa, T., Hayashi, T., Mizuno-Matsumoto, Y.: Evaluation of the autonomic nervous function with plethysmography under the emotional stress stimuli. Jpn. Soc. Med. Biol. Eng. **49**(1), 91–99 (2011)
4. Miyagawa, D., et al.: Evaluation of autonomic nervous function using photoplethysmography under emotional stress stimuli on a cellular phone. Jpn. Soc. Clin. Neurophysiol. **40**(6), 540–546 (2012)

Investigation of Psychological Evaluation and Estimation Method Using Skin Temperature of Lower Half of Face

Tota Mizuno[✉], Kazuyuki Mito, and Naoaki Itakura

The University of Electro-Communications,
1-5-1 Chofugaoka, Chofu, Tokyo 180-8585, Japan
mizuno@uec.ac.jp

Abstract. This study is aimed at establishing a mental workload (MWL) estimation method that can be used in work sites.

Advancements in information society have resulted in an increase in MWL mainly caused by using computers daily. Long-term excessive MWL can cause fatigue and lead to a drop in concentration and mental saturation. Therefore, it is important for workers to evaluate their MWL to prevent and reduce human errors and associated health hazards. We examine the correspondence between autonomic nervous activities and MWL using facial skin temperature with infrared thermography. Consequently, the ability to evaluate MWL according to the skin temperature of a face is shown.

In an actual environment, the forehead is often hidden by hair or wearing glasses. This hinders the measurement of the temperature of an entire face. This study focuses on the lower half of the face area. This is the area with less glass and hair effects. MWL was evaluated using the variance of the entire face, nose, and forehead in existing studies. However, detailed analysis of the temperature distribution information, such as the variance value of the nose only or the area other than the nose is scarce.

We examined the characteristics of the nose, cheeks, lips, and lower half of the face.

Keywords: Mental work load · Facial thermal image · Nasal skin temperature · Face detection · Lower half of face

1 Introduction

The proportion of mental work in everyday life is increasing in the advanced information society. The load and burden owing to mental work is called mental work-load (MWL) [1]. Appropriate evaluation and management of MWL is important for reducing human error and health damage [2–5].

Appropriate evaluation and management of MWL is important to reduce human error and health damage [2–5]. Because MWL affects autonomic nervous

C. Stephanidis and M. Antona (Eds.): HCII 2020, CCIS 1224, pp. 372–377, 2020.
https://doi.org/10.1007/978-3-030-50726-8_49

activity, estimating MWL by evaluating autonomic nervous activity has been investigated. Some studies have reported on measuring nasal skin temperature (NST) using infrared thermography and evaluating autonomic nervous activity during MWL. NST is an indicator that reflects autonomic nerve activity and the effectiveness of MWL evaluation. This method extracts the forehead and nose from the facial thermal image to determine the temperature difference using NST to evaluate and estimate autonomic nervous activity. Skin temperature is measured with less restraint and non-contact compared to other bioelectric signal indices. Therefore, it is suitable for measurement in a real work scene. Existing studies have reported that MWL may affect NST and the skin temperature of the lips [6–9]. Therefore, the analysis range was extended from the nose to the entire face. Then, the variance of the skin temperature of the entire face was used as an index of autonomic nervous activity. This can estimate and evaluate autonomic nervous activity with higher accuracy than the approaches used in existing studies. However, because the index uses a thermal image of the entire face, its effect on hair and wearing glasses is not considered. In an actual environment, it is difficult to evaluate the temperature of an entire face if the forehead is covered by hair or wearing glasses.

Therefore, this study considers the lower half of the face area; the area with less effect from glasses and hair. Temperature analysis was performed on the characteristic areas such as nose, cheeks, lips, and the entire area under the face. Additionally, we compared the temperature distribution characteristics of these areas with psychological and behavioral indices and evaluated the MWL status of the subjects.

2 Experiment

Experiments were carried out to acquire facial thermal images of different MWL states. Subjects performed a consuming MWL task.

2.1 Experimental Procedure

Figure 1 shows the experimental system is shown in Fig. 1. Thermal images were taken when after a subject solved the a mental arithmetic calculation. An infrared thermography device (ViewOhreIMAGING XA0350) was placed at a distance of 1 m horizontally from the nose of the subject. The thermal image size was 320 * 240 pixels, and the sampling period was 1 s. A PC display and numeric keypad were placed uponon the desk.

Figure 2 shows the experimental protocol is shown in Fig. 2 shows. Subjects rested for were given a 3 min rest, period in a sitting position. After this initial rest period. Subsequently, subjects began the mental arithmetic calculation task and continued this task that lasts for 10 min. After completion of the task, subjects again rested for took 3 min rest, thereby completing the experiment. The calculation involved the addition of two integers, each of which was between 10 and 99. The subject inputs the answer of the 4 calculations displayed on the

PC by using the numeric keypad. The calculation was performed and displayed for 20 s. After 20 s, the following calculation will displayed on the PC, regardless of whether the subject answers the calculation within 20 s or not. The subjects were 6 healthy adults, from 22 to 28 years old, who were well had adequate rested the night before the experiment.

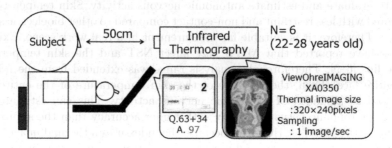

Fig. 1. Experimental system.

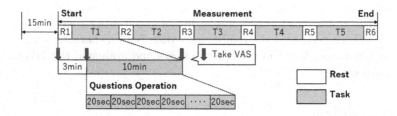

Fig. 2. Experimental procedure.

2.2   Analysis Area of Lower Half of Face

The analysis area is shown in Fig. 3. From Fig. 3, (a) the nose tip, (b) the right cheek, (c) the left cheek, (d) the lip, and (e) the lower half of the face, the average temperature and the variance of each area is calculated. The nose tip denotes the width of the nose, the height denotes the center of the back of the nose that did not interfere with the glasses. The width of the lip region was approximately the same as in (a), and the height was extracted as an ellipse from the chin to the nose tip. The cheek was set in the remaining area and analyzed. Additionally, for the evaluation values of the average and variance values, the average value from the start to the end of each mental arithmetic calculation task was calculated, and the tendency of the temperature transition in each trial was examined.

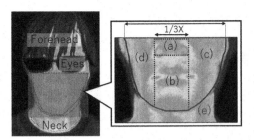

(a): Nose tip

(b): Left Cheek

(c): Right Cheek

(d): Mouth

(e): The Lower of Face

Fig. 3. Analysis area.

2.3 Behavioral and Psychological Indicators

As behavior indicators, the average, and standard deviation of the time taken to answer, and the number of incorrect answers were calculated for each trial of the mental arithmetic calculation task. For psychological indicators, VAS was used. The VAS evaluates the subjective degree by marking it on a straight line. In this study, the evaluation was given on a scale of 100 according to the psychological score at the start of the experiment.

Five evaluation items were used: pleasure, concentration, fun, energy, and cold. For each subject, the items of each scale were converted into a standardized score T using Eq. (1), and the average scores and standard deviations were calculated for each individual by the psychological score during the task. The psychological score at the start of the experiment was set as a reference value, and the difference value from the psychological score after the task was set.

$$T = (VAS\ value - Average)SD \tag{1}$$

2.4 Results and Discussion

Behavioral Performance. Behavioral performance was divided into subjects whose answer time and number of errors increased and those whose answer time decreased. The former is influenced by monotonous feelings and fatigue from the task over time. The latter is influenced by habituation.

Psychological Evaluation. The results of VAS are shown in Fig. 4. Considering the psychological effect of the computational task, most subjects exhibited negative emotions such as discomfort, distraction, and fatigue over time. Some subjects changed to positive emotions such as pleasantness and concentration.

Physiological Evaluation. The results of the subject A are shown in Figs. 5 and 6.

A temperature fluctuation caused by the calculation task in other areas is indicated in Fig. 5. However, the area with high changes in the average

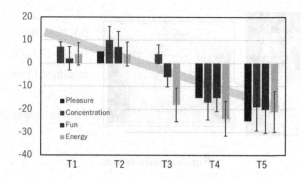

Fig. 4. Analysis area.

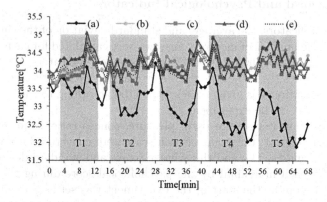

Fig. 5. Average temperature (Sub. A).

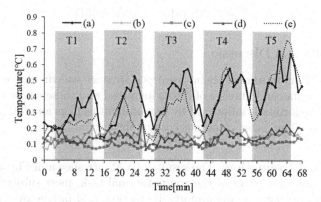

Fig. 6. Variance (Sub. A).

temperature is on the nose (a). Each time the task was performed, area (a) fell below the other areas. However, some subjects exhibited small changes, and there were individual differences.

In Fig. 6, areas (a) and (e) are shown as those with high changes in the variance of temperature. Although there were individual differences in the magnitude of the values, the tendency was similar. From above, it was suggested that the nose and lower half of the face can affect the variance of temperature by MWL. In other subjects, the variance increased with each trial.

Conclusion. This study considers the lower half of the face area that is less affected by glasses and hair. We compared the temperature distributions of these areas with psychological and behavioral indices and evaluated the MWL status of the subjects. Consequently, the effect of MWL can be estimated using the variance of the nose and lower half of the face. In further studies, we will develop a system that can perform real-time processing.

References

1. Haga, S.: Theory and Measurement of Mental Work-Load. Japan Publication Service (2001)
2. Murata, A.: Measurement of mental workload by heart rate variability indexes. Jpn. Ergon. Soc. **28**(2), 91–99 (1992)
3. Hirayanagi, K., Iwasaki, K., Kanda, S., Yajima, K.: An experimental study on the measurement and assessment of mental workload (MWL). Jpn. Ergon. Soc. **32**(5), 251–259 (1996)
4. Morgan, J.F., Hancock, P.A.: The effect of prior task loading on mental workload: an example of hysteresis in driving. Hum. Factors **53**(1), 75–86 (2011)
5. Tokunaga, R., Hagiwara, T., Kagaya, S., Onodera, Y.: Effects of talking through cellular telephone on driving behavior. Jpn. Soc. Civil Eng. **17**, 995–1000 (2000)
6. Zenju, H., Nozawa, A., Tanaka, H., Ide, H.: The estimation of unpleasant and pleasant states by nasal thermogram. Inst. Electr. Eng. Jpn. Trans. Electron. Inf. Syst. **124**(1), 213–214 (2004)
7. Hioki, K., Nozawa, A., Mizuno, T., Ide, H.: Evaluation of the effect of intermittent mental work-load by nasal skin temperature. Inst. Electr. Eng. Jpn. Trans. Electron. Inf. Syst. **127**(7), 1000–1006 (2007)
8. Mizuno, T., Nomura, S., Nozawa, A., Asano, H., Ide, H.: Evaluation of the effect of intermittent mental work-load by nasal skin temperature. IEICE Trans. Inf. Syst. **J93–D**(4), 535–543 (2010)
9. Mizuno, T., et al.: Measuring facial skin temperature fluctuation caused by mental work-load with infrared thermography. Inst. Electr. Eng. Jpn. Trans. Electron. Inf. Syst. **136**(11), 1581–1585 (2016)

Tracking and Evaluation of Human State Detections in Adaptive Autonomous Vehicles

Dario Niermann$^{(\boxtimes)}$, Alexander Trende, and Andreas Luedtke

OFFIS e.V., Escherweg 2, 26121 Oldenburg, Germany
dario.niermann@offis.de

Abstract. Autonomous Vehicles (AVs) take away the control of their passengers, which could result in uncomfortable or stressful situations through inappropriate driving styles, reducing the overall acceptance of AVs [1]. The detection of such situations through sensory measurements could improve driving quality through intelligent driving style adaptations, leading to an overall more personalized and satisfying driving experience [2, 5]. Such adaptive autonomous vehicles (AAVs) promise great increase of trust and better quality of human machine interaction, leading to more acceptance and higher safety in driving. We propose a software framework that allows an easy recording of various sensor measurements, statistical analysis of the data and generating easy to understand user interfaces. Since the sensory data is collected at time scales of milliseconds and changes in the user and vehicle behavior can stretch over multiple months, an efficient analyses and transparent representation of the recorded data is crucial. Enabling the passenger to see how well the vehicle adapted to his or her needs can further increase trust, while providing in depths analysis of long-term changes to the manufacturer can help to track and improve the vehicles adaption models. The graphical user interface (GUI) allows passengers to access comprehensive metrics, the history of the recorded data and to make changes to the car's behavior.

Keywords: Automated vehicles · Human-machine-interaction · Intention detection · Human centered design · User state detection

1 Introduction

Automated driving will be a completely new experience for all users and unpleasant experiences during the usage of this novel technology can hinder its acceptance. Since all humans are subjective in nature, a single optimal design to avoid these negative experiences does not exist, thus an adaptive approach seems promising. This would require to assess the user state during the usage of the adaptive autonomous vehicle (AAV) and adapt the vehicles behavior accordingly [1, 3]. This concept is explained graphically in Fig. 1. The user state is assessed using in-vehicle sensors that monitor the user (heart rate, skin response, pose, ...) and a classification algorithms, e.g. a pre-trained neural network [1, 3]. In the following the user state will be represented by discomfort and stress, since it has been shown that this state can be measured [1] but other states like joy, confusion, activity and so on can also be considered. The classification algorithm can also use

© Springer Nature Switzerland AG 2020
C. Stephanidis and M. Antona (Eds.): HCII 2020, CCIS 1224, pp. 378–384, 2020.
https://doi.org/10.1007/978-3-030-50726-8_50

additional traffic context [4]. The user state is then passed to the maneuver model, which can choose to adapt the current driving style based on traffic context and user state. All these decisions and measurement are passed to the proposed tracking framework for later analysis.

Many researchers worked on software frameworks to combine physiological measurements from different sensors [7–10]. The ARISTARKO framework [8] for physiological data acquisition combines measurements from wearable electrodermal, electrocardiogram, electromyogram and skin temperature sensors. It features a graphical user interface (GUI) and safes recordings to a database. After recording, the sensor measurements can be used to classify arousal in the user.

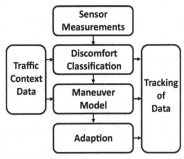

Fig. 1. Concept of adaptive autonomous vehicle

In the case of automated driving, the user state is related to the driving behavior and current traffic situation. This means that information about the vehicle's behavior and contextual information about the situation has to be taken into account when assessing the user state [5, 14]. This could allow the automation to adapt according to the given traffic situation.

In this paper we introduce a framework to collect measurements from physiological sensors, vehicles and driving simulators. The framework collects the data to detect the state of the user and tracks the user state over longer periods of time. This can help to adapt the autonomous vehicle's behavior to reduce negative user states and improve the driving experience. Furthermore, the framework can be used to collect and synchronize data during driving studies.

2 Concept

2.1 Architecture

Figure 2 shows a schematic overview over the proposed framework. The framework consists of six main components, which are explained in detail in the following subsections.

The key idea is explained in the following. The collection of data happens through both physiological and vehicle sensors, which are combined, synchronized and preprocessed by the backend. The data is continuously saved to a database. The inference engine has read and write access to the database through the backend, such that it can expand and filter the data considering long time scales, multiple maneuvers and the like. Finally, the GUI can read the processed and simplified data to display status developments to the user.

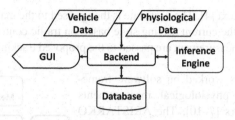

Fig. 2. Schematic overview of the framework's architecture. Vehicle and physiological sensor data are collected and processed in the backend and saved in a database. The inference engine and graphical user interface (GUI) can request data from the database via the backend.

2.2 Data Collection and Backend

Collecting gigabytes of data using multiple real-time sensors usually happens within hours or minutes of driving, leading to the need of extracting meaningful information as quickly as possible to remove unnecessary data. An exemplary subset of previous recorded physiological data is displayed over time in Fig. 3 left.

Besides the data from physiological sensor the framework will receive data input from the vehicle or the driving simulator software. The backend parses all incoming data from sensors and reduces the amount of data needed to be saved. This is done by preprocessing all incoming data, using pre-trained algorithms to filter out unnecessary events and measurements, grouping multiple value-pairs into semantic relations, synchronizing data to a common time-scale and removing redundant data. This reduced data format is then saved into the vehicle's internal database and can be used by the inference engine and the GUI.

2.3 Inference Engine

Since the direct sensory measurements are simple time series without any context or a shared reference to other context information, further post processing needs to be applied to the collected data.

Coming from direct measured values like the ones seen in Fig. 3 (left), the inference engine can use the recorded context, like driven maneuver, to infer more general representations, like the distribution of assessed discomfort over driving maneuver (Fig. 3 right). Further processing can then fit statistical distributions over the data, allowing to make more sophisticated predictions. For example, fitting a normal distribution would reduce all data points to just an average and a standard deviation. These numbers could then be saved to the database to allow faster subsequent processing.

Additionally, a risk assessment of the current traffic context can be calculated based on recorded passenger discomfort and more objective measures, like the number of road users in close proximity, road type, ego speed, time head ways and so on. These processing steps are done parallel to the recording of data and driving of the vehicle to continuously update the dataset.

Using the acquired probabilities from such statistical fits, the inference engine can also be used to predict passenger discomfort for certain maneuvers before the maneuver is executed. Taking into account the traffic context, future maneuver, driving style settings and comparing it with previous data or extrapolating from previous data, these predictions could potentially help to adapt to novel situations. The inference engine could not only know that e.g. overtaking induces discomfort because of previous recorded overtaking maneuvers, but also because it recorded statistics on how speed and lane changes induce discomfort, using that information to deduce how a planned overtaking maneuver would induce discomfort.

One of the most important tasks of the inference engine is the calculation of correlations between context parameters and measured discomfort. As a context parameter we define all parameters that can be changed through driving style adaptations, like g-forces, top speed, distance to vehicle in front, and the like. These parameters change during driving through varying interactions with surrounding traffic. This allows to calculate correlations between all measured parameters and the respective measured discomfort, creating a score of how important each parameter for reducing discomfort is.

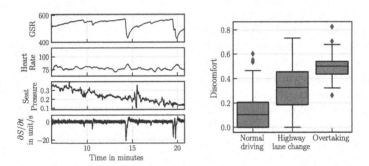

Fig. 3. (Left) Time series of various physiological data collected during driving. No direct information can be read out of this data. (Right) Distribution of moments of discomfort over driven maneuver. Out of this data, meaningful information can be extracted.

Highly correlating parameters can be considered in the maneuver and route planning of the vehicle and therefore help to reduce discomfort. For example, if the passengers discomfort correlates with lateral g-forces, the vehicle needs to reduce these forces to reduce discomfort. This can lead to adaptations in every maneuver, e.g. the overtaking needs to reduce the lateral movement when switching lanes. Which in turn increases the time needed to overtake and reduces the times overtaking may take place.

After the vehicle has adapted to change the parameter, the newly created data shows less significant correlation of that parameter, since extreme values did not appear in the new driving style. This leads to another parameter that has the highest correlation, again demanding for a new adaption of driving style. This leads to cyclic process that changes the user state over time.

2.4 User Information

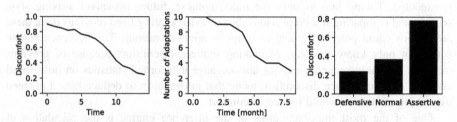

Fig. 4. Three example plots that users could see in the framework: development of discomfort over time (left), number of behavior adaptations performed by the system (center) and the average discomfort for given driving styles (right).

The graphical user interface (GUI) allows the passenger to access visualizations of the system's properties, statistics over performed system adaptations and to make changes to the system's preferences manually. Depending on the data needed by the user, the GUI sends a request to the backend, which itself will send a query to the database to fetch the necessary data. Figure 4 shows some example visualizations that might be of interest for the user. This could include time-series of measured or inferred data like heart rate or discomfort, but also how often the system has changed its behavior over time. Through control elements the user might also be able to make changes to the system

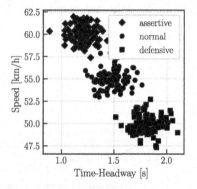

Fig. 5. Based on the inferred driving style parameters different driving styles and user groups can be determined. As an example, three clusters for a speed vs. Time-Headway are shown. These clusters can be used to serve users better preset driving styles.

manually [6]. This could include preferences regarding driving style or routing.

A possible extension of the framework could be to use a cloud-based database to store data from multiple vehicles and users. Statistical modeling based on this data could be used to generate more abstract user models. A simple example would be to collect driving style related parameters over multiple users to derive common driving style groups (Fig. 5). Based on empirical user studies this has already been done [11–13]. A lot of these studies feature relatively small sample sizes (N = 20–50) and focus on just specific traffic use cases (e.g. lane-following [11] or overtaking [13]). However, a cloud-based approach could potentially fetch data from thousands of drivers, allowing to generate reasonable data sizes to group passengers into specific driving styles. The derived driving styles may be used as presets for new users and could help to recommend the optimal driving style for a person based on the similarity with respect to the manual configuration of the system or demographic information of the user.

3   Conclusion

We presented a framework for tracking and evaluating physiological and vehicle data in adaptive autonomous vehicles (AAV). It can be used to record and synchronize physiological sensor measurements like electrodermal activity or electrocardiography and automatically combines this data with contextual information about the traffic situation and the vehicles driving behavior. This allows the framework to calculate user statistics and assess the user state in real-time, while also featuring a graphical user interface that visualizes these statistics to the user. This gives the opportunity to change the vehicles driving behavior based on statistical analysis of previous driven maneuvers and to increase trust between human and machine through a driving style tailored to the user. We plan to use the framework in upcoming real-world and driving simulator studies [6].

Acknowledgment. This work was supported by the German Federal Ministry of Transport and Digital Infrastructure in the funding program Automated and Connected Driving, AutoAkzept and by the DFG-grant "Learning from Humans – Building for Humans" (project number: 433 524 510).

Supported by:

Federal Ministry
of Transport and
Digital Infrastructure

on the basic of a decision
by the German Bundestag

References

1. Niermann, D., Lüdtke, A.: Measuring driver discomfort in autonomous vehicles. In: Ahram, T., Karwowski, W., Vergnano, A., Leali, F., Taiar, R. (eds.) IHSI 2020. AISC, vol. 1131, pp. 52–58. Springer, Cham (2020). https://doi.org/10.1007/978-3-030-39512-4_9
2. Hartwich, F., Beggiato, M., Krems, J.F.: Driving comfort, enjoyment and acceptance of automated driving–effects of drivers' age and driving style familiarity. Ergonomics **61**(8), 1017–1032 (2018)
3. Drewitz, U., et al.: Automation ohne Unsicherheit: Vorstellung des Förderprojekts AUTOAKZEPT zur Erhöhung der Akzeptanz automatisierten Fahrens (2019)
4. Beggiato, M., Hartwich, F., Krems, J.: Using smartbands, pupillometry and body motion to detect discomfort in automated driving. Front. Hum. Neurosci. **12**, 338 (2018)
5. Trende, A., Hartwich, F., Fränzle, M.: Improving the detection of user uncertainty in automated overtaking maneuvers by combining contextual, physiological and individualized user data. In: International Conference on Human-Computer Interaction (2020, submitted)
6. Trende, A., Gräfing, D., Weber, L.: Personalized user profiles for autonomous vehicles. In: Proceedings of the 11th International Conference on Automotive User Interfaces and Interactive Vehicular Applications: Adjunct Proceedings, pp. 287–291, September 2019
7. Bar-Or, A., Healey, J., Kontothanassis, L., Van Thong, J.M.: BioStream: a system architecture for real-time processing of physiological signals. In: The 26th Annual International Conference of the IEEE Engineering in Medicine and Biology Society, vol. 2, pp. 3101–3104. IEEE, September 2004

8. Martínez-Rodrigo, A., Pastor, J.M., Zangróniz, R., Sánchez-Meléndez, C., Fernández-Caballero, A.: ARISTARKO: a software framework for physiological data acquisition. Ambient Intelligence- Software and Applications – 7th International Symposium on Ambient Intelligence (ISAmI 2016). AISC, vol. 476, pp. 215–223. Springer, Cham (2016). https://doi.org/10.1007/978-3-319-40114-0_24

9. Kang, K., Bae, C., Lee, J., Han, D.: UHaS: ubiquitous health-assistant system based on wearable biomedical devices. IJIPM: Int. J. Inf. Process. Manag. 2(2), 114–126 (2011)

10. Kemper, D., Davis, L., Fidopiastis, C., Nicholson, D.: A first step towards a generalized physiological measurement framework. In: Proceedings of the Human Factors and Ergonomics Society Annual Meeting, vol. 52, no. 7, pp. 615–618. SAGE Publications, Los Angeles, September 2008

11. Siebert, F.W., Oehl, M., Pfister, H.-R.: The influence of time headway on subjective driver states in adaptive cruise control. Transp. Res. Part F: Traffic Psychol. Behav. 25, 65–73 (2014)

12. Scherer, S., Schubert, D., Dettmann, A., Hartwich, F., Bullinger, A.C.: Wie will der "Fahrer" automatisiert gefahren werden? Uberpr¨ufung verschiedener Fahrstile hinsichtlich des Komforter- lebens, in 32. VDI/VW-Gemeinschaftstagung Fahrerassistenzsystemeund automatisiertes Fahren (2016)

13. Bellem, H., Thiel, B., Schrauf, M., Krems, J.F.: Comfort in automated driving: an analysis of preferences for different automated driving styles and their dependence on personality traits. Transp. Res. Part F: Traffic Psychol. Behav. 55, 90–100 (2018)

14. Telpaz, A., Baltaxe, M., Hecht, R.M., Cohen-Lazry, G., Degani, A., Kamhi, G.: An approach for measurement of passenger comfort: real-time classification based on in-cabin and exterior data. In: 2018 21st International Conference on Intelligent Transportation Systems (ITSC), pp. 223–229. IEEE, November 2018

Proof of Concept for an Indicator of Learner Anxiety via Wearable Fitness Trackers

Jonathan Shachter[1(✉)], Maria Kangas[2], Naomi Sweller[2], and Jeffrey Stewart[3]

[1] Kyushu Sangyo University, Fukuoka, Japan
jonathanshachter@gmail.com
[2] Macquarie University, Sydney, NSW, Australia
{maria.kangas,naomi.sweller}@mq.edu.au
[3] Tokyo University of Science, Tokyo, Japan
jeffjrstewart@gmail.com

Abstract. The Fitbit Data Collection System (FDCS) is designed to facilitate measuring heart rate response related to Language Learning (LL) anxiety. Using Fitbit Wristbands and the Fitbit Cloud, the FDCS can track the heart rates for multiple test subjects on-demand or automatically. This data can be aggregated, synchronized and transferred directly to a statistical program for further analysis. This paper provides researchers with an explanation of why the tool was built, its functionality and how it will be used in a forthcoming LL anxiety study.

Keywords: Language Learning anxiety · Fitbit · Heart rate

1 Introduction

In the broader field of anxiety, researchers often use a combination of physiological and self-reported methodology [1, 2]. The most common physiological measurements involve cortisol (via saliva), heart rate (HR), blood pressure, skin conductance and in some cases muscle tension [3]. Correlating self-reported assessments with a physiological measure, however, can be expensive for Language Learning (LL) anxiety researchers and may be obtrusive in classroom data collections [4]. In previous empirical studies outside of LL anxiety [5–7], self-reported anxiety measurements were found to have a significant correlation with HR responses.

In recent years, personal fitness trackers such as Fitbit™ have made measurement of a user's HR more affordable for consumers. However, since these products are designed for personal use, it is difficult for researchers to aggregate results across multiple participants to compute averages by given points in time that coincide with stimuli introduced by researchers. Fortunately, Fitbit offers an Application Programming Interface (API) for researchers to create data collection systems and tools. A "web-API" is a set of protocols that allows one computer to request and extract information from another computer, over the web (via a gateway). Using this, it is possible to build a tool that can track heart rate data for multiple users simultaneously, permitting second language acquisition researchers to monitor and measure anxiety on a group level. The following paper will describe such a tool, the Fitbit Data Collection System (FDCS).

C. Stephanidis and M. Antona (Eds.): HCII 2020, CCIS 1224, pp. 385–392, 2020.
https://doi.org/10.1007/978-3-030-50726-8_51

2 Language Learning Anxiety and the Need for Objective Measures

LL anxiety is commonly categorized as situational-specific [8], whereby anxiety occurs when individuals are learning a new language and are anxious about their performance (e.g., during a foreign language class). LL anxiety can affect both cognition and oral production [9]. The Foreign Language Classroom Anxiety Scale (FLCAS) [10] is one of the most commonly used self-report questionnaires in the field of LL anxiety. Validated through the use of factor analysis [11], the FLCAS is a lengthy 33-item survey, which measures self-reported LL anxiety assessments on a scale from 5 (strongly agree) to 1 (strongly disagree). The FLCAS contains a range of statements (i.e. I feel confident when I speak in English class), which aim to identify self-reported levels of state anxiety, task-irrelevant thinking and feelings of insecurity regarding various aspects of English language learning, oral performance and testing. To date, LL anxiety has primarily been assessed using self-report methods (e.g., via the FLCAS) to further understanding of the incidence and mechanisms of LL anxiety. A limitation of retrospective studies (which draw data exclusively from subjective measures) is the possible existence of "inaccurate recall"—data and/or conclusions drawn in such studies may be biased or inaccurate [12]. Therefore, the introduction of a framework for inexpensively and conveniently measuring classroom anxiety via heart rate could be of great benefit to second language acquisition researchers.

3 Forthcoming Research Using the Fitbit Data Collection System

In a forthcoming study led by the first author [13], the aim is to use a physiological measure, namely HR response, to evaluate the association between HR and self-reported nervousness feelings related to LL anxiety. To that end, IT Specialist (Nick May, Cogito Ltd.) was contracted to develop and test a proof of concept software measurement tool that can collect HR measures using Fitbit™ "smart watches" and a software Web Application Programming Interface (API) provided by FitBit, Inc. This research tool has been designed to effectively, unobtrusively and cost-effectively collect HR responses before, during and after a speaking activity of Japanese English learners in a university classroom in Japan.

In the forthcoming study, the aim is to evaluate the feasibility of using the FDCS to capture undergraduate students' LL anxiety responses by correlating their physiological/HR data with their state affective self-report data in a classroom setting over 3 consecutive weekly classes. To aid researchers and teachers to detect "real time" patterns of LL anxiety within a lecture and/or term, Shachter (2018) developed the Nervousness Metric (NM) as a self-reporting tool [14] (Fig. 1).

How nervous are you feeling right now?

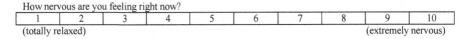

1	2	3	4	5	6	7	8	9	10
(totally relaxed)								(extremely nervous)	

Fig. 1. The nervousness metric

The NM is a 1-item instrument designed to measure student self-reports of state levels of anxiety on a scale from 1 (totally relaxed) to 10 (extremely nervous). Although formal validity and reliability tests on the NM were not conducted, the instrument is similar in function to the 11-point Numerical Rating Scale (NRS) used by doctors and nurses to measure self-assessments of pain intensity [15]. The NRS ranges from 0 to 10 with 0 being "no pain" and 10 being "the worst possible pain". A 10-point scale was chosen to more easily compute average ratings across multiple classes. The NM is also similar in function to the Subjective Units of Distress Scale [16] and the Positive and Negative Affect Schedule [17]. In a forthcoming study by the first author, the NM will be modified to ensure the descriptors for the numeric rating scale is consistent for affect state assessed (e.g., not at all nervous to extremely nervous).

As it will not be feasible for the purposes of this forthcoming study to collect data on participants' resting HRs outside of the classroom context, relative baseline HR data will be collected approximately 10 min prior to performance. To the best of the researchers' knowledge, this would be the first such study to simultaneously measure HR via Fitbit technology with self-reported LL assessments over time.

4   Fitbit Wearable Heart Rate Monitors

Fitbit Smart watches specialize in HR monitoring and have gone through performance testing in clinical trials. Regarding accuracy, Shcherbina et al. (2017) concluded that the Fitbit's HR measurements were within an "acceptable error range" [18]. A separate study by Wang et al. (2017) found that the accuracy of wrist-worn monitors was best at lower heart rates (i.e. not during strenuous activity) [19]. While there is still an ongoing debate regarding the reliability of wearable HR monitors in clinical settings, their usage in human physiology research has been accepted since 2016 [20].

5   Functionality of the Fitbit Data Collection System

5.1   Overview

The Fitbit Data Collection System (FDCS) has been successfully tested to (1) collect participant HR data using the Fitbit 'smart watch' (via the FitBit Cloud), (2) automatically synchronize the HR data by 'start of test' time for each student, and (3) transfer the synchronized HR data to a secure database. From the researcher's database, data can be transferred into a statistical program of choice for analysis via Excel or csv file. Figure 2 shows the flow of data from the user's own heart beat through to the researcher's computer.

User heart beat => Fitbit Wristband = [Smartphone App] => Fitbit Cloud Account = [WebAPI] => Fitbit Data Collection System = Browser = > Researcher's Computer.

Fig. 2. Data flow

5.2 Setting Up Accounts

The FDCS facilitates the semi-automatic creation and authorization of hundreds of accounts in the FitBit Cloud and configures those accounts to permit HR data-extraction to the researcher's secure server. As part of the account setup process an email address, name, date of birth, weight and height must be entered. The email address entered must be unique and the user's name must not include digits or underscores. Due to ethical issues, we used generic values for the date of birth [2002/02/30], height and weight [59 kg; 166 cm]. Fitbit has stated that although such details are needed for setup, the type of activity or person's personal information has no effect on how HR is detected [21]. We then made email addresses using the word representation of a number (e.g. 1 Male becomes one@ourdomain.com). The first name was entered into the Fitbit system as 'one' and the surname 'm'. Even though 'm' is not shown in the registered e-mail address, sex information is displayed on the registered Fitbit account.

Figure 3 shows account **one m.** on the researcher's smartphone Fitbit application. After data collection, researchers need to manually 'sync' data from each individual wristband. The researcher can use the same smartphone for the syncing of all wristbands, but this involves logging in and out for each Fitbit account. Once synced, the FDCS can access data via the Fitbit server.

Fig. 3. Logging-in to a pre-registered fitbit account for data sync

Figure 4 shows **one m.'s** account information as displayed in the FDCS. Manual setup of Fitbit accounts takes place through a web-interface and is a complex, time-consuming and error-prone process. To address this, we used the browser extension TamperMonkey to automatically set up Fitbit accounts. Previous research has been conducted [22] on the usefulness of TamperMonkey to assist in the modification and handling of webpage user-interfaces. The FDCS includes a TamperMonkey script that can automatically create Fitbit User accounts in the Fitbit Cloud and authorize them to permit data extraction via the web-API. Note the 7-digit code '7R5PND' in Fig. 4. This is the Fitbit Account ID and is used to tell Fitbit which account we are extracting data from.

```
□ Devices: 1 : 7R5PND Charge 3 [100%]
Wristband→F.Ac@11:59:49 Wed 25 Sep [2019]
Collections:1 [heart-data : account : update : devices]
Live updates: Off [switch on]
heartdata: FDCS←F.Ac@12:45:21 Tue 10 Mar [2020]
account: FDCS←F.Ac@ 12:45:21 Tue 10 Mar [2020]
devices: FDCS←F.Ac@12:45:21 Tue 10 Mar [2020]
email: oneone@ksu-lla2018.com
fitbit website I force new grant I validate
download
```

Fig. 4. Account generated via TamperMonkey with data imported into the FDCS

5.3   Managing Data in the FDCS Interface

Figure 5 shows the FDCS Interface as seen by the researcher. In Column 1 of Fig. 5, we have a list of 'people' (i.e. researchers or research assistants). People are linked with 'collections' of Fitbits that will be used with a particular group or class. A collection is associated with a particular class time. In column 4, we have a list of all the Fitbit Accounts (and linked wristbands) registered in the system. The '79TYLN' account has 'Devices 0' indicating that a physical wristband is not currently linked to that Fitbit Account. One can add or remove a Fitbit Account (and linked wristband) from a collection by selecting its checkbox and clicking the 'move' or 'remove' button. A single 'wristband' can appear in several collections (always linked to the same Fitbit account). It can thus be used in several classes and the HR data for each participant is held separately by the system.

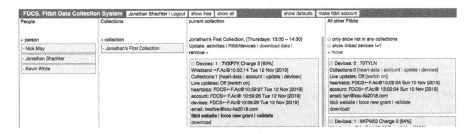

Fig. 5. The FDCS interface

5.4   Downloading Data from the FDCS Interface

Figure 6 shows the process of downloading HR data for those FitBit Accounts generated between 13:00 and 14:30 on Thursdays - the defaults for that particular collection. These defaults can be over-ridden, and if needed, we can specify a particular date range. Furthermore, we can also specify for how many minutes before and after the test activity we want HR data.

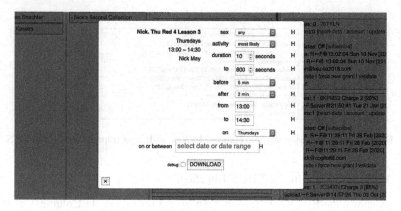

Fig. 6. Download settings

5.5   Heart Rate Data Output via csv or Excel File

Figure 7 displays csv-formatted output for the heart rates of a group of 4 test subjects (–60 s to –52 s in the top panel; 0 to 11 in the bottom panel). It is formatted relative to the START (0 s) of the test (when a participant presses 'run' on the Fitbit) for each test subject, and (in this particular test) includes readings for the 60 s prior to test start through to 60 s after test end (when a participant presses 'stop run' on the Fitbit). These settings can be adjusted in the FDCS. Detailed heart rate data is not standardly available to users in the Fitbit Cloud Account web interface; the availability of this level of detail is a key feature of the FDCS. The 'identifier' is a wristband's associated code on the Fitbit server.

Identifier	Date	Duration	-60s	-59s	-58s	-57s	-56s	-55s	-54s	-53s	-52s
7NVHDX	2019-10-03T	0:00:14				87				86	
7O34XN	2019-10-03T	0:00:13							82		
7Q3NQT	2019-10-03T	0:01:48			84				83		
7Q43ZH	2019-10-03T	0:02:28					82				83

Identifier	Date	Duration	START(0s)	1s	2s	3s	4s	5s	6s	7s	8s	9s	10s	11s
7NVHDX	2019-10-03T	0:00:14			82			82	89			89		93
7O34XN	2019-10-03T	0:00:13			84			84	88			88		88
7Q3NQT	2019-10-03T	0:01:48			77			77	81			81		80
7Q43ZH	2019-10-03T	0:02:28			83			83	86			86	82	

Fig. 7. Heart rate data output via csv or excel file

6   Summary

The Fitbit Data Collection System (FDCS) has the scope to provide an efficient and cost-effective method to objectively measure and track LL anxiety. In doing so, this will facilitate and further our understanding of the association between LL anxiety self-reports and how strongly this is related to people's heart rate responses in ecologically valid settings (i.e., classroom contexts). Unlike self-report methods, the FDCS facilitates the tracking of heart rate in real time. This has the scope to serve two purposes: 1) enhancing anxiety and arousal awareness in individuals, and 2) for educators to become mutually aware when students are experiencing heightened anxiety or arousal whilst learning a new language. This method can also extend to evaluating anxiety in other contexts (such as social anxiety disorder). Moreover, if the FDCS is proven effective to track anxiety and arousal changes, it has the scope to be used as a validated method to assess efficacy of treatment interventions for anxiety related conditions. For a more detailed description of the API application, data request/authorization/authentication processes, security and coding, please refer to [23].

Acknowledgements. The Fitbit Data Collection System was made possible by a grant awarded by the Kyushu Sangyo University (KSU) Computer Network Center (CNC). Thank you to Nick May of Cogito Ltd. (cogitoltd.com - nick@cogitoltd.com) for helping with the design, writing the code and supervising all IT aspects of this project.

References

1. Busscher, B., Spinhoven, P., van Gerwen, L.J., de Geus, E.J.: Anxiety sensitivity moderates the relationship of changes in physiological arousal with flight anxiety during in vivo exposure therapy. Behav. Res. Ther. **51**(2), 98–105 (2013)
2. Wild, A., Freeston, M.H., Heary, S., Rodgers, J.: Diminished physiological flexibility is associated with intolerance of uncertainty during affective decision making in adolescence. J. Exp. Psychopathol. **5**(4), 503–513 (2014)
3. Ganster, D.C., Crain, T.L., Brossoit, R.M.: Physiological measurement in the organizational sciences: A review and recommendations for future use. Ann. Rev. Organ. Psychol. Organ. Behav. **5**, 267–293 (2018)
4. Gregersen, T., Macintyre, P.D., Meza, M.D.: The motion of emotion: idiodynamic case studies of learners' foreign language anxiety. Mod. Lang. J. **98**(2), 574–588 (2014)
5. Daly, A.L., Chamberlain, S., Spalding, V.: Test anxiety, heart rate and performance in A-level French speaking mock exams: an exploratory study. Educ. Res. **53**(3), 321–330 (2011)
6. Hahn, H., Kropp, P., Kirschstein, T., Rücker, G., Müller-Hilke, B.L.: Test anxiety in medical school is unrelated to academic performance but correlates with an effort/reward imbalance. PLoS ONE **12**(2) (2017)
7. Kantor, L., Endler, N.S., Heslegrave, R.J., Kocovski, N.L.: Validating self-report measures of state and trait anxiety against a physiological measure. Curr. Psychol. **20**(3), 207–215 (2001). https://doi.org/10.1007/s12144-001-1007-2
8. Woodrow, L.: Anxiety and speaking English as a second language. RELC J. **37**(3), 308–328 (2006)
9. Young, D.J.: The relationship between anxiety and foreign language oral proficiency ratings. Foreign Lang. Ann. **19**(5), 439–445 (1986)

10. Horwitz, E.K., Horwitz, M.B., Cope, J.: Foreign language classroom anxiety. Mod. Lang. J. **70**(2), 125–132 (1986)
11. Vitasari, P., Wahab, M.N.A., Herawan, T., Othman, A., Sinnadurai, S.K.: Validating the instrument of study anxiety sources using factor analysis. Procedia Soc. Behav. Sci. **15**, 3831–3836 (2011)
12. Coughlin, S.S.: Recall bias in epidemiologic studies. J. Clin. Epidemiol. **43**(1), 87–91 (1990)
13. Shachter, J.: Using fitbits to physiologically measure Japanese English language learner speaking anxiety. Master's thesis. Macquarie University (2021, forthcoming)
14. Shachter, J.: Tracking and quantifying Japanese English language learner speaking anxiety. Lang. Teach. **42**, 3–7 (2018)
15. Williamson, A., Hoggart, B.: Pain: a review of three commonly used pain rating scales. J. Clin. Nurs. **14**(7), 798–804 (2005)
16. Wolpe, J., Lang, P.J.: Fear Survey Schedule. Educational and industrial testing service, San Diego (1969)
17. Watson, D., Clark, L.A.: The PANAS-X: Manual for the Positive and Negative Affect Schedule-Expanded Form (1999)
18. Shcherbina, A., et al.: Accuracy in wrist-worn, sensor-based measurements of heart rate and energy expenditure in a diverse cohort. J. Pers. Med. **7**(2), 3 (2017)
19. Wang, R., et al.: Accuracy of wrist-worn heart rate monitors. JAMA Cardiol. **2**(1), 104–106 (2017)
20. Wright, S.P., Hall Brown, T.S., Collier, S.R., Sandberg, K.: How consumer physical activity monitors could transform human physiology research. Am. J. Physiol. Regul. Integr. Comp. Physiol. **312**(3), R358–R367 (2017)
21. Fitbit Developer Homepage. Heart-rate sensor - does it use height/weight/gender etc to produce continuous heart rate values? 5 March 2020. https://community.fitbit.com/t5/Web-API-Development/Heart-rate-sensor-does-it-use-height-weight-gender-etc-to-produce/m-p/4126895#M11592
22. May, N.: Adding functionality to online educational systems using browser Scripting tools. Lang. Educ. Res. Center J. **15**, 63–77 (2020)
23. Shachter, J., Stewart J.: Designing and building the fitbit data collection system. Kyushu Sangyo Univ. Comput. Network. Center J. (2021, in Press)

Assessment of Mental Fatigue
on Physiological Signals

Guilei Sun[(⊠)] and Yanhua Meng[(⊠)]

Department of Safety Engineering,
China University of Labor Relations, Beijing 100048, China
sunguilei@culr.edu.cn, mengyh2008@126.com

Abstract. In order to evaluate the value of mental fatigue, a method for assessing the intensity of mental fatigue was supposed to obtain from the physiological signals. 30 subjects were selected to participate in the experiment process. The questionnaire survey was used to ensure that the participants were all in a non-fatigue state before the test. 5 min, 10 min, and 15 min of high-intensity mental work was used to control the fatigue level of the participants, while the man-machine-environment system was used to obtain the participants' electrocardiogram (ECG) signals, electromyography (EMG) signals, photoplethysmography (PPG) signals, and respiration (RESP) signals. SPSS 26 was used for peak amplitude analysis. The results indicate that the mean peak amplitude of RESP is significantly affected ($P = 0.017$) by the time of mental work. And it has a non-linear correlation with mental work time ($R^2 = 1$). The mean peak amplitude of EMG is also affected, but it is not statistically significant at the standard level of 0.05. The mean peak amplitudes of ECG and PPG are less affected by the mental work. The peak amplitude of the RESP signal can be used to evaluate the level of mental fatigue so that the probability of accidents caused by mental fatigue could be reduced.

Keywords: Fatigue assessment · Mental fatigue · Physiological signal · Correlation analysis · Photoplethysmography (PPG)

1 Introduction

In recent years, people have more and more mental work along with the rapid development of the economy. When people are fatigued, they often have poor physical coordination. The brain's dominance of limbs declines, and people have slow thinking and slow movements, so it is easy for people's judging mistakes and operational errors which will led to accidents [1]. At present, common fatigue testing methods mainly include subjective sensory evaluation method, physiological parameter test method, biochemical test method, psychological test method, and a combination of several methods [2, 3]. For example, Niu [4] used physiological signals such as ECG signals when constructing driving fatigue recognition models. Wu et al. [5] used EEG signals in driving fatigue detection research. Zhao et al. [6] used a combination of subjective questionnaires and physiological data detection of the drivers to determine driving fatigue. Yang [7] studied the impact of VDT mental fatigue status on the physiological

© Springer Nature Switzerland AG 2020
C. Stephanidis and M. Antona (Eds.): HCII 2020, CCIS 1224, pp. 393–402, 2020.
https://doi.org/10.1007/978-3-030-50726-8_52

electrical signals, and the electrocardiographic signals, pulse signals, analysis of physiological signals, and temperature signals. Cai [8] demonstrated the influence of human pulse signals in the detection of visual fatigue when studying the effects of visual fatigue on human physiological electrical signals and believed that pulse signals could achieve objective detection of visual fatigue. Zhang [9] used eye movement equipment to measure the relationship between pilot fatigue and PERCLOS and blink frequency. Wang et al. [10] used the change of heart rate index and subjective fatigue to study the effect of noise on construction fatigue and measured the level of fatigue of the subjects with evaluation table. Regarding the relationship between fatigue work and physiological signals, Jiang [11] mentioned in the experimental study of fatigue on physiological electrical signals that human fatigue can be intuitively reflected by changes in physiological parameters. Compared with domestic scholars, foreign scholars like to conduct in-depth exploration in many fields from ergonomics, physical mechanics, and medical biology. For example, Trejo [12] evaluates and classifies mental fatigue based on EEG. Borghini [13] measures the neurophysiological signals of aircraft pilots and car pilots to assess mental workload, fatigue and lethargy with EEG index, which controls the operator for brain fatigue monitoring through interactions between brain regions.

At present, many scholars' research on mental fatigue mainly focuses on driver' fatigue, psychological fatigue, visual fatigue, etc. [14]. Few studies are only related to mental work fatigue, and most scholars are focusing on EEG signals in the study of fatigue research. Strictly speaking, these researches are just some branches of mental fatigue. For example, driving fatigue includes mental fatigue and fatigue caused by static work, etc., while they are not the same type of mental fatigue. This paper mainly deals with mental work, which reflects mental fatigue from the perspective of physiological signals.

2 Experiment

2.1 Subjects Selection

The subjects were selected before the test, and 30 subjects (15 male and 15 female), aged 20–45 years old were invited. All the subjects, without physical discomfort, mental work, exercise, video work, entertainment, or using drugs, and so on before the test, were in good mental conditions.

2.2 Experiment Equipment

Wireless and wearable sensors were used to obtain the physiological parameters of the subjects, including: electrocardiograph monitoring sensor was used for electrocardiograph (ECG), myoelectric sensor was used to get electromyogram (EMG), pulse rate sensor was used to obtain photoplethysmographic (PPG) pulse waveform, and respiratory sensor was used to get respire (RESP) signals. Microsoft camera was used to capture the process of experiment. Human-machine-environment synchronization platform system, which was running on a computer, was used to collect data of physiological signals.

2.3   Experiment Procedure

Before the test was performed, the subjects were asked to rest for 20 min to fully ensure the stability of the test physiological signal. The temperature of the environment was constant at 23 °C and the procedures were as shown in Fig. 1.

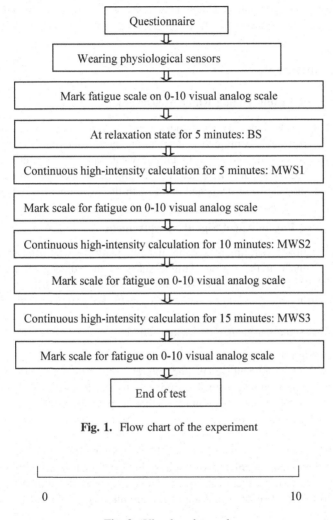

Fig. 1. Flow chart of the experiment

Fig. 2. Visual analog scale

In Fig. 1, the questionnaire was mainly used to determine that the participants were fitting for participating in the test in order to avoid the outer factors that may affect physiological signals before the experiment and in the procedure. The relaxed state before the test was defined as the "basic state" (BS), which was mainly used to obtain the basic physiological signal data of the subject in a stable state. The state after the

5-min continuous high-intensity calculation test was defined as the "mental working state 1" (MWS1). After the visual fatigue scale test, another 10 min continuous high-intensity calculation test was carried on, and this state was defined as "mental working state 2" (MWS2). After the third visual fatigue scale test, a 15-min high-intensity calculation test was performed again, and this state was defined as "Mental Working State 3" (MWS3). In the flowchart, the visual simulation scale, in which "0" represents no fatigue and "10" represents very fatigue, was shown in Fig. 2. It was mainly used to provide subjective assessment for the fatigue levels of the subjects.

3 Data Analysis

3.1 Analysis of Visual Analog Ruler Measurement

According to the scale drawn by the subjects after each test, 30 subjects, of which 28 participates' fatigue levels continued to deepen, one person's fatigue level change was small, and one person showed signs of fatigue weakening as the mental work time increased due to the individual differences of the subjects. In a conclusion, the levels of fatigue to most subjects were deepened along with the experiment.

3.2 Analysis of Physiological Signal Measurement

The human-machine-environment synchronization platform was used to extract the physiological signals of the various fatigue states of the subjects. Since the sitting operation was used during the experiment, only mental work was performed, the operating environment was quiet, and there were no external influence factors. Therefore, the amplitude of physiological signals could be studied for further research of physiological signals influence on mental fatigue.

Physiological Signal Amplitude Changes. In order to observe the peak amplitude variation of each physiological signals, the difference between the maximum value and the minimum value is subjected to descriptive statistical analysis, and the results are shown in Fig. 3, 4, 5 and 6. It shows in Fig. 3 that the peak amplitude variation of ECG signal increases gradually with the deepening of the fatigue. In Fig. 4 and Fig. 5, the amplitude variations of the EMG and PPG peak amplitudes increase at first and then decrease, while in Fig. 6 the change of the RESP peak amplitude is relatively stable. It indicates that there may be differences in physiological signals under different levels of fatigue. However, whether this difference is statistically significant or not and whether it is related to the level of brain fatigue or not are all needs further analysis.

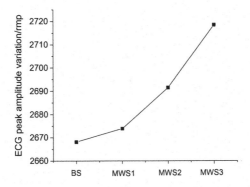

Fig. 3. Curve of ECG peak amplitude variation

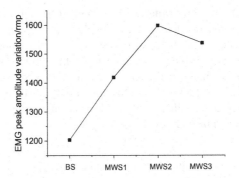

Fig. 4. Curve of EMG peak amplitude variation

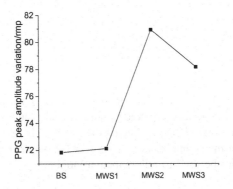

Fig. 5. Curve of PPG peak amplitude variation

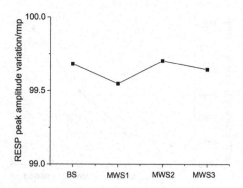

Fig. 6. Curve of RESP peak amplitude variation

Differences in the Mean Amplitude of Physiological Signals. Multiple independent sample tests are performed on physiological signals under different working conditions. The results of the significance (2-tailed test) of the physiological signals in the experiments are shown in Table 1. It demonstrates that three states in the EMG test results do not meet normal distribution. And one of RESP signals also does not conform to the normal distribution. For data with normal distribution, the sample paired t test is used to analyze the difference, and for data that does not meet the normal distribution, Wilcoxon sign rank test is used.

Table 1. Shapiro-Wilk test results

Physiological signals	BS	MWS1	MWS2	MWS3
ECG	0.361	0.998	0.142	0.208
EMG	0.000	0.025	0.073	0.017
PPG	0.750	0.684	0.062	0.304
RESP	0.302	0.573	0.149	0.047

a. ECG Paired Sample Test

The differences in ECG amplitudes are in line with the normal distribution. Paired sample t-tests are used to perform a paired test on the four groups of data and Table 2 is obtained. It shows that there is no significant difference between the data of all paired tests. That is, whether the mental work is in level of fatigue or not, the mean amplitude of ECG signals cannot be used to reflect mental fatigue.

Table 2. ECG paired sample t test

	Paired differences					t	Sig. (2-tailed)
	Mean	Std. deviation	Std. error mean	95% Confidence interval of the difference			
				Lower	Upper		
BS & MWS1	17.602	715.013	178.753	−363.402	398.606	0.098	0.923
BS & MWS2	−121.959	704.022	176.005	−497.105	253.188	−0.693	0.499
BS & MWS3	−305.031	972.364	243.091	−823.167	213.105	−1.255	0.229
MWS1 & 2	−139.561	426.078	106.520	−366.602	87.481	−1.310	0.210
MWS1 & 3	−322.633	819.728	204.932	−759.436	114.169	−1.574	0.136
MWS2 & 3	−183.073	794.629	198.657	−606.501	240.356	−0.922	0.371

b. EMG Wilcoxon Rank Test

As it is shown in Table 3, although there is no statistical significance at the test level of 0.05 for all paired samples, p value of BS & MWS1, BS & MWS2, and BS & MWS3, getting by Wilcoxon rank test, are decreasing gradually.

The decrease indicates that the differences in EMG signals gradually appear as the levels of mental fatigue increases. EMG responds better to changes in mental fatigue, but it still lacks sensitivity.

Table 3. EMG Wilcoxon Rank Test Statistics

	BS & MWS1	BS & MWS2	BS & MWS3	MWS1 & 2	MWS1 & 3	MWS 2 & 3
Z	−0.621	−1.551	−1.913	−0.776	−0.776	−0.052
Asymp. Sig. (2-sided)	0.535	0.121	0.056	0.438	0.438	0.959

Table 4. PPG paired sample t test

	Paired differences					t	Sig. (2-tailed)
	Mean	Std. deviation	Std. error mean	95% confidence interval of the difference			
				Lower	Upper		
BS & MWS1	−1.076	14.427	3.607	−8.764	6.611	−0.298	0.769
BS & MWS2	−12.865	13.925	3.481	−20.285	−5.445	−3.696	0.002
BS & MWS3	−9.675	20.412	5.103	−20.552	1.202	−1.896	0.077
MWS1 & 2	−11.789	17.431	4.358	−21.077	−2.500	−2.705	0.016
MWS1 & 3	−8.599	16.621	4.155	−17.456	0.258	−2.069	0.056
MWS2 & 3	3.191	17.468	4.367	−6.118	12.498	0.730	0.476

c. PPG Paired Sample t Test

According to the test results of the paired samples shown in Table 4, there is statistically significant for BS & MWS2, which indicated that mental fatigue has affected PPG. The p value of BS & MWS2, MWS1 & MWS2 are all show significant differences at the test level of 0.05, while BS & MWS1, MWS2 & MWS3 do not show significant differences. It demonstrates that the MWS2 may be in fatigue state. However, the test results of BS & MWS3 does not appear significant differences. Therefore, the mean amplitude of the PPG peak should not be used to evaluate the level of mental fatigue.

d. RESP Data Analysis

The RESP data distribution of BS, MWS1, and MWS2 obey the normal distribution, and the paired sample t test is used for analysis. The results are shown in Table 5. BS & MWS3, MWS1 & MWS3, and MWS2 & MWS3 are analyzed using Wilcoxon rank test, as shown in Table 6.

Table 5. Paired sample t test

	Paired differences					t	Sig. (2-tailed)
	Mean	Std. deviation	Std. error mean	95% Confidence interval of the difference			
				Lower	Upper		
BS & MWS1	−3.59625	25.27511	6.31878	−17.06441	9.87191	−0.569	0.578
BS & MWS2	−10.63000	26.51541	6.62885	−24.75906	3.49906	−1.604	0.130
MWS1 & 2	−7.03375	33.84394	8.46098	−25.06791	11.00041	−0.831	0.419

Table 6. Wilcoxon Rank Test Statistics

	BS & MWS3	MWS1 & 3	MWS2 & 3
Z	−2.379	−1.862	−0.454
Asymp. Sig. (2-tailed)	0.017	0.063	0.650

From the results of data analysis shown in Table 5 and Table 6, it appears that the significance (2-tailed) of BS & MWS1, BS & MWS2, and BS & MWS3 are gradually increases with the decrease of p value. And there is significant difference between BS and MWS3, which has statistical significance. There is no significant difference on MWS2 & MWS3, while there is more difference on MWS1 & MWS3 because the level of fatigue in MWS3 is higher. It proves that the RESP signals show clear correlation and regularity with the level of mental fatigue. Hence, the RESP signal can be used to reflect the level of mental fatigue and detect mental fatigue.

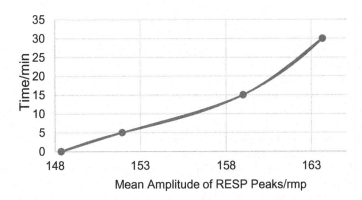

Fig. 7. Relationship between high-intensity mental work time and mean amplitude of RESP peaks

The non-linear fitting of the mean value of RESP amplitude and the mental time of work yields the equation:

$$T = 0.0099 \text{ RESP}^3 - 4.5313 \text{ RESP}^2 + 694.44 \text{ RESP} - 35526, R^2 = 1$$

$R^2 = 1$, which shows that the formula has highly corresponding with actual value, as shown in Fig. 7. Therefore, the formula, which can be used to calculate the level of mental work under different intensities by RESP amplitude, provides a very useful evaluation mode for the evaluation of mental work.

4   Conclusions

1. As the level of mental fatigue gradually increases, the mean amplitude of the RESP peaks gradually increases. When the high-intensity mental work last 30 min, the mean amplitude of the RESP peaks shows a significant difference at the test level of 0.05 (0.017).
2. The difference of EMG (ECG the same) mean amplitude increase gradually with levels of mental fatigue deepening, but it does not show statistical significance at the test level of 0.05. There are no significant correlations between the mean amplitude of PPG signals and mental fatigue.
3. A non-linear fitting of the mean amplitude of the breathing peak RESP and the mental work time T is performed, and a cubic polynomial is obtained.

$$T = 0.0099 \text{ RESP}^3 - 4.5313 \text{ RESP}^2 + 694.44 \text{ RESP} - 35526, R^2 = 1$$

According to this formula, $R^2 = 1$, the high-intensity mental work time can be evaluated by the mean amplitude of the breathing peaks.

References

1. Li, H.P., Ji, N.: Fatigue impact of staff on safety production and protection. Electr. Power Saf. Technol. **9**, 21–22 (2007)
2. Chen, J.W., Bi, C.B., Liao, H.J., Li, J., Guo, J.Y., Liu, B.L.: Comparative research on measurement methods of work fatigue. J. Saf. Sci. Technol. **7**(5), 63–66 (2011)
3. Sun, G.L.: Visual Fatigue Detection Technology and Application. China Meteorological Press, Bejing (2019)
4. Niu, L.B.: Study on driving fatigue recognition method based on ECG signal (Master's thesis, Southwest Jiaotong University) (2017)
5. Wu, S.B., Gao, L., Wang, L.A.: Detecting driving fatigue based on electroencephalogram. Trans. Beijing Inst. Technol. **29**(12), 1072–1075 (2009)
6. Zhao, X.H., Fang, R.X., Mao, K.J., Rong, J.: Test effectiveness of sound as countermeasure against driving fatigue based on physiological signals. J. Southwest Jiaotong Univ. **45**(3), 457–463 (2010)
7. Yang, H.: The research of VDT mental fatigue estimated method based on ECG and pulse signal (Master's thesis, Lanzhou University of Technology) (2011)
8. Cai, H.Y.: The research of VDT visual fatigue of based on pulse signal (Master's thesis, Lanzhou University of Technology) (2012)
9. Zhang, L., Zhou, Q., Yin, Q., Liu, Z.: Assessment of pilots mental fatigue status with the eye movement features. In: Nunes, I.L. (ed.) AHFE 2018. AISC, vol. 781, pp. 146–155. Springer, Cham (2019). https://doi.org/10.1007/978-3-319-94334-3_16
10. Wang, C.X., Lu, S.R.: Experimental study on influence of noise on work fatigue of construction personnel. J. Saf. Sci. Technol. **11**, 156–160 (2015)
11. Jiang, F.: Effect of sensory stimulation on fatigue based on physiological signals (Master's thesis, Henan Polytechnic University) (2016)
12. Trejo, L.J., Kubitz, K., Rosipal, R., et al.: EEG-based estimation and classification of mental fatigue. Psychology **6**, 572–589 (2015)
13. Borghini, G., Astolfi, L., Vecchiato, G., Mattia, D., Babiloni, F.: Measuring neurophysiological signals in aircraft pilots and car drivers for the assessment of mental workload, fatigue and drowsiness. Neurosci. Biobehav. Rev. **44**(Sp. Iss. SI), 58–75 (2014)
14. Charbonnier, S., Roy, R.N., Bonnet, S., Campagne, A.: EEG index for control operators' mental fatigue monitoring using interactions between brain regions. Expert Syst. Appl. **52**, 91–98 (2016)

User Experience Studies

Using Sugiyama-Styled Graphs to Directly Manipulate Role-Based Access Control Configurations

Anja Bertard(✉)[iD] and Jennifer-Kathrin Kopp(✉)

German Aerospace Center (DLR), Albert-Einstein-Str. 16, 12489 Berlin, Germany
{anja.bertard,jennifer-kathrin.kopp}@dlr.de

Abstract. Classical Role-Based Access Control (RBAC) software lacks options to allow users to gain a deeper understanding of RBAC configurations. Users need to comprehend a configuration to efficiently maintain and manipulate it. We developed a RBAC visualization based on a Sugiyama-styled graph. Our visualization allows RBAC untrained users to understand and manipulate RBAC configurations.

Keywords: Role-Based Access Control · RBAC · Sugiyama-styled graph · Voice communication systems · VoCS

1 Introduction

Role-Based Access Control (RBAC) configuration software focuses on editing individual entries of the RBAC data. Connections and dependencies between entries are usually displayed as attributes inside entries. The underling configuration structure is hidden behind a multitude of individual entries and therefore difficult for users to mentally reconstruct. We believe that understanding the structure of an RBAC system supports users to make better design choices. We further discuss this topic in Sect. 2.

Interactive creation and manipulation of graphs is a common technique for conceptual modeling. In configuration modelling this technique is rarely used. We show an approach using graph representations to display and edit RBAC configurations and how user experience is enhanced by the visualization:

- We discuss advantages of using a graph representation as base for a RBAC configuration interface in comparison to the classical entries based approach (Sect. 3).
- We explore different design choices to represent a RBAC configuration graph. We conducted a user study (Sect. 4) for two representations: One is based on biadjacency matrices (Sect. 3.1) and one on Sugiyama-styled graphs (Sect. 3.2).
- We discuss edit options we integrated in our visualization and improvements we implemented, after receiving feedback from the user study (Sect. 3.4).

© Springer Nature Switzerland AG 2020
C. Stephanidis and M. Antona (Eds.): HCII 2020, CCIS 1224, pp. 405–412, 2020.
https://doi.org/10.1007/978-3-030-50726-8_53

– We analyse limitations of our current approach and present ideas to further improve our interface. In addition we discuss options to make it viable for a wider range of configuration schemata (Sect. 5).

As basis for our considerations and tests we use the RBAC configuration of our software suite OPENVOCS [6], a voice communication system for mission control centers.

2   Role-Based Access Control and Role-Based Access Control Software—State of the Art

Role-based access control (RBAC) [2] is used in many commercial or governmental organizations to manage user permissions by enforcing *user—role*, *role—role*, and *role—permission* relationships. Main advantage is the permission intermediate role object: Instead of defining a set of permissions for each user, permissions are bound to a much smaller number of roles. Users receive roles that fit their needs.

Directory services of large organizations commonly use RBAC. User access is implemented over the *Lightweight Directory Access Protocol (LDAP)*.

LDAP is a non-trivial protocol, which takes effort to learn. It is created for administrators and their processes. LDAP software is not developed to enable its users to get a quick overview over the configuration and comprehend its content. It focuses on displaying entries. Relationships between entries are saved and displayed as lists inside entries. This handicaps users in their attempt to build a mental image of the configuration. For complex system, with many role and permission combinations this may result in involuntary redundant or faulty configurations.

RBAC configurations for *Voice communication systems (VoCS)* in mission control centers are a good example for such complex systems. As example the VoCS core project to supervise the COLUMBUS science laboratory on the International Space Station (ISS) contains 27 roles with access configurations for 96 virtual voice conference rooms, so called *voice loops*.

In context of VoCS, we encountered an additional problem. To design the access configuration of a VoCS user, many different factors need to be considered—from team dynamics to politics at space agency overlapping projects. It is the responsibility of selected project staff members to create that configuration. They usually lack domain and tool knowledge to work directly with RBAC configurations. Instead they note down the configuration in matrices and communicate all changes to administrators.

3   Graph-Based Role-Based Access Control Configuration Modelling

We propose to use a visualisation to help users to better understand and validate the configuration. Giving insight in complex data sets is one of the main tasks of information visualization. In this section, we will describe and analyze two visual representations which are understandable even without administrator domain knowledge. We prove this in our user study (Sect. 4).

We enhance our visualization with the necessary edit options to allow users to change the user access configuration. The resulting user interface can serve as an RBAC edit tool to a multitude of users with different backgrounds and enables a sleeker workflow in VoCS RBAC projects.

On a rudimentary level, directory services can be imagined as graphs. There are entries and connections between them. Interactive graph modelling is often used for workflow or conceptual modeling. Graphs can be displayed in a multitude of ways. Which one we use depends on the structure of the graph.

Each entry of an RBAC configuration belongs to at least one object class. We use the RBAC configuration of our VoCS software OPENVOCS as basis for our considerations. The RBAC structure of OPENVOCS is straight forward and relatively simple. We have only three different object classes: *user*, *role*, and *voice loop*. Each entry has exactly one object class. Connections exist between *users* and *roles* as well as between *roles* and *voice loops*. *Roles* can have two different types of access rights to voice loops: *TALK* or *MONITOR*. In the remainder of this section, we want to have a closer look at two possible graph representations for our interface: *biadjacency matrices* and *Sugiyama-styled graphs*.

3.1 Two Biadjacency Matrices

The staff of VoCS projects at the German Space Operation Center (GSOC) currently uses biadjacency matrices to keep track of the configuration state of their projects. One matrix shows the *role* assignment for each *user*. The second defines which *roles* have which type of access to which *voice loops*. We outline a biadjacency matrix for *voice loop-role* connections in Fig. 1.

In both matrices the columns are used to encode *roles*. In the first matrix the rows represent *voice loops*. To encode a link between a *role* and a *voice loop* we write down "*M*" for *MONITOR* or an "*T*" for *TALK* in the cell for the specific column and row combination. Otherwise the cell is left empty.

The rows of the second matrix represent *users*. We assign a *role* to a *user* by inserting an "*X*" in the specific column and row combination.

3.2 Sugiyama-Styled Graph

We can separate the nodes of our graph in three distinctive groups. Connections exists between the groups *users* and *roles* as well as *roles* and *voice loops*. This structure fits a Sugiyama-styled graph [5]. The Sugiyama-styled graph is also called *layered graph* because nodes are grouped and drawn on different layers. Our visualization (Fig. 2) is based on the same concept. We display each node as a rectangle and label them with the name of the node. We group nodes for *users*, *roles*, and *voice loops*, each on separate layers. This creates the impression of a three columned table with one column for each kind of node. Links between nodes are visualized by lines.

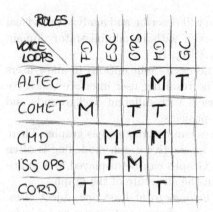

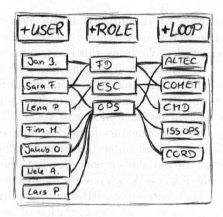

Fig. 1. Configuration matrix for loop-role connections

Fig. 2. Sugiyama-styled graph for user-role-loop connections

3.3   Analysis of the Approaches

With biadjacency matrices we split the interface in two separate visualizations. Each visualization on its own contains only a part of the data. Each visualization has to display less content and is possibly less complex and easier to understand. On the other hand is it necessary to work with two visualizations. VoCS project staff at the GSOC currently use MICROSOFT EXCEL to write down biadjacency matrices. We have used their biadjacency matrices visualizations as reference to test which kind of interface works best for users without administrative background.

The recent work of Okoe et al. [3] indicates node-link graphs are usually more intuitive than adjacency matrices. Sugiyama-styled graphs are a sub class of node-link graphs, like biadjacency matrices are a sub class of adjacency matrices. In addition we have the advantage to visualize the complete data set in one visualization, which allows to easily trace indirect connections between entries.

The *user–role–voice loop* sequence of the Sugiyama-styled graph highlights the separation between users and permissions via roles. Grouping of nodes on layers helps to identify the type of each node. In addition it cleans up the display by removing unnecessary clutter. There are no direct connections between *users* and *voice loops*. The sequence of the layers ensures that no line is ever crossing a node.

With interactive elements both visualizations can be further improved. We use highlighting on mouse-over for better connection tracing between nodes. To further enhance readability we group *users* who are assigned to the same *roles*. This is also done for *voice loops* sharing the same *role* configuration.

Content grouping and connection visualization may support users in their decision making process by presenting additional, otherwise hidden, information data. Grouped *users* will have the same access rights and may work in shifts or replace colleagues in case of sickness. Possible duplicates of *voice loops* become visible. All *voice loops* in a group can be accessed by the same set of *roles* with the same access rights. This raises the question if all of those *voice loops* are really necessary or if they could be merged.

To be able to compare both approaches we implemented an interactive version of our Sugiyama-styled graph design.

3.4   Interactive Sugiyama-Styled Graph Configuration Modelling

In our layout, we integrate all required edit options to enable project staff to change the access configuration of their VoCS project (Fig. 3). An user may edit or delete entries after selection. A selected node and its directly linked nodes are highlighted in blue.

Icons are displayed to change the attributes of the selected node or change its connections to other nodes. The cogwheel symbol triggers a dialog to change a nodes attributes. Opened or closed link icons in the nodes on adjacent layers indicate a node's connection state to the selected node. A click on the icon will toggle the connection state. The headphone icon for MONITOR or microphone icon for TALK indicates the access rights of a *role* within a *voice loop*. The user can toggle the access rights by clicking the icon. In the head of each layer is a plus symbol. The user can click it to create new entries for the corresponding object class.

The user study (Sect. 4) we conducted gave us valuable feedback of the usability of our interface. After the study we decided to rework the mechanic on creating and deleting connections based on the user input. As an example, some users found it cumbersome to have to click exactly on the symbols. They would have preferred to be able to click on the whole node to toggle a connection. In addition our interface did not allow to directly assign a connection with the permission TALK between a *role* and a *voice loop*. Connecting a *voice loop* and a *role* creates a connection with the permission MONITOR. The users need to perform a second step to change the permission to TALK.

In our reworked interface design nodes are split in two parts: left and right. Each part acts as a button. Icons, displayed on the left or right side of the node, indicate the function of the button. The icons change depending on the current scenario.

To change the connection of a node the user needs to click first on the button with the network icon (Fig. 4a). The node is selected (Fig. 4b). Connected nodes are highlighted. The permission state for each connection is displayed. If the user hovers over a node on an adjacent layer one or two of the following option are displayed (Fig. 5):

- connect to this node
- connect to this node with the permission MONITOR
- connect to this node with the permission TALK
- toggle the permission for the link to this node
- disconnect from this node

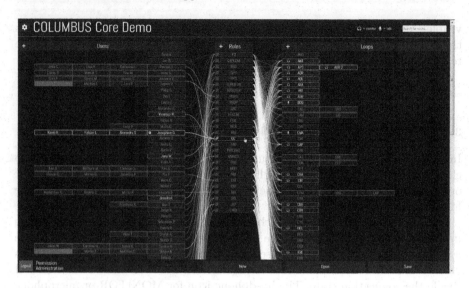

Fig. 3. Implementation of our interface, original design: The *user Josephine D.* is selected. This node as well as directly connected nodes and links are highlighted in blue. The mouse hovers over the *role GC*. All connected nodes and links are highlighted in white color. (Color figure online)

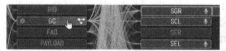

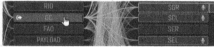

Selecting a node.
Left side: edit node attributes.
Right side: change node connections.

Deselecting a node.
The user needs to click a second time on the node.

Fig. 4. Reworked interaction design: Selecting a node to change its connections.

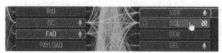

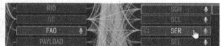

Modifying existing connections.
Left side: toggle permission.
Right side: delete connection.

Creating a new connection.
Left side: with permission MONITOR.
Right side: with permission TALK

Fig. 5. Reworked interaction design: modifying the connections of a node.

4 User Study

We conducted a user study to evaluate the usability of the Sugiyama-styled graph visualization. In the study we compare the currently used biadjacency matrices (Sect. 3.1) in MICROSOFT EXCEL and our visualization (Sect. 3.2).

We defined three different tasks participants had to perform with both visualizations. The tasks were developed in consultation with project staff responsible for defining the access rights and VoCS administrators responsible for applying the changes. The following tasks correspond to their usual tasks:

(1) Change the access rights of a *role* within some *voice loop*.
(2) Create or delete a *user* and assign or change his *roles*.
(3) Change a *role* or *voice loop* name to improve descriptiveness.

The order of the used visualisation was randomized. We used the COLUMBUS core configuration (27 *roles*, 96 *voice loops*) as demo data for the study. We auto-generated 120 *users*, which were randomly assigned to 1–5 *roles*. We used the same data for both systems but with different naming schemes to prevent training effects. The COLUMBUS core configuration is currently the biggest VoCS RBAC project at the GSOC. Most GSOC configurations contain about 10–15 *roles* and *voice loops*.

There were 19 participants (79% male) with an average age of 31 years (Standard deviation $SD = 10.94$). All of them have their higher education entrance qualification.

We used the System Usability Scale (SUS) [1] to evaluate the usability of these two systems. We analyzed the data with the open source Software RSTUDIO [4]. We performed paired two-sample t-tests. The SUS showed no differences between both visualizations ($t = -1.31$, $df = 18$, $p = .21$). Satisfaction ($t = -1.36$, $df = 18$, $p = 0.19$), and efficiency ($t = -0.81$, $df = 18$, $p = 0.43$) were rated equally as well. 59% of the participants would prefer working with the graph visualisation.

As results show, there is no difference between the two systems except for the efficiency aspect of usability. This could be explained by the common usage of Microsoft Excel, but no previous knowledge of the Sugiyama-styled graph. In our sample, every participant had prior knowledge in working with Excel. Although there are no significant effects, computing a Spearman's correlation test indicated that the experience with Excel could have a negative effect on the ratings for the Sugiyama-styled graph ($r_{sp} = -.45$, $p = .05$). Nonetheless it would be advisable to explore these differences with a more heterogeneous sample or a prior training with the Sugiyama-styled graph to compensate for previous experience with Excel.

The user study indicates that our interface has a similar usability as the configuration matrices currently used. Both were rated with good scores. We can conclude that our Suigyama-styled graph implementation is comprehensible and usable for users without administrative background.

5   Conclusions and Future Work

We presented an interactive Sugiyama-styled graph visualization to allow users without administrative backgrounds to access and manipulate RBAC configurations for VoCS projects. The interface gives a comprehensible overview over the configuration and enhances the notion of the *user-role-permission* relationships of RBAC systems. The visualization allows its user to easily identify possible duplications. We identified with our interface several identical *role-voice loop* configurations in the COLUMBUS source data set. These double entries are hard to find within traditional RBAC software, but easy to identify with our graph representation.

The feedback from our user study gave us valuable pointers where we need to improve the interface. We already described our improvements of the edit options. In addition we plan to improve the clarity of our interface for big data sets like the COLUMBUS data. We received the feedback that connections were sometimes hard to follow, especially if the connected nodes were not in the same scroll frame. We need to take additional measures to improve the clarity for data sets with many nodes and lines. For example, by rearranging nodes on a layer to minimize line crossings.

The VoCS RBAC projects we used to design our interface, have a rather simple structure. There are no *role-role* relationships and entries only ever have one object class, not several. In a next step we need to evaluate if and how a Sugiyama-style graph could be used to also visualize more complex configurations.

References

1. Brooke, J., et al.: Sus-a quick and dirty usability scale. Usability Eval. Ind. **189**(194), 4–7 (1996)
2. Ferraiolo, D., Kuhn, R.: Role-based access control. In: In 15th NIST-NCSC National Computer Security Conference, pp. 554–563 (1992)
3. Okoe, M., Jianu, R., Kobourov, S.: Node-link or adjacency matrices: old question, new insights. IEEE Trans. Vis. Comput. Graph. **25**(10), 2940–2952 (2019). https://doi.org/10.1109/TVCG.2018.2865940
4. R Core Team: R: a language and environment for statistical computing. R foundation for statistical computing (2019)
5. Sugiyama, K., Tagawa, S., Toda, M.: Methods for visual understanding of hierarchical system structures. IEEE Trans. Syst. Man Cybern. **11**(2), 109–125 (1981). https://doi.org/10.1109/TSMC.1981.4308636
6. Töpfer, M., Sonnenberg, A., Kozlowski, R.A.: Opensource based voice communication for mission control. In: SpaceOps Conferences. American Institute of Aeronautics and Astronautics, May 2016. https://doi.org/10.2514/6.2016-2437

Google Indoor Maps or Google Indoor No Maps? Usability Study of an Adapted Mobile Indoor Wayfinding Aid

Laure De Cock[(✉)], Kristien Ooms, Nico Van de Weghe,
and Philippe De Maeyer

Department of Geography, Ghent University, Ghent, Belgium
laudcock.decock@ugent.be

Abstract. ARC is an adaptive indoor mobile wayfinding system, which was developed based on the results of a previous online survey. The ARC system links data from several sources to enable a route guidance adapted to the environment: the type of route instruction is adapted to the location of the user. In this study, the usability of the system was tested in a smart building by use of a mobile eye-tracker. Five eye tracking measures were analyzed and compared with the space syntax values of the decision points. The results confirm that video instructions can improve support at complex decision points, while symbols might not be supportive enough at these points in the indoor environment. These findings enhance our understanding of the relationship between environment and complexity perception during route guidance, which is essential for supportive indoor route guidance.

Keywords: Adaptive route guidance · Indoor · Space syntax · Complexity perception · Route instruction type

1 Introduction

Numerous studies have investigated the influence of the environment on people's indoor wayfinding behavior [1–3]. Moreover, the structure and layout of buildings has been identified as a major contributing factor in the mental map that is formed during wayfinding [4]. However, technology in the built environment is evolving fast and little is known about the influence of new factors, such as positioning sensors, mobile indoor wayfinding aids and 3D-technology. There is an unambiguous relationship between the environment and explorative wayfinding behavior, but when people are being guided by a system, their perception of the environment might be different. Understanding this perception during route guidance and the elements that affect it is crucial for the usability of the wayfinding systems of the future. Therefore, this study aims to link complexity perception during route guidance with building architecture. To this end, an Adaptive Route Communication (ARC) system has been developed, which links architectural data of several sources, such as ultra-wideband (UWB) sensors and the building information model (BIM). A usability study was conducted in which the cognitive load imposed by the ARC system during route guidance was monitored with

C. Stephanidis and M. Antona (Eds.): HCII 2020, CCIS 1224, pp. 413–420, 2020.
https://doi.org/10.1007/978-3-030-50726-8_54

mobile eye tracking glasses. The major objective of this experiment is to study the link between the cognitive load imposed by a wayfinding system and building architecture, quantified with spacy syntax.

1.1 Space Syntax

Indoor wayfinding can be very challenging as the indoor environment can be very complex [5]. A well-established theory to quantify building complexity, which is known to correlate with wayfinding performance, is space syntax [6]. Space syntax is a collection of theories and methods to quantify the relation between both indoor and outdoor space on the one hand and society on the other hand. One of these methods are isovists, which are areas in space that can be seen simultaneously from a certain viewpoint. The visibility at viewpoints can be compared through the properties of the isovists at these points, such as area and longest line of sight [7]. Another space syntax method which uses visibility as a complexity measure is the visibility graph analysis (VGA). In this approach, a grid is drawn on the floorplan and in every point of the grid an isovist is drawn. Analogue to isovists, several metrics can be calculated of a VGA, such as the mean visual depth (MVD) which is the mean number of isovists you have to cross to reach a certain point of the grid from every other point [8]. De Cock *et al.* (2020) studied the relationship between space syntax and complexity perception during route guidance by conducting an online survey [9]. Results showed that this relationship depended a lot on the given route instruction at a decision point: taking turns was most complex at convex, central spaces, while this was reversed to start and end a route and to change levels. These findings indicate that the link between space syntax and perception might be different during route guidance compared to explorative wayfinding. This study seeks to test the findings of the online survey by De Cock *et al.* (2020) in the real-life environment with a real-life adapted mobile wayfinding system.

1.2 Adapted Mobile Wayfinding Systems

Because the indoor environment can be very complex, users could benefit from route guidance systems that adhere better to the user's spatial cognition. One way of making route guidance systems cognitively supportive is by adapting the given information to the environment [10]. The ARC system puts this theory into practice by adapting the type of route instruction (e.g. photo, symbol, video) to the decision point. Every decision point is different so the needs of the users also change at every decision point. Changing the instruction type can support these needs, as every instruction type has specific characteristics and induces a different cognitive load [11]: Symbols impose a low cognitive load as they show abstracted information as opposed to photos and 3D-simulations, but at complex decision points abstracted information can also impose a high cognitive load when the translation to the environment is more difficult. The ARC system, developed for this study, adapts the route instruction types according to the results of the online survey carried out by De Cock *et al.* (2020) [12]: symbols + text to start and end a route, 3D-simulations + text at central decision points and photo + text at other decision points.

A number of studies have developed adaptive systems for specific users, such as impaired people or tourists [13–16], but few were developed for everyday life, even though in this case people are often rushed. For example when you have to attend a meeting, you want to find the meeting room as efficiently as possible. Recent technologies in smart buildings enable the development of wayfinding systems that use linked data. The Find Me! App is an example of such a system where sensor data is linked to the BIM of the building to enable accurate route guidance [17]. With these systems on your smartphone, you can be guided indoors, from your own office to the meeting room. So far, however, research on these systems was mostly limited to the development and installation instead of the usability [18].

1.3 Eye Tracking

The usability of wayfinding systems can be tested by use of an eye tracker, which renders information on where and how long the visual attention of users is directed [19]. By using a mobile eye tracker, wayfinding experiments can be conducted in real indoor environments, which enables cross-validation of less immersive, more controlled experiments [20]. A number of studies have used mobile eye tracking to measure the cognitive load induced by wayfinding systems, such as [21–23]. Most of them use fixation measures to analyze cognitive load, for example a longer fixation duration implies a higher cognitive load, while a higher fixation rate implies a lower cognitive load. Saccadic duration and rate measure the same effect as fixation duration and rate, but additionally saccadic amplitude can be calculated, which decreases when cognitive load increases because of a difficult search task or a careful inspection of the stimulus [24].

2 Materials and Methods

2.1 ARC

For this case study, the ARC mobile wayfinding aid has been developed (Fig. 1).

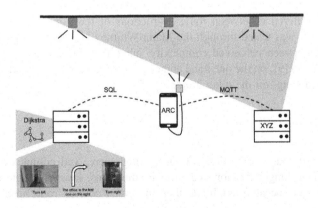

Fig. 1. Schematic overview of the ARC system.

ARC uses the low-cost and open source UWB hardware platform Wi-PoS for positioning, installed in the smart building iGent (Belgium) [25]. The location of the mobile UWB tag, connected to the smartphone, is calculated through a particle filter and sent to the webplatform through the MQTT protocol. For the route planning Dijkstra's shortest path algorithm is used on a graph of the building, extracted from the floorplans. The photos for the photo + text type were taken beforehand in the building and arrows were placed on top of them to create augmented photographs [18]. For the 3D-simulations, the BIM of the building was imported in Unity and graphics were added. The symbol + text type requires least resources as only 4 symbols have to be designed to cover all actions. Depending on the decision point and the demanded turn, the right route instruction is fetched from the server and combined with a text line. When the user reaches the decision point with the smartphone and UWB tag, a short sound will be played and the route instruction will automatically appear on the screen.

2.2 Eye Tracking Experiment

33 participants were asked to walk three routes in the building (Fig. 2), guided by the ARC system, while wearing the SMI ETG 2.1 mobile eye tracking device (60 Hz/30 FPS). During route guidance they received 12 route instructions: 3 to change levels (Level 1, Level 2 and Level 3), 4 to take turns (Turn 1, Turn 2, Turn 3 and Turn 4), 2 to start a route (Start 1 and Start 2) and 3 to end a route (End 1, End 2 and End 3). The first route is started by taking the stairs at Level 1, from then on each new route starts at the endpoint of the previous route. The color of each route instruction on Fig. 2 is determined by the space syntax value and visualizes how complex this instruction would be perceived compared to other instructions of the same category, according to the results of De Cock *et al.* (2020) [9]. For example, the route instruction to take the stairs at Level 2 (red color) would be perceived as more complex than the instruction to take the elevator at Level 3 (green color), because of a higher mean visual depth value.

2.3 Statistical Analysis

Five eye tracking measures were calculated for every decision point: fixation duration, saccadic duration, fixation rate, saccadic rate and saccadic amplitude. For each of these measures the difference between route instructions of the same category (Start/End, Level and Turn) was tested through the Mann-Whitney U test. This way, the relation was analyzed between perceived complexity, quantified through space syntax by De Cock *et al.* (2020) [9], on the one hand and cognitive load imposed by ARC, quantified through eye tracking, on the other hand.

3 Results

The red colored route instructions of Fig. 2 (high perceived complexity) would be expected to have longer fixation and saccadic durations, lower fixation and saccadic rates and a lower saccadic amplitude than the green colored route instructions (low

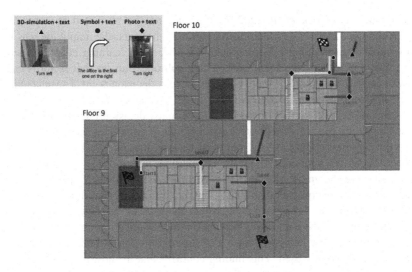

Fig. 2. The 12 route instructions, given by ARC, with instruction type (symbol) and perceived complexity level (color). (Color figure online)

perceived complexity). For most comparisons, this seems to be the case, confirming the findings of De Cock *et al.* (2020) [9], except for the following route instructions:

- The video instruction of Turn 3 resulted in smaller saccadic durations, higher saccadic rates and a smaller saccadic amplitude than the photo instruction of Turn 2.
- Turn 3 induced a higher fixation and saccadic rate than Turn 1, resulting in a lower cognitive load.
- Level 1 induced a higher saccadic amplitude than Level 3, resulting in a lower cognitive load.
- End 1 induced a higher saccadic rate than End 3, resulting in a lower cognitive load

4 Discussion

The first two findings were most likely caused by the experimental setup. In the first, a video type is compared to a photo type, which can render ambiguous results in eye tracking research. When dynamic stimuli, such as videos, are used, smooth pursuit eye movements can occur, in which the eye follows a moving object. These smooth pursuit movements are not easily detected by standard event detection algorithms, and even less so with mobile eye tracking glasses. As a result, smooth pursuit movements are often misclassified as long fixations or small saccades [26], which might explain the small saccadic duration, high saccadic rate and small saccadic amplitude of Turn 3. The second finding involves two videos, which should render more comparable results. However, all participants did the three routes in the same order, thus all participants saw Turn 1 before Turn 2. Both route instructions were very alike so the lower cognitive load at the second turn instruction might be caused by a learning effect. The last two findings that contradict De Cock *et al.* (2020) [9], could not be attributed to experimental setup. Although Level 1 is a video instruction, a higher saccadic amplitude was registered compared to the photo instruction of Level 3. Both learning effect and smooth pursuit would have caused a smaller saccadic amplitude, thus another factor is causing the lower cognitive load on the more complex Level 1 decision point. The adapted ARC system showed a video instruction at Level 1, as De Cock *et al.* (2019) [12] found that this instruction type was more appreciated at complex decision points. Therefore, this eye tracking study confirms the positive effect of video instructions on complex decision points: the imposed cognitive load can even be less than on a less complex decision point with a photo instruction. As for the last finding, both at End 1 and End 3 symbol instructions were shown by ARC. According to De Cock *et al.* (2020) [9], End 3 should be perceived as more complex than End 1, but the findings of the usability study do not support this. Moreover, it seems that the use of the symbol instruction type can have a reversed influence on the complexity perception of decision points: route instructions to end a route in a narrow hallway induce a lower cognitive load than at a convex space when the symbol type is used. This finding confirms that the abstracted information of symbols might not be sufficient for effective wayfinding at convex spaces [27].

5   Conclusions and Future Research

For this usability study, an adapted mobile wayfinding system (ARC) has been developed, which combines several data sources to facilitate a mobile route guidance system adapted to the environment. The cognitive load imposed by the system was determined by measuring the eye movements of participants during a wayfinding experiment. This imposed cognitive load was then compared to the space syntax values of the indoor environment. The results confirm that adapting the route instruction type can have a significant influence on the cognitive load at decision points. More specifically, this study has shown that using a video instruction at complex decision points can decrease cognitive load, while using a symbol instruction can increase cognitive load at convex spaces. Understanding the association between space syntax, route instruction types and cognitive load is crucial to facilitate efficient route guidance. Therefore, this information should be included in the linked data systems of smart indoor environments, which is to date not yet the case.

References

1. Li, R., Klippel, A.: Using space syntax to understand knowledge acquisition and wayfinding in indoor environments. In: Proceedings of the 9th IEEE International Conference on Cognitive Informatics, pp 302–307 (2010). https://doi.org/10.1109/COGINF.2010.5599724
2. Meilinger, T., Franz, G., Bülthoff, H.H.: From isovists via mental representations to behaviour: first steps toward closing the causal chain. Environ. Plan. B Plan. Des. **39**, 48–62 (2012). https://doi.org/10.1068/b34048t
3. Peponis, J., Zimring, C., Choi, Y.K.: Finding the building in wayfinding. Environ. Behav. **22** (5), 555–590 (1990)

4. O'Neill, M.J.: Evaluation of a conceptual model of architectural legibility. Environ. Behav. **23**(3), 259–284 (1991)

5. Giudice, N.A., Walton, L.A., Worboys, M.: The informatics of indoor and outdoor space: a research agenda. In: Proceedings of the 2nd ACM SIGSPATIAL International Workshop on Indoor Spatial Awareness, pp 47–53. ACM, New York (2010). https://doi.org/10.1145/1865885.1865897

6. Montello, D.R.: Spatial cognition and architectural space: research perspectives. Archit. Des. **84**(5), 74–79 (2014)

7. Benedikt, M.L.: To take hold of space: isovists and isovist fields. Environ. Plann. B Plann. Des. 47–65 (1979). https://doi.org/10.1068/b060047

8. Turner, A., Doxa, M., O'Sullivan, D., Penn, A.: From isovists to visibility graphs: a methodology for the analysis of architectural space. Environ. Plan. B Plan. Des. **28**(1), 103–121 (2001). https://doi.org/10.1068/b2684

9. De Cock, L., et al.: Identifying what constitutes complexity perception of decision points during indoor route guidance. Int. J. Geogr. Inf. Sci. 1–19 (2020). https://doi.org/10.1080/13658816.2020.1719109

10. Reichenbacher, T.: Adaptive methods for mobile cartography. In: Proceedings of the 21st ICC, Durban, 10–16 August 2003. https://doi.org/10.1044/1092-4388(2010/10-0131)

11. Gartner, G.: Location-based mobile pedestrian navigation services – the role of multimedia cartography. In: ICA UPIMap, Na, Tokyo, Japan, pp 155–184 (2004). https://doi.org/10.1017/S0373463302001790

12. De Cock, L., Ooms, K., Van de Weghe, N., Vanhaeren, N., De Maeyer, P.: User preferences on route instruction types for mobile indoor route guidance. ISPRS Int. J. Geo-Inf. **8**(482), 1–15 (2019). https://doi.org/10.3390/ijgi8110482

13. Chang, Y.J., Wang, T.Y.: Indoor wayfinding based on wireless sensor networks for individuals with multiple special needs. Cybern. Syst. **41**(4), 317–333 (2010). https://doi.org/10.1080/01969721003778584

14. Abowd, G.D., et al.: Cyberguide: a mobile context-aware tour guide. Wirel. Networks **3**(5), 421–433 (1997). https://doi.org/10.1023/A:1019194325861

15. Cheverst, K., Davies, N., Mitchell, K., Friday, A., Efstratiou, C.: Developing a context-aware electronic tourist guide: some issues and experiences. CHI Lett. **2**(1), 17–24 (2000). https://doi.org/10.1145/332040.332047

16. Malaka, R., Zipf, A.: DEEP MAP challenging IT research in the framework of a tourist information system. In: Fesenmaier, D.R., Klein, S., Buhalis, D. (eds.) Information and Communication Technologies in Tourism 2000, pp. 15–27. Springer, Vienna (2000). https://doi.org/10.1007/978-3-7091-6291-0_2

17. Ferreira, J.C., Resende, R., Martinho, S.: Beacons and BIM models for indoor guidance and location. Sensors (Switzerland) **18**(12) (2018). https://doi.org/10.3390/s18124374

18. Walther-Franks, B., Malaka, R.: Evaluation of an augmented photograph-based pedestrian navigation system. In: Butz, A., Fisher, B., Krüger, A., Olivier, P., Christie, M. (eds.) SG 2008. LNCS, vol. 5166, pp. 94–105. Springer, Heidelberg (2008). https://doi.org/10.1007/978-3-540-85412-8_9

19. Kiefer, P., Giannopoulos, I., Raubal, M., Duchowski, A.: Eye tracking for spatial research: cognition, computation. Challenges. Spat. Cogn. Comput. **17**(1–2), 1–19 (2017). https://doi.org/10.1080/13875868.2016.1254634

20. Ooms, K.: Cartographic user research in the 21st century: mixing and interacting. In: 6th International Conference on Cartography and GIS Proceedings, no. June, pp. 367–377 (2016)

21. Ohm, C., Müller, M., Ludwig, B.: Evaluating indoor pedestrian navigation interfaces using mobile eye tracking. Spat. Cogn. Comput. **17**(1–2), 89–120 (2017). https://doi.org/10.1080/13875868.2016.1219913
22. Schnitzler, V., Giannopoulos, I., Hölscher, C., Barisic, I.: The interplay of pedestrian navigation, wayfinding devices, and environmental features in indoor settings. In: Proceedings of the Ninth Biennial ACM Symposium on Eye Tracking Research & Applications - ETRA 2016, pp. 85–93 (2016). https://doi.org/10.1145/2857491.2857533
23. Li, Q.: Use of Maps in Indoor Wayfinding (2017)
24. Holmqvist, K., et al.: Eye Tracking A Comprehensive Guide to Methods and Measures. Oxford University Press, New York (2011)
25. Van Herbruggen, B., et al.: Wi-Pos: a low-cost, open source ultra-wideband (UWB) hardware platform with long range sub-GHZ backbone. Sensors (Switzerland) **19**(7), 1–16 (2019). https://doi.org/10.3390/s19071548
26. Larsson, L., Nyström, M., Andersson, R., Stridh, M.: Detection of fixations and smooth pursuit movements in high-speed eye-tracking data. Biomed. Signal Process. Control **18**, 145–152 (2015). https://doi.org/10.1016/j.bspc.2014.12.008
27. Chittaro, L., Burigat, S.: Augmenting audio messages with visual directions in mobile guides. In: Proceedings of the 7th International Conference on Human Computer Interaction with Mobile Devices & Services, Salzburg, pp 107–114 (2005). https://doi.org/10.1145/1085777.1085795

An Interactive Coffee Table: Exploring Ludic Engagement During Lunch Breaks

Hamza Zubair Gondal$^{(\boxtimes)}$, Magnus Over-Rein$^{(\boxtimes)}$,
Sumayya Munir$^{(\boxtimes)}$, Mohsin Afzal$^{(\boxtimes)}$, Aqsa Khalid$^{(\boxtimes)}$,
and Klaudia Çarçani$^{(\boxtimes)}$

Faculty of Computer Science, Østfold University College, Halden, Norway
{hamza.z.gondal,magnus.s.over-rein,sumayya.munir,
mohsin.afzal,aqsa.khalid,klaudia.carcani}@hiof.no

Abstract. University classes may be demanding and tiring. The lunch/coffee breaks are the opportunities to reload energies for the next hour by interacting with other students and have fun together. Technology can help in enhancing this positive experience. Thus, we used the Interaction Design process to study the needs for a digital solution, which can enhance a ludic experience during lunch breaks in schools and developed an interactive prototype. Through interviews and observations, we explored what students considered ludic during breaks. Socializing in common areas and being involved in activities that require collaborative engagement, was highlighted. We used the assumptions of ludic design discussed by Gaver et al. [1] for designing our prototype, an Interactive Coffee Table, called Willy's Pond. The solution consists of a tabletop transformed into a digital pond for Willy, the fish, to swim around. The prototype was tested in a natural setting with approximately 25 students in groups and individually. We found that the Interactive Coffee table enhances the ludic experience. Moreover, a relevant finding was that collaborative engagement was seen as a critical element for ludic design in addition to Gaver et al. [1] assumptions for designing for a ludic experience.

Keywords: Coffee table · Ludic · Engagement · Lunch break · Student · Interactive · Human-computer interaction · Playfulness · Interaction design

1 Introduction

University classes require concentration and devotion. The lunch/coffee breaks provide opportunities to relax, take time away from studies, and meet students from outside the class. However, in some cases, students spend breaks sitting in the classroom on their phones and not interacting with each other. In some other cases, they sit with each other in common areas, but the full potential of the break is not explored. As Fuchs [2] and Liu et al. [3] state, "we have a society with a 'high lusory attitude'". Thus, the lack of ludic and collaborative opportunities at school can decrease the interest of the student in engaging in activities during their lunch breaks. Fuchs [2] also states that "an essential quality of the digital medium is its ludic potential." Hence, laptops and more recently, smartphones have become a center point for ludic engagement with their almost endless number of apps. This makes it easy to connect with people from all parts of the world to facilitate individuals' ludic needs. Thus, in the study presented in this paper, we took a design approach to explore how technology can contribute to creating a ludic experience during lunch breaks among students within the school area. We used Østfold University College (ØUC) in Halden, Norway, as the venue for conducting our study. We used the interaction design process described by Sharp et al. [4] to investigate needs and design an interactive prototype, which we called "Willy's Pond". The design was inspired by the elements of ludic design by Gaver et al. [1]. The prototype was then evaluated in a natural setting. Observations and semi-structured interviews were used to capture the users' experience.

This paper has the following outline. In Sect. 2, we root our study in the literature. In Sect. 3, we present the design process, which is then followed by the Findings from the evaluation of the prototype in Sect. 4. The findings are then briefly discussed, and together with conclusions are presented in Sect. 4.

2 Background

Ludic engagement, playfulness/fun, and enjoyment have been extensively discussed in the literature. In HCI, ludic design or designing for ludic experiences has been initially discussed by Gaver et al. [1] in their classic paper "The Drift Table: Designing For Ludic Engagement". In the paper, they explored ludic design in a home context and designed a coffee table with a viewing port in the middle that shows photos of a landscape moving in directions according to weight distribution on the table. It offers an experience that can be shared between the people sitting around the table. The design has no other purpose than to engage in a ludic activity. However, according to Gaver et al. [1], "such activities are not a simple matter of entertainment or wasting time. On the contrary, they can be a mechanism for developing new values and goals, for learning new things, and for achieving new understandings". Designing for the non-utilitarian part of ludic engagement can be just as important as designing for any other utilitarian activity [5]. Gaver et al. [1] assumptions for a design for ludic activities were:

- To promote curiosity, exploration, and reflection systems should provide resources for people to appropriate, rather than content for consumption.
- It should not achieve a practical task, as this will distract the user from a more playful engagement.
- It should maintain openness and ambiguity. The design should avoid a clear narrative so people can find their own meaning.

There are also other approaches to ludic design or designing for ludic experiences. According to Selander [6] in his paper "Designs for learning and ludic engagement," ludic engagement is associated with learning. According to him, learning and ludic both involve human interest and participation. People interact with each other to collaborate, experience, negotiate, and share their ideas to achieve a specific goal. Therefore, both processes are interlinked with each other.

Moreover, Selander [6] relates the ludic experience to play referring to play, as studied in Caillois [7]. According to Caillois's, playing is all about competition and struggling to win. He gave four aspects of play in four different forms, such as competition, chance, danger, and role-play. Selander [6] also emphasizes how ludic activities in analogy with play are activities that do not have a specific purpose.

Moreover, in another study, Gadamer [8] relates ludic with fun. He says we play for fun, not for a specific purpose. So, according to him, we play for ourselves and not to perform any specific task.

In this paper, we draw on Gaver et al. [1] design principles for designing for a ludic experience of students' during lunch breaks. We have investigated how such design can help students socialize and engage in collaborative activities during lunch breaks.

3   Design Process

We adopted the interaction design process by Sharp et al. [4] in order to explore what to design to enhance student's ludic experience during lunch breaks in schools. They have identified four phases of the interaction design process:

1. Identify needs and requirements - the needs of the studied user groups are investigated and mapped through different methods.
2. (Re) Design - based on the identified needs and requirements, different design alternatives are created and critically evaluated through different methods.
3. Build an interactive system (Prototype) - a representation of one of the design alternatives is created as a proof of concept. There are different categories of prototypes that can be built [9].
4. Evaluate - the prototype is evaluated. The evaluation can be used to research further the user requirements or evaluating the usability of the prototype.

3.1   Identify Needs and Requirements

The following methods were used for data gathering, and the main goal was to understand the aspects and opportunities most of the students were lacking for having ludic experience during their lunch breaks.

Unstructured Interviews. We conducted unstructured interviews, which are characterized by open questions around an issue that the interviewer wants to discuss with the interviewee [10]. Considering the design approach of our study, we wanted to know the students' unbiased opinions regarding their experience during lunch breaks.

We conducted interviews on different days at ØUC, with twenty-five randomly chosen students. The students interviewed were initially asked for consent. Two of the researchers took handwritten notes of the answers. The topic discussed was "what students did during lunch breaks at the college and what changes would they need to have a more ludic experience during the lunch breaks". Zhang and Wildemuth [10] say that unstructured interviews are primarily incorporated into a study through participant observations. Thus, we followed their advice and supplemented our interviews with observations.

Observations. The observations were conducted at four different places at the university, in the café, library, classroom, and lobby area. Our framework was to look for activities the students do, objects they use or interact with, and feelings among the students. The data was collected by splitting up in two groups and sitting for 20 min at each place and passively observing students during their lunch breaks. We observed for two days for a total of four hours. We asked students for consent prior to observations and observed both students alone and in groups. The most notable things we learned from these observations were that all of the persons sitting alone were occupied with either a mobile or a laptop, and their mood was more sedated. Many of the group observations also had laptops or mobiles present, but they were more interested in interacting with each other than using the devices. The groups that were having lunch in the café and the groups sitting in the lobby area were in a happy and playful mood where they were laughing, chatting, or playing ping-pong.

Results. The data collected from the interviews and observations, was analyzed with a grounded theory [11] approach and the findings were that most people like to:

1. Spend the lunch break out of the classroom - visiting the café, eat lunch, or sit and chat in the common areas until the next class starts. Moreover, the socializing and spending time with friends involves a few activities and is mostly sedentary with phone on their hands.
2. Students were looking for more opportunities in terms of collaborative engagement in playful activities during lunch breaks.

3.2 Design

The findings from the first phase were evaluated and discussed. The discussion was followed by brainstorming sessions in which we started to ideate a design solution that would satisfy the findings from the first phase. The iterative brainstorming sessions resulted in four different ideas. For each of the ideas, we created possible scenarios [12] and storyboards [13], which helped in further refining the ideas.

Considering the focus on lunch breaks and the observation of students sitting around a table in groups during breaks, we focused on tabletop solutions that could contribute to a ludic experience that would require a collaborative engagement. Designing for a ludic experience was drawn on Gaver et al. [1] principles, and further findings from the literature described in Sect. 2. Finally, we concluded with the idea of an interactive coffee table, as shown in Fig. 1 and described in detail in the next subsection.

3.3 Prototype

Our prototype was inspired by the findings in requirements gathering. We designed an Interactive Coffee Table, which we called "Willy's Pond".

The prototype is a circular tabletop transformed into a pond for Willy, a fish, to swim around in. Willy swims around by his own will, but the users can interact and socialize with him by touching the screen. Three main functionalities are implemented in the prototype.

Fig. 1. The interactive table

- Expanding and contracting the pond area based on the number of people sitting around the table.
- Influencing Willy's movement in the pond by touching the screen.
- Feeding Willy.

The pond surface has levels, ranging from 1–5, that change according to the number of people at the table (see Fig. 2). When there is no one at the table, the pond is small, and Willy is sad and moves slowly. When more people join the table, the pond area will expand, making Willy happier, and moving faster. In the last level, food for feeding Willy is available, and the user can drag and drop into the pond to feed the fish. Willy will then eat the food and grow in size. If Willy has not been fed for a while, he will become smaller.

Fig. 2. The prototype with Fish, Five levels (1–5), and food for fish

To develop the prototype, we used a laser cutter for making a round tabletop shape that had a square in the middle where a computer screen was inserted. Sensors were supposed to be installed on each side of this tabletop to detect people approaching the table as well as speakers for sound feedback. Due to time constraints, we had to connect the screen to a laptop that provided sound, and also, the sensor detection and fish movement were simulated during evaluations on the laptop. For graphics, we used: Javascript, HTML. CSS and GIF animations.

3.4   Evaluation

Inspired by the "Turn in the Wild" movement in HCI [14], we decided to place the prototype in natural settings in order to conduct what in the interaction design process is called evaluation. We positioned the prototype in the cafe and leisure room at ØUC for three days in a row during lunch breaks. Meanwhile, we conducted observations on how people interacted with the prototype and interviewed them through semi-structured interviews afterward to gain better insight regarding their experience. We had four groups (four to five students) and five individual students who engaged with the prototype and consented our observations and our interviews. The evaluation in the natural setting had two aims: 1) look into the user experience and if the prototype was enhancing a ludic experience for the students during lunch breaks, 2) which elements of the design were contributing to having a ludic experience.

Thus, from the observations and interviews, we had written notes, which we analyzed with a qualitative interpretive approach [15]. Regarding users' experience, we interpreted testers' behavior and answers from the interviews. Instead, for the design elements enacting a ludic experience, we used as a basis for our interpretative analysis, Gaver et al. assumptions, for a design for ludic activities. Our analysis is limited due to the small number of people participating in the evaluation. Thus, further investigations are planned in the future.

4   Findings

Below we list some of our findings grouped in main categories.

- **Users found the prototype ludic & less task-oriented.** Almost all participants in the evaluation found the prototype ludic. They had fun interacting with it and took it as a game, which almost needed no effort. Two of the groups emphasized how much they loved the fish and felt good after playing/interacting with the table-top. Only one participant found the prototype concept hard to understand.
- **Users were curious to explore the prototype.** Apart from one student, all participants described their reactions as of surprise and curiosity. When they first saw the prototype they asked amongst themselves, "What is this? Why does this table look different?" and were inquisitive about checking out the prototype.
- **Openness and ambiguity.** The open structure and avoidance of a clear narrative gave users the possibility to explore without a specific meaning and a clear goal to achieve. This ambiguity allowed each of them to find his/her own meaning to the interaction. This is in line with Gadamer [8], who states, as mentioned earlier, "we play for fun, not for a specific purpose".
- **Users found ludic the need for collaborative engagement.** Many students said they would love to sit around this table with other students and have their lunch together as well as making Willy happy. Three students distinctively mentioned that they empathized with Willy after they saw he needed more breathing space and food. They decided to invite other students to join them at the table. In comparison to Gaver et al. [1] "Drift Table", where the interactions are triggered individually by people putting weight on the table, our prototype has a requirement for collaborative interaction. People need to join forces to enjoy the ludic experience while still having individual elements of interaction.

- **Users wanted more interaction on the table.** Even though almost all the students found the current prototype interesting and playful, the general consensus was that in the future they would prefer additional interaction with the table. Some students suggested having more fish on the last level (allow all students at the table to have their personalized fish), while others loved the idea of having more food options as well as different feeding methods (like dragging the food toward the fish).

5   Conclusion

In this paper, we presented the design of a prototype, which can enhance a ludic experience during lunch breaks in school. The prototype consisted of a tabletop, turned into an interactive pond, where a fish swims around, through the usage of a touch-based screen. The prototype was inspired by the students' needs investigated through interviews and observations and findings for designing for a ludic experience from the literature [3, 7–9].

In our evaluation, we found that all the students valued the experience of sitting around the table with their friends and playing with the fish ludic in the sense of being playful and fun. This is in analogy with Selander [6]. Students also highlighted that the non-task oriented approach, the openness, and ambiguity of the prototype triggered their curiosity. Drawing in these elements of ludic design by Gaver et al. [1] contributed to the ludic experience of students during the lunch break. Moreover, an important element of the ludic experience mentioned during our identifying needs and requirements phase of the design process and during evaluations was the need for collaborative engagement of the users (students in our case) in exploring the whole ludic experience. The findings show that the prototype model motivates people to interact with each other by physically sitting together and joining their actions.

This paper offers three main contributions. Firstly, we identified some problems after researching what students lack during their free time in between classes, which we refer to as the lunch/coffee breaks. Secondly, we proposed a new design solution to address the issues identified in the identify needs and requirements phase. Thirdly, we took a research through design approach when evaluating the solution designed. Thus, we used the prototype to provoke students' reactions and, as Gaver et al. [1] suggests, create new understandings on what can contribute to students' ludic experience during lunch breaks. We evaluated the user experience with infield testing, qualitative observations, and semi-structured interviews to finally get on the conclusions using a qualitative interpretive approach. In addition to Gaver et al. [1] three characteristics of ludic design, we found out that the feeling of collaboration in the table enhanced the ludic experience. Thus, we can highlight collaborative engagement as a characteristic of the ludic design.

In the future, we want to improve the prototype described in this paper based on the students' recommendations. Moreover, we want to explore with more design alternatives that can be used to motivate people in other contexts to engage collaboratively in ludic activities.

Acknowledgments. We would like to thank all the students that participated in our research. Moreover, we want to thank Østfold University College for providing the MakerSpace and Rapid Prototyping Lab, which created us the right environment to experiment with designs and different prototypes.

References

1. Gaver, W.W., et al.: The drift table: designing for ludic engagement. In: CHI 2004 Extended Abstracts on Human Factors in Computing Systems (2004)
2. Fuchs, M.: Ludic interfaces. Driver and product of gamification, vol. 1, no. 1. G|A|M|E Games as Art, Media, Entertainment (2012)
3. Liu, M., Horton, L., Kang, J., Kimmons, R., Lee, J.: Using a ludic simulation to make learning of middle school space science fun. Int. J. Gaming Comput. Mediated Simul. (IJGCMS) **5**(1), 66–86 (2013)
4. Sharp, H., Rogers, Y., Preece, J.: Interaction design: Beyond Human-Computer Interaction, 5th edn. Wiley, Indianapolis (2019)
5. Isomursu, M., Tähti, M., Väinämö, S., Kuutti, K.: Experimental evaluation of five methods for collecting emotions in field settings with mobile applications. Int. J. Hum Comput Stud. **65**(4), 404–418 (2007)
6. Selander, S.: Designs for learning and ludic engagement. Digital Creativity **19**(3), 145–152 (2008)
7. Caillois, R.: Les jeux et les hommes (1958)
8. Gadamer, H.-G.: Truth and Method, trans. Glen-Dopel, W. Sheed and Ward, London (1975)
9. Houde, S., Hill, C.: What do prototypes prototype? In: Handbook of Human-Computer Interaction, pp. p. 367–381. Elsevier (1997)
10. Zhang, Y., Wildemuth, B.M.: Unstructured interviews. In: Applications of Social Research Methods to Questions in Information and Library Science, pp. 222–231 (2009)
11. Chong, C.-H., Yeo, K.-J.: An overview of grounded theory design in educational research. Asian Soc. Sci. **11**(12), 258 (2015)
12. Carroll, J.M.: Scenarios and design cognition. In: Proceedings IEEE Joint International Conference on Requirements Engineering. IEEE (2002)
13. Andriole, S.J.: Storyboard Prototyping: A New Approach to User Requirements Analysis. QED Information Sciences Inc., Wellesley (1989)
14. Crabtree, A., et al.: Introduction to the Special Issue of "The Turn to The Wild". ACM, New York (2013)
15. Willis, J.W., Jost, M., Nilakanta, R.: Foundations of Qualitative Research: Interpretive and Critical Approaches. Sage, Thousand Oaks (2007)

How Consumers Utilize Healthcare Apps? – Focusing on Samsung Health

Hee Ra Ha, Jaehye Suk$^{(\boxtimes)}$, YuanZhou Deng, Yue Huang,
and Seonglim Lee

Department of Consumer Science, Sungkyunkwan University, Seoul, Korea
jaehye.s@skku.edu

Abstract. Samsung Health, Samsung's primary health-related app, is now one of the most comprehensive wellness applications, as it offers a personalized health coach, tracks daily activities according to users' goals, and charts users' activity to promote regular exercise. This study aimed to examine Korean consumers' responses to healthcare apps, specifically Samsung Health, to enhance consumer satisfaction with such apps. From April 21, 2015 to January 3, 2020, 11,361 user reviews of the application were collected from the Google Play website. The final tidy dataset was composed of 7,407 reviews. We conducted hierarchical clustering, CONCOR analysis, and semantic network analysis with R.3.5.3 and Ucinet6. First, the hierarchical clustering analysis resulted in 39 clusters. Second, the CONCOR analysis revealed four clusters: benefits, costs, health care, and system error. Third, the betweenness centrality of each node was reviewed to identify the importance of terms in the semantic network. Consumers appreciated the benefits of being able to achieve their goals through the measurement of their physical activities and competition with others. However, consumers pointed out inaccurate measurements, synchronization errors, and a lack of information as points for improvement for Samsung Health. Health is an essential factor in improving consumers' quality of life, and while Samsung Health provides useful functions, the improvement of basic errors in the application could enhance consumer satisfaction.

Keywords: Healthcare apps · Samsung Health · Hierarchical cluster analysis · Semantic network analysis

1 Introduction

With the development of the Internet and information technology, access to beneficial health information has gradually been increasing. The introduction of smartphones has allowed consumers to access personal data with a simple touch of their keypads. It has been estimated that there were 2.71 billion smartphone users worldwide in 2019 [1], with this number increasing yearly. Smartphones, such as Android devices and iPhones, provide users with access to numerous health-related apps with various functions including tracking and calculators. The sensors integrated into smartphones and their computational power enable wide applications in many areas of daily life, including health and activity monitoring. Parameters such as heart rate [2, 3], blood

© Springer Nature Switzerland AG 2020
C. Stephanidis and M. Antona (Eds.): HCII 2020, CCIS 1224, pp. 429–437, 2020.
https://doi.org/10.1007/978-3-030-50726-8_56

oxygen saturation [3, 4], blood pressure [5–7], number of walking steps [8], and activity types [9] can be measured using a smartphone. Smartphone health monitoring does not replace certified medical devices, but it can still serve as a useful alternative. Its advantages include its multi-functionality, mobility, and non-invasiveness [10]. Healthcare apps for mobile and wearable devices are proliferating. Most users employ these apps in stand-alone and unsupervised modes, e.g. for personal goal tracking or assistance in changing unhealthy habits or to gain an awareness of their own health and fitness [11].

Samsung Health has become one of the most comprehensive healthcare apps and had been downloaded more than 100 million times from Google Play by January 2020. Samsung Health allows users to intuitively check health data collected via smartphones or smart watches and to easily determine strategies to improve their health and physical strength. Although a growing body of research has evaluated mobile health and fitness apps, no studies have examined users' actual responses to healthcare apps. Existing evaluations of generic mobile platforms are often at a technical programming level, and focus on mobile devices apart from their practical applications [12, 13].

This study aimed to examine Korean consumers' responses to healthcare apps, focusing on Samsung Health. This study's findings present implications for product development with the aim of helping manufacturers enhance consumer satisfaction.

2   Research Methods

We employed the following data analysis procedures:

From April 21, 2015 to January 3, 2020, 11,361 user reviews of the application were collected from the Google Play website. Text not related to the services provided by Samsung Health was excluded, and words with the same meaning in the text were unified as the same words. The final tidy dataset consisted of 7,407 reviews. Next, term extraction through stop-word elimination, part-of-speech tagging, and stemming was conducted using a Korean morphological analyzer and the KoNLP package in R 3.5.3. Through this process, we identified 5,214 terms. We then performed a word frequency analysis to identify users' general responses to Samsung Health. We selected 283 terms that appeared more than 30 times and then eliminated 165 terms that were irrelevant or too general to infer consumers' responses to Samsung Health, resulting in a dataset with 118 terms. To ensure reliability, we crosschecked the results. We further conducted a hierarchical cluster analysis to identify terms associated with similar topics and to summarize the data. Among the 118 terms selected earlier, 81 nouns with similar meanings were placed into 39 groups, leaving a total of 76 terms including verbs and adjectives for the semantic network analysis. To identify sub-dimensional cost and benefit factors for users, 39 clusters and 37 verbs and adjectives were used to perform a CONCOR analysis and semantic network analysis using Ucinet6. In addition, R 3.5.3 was used to identify the role of each keyword within the network structure based on four centralities: degree, closeness, betweeness, and eigenvector centrality.

3 Results

3.1 Word Frequency Analysis

A word frequency analysis was conducted to examine overall consumer perceptions of Samsung Health; the top 50 nouns, verbs, and adjectives are shown in Table 1. Words such as "help" (n = 436) and "usefulness" (n = 374) were categorized as positive responses and "error" (n = 288) and "shut down" (n = 59) as negative responses.

Table 1. Word frequency results

Noun						Verb/Adjective					
No.	Keyword	Freq	No.	Keyword	Freq	No.	Keyword	Freq	No.	Keyword	Freq
1	Workout	1579	26	Input	228	1	Can	2454	26	Shut down	59
2	Use	1187	27	Request	211	2	Good	2168	27	Disappear	55
3	Number of steps	848	28	10,000 steps	210	3	Walk	1266	28	Run applications	54
4	Measurement	823	29	Best	208	4	Can't	1258	29	Feel	49
5	Record	706	30	Food	205	5	Same	770	30	Move	48
6	Health	662	31	Deletion	205	6	Do	724	31	Different	46
7	Function	635	32	Goal	204	7	Pop up	311	32	Vanish	46
8	Samsung health	629	33	Information	202	8	Doesn't	223	33	Sleep	42
9	Linkage	581	34	Friend	198	9	Big	210	34	Difficult	38
10	Wearable devices	528	35	Mark	197	10	Know	198	35	Application crash	38
11	Confirmation	470	36	Heart rate	189	11	Turn off	192	36	Be essential	37
12	Help	436	37	Problem	183	12	Ascend	158	37	Enjoy	33
13	Management	426	38	Gratitude	183	13	Ride	153	38	Slow	31
14	Update	404	39	Stress	180	14	Change	129	39	Eliminate	30
15	Galaxy	398	40	Fun	179	15	Run	107	40	Small	30
16	Addition	385	41	Modification	178	16	Eat	101	41	Protect	28
17	Usefulness	374	42	Bicycle	177	17	Find	100	42	Don't know	28
18	After update	366	43	Awareness	174	18	Stop	98	43	Fall	27
19	Practice	341	44	Synchronization	170	19	Showed	95	44	Have	27
20	Data	305	45	Beginning	166	20	Comfortable	95	45	Drink	26
21	Set-up	290	46	Possibility	162	21	Press	93	46	Thank	25
22	Error	288	47	Item	160	22	Fast	81	47	Happen	24
23	Samsung	251	48	Challenge	156	23	Feel the lack of	81	48	Help	24
24	Pedometer	247	49	Distance	152	24	Easy	67	49	High	24
25	Auto	230	50	Ways	150	25	Correct	65	50	Omit	24

3.2 Hierarchical Cluster Analysis

Among the terms derived earlier, a hierarchical cluster analysis was conducted on 81 nouns that appeared more than 30 times to identify the benefits and costs of using the Samsung Health application.

The hierarchical cluster analysis resulted in 39 clusters, as shown in Fig. 1. Specially, the clusters concerned functions experienced by users of Samsung Health. These included clusters of health-related indicators such as "oxygen saturation," "heart rate," and "stress," as well as clusters related to tracking activities through links with other apps, including words such as "Strava," "bicycle," and "route." There were also clusters concerning various system errors, including words such as "compatibility" and "going dead," that could arise from the app.

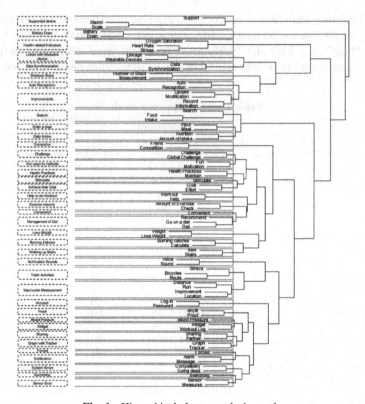

Fig. 1. Hierarchical cluster analysis results

3.3   CONCOR Analysis

To examine the dimensions of the benefits and costs associated with using Samsung Health, 76 words, including 39 noun clusters and 37 verbs and adjectives; the results are shown in Fig. 2. Four dimensions were derived and named as follows.

The first dimension was named *benefits* and included "enjoy," "good," and "fun ways to motivate." The second was *costs* and included "eliminate," "forced," "shut down," and "inaccurate measurement." The third dimension was *health care* and included "lose weight," "enter a meal," and "daily intake." The fourth was *system error* and included "data synchronization" and "system error."

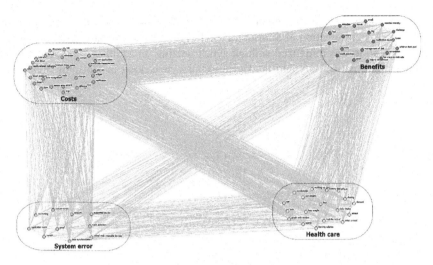

Fig. 2. CONCOR analysis results

3.4   Semantic Network Analysis

A semantic network analysis was conducted on 76 clusters, adjectives, and verbs to examine the contents and structure of the benefits and costs felt by users when using Samsung Health. In addition, the role of specific keywords within the network structure was identified based on the following four centralities.

Degree centrality characterizes how nodes are connected to other nodes in the network, measured its number of connections [14]. In Fig. 3, the size of each node reflects the degree centrality. Betweenness centrality measures the frequency of a given node on the shortest path to all other connected pairs [14, 15]. The colors of the nodes indicate the degree of betweeness centrality, and the ordering of red, orange, yellow and white represents a high level of betweenness centrality. Closeness centrality measures closeness, calculated as the sum of the shortest paths between nodes to all other nodes in the network [14]; a node with a shorter path demonstrates higher closeness and is considered important relative to nodes with longer paths [16]. Lastly, eigenvector centrality indicates the most influential nodes in the network by assigning relative scores to all concepts in the network based on the number and quality of their relationships [17]. The degree of centrality of nodes in the network is shown in Table 2.

The betweenness centrality of each node was assessed to identify the importance of the role of terms in the semantic network. "Good," which was linked to various items, had the highest level of betweenness centrality. The expression "good" was connected to "help to do workout," "measure steps," "competition," and "achieve their goals," indicating that consumers experienced the benefits of being able to achieve their goals through monitoring their physical activities and competing with others. "Improvement" showed the highest level of betweenness centrality, which was linked to "measure steps," "walk," "inaccurate measurement," "track activities," "linked with wearable devices," "data synchronization," "search," and "enter a meal." This indicates that consumers suffer from inconveniences such as inaccurate measurements of physical activities, the main function of Samsung Health. It also showed that information stored in the application was initialized without synchronizing. In addition, this indicates that consumers feel that activity and intake information is lacking in Samsung Health.

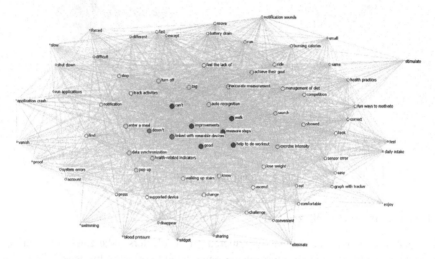

Fig. 3. Semantic network analysis results (Color figure online)

Table 2. Centrality results

Node.	Degree centrality (Average: 0.360055769)	Betweenness centrality (Average: 59.13157895)	Closeness centrality (Average: 0.003753436)	Eigenvector centrality (Average: 0.757266418)
Good	0.503311258	124.8472156	0.004424779	1
Improvements	0.503311258	124.8472156	0.004424779	1
Measure steps	0.503311258	124.8472156	0.004424779	1
Help to do workout	0.496688742	119.3395307	0.004385965	0.992685371
Walk	0.496688742	119.4055142	0.004385965	0.992524953
Linked with wearable devices	0.496688742	117.7523012	0.004385965	0.994094809
Can't	0.496688742	119.7837624	0.004385965	0.99203995
Doesn't	0.483443709	108.8688129	0.004310345	0.976382229
Inaccurate measurement	0.476821192	107.2186247	0.004273504	0.962521004
Data synchronization	0.470198675	103.557085	0.004237288	0.950977889
Auto recognition	0.470198675	100.8558059	0.004237288	0.957542374
Big	0.470198675	98.73245427	0.004237288	0.960088879
Enter a meal	0.450331126	91.13741595	0.004132231	0.922082882
Turn off	0.450331126	88.98819392	0.004132231	0.927097782
Health-related indicators	0.443708609	85.16708348	0.004098361	0.918838204
Search	0.443708609	86.75429698	0.004098361	0.915512323
Pop up	0.443708609	89.23005744	0.004098361	0.908744291

(continued)

Table 2. (*continued*)

Node.	Degree centrality (Average: 0.360055769)	Betweenness centrality (Average: 59.13157895)	Closeness centrality (Average: 0.003753436)	Eigenvector centrality (Average: 0.757266418)
Exercise intensity	0.443708609	85.74134775	0.004098361	0.918616251
Know	0.443708609	83.61762953	0.004098361	0.921658406
Achieve their goal	0.437086093	86.03956112	0.004065041	0.900341218
Management of diet	0.42384106	79.52404605	0.004	0.877177225
Walking up stairs	0.42384106	76.92549441	0.004	0.881462793
Lose weight	0.42384106	74.43494645	0.004	0.886953149
Ascend	0.417218543	76.13458822	0.003968254	0.870199689
Change	0.417218543	77.19661787	0.003968254	0.863876407
Showed	0.417218543	74.85254371	0.003968254	0.867852651
Feel the lack of	0.417218543	70.53232443	0.003968254	0.880284159
Track activities	0.410596026	71.39909819	0.003937008	0.859177191
Competition	0.40397351	68.89008586	0.00390625	0.852170575
Stop	0.40397351	70.15109286	0.00390625	0.844009521
Notification	0.397350993	64.68332401	0.003875969	0.835807166
Find	0.397350993	67.15597373	0.003875969	0.831230605
Ride	0.390728477	63.61375592	0.003846154	0.823312988
Look	0.38410596	61.12417744	0.003816794	0.816592514
Supported device	0.370860927	54.27565647	0.003759398	0.793644216
Challenge	0.370860927	63.2251288	0.003759398	0.768414095
Run	0.364238411	52.23661008	0.003731343	0.781519036
Fun ways to motivate	0.357615894	54.54344139	0.003703704	0.753794815
Eat	0.357615894	51.22580491	0.003703704	0.763622169
Sensor error	0.357615894	50.19397887	0.003703704	0.765952483
Press	0.357615894	53.80972458	0.003703704	0.750895424
Battery drain	0.350993377	46.31973074	0.003676471	0.760083825
Burning calories	0.350993377	46.24306545	0.003676471	0.762070965
Correct	0.344370861	44.8366512	0.003649635	0.747297666
Fast	0.337748344	47.29036989	0.003623188	0.714281411
Health practices	0.337748344	42.43036686	0.003623188	0.727832538
Comfortable	0.331125828	39.86959128	0.003597122	0.721429161
Graph with tracker	0.331125828	39.48302983	0.003597122	0.725788269
Easy	0.331125828	39.23334041	0.003597122	0.726901461
Move	0.331125828	44.45972593	0.003597122	0.703846192
Except	0.324503311	39.03221391	0.003571429	0.708832506
Same	0.317880795	40.28114441	0.003546099	0.684590885
Convenient	0.311258278	39.08502269	0.003521127	0.664982667
Account	0.304635762	37.2624355	0.003496503	0.649941038
Disappear	0.304635762	35.68556395	0.003496503	0.65937386
Different	0.304635762	31.5939197	0.003496503	0.679239659
Difficult	0.304635762	35.43333521	0.003496503	0.658164844
Notification sounds	0.291390728	32.66842637	0.003448276	0.632019017
System errors	0.291390728	35.87076581	0.003448276	0.618147563
Widget	0.284768212	30.5694184	0.003424658	0.619815878
Run applications	0.278145695	29.58828556	0.003401361	0.601456158

(*continued*)

Table 2. (*continued*)

Node.	Degree centrality (Average: 0.360055769)	Betweenness centrality (Average: 59.13157895)	Closeness centrality (Average: 0.003753436)	Eigenvector centrality (Average: 0.757266418)
Shut down	0.271523179	30.30042136	0.003378378	0.578414681
Daily intake	0.264900662	25.63043739	0.003355705	0.585541208
Sharing	0.258278146	24.0566326	0.003333333	0.571479267
Small	0.258278146	24.90435073	0.003333333	0.561280045
Feel	0.251655629	21.32868243	0.003311258	0.560344054
Proof	0.238410596	21.41369941	0.003267974	0.516448586
Vanish	0.231788079	19.47864816	0.003246753	0.511896007
Blood pressure	0.225165563	17.96555215	0.003225806	0.497940132
Forced	0.218543046	17.82272147	0.003205128	0.479760791
Eliminate	0.205298013	14.78355416	0.003164557	0.458118744
Application crash	0.198675497	15.62321866	0.003144654	0.430205753
Swimming	0.185430464	11.48599015	0.00310559	0.421731645
Slow	0.185430464	11.34170507	0.00310559	0.420973314
Enjoy	0.165562914	9.528469551	0.00304878	0.372463281
Stimulate	0.152317881	8.239975178	0.003012048	0.339857013

4   Conclusions

This study examined Korean consumers' responses to Samsung Health using hierarchical cluster analysis and semantic network analysis. By collecting consumers' opinions from their reviews of the app, this study provided an in-depth understanding of consumer opinions on Samsung Health. While Samsung Health has helped consumers enjoy health benefits by providing useful wellness-related functions and providing incentives for healthy behavior based on competition with others, consumers still experiencing drawbacks such as the inaccurate measurement and recording of physical activity and flawed data initialization. As health is the most important factor in improving consumers' quality of life, improving basic errors in health-related applications is expected to markedly enhance consumer satisfaction.

References

1. Statista Homepage. https://www.statista.com/statistics/330695/number-of-smartphone-users-worldwide. Accessed 10 Mar 2020
2. Siddiqui, S.A., Zhang, Y., Feng, Z.Q., Kos, A.: A pulse rate estimation algorithm using PPG and smartphone camera. J. Med. Syst. **40**(5), 126 (2016)
3. Tayfur, İ., Afacan, M.A.: Reliability of smartphone measurements of vital parameters: a prospective study using a reference method. Am. J. Emerg. Med. **37**(8), 1527–1530 (2019)
4. Ding, X., Nassehi, D., Larson, E.C.: Measuring oxygen saturation with smartphone cameras using convolutional neural networks. IEEE J. Biomed. Health Inf. **23**(6), 2603–2610 (2018)
5. Junior, A.D., Murali, S., Rincon, F., Atienza, D.: Methods for reliable estimation of pulse transit time and blood pressure variations using smartphone sensors. Microprocess. Microsyst. **46**, 84–95 (2016)

6. Gesche, H., Grosskurth, D., Küchler, G., Patzak, A.: Continuous blood pressure measurement by using the pulse transit time: comparison to a cuff-based method. Eur. J. Appl. Physiol. **112**(1), 309–315 (2012)
7. Gaurav, A., Maheedhar, M., Tiwari, V.N., Narayanan, R.: Cuff-less PPG based continuous blood pressure monitoring—A smartphone based approach. In: 2016 38th Annual International Conference of the IEEE Engineering in Medicine and Biology Society (EMBC), pp. 607–610. IEEE (2016)
8. Gu, F., Khoshelham, K., Shang, J., Yu, F., Wei, Z.: Robust and accurate smartphone-based step counting for indoor localization. IEEE Sens. J. **17**(11), 3453–3460 (2017)
9. Menhour, I., Fergani, B., Abidine, M.B.: E-health human activity recognition scheme using smartphone's data. In: Hajji, B., Tina, G.M., Ghoumid, K., Rabhi, A., Mellit, A. (eds.) ICEERE 2018. LNEE, vol. 519, pp. 128–134. Springer, Singapore (2019). https://doi.org/10.1007/978-981-13-1405-6_17
10. Nemcova, A., et al.: Monitoring of heart rate, blood oxygen saturation, and blood pressure using a smartphone. Biomed. Signal Process. Control **59**, 101928 (2020)
11. Farshchian, Babak A., Vilarinho, T.: Which mobile health toolkit should a service provider choose? A comparative evaluation of Apple HealthKit, Google fit, and Samsung digital health platform. In: Braun, A., Wichert, R., Maña, A. (eds.) AmI 2017. LNCS, vol. 10217, pp. 152–158. Springer, Cham (2017). https://doi.org/10.1007/978-3-319-56997-0_12
12. Gavalas, D., Economou, D.: Development platforms for mobile applications: Status and trends. IEEE Softw. **28**(1), 77–86 (2011)
13. Anvaari, M., Jansen, S.: Evaluating architectural openness in mobile software platforms. In: Proceedings of the Fourth European Conference on Software Architecture: Companion, pp. 85–92 (2010)
14. Freeman, L.C.: Centrality in social networks conceptual clarification. Soc. Netw. **1**(3), 215–239 (1978)
15. Stanley, W., Faust, K.: Social Network Analysis: Methods and Applications. Cambrigdge University, Cambridge (1994)
16. Raad, E., Chbeir, R.: Socio-graph representations, concepts, data, and analysis. In: Alhajj, P. R., Rokne, P.J. (eds.) Encyclopedia of Social Network Analysis and Mining, pp. 1936–1946. Springer, New York (2014). https://doi.org/10.1007/978-1-4939-7131-2_402
17. Heymann, S.: Gephi. In: Alhajj, P.R., Rokne, P.J. (eds.) Encyclopedia of Social Network Analysis and Mining, pp. 612–625. Springer, New York (2014). https://doi.org/10.1007/978-1-4614-6170-8_299

Perceived Usability Evaluation of 360° Immersive Video Service: Empirical Evaluation of the System Usability Scale

Fei-Hui Huang[✉]

Department of Marketing and Distribution Management, Oriental Institute
of Technology, Banciao. 58, New Taipei City 22061, Taiwan R.O.C.
Fn009@mail.oit.edu.tw

Abstract. An experience system using virtual reality (VR) devices and applying 360-degree panoramic formats for the experiential service of the vehicle is proposed. In this experimental study, the research goal is to analyze the effectiveness of using a head-mounted display (HMD) VR devices and applying 360° panoramic formats in eliciting positive user-perceived usability and to compare these to usability evoked in physical scooter ride settings. Data were collected from an experiment involving a total of 56 individual scooter commuters. The participants were asked to complete a System Usability Scale (SUS). The results verified that using a VR service may create an okay impression concerning usability. Furthermore, easy to learn, easy to use, and confident play a big part in positively influencing user's perception of VR service usability. Based on these results, a VR service may be used as an experienced tool to create reality-like scooter riding experiences for users.

Keywords: Human-computer interaction · Usability · System usability scale · Electric two-wheelers

1 Introduction

Taiwan is an island nation with the highest density of scooter-riding populations in the world. For improving air quality and public health, the Taiwanese government proposes an eco-friendly environmental protection policy to replace scooters with electric two-wheelers (E2Ws) in the Taiwanese two-wheeler market. Providing E2W trial ride services has a positive impact on the user's acceptance level of the E2W product [1–3]. Direct product or service experiences may create stronger associations in memory, given its inherent self-relevance [4]. Experiential benefits generally correspond to product-related attributes, and the experience of using the product or service, and satisfying needs such as sensory pleasure, variety, and cognitive stimulation [5]. Therefore, E2Ws industries are becoming increasingly interested in applying experiential marketing, to positively stimulate people's willingness to accommodate E2Ws. Thus, an experience system using virtual reality (VR) devices and applying 360-degree panoramic formats for the experiential service of vehicle is proposed. In this experimental study, the research goal is to analyze the effectiveness of using head-mounted

© Springer Nature Switzerland AG 2020
C. Stephanidis and M. Antona (Eds.): HCII 2020, CCIS 1224, pp. 438–444, 2020.
https://doi.org/10.1007/978-3-030-50726-8_57

display (HMD) virtual reality (VR) devices and applying 360° panoramic formats in eliciting positive user perceived usability and to compare these to usability evoked in physical scooter ride settings. Within the usability evaluation methods described in the literature [6], questionnaires assume a significant importance for qualitative self-reported data collection about the characteristics, thoughts, feelings, perceptions, behaviors or attitudes of users [7]. Questionnaires have the advantage of being low budget techniques, they do not require test equipment, and their results reflect the users' opinions. They also provide useful information about what are the strengths and weaknesses of a product or service. The System Usability Scale (SUS) is one of the usability evaluation questionnaires most widely used [8]. The SUS is a widely used self-administered instrument for the evaluation of usability of a wide range of products and user interfaces. The principal value of the SUS is that it provides a single reference score for participants' view of the usability of a product or service. Therefore, SUS has been adopted in this study.

2 Literature Review

2.1 Virtual Reality

Virtual reality (VR) has typically been portrayed as a medium. Computer hardware and software and its peripheral devices, that are used to create a VR system, are designed to replicate the information available to the sensory/perceptual system in the physical world and to produce outputs that impinge upon the body's various senses, resulting in convincing illusions for each of these senses and thus a rich, interactive multimedia facsimile of real-life [9]. With regard to hardware, VR is a particular collection of technological hardware, including computers, head-mounted displays, headphones, and motion-sensing controllers. With regard to content, two major types of VR content are realistic images or videos, in 360-degree and three-dimensional (3D) digital representations. In the past, the format most used has been 3D. The 3D format is created digitally through computer vision software, the navigation is continuous, and it must be connected to a computer. Now, panoramic videos are a new and rapidly growing approach that can display the power of sight, sound, and motion in an entirely new way, and allows viewers to sense action from all angles and directions. Experiences created by the VR system, which including computer hardware and software and video contents, are expected to provide sensory, emotional, cognitive, and behavioral values that replace functional values. Related simulations have been verified to evoke user responses, similar to those in physical environments [10].

2.2 System Usability Scale

The System Usability Scale (SUS) is one of the most widely adopted usability evaluation questionnaires to measure users' subjective assessments of a system's usability [11]. The SUS was developed by John Brooke more than 25 years ago as part of a usability engineering program (1986) as a "quick and dirty" survey scale that would allow the usability practitioner to quickly and easily assess the usability of a given product or service. The main advantage of SUS is that it comprises only 10 items to be rated on a five-point scale ranging from strongly disagree to strongly agree, among which five are positive statements and the rest are negative. The SUS items have been developed according to the usability criteria defined by the ISO 9241-11, including the ability of users to complete tasks using the system, and the quality of the output of those tasks, i.e., effectiveness; the level of resource consumed in performing tasks, i.e., efficiency; how easily users can learn to use the system, i.e., learnability; and the users' subjective reactions using the system, i.e., satisfaction. In addition, the SUS score is single and ranges from 0 to 100. The results of the SUS can be comprehensible even to non-experts. A SUS score above 68 would be considered above average and anything below 68 is below average [12]. SUS has a remarkably robust measure of system usability, even with a small sample size [13].

3   Methods

This study conducted with two experiential services, including 360° immersive video service and panoramic video service. We investigated paths through which VR and/or 360° panoramic video technologies impacted user perceived usability. The service presented actual situations of riding scooters on the road, which allowed us to make valid comparisons. The responses from participants were collected to understand user's usability all in using 360° immersive video service, using panoramic video service, and riding a scooter on the road.

3.1   Participants

Fifty-six individual scooter commuters took part in the experiment and completed surveys. There were 36 males and 20 females aged 18–62 years ($\bar{X}$ = 23.53; σ = 7.31). No participant experienced simulator sickness or had technical difficulties with the VR system.

3.2   Procedures

At the beginning of the experiment, participants were required to read and sign an IRB-approved consent form, which provided details regarding the experiment. They were allowed to opt out of the study at any time during their participation. Then, participants were instructed regarding the use of the VR equipment. In the experiment, participants experienced a scooter ride on the road. The overall experience of the participant is based on the VR using HMD of VR for transmission of panoramic video data. At the end of the experiment, participants completed the SUS.

3.3   Data Analysis

Analyses were conducted using SPSS software, Version 22.0. The two-tailed significance level was set at $p < .05$.

4   Results

4.1   Descriptive Statistics

The results of each question item for SUS is listed in Table 1.

Table 1. Descriptive statistics of SUS scores

SUS items	Riding a scooter		Using VR system	
	X̄	σ	X̄	σ
SUS1. I think that I would like to use this system frequently	3.16	1.02	1.98	1.17
SUS2. I found the system unnecessarily complex	3.04	0.91	1.86	1.15
SUS3. I thought the system was easy to use	3.30	0.83	2.70	1.03
SUS4. I think that I would need the support of a technical person to be able to use this system	2.52	1.19	1.02	0.86
SUS5. I found the various functions in this system were well integrated	2.77	0.83	2.55	0.93
SUS6. I thought there was too much inconsistency in this system	2.14	0.98	2.23	0.89
SUS7. I would imagine that most people would learn to use this system very quickly	2.50	1.03	2.84	0.85
SUS8. I found the system very cumbersome to use	2.88	0.76	2.52	0.95
SUS9. I felt very confident using the system	3.18	0.88	2.59	0.99
SUS10. I needed to learn a lot of things before I could get going with this system	2.02	1.20	2.30	1.14
Score	68.75	12.84	56.47	8.75

4.2   T Test

The T-test results indicated that SUS items for riding a scooter had significantly different findings for 'I would like to use this system frequently' ($F = 4.63$, $p < .05$; $t = 3.24$, $p < .05$) between men ($\bar{X} = 3.5$, $\sigma = 1.00$) and women ($\bar{X} = 2.55$, $\sigma = 1.19$) and 'easy to use' ($t = 2.49$, $p < .05$) between men ($\bar{X} = 3.5$, $\sigma = .56$) and women ($\bar{X} = 2.95$, $\sigma = 1.1$). In addition, SUS items for using VR service had significantly different findings for 'easy to use' ($F = 6.35$, $p < .05$; $t = 2.19$, $p < .05$) between women ($\bar{X} = 3.05$, $\sigma = .76$) and men ($\bar{X} = 2.5$, $\sigma = 1.11$) and 'needed to learn a lot of things before I could get going with this system' ($t = 2.02$, $p < .05$) between men ($\bar{X} = 2.53$, $\sigma = 1.06$) and women ($\bar{X} = 1.9$, $\sigma = 1.21$).

4.3   Wilcoxon Signed-Rank Test

The Wilcoxon signed-rank test revealed that there were statistically significant difference for SUS1, SUS2, SUS3, SUS4, SUS8, and SUS9 items (P 2 0.05). These results indicate that:

- Users are perceived themselves more frequently to ride the scooter (Mdn = 3) than to use the VR system (Mdn = 2)
- Users are perceived more easy to use when riding a scooter (Mdn = 3) than when using VR system (Mdn = 3)
- Users are perceived more confident when riding a scooter (Mdn = 3) than when using VR system (Mdn = 3)
- Users are perceived themselves more needs to have support from technical person when riding a scooter (Mdn = 3) than when using VR system (Mdn = 1)
- Users are perceived more cumbersome to use when riding a scooter (Mdn = 3) than when using VR system (Mdn = 2.5)
- Users are perceived more complex to use when riding a scooter (Mdn = 3) than when using VR system (Mdn = 2)

5   Discussion

In this study, a quantitative analysis of the usability while riding a scooter and usability while using VR service to watch the panoramic scooter ride video was carried out using a SUS scale. SUS is an easy scale to administer to participants. Also, SUS can effectively and quickly differentiate between usable and unusable systems. The results revealed that the average score of SUS for riding a scooter is 68.75, which is above average. This means that most of the participants consider the usability of riding a scooter is acceptable. In other words, riding a scooter created a positive impression concerning usability. However, the 68.75 score expresses somewhat negative subjective usability impressions about scooters as well. In addition, the results revealed that the average score of SUS for using the VR system is 56.47, which is below average. This means that most of the participants consider the usability of using VR system is marginally acceptable. Such a score expresses a few negative subjective usability impressions about VR service applying in scooter products as well. The results verified that both the scooter product and the VR scooter ride service are acceptable and useful systems for users. However, the functionality provided by scooter and VR service to users is different. Riding a scooter is mainly based on the usefulness of transportation vehicles, while the VR scooter ride service is mainly about to create like the reality of riding a scooter.

The influence of a scooter ride and a scooter VR service on user-perceived usability when riding a scooter or watching 3600 scooter ride videos was investigated. With regard to riding a scooter, easy to use, confident, and intention of using frequently play a big part in positively influencing user's perception of scooter usability. In addition, the values of these three factors for user-perceived usability when riding a scooter are significantly higher than using VR service. With regard to using VR service, easy to learn, easy to use, and confident play a big part in positively influencing user's perception of VR service usability. Compared with riding a scooter, user perceived fewer needs of the support for a technical person and lower feel of cumbersome and complex when using VR service.

There is a gender-based variation in usability while riding a scooter and using VR service. This gender-based difference has been found to be due to the user's general response toward the scooter as a product and the VR service as an experience tool to create reality-like scooter riding experiences for users. The results indicated that most of the male participants tended to use frequently and feel easy to use for scooter products, while female participants tended to have slightly negative feelings. This means that male users perceived better usability of riding a scooter than female users. In addition, the results indicated that most of the female participants tended to feel easy to use for VR service, while male participants tended to have slightly negative feelings. Men participants tended to need learning a lot of things before they could get going with VR system, while female participants tended to have slightly less feelings. This means that female users perceived better usability of using VR service to create reality-like scooter riding experiences than male users.

6   Conclusion

The main aim of this study was to use SUS evaluation methods to investigate the usability and the differences in user-perceived usability between riding a scooter and using VR service. Results of the surveys, conducted with scooter commuters in the country of Taiwan, provide evidence to understand that users perceived usability for both scooter product and VR service are acceptable and tend to be marginally acceptable. Comparing with VR service, user-perceived easy to use, confident, and intention of using frequently play a big part in positively influencing user's perception of scooter usability. In contrast, using VR service to create an experience of scooter ride may have fewer needs of the support for a technical person and lower user's feel of cumbersome and complex then riding a scooter. Hence, VR service is an innovating idea applying to two-wheeler products for creating a rider experiences. Furthermore, female users perceived better usability of using VR service to create reality-like scooter riding experiences than male users. Finally, designers and developers of VR systems for experiencing scooter products would need further research to improve the effectiveness of applying on two-wheeler products and implement permanent versions of the public VR two-wheeler service.

References

1. Huang, F.H.: Exploring the environmental benefits associated with battery swapping system processes. Adv. Environ. Biol. **9**(26 SI), 87–93 (2015)
2. Huang, F.-H.: Measuring user experience of using battery swapping station. In: Ahram, T., Falcão, C. (eds.) AHFE 2017. AISC, vol. 607, pp. 656–664. Springer, Cham (2018). https://doi.org/10.1007/978-3-319-60492-3_62

3. Huang, F.H.: System acceptability evaluation of battery swapping system for electric two wheelers. In: Soares, M., Falcão, C., Ahram, T. (eds.) Advances in Ergonomics Modeling, Usability & Special Populations, vol. 486, pp. 325–337. Springer, Cham (2017). https://doi.org/10.1007/978-3-319-41685-4_29

4. Millar, M., Thomas, R.: Discretionary activity and happiness: the role of materialism. J. Res. Personal. **43**(4), 699–702 (2009)

5. Nicolao, L., Irwin, J.R., Goodman, J.K.: Happiness for sale: do experiential purchases make consumers happier than material purchases? J. Consum. Res. **36**(2), 188–198 (2009)

6. Martins, A., Queirós, A., da Rocha, N.P.: Usability evaluation of products and services: a systematic review. In: e-society 2013, p. 299 (2013)

7. Hanington, B., Martin, B.: Universal Methods of Design: 100 Ways to Research Complex Problems, Develop Innovative Ideas, and Design Effective Solutions. Rockport Publishers, Beverly (2012)

8. Lewis, J.R.: Usability testing. Handb. Hum. And Ergon **12**, e30 (2006)

9. Burdea, G., Coiffet, P.: Virtual Reality Technology. Wiley-Interscience, Hoboken (2003)

10. Villa, C., Labayrade, R.: Multi-objective optimisation of lighting installations taking into account user preferences–a pilot study. Lighting Res. Technol. **45**(2), 176–196 (2013)

11. Brooke, J.: SUS: a 'quick and dirty' usability scale. In: Jordan, P.W., Thomas, B., Weerdmeester, B.A., McClelland, I.L. (eds.) Usability Evaluation in Industry, pp. 189–194. Taylor & Francis, London (1996)

12. From, W.: SUS: a retrospective. J. Usability Stud. **8**(2), 29–40 (2013)

13. Tullis, T.S., Stetson, J.N.: A comparison of questionnaires for assessing website usability. In: Proceedings of UPA, Minneapolis, 7–11 June 2004

Consumer Experiences of the World's First 5G Network in South Korea

Hyesun Hwang$^{(\boxtimes)}$, Xu Li, Muzi Xiang, and Kee Ok Kim

Department of Consumer Science, Sungkyunkwan University, Seoul, Korea
h.hwang@skku.edu

Abstract. The purpose of this study is to investigate South Korean consumers' feelings and experiences of the 5G network. Using R3.5.3 topic modeling, we text mined 38,649 tweets from April to December 2019 to identify key experiences. The results of the topic modeling indicated that South Korean consumers are proud of having the world's first deployment of a nationwide 5G network, and welcome the promises of 5G. Additionally, the results revealed that consumers enjoyed live streaming and immersive content using technologies such as virtual reality, augmented reality, and 360° video. Data plans and speeds have resulted in these consumers being at the forefront of cellular technology deployment. Noticeable negative opinions were found on the performance and stability of the service, and included service disruptions and slower speeds than expected. Due to the slow installation progress of the 5G base stations and the non-standalone versions of the 5G network, delays in the non-standalone 5G version are inevitable the standalone 5G version may be run. This study shows that Korean consumers are receiving the chance to experience the future via new 5G technologies. As standalone 5G networks become widely deployed and more 5G capable devices and infrastructure becomes available, 5G will transform consumer lifestyles.

Keywords: 5G · Consumer experience · Twee · Tweeter · Topic modeling · Network analysis

1 Introduction

The world's first 5G radio wave was transmitted from South Korea on December 1, 2018, and the first commercialization of 5G commenced on April 5, 2019 for the purpose of three servicing blueprints: ultra-fast speed, extremely low latency rates, and hype-connections [1]. Besides updating the existing mobile communications based on the above three characteristics, the 5G network will help more services target different consumers, enterprises, and public sectors in many other fields [2]. Therefore, based on actual consumers' responses and attitudes toward 5G in South Korea, this paper further explores a variety of these consumers' experiences and suggestions in the process of using 5G.

© Springer Nature Switzerland AG 2020
C. Stephanidis and M. Antona (Eds.): HCII 2020, CCIS 1224, pp. 445–449, 2020.
https://doi.org/10.1007/978-3-030-50726-8_58

2 Background

According to a survey conducted before the official commencement of the 5G's commercialization in 2018 [2], only 9.8% of consumers intended to use 5G services immediately after commercialization, and only 35.6% of consumers intended to use 5G services within one year. One of the main reasons for this result was because consumers are more familiar with the operation of 4G services and do not think 4G has any shortcomings, thus they do not think it necessary to change to 5G [3]. Therefore, in order to provide consumers with more information about 5G and to increase the 5G market before the official commencement of 5G's commercialization, Korean telecommunications companies KT, SK Telecom (SKT), and LG Uplus (LGU+) held many 5G content service experience activities, and organized several groups to experience 5G services in advance.

As the first country to begin commercializing 5G services, Korean consumers' comments and feedback are crucial in solving the existing shortcomings of 5G services and in improving their quality. The results of this study can also provide a reference for 5G deployment in other countries.

3 Methods

3.1 Text Data

Using the Trendup 4.0 program, we collected 38,649 Twitter mentions that were related to the 5G service from April 3, 2019 to December 31, 2019, when the 5G service began. Using the R3.5.3 program, the collected data were further cleaned by deleting meaningless punctuation marks, words, and suffixes; at the same time, advertisements, product names, and brand names related to 5G were also deleted. To explore consumers' responses on 5G technology, nouns and adjectives in the cleaned data were extracted using the SimplePos22 function in the KoNLP package in the R3.5.3 program. Finally, Latent Dirichlet Allocation (LDA) topic modeling and a bigram network analysis were used to analyze the data.

3.2 Topic Modeling

To understand consumers' experiences with the 5G network, topic modeling was performed using the LDA package in the R3.5.3 version. Topic modeling algorithms have been widely used with good success rates in discovering the hidden semantic topical structure in a large corpus of documents [4]. Topic modeling algorithms are used to find patterns in the words in a collection of documents, and categorizes them under different topics [5].

3.3   Network Analysis

Network analysis offers an intuitive and visual way of thinking about relationships and interactions. We extracted a tokenized text dataset by pairs of adjacent words. In addition, the results of network analysis were visualized using R 3.5.3 [6].

4   Results

Topic modeling derives topics and identifies key issues by classifying user comments, and network analysis describes, in detail, the relationship based on topic modeling. We can obtain the positive and negative experiences of consumers in the process of using 5G through network analysis and topic modeling. Table 1 lists the six topics obtained by topic modeling and the top 15 keywords in each topic.

Table 1. Results of topic modeling

	Topic 1	Topic 2	Topic 3	Topic 4	Topic 5	Topic 6
1	World	Mobile-service company	Slow	Era	Fail	Model
2	Phone plans	World	Phone plans	Service	The first	Technology
3	Era	Nice	Era	Game	Phone plans	Market
4	Service	Smart phone	Data	Korea	Qualcomm	The first
5	Launch	Fast	Internet	Data	Fast	Data
6	Big	Era	Nice	Technology	Problem	Fast
7	Price	Activate phone plan	Basis	Many	Commercialization	Network
8	Wi-Fi	Wi-Fi	Usage	Unlimited data plan	Big	Launch
9	News	Big	Person	4G	Era	Future
10	Beginning	Commercialization	The first	Phone plans	Support	Era
11	Smart phone	Launch	Smart phone	World	Korea	World
12	Domestic	Data	Think	Big	Slow	Smart phone
13	5G experience group	5G mobile phone	Big	Person	Investment	Commercialization
14	Equipment	Modem	Source	Commercialization	Subscriber	Big
15	Usage	Speed	Picture	Properly	Technology	Communication

Among these six topics, topics 1, 2, 4, and 6 showed positive experiences of the consumers in the process of using 5G. These topics included the pride that South Koreans have as being the first country to commercialize the 5G service, the enjoyment of 5G content services such as virtual reality (VR), augmented reality (AR), and 360° video, and the anticipation they have regarding 5G's potential.

The negative experiences of consumers mainly included the high price data traffic packages and the problems of the 5G communication network, because the consumption of 5G data traffic is larger than 4G, and the investment cost of communication companies for 5G technology is 1.5 to 2 times that of 4G [7]. Therefore, the price of 5G data traffic packages are higher than those of 4G. This has become one of the most important negative experiences of consumers' using 5G services, and has hindered the pace of consumers who want to register for 5G services. Problems of the 5G communication network included connection instability and slow network speed, and the consumers said that the 5G network speed was not as fast as that which was promoted, and that there is no signal in many places, which is a very serious problem for 5G users. These problems also reveal the demand for network speed and stability from contemporary consumers.

The results of the network analysis in Fig. 1 can help us understand the relationship among the keywords in the 5G users' comments. For example, consumers enjoy using 5G Multiview to watch games and sports competitions. Due to the large data consumption of 5G, they anticipate an unlimited monthly package with an appropriate price, more 5G models, more 5G content services, and feedback on the fast power consumption of 5G mobile phones.

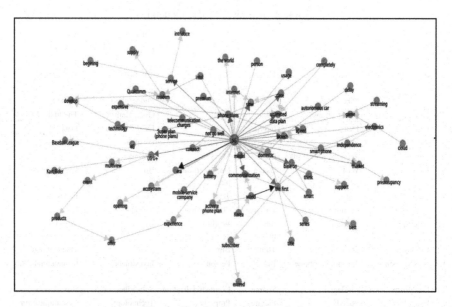

Fig. 1. Result of network analysis

5 Conclusion

In this study, we explored a wide range of consumer responses to 5G services by analyzing texts on Twitter. Our results show that South Korean consumers are proud for their country to be the first 5G commercialized country in the world. They enjoy 5G content services, and are in anticipation of 5G's potential. On the contrary, there is dissatisfaction caused by the high price of the 5G data plan and the negative experiences caused by the delay and instability of the 5G network. These points appear inevitable due to the slow installation progress of 5G base stations and the non-standalone (NSA) version of the 5G network. Up-switching latency issues will occur in future 5G regions using the NSA version of the 5G network until the standalone (SA) 5G version is running. The results of the present study have shown that, as the first country to use 5G, South Korea still faces some problems in 5G service technology at this stage. Technicians need to continue to work hard to improve and perfect 5G's service quality to improve the negative experience of consumers.

This study used network analysis and topic modeling to mine a large number of comments to help technicians improve 5G's service quality, which shows the importance of consumer feedback. At the same time, as the first 5G commercialized country, this study from South Korea provides practical significance for 5G deployment in other countries.

In future research, it will be necessary to derive practical implications to discover specific improvements of the service by analyzing data based on the experience of actual 5G service users. In addition, future research needs to track what kind of consumer experience will change alongside the stabilization of 5G services. Future research should also adopt a broad perspective on technological advancements, not just by examining the changes in the speed or breadth of telecommunications services, but by broadly examining the expansion of the numerous services derived from the changing technological environment and, consequently, the impact on consumers' lives.

References

1. Shin, J., Shin, J.: 5th generation mobile telecommunication. Korea Robot. Soci. Rev. **16**(2), 14–21 (2019)
2. Kim, H., Kim, J., Lee, Y., Shin, J.: Factors affecting 5G mobile communication market diffusion: focusing on non-use intention of 5G based services. J. Korea Manage. Eng. Soc. **24**(3), 113–128 (2019)
3. Oh, Y.: A study on the influence of customer value and switching barriers on the attitude toward 5G service. Korea Res. Acad. Distrib. Manage. Rev. **22**(4), 101–108 (2019)
4. Yi, F., Jiang, B., Wu, J.: Topic modeling for short texts via word embedding and document correlation. IEEE Access **8**, 30692–30705 (2020)
5. George, L.E., Birla, L.: A study of topic modeling methods. In: 2018 Second International Conference on Intelligent Computing and Control Systems (ICICCS), pp. 109–113 (2018)
6. Kurt, H., Ingo, F., David, M.: Text mining infrastructure in R. J. Stat. Softw. **25**(5), 1–54 (2008)
7. Kim, Y.: [Hot News] 5G is a 'charge bomb'? 1 GB consumed in 10 minutes of game. Midas **2019**(4), 88–89 (2019)

Survey on Dining Experiences of Overseas Travelers

Rieko Inaba^(⊠) and Naoko Fujimaki

Department of Computer Science, Tsuda University, Tokyo, Japan
inaba@tsuda.ac.jp

Abstract. Although the number of foreign visitors to Japan is increasing steadily, it has been reported that there is a need to improve the environment for accepting foreigners. According to a survey conducted by the Japan Tourism Bureau on foreign tourists visiting Japan in 2009, there were many complaints regarding the lack of foreign language display on signposts and multilingual support at places such as restaurants. Most of all, the dietary pattern, which people display during a trip, is an important aspect for improving their satisfaction when staying in Japan. The aim of this study is to solve the communication problems at dining facilities in Japan by developing a communication support system for foreign people to easily communicate in any language. To better understand user needs, we conducted an online survey on more than 400 people. The elements for system construction were extracted from the results of the survey.

Keywords: Multilingual communication tool · Foreign tourist · Dietary restrictions

1 Introduction

Japan continues to break the record for the number of visitors and aims to achieve 40 million annual inbound tourists by 2020 [1]. Despite the increasing number of visitors, there are some problems that need to be solved to accept more people from abroad than previously. One of those problems is the lack of signposts or displays in English or other languages at dining facilities. It is difficult for visitors to communicate at restaurants without such signs because even staff members are rarely able to use languages other than Japanese [2]. Moreover, we need to create an environment that can accept the diversity of dietary preferences. Considering the fact that the number of visitors from Southeast Asia and South Asia, where people have a variety of dietary restrictions according to several religions, has increased, the dietary habit of visitors has diversified in Japan. Hence, it is important to support communication regarding dietary preferences because miscommunication over the same might cause life-threatening problems or identity infringement.

Therefore, we aimed to solve these problems by developing a mobile application that would allow foreigners to easily communicate in multiple languages in Japanese restaurants. First, we conducted an online survey of approximately 429 persons to better understand user needs. We asked questions such as: Are there dietary restrictions

© Springer Nature Switzerland AG 2020
C. Stephanidis and M. Antona (Eds.): HCII 2020, CCIS 1224, pp. 450–454, 2020.
https://doi.org/10.1007/978-3-030-50726-8_59

for health or religious reasons? If so, how do they deal with the restrictions during travel? In addition, based on their experience, have they ever had any problems with restaurants and meals while traveling abroad? From the results of the survey, the necessary elements of the application were extracted.

2 Survey Overview

We conducted a questionnaire survey on foreigners living in Japan and abroad (non-Japanese nationals) to understand the user needs and dining experiences when traveling overseas. The survey was conducted as an online questionnaire from June to July 2016. The questionnaire was prepared in both Japanese and English. The total number of valid responses was 429.

Figure 1 shows the distribution of respondents' nationalities by region. Despite the bias, answers were obtained from all regions.

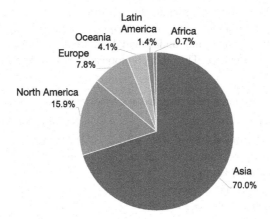

Fig. 1. Distribution of respondents' nationalities by region.

3 Survey Results

- This section presents the items that have been revealed by the survey.
- Dietary restrictions
- Information on food required by travelers
- Dissatisfaction and inconvenience felt at restaurants during travel
- Internet usage environment when traveling overseas

3.1 Dietary Restrictions

People with any dietary restrictions were 30.8% of the total. The types of dietary restrictions are shown in Fig. 2.

In addition, for dietary restrictions under "discipline of religion," we asked questions regarding the manner in which such disciplines are handled when traveling abroad. "Respond as if you were in your home country" was the most common

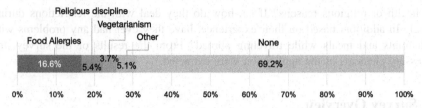

Fig. 2. Dietary restrictions.

response at 71.0%; however, 29% said they would "make some compromise." From these responses, it was found that there is a difference in individual approaches to "discipline of religion," and it is necessary to set an approach for each individual.

3.2   Information on Food Required by Travelers

We asked the question: what type of information is needed at restaurants when traveling abroad? Table 1 shows the responses to this question. These results indicate that the demand for "menus with photos" and "menu display in multiple languages" is high. In other words, foreign tourists cannot understand the ingredients and taste of dishes using only menus written in Japanese. The other common answer was "raw material labeling."

Table 1. Responses for information required at overseas restaurants (Total number = 429).

Responses	No. of respondents
Menu with photos	322 (75.1%)
Menu display in multiple languages	266 (52.7%)
Raw material labeling	142 (33.1%)
English speaking employees	137 (31.9%)
Description of the taste of dishes	70 (16.3%)
Information on ingredients causing allergies	41 (9.6%)
Other	18 (4.2%)

Furthermore, 93.5% of respondents said that "they would like to eat local food," which is unique to the country or region where they are traveling to. Meanwhile, some respondents said, "I am reluctant to eat unfamiliar food."

In other words, it turned out that many travelers not only seek the "name of the dish", but also information on what kind of dishes such as taste, ingredients, and quantity.

3.3   Dissatisfaction and Inconvenience Felt at Restaurants During Travel

The dissatisfactions that travelers felt at restaurants when traveling abroad could be broadly divided into four types:

(1) Language barriers

Many respondents answered: "I cannot communicate with the clerk at the restaurant," or "I didn't understand the menu table and ingredients, so I felt inconvenient when ordering."

(2) Insufficient explanation of menu

The common answers were: "I can't tell what the taste is just by the name of the dish," or "I was not able to imagine what was in it."

(3) Lack of awareness at restaurants

A restaurant clerk misunderstood "food allergies" as "likes and dislikes."
Many respondents reported that they faced problems at restaurants owing to the lack of awareness about dietary restrictions.

(4) Differences in restaurant systems

Some of the respondents commented that they were puzzled by the restaurant rules of "I do not know how to wait," and "I do not know how to order."
Therefore, it was established that the system to be developed needed a design that could cope with situations where travelers could be confused.

3.4 Internet Usage Environment When Traveling Overseas

We surveyed the Internet usage environment of travelers. Table 2 shows the results. It was observed that 70.2% of overseas travelers used only free public Wi-Fi for Internet connection. In other words, it was found that an Internet connection that is hassle-free and does not require any specification for usage is preferable.

Table 2. Internet usage environment (Total number = 429).

Type of internet connection	No. of respondents
Use free public Wi-Fi	301 (70.2%)
Buy SIM card	152 (25.9%)
Use portable Wi-Fi	109 (18.6%)
Other	24 (4.1%)

4 Consideration

For developing a support system, it is necessary to consider the following three aspects based on the knowledge obtained from the survey results and the drawbacks in existing communication support tools.

(1) Achieve smooth two-way communication between foreign customers and restaurants.
(2) Enable detailed conversation about dietary restrictions.
(3) Provide the system as a mobile application that does not require an Internet connection for usage.

In particular, it was shown that it is necessary to address dietary restrictions based on "food allergies," "religious discipline," and "vegetarianism."

5 Conclusion

In this study, we aimed to develop a multilingual communication support application to solve problems such as delays in foreign language support at restaurants in Japan and lack of understanding and response to various dietary preferences. For the purpose of determining the requirements of the application, we conducted a survey on the real dining experiences of people when traveling abroad.

References

1. Japan National Tourism Organization Press Release (in Japanese). https://www.jnto.go.jp/jpn/news/press_releases/pdf/200117_monthly.pdf. Accessed 16 Mar 2020
2. Japan Tourism Agency, Ministry of Land, Infrastructure, Transport and Tourism, The JTA conducted a survey of foreign travelers visiting Japan about the welcoming environment (in Japanese). http://www.mlit.go.jp/common/001171594.pdf. Accessed 16 Mar 2020

Mental Effort and Usability of Assistance Systems in Manual Assembly – A Comparison of Pick-to-Light and AR Contours Through VR Simulation

Annemarie Minow[1(✉)], Stefan Stüring[2], and Irina Böckelmann[1]

[1] Occupational Medicine, Medical Faculty, Otto-von-Guericke-University,
Leipziger Straße 44, 39120 Magdeburg, Germany
{annemarie.minow,irina.boeckelmann}@med.ovgu.de
[2] LIVINGSOLIDS GmbH, Schilfbreite 3, 39120 Magdeburg, Germany
info@livingsolids.de

Abstract. In our experimental user test, 25 healthy participants assembled hydraulic valves and geometric figures using two assistive functions (Pick-to-light (PtL) and Augmented Reality (AR) contours at the place of installation). We used virtual reality (VR; HTC Vive) to simulate the workplace and the assistance functions and compared the mental effort and the usability between PtL and AR. We also examined the applicability of our methodology to further studies in this field. The mental effort was higher when using the AR contours than when using the Pick-to-light. The participants rated the usage suitability of both alternatives as approximately equal regarding the perceived usefulness, perceived ease of use and dialogue principles of the ISONORM. However, the System Usability Scale (SUS) showed a better usability with the PtL. We found low to medium negative correlations of mental effort with usability dimensions. In general, VR simulations and the methods applied appear to be suitable to investigate user-centric aspects of the use of digital assistance systems in manual assembly. However, in order to broaden our understanding of health standards and productive work, we recommend further field studies and participants of more varied ages.

Keywords: Assistance system · Usability · User test

1 Introduction

Work 4.0 changes almost all areas of production and industry today. Even manual assembly is facing upheavals such as new forms of work organization, changing competence requirements and increasing digitalization.

It is a challenge that customers place more and more individual and specific demands on the manufacturing companies. The necessary flexibility in industrial assembly processes, the complexity and variety of products not only place new strain on the company itself, but also on the cognitive performance of employees.

© Springer Nature Switzerland AG 2020
C. Stephanidis and M. Antona (Eds.): HCII 2020, CCIS 1224, pp. 455–461, 2020.
https://doi.org/10.1007/978-3-030-50726-8_60

In this context, assistance systems can help to support employees in carrying out their work, to achieve their quantitative and qualitative goals and to promote ergonomic and humane work design. Here, on the micro-level of the work system, mental stress and usability aspects, among other things, must be recorded and assessed.

The objectives of the user test presented here included the assessment of mental effort and usability of two possible assistance systems (Pick-to-light and AR contours) for manual assembly. We selected Pick-to-Light and AR-contours as two possible functions, because from the point of view of the application companies involved in the joint project they promise the greatest chances of employee support.

In terms of mental effort, some trials show a lower workload with the HMD, or the combination of HMD and Pick-to-Light, compared to using Pick-to-Light alone [1–3]. Wu et al. [3] could not identify any differences in usability between HMD and pick-to-light, while Guo et al. [1] and Wu et al. [2] identified the HMD as the preferred system.

We conducted the user test by means of VR simulation, as this allows the investigation of assistance modalities and their effects on humans at an early stage of the project, even without a fully functional real prototype.

2 Materials and Methods

2.1 Experimental Setup

On the hardware side, the experimental setup consisted of an HTC Vive (HMD) with two base stations for recording the position and orientation of the HMD.

In order to record the user inputs relevant for the assembly tasks (gripping components, moving components and releasing the components when reaching the assembly position), we equipped the HMD with a Leap Motion Sensor, which detects the hand position and thus enables intuitive interaction with virtual objects.

For the simulation of the working environment, we designed and simulated a room and a real workplace in it with the help of 3D models of the individual objects. We integrated all containers, necessary devices and components into the scenario as 3D objects.

For the experiments, we equipped the interactive VR application with functions that support the execution of the experiments. This includes the possibility of a simple configuration of the test procedure as well as the acquisition of essential measured values for the evaluation of the user performance.

2.2 Questionnaires

We measured the mental effort using the Rating Scale Mental Effort (RSME). The RSME [4, 5] describes a one-dimensional scale for assessing the effort experienced, with a scale from 0 to 220. The RMSE has anchor points with the degrees of effort operationalized as hardly, somewhat, reasonably, fairly, strongly, very strongly and extraordinarily.

To measure usability, we used the System Usability Scale (SUS), the ISONORM questionnaire and two sub-scales of the Technology Acceptance Model (TAM).

Brooke's SUS [6], as a "quick and dirty" method, consists of five positive and five negative questions, in which the respondents assess how user-friendly they perceive a system using a five-point Likert scale from "strongly disagree" (1) to "strongly agree" (5). The result is a one-dimensional global SU score between 0 and 100.

Because a low SU score may indicate a problem of the assistance system but does not elucidate the exact problem more precisely, we also used the ISONORM questionnaire in the user test [7, 8]. A long and short form of a questionnaire based on the seven principles of dialogue design according to DIN EN ISO 9241-110 exists. For reasons of time economy, we selected the short version for our test series [9]. The positively and negatively formulated statements on software are presented in a bipolar question format with seven levels (− − − to + + +).

Furthermore, two subscales of the TAM were used: perceived usefulness and perceived ease of use [10].

2.3 Experimental Procedure

In two randomized trials (simulation of PtL and AR contours), the test participants mounted a hydraulic valve, three geometric figures and again the same hydraulic valve, so that each participant used both assistance functions (see Fig. 1).

Fig. 1. Virtual workspace with assistance systems

There were two variants of the geometric figures, each with three randomized figures. The user-test is a crossover study.

The PtL showed the participant with a green light on the box that contained the next component to be mounted.

The second assistance function was the simulation of AR contours. Here, the participant saw contours at the installation location of the components.

In both simulated modalities, a display was running in the background showing video sequences of the next assembly step. An acoustic signal confirmed the correct installation of a component during assembly. After the assembly runs, the participants each filled out the questionnaires RSME, SUS, TAM and ISONORM.

2.4   Data Evaluation

We collected and analyzed the data using IBM SPSS Statistics 26. To check the interval-scaled data for normal distribution we used the Shapiro-Wilk test. Because most variables were not normally distributed, we used the nonparametric Wilcoxon test to analyze the data.

In the results, we show the mean value and standard deviation (MV ± SD) and, for ordinal variables, the median (MD), minimum (min) and maximum (max). The test decisions rest on a significance level of 5%.

3   Results and Discussion

13 of the 25 volunteer healthy study participants were men (52%) and 12 women (48%). The average age of the volunteers was 26.8 ± 8.93 years (min. 21, max. 59). The average age of the women was 25.9 ± 10.54 years, the average age of the men 27.6 ± 7.49 years. The majority of the participants were students or university graduates.

52% of the participants (n = 13) had no experience with HMDs before the test. The other 48% had already briefly tried VR-HMDs (e.g. in other research studies or in video games).

3.1   Mental Effort

Mental effort, as determined by the RSME, was significantly higher after working with the AR contours compared to the Pick-to-light system (47.8 ± 37.11 vs. 37.9 ± 22.6 points; $p_{Wilcoxon} = 0.004$).

Thus, the participants estimated the stress during assembly with the contours to be higher than with the Pick-to-light variant.

3.2   Usability

SUS. The results from the SUS showed a higher and therefore better evaluation of the Pick-to-light system compared to the AR contours (Pick-to-light: 78.7 ± 11.99 points vs. AR contours: 75.6 ± 13.84 points; $p_{Wilcoxon} = 0.031$). Both variants lay in the range good to excellent according to [11].

ISONORM. In contrast to the SUS, the mean values of both assistance functions in the seven dialogue principles of the ISONORM questionnaire were not statistically significantly different ($p_{Wilcoxon} > 0.05$). Therefore, we cannot make a clear statement about which assistance function the participants preferred (see Table 1). However, due to the positive mean values in all dimensions of the questionnaire, we assume that both functions were sufficiently usable.

Table 1. Results for ISONORM questionnaire

Variable	AR contours	Pick-to-light	$p_{Wilcoxon}$
	MV ± SD MD (Min - Max)		
Suitability for the task	1.4 ± 1.19 1.7 (–1 – 3)	1.6 ± 0.95 1.7 (–0.3 – 3)	0.332
Self-descriptiveness	1.1 ± 1.28 1 (–1.7 – 3)	1.0 ± 1.30 1 (–2.3 – 3)	0.541
Controllability	0.8 ± 1.44 0.5 (–2 – 3)	0.7 ± 1.26 0.5 (–1.5 – 3)	0.529
Conformity with user expectations	2.1 ± 0.65 2 (0.7 – 3)	2.0 ± 0.79 2 (0.3 – 3)	0.753
Error tolerance	0.6 ± 1.24 0.3 (–1.3 – 3)	0.8 ± 0.94 0.7 (–0.7 – 2.7)	0.671
Suitability for individualization	1.1 ± 1.00 1 (–1.5 – 2.5)	0.6 ± 0.99 0.5 (–1 – 3)	0.123
Suitability for learning	2.0 ± 0.87 2 (–0.7 – 3)	2.2 ± 0.76 2.3 (0 – 3)	0.105

Perceived Usefulness and Perceived Ease of Use. The perceived usefulness and perceived ease of use of the TAM did not show statistically significant differences between the assistance functions.

3.3 Correlations

We found low to medium negative correlations of RSME with SUS, Perceived Usefulness and Perceived Ease of Use and the dialogue principles controllability and suitability of the task (see Fig. 2). This indicates that with an increase in mental effort comes a decrease in the assessment of usability. Conversely, the mental effort decreases with a high, and therefore good, usability.

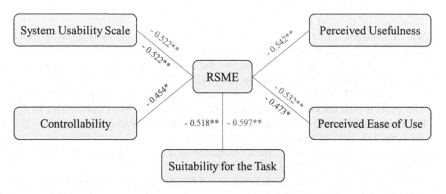

Fig. 2. Correlations of Mental Effort and Usability for the AR contours (purple correlation coefficient) and Pick-to-Light (orange correlation coefficient) (* = p < 0.05; ** = p < 0.01) (Color figure online)

4 Conclusion

Finally, we want to discuss the limitations of the study.

These include the short duration of application of the assistance systems and the fact that the experiments took place in a virtual environment. The usability of the HTC Vive itself may also have had an impact on the results. Further experiments within the scope of the project are to take place at the real model workplace or in the application company.

Our sample was relatively young. Perhaps it is easier for them to use VR as they are generally more used to technology compared to older people. Therefore, it might be important to get older workers in these tests as well to ensure that we can generalize the results to workers of all ages.

Furthermore, the participants of the user test were not trained assembly workers.

The result indicates that the participants found the use of the Pick-to-Light system more helpful. Perhaps finding the next component was more difficult for the participants than finding the correct position of the component. Therefore, the Pick-to-Light system offered more support to the participants.

However, the Pick-to-light system does not usually help to find the next part. This is where AR contours can provide support. A combination of both assistance systems is also conceivable. If necessary, the difficulty of the task or the display types (shapes, colors, etc.) must be adapted in further experiments.

It is possible to transfer the methodology used here to other studies.

Acknowledgments. The Federal Ministry of Education and Research have funded this research in the project "3D-basierte Assistenztechnologien für variantenreiche Montageprozesse – Menschzentrierter Arbeitsplatz der Zukunft '3D-Montageassistent'" (project number 03ZZ0441E).

References

1. Guo, A., et al.: A comparison of order picking assisted by head-up display (HUD), cart-mounted display (CMD), light, and paper pick list. In: Dunne, L., Martin, T., Beigl, M. (eds.) Proceedings of the 2014 ACM International Symposium on Wearable Computers - ISWC 2014, pp. 71–78. ACM Press, New York (2014)
2. Wu, X., Haynes, M., Guo, A., Starner, T.: A comparison of order picking methods augmented with weight checking error detection. In: Beigl, M., Lukowicz, P., Blanke, U., Kunze, K., Lee, S.C. (eds.) Proceedings of the 2016 ACM International Symposium on Wearable Computers - ISWC 2016, pp. 144–147. ACM Press, New York (2016)
3. Wu, X., et al.: Comparing order picking assisted by head-up display versus pick-by-light with explicit pick confirmation. In: Mase, K., Langheinrich, M., Gatica-Perez, D. (eds.) Proceedings of the 2015 ACM International Symposium on Wearable Computers – ISWC 2015, pp. 133–136. ACM Press, New York (2015)
4. Zijlstra, F.R.H., van Doorn, L.: The Construction of a Scale to Measure Perceived Effort. Delft University of Technology, Delft (1985)
5. Zijlstra, F.R.H.: Efficiency in Work Behaviour. A Design Approach for Modern Tools. Delft University Press, Delft (1993)

6. Brooke, J.: SUS: a "quick and dirty" usability scale. In: Jordan, P.W., Thomas, B., Weerdmeester, B.A., McClelland, A.L. (ed.) Usability Evaluation in Industry, pp. 189–194. Taylor and Francis, London (1986)

7. Prümper, J., Anft, M.: Die Evaluation von Software auf Grundlage des Entwurfs zur internationalen Ergonomie-Norm ISO 9241 Teil 10 als Beitrag zur partizipativen Systemgestaltung – ein Fallbeispiel. In: Rödiger, K. (ed.) Software-Ergonomie 1993 – Von der Benutzungsoberfläche zur Arbeitsgestaltung, pp. 145–156. Teubner, Stuttgart (1993)

8. Prümper, J.: Der Benutzerfragebogen ISONORM 9241/10: Ergebnisse zur Reliabilität und Validität. In: Liskowsky, R., Velichkovsky, B.M., Wünschmann, W. (ed.) Software-Ergonomie 1997 - Usability Engineering: Interaktion von Mensch-Computer-Interaktion und Software-Entwicklung, pp. 253–262. Teubner, Stuttgart (1997)

9. Pataki, K., Sachse, K., Prümper, J., Thüring, M.: ISONORM 9241/110-Short: Kurzfragebogen zur Software-Evaluation. In: Lösel, F. (ed.) Berichte über den 45. Kongress der Deutschen Gesellschaft für Psychologie, pp. 258–259. Pabst Science Publishers, Lengerich (2006)

10. Venkatesh, V., Davis, F.: A model of the antecedents of perceived ease of use: development and test. Decis. Sci. **27**(3), 451–481 (1996)

11. Bangor, A.W., Kortum, P., Miller, J.: Determining what individual SUS scores mean: adding an adjective rating scale. J. Usability Stud. **4**(3), 114–123 (2009)

Exploring the Value of Shared Experience in Augmented Reality Games

Hye Sun Park[1]([✉]), Byung-Kuk Seo[1][iD], Gun A. Lee[2][iD], and Mark Billinghurst[2][iD]

[1] Electronics and Telecommunications Research Institute, Daejeon, Korea
{hspark78,byungkuk.seo}@etri.re.kr
[2] University of South Australia, Adelaide, Australia
{Gun.Lee,Mark.Billinghurst}@unisa.edu.au

Abstract. Augmented reality (AR) games have provided positive, fun, and enjoyable user experiences in various ways. While these experiences are mostly oriented to single users, AR technology naturally supports face-to-face interaction, so it is valuable to take into account shared experience in sketching game scenarios, designing user interfaces and interaction schemes, and developing technical features. In this study, we explore a novel shared experience by designing a compelling user journey and good affordance in a game called SHYGER, which is a new type of AR game interacting with 3D real objects. We also report a user study and discuss how the shared AR experience could improve the overall user experience and satisfaction.

Keywords: Shared experience · User journey · User affordance · Augmented reality game

1 Introduction

Augmented reality (AR) is a technology that superimposes virtual information on a user's view of the real world, thus providing the user with both virtual and real experiences [1]. Compared to virtual reality (VR) in which the user is fully immersed in the virtual world, AR allows the user to interact with virtual contents in the real world where the user is present. Taking advantage of these benefits, AR has been applied to various fields such as gaming, education, medicine, and industry.

Different from the typical user experiences (UX) and user interface (UI) design, AR provides users with unique and interactive experiences blending the real and virtual worlds, so there is a need for different approaches and more considerations when it comes to designing AR experiences. One of the common practices is based on a user-centered UI design, which allows users to easily understand and use AR UIs against not only augmented 3D virtual contents, but also a 3D real space [4,8,9]. Another one is designing a compelling user journey, which drives users to follow a designer's hidden intention and hence

© Springer Nature Switzerland AG 2020
C. Stephanidis and M. Antona (Eds.): HCII 2020, CCIS 1224, pp. 462–469, 2020.
https://doi.org/10.1007/978-3-030-50726-8_61

experience AR in a complete and natural manner [11,15]. Instead of taking a user's learning process, inducing user behavior is also a key design factor for improving the user's usability and providing better affordance [5,6,13].

While most AR applications have been designed for single-user experiences, early researches in AR highlighted its potential for supporting multi-user experiences where people collaborate with each other while naturally interacting with the same virtual content in the same physical space [2,10,12]. Furthermore, recent advances in technologies such as cloud computing or 5G networking has been triggering sharing multi-user experiences to become a major feature of AR applications. For example, popular AR engines, such as Apple ARKit or Google ARCore to name a few, recently unveiled new updates to support collaborative and shared experiences. One of the most beloved AR games, Pokémon GO also rolled out the new shared AR experience feature, allowing multiple users to place their virtual characters in the same place and take a photo together.

In this study, we delve into these aspects to enrich user experience in AR applications and explore a new approach of designing AR experiences contemplating their usage as shared experience across multiple users. To achieve it, we design a compelling user journey and good affordance in a new type of AR game called SHYGER where an augmented virtual character is capable of hiding behind 3D real objects. In particular, SHYGER uses 3D real objects as hiding places, so the user journey reflects on how users arrange the real objects in a physical space as game strategies before and after the game. For better affordance during the game, we adopt a natural and stepwise approach through nudging, inducing the user's movement to easily adapt. In this paper, we report a user study to explore the value of shared AR experience in the AR game and demonstrate that our approach of considering shared experience in designing AR games could improve the overall user experience.

2   Designing a Shared Experience: SHYGER

2.1   Concept

SHYGER is an AR game we developed as an exploration of applying a user-centered design methodology considering shared experience. As a kind of AR hide-and-seek game, SHYGER leverages the characteristics of AR technology, making 3D real objects into hiding places for a virtual character called 'shyger' (shy+tiger). In the game, players try to find the shyger hiding behind the real objects by moving around the physical environment. As one of promising features for the next level of AR applications, the game uses 3D real objects as hiding places of the virtual character, so the gameplay changes based on how the real objects are arranged in the physical game space. In this study, we design shared AR experience on such interactive feature of SHYGER where players can establish game strategies to place the real objects on their own advantages and share experiences before, during, and after the game. While arranging the real objects works well on a single-player condition, we also extend the gameplay for multiple users and compare with each other.

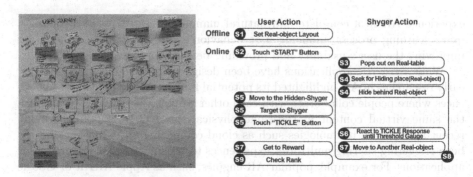

Fig. 1. Designing a shared experience: (Left) User journey, (Right) Game scenario.

2.2 User Journey Design and User Affordance Approach

Following a designer's intention is one of the indications of good user experience [11,15]. To achieve this, it is necessary to design a compelling user journey and provide a user with good affordance, inducing and guiding the user's behavior [5,6,13]. As shown in Fig. 1-(Left), a user journey for SHYGER is designed through three parts: before the game begins, during the game, and after the game. Before starting the game, all players establish their own game strategies to arrange 3D real objects in the game space. When a single user plays the game, the experience of establishing a "strategy for winning the game" offers various benefits, e.g., inducing the user's curiosity, making him/her be fully immersed in the game, and having more fun. When multiple players are involved in the game, particularly, arranging physical objects delivers more variety to the game. When collaborating with each other, for example, players can coordinate to arrange the real objects in a way that they can play well together, or for playing in competition, players can strategically place the real objects where it becomes difficult for the other player to find the shyger.

When users start playing the game, they need to move around the physical environment to have compelling game experience. However, the players who are used to 2D interaction are not familiar with the game concept of SHYGER, and they tend not to move. In order to easily adapt the players to the AR environment, a natural and stepwise approach is necessary through nudging. Nudging is a UX technique to encourage positive changes in behaviors of users through gentle intervention [14]. In AR, unlike 2D interfaces, users can recognize disparity in the height and distance of a virtual content as if it were a real object in 3D space. We leverage this disparity as a key to induce the user's movement through nudging. When the game starts, the shyger, a virtual character, first appears on a real table in front of the players, then hides itself behind the real objects on the table (e.g., a cup, a stack of books, etc), and the players try to find the shyger by centering it on a touch screen that shows a live video feed of the real world. This type of interaction involving device motion induces the user's movement, and may enhance user engagement and experience. In addition, the user's movement could be further encouraged by involving multiple players and sharing the game experience.

After finishing playing the game, players can share their experiences with each other about the gameplay or game rules; or they can also play another round of the game to try different strategies of arranging physical objects in the game space. Figure 1-(Right) shows the game scenario design for SHYGER that reflects the user journey design.

2.3 Spatiotemporal Requirements

Games are a good tool to induce social interaction and individual connection between players [3,7]. In particular, an AR game allows players to have shared experience in a natural manner, as long as they share the same physical game space. This may elicit close social interaction between players. To fulfill this, there are requirements in terms of setting up the space and time for the gameplay. The game, SHYGER, requires a flat surface (e.g., floor or table) with a diameter of 3 m or less with good lighting. The game space must also have 3 to 4 physical objects that are solid, opaque, and big enough for the shyger to hide. In terms of the temporal requirement, AR games are preferred to be shorter because they involve a lot of physical movements of the player which can be tiring; thus, keeping the game period short may lead to a positive game experience. SHYGER is designed to let users complete a game mission in 3 min, taking into consideration various internal and external factors such as the user's proficiency in handling a device.

3   User Study

3.1 Setup

For our user study, we developed SHYGER based on our custom developed computer vision based AR engine, which is capable of the following technical features: simultaneous localization and mapping (SLAM), real-time dense 3D reconstruction using a stereo RGB camera with an efficient fusion algorithm, handling scene changes by incrementally updating and recovering the reconstructed 3D scenes, and occlusion-aware augmentation, which allows virtual contents to be occluded by real objects (e.g., the shyger can hide behind the real objects).

SHYGER is designed as a handheld AR game that uses a touch screen large enough (13-in.) to be shared by multiple users. To meet high performance requirements of our AR engine, the prototype uses a backpack PC. SHYGER is played by using both the user's movement and touch interaction. Namely, the user needs to move around the physical environment to find the hiding shyger and aim at it, and then presses a button to interact with the shyger (see Fig. 2-(Left)). When the user finds the shyger hiding behind a physical object, the user can entice it to get out of the hidden place by tickling the shyger with a virtual feather. This is done by pressing the button on the touch screen, and

Fig. 2. User study setup: (Left) Multi-player condition, (Right) Gameplay and UIs.

the number of times the user touches the button is expressed as the intensity of the action. The shyger reacts to tickling by rolling on the floor and laughing (see Fig. 2-(Right)). If the tickling intensity goes above a predefined threshold, it moves to another location, finding a place to hide again. After successfully finding the hiding shyger three times, the user finally gets a reward and the score on the leader board. In addition, SHYGER is implemented to provide rich visual feedback and the UIs are designed and laid out to be easy and intuitive to use the following user-centered design aspects such as the reminiscence of childhood, the gameplay of traditional games, and human behavior characteristics.

3.2   Study Design and Procedure

We conducted a user study that compares single- and multi-player experiences of our AR game. The study was in a within-subject design where participants tried SHYGER in both conditions, and collected feedback from the participants through questionnaires, observation, and interview. A user study session took about 40 min including a 20-min interview. We recruited 10 participants (8 males and 2 females at the age between 25 and 54). All participants had previous experiences of playing PC or mobile games, and six of them had played AR games like Pokémon GO. Two participants have never experienced AR applications, while the other eight had prior experiences of mobile AR applications.

Two researchers coordinated to conduct the studies and observe the participants, taking notes of various aspects of user experience in SHYGER, including user's facial expressions, interaction between the participants while placing physical objects prior to the game (e.g., playing rock-paper-scissors to decide who will go first, dialogue to negotiate on how to arrange physical objects, etc.), and the user's movement to check the effect of user affordance. We compared and analyzed these observations with the user feedback from interviews. After the participants played the game in both conditions, we conducted a face-to-face semi-structured interview, and collected subjective feedback on overall user satisfaction, fun, usability, and experience sharing. In addition to collecting qualitative feedback, interviews also asked rating questions (1: negative–10: positive). Finally, we investigated whether the user has experienced the intended user journey design, and whether the usability has improved through the user affordance approach focusing on shared experience.

3.3   Results and Discussion

The main focus of our study is to explore how the shared AR experience could improve the overall user experience and satisfaction. Figure 3 summarizes the results of observation and interview, comparing various aspects of user experience between single- and multi-player conditions. The results of the observation are based on the following measurements: facial expressions during the game, asking questions about the game, and changes in the range of motion when searching for the shyger during the game, summarized into a rating scale of 1 to 10.

As shown in Fig. 3, the participants had better user experiences when playing SHYGER with other participants and being involved in more physical movement and higher engagement. From the results of the interview, the participants rated the multi-player condition significantly higher ($W = 45$, $p < 0.01$) than the single-player one in terms of affordance, interest, immersive experience, and experience sharing. While most participants perceived the shared experience as being more intuitive, interesting, and immersive, some of them gave feedback on how the single-player experience could be also improved to be more engaging. In addition, suggested improvements included: allowing users to choose from various characters to play with, making game logic more complex (such as hiding algorithms), and making games more versatile (e.g., various levels in missions).

The results of user satisfaction on the game elements and UIs are shown in Fig. 4. The participants mostly rated the user interface design as being significantly positive ($W = 55$, $p < 0.01$) in terms of the ease of use, intuitive, and design satisfaction. However, the results revealed that there is room for improvement in terms of game elements such as fun factor, game character, and game scenario, especially when compared to other AR and non-AR games. To sum up qualitative feedback, most participants mentioned that SHYGER is simpler than other similar PC or mobile shooting games. Some wanted more variety to interactions with the virtual character (e.g., lure with toy or food), while others suggested using more intuitive interactions like touch gestures (e.g., rubbing on the screen to tickle the shyger). The satisfaction was high in terms of ease of use, character suitability, and intuitive design.

Overall, the results of our user study indicated that users had satisfactory experiences while playing SHYGER. Design principles applied to the development process appeared to be effective in terms of nudging the user's physical movement and providing an intuitive touch interface. Our design approach of considering shared experience was constructive as most participants' feedback showed improved user experiences when playing the game together with another participants. Using the pre-game activities of arranging physical objects as a strategical element for collaboration/competition was also considered as novel and interesting. Finally, our observations suggested that future AR game development projects should consider shared experience in design scenarios, thinking

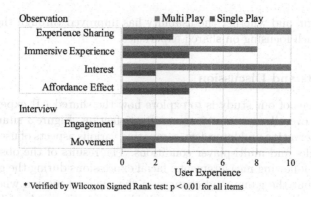

Fig. 3. Results of user experience on observation and interview.

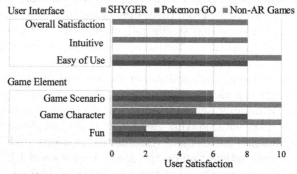

Fig. 4. Results of user satisfaction on user interface and game element.

of how the game in development could be played and enjoyed by multiple users even when technical features are focusing on a single user scenario.

4   Conclusion

In this paper, we presented the methodology and scenario of a user-centered design especially focusing on AR shared experience by applying them to a case of developing an AR game named SHYGER. We described our design process and decisions including the user journey, user affordance, and design requirements. We also conducted a preliminary user study and observed that our approach of considering shared experience in designing AR games could improve the overall user experience and satisfaction. For future works, we envision further developing SHYGER for a lightweight AR glasses, using a natural gesture interface.

Acknowledgements. This work was supported by Institute of Information & communications Technology Planning & Evaluation (IITP) grant funded by the Korea government (MSIT) (No. 2017-0-01849, Development of Core Technology for Real-Time Image Composition in Unstructured In-outdoor Environment).

References

1. Billinghurst, M., Clark, A., Lee, G.: A survey of augmented reality. Found. Trends Hum. Comput. Interact. **8**(2–3), 73–272 (2015)
2. Billinghurst, M., Kato, H., Poupyrev, I.: The magicbook: a transitional AR interface. Comput. Graph. **25**(5), 745–753 (2001)
3. Eklund, L., Johansson, M.: Played and designed sociality in a massive multiplayer online game. Eludamos J. Comput. Game Cult. **7**(1), 35–54 (2013)
4. Garrett, J.J.: The Elements of User Experience: User-Centered Design for the Web and Beyond. New Riders Publishing, San Francisco (2010)
5. Kaptelinin, V.: The Encyclopedia of Human-Computer Interaction. The Interaction Design Foundation. https://www.interaction-design.org/literature/book/the-encyclopedia-of-human-computer-interaction-2nd-ed/affordances
6. Kaptelinin, V., Nardi, B.: Affordances in HCI: toward a mediated action perspective. In: Proceedings of the SIGCHI Conference on Human Factors in Computing Systems, CHI 2012, pp. 967–976 (2012)
7. Meakin, B.: Gaming as a shared experience: Fortnite and Pokémon Go, July 2018. https://medium.com/the-megacool-blog/gaming-as-a-shared-experience-fortnite-and-pok%C3%A9mon-go-35f39546c9f7
8. Miaskiewicz, T., Kozar, K.A.: Personas and user-centered design: how can personas benefit product design processes? Des. Stud. **32**(5), 417–430 (2011)
9. Perez, L.: Designing intuitive UI/UX for AR, January 2019. https://www.zappar.com/blog/designing-intuitive-uiux-ar
10. Poupyrev, I., Tan, D.S., Billinghurst, M., Kato, H., Regenbrecht, H., Tetsutani, N.: Developing a generic augmented-reality interface. Computer **35**(3), 44–50 (2002)
11. Rohrer, C.: When to use which user-experience research methods, October 2014. https://www.nngroup.com/articles/which-ux-research-methods
12. Schmalstieg, D., et al.: The studierstube augmented reality project. Presence Teleoper. Virtual Environ. **11**(1), 33–54 (2002)
13. Soegaard, M.: The Glossary of Human Computer Interaction. The Interaction Design Foundation. https://www.interaction-design.org/literature/book/the-glossary-of-human-computer-interaction/affordances
14. Somerville, D.: Using nudge theory to achieve a competitive edge with your UX, talk at the CharityComms conference (2018)
15. Wilson, T.: The principles of good UX for augmented reality, November 2017. https://uxdesign.cc/the-principles-of-good-user-experience-design-for-augmented-reality-d8e22777aabd

Evaluating Character Embodiment and Trust Towards AI Based on a Sleep Companion

Andreas Schmid[1]([✉]), Maximilian Fuchs[1], Dominik Anhorn[1],
Mareike Gabele[1,2], and Steffi Hußlein[1]

[1] Magdeburg-Stendal University of Applied Sciences, Magdeburg, Germany
andreas.schmid@stud.h2.de
[2] Otto von Guericke University Magdeburg, Magdeburg, Germany

Abstract. Artificial Intelligence (AI) enables new ways of user interaction with tech products. Due to their design, the systems appear as a black box to the user, which leads to a lack of trust towards the AI. This work answers the questions: 1) How can the character of an AI be embodied through shape, tactility and movement? 2) How can a combination of this embodiment and tangible user interaction enhance the relationship of trust of the user towards an AI? An AI-enhanced sleep companion ("SleepMate") is used to specify the field of application in a scenario that affects a variety of user groups. A preliminary study (n = 22) was conducted to identify key points in the context of sleeping and waking-up using the Diary Method. A structured interview was conducted to evaluate how users react to the execution of the prototype and the concept of tactility, movement, light and sound in the context of AI and to study how embodiment changes trust towards smart assistants. When using SleepMate, the results show that 76.5% of the participants feel more involved in the AI decision-making process. They have a better understanding of the system's behaviour and greater trust in the correct execution of tasks and respect for privacy. 64.7% see advantages in physical interaction and embodiment of AI compared to voice control. The results provide a basis for future research on the effects of user interaction and embodiment in AI relationships.

Keywords: Artificial Intelligence · Interaction Design · Tactile interaction

1 Introduction

The number of devices in homes and personal lives of people using artificial intelligence (AI) seems to increase [1, 2]: Voice-activated assistants featuring AI, e.g. Alexa [3, 4], reach a wide range of customers and nearly everyone knows personalized suggestions [1, 5]. This is changing the way of how people interact with their devices.

People tend to assign a character to objects because it helps to categorize them and adjust the expectations on it. It also masks some of the complexity of the object, which supports the interaction process [6].

However, this cannot be transferred directly to the digital world. Most digital devices resemble each other in their physical appearance as well as in their usability. Data Processing is neither understandable to the average user, nor is it communicated

© Springer Nature Switzerland AG 2020
C. Stephanidis and M. Antona (Eds.): HCII 2020, CCIS 1224, pp. 470–479, 2020.
https://doi.org/10.1007/978-3-030-50726-8_62

through the device [7]. Because of that, most of today's AI systems appear like a Black Box [8] to the user which leads to a lack of transparency in how the system works due to missing feedback. This leads to a lack of trust from the user towards the AI. To approach these issues, the following research questions were developed:

1) How can the character of an AI be embodied through shape, tactility and movement? 2) How can a combination of this embodiment and tangible user interaction enhance the relationship of trust of the user towards an AI?

Thereby, the scope was narrowed down to the concept and functional prototype of a sleep companion ("SleepMate"). It is backed by an AI concept giving context for the scenario of waking up and going to sleep. Tangible user interaction is achieved by using three different caps, which can be put on the body of SleepMate and influence the character of the AI. The study carried out with the prototype shows, that 76,47% of the people like the idea of participation in the decision-process of AI. Also, 58,82% of the participants trust SleepMate more than other digital assistants.

The main contributions are the results of a small-scale study on the prototype SleepMate. The results show, that the participants of the study see advantages in SleepMate at physical interaction and embodiment of AI compared to voice control. They also confirmed the tendency that embodiment can enhance trust relationships between users and AI.

2 Related Work

Actual assistants, regardless of their implementation, mainly communicate through voice or text interfaces. This communication is supported by sound notifications, visual feedback (e.g. lights, screens) and the design of the product the assistant is embedded in. The design mostly resembles to brand guidelines, with little differences between the tactile elements of different brands. Most devices feature a minimalistic shape, some are partly covered in fabric [9, 10].

There are a lot of devices and apps that promise to tackle the problem of bad sleep and sleeping behaviour [11–14]. Some of them are simple data trackers, others are AI-enhanced. For alarm clocks, haptic, visual and tactile feedback was the most desired features. Also, simplicity in use was an often-mentioned feature [15].

Researchers at Microsoft proposed 18 Guidelines which are applicable for Human-AI interaction and were tested and verified with AI professionals on various projects [16]. Also, patterns developed by Smarter Patterns concerning form, functional approach and ethics are used to develop the AI-concept of SleepMate [17].

Enhancing transparency is not inevitably enhancing trust. When systems are designed for transparency they give up on trust and focus on control. Marisa Tschopp distinguishes between reliance and trust over the feeling of betrayal [18]. In this work, this distinction is not made, when the word "trust" is used, it carries both meanings. This helps to focus on the aspect of how the embodiment and interaction can affect trust relationships, which includes both, reliance and trust. Trust can define the way people interact with technology [7].

3 Design Process

According to research question 1, a set of interaction patterns is developed and applied to a prototype in the design process.

The process is split into three main steps: 1) conduction of a preliminary study to gather insight on sleeping behaviour and habits to examine the field in which the prototype will be domiciled, 2) development of the interaction patterns and their merge into a functional prototype, 3) evaluation of the patterns using the prototype.

3.1 Preliminary Study

To gather insight about sleep behaviour, a preliminary study was conducted, using the diary method [29, 30]. The group of participants consisted of 22 people (M = 32.8 yrs.; SD = 14.9) with various socio-demographic backgrounds. Over one week, they were given the same five questions about their habits and sleep behaviour every day via a WhatsApp text message at the same time in the morning [19].

The main results were, that the average sleep time of all participants exceeded 7 h on just two days within the study period of one week. This is less than the recommended [20]. A major part does not sleep a continuous amount during the week with no indications for an established rhythm. 11 of 22 participants set more than one alarm clock or snoozed on at least 3 of 7 days.

3.2 Interaction Patterns and Prototype

Information used to develop the patterns and the prototype was gathered from the preliminary study on sleeping behaviour and habits, a market analysis of devices connected to sleep and behaviour tracking as well as smart devices with and without AI and relevant scholarly papers and books on AI, sleeping behaviour and HMI [21, 22]. Additionally, the lecturing notes and workshop-results of the courses "Design Methods" and "Into Things" of the Magdeburg-Stendal University of Applied Sciences were compiled and accounted.

Based on a first Low-Fi-Prototype a basic shape for the device was developed. It is a cylindrical object with an average height of about 7 cm and a diameter of 14 cm to fit the diameter of the palm of an average hand (Fig. 1). It is divided into two parts, a base part which contains the electronic components and a top part which features exchangeable heads with different surfaces, so-called "caps". It is assumed that SleepMate can detect if a person is in the same room using appearance sensors.

Because the caps are the main instrument of tactile interaction, a variety of materials was gathered, and 16 samples were 3D-printed to research different haptic experiences of surfaces. For the final prototype 3D printing was used, allowing for the incorporation of different tactile experiences into the design that has proven particularly suitable.

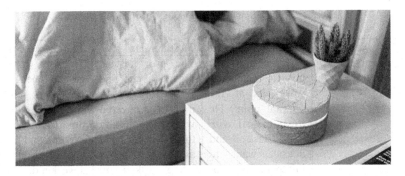

Fig. 1. SleepMate with the AI-Cap, one of the three interaction-elements

In addition to the prototype, an AI-concept was developed. It involves the acquisition of the user's fitness, social, productivity, calendar, health, and sleep data, as well as data about the usage of technical devices and services the user already owns (e.g. Wearables, Smartphones, Online Services) as well as built-in sensors of SleepMate (appearance sensors, light sensor). Additionally, external databases (like public health databases) are used as a reference. Based on that, the AI generates personalized recommendations for going to sleep, the duration of sleep and waking up, which are improved by continuous machine learning [21, 23].

The interaction mechanism with the device and the character of the AI are focused on tactile interaction. The character trait of the AI is influenced based on the caps that are put on the top part of SleepMate [24–26]. This significantly affects the behaviour of SleepMate by shifting different scales of character traits (e.g. energy or strictness) and enables or disables certain functions e.g. when waking up its user [24]. To develop and test the interaction mechanisms, three different scenarios, as well as the corresponding instances of caps and interaction patterns were developed (See Table 1).

Construction. For the movement patterns, three servo motors with gears and gear racks were integrated into the base part. Also, a NeoPixel RGB LED Ring for the light patterns is located there. The 3D-printed parts are built of white matte and transparent PLA-Filament. This enabled to illuminate the gap between the top and bottom part (See Fig. 2). The NeoPixel Ring, the servo motors and a Bare Conductive Touch-Board for external speakers, are connected to an Arduino ESP-32. Through a Bluetooth connection between the ESP-32 and an Android device, it is possible to remotely control the prototype and execute the scenarios repeatedly for the Wizard-of-Oz (WOz) evaluation [27, 28].

For a video of the described expressions, please refer to: https://youtu.be/SXLBkJXhFH4

Table 1 Scenarios and corresponding interaction patterns.

	1) AI-driven cap	2) Strict cap	3) Relaxed cap
Requirements of the user	The user wants to go to bed and wake up at the optimal point. He trusts the AI with that task and doesn't want to influence the process.	The user has an urgent event and wants to be optimally recovered while not missing this event, and assure that he is being woken on time.	The user wants to go to bed and wake up relaxed and with flexible time frames in the evening and morning, for example at a weekend.
Influence on AI character traits	default, neutral character traits	character traits shift to stricter behaviour	character traits shift to more relaxed behaviour
Expression of the AI character	Movement, light and sound patterns are minimalistic and balanced. Snoozing disabled.	Faster and bigger movements. Brighter and more frequent light sequence. Pushing sounds. Snoozing disabled.	Slower, smaller movements. More dim and slower light sequence. Relaxing sounds. Snoozing enabled.
Appearance of the cap	Neutral design with a pattern resembling a neuronal network. Communicates neutrality.	Surface covered in cone-shaped peaks. Communicates strictness and energy. Physically prevents snoozing.	Soft and wave-like surface. Communicates relaxedness and lightness. Invites the user to touch its surface.
Image of the cap			

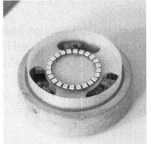

Fig. 2. From left to right: Internal construction, middle layer with NeoPixel LED ring and AI-driven cap on the device.

4 Evaluation

According to our research questions, a structured interview was conducted to 1) evaluate how users react to the execution of the prototype and the concept of tactility, movement, light and sound in the context of AI and 2) study how embodiment changes trust towards smart assistants.

4.1 Apparatus and Procedure

After an initial study (n = 6) at an exhibition, the evaluation was adjusted. The final survey form consisted of four parts: 1) questions about the socio-demographic background, the preferred waking-up device and the previous experience with AI; 2) specific questions regarding trust towards existing AI devices, their reliability and possible application in exemplary situations; 3) is based on the AttrakDiff 2 short questionnaire [29] which uses the semantic differential to determine the handling and appearance of the prototype; 4) questions about the participant's opinions on Sleep-Mate. Part 4 included five questions about trust towards AI that were already asked in part 1 and 2 of the survey, which allowed for a direct comparison between existing smart devices and SleepMate.

The study was conducted in a seminar room, where SleepMate with its nightstand (Fig. 1) was placed on a desk with the neutral cap on the top and the other caps beside. To allow for an easier analysis a digital survey form was used.

After filling part 1 and 2 of the survey, participants were encouraged to investigate the prototype and the caps on their own and try possible interaction. After that, the participants were given an explanation on the functions of the device and told to complete the survey (part 3 and 4) [30].

Seventeen persons, ranging in age from 14 to 55 years (M = 31.4 yrs; SD = 12.7) participated. Since the usage of an alarm clock (or comparable devices) is a normal behaviour, no further exclusion criteria were used.

4.2   Analysis

Simple "scheme-checking" was eliminated through alternation of the position of the positive and the negative word pairs. Also, the AttrakDiff 2 short questionnaire was used to reduce bias [29]. The survey forms were evaluated after all participants had given in their forms.

For closed questions 5- and 7-point Likert scales were used. In the evaluation Top and Bottom Box scorings were grouped, leaving out the midpoint, and converted into percentage values [31, 32].

4.3   Results

52.9% of the participants use digital assistants at least once a week. 70,59% use smartphone alarms for waking up. But only 29.41% could image using digital assistants in their bedroom. Reasons are, inter alia, bad control surfaces and privacy concerns.

The short AttrakDiff has shown mainly positive feedback towards the appearance of SleepMate, with ratings towards the adjectives elegant (M = 1.4), good (M = 1.5), simple (M = 2.2), practical (M = 2.3) and predictable (M = 3.2).

Participants stated the following reasons for using SleepMate in their bedroom: Better interaction than smartphones, no usage of smartphones in the bedroom, functionality is aimed at supporting sleep, aesthetic reasons.

All participants stated that light and movement clearly support the character of the AI. Furthermore, 64.7% see advantages in physical interaction and embodiment of AI compared to voice control. Stated reasons being more unambiguous control, no usage of microphones, no need to talk, possible usage with closed eyes. In addition, 58,82% of the participants would trust SleepMate more than other assistants, because it is more personal, more tangible and less concerning when it comes to privacy.

Table 2. Results of comparable questions in pars 1/2 and 4.

Question	Digital assistants	SleepMate
The device understands the assigned task	70.59%	88.24%
The device will perform the assigned task in a satisfactory manner	76.47%	88.24%
The device respects my privacy	23.53%	58.82%
Do you feel involved in the decision-making of the AI?	41.18%	76.47%
Could you imagine using (1) digital assistants/(2) SleepMate in your bedroom?	29.41%	64.71%

5 Discussion

The results of this work show, that an enhancement of trust from the user towards the AI is favourable. It also shows that there is mistrust and privacy concerns against companies that acquire personal data. A connection between privacy-related trust concerns and bedrooms is suspected. Still, character and embodiment can have an influence on trust relationships with AI. The user feels more involved in the decision-making process (Table 2). A similar effect of tangible interaction is described by the Interaction Design Foundation for interaction that focuses on "doing" instead of "receiving" [33].

Also, there are indications that the embodiment of AI can be attained through shape, tactility and movement. This is shown by mainly positive feedback on Sleep-Mate with tendencies to the attributes "predictable", "practical", "simple" and "good", as mentioned in the results. The radical approach of not giving control by design shows the need for a balance between transparency and control to earn trust. There remains a gamble between trust and control when transparency in design is focused [18].

58,82% of the participants of the study said that they would trust SleepMate more than other digital assistants. They also ranked SleepMate more positive than other digital assistants even though the rehearsals did not use it for quite a long time. It remains to be noted, that building up trust is a complicated and delicate process [7] and that over time relationships of trust can change in a positive and negative direction.

Also, the participants stated that tactility, light and movement support the character of the AI, with 64.7% seeing advantages in physical interaction and embodiment of AI compared to voice control. This shows, that a combination of embodiment and tangible user interaction can enhance the relationship of trust of the user towards an AI, as predicted in the research question.

6 Future Work

An evaluation in a sleep environment, either by using a WOz-approach or implementation of alarm clock functionality into the prototype, would enable to gain more insight into Human-AI relationships in the given scenario. To verify the evaluation and find effects on long-term trust-building [7] this evaluation could be extended over a longer period of time. Because the approach was narrowed down to one specific scenario and use-case there is room for improvement in the prototypic approach as well as a generalisation for a broader range of application. This allows for the design patterns to be transferred to other use-cases.

7 Conclusion

This paper contributed to the evaluation process on how the character of an AI can be embodied through shape, tactility and movement and how the combination of this embodiment and tangible user interaction can enhance the relationship of trust of the user towards an AI. The main contributions are the results of a small-scale study on the prototype SleepMate. The results show, that the participants of the study see advantages in SleepMate at physical interaction and embodiment of AI compared to voice control. Also, the embodiment is described with positive adjectives which indicates positive character-shaping effects. They also confirmed the tendency that embodiment can enhance trust relationships between users and AI, with 58,82% of the participants saying, that they trust SleepMate more than other digital assistants. The developed interaction patterns can be used in projects in the field of human-AI-interaction to build up trust and communicate character.

It can be assumed, that the character and embodiment of an AI, as well as tangible interaction, can increase the trust of the user towards the AI.

Acknowledgments. We would like to thank BMW Designworks (especially Yedan Qian and Claudia Berger) for their support, feedback and cooperation.

References

1. Nadimpalli, M.: Artificial intelligence – consumers and industry impact. Int. J. Econ. Manage. Sci. **06**, 429 (2017)
2. Pettey, C.: Gartner Says Artificial Intelligence Is a Game Changer for Personal Devices (2018).   https://www.gartner.com/en/newsroom/press-releases/2018-01-08-gartner-says-artificial-intelligence-is-a-game-changer-for-personal-devices. Accessed 19 Mar 2020
3. Amazon Alexa Offizielle Webseite: Was ist Alexa?. https://developer.amazon.com/de/alexa. Accessed 19 Mar 2020
4. Google Home. https://store.google.com/de/product/google_home. Accessed 19 Mar 2020
5. Sen, I.: How AI helps Spotify win in the music streaming world (2018). https://outsideinsight.com/insights/how-ai-helps-spotify-win-in-the-music-streaming-world/. Accessed 19 Mar 2020
6. Janlert, L.-E., Stolterman, E.: The character of things. Des. Stud. **18**, 297–314 (1997)
7. Siau, K., Wang, W.: Building trust in artificial intelligence, machine learning, and robotics. Cutter Bus. Technol. J. **31**, 47–53 (2018)
8. Latour, B.: Die Hoffnung der Pandora: Untersuchungen zur Wirklichkeit der Wissenschaft. Suhrkamp Taschenbuch Wissenschaft (2002)
9. Apple Inc.: Accessory Design Guidelines for Apple Devices (2019). https://developer.apple.com/accessories/Accessory-Design-Guidelines.pdf. Accessed 19 Mar 2020
10. Pyae, A., Joelsson, T.N.: Investigating the usability and user experiences of voice user interface: a case of Google home smart speaker. In: Proceedings of the 20th International Conference on Human-Computer Interaction with Mobile Devices and Services Adjunct, MobileHCI 2018. Association for Computing Machinery, New York (2018)
11. Apple: Use bedtime to track your sleep on your iPhone (2019). https://support.apple.com/en-us/HT208655. Accessed 19 Mar 2020
12. Sleep cycle alarm clock, https://www.sleepcycle.com/. Accessed 19 Mar 2020
13. Artashyan, A.: Xiaomi Xiao AI Smart Alarm Clock Review (2018). https://www.xiaomitoday.com/xiaomi-xiao-ai-smart-alarm-clock-review/. Accessed 19 Mar 2020
14. Bonjour | Smart Alarm Clock with Artificial Intelligence. https://www.kickstarter.com/projects/1450781303/bonjour-smart-alarm-clock-with-artificial-intellig. Accessed 19 Mar 2020
15. Lim, R.W., Wogalter, M.S.: Human factors design considerations of alarm clocks. In: Proceedings of the Human Factors and Ergonomics Society Annual Meeting, vol. 46, pp. 705–709 (2002)

16. Guidelines for Human-AI Interaction (2019). https://www.microsoft.com/en-us/research/uploads/prod/2019/01/Guidelines-for-Human-AI-Interaction-camera-ready.pdf. Accessed 19 Mar 2020

17. Myplanet: Design for AI (2019). https://smarterpatterns.com. Accessed 19 Mar 2020

18. Tschopp, M., Ruef, M.: AI & Trust - Stop asking how to increase trust in AI (2020). https://www.researchgate.net/publication/339530999_AI_Trust_-Stop_asking_how_to_increase_trust_in_AI. Accessed 19 Mar 2020

19. Yakubu-Sam, T.: Whatsapp diary study (2017). https://www.tobyys.com/blog-1/whatsappdiarystudy. Accessed 19 Mar 2020

20. Blackham, A., Mcdaniel, J.R., Chauvin, I.A., et al: Annals of sleep medicine sleep disruptions and disorders in children and adolescents: a review of the impact of parents and family on sleeping behaviors (2019). https://www.researchgate.net/publication/335703000_Annals_of_Sleep_Medicine_Sleep_Disruptions_and_Disorders_in_Children_and_Adolescents_A_Review_of_the_Impact_of_Parents_and_Family_on_Sleeping_Behaviors. Accessed 19 Mar 2020

21. Mainzer, K.: Künstliche Intelligenz – Wann übernehmen die Maschinen? Technik im Fokus (2019)

22. Peever, J., Fuller, P.M.: Neuroscience: a distributed neural network controls rem sleep. Curr. Biol. 26, R34–R35 (2016)

23. Sambasivan, N., Holbrook, J.: Toward responsible AI for the next billion users. Interactions 26, 68–71 (2018)

24. Mugge, R., Govers, P.C.M., Schoormans, J.P.L.: The development and testing of a product personality scale. Des. Stud. 30 (2009). https://doi.org/10.1016/j.destud.2008.10.002

25. Mateas, M., Sengers, P.: Narrative intelligence. AAAI Technical report FS-99-01 (1999)

26. Mostafa, M., Crick, T., Calderon, Ana C., Oatley, G.: Incorporating emotion and personality-based analysis in user-centered modelling. In: Bramer, M., Petridis, M. (eds.) Research and Development in Intelligent Systems XXXIII, pp. 383–389. Springer, Cham (2016). https://doi.org/10.1007/978-3-319-47175-4_29

27. Munteanu, C., Boldea, M.: MDWOZ: a wizard of oz environment for dialog systems development. In: Proceedings of LREC (2000). http://www.lrec-conf.org/proceedings/lrec2000/pdf/104.pdf. Accessed 19 Mar 2020

28. Benzmüller, C., Fiedler, A., Gabsdil, M., et al: A wizard of oz experiment for tutorial dialogues in mathematics. In: Proceedings of AI in Education (AIED 2003) Workshop on Advanced Technologies for Mathematics Education (2003)

29. Hassenzahl, M., Burmester, M., Koller, F.: AttrakDiff: Ein Fragebogen zur Messung wahrgenommener hedonischer und pragmatischer Qualität. In: Ziegler, J., Szwillus, G. (eds.) Mensch & Computer 2003. Interaktion in Bewegung, pp. 187–196. B.G. Teubner, Stuttgart, Leipzig (2003). https://doi.org/10.1007/978-3-322-80058-9_19

30. Finding Usability Problems through Heuristic Evaluation. http://www.csc.villanova.edu/~beck/csc8570/jim2.htm. Accessed 20 Mar 2020

31. Likert Skala | Auswertungsmöglichkeiten und Einflusskomponenten (2018). https://novustat.com/statistik-blog/likert-skala-auswertungsmoeglichkeiten.html. Accessed 19 Mar 2020

32. Kirchhoff, S.: Der Fragebogen: Datenbasis, Konstruktion und Auswertung. 5. Auflage. VS Verlag für Sozialwissenschaften | Springer Fachmedien Wiesbaden GmbH (2010). https://doi.org/10.1007/978-3-531-92050-4

33. Challis, B.: The Encyclopedia of Human-Computer Interaction, 2nd edn. In: The Interaction Design Foundation. https://www.interaction-design.org/literature/book/the-encyclopedia-of-human-computer-interaction-2nd-ed/tactile-interaction. Accessed 19 Mar 2020

Usability Study of a Pre-anesthesia Evaluation App in an University Hospital: Before the Revision of User Interface

Po-Yuan Shih[1,2] and Meng-Cong Zheng[1(✉)]

[1] Department of Industrial Design, National Taipei University of Technology,
Taipei, Taiwan
zmcdesign@gmail.com
[2] Department of Anesthesiology, National Taiwan University Hospital,
Taipei, Taiwan

Abstract. A pre-anesthesia evaluation app named EVAN was developed to facilitate anesthesiologists in their daily practice. EVAN contained a well-organized interface for medical records and an evaluation entry page. The purpose of this study is to assess the usability of EVAN and to find the weakness in the user interface before the revision. Twenty participants were recruited in this study with three components: user task analysis, questionnaires, and semi-structured interview. During the user task analysis, participants were asked to complete 16 tasks under monitoring. The second component of the study is questionnaires, consisted of SUS and AttrakDiff-Short. According to the results, seven participants completed all the tasks successfully. Two tasks had the most failures (8 and 7 failures, respectively). Participants were unable to find a specific function due to inadequate clues on the interactive buttons. Results of task analysis also revealed that the current logic of data storage which aimed to prevent accidental deletion, was not intuitive for most participants. Despite the drawbacks, the gradings of SUS questionnaire was 80.6 ± 14.4, which is an above average result. Scores from the AttrakDiff-Short were all positive, for both pragmatic quality, hedonic quality, and attractiveness. The results of this study are summarized and integrated for the revision of EVAN.

Keywords: User interface · Usability · Anesthesia · Electronic medical record

1 Introduction

A successful surgery requires a high-quality anesthesia. A good pre-anesthesia evaluation is a crucial step for high-quality anesthesia. To complete the evaluation, anesthesiologists must check the medical records, including laboratory examinations and image studies, perform the physical examination, and fill in the evaluation document. Previously in National Taiwan University Hospital (NTUH), a top-notch medical center in Taiwan, anesthesiologists have to write down the evaluation results in paper. To improve the evaluation efficiency of the above meticulous process, an intuitive electronic medical record viewing system and a convenient data entry page are needed. In 2018, a pre-anesthesia evaluation information system was launched. It consisted of a

C. Stephanidis and M. Antona (Eds.): HCII 2020, CCIS 1224, pp. 480–487, 2020.
https://doi.org/10.1007/978-3-030-50726-8_63

web page and a mobile application(app). The web page was only for filling in the electronic version of the evaluation form. The app was named EVAN, as "EValuation for ANesthesiologist". It was an iOS-running app on iPad mini, and its user interface (UI) was designed by the Design Psychology Lab of National Taipei University of Technology. EVAN featured an electronic medical record system and an evaluation entry interface. This empirical study is held to evaluate the usability and the reference of future updates of UI design.

2 Methods

2.1 Design Concepts

Two main methods were used to clarify the user needs. Clinical shadowing, where the designers followed and observed the anesthesiologists undergoing the pre-anesthesia evaluation, was used to understand the usage scenarios. After clinical shadowing, the anesthesiologists were interviewed. With these methods, designers could understand the details of pre-anesthesia evaluation and expectations from the users.

The users, in this case anesthesiologists, used EVAN for two major purpose. First, EVAN was used to check the patients' medical records, laboratory examinations, and image studies. Thus, EVAN should contain a well-organized interface for all types of medical data. (Figure 1) The categories were organized according to the users' preference. Second, EVAN was used to fill the pre-anesthesia evaluation form. A questionnaire-like interface with clear hierarchy is essential. (Figure 2) When anesthesiologists filled the form in front of the patient, they were easily interrupted. To prevent the unsaved evaluation from accidental deletion, we designed a "Confirm" button for every category of the questionnaire. In addition, the questionnaire was saved automatically when the users exited the questionnaire page with the top right button.

2.2 Participants

Twenty participants were recruited in this study. All the participants were the attending anesthesiologists or anesthesia residents of NTUH who were authorized to perform the pre-anesthesia evaluation.

2.3 Procedures

This study composed of three components, including task analysis, questionnaires, and semi-structured interview. All procedures were conducted in an isolated room with a researcher and a research assistant.

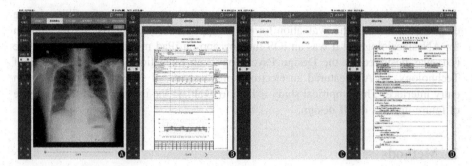

Fig. 1. The interface for different types of medical reports and records. A, medical image; B, previous medical record; C, the list of previous pre-anesthesia evaluation; D, the document of the pre-anesthesia evaluation.

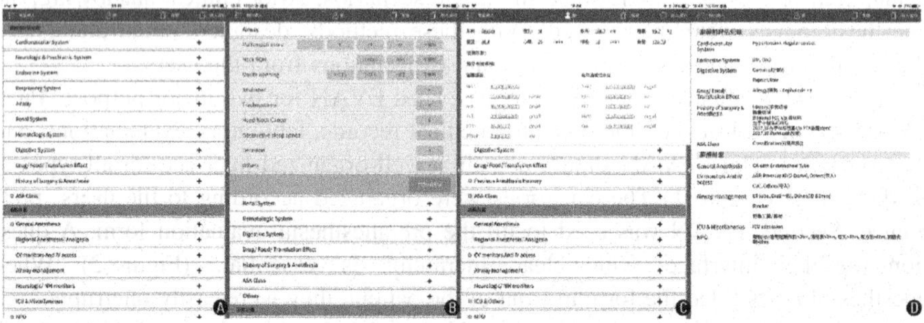

Fig. 2. The evaluation questionnaire entry page. A, the major topics of the evaluation; B, the hierarchy of the evaluation; C, the basic data window by pressing the top middle icon with the patient's name; D, the preview page by pressing the right second icon with the word preview in Traditional Chinese.

2.4 Task Analysis

Participants were asked to use an iPad mini to perform 16 tasks, with instructions projected on screen. The iPad mini was connected to a computer for surveillance and screen recording. The researcher also judged the completeness of every single task via the connected computer. Tasks were marked as failure when participants waived the task or when the completion time for each task was greater than 2 min. The results including failure and task time was recorded by the research assistant. Sixteen tasks consisted of three parts. The detailed tasks were shown in Table 2.

1. Searching the patient with specified conditions. (Task 1) Participants were given a date and a specific operating room number to find the patient.
2. Checking the patient data. (Task 2–8) Participants were asked to check the specified information, including previous pre-anesthesia evaluation, medical records, and laboratory examination results. The tasks were marked as a success only when they were performed in the expected manner.

3. Filling, saving, and previewing the pre-anesthesia evaluation under a paper instruction. (Task 9–16) Participants were asked to perform the tasks three times (first time: task 9–11, second time: task 13–15, and the third time: task 16).

The in-app activity was recorded with the connected computer and with the service from UXCAM.

2.5   Questionnaire

In the first part of the questionnaire, we investigate the participants' experience for EVAN. If the participants had used EVAN during any steps of their daily evaluation work, they were marked as experienced users. We used System Usability Scale (SUS), one of the most popular and standardized questionnaires, to assess the usability of EVAN. SUS consisted of 10 questions with alternating tone. [1]

We used AttrakDiff-Short to assess hedonic quality of user experience, the aspect that could not be evaluated with SUS. AttrakDiff-Short is extracted from the original AttrakDiff. The original AttrakDiff was developed by Hassenzahl and aimed to evaluate the hedonic quality of user interface.[2] Hassenzahl proposed that the perceived attractiveness of a user interface could be separated into two distinct factors: hedonic and pragmatic quality (HQ and PQ). While HQ is related to the quality and aesthetic aspects, PQ can be taken as the perceived usability. The AttrakDiff-Short questionnaire rated 10 pairs of contrasting adjectives in 7 scales. It consisted of 4 questions on PQ, 4 questions on HQ and 2 questions on the general attractiveness.

Table 1. Demographics of participants enrolled in this study

Participant demographics	Number
Total participants enrolled	20
Male	13
Female	7
Attending anesthesiologist	12
Anesthesia resident	8
Experienced user	8
Non-experienced user	12

2.6   Semi-structured Interview

The last component of the study was a semi-structured interview. The participants reviewed previous tasks and were urged to elaborate on their thinking process while performing the tasks. The researcher would make a detailed inquiry when the participants made mistakes or hesitate during the user tasks. After reviewing the tasks, participants were asked to share their opinions on EVAN in all aspects, including the pros and cons.

3 Results

Table 2. The results of SUS and task analysis

Results			
SUS	80.6 ± 14.4		
Experienced user	85.3 ± 13.5		
Non-experienced user	77.5 ± 12.8		
Task results	Task time (sec)	Number of failures	
Task 1: Find the patient under instruction	53.5 ± 14.8	0	
Task 2: Find specific data in previous pre-anesthesia evaluations	60.6 ± 30.7	7	
Task 3: Find specific data in medical records	30.2 ± 10.9	0	
Task 4: Find specific data in medical records	21.0 ± 5.9	0	
Task 5: Find specific data in medical records	33.4 ± 18.8	0	
Task 6: Find specific data in medical records	23.9 ± 17.2	0	
Task 7: Enter the evaluation entry page	10.7 ± 4.8	0	
Task 8: Find specific data in basic data window	16.5 ± 10.9	8	
Task 9: Fill the evaluation form (first time)	110.7 ± 38.1	2	
Task 10: Save the document (first time)	35.7 ± 33.5	4	
Task 11: Preview the results (first time)	52.1 ± 41.3	2	
Task 12: Find specific data in medical records	18.8 ± 9.4	1	
Task 13: Fill the evaluation form (second time)	115.7 ± 32.4	1	
Task 14: Save the document (second time)	11.2 ± 16.0	3	
Task 15: Preview the results (second time)	20.5 ± 14.0	1	
Task 16: Fill, save, and preview the document (third time)	21.0 ± 11.5	0	
Observational results in repeat tasks:	First time	Second time	Third time
Negligence of "Confirm"	11	3	0
Failed to save the document	4	3	0
Preview the document	2	1	0

3.1 Demographic Results

Twenty participants completed this study including 7 females and 13 males. The demographic data were shown in Table 1. Eight participants were experienced users, while 12 participants did not use EVAN in their daily practice. The mean age of the participants was 38.6 ± 11.0-year-old. The mean working experience was 13.4 ± 10.8 years.

3.2   Usability and User Experience

The average score of SUS was 80.6 ± 14.4. According to the Sauro-Lewis curved grading scale (CGS), EVAN was graded as A-, which was an above-average usability. We performed a subgroup analysis according to the participants' experience of EVAN. The scores of experienced and non-experienced users were 85.3 ± 13.5 and 77.5 ± 12.8, respectively. However, there were no differences in the SUS scores between experienced and non-experienced users. The AttrakDiff results were shown in Fig. 3. All the 10 adjectives in PQ, HQ, and ATT were positive, which showed a favorable attitude from the participants. The mean PQ, HQ, and ATT gradings were 1.2, 1.0, and 1.6 respectively.

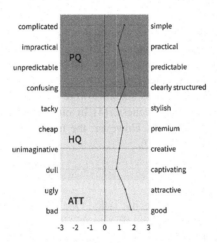

Fig. 3. The results of AttrakDiff Short questionnaire.

3.3   Task Analysis

The task time and the number of tasks failed was shown in Table 2. Eight participants completed all the tasks without failure. Among them, 5 participants were experienced users. Task 8 had the most failures, followed by task 2; 8 and 7 participants failed respectively. Eight participants failed in the task 8, and seven participants failed in task 2. Among eight participants who failed in task 8, three waived the task, while the other five completed the task with incorrect methods. Similar situations were noted in task 2, five out of seven participants completed the task in incorrect ways.

As mentioned previously, we asked the participants to fill, save, and review the evaluation form three times. One behavior noted during filling the evaluation was that the negligence of the "Confirm" button. (Figure 2B) Eleven out of twelve non-experienced users shared the same behavior in their first time. As shown in Table 2, the number of failures decreased as the participants gained experience while performing tasks.

4 Discussion

4.1 Perceived Usability

In the questionnaire, we used SUS to assess perceived usability. The average rating of EVAN, a business app, was 80.6 ± 14.4. In a previous study by Kortum et al. [3], the top 10 mobile apps in platforms were rated 77.7 in SUS. It is surprising that a business app was rated higher than that of 10 popular apps. Part of the reason might be that EVAN was inadvertently compared with the hospital information system (HIS) in NTUH, and the UI design of HIS was not user-oriented designed. On the other hand, the high rating could also indicate the improved workflow while undergoing pre-anesthesia evaluation with EVAN. These steps might be cumbersome, and some non-experienced users said that they would incorporate EVAN in their workflow after the study. The AttrakDiff-Short ratings from the participants were positive in all PQ, HQ and ATT. Reasons for these results were similar with that of SUS. Participants pointed out that the most distinguish difference between the two was the well-organized information layouts with distinct hierarchy. In the past, the hedonic quality was more emphasized in web page and entertaining software. A study held by Schrepp et al. showed that PQ and HQ of business software were perceived independently by users and contributed equally to attractiveness. [4] In our study, EVAN was taken as an evaluation tool with high PQ (1.2). However, the high ATT gradings (1.6) could be partially owing to the high HQ (1.0).

4.2 Task Analysis

Many participants failed in two specific tasks. One of them was to find the patient's body weight in the basic data window. (Figure 2C) This information could be found in the "personal basic data page" after tapping button consisted of the patient's name and icon. However, eight participants could not recognize this functional button. During the interview, all the non-experienced users who successfully completed this task said that they found this function by accident. Although similar design was used for the "preview page", (Fig. 2D) almost all participants thought that the button with the word "preview" (in Traditional Chinese) made it easier to predict the function of the button. Thus, the number of participants failed to preview was far less than that of participants failed to find patient's body weight. Most of them agreed that it is an easy-to-remember function, but they thought the hint of the functional area should be more recognizable. This is one of the designs to be changed in the future updates.

The other task, in which seven participants failed, was to find a specified information from a list of previously assessed pre-anesthesia evaluation. The standard procedure was to look for the most recent evaluation, tap the list (white rectangle in Fig. 1C) to open the evaluation form and find the specified data in a previous evaluation report. Five of the failed participants did not picture an interactive bar for each evaluation. Instead, they pressed the "Ditto" button (the green button in the white rectangle in Fig. 1D), which function was to copy the content and paste it to a new evaluation form. Although they still have the right data, this task would still be viewed as a failure. Participants later revealed that they neglected the bar when seeing the

"Ditto" button. To improve the performance, the "Ditto" button should only be seen after viewing the content of the previous evaluation.

The most important finding in the screen recording was that the "Confirm" button was neglected initially by eleven participants. To prevent the whole entries being deleted without saving, we designed the "Confirm" button in every major topic. Once the users completed the questions under a major topic, they should click on the "Confirm" button to save the content within this topic. This logic was intended to save the whole entries in small parts instead of the whole document as pre-anesthesia evaluation rarely go uninterrupted. However, neglecting the "Confirm" button meant that all current entries in this topic were futile. During the interview, most participants, even those who completed this task successfully, mentioned that the button was easily neglected and impractical. On the other hand, they appreciate the concept of saving the document in small parts. These evidences gave us clues for future UI updates.

5 Conclusions and Future Works

In the current study, the UI design of EVAN was satisfactory for users in NTUH, but with minor flaws. These empirical results could be concluded into two major directions for future design:

1. Improve the hint of interactive areas: Most failures in the user tasks resulted from inadequate clues of the interactive buttons. One of the solutions is to enhance the metaphor of the interactive areas with icon and its adjacent keywords (as in the case of Fig. 2C). Another way is to increase the contrast between the interactive area and the background (as in the case of Fig. 1C).
2. Adjust the workflow for data storage to be more intuitive: The rationale of the "Confirm" button was to prevent accidental deletion. However, the logic of "saving document in parts" was not intuitive for many users. To correct the design flaw, the "Confirm" button will be cancelled. The mechanism of saving will be shifted to "automatic mode", with every change saved.

References

1. Lewis, J.R.: The system usability scale: past, present, and future. Int. J. Hum. Comput. Interact. **34**(7), 577–590 (2018)
2. Hassenzahl, M.: The interplay of beauty, goodness, and usability in interactive products. Hum. Comput. Interact. **19**(4), 319–349 (2004)
3. Kortum, P., Sorber, M.: Measuring the usability of mobile applications for phones and tablets. Int. J. Hum. Comput. Interact **31**(8), 518–529 (2015)
4. Schrepp, M., Held, T., Laugwitz, B.: The influence of hedonic quality on the attractiveness of user interfaces of business management software. Interact. Comput. **18**(5), 1055–1069 (2006)

Moral Robots? How Uncertainty and Presence Affect Humans' Moral Decision Making

Carolin Straßmann[✉][iD], Alina Grewe, Christopher Kowalczyk,
Alexander Arntz, and Sabrina C. Eimler[iD]

Institute of Computer Science, University of Applied Sciences Ruhr West,
Lützowstraße 5, 46236 Bottrop, Germany
{carolin.strassmann,alexander.arntz,sabrina.eimler}@hs-ruhrwest.de
{alina.grewe,christopher.kowalczyk}@stud.hs-ruhrwest.de

Abstract. Robots are ubiquitously embedded in today's work life and are increasingly applied in scenarios where they take moral decisions or at least give recommendations. Accordingly, this study investigates how physical presence and robot's uncertainty expression affect humans' moral decision-making and robot perception. In a 2 (uncertainty expression: certain/uncertain) × 2 (physical presence: present/video) between-subjects lab experiment (N = 91) the robot Pepper presented a moral dilemma and expressed its decision. It was then tested if participants align with this decision and how certain they are. Moreover, their judgment on the robot's decision as well as their perception of the robot were assessed. This study provides important implications for the human-robot interaction. Based on the present results, humans' decision-making was not affected by behavioral variations of the robot (at least for the dilemma used). However, those variables clearly influence humans' perception of the robot and therefore the interaction with it.

Keywords: Robots · Moral decision · Persuasion · Trolley problem · Social robotics

1 Introduction

The impact of robots on today's work life increases strongly. Robots and AI-based systems are increasingly applied in scenarios where they take moral decisions or at least give recommendations [10]. As humans tend to see robots as moral entities [8] and prior research already presented the persuasive impact of robots on humans' perceptions [6], it is important to investigate how they can influence our moral decision-making. Based on prior work [13,14], this study investigates how physical presence and robot's uncertainty affect humans' moral decision-making and robot perception.

© Springer Nature Switzerland AG 2020
C. Stephanidis and M. Antona (Eds.): HCII 2020, CCIS 1224, pp. 488–495, 2020.
https://doi.org/10.1007/978-3-030-50726-8_64

1.1   The Effect of Uncertainty Expression

Uncertainty expression enhances persuasive effects in human-human interaction [15]. According to [15], expressing uncertainty can be used to evoke deeper message processing and foster people's need for information. On the opposite, expressing certainty leads to stronger attitudes and more attitude congruent actions [15]. With regard to human-robot interaction, [5] investigated the effect of multi-modal uncertainty expression by a robotic system (virtual human). When a virtual human marks uncertainty using multi-modal utterances, users' recall ability of the presented content is negatively affected. Thus, uncertainty seems to lower the number of recalled arguments presented by the virtual human. This may be decisive when robots present moral dilemmas and decision recommendations, as the users might remember less of the presented scenarios and arguments. Accordingly, while presenting a moral dilemma and a decision recommendation, a robot is assumed to be less persuasive. Conducting two studies, [13,14] found that a humanoid robot expressing uncertainty leads to higher blame attribution, when the dilemma is unknown, but does not affect the evaluation of moral wrongness. As uncertainty is an emotional reaction that induces human-likeness perception [4], [13] assumed that robot's expressing uncertainty evoke a different person perception. Against their hypothesis, [13] did not find an influence of uncertainty expression on users' impression of the robot. This might be caused by the fact that both studies were observation studies and people evaluated videos of the robot instead of interacting with it.

1.2   The Effect of Physical Presence

The way robotic systems are embodied can be described by two different dimensions: presence and embodiment [9]. Embodiment describes the way the robot is manifested in the physical world. In contrast to being present in the same room, it might as well be mediated via a virtual environment or in a video. The effect of a robot's embodiment and presence are discussed controversially [7]. A review study concluded that physical presence evokes stronger effects in user's reactions and evaluations than the embodiment [9]. Thus, a robot that is telepresented via video evokes less reactions than a physical present robot. [7] argue that a physically co-present robot is taken more seriously, because the robot is potentially able to touch or even harm the user.

Building on those findings, the present work investigates the following hypotheses:

H1: Expressing uncertainty affects the persuasive effect of robot's in a moral decision scenario negatively.

H2: A physically present robot has a stronger persuasive effect than a telepresent robot.

H3: Expression uncertainty and the physical presence of the robot affect the perception of the robot positively.

2   Method

In a lab study with a 2×2 between-subjects design the effect of robot's certainty expression (certain vs. uncertain) and physical presence (present vs. video) on the participants' moral decision and robot perception were assessed.

2.1   Procedure

One week before the lab-part of the experiment, participants filled in a pre-questionnaire to assess person variables. At the beginning of the lab-part, participants signed informed consent and were introduced to the procedure. Afterwards, Pepper presented the moral dilemma in one of the four different experimental variations (certain and present, uncertain and present, certain and video, uncertain and video). When Pepper finished its explanation and stated its decision, participants filled in the second questionnaire and stated their own moral decision, decision certainty and their perception of the robot. At the end, the experimenter debriefed the participants and explained the detailed study goals that were not presented in the beginning.

2.2   Experimental Conditions

In the experiment the robot Pepper from SoftBank Robotics presented the so called trolley problem. In this moral dilemma five people on a rails track could be saved by pushing a big man on the rail road. In all conditions, the robot declared that his decision would be pushing the big man. Pepper explains the dilemma verbally and additionally presents a scribbled scenario on its tablet (see Fig. 1). To manipulate the expressed certainty of the robot, the verbal expression of the robot's decision with regard to the trolley problem was varied. In the certainty condition Pepper says "If I were in this situation I would push the fat man off the bridge to save more lives." and in the uncertainty condition uncertainty cues were added ("hm... I'm not sure. If I were in this situation and had to decide I would probably push the fat man off the bridge. Maybe this would be a better decision because more lives could be saved."). This variation was closely aligned with the manipulation described by [13]. Moreover, in terms of variation of the physical presence of the robot, Pepper was either present in the same room with the participants and explained the dilemma or a video of Pepper was presented. The video was recorded in the exact same position in which Pepper stands in the other condition. The screen, on which the video was displayed, was chosen and positioned in a manner in which the robot had the same size and distance to the participants as in the presence condition.

2.3   Measures

To measure the effect of the robot on human's decision making and evaluation of the robot, self-reported questionnaire-data were used. Participants rated their

Fig. 1. Pepper with the presented scenario on its tablet.

perception of the robot using the likeability (5 items, $\alpha = .815$), anthropomorphism (5 items, $\alpha = .725$), animacy (5 items, $\alpha = .756$) and perceived intelligence (5 items, $\alpha = .793$) sub-scale of the godspeed questionnaire [1]. Additionally, the perceived presence of the robot was measured with the physical presence sub-scale (9 items, $\alpha = .869$) and the social presence sub-scale (11 items, $\alpha = .776$) adapted from the Multimodal Presence Scale [11]. Moreover, the negative attitude towards robots scale (interaction (5 items, $\alpha = .751$), social (3 items, $\alpha = .755$) and emotion (6 items, $\alpha = .663$)) [12] was used. To analyse the effect of the robot on participants' moral decision, participants stated their decision (push the man or do nothing). Their answers were coded with regard to congruence to the robot's decision (congruent = pushing the man and in-congruent = do nothing). Using a 5-point Likert-scale participants stated their decision certainty (1 = "not certain at all", 5 = "completely certain"). In the end, participants' socio-demographic variables were queried.

2.4 Sample

Overall, 91 individuals volunteered in the experiment. 69 were male, while 22 were female. The average age was 22 ($M = 21.60$, $SD = 3.46$). All participants were students recruited from the University of Applied Sciences Ruhr West, where they received course credits for their participation. Gender was equally distributed across the experimental conditions. 68 people of the sample stated to be familiar with the presented trolley problem, whereas 23 participants where not familiar. As this turned out to be a decisive factor [13], the distribution among the conditions was checked. Again, people, who are familiar with the trolley problem, are equally spread among the groups.

3 Results

The moral decision of the participants (pushing the man or not) was coded with regard to the congruence to the robot's decision. To analyse whether participants were persuaded by the robot's decision statement (H1; H2), a chi-square test was calculated. The analysis revealed no significant differences between the experimental conditions. Table 1 presents the frequency values separated by the experimental groups. Thus, under the given circumstances of this study, no impact of the robot's characteristics (presence and certainty) on participant's moral decision was obtainable. Further, participants certainty of their moral decision was evaluated. Results of a 2-factorial ANOVA (Analysis of Variance) indicated no significant differences between the experimental conditions (see Table 2 for descriptive values). Thus, the hypotheses H1 and H2 have to be neglected based on the present data.

Table 1. Participants' moral decision in congruence with the decision of the robot.

	Present		Video		
	Certain	Uncertain	Certain	Uncertain	Total
Congruent	10	10	8	6	34
Incongruent	16	13	12	16	57

Multiple 2-factorial ANOVAs were calculated to analyse the effect of uncertainty expression and presence on participants' perception of the robot's animacy, likeability, perceived intelligence and anthropomorphism. Analyses for perceived anthropomorphism revealed a main effect of the robots' presence (H3). Pepper is rated as more anthropomorphic ($F(1, 87) = 5.963$, $p = .017$), when it is physically present in the room compared to the video condition. No effect of presence or uncertainty expression on perceived likeability was found. Furthermore, the analyses showed a significant interaction effect for the robot's presence and certainty. The robot is perceived as more alive ($F(1, 87) = 4.415$, $p = .039$) and intelligent ($F(1, 87) = 4.415$, $p = .039$) when it is physically present and uncertain about its decision compared to present and certain, video and certain and video and uncertain. Against this background, hypothesis H3 is supported by the given results.

Additionally, the effect of the experimental conditions on perceived presence was analyzed using 2-factorial ANOVAs. The ANOVA showed a significant effect for the robot's presence. The robot was rated as more present when it was physically present compared to being seen in the video ($F(1, 87) = 12.440$, $p = .001$). This supports a successful manipulation of physical presence. Please consult Table 2 for descriptive values.

Table 2. Descriptive values of the dependent variables in dependence of the experimental conditions.

	Present		Video	
	Certain	Uncertain	Certain	Uncertain
	M(SD)	*M(SD)*	*M(SD)*	*M(SD)*
Decision certainty	3.19 (1.20)	3.48 (1.38)	3.40 (1.23)	3.05 (1.40)
Likeability	3.80 (0.75)	4.11 (0.66)	3.72 (0.65)	3.66 (0.63)
Anthropomorphism	2.27 (0.88)	2.53 (0.54)	2.13 (0.64)	1.96 (0.60)
Animacy	2.72 (0.79)	3.03 (0.62)	2.68 (0.50)	2.40 (0.70)
Intelligence	3.51 (0.71)	3.46 (0.66)	3.64 (0.66)	3.20 (0.62)
Presence	3.41 (0.67)	3.61 (0.61)	3.04 (0.58)	3.00 (0.40)

4 Discussion, Limitations and Future Work

The present work investigated the effect of robot's uncertainty expression and presence on human's moral decision making and robot perception. Based on the present results, neither the robot's behavior nor it's physical presence affected the robots persuasive effect. However, physical presence and uncertainty expression affected human's perception of the robot. The robot was perceived as more human-like when it was physically present compared to a tele-present robot via video. In line with prior findings [9], this shows that the difference between face-to-face communication and video communication plays also a role when it comes to the interaction with a robot. Moreover, the robot's animacy was also rated higher when it was physically present and expressed uncertainty. Gestures are an important part of communication. These results are probably due to the fact that gestures are perceived more clearly in a face-to-face communication scenario. Further on, the participants rated the robot as the more intelligent when it was physically present and expressed uncertainty compared to the other three groups. This could have two reasons: First, like mentioned before, the face-to-face scenario and second, the uncertainty conveys a form of reflection of the situation which could be interpreted as intelligence. Differences between the present findings and those of prior work [13] are most likely caused by the physical presence of the robot. As [7] stated, physically present robots are taken more seriously. Consequently, the effect of uncertainty on robot perception only occurs for a physically present robot.

A central limitation of this study can be found in the comparably high affinity towards technology that can be assumed for students of a STEM-university, in which the study was conducted. This might go along with a more realistic view of the robot's capabilities and thus generally lead to lower levels of suggestibility. Also, the uneven distribution of men and women in the sample is a limitation. Since, however, it did not differ between the experimental conditions, potential gender effects are unlikely to have influenced the present findings systematically. Because of the distribution, differential effects could not be calculated, but they represent an important aspect for future studies because of gender differences in moral sensitivity [16] as well as conformity behavior [2,3]. Also, the dilemma as such might be extremely well-known, which impacts the decision-making process [13,14]. It needs to be discussed if a less known decision scenario with higher complexity would lead to different findings. Instead of using a moral dilemma that is a binary decision-task, future studies should investigate the persuasive effect of robots with a moral decision where people have to take multiple small decisions. Within more subtle decisions the persuasive effect of robots on human's decision making might be stronger.

5   Conclusion

This study provides important implications for the human-robot interaction. Based on the present results humans' decision-making was not affect by robots expression behavior and physical presence. However, those variables clearly influence humans' perception of the robot and therefore the interaction with it.

References

1. Bartneck, C., Kulić, D., Croft, E., Zoghbi, S.: Measurement instruments for the anthropomorphism, animacy, likeability, perceived intelligence, and perceived safety of robots. Int. J. Soc. Robot. **1**(1), 71–81 (2009)
2. Eagly, A.H.: Sex Differences in Social Behavior: A Social-Role Interpretation. Psychology Press, London (2013)
3. Eagly, A.H., Carli, L.L.: Sex of researchers and sex-typed communications as determinants of sex differences in influenceability: a meta-analysis of social influence studies. Psychol. Bull. **90**(1), 1–20 (1981)
4. Eyssel, F., Hegel, F., Horstmann, G., Wagner, C.: Anthropomorphic inferences from emotional nonverbal cues: a case study. In: 19th International Symposium in Robot and Human Interactive Communication, pp. 646–651. IEEE (2010)
5. Freigang, F., Kopp, S.: This is what's important – using speech and gesture to create focus in multimodal utterance. In: Traum, D., Swartout, W., Khooshabeh, P., Kopp, S., Scherer, S., Leuski, A. (eds.) IVA 2016. LNCS (LNAI), vol. 10011, pp. 96–109. Springer, Cham (2016). https://doi.org/10.1007/978-3-319-47665-0_9
6. Ham, J., Cuijpers, R.H., Cabibihan, J.J.: Combining robotic persuasive strategies: the persuasive power of a storytelling robot that uses gazing and gestures. Int. J. Soc. Robot. **7**(4), 479–487 (2015)
7. Hoffmann, L., Bock, N., Rosenthal vd Pütten, A.M.: The peculiarities of robot embodiment (emcorp-scale) development, validation and initial test of the embodiment and corporeality of artificial agents scale. In: Proceedings of the 2018 ACM/IEEE International Conference on Human-Robot Interaction, pp. 370–378 (2018)
8. Kahn Jr., P.H., et al.: "Robovie, you'll have to go into the closet now": children's social and moral relationships with a humanoid robot. Dev. Psychol. **48**(2), 303–314 (2012)
9. Li, J.: The benefit of being physically present: a survey of experimental works comparing copresent robots, telepresent robots and virtual agents. Int. J. Hum. Comput. Stud. **77**, 23–37 (2015)

10. Liptak, A.: Sent to prison by a software program's secret algorithms, May 2017. https://www.nytimes.com/2017/05/01/us/politics/sent-to-prison-by-a-software-programs-secret-algorithms.html

11. Makransky, G., Lilleholt, L., Aaby, A.: Development and validation of the multimodal presence scale for virtual reality environments: a confirmatory factor analysis and item response theory approach. Comput. Hum. Behav. **72**, 276–285 (2017)

12. Nomura, T., Suzuki, T., Kanda, T., Kato, K.: Measurement of negative attitudes toward robots. Interact. Stud. **7**(3), 437–454 (2006)

13. Stellmach, H., Lindner, F.: Perception of an uncertain ethical reasoning robot: a pilot study. Mensch und Computer 2018-Tagungsband (2018)

14. Stellmach, H., Lindner, F.: Perception of an uncertain ethical reasoning robot. i-com **18**(1), 79–91 (2019)

15. Tormala, Z.L.: The role of certainty (and uncertainty) in attitudes and persuasion. Curr. Opin. Psychol. **10**, 6–11 (2016)

16. You, D., Maeda, Y., Bebeau, M.J.: Gender differences in moral sensitivity: a meta-analysis. Ethics Behav. **21**(4), 263–282 (2011)

Maritime Navigation: Characterizing Collaboration in a High-Speed Craft Navigation Activity

Tim Streilein[1]([✉]) [iD], Sashidharan Komandur[1] [iD], Giovanni Pignoni[1] [iD], Frode Volden[1] [iD], Petter Lunde[2] [iD], and Frode Voll Mjelde[2] [iD]

[1] Institutt for design, Norwegian University of Science and Technology, Gjøvik, Norway
timst@stud.ntnu.no, postmottak@ntnu.no
[2] Royal Norwegian Naval Academy, Norwegian Defence University College, Bergen, Norway
forsvaret@mil.no
https://www.ntnu.edu/design

Abstract. Communication is an important factor in teamwork and collaboration in safety-critical systems. Operating a safety-critical system such as a military vessel requires maintaining high levels of safety. In maritime navigation, communication is key and collaboration as a team is paramount for safety during navigation. Characterizing this is essential for training and bridge design purposes. Characterizing requires objective tools in addition to visual observation of the navigational exercise. Eye-trackers can fill this gap. Eye-trackers enable measurement of eye movements and dilation measures of the pupil in real time. This can help locate design issues and assist designing training paradigms. In this study two eye-trackers were used to measure joint vision of two navigator simultaneously. Through data of visual attention communication patterns can be characterized with greater richness than just visual observation. As for this case study, in an simulator at the Royal Norwegian Naval Academy in Bergen (Norway), understanding the kind of communication and finding a way to formulate the collaboration will help to characterize communication pattern as a first attempt. This study builds up upon a previous study that improved an off the shelf eye-tracker through hardware additions and software enhancements to accurately measure pupil dilation despite changing ambient light. This study is expected to be a key landmark study that shows the potential of objective tools such as eye-trackers to characterize communication in safety critical systems such as a high-speed navigational environment.

Keywords: Maritime · Eye-tracker · Military vessel · Communication · Teamwork

1 Introduction

Communication is key-element of safety-critical systems involving multiple operators, such as navigation of an high-speed military vessel. Efficient bridge

© Springer Nature Switzerland AG 2020
C. Stephanidis and M. Antona (Eds.): HCII 2020, CCIS 1224, pp. 496–503, 2020.
https://doi.org/10.1007/978-3-030-50726-8_65

teamwork is ensured through precise and established communication. Operations on a military vessel and its performance is highly dependent on the communication (humans interaction) as it is between human-computer interaction. As pointed out by Macrae [8], 42,2% of naval accidents are caused by poor communication between the team members. The recent accident report of the Norwegian Helge Ingstad (frigate) also shows concerns regarding sufficient bridge communication, and failure to build a shared mental model and situational awareness [1].

McCallum [9] notes how sailors do often not ask other crew members for help and often interpret situations on their own; leading to a lack of verified information-flow as more and more things are taken for granted. This behaviour can, therefore, lead to cases such as the accident of Helge Ingstad in 2018 and demonstrates the importance of communication as a tool for improving the team's general awareness of a situation and human errors. Human error happens on the bases of false and incorrect interpretation of the situation; which leads to wrong decision making or improper actions [18]. Therefore, a communication failure can lead to a diverging mental representation of the ship's situation. This representation also has the potential of wrong decision making and might become a safety-critical situation [4].

In the field of control rooms for safety-critical industrial applications, automation is an approach that has proven capable of lowering the chance of human error [2]. Compared to other domains, such as aviation, maritime bridge design still lags in technology adoption [15]. Even though automation should improve the workload during operations, it still has limitations. It can support navigators in their routine, but in case of failure, it can also generate an instant performance demand which could increase stress for the operators [11]. Despite that, it also has been shown that situational awareness could be lowered by the adoption of automation processes [13]. Therefore, the benefits of an automated system depend on how the system is designed or the navigators are trained to overtake in such a safety-critical situation [12]. It is urgent to understand how different situations change human behaviour. The definition of communication patterns is capable of improving the development of automation systems in a safety-critical system such as in military vessels. Prospectively it will help to lower human error and therefore, the safety of the crew.

1.1 Related Work

Although the essential communication, in the collaborative environment of safety-critical systems, has been covered by a multitude of studies. For instance, on fields such as aviation and nuclear power plants, showing that understanding and improvement of communication is of high importance [6,14,15], there has been a lack of focus on the maritime environment.

A recent study focused on the crew's workload on board of a shipping vessel, including guided tug boats and VTS. It partially shows how communication depends on workload [7]. It is highlighted how communication patterns in the communication dynamics helped to indicate events of interest with a connection to mental workload. Besides conversations recordings (audio analysis), gaze behaviour has shown its importance, as it is associated with performance [16]. This study showed how gaze patterns could measure the performance of athletes in a specific situation, indicating that also gaze tracking could support the analysis of patterns in communication. Weibel et al. [17] have used two wearable eye trackers to track the joint attention of two pilots operating an aeroplane. The study revolves around the development of an effective method to analyze simultaneously multiple data streams in collaboration activities, enabling the tracking of a pilot's behaviour in flight operations. Despite that, Ziv [19] points out that there is still a high demand for analyzing dual (two participants) eye-tracking data. Safety-critical systems often involve more than one operator at a time. Therefore, future research on the topic should focus more on the collaborative aspect as mobile eye-trackers technology becomes more accessible.

1.2   Research Question

With this case-study i.e. communication in a military vessel during a navigational activity will be analyzed. The utility of eye-tracking data to understand the communication patterns in this context will also be explored. It will be investigated if the operator's communication can be described and put into a communication pattern in the military vessel background. Using wearable eye-trackers during a routine task will help to get a better understanding of verbal and non-verbal communication. With that as a base, more data can be used to conclude the further behaviour of the operators in that study. The result might be helpful to create new methodologies to evaluate collaboration for training purposes in large vessel simulators.

2   Experiment

2.1   Method Background

The experiment has been conducted in collaboration with the Norwegian Defence University College (at the Royal Norwegian Naval Academy in Bergen, Norway), which provided participants (cadets) and use of the simulator facility. Fifteen cadets took part in the experiment plus one member of staff. Each round required two participants (excluding the helmsman) at a time and there were total eight teams. The cadets were graduating students in the operational branch. This implies they have about 300 h on board the training vessels prior to the data collection.

2.2   Royal Norwegian Navy Simulator

The simulator is equipped with the same Integrated Navigation System (INS) as onboard larger vessels (e.g. Corvettes, Frigates, Submarines or Platform Support Vessel), and is used for navigation training. Figure 1 shows the general setup without the ODB (Optical Bearing Device) lowered. The INS and simulator is provided by a major Original Equipment Manufacturer (OEM), and replicates of the traditional setup with Electronic Chart Display and Information System (ECDIS), Radar, and Conning. The simulator has eight projectors providing a 210° field of view (FOV) in front and 30° FOV astern. For this experiment, the radar was kept off. The team onboard the simulated vessel:

1. **Navigator:** In charge of safe navigation and the leader of the team.
2. **Navigator's Assistant:** Provides the navigator with navigational information, which is aligned with Standard Operating Procedure (SOPs). Conducts nav. tasks for the navigator, e.g. position fixes (are aligned with SOPs).
3. **Helmsman:** responsible for the wheel and throttle of the vessel. Sets speed and steers course as ordered by the navigator.

The Navigator and the Assistant are required to work very closely with explicit closed-loop communication, as neither one of them have the entire picture, thus being dependant on each other. Each run involved two participants, a Navigator and an Assistant. The first run (pilot) involved a staff member as the Assistant. The use of a simulator allows high repeatability of the scenario, traffic and environmental conditions. All experiments were conducted in morning, clear daylight conditions.

2.3   Route

The route starts and ends under the Sotra Bridge near the RNoNA harbour, running clockwise around the Bjorøy island. This route was chosen as it is part of standard training activities and the participants would be in general already familiar to the area. All the participants were given the same navigation plan, which was created by an instructor using standard RNoNA Notations. All Navigators were given five minutes for the team preparation as well as to look through the navigation plan with the Assistant. The scenario was run at the almost constant speed of thirty knots and created with different appearing situations (phases) in order to create a variation in workload:

1. **Phase:** No traffic and easy navigation (baseline).
2. **Phase:** Simple single ship traffic with easy navigation.
3. **Phase:** No traffic and easy navigation (return to baseline).
4. **Phase:** Sudden appearing traffic/near-collision course during narrow and challenging navigation.
5. **Phase:** Complex traffic & easy navigation; the traffic does not require significant actions (compared to phase 4) if the participant acts reasonably.

2.4   Experimental Procedure

The experiment was set up in one of the of the simulators of the Royal Norwegian Naval Academy. Data was recorded using multiple devices: overview video of the bridge recorded by a scene camera, eye tracking from both the Navigator and the Assistant (this includes an egocentric video form each participant) and voice recordings.

Fig. 1. Royal Norwegian Navy Simulator in Bergen, assistant (left), navigator (centre) and helmsman (right)

The Pupil Pro eye-tracking glasses [5], was equipped with an egocentric video camera and video tracking of the right eye. It uses infrared technology to record the movement of the eye by the reflecting iris/pupil. Both cadet's eye-movements were recorded at the same time. This particular eye tracker was found suitable for such study as it impedes vision only in minimally thanks to a small eye camera and no frame. The eye-trackers were wired to two different computers with sufficient length to allow the navigator to move freely in the simulator; it has been ensured that the participant would not risk tripping or yanking on the cable. The cadets also were equipped with a clip-on microphone, which wireless recorded each voice separately. Besides the automated data gathering, the experiment involved extensive note-taking and a questionnaire. The questionnaire was administered before the debriefing, and after the session in the simulator. The questionnaire contained questions regarding the route, communication and workload. Most questions were answered by coloring a template of the course.

2.5   Performance Evaluation

The Royal Norwegian Navy (RNoNA) evaluates the performance of high-speed navigation teams by assessing both technical navigation skills (taskwork), and their ability to interact through communication and coordination (teamwork) to support mission objectives. Research on team performance assessment indicates that scoring of performance metrics are best met by balancing teamwork and taskwork constructs [10]. RNoNA subject matter experts have constructed an assessment form that reflects mission essential competencies necessary for safe and efficient high-speed navigation. This observational tool was used to assess each teams' taskwork and teamwork behaviours as they performed the experiment. The route used in the experiment can be broken down into smaller segments labelled with different levels of navigational difficulty. It is expected that teams receiving a low score on observed taskwork and teamwork behaviour within a particular segment also will receive a low score on mission success in the same segment, and vice versa for high performing teams. Additionally, the effect of team performance has on mission success is expected to be more observable in the hardest segments than in segments that are easier to navigate.

2.6   Initial Impressions

Emerging communication patterns can be seen in the notes, indicating standardisation in communication and procedures happening on the bridge. Verbal communication is generally preferred to non-verbal. Still, non-verbal communication is used to specify and support verbal communication e.g. to pinpoint dangerous elements in the environment or on the ECDIS. Such instances should have a high chance of joint vision (JV) that will be further investigated. Other cues, such as head movement or eye contact, are used to get attention or confirmation from another crew member. The communication patterns observed during the experiment have been initially organised in four recurring sequences (Table 1).

Table 1. Observed sequences incl. repeating patterns (N.: Navigator; A.: Assistant)

Briefing	Initialize
ECDIS gets inspected	Check status of everyone
Situations are discussed	N. initialize and takes over the lead
Non-verbal actions to point out situations	Everyone stays in their position
Set the system and settings e.g. AIS	Using non-verbal cues (e.g. pointing and look back)
	A. and N. look often outside
Prepare	Turning
A. provides coordinates from ECDIS, N. replies	N. commands the bridge (actively walks around)
N. uses the Conn and checks other instruments	The voice rises often
N. looks outside mostly	A looks more often outside and at the N
A looks outside or on ECDIS	N. looks together at ECDIS with A
A wants attention (by pointing or turning head)	N. mentions s.th outside (both look and discuss)
A. points out a situation (outside)	Rarely A. points at the ECDIS (4th turn)
Arrive	
N. mostly stays at middle position	
Everyone looks mostly outside	
Non-verbal communication rises	
A. and N. still discuss situation on ECIDIS	

2.7 Future Work

Further analysis of the notes will be followed an integrated with eye-tracking and video recording as well as speech analysis. Areas-of-interest will be used to analyse the eye-tracking data and JV can be identified as the overlap of the dwell time of both navigators. The communication will be analysed through the newly defined pattern set and categorised. Speech analysis and recognition (e.g. words per minute) will be used to support or identify other patters. Still, the content of the conversation will not be analyzed as the content should not correlate with the performance of the operator [20]. The RNoNA will analyze the collected team performance observations with respect to the scores for mission success, both for the overall mission and for each individual segment. It is of interest to the Navy to compare the SME ratings with the data presented by the eye-tracking analysis to identify how eye-tracking tools can assist in performance assessment of teams collaborating in a challenging maritime environment.

3 Conclusion

Even though communication frequency may not linearly relate to performance (e.g. an increase of communication may result in an inferior performance [3]), the definition of communication patterns will help to understand how communication can become more or less beneficial in an operational environment. The eye-tracking data should help to quantify the effect of communication on JV and the relation between workload (pupillometry) and other communication variables such as words per minutes. The first outcome of this research is the list of recurring communication patterns extracted from the observation notes. These patterns will be objectively verified through the analysis of the eye-tracking data and speech recordings. This effort should indicate whether such tools can be used to characterize communication in a high-speed navigational environment. Determining standards in communication and procedures could help to identify any abnormal behaviour at an early stage and aid the training process.

References

1. AIBN, DAIBN: Part one report on the collision on 8 november 2018 between the frigate Hnoms Helge Ingstad and the oil tanker Sola TS outside the sture terminal in the HJeltefjord in Hordaland country. Technical report, November 2019
2. Hadnett, E.: A bridge too far? J. Navig. **61**(2), 283–289 (2008)
3. Hutchins, E.: Cognition in the Wild. MIT Press, Cambridge (1995)
4. John, P., Brooks, B., Schriever, U.: Speech acts in professional maritime discourse: a pragmatic risk analysis of bridge team communication directives and commissives in full-mission simulation. J. Pragmat. **140**, 12–21 (2019)
5. Kassner, M., Patera, W., Bulling, A.: Pupil: an open source platform for pervasive eye tracking and mobile gaze-based interaction. In: Adjunct Proceedings of the 2014 ACM International Joint Conference on Pervasive and Ubiquitous Computing, pp. 1151–1160. UbiComp 2014 Adjunct, New York, NY, USA. ACM (2014)

6. Kim, S., Park, J., Kim, Y.J.: Some insights about the characteristics of communications observed from the off-normal conditions of nuclear power plants. Hum. Factors Manuf. **21**(4), 361–378 (2011)
7. Lochner, M., Duenser, A., Lutzhoft, M., Brooks, B., Rozado, D.: Analysis of maritime team workload and communication dynamics in standard and emergency scenarios. J. Shipp. Trade **3**(1), 1–22 (2018). https://doi.org/10.1186/s41072-018-0028-z
8. Macrae, C.: Human factors at sea: common patterns of error in groundings and collisions. Marit. Policy Manage. **36**(1), 21–38 (2009)
9. McCallum, M.C., Raby, M., Forsythe, A.M., Rothblum, A.M., Smith, M.W.: Communications problems in marine casualties: development and evaluation of investigation, reporting, and analysis procedures. In: Proceedings of the Human Factors and Ergonomics Society Annual Meeting, vol. 44, no. 27, pp. 384–387 (2000)
10. McIntyre, R.M., Salas, E.: Measuring and managing for team performance: emerging principles from complex environments. In: Guzzo, R.A., Salas, E., Goldstein, I.L. (eds.) Team effectiveness and decision making in organizations, pp. 149–203. Jossey-Bass, San Francisco (1995)
11. Onnasch, L., Wickens, C.D., Li, H., Manzey, D.: Human performance consequences of stages and levels of automation: an integrated meta-analysis. Hum. Factors **56**(3), 476–488 (2014)
12. Parasuraman, R., Manzey, D.H.: Complacency and bias in human use of automation: an attentional integration. Hum. Factors **52**(3), 381–410 (2010)
13. Pazouki, K., Forbes, N., Norman, R.A., Woodward, M.D.: Investigation on the impact of human-automation interaction in maritime operations. Ocean Eng. **153**, 297–304 (2018)
14. Salas, E., Wilson, K.A., Burke, C.S., Wightman, D.C.: Does Crew resource management training work? An update, an extension, and some critical needs. Hum. Factors **48**(2), 392–412 (2006)
15. Schager, B.: When technology leads us astray: a broadened view of human error. J. Navig. **61**(1), 63–70 (2008)
16. Vickers, J.N.: Advances in coupling perception and action: the quiet eye as a bidirectional link between gaze, attention, and action. In: Progress in Brain Research, vol. 174, pp. 279–288. Elsevier (2009)
17. Weibel, N., Fouse, A., Emmenegger, C., Kimmich, S., Hutchins, E.: Let's look at the cockpit: exploring mobile eye-tracking for observational research on the flight deck. In: Proceedings of the Symposium on Eye Tracking Research and Applications - ETRA 2012,Santa Barbara, California, p. 107. ACM Press (2012)
18. Wickens, C.D., Hollands, J.G.: Engineering Psychology and Human Performance, 3rd edn. Prentice Hall, Upper Saddle River (2000)
19. Ziv, G.: Gaze behavior and visual attention: a review of eye tracking studies in aviation. Int. J. Aviat. Psychol. **26**(3–4), 75–104 (2016)
20. Øvergård, K.I., Nielsen, A.R., Nazir, S., Sorensen, L.J.: Assessing navigational teamwork through the situational correctness and relevance of communication. Proc. Manuf. **3**, 2589–2596 (2015)

When Imprecision Improves Advice: Disclosing Algorithmic Error Probability to Increase Advice Taking from Algorithms

Johanna M. Werz[✉], Esther Borowski, and Ingrid Isenhardt

IMA, RWTH Aachen University, Dennewartstr. 27, 52068 Aachen, Germany
johanna.werz@ima.rwth-aachen.de

Abstract. Due to the increasing number and complexity of information and available data, people use algorithmic decision support systems to improve the quality of their decisions. However, research has shown that despite an increasing "algorithm appreciation", people still abandon algorithmic decision support when they see it fail – even if they know that the alternative, the human advisor, is advising worse. As algorithms consist of statistical models and never mirror the reality completely, mistakes of algorithms are inevitable – and as described, the following algorithmic refusal posts a threat to the quality of subsequent decision-making. With human advisors, people use the confidence of the advisor, often operationalized as a probability or Likert-scale estimate, as an indicator for correctness. The question arises whether information about algorithmic insecurities, e.g., their error probabilities, can serve a similar goal: to increase the transparency for human users and eventually counteract algorithmic refusal.

Therefore, the authors are currently developing a study design that compares how algorithms that indicate vs. do not indicate an estimated accuracy influence participants' advice taking. To investigate the effect on algorithmic refusal, participants get wrong information from an algorithm that indicates vs. does not indicate its error probability and in a second round, participants can decide whether they will use it again. The poster will describe open questions and limitations and provide a basis for further discussion on the ongoing research.

Keywords: Algorithm aversion · Accuracy · Decision-making · Forecasting · Human computer interaction

1 Algorithm Usage for Advice

Nowadays, we more and more realize that humans alone cannot process the growing number of available information and its (global) dependencies and interrelations, e.g. data of people's movements [1], buying decisions [2], or career trajectories [3]. This is why the market of algorithmic advice systems is growing and people increasingly turn towards these systems for structure and advice in all different kinds of ways. In their private live, many people rely on algorithmic support of some kind, e.g. choosing music to hear or movies to watch or even selecting a future partner (Spotify, Netflix, OkCupid). In the working world, expert systems offer support for more complex

© Springer Nature Switzerland AG 2020
C. Stephanidis and M. Antona (Eds.): HCII 2020, CCIS 1224, pp. 504–511, 2020.
https://doi.org/10.1007/978-3-030-50726-8_66

decisions, e.g. for career planning [4], in the medical domain [5], or for the maintenance of machines [6]. Despite their broad application, 46% of Germans state that they cannot judge whether algorithms are a win or a threat [7].

Decision support by computer and algorithms is nothing new and its strength in supporting humans has long been known. Especially in tasks of predictive nature or those that are objectively right or wrong, researchers compare the results or algorithms to human advice. Already in 1954, Meehl [8] showed that clinical diagnoses by statistical methods were more accurate than those by human doctors. In addition, in different examples like diagnosing patients in a psychiatric clinic or predicting academic success of first-year graduate students, linear regression models were more accurate than humans [9] – and nonetheless people did not use the algorithmic advice. These old papers document the distrust people held against algorithms. Still today, research shows that when humans can choose between advice by people or an algorithm, there are different reasons why humans (do not) choose the latter. In respective studies, participants prefer other humans to an algorithm when predicting joke funniness [10] and reject automated advice in medical domains [11], although in both cases, when put to the test the algorithmic advice outperforms human advice. On the other hand, recent research shows that depending on the type of task people increasingly use algorithms, an effect called "algorithm appreciation". When confronted with objective (vs. subjective) tasks [12] or numerical questions [13], nowadays users prefer algorithmic advice to human advice.

At the same time, an effect called "algorithm aversion" (see [12] for an overview) emerges: When users experience an algorithm giving wrong advice, they abandon it – even if they know, that overall the algorithm is performing better than the human alternative [14–17]. Thus, as the number of decision support systems is growing and as they prove to be precious support for human reasoning, understanding how to overcome this rigid algorithm refusal is mandatory to improve decision quality. This question is even more pressing as all algorithms and automated advice systems somehow base on statistical models. Such models, from their very nature, are not able to mirror the reality completely but inevitably make a wrong prediction at some point.

2 Confidence and Error Probability in Advice Taking

In comparison to automation and algorithm research, research on human advice taking is splendid. On the one hand, human-to-human advice works in different ways than algorithm-to-human advice. On the other hand, the point that a human has to decide whether to take or not to take the advice, justifies a look into which reasons people have for accepting advice by others. What is more, research shows that humans apply their ways of interacting interpersonally to interactions with "intelligent machines" [16]. Several factors influence to which extend someone takes another person's advice. The fact whether the advisor is considered an expert [18], delivers an explanation for the advice [19], or how extremely the advice differs from my point of view [20] influence advice taking. However, the strongest relation with advice taking is the advisor's expressed confidence or a person's notion of it [21, 22]. Simply put, people assume that the higher the advisor's confidence the higher the probability, that the advice is correct.

Human have countlessly experience with human advisors, which is why everybody knows that people can err. Therefore, people use confidence to imply the accuracy of advice. In research, human confidence is often operationalized as a probability estimate or a rating of the extent to which one expects the advice to be correct [23]. To the contrary, when using algorithms, research shows that users assume "algorithms make no mistakes" [14]. When they nevertheless do, this instance violates their expectation a lot more than seeing humans err. Cognitive psychology knows people remember such unexpected experiences very well or even magnify them in their memory [24]. Indeed, some studies show that when participants newly interact with a system, they overestimate the performance of the automated advisor [14, 16]. But as soon as they see the system err, algorithm aversion occurs and they discount the system, even if they know it performs better than the alternative human advisor [14, 15].

The question arises whether one can transfer the human confidence estimate to automation. Whereas for humans, everybody knows that people can err and confidence implies lesser probability for mistakes, disclosing how *sure* an algorithm is about an advice or rather, how unsure, this prepares its user to the possibility it could be wrong. And indeed: When Dzindolet et al. [14] inform participants that the system may err ("in 10 of 200 cases") before actually seeing it err, participants kept using it more often that participants that get no such information or that get a positively framed message (the system "made about half as many mistakes than most participants"; [14]). It has to be noted, however, that in the study participants used both the human and the algorithmic advice very rarely. Another point speaks to the fact that information about a possible mistake improves algorithm usage: humans use human confidence to predict advice accuracy. At the same time, they prefer systems they can understand and that are transparent [10], a reason why transparency in artificial intelligence is a currently boosting topic. Building on that, the current study has two aims: First, nearly twenty years later, we are trying to replicate the effect that information about a possible mistaken algorithmic system will protect it from algorithm aversion (building on [14]). Second, rather than vaguely warning the users of a possible mistake, we investigate the effect of "algorithm's confidence". The question is whether an algorithm's error probability is considered both an indicator for its accuracy and works as a shield against algorithm aversion. As most existing expert systems are based on statistical models, by default they produce error probabilities of some kind in addition to their results. In the end, such an information should not only help to manage users' expectation of an algorithm's performance but also improve the decision quality of experts when evaluating the advice.

Based on this reasoning, when participants have to solve numerical estimation tasks and get advice by algorithms, the expected hypotheses are the following:

- Participants that get error information for the algorithm's results use the algorithm's advice more than those without such information do.
- When participants get error information, a higher error probability will lead to lower advice taking.
- In tasks following an error, participants that get information about the error probability will use the advice more than those without this information will.

3 Suggested Method

3.1 Design

To investigate these effects, an online game is set up, in which participants have to estimate the height of people on pictures. Within the study, both information about the algorithm's insecurity (between subject: various levels vs. not present) and the error experience (within subject: before vs. after error) are manipulated.

As in several previous studies [13, 15], the Judge Advisor System (JAS) paradigm will be used to measure the extent to which users adapt to human vs. algorithmic advice under different conditions. The JAS consists of a judge that has to give an initial and a final decision, and an interaction with an advisor happening in between (see Fig. 1).

Fig. 1. Judge Advisor System paradigm. (Icon by Smartline of flaticons.com)

In this part of the study, participants interact with the algorithmic advisor. The dependent variables in the JAS paradigm is the adaption value, meaning the delta between the judge's initial and final estimation. For example, when the judge estimates a body height of 1.65 m in the first round, the advisor states an height of 1.77 m, and the judge then changes her initial estimate to 1.72 m, the adaption value is 0.07.

3.2 Procedure

The participants will enter the online-study from their own computer. Without their knowledge, participants will be allocated to the group "error probabilities" or the one "no error probability" (see Fig. 2). First, they will read that they have to solve several estimation tasks in which different algorithms will be tested. Depending on their performance, their probability to win a voucher raises. The estimation game consists of sixteen tasks (four tasks in four rounds) in which they have to estimate the height of a person from a picture. For each correct estimation of the height plus/minus two cm, their name will be added to a lottery. In total, they can reach a sixteen times higher probability to win the voucher. They will then learn that in each phase a different algorithm that was developed to evaluate such tasks will give them advice. Each phase consists of four tasks, that is, participants will always get advice by the same algorithm four times, before allegedly a new algorithm is used. Without their knowledge, the advice will be wrong in each phase in the second or third task. That is, participants will have not experienced errors by the advisor in the beginning, but in the end. In the insecurity information-condition, each algorithm will keep "its" error probability for the whole phase, and it will randomly vary between 5 and 15%. In each task, participants will see a picture of a person and indicate their estimation of the person's height. Then

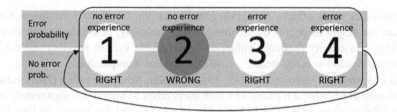

Fig. 2. Conditions (insecurity information × error experience) and procedure within one phase. In total participants will run through four phases.

they get advice by the algorithm that, depending on their condition, either contains or does not contain an error probability estimate. On a next screen, the participants see their initial estimate and fill in their final estimate below it. What is more, they indicate on a scale how much they trust the advisor. After that, they are informed about the actual height of the person and about whether they are added to the lottery and they are reminded of their estimate and the advisors estimate. Then the second round with the same advisor begins. In the wrong advice-task, the system's estimate will be off by 5–10 cm. In the following tasks, the estimations will again be off by less than 2 cm. After each phase, participants read that now the phase is over and a differently developed algorithm will be used for the next phase.

4 Limitations and Further Thoughts

There are some limitations to that design. First, the height of insecurity value seems to be critical: One could assume that insecurity information – as it might imply more insecurity than no information – always deteriorates the usage. It is reasonable to use an algorithm more if its "confidence" is 95% that 85%. The single effect of error probability has to be considered. One approach to this problem is to keep the value constant across tasks – but then effects are limited to this specific level. Dzindolet et al. [14] handled this problem by making sure that the information underlying the framing (negative framing: "system is wrong in 10 of 200 cases" vs. positive framing: "half as many mistakes as participants") was equal. However, when comparing error probabilities this is not possible. In addition, the refusal could be differently strong after an error with an error probability of 5% and one of 15%. On the other hand, transparency is supposed to increase the usage of technology [10]. This is why many recommendation systems that are in use today already add information about the match (e.g. "The following recommendation matches your previously inserted information to 90%") or accuracy ("The probability that you'll like the suggestion is 90%"). A high number of security, i.e. 99% or 95%, should therefore outperform the no-information condition. Concerning the lower numbers, i.e. 85%, the effect is yet unclear.

Another limitation is that until now algorithm aversion has always been tested by comparing the choice of algorithmic and human advice. On the one hand, this comparison demonstrates the irrationality of declining algorithmic advice. On the other hand, the type of task and the choice of advice medium are highly intermingled. People prefer algorithms for objective tasks, i.e. tasks that have an objectively right (or wrong) solution. This is why, in this study, we also concentrate on such tasks. Whether the effect of algorithm aversion also applies to subjective tasks (e.g. liking a movie or the choice of a future partner), this study does not investigate.

What is more, in the study no individual factors that influence human-technology-interaction are assessed. These include, e.g., experience with technology and acceptance of technology, moderating variables from previous research [25, 26], or perceived usefulness or ease of use, variables from the prominent Technology Acceptance Model (TAM; [27]). On an individual level, these factors influence how people interact with different technologies. At the same time, no relation of these individual factors to algorithm aversion have yet been investigated. They could, nevertheless, be added and tested exploratively.

5   Conclusion

Despite advice taking by algorithms has increased, when an algorithm errs, users refuse to use its advice any longer, even if they know that overall the algorithm is superior to them or an alternative person's advice [15]. This effect is called "algorithm aversion". One reason for this effect is the assumption that algorithms do not err (in comparison to humans) [14]. When using human advice, people use the advisor's confidence as an indicator for accuracy [23]. In these studies, confidence is often operationalized as a probability or rating value. Confidence, transferred to algorithms, corresponds to their error probability. Indeed, several popular recommender systems (e.g. Amazon or Netflix) already use numbers to express the expected accuracy of their recommendations. The question emerges, whether such an error probability can shield against algorithm aversion. First, because it will manage the expectations users have when using an algorithm and second, because it will increase transparency of the results. The paper proposed a study to investigate this effect in with a 2 (information about algorithm confidence vs. none) × 2 (usage before vs. after error) design. Limitations of the concept are the missing comparison to a human advisor and the inherent effect of different insecurity values. Nevertheless, overcoming the irrational algorithm aversion is an important step to increase decision quality and to use the full potential of algorithmic support. Knowing how to overcome it is both relevant for managers that want their employees to decide in the best possible way and for designers of decision support systems that want to improve users' decision-making.

References

1. Shih, C., Chen, F.-C., Cheng, S.-W., Kao, D.-Y.: Using google maps to track down suspects in a criminal investigation. Proc. Comput. Sci. **159**, 1900–1906 (2019). https://doi.org/10.1016/j.procs.2019.09.362
2. Mishra, M., Chopde, J., Shah, M., Parikh, P., Babu, R.C., Woo, J.: Big data predictive analysis of amazon product review. In: KSII The 14th Asia Pacific International Conference on Information Science and Technology, APIC-IST, KSII, Beijing, China (2019)
3. Werz, J.M., Varney, V., Isenhardt, I.: The curse of self-presentation: Looking for career patterns in online CVs. In: Proceedings of the 2019 IEEE/ACM International Conference on Advances in Social Networks Analysis and Minging, ASONAM, pp. 733–736., Vancouver, BC, Canada (2019). https://doi.org/10.1145/3341161.3343681
4. Werz, J.M., Stehling, V., Haberstroh, M., Isenhardt, I.: Promoting women in STEM: requirements for an automated career-development recommender. In: Paoloni, P., Paoloni, M., Arduini, S., (eds.) Proceedings of the 2nd International Conference on Gender Research, ICGR 2019, Rome, Italy, pp. 653–660(2019)
5. Sim, L.L.W., Ban, K.H.K., Tan, T.W., Sethi, S.K., Loh, T.P.: Development of a clinical decision support system for diabetes care: a pilot study. PLoS ONE **12**, e0173021 (2017). https://doi.org/10.1371/journal.pone.0173021
6. Posada Moreno, A.F., Klein, C., Haßler, M., Pehar, D., Solvay, A.F., Kohlschein, C.P.: Cargo wagon structural health estimation using computer vision. In: 8th Transport Research Arena, TRA2020, 2020-04-27 - 2020-04-30, Helsinki, Finland (2020)
7. Fischer, S., Petersen, T.: Was Deutschland über Algorithmen weiß und denkt. Bertelsmann Stiftung, Gütersloh (2018)
8. Meehl, P.E.: Clinical versus statistical prediction: a theoretical analysis and a review of the evidence. University of Minnesota Press, Minneapolis (1954). https://doi.org/10.1037/11281-000
9. Dawes, R.M., Corrigan, B.: Linear models in decision making. Psychol. Bull. **81**, 95–106 (1974). https://doi.org/10.1037/h0037613
10. Yeomans, M., Shah, A., Mullainathan, S., Kleinberg, J.: Making sense of recommendations. J. Behav. Decis. Mak. **32**, 403–414 (2019). https://doi.org/10.1002/bdm.2118
11. Longoni, C., Bonezzi, A., Morewedge, C.K.: Resistance to medical artificial intelligence. J. Consum. Res. **46**, 629–650 (2019). https://doi.org/10.1093/jcr/ucz013
12. Castelo, N., Bos, M.W., Lehmann, D.R.: Task-dependent algorithm aversion. J. Mark. Res. **56**, 809–825 (2019). https://doi.org/10.1177/0022243719851788
13. Logg, J.M., Minson, J.A., Moore, D.A.: Algorithm appreciation: people prefer algorithmic to human judgment. Organ. Behav. Hum. Decis. Process. **151**, 90–103 (2019). https://doi.org/10.1016/j.obhdp.2018.12.005
14. Dzindolet, M.T., Pierce, L.G., Beck, H.P., Dawe, L.A.: The perceived utility of human and automated aids in a visual detection task. Hum. Factors **44**, 79–94 (2002). https://doi.org/10.1518/0018720024494856
15. Dietvorst, B.J., Simmons, J.P., Massey, C.: Algorithm aversion: people erroneously avoid algorithms after seeing them err. J. Exp. Psychol. Gen. **144**, 114–126 (2014). https://doi.org/10.1037/xge0000033
16. Madhavan, P., Wiegmann, D.A.: Similarities and differences between human–human and human–automation trust: an integrative review. Theor. Issues Ergon. Sci. **8**, 277–301 (2007). https://doi.org/10.1080/14639220500337708
17. Prahl, A., Swol, L.V.: Understanding algorithm aversion: when is advice from automation discounted? J. Forecast. **36**, 691–702 (2017). https://doi.org/10.1002/for.2464

18. Jungermann, H., Fischer, K.: Using expertise and experience for giving and taking advice. In: Betsch, T., Haberstroh, S. (eds.) The Routines of Decision Making, pp. 157–175. Psychology Press, New York (2005)
19. Yates, J.F., Price, P.C., Lee, J.-W., Ramirez, J.: Good probabilistic forecasters: the 'consumer's' perspective. Int. J. Forecast. **12**, 41–56 (1996)
20. Yaniv, I., Milyavsky, M.: Using advice from multiple sources to revise and improve judgments. Organ. Behav. Hum. Decis. Process. **103**, 104–120 (2007). https://doi.org/10.1016/j.obhdp.2006.05.006
21. Van Swol, L.M., Sniezek, J.A.: Factors affecting the acceptance of expert advice. Br. J. Soc. Psychol. **44**, 443–461 (2005). https://doi.org/10.1348/014466604X17092
22. Van Swol, L.M.: Forecasting another's enjoyment versus giving the right answer: trust, shared values, task effects, and confidence in improving the acceptance of advice. Int. J. Forecast. **27**, 103–120 (2011). https://doi.org/10.1016/j.ijforecast.2010.03.002
23. Bonaccio, S., Dalal, R.S.: Advice taking and decision-making: an integrative literature review, and implications for the organizational sciences. Organ. Behav. Hum. Decis. Process. **101**, 127–151 (2006). https://doi.org/10.1016/j.obhdp.2006.07.001
24. Stangor, C., McMillan, D.: Memory for expectancy-congruent and expectancy-incongruent information: a review of the social and social developmental literatures. Psychol. Bull. **111**, 42–61 (1992). https://doi.org/10.1037/0033-2909.111.1.42
25. Fishbein, M., Ajzen, I.: Attitudes towards objects as predictors of single and multiple behavioral criteria. Psychol. Rev. **81**, 59–74 (1974). https://doi.org/10.1037/h0035872
26. Venkatesh, V., Morris, M.G., Davis, G.B., Davis, F.D.: User acceptance of information technology: toward a unified view. MIS Q. **27**, 425–478 (2003)
27. Davis, F.D.: Perceived usefulness, perceived ease of use, and user acceptance of information technology. MIS Q. **13**, 319–340 (1989). https://doi.org/10.2307/249008

An Interactive Game for Changing Youth Behavior Regarding E-cigarettes

Angela Xu[1], Muhammad Amith[2], Jianfu Li[2], Lu Tang[3], and Cui Tao[2(✉)]

[1] St. John's School, Houston, TX 77019, USA
[2] School of Biomedical Informatics, The University of Texas Health Science Center at Houston, Houston, TX 77030, USA
cui.tao@uth.tmc.edu
[3] Department of Communication, Texas A&M University, College Station, TX 77843, USA

Abstract. The aim of this study is to develop an educational video game and to assess its feasibility to influence youths' interest in e-cigarettes. We first built a prototype storytelling game with facts about e-cigarettes, and then recruited 30 participants to evaluate the game. Each participant took pre- and post-game surveys on their knowledge, risk awareness, and susceptibility to using e-cigarettes. In addition, usability of the game was also evaluated in post-game survey. After playing the game, the participants demonstrated increased knowledge and perceived risk of e-cigarettes. The non-e-cigarette users reduced willingness to use e-cigarettes in post-game surveys. Results from this study demonstrated that using interactive video games can increase the users' perception of vaping risk and thus potentially lower nicotine interest in youth.

Keywords: Electronic cigarettes · Vaping · Video game · Youth · Intervention

1 Introduction

The number of people using electronic cigarettes (e-cigarettes), or vaping, has increased dramatically in recent years, especially in adolescents and young adults. The National Youth Tobacco Survey estimated current e-cigarette use among high school students at 20.8% in 2018, compared to 1.5% in 2011 and 11.7% in 2017 [1]. For young U.S. adults aged 18–24 years, the ever-used and current-use rate of e-cigarettes were 35.8% and 13.6%, respectively [2]. Past 30-day use of e-cigarettes in college students rose from 5.9% in 2016 to 27.7% in 2018 [3]. The growing e-cigarette usage has resulted in the reversing of the previous decline in usage of nicotine products by teens, and may result in a new generation of nicotine addicts.

Evidence from recent studies suggested that the increasing popularity of e-cigarettes is related to a lower perceived risk and knowledge of e-cigarettes [4–6]. Approximately two thirds of the adolescent e-cigarettes users did not know vaping products, such as JUUL, contain nicotine [6]. One in three adolescents considered e-cigarettes to be less harmful than conventional combustible cigarettes [1, 7]. Therefore

© Springer Nature Switzerland AG 2020
C. Stephanidis and M. Antona (Eds.): HCII 2020, CCIS 1224, pp. 512–518, 2020.
https://doi.org/10.1007/978-3-030-50726-8_67

it is important to educate youth about the harm from e-cigarettes, to increase their awareness of risk, and eventually to influence their health behaviors.

Storytelling video games have been used as an effective method to improve health outcome by educating users about health problems through an interactive and memorable experience [8]. It has demonstrated its efficiency in influencing health behaviors in the area of HIV management, vaccination promotion, and substance use, etc [9–12]. Therefore, an educational video game intervention that targets youth for e-cigarette risk awareness could positively influence their behavior.

The goal of this study is to develop an interactive storytelling game (The E-Cig Report) and to evaluate its potential in educating youth on the health risks of e-cigarettes and influencing their behaviors. To the best of our knowledge, besides this study, smokeSCREEN is the only other videogame that have been developed as a prevention invention with a target for e-cigarettes [13, 14]. While the evaluation of smokeSCREEN mainly focused on adolescents aged 10 to 16, the current study reported the effectiveness of video game in educating young adults.

2 Methods

2.1 Game Design and Development

We first created a prototype storytelling video game using GameMaker Studio 2. The design principle was based on the health belief model focusing on *perceived severity*, which pertains to an individual's perception of succumbing to a disease or illness [6].

In the game, the user takes the role of an employee at an e-cigarette company, whose goal is to find various items around the building that are related to vaping. The game consists of 3 rooms (e.g. Fig. 1A), where the participants would look for the objects. Upon discovery, the objects would offer further information about e-cigarettes based on published facts from reliable sources such as US Department of Health and Human Services and Centers for Disease Control and Prevention [15, 16]. For example, a list of ingredients used in e-cigarettes liquid explains what kinds of harmful chemicals are present in e-cigarettes, or an ad for e-cigarettes revealing the different types of restrictions on cigarettes versus e-cigarettes advertising (Fig. 1B).

2.2 Game Evaluation

Thirty young adults aged 18–25 (mean 19.7) were recruited from Texas A&M University (TAMU, College Station, TX) to evaluate the game (TAMU IRB# 2019-0974D, and UTHealth IRB#: HSC-SBMI-19-0629), among which there are 12 females and 18 males. Participants took a pre-game survey, played the game, and then took a post-game survey with the same questions. Survey questions were adapted from previous studies, [17, 18] and included vaping history, measures for e-cigarettes knowledge, willingness-to-use (e-cigarettes susceptibility), perceived risk of e-cigarettes, and cognitive elaboration about e-cigarettes.

Vaping History: The participants were asked whether they "have ever used e-cigarettes or other vaping devices..." "in the lifetime" or "in the past 30 days" [18].

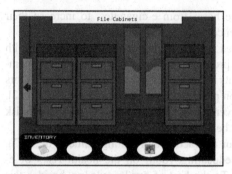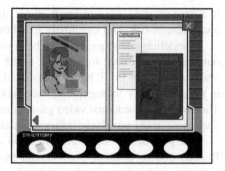

Fig. 1. Screenshots of the game. A) one of the rooms inside the building, B) the completed file of objects users are required to find.

E-cigarettes knowledge: The participants were provided with 5 statements about the facts of e-cigarettes, and responded with "True", "False", or "Don't know" [17, #15]. Each correctly answered question will be graded "1", otherwise graded "0". The score for all 5 questions will be summed to yield the measure for e-cigarettes knowledge.

Perceived Relative Risk was measured by asking the participants to rate the health risk of e-cigarettes compared to conventional cigarettes on a scale of "1: much less harmful" to "5: much more harmful" [17].

Perceived Risks. The measures for perceived risks were adapted from the scale developed by Noar et al. [17]. The participants were asked to rate the severity of risk in "damage my brain" or "get addicted" if they were to use an e-cigarettes on a 5-point scale of "1: definitely wouldn't" to "5: definitely would". Answers to all the questions were averaged to yield the measure for perceived risks.

Willingness-to-Use (e-Cigarettes Susceptibility): The participants' intention to use e-cigarettes was measured by responding in a 5-point scale to questions such as "when offered an e-cigarette or vaping device, how willing would you be to take one puff?" [17, 19].

Cognitive Elaboration: This measure evaluated how often the participants thought of "the harmful effects" or "addictiveness" of e-cigarettes by choosing a value between 1 (not at all) to 5 (very much) [17].

After playing the game, the participants also took a usability survey to assess the game playing experience following the validated System Usability Survey (SUS) scale [20–22]. The SUS scale employs a 10-item survey that produces a composite score to attain a quantifiable usability assessment. Each survey item was scaled between 1 to 5 for a range of items indicating whether the user perceived the game to difficult, easy, integrated, learnable, etc.

2.3   Data Analysis

Paired t-test on pre- and post-game survey questions were used to measure significance of any changes in the participants' awareness and knowledge of e-cigarettes risks.

3   Results

The survey on history of e-cigarettes use revealed that 16 participants used or tried e-cigarettes including 11 males and 5 females. Six out of the 16 self reported to be current e-cigarettes users, i.e. used in the past 30 days. The remaining 14 participants chose 'did not use e-cigarettes in the lifetime' in the survey, and were considered 'non-user' in this study.

Game Survey on E-cigarettes. We compared participants' susceptibility, knowledge about vaping, perceived risks, willingness to vape, and cognitive elaboration before and after playing the game using paired t-test. As shown in Table 1, the participants demonstrated significantly more knowledge about e-cigarettes ($p < 0.05$) after playing the game than before. There was a significant increase in the perceived risk ($p < 0.01$) from pre-game to post-game survey. When offered an e-cigarette by their friends, the participants responded with reduced willingness to use e-cigarettes in post-game surveys compared to before ($p = 0.1$). No significant difference was observed in cognitive elaboration, or perceived relative risk (data not shown).

When the participants were grouped based on vaping history, the non-user group showed significant increase in perceived risk ($p < 0.01$) and knowledge ($p < 0.05$) as well as decreased willingness to use e-cigarettes ($p = 0.06$) after playing the game. The e-cigarette user group also demonstrated increased the perceived risk in the post-game survey ($p < 0.05$), but no significant differences were observed in other survey measures (Table 2).

User Experience. Based on the participants' response to the game experience survey, we calculated the overall SUS score for this game is 70 out of 100 ($\sigma = 16$), which is slightly above 68, the standard average noted by researchers [23]. The lowest ratings for the game were willingness to use the game repeatedly *"I think that I would like to use this game frequently"* (score 43[1]) and *"I found the game very awkward to use"* (score 41[1]). The higher ratings for the game were the perception that others may learn to use the game quickly *"I would imagine that most people would learn to use the game very quickly"* (score 83[1]), the perception of ease of use *"I thought the game was easy to use"* (score 79[1]), and feeling confident about using the game (*"I felt confident using the game"* (score 75[1]).

Table 1. Survey measures before and after playing the game for all participants

Game survey measures	All participants		
	Pre-game	Post-game	T statistics (p)
Knowledge	3.87 ± 0.86	4.30 ± 1.12	**−2.28 (*0.03*)**
Perceived risk	3.46 ± 0.94	3.77 ± 0.90	**−3.62 (*0.001*)**
Willingness-to-use	1.83 ± 1.18	1.62 ± 1.07	1.67 (*0.1*)

---

[1] Value was normalized to percentages. Some scores that were reversed and normalized to the percentages.

Table 2. Survey measures from pre- and post-game for e-cigarette users and non-users

Game survey measures	E-cigarettes user			Non-user		
	Pre-game	Post-game	T statistics (*p*)	Pre-game	Post-game	T statistics (*p*)
Knowledge	3.88 ± 1.02	4.13 ± 1.41	−0.78 (*0.45*)	3.86 ± 0.66	4.50 ± 0.65	**−3.80 (*0.002*)**
Perceived RIsk	3.65 ± 0.90	3.96 ± 0.88	**−2.46 (*0.03*)**	3.24 ± 0.98	3.55 ± 0.91	**−2.62 (*0.02*)**
Willingness-to-use	1.46 ± 0.84	1.35 ± 0.77	0.55 (*0.59*)	2.26 ± 1.39	1.93 ± 1.30	2.03 (*0.06*)

4   Discussion and Conclusion

The present study showed that playing the educational video game increased the participants' knowledge of e-cigarettes and their risk awareness, which are important predictive factors for future e-cigarette use [24, 25]. Moreover, the non-user group demonstrated less willingness to use e-cigarettes after playing the game. These results supported the initial game design that aimed to influence behavior by changing perceived risk. Recent reports on the smokeSCREEN game in adolescents also showed significant increase in the knowledge and belief of e-cigarette use, proving the potential of videogame playing in delivering e-cigarettes information to the young population [13, 14]. Previous studies using health communication messages to educate youth about health risks of e-cigarettes observed similar effects [17, #15, #26, #27]. The aforementioned findings suggested the importance of education and information delivery in improving the perception of risks which could lead to positive behavior change. Compared to messages, video games have additional advantages in that they are more entertaining and interactive, and many adolescents and young adults play video games.

Despite the promising results, there are several limitations in the current study. First, the prototype of the videogame requires more interactive features and improvement in user experience. According to Bangor, the overall SUS score of 70 would be classified as "OK" which is the median classification [23]. There are challenges in designing interfaces with video games since we observed that most games tend to vary on how the arrange and cluster widgets or have their own unique way to interact with the playability. The results from usability survey could serve as a guide in developing the next version of the game. Second, in this small-scale pilot study, we were not able to investigate the contribution of other factors such as age, gender, and education in the effect of video game. Hieftje et al. [14] found that gender and age were likely associated with the belief or knowledge about e-cigarettes in adolescents. Education could also be a confounding factor as the current participants were all college students. Future study will recruit more participants to achieve enough power for correlation analysis with these variables.

In summary, playing video game could increase the perceived risk and knowledge about e-cigarettes, and thus offers an effective prevention method to fight the epidemic e-cigarette usage in the young generation.

References

1. Cullen, K., Ambrose, B., Gentzke, A., et al.: Notes from the Field: Use of Electronic Cigarettes and Any Tobacco Product Among Middle and High School Students—United States, 2011–2018. MMWR and Morbidity and Mortality Weekly Report 2018. vol. 67, p. 2 (2018)

2. Centers for Disease Control and Prevention: National adult tobacco survey (NATS) 2013–2014. https://www.cdc.gov/tobacco/data_statistics/surveys/nats/index.htm

3. Roberts, M.E., Keller-Hamilton, B., Ferketich, A.K., et al.: Juul and the upsurge of e-cigarette use among college undergraduates. J. Am. Coll. Health, 1–4. (2020). https://doi.org/10.1080/07448481.2020.1726355

4. Cooper, M., Loukas, A., Case, K.R., et al.: A longitudinal study of risk perceptions and e-cigarette initiation among college students: Interactions with smoking status. Drug Alcohol Depend. **186**, 257–263 (2018)

5. Choi, K., Forster, J.L.: Beliefs and experimentation with electronic cigarettes: a prospective analysis among young adults. Am. J. Prev. Med. **46**(2), 175–178 (2014). https://doi.org/10.1016/j.amepre.2013.10.007

6. Fadus, M.C., Smith, T.T., Squeglia, L.M.: The rise of e-cigarettes, pod mod devices, and JUUL among youth: factors influencing use, health implications, and downstream effects. Drug Alcohol Depend. **201**, 85–93 (2019). https://doi.org/10.1016/j.drugalcdep.2019.04.011

7. Amrock, S.M., Zakhar, J., Zhou, S., et al.: Perception of e-cigarette harm and its correlation with use among U.S. adolescents. Nicotine Tob. Res. 17(3) 330–6. 2015. https://doi.org/10.1093/ntr/ntu156

8. Lugmayr, A., Sutinen, E., Suhonen, J., Sedano, C.I., Hlavacs, H., Montero, C.S.: Serious storytelling – a first definition and review. Multimedia Tools Appl. **76**(14), 15707–15733 (2016). https://doi.org/10.1007/s11042-016-3865-5

9. Enah, C., Piper, K., Moneyham, L.: Qualitative evaluation of the relevance and acceptability of a web-based HIV prevention game for rural adolescents. J. Pediatr. Nurs. **30**(2), 321–328 (2015). https://doi.org/10.1016/j.pedn.2014.09.004

10. Montanaro, E., Fiellin, L.E., Fakhouri, T., et al.: Using videogame apps to assess gains in adolescents' substance use knowledge: new opportunities for evaluating intervention exposure and content mastery. J. Med. Internet Res. **17**(10), e245 (2015). https://doi.org/10.2196/jmir.4377

11. Cates, J.R., Crandell, J.L., Diehl, S.J., et al.: Immunization effects of a communication intervention to promote preteen HPV vaccination in primary care practices. Vaccine **36**(1), 122–127 (2018). https://doi.org/10.1016/j.vaccine.2017.11.025

12. Ohannessian, R., Yaghobian, S., Verger, P., et al.: A systematic review of serious video games used for vaccination. Vaccine **34**(38), 4478–4483 (2016). https://doi.org/10.1016/j.vaccine.2016.07.048

13. Pentz, M.A., Hieftje, K.D., Pendergrass, T.M., et al.: A videogame intervention for tobacco product use prevention in adolescents. Addict. Behav. **91**, 188–192 (2019). https://doi.org/10.1016/j.addbeh.2018.11.016

14. Hieftje, K.D., Fernandes, C.F., Lin, I.H., et al., Effectiveness of a web-based tobacco product use prevention videogame intervention on young adolescents' beliefs and knowledge. Substance abuse, p. 1–7 (2019). https://doi.org/10.1080/08897077.2019.1691128

15. US Department of Health and Human Services: E-Cigarette Use Among Youth and Young Adults: A Report of the Surgeon General, US Department of Health and Human Services, Centers for Disease Control and Prevention (US): Atlanta, GA (2016)

518   A. Xu et al.

16. Centers for Disease Control and Prevention: Quick facts on the risks of e-cigarettes for kids, teens, and young adults, 28 August 2019. https://www.cdc.gov/tobacco/basic_information/e-cigarettes/Quick-Facts-on-the-Risks-of-E-cigarettes-for-Kids-Teens-and-Young-Adults.html

17. Noar, S.M., Rohde, J.A., Horvitz, C., et al.: Adolescents' receptivity to E-cigarette harms messages delivered using text messaging. Addict. Behav. **91**, 201–207 (2019). https://doi.org/10.1016/j.addbeh.2018.05.025

18. Rohde, J.A., S.M. Noar, C. Horvitz, et al.: The role of knowledge and risk beliefs in adolescent e-cigarette use: a pilot study. Int. J. Environ. Res. Pub Health, **15**(4), 380 (2018). https://doi.org/10.3390/ijerph15040830

19. Wills, T.A., Sargent, J.D., Knight, R., et al.: E-cigarette use and willingness to smoke: a sample of adolescent non-smokers. Tob. Control **25**(e1), e52–e59 (2016). https://doi.org/10.1136/tobaccocontrol-2015-052349

20. Brooke, J.: SUS-A quick and dirty usability scale. In: ordan, P.W., Thomas, B., McClelland, I.L., Weerdmeester, B., (eds) Usability Evaluation in Industry, vol. 189, no. 194, pp. 4–7. CRC Press, Ohio (1996)

21. Brooke, J.: SUS: a retrospective. J. Usability Stud. **8**(2), 29–40 (2013)

22. Lewis, J.R.: The system usability scale: past, present, and future. Int. J. Hum. Comput. Interact. **34**(7), 577–590 (2018)

23. Bangor, A., Kortum, P., Miller, J.: Determining what individual SUS scores mean: adding an adjective rating scale. J. Usability Stud. **4**(3), 114–123 (2009)

24. Lechner, W.V., Murphy, C.M., Colby, S.M., et al.: Cognitive risk factors of electronic and combustible cigarette use in adolescents. Addict. Behav. **82**, 182–188 (2018). https://doi.org/10.1016/j.addbeh.2018.03.006

25. Jones, K., Salzman, G.A.: The vaping epidemic in adolescents. Mo. Med. **117**(1), 56–58 (2020)

Human Perception and Cognition

Research on the Monitoring of Human Auditory and Visual Stimulation Based on Brain Wave Visualization System

Qi Chen[✉]

Wuhan Textile University, Wuhan, China
592197305@qq.com

Abstract. Currently there is no standard treatment for vegetative patients. The treatment mainly focuses on the traditional medical treatment. However, the daily rehabilitation training of vegetative patients also needs the support of various scientific and technological systems. For example, a rehabilitation monitoring system can help observe the status of the patients during the stimulation treatment. However, currently the market lacks such system for clinic usage. The purpose of the research is to develop a brain wave visualization system that can be used for monitoring vegetative patients. Two versions of the system were developed. The first version can collect brain waves from normal people. The second version can successfully collect brain waves of vegetative patients and detect changes in the patient's brain wave data when the patient receives and auditory stimulation, it is verified that our brainwave visualization system can be used as a rehabilitation monitoring system of vegetative patients. In the future, more experimental data needs to optimize the accuracy of the brain-computer interface algorithms, thereby improving the rehabilitation monitoring system.

Keywords: Brain wave visualization · Audio visual stimulation · System development

1 Research Background

1.1 Medical Premise of Vegetative Patients Rehabilitation

According to incomplete statistics, there are about one million "vegetative patients" in China. Through treatment, some patients will change from vegetative state to minimal consciousness state (MCS). Patients in MCS have physiological potential to be awakened [1]. It is a new way to use the visualization of brain wave information to stimulate the patients' visual and audio senses, and to show patients' families their brain activity state.

1.2 The Effect of Visual and Auditory Stimulation on Human Brain

In some studies, images in the International Affective Picture System database (IAPS) [2] with different emotional contents (pleasant, unpleasant and neutral) were widely

© Springer Nature Switzerland AG 2020
C. Stephanidis and M. Antona (Eds.): HCII 2020, CCIS 1224, pp. 521–525, 2020.
https://doi.org/10.1007/978-3-030-50726-8_68

used. The common finding in these studies was that the responses of brain to unpleasant and neutral stimuli are different. The brightness of visual stimuli has the potential to affect sensory and cognitive processes in visual processing studies. Some visual processing studies found that the brightness of visual stimuli could be represented by the change of the activity power of the brain cortex. Therefore, our study starts from visual stimulation combined with brain wave visualization system. The aim of the study is to find what types of visual style, color and shape can have a better effect on stimulate vegetative patients.

In addition to visual stimulation, auditory stimulation can also help patients with rehabilitation training. Auditory stimulation can enrich the environment and improve the awakening and consciousness state of vegetative patients. Clinical studies believe that the generation of consciousness is the result of the joint action of multiple brain networks. The auditory cortex is an important part of some brain networks (Default mode network). Auditory stimulation is also effective in the recovery of consciousness, and a recent study focusing on the impact of sensory stimulation programs (SSP) in the recovery of Disorders of consciousness (DOC)highlighted that SSP may not be sufficient to restore consciousness but it may lead to improved behavioral responsiveness in patients in MCS. Our study uses family calling as an important means of auditory stimulation. We use brain wave visualization system to visualize the change of attention level when patients hear the family calling, so that patients' families can understand the response of patients to different auditory stimulation more directly and cost effectively. The purpose of this research is to help families to carry out auditory and visual stimulation for patients in a long term and more effectively way.

2 Research Methods

2.1 Research Equipment

The wearable EEG acquisition equipment used in this study is from company named Intraexon. The device has seven electrodes. Data acquisition mode belongs to bipolar mode. The equipment measures the potential difference between two electrodes. The advantages include its mature technology, low price, portability and simplicity of operation.

2.2 Brain Computer Interface Algorithm Scheme

According to different frequencies, human brain waves can be divided into δ wave, θ wave, α wave, SMR wave, β wave, high β wave and other types. Each of them respectively represents a different type of brain activity. The following Table 1 gives a summary of all analysis.

Based on the principle of brain wave activities, this research collected the brain wave of five normal healthy people in three states which include calm, concentration and relaxation. We obtain the algorithm of these three different states of brain by test and calculate.

Table 1. Relationship between brain wave and brain activity

Brain wave type	Brain wave frequency (HZ)	Brain activity
δ wave	0.1–3	Deep sleep, sober, attentive.
θ wave	4–7	Sleep, idle
α wave	8–12	Relax
SMR wave	12–15	Concentrate
β wave	15–20	Think positively and focus
High β wave	20–35	Nervousness, anxiety

2.3 Steps of Brain Wave Visualization

The system uses our algorithm to process the user's real-time brain wave data. First, the EEG wearable equipment can help us to obtain δ wave, θ wave and α wave. Second, we filter out useless data with mass signals by weighting the quality signal. Then, the patient's attention degree will be obtaining in real time through special algorithm processing. Finally, the attention degree could be visualized through the changing of color, shape, animation speed and movement direction.

3 Research Results

3.1 Brainwave Visualization System Version 1.0

The version 1.0 of brain wave visualization system collected 5 healthy volunteers (control group). First, we used the brain wave data of these normal healthy people to improve algorithm of the attention level. After that, five volunteers took part in the text of the system. They all gave subjective feedback on the use experience of brain wave visualization system version 1.0.

3.2 Brainwave Visualization System Version 2.0

Based on the summary of the research, we have improved the system. The main contents of improvement: First we improved the sound correlation. Then, we increased the image richness and correlation. Next, we improved accuracy of the algorithm. Finally, we changed wo-dimensional and three-dimensional graphics. A right-hand paralyzed patient (experimental group) from China Rehabilitation Center was invited to the test the version 2.0 in order to collect data. We guide the patient to do hand drawing, and the brainwave visualization system successfully collected the real-time brainwave of the patient when he was drawing. In order to further study the effect of auditory to vegetative patients, we included 4 patients with good hearing to join the test of brain wave visualization system. First, we organized the family members of the patients, and help the patients to wear the EEG equipment. Next, we encourage the family members to praise, interact with the patients. Then, the monitoring system showed that the patients' attention intensity was increased to a certain extent compared with the quiet state. This means that the vegetative patients can perceive the external sound stimulation and cause the change of attention.

4 Discussion

Vegetative patients are not only a medical problem, but also the impact to the whole family members, finally it will turn into a social problem. It is urgent to solve the problem of recovery and rehabilitation of vegetative patients. Nowadays, clinical "wake-up promotion" treatment and life support are still the main means of treatment for vegetative patients, but the proportion of the patients in MCS who finally wake up successfully is rare. With the passage of time, lots of family members will have to give up treatment within two years for the patient because of the heavy economic burden. Some patients will change from vegetative state to MCS through clinical treatment, and these patients have physiological potential to be awakened. It has become the core problem of the treatment of "waking up" for the vegetative patients to recover from MCS. With the development of information technology, it is a new method to use brainwave visualization to show families members the patients' brain activity state. This method can help patients be trained by more effective visual and auditory stimulation. In this study, wearable EEG acquisition equipment was used to transform the collected EEG into attention degree. The way to calculate attention degree is according to the relationship between EEG frequency and real-time brain activity. Visualization image of the system was formed through brain computer interface algorithm in real time to reflect the conscious state of vegetative patients. Through the optimization of the version 1.0, the upgraded version 2.0 of brain wave visualization system can successfully collect brain waves of vegetative patients and convert their real time brain data into visual images. The version 2.0 of brain wave visualization system can monitor and record these changes well.

5 Conclusion

The brain wave of human body can be monitored by a simple wearable device. The brain wave visualization system developed in this study can be used to monitor the audio-visual stimulation of human body (healthy people and vegetative patients). This study found that visualizing the brain wave activity of patients can help to find the role of specific visual or auditory stimuli. The brain wave data of patients show different degree of positive correlation response. Therefore, patients with normal function of hearing and seeing can use the brain wave visualization system to assist in the daily rehabilitation training of visual and auditory stimulation. Of course, we need more experimental data and more optimized brain computer interface algorithm to further explore this field to help vegetative patients with a better rehabilitation training system.

References

1. Di, H.: Plant man perspectives for consciousness research. 意识研究的植物人视角, Science, **4**, 22–26 (2016)
2. Lang, P.J., Bradley, M.M., Cuthbert, B.N.: International affective picture system (IAPS): technical manual and affective ratings. NIMH Cent. Study Emot. Atten. **1**, 39–58 (1997)

Comparison of the Remembering Ability by the Difference Between Handwriting and Typeface

Risa Ito[1(✉)], Karin Hamano[1(✉)], Kosuke Nonaka[1(✉)],
Ippei Sugano[1(✉)], Satoshi Nakamura[1(✉)], Akiyuki Kake[2(✉)],
and Kizuku Ishimaru[2(✉)]

[1] Meiji University, Nakano 4-21-1, Nakano-Ku, Tokyo, Japan
ev170504@meiji.ac.jp
[2] Wacom, Toyonodai 2-510-1, Kazo-Shi, Saitama, Japan

Abstract. When people study something, it is common to memorize textbooks, reference books, and notes that are handwritten or typed. Those memorization tasks are known to be effectively done with typefaces that are hard to read. Then, it is assumed that handwriting would help you memorize things better than typed letters as it is often difficult to read and the form of letters is not uniform. In this research, we conducted experiments on handwritten characters and typefaces that have different features from each other to verify whether they work differently for memorization. The result found that handwritten characters are more likely to be retained in memory than typefaces. Specifically, familiar handwritten characters are more likely to be retained in memory.

Keywords: Handwriting · Typeface · Memory · Character shape · Memory easiness

1 Introduction

When people study something, they use textbooks, reference books, lecture slides, and notes in which the contents of the lectures and the textbooks are organized. These books, slides, and notes are written with various forms of characters. Usually, typefaces are used in textbooks and reference books. On the other hand, notes are handwritten or typed.

According to the study of Mueller et al. [1] concluded that students who took notes on a laptop performed worse on conceptual questions than students who took notes by hand. Mendizábal et al. [2] also concluded that students who took notes by hand performed better on memory tests than those who took notes by computer. These studies focused on the comparison of writing and typing, but it has not been clarified which form of characters, handwriting or typeface, is more effective for memorization.

Various studies have been conducted on the influence of the character style used when memorizing. For example, Diemand-Yauman et al. [3] have clarified that it is easy to remember the contents when they are written in a typeface that is difficult to read. In addition, Sungkhasettee et al. [4] showed that it is easier to memorize words

© Springer Nature Switzerland AG 2020
C. Stephanidis and M. Antona (Eds.): HCII 2020, CCIS 1224, pp. 526–534, 2020.
https://doi.org/10.1007/978-3-030-50726-8_69

that are rotated 180° to make them difficult to read. These results suggest that unrecognizable characters are more likely to be retained in memory. Then, since handwritten characters are often difficult to read and the form of letters is not uniform compared to characters in typefaces, it is expected that memorization would be easier with handwritten characters than characters in typefaces. However, it has not been clarified whether memorization can be done more easily with handwritten characters or typefaces. Given that typefaces are easier to read due to the uniform style of characters, it is expected that handwritten characters are more helpful for memorization.

In this research, in order to realize a style of note which makes it easy to memorize things, we examine what form of characters has high effect for memorization when learning. We hypothesize that handwriting is more effective for memorization than uniform, relatively readable typed characters. We also focus on features of handwriting and typed characters, and carry out a memory task experiment to verify which one helps memorization more.

2   Characteristic Memory Experiment

2.1   Outline of the Experiment

In order to verify the hypothesis that handwriting is more effective for memorization than uniform, relatively readable typed characters, we conducted a feature-memory experiment to see if memorization can be influenced by whether the information to memorize was handwritten or typed. The experiment was designed based on the study by Diemand-Yauman et al. [3], in which the participants were asked to memorize features of imaginary things. In the experiment, two types of typefaces, MS Gothic and MS Mincho, and two types of handwritten characters were compared. Though handwriting characters necessarily have various types of individual differences, two types of handwritten characters with different features were used for the current study. The features of the two kinds of handwritten characters (hereinafter referred to as handwritten A and handwritten B) are as follows (see Fig. 1).

- handwriting A: Round, wide, and angular
- handwriting B: Angled, long, and chained

2.2   Experimental Procedure

In this experiment, participants were provided with a document in which three imaginary proper nouns and seven features for each noun were written, and were asked to memorize them in 90 s. The text was written in one of the four forms shown in Fig. 1 and Fig. 2. The order effect was considered for the presentation of the character style. After the memorization session, we asked the participants to watch a 15-min-long video clip to take a rest. After that, the participants were asked to answer 10 questions about 21 items (3 nouns × 7 features). An example of the question is shown in Fig. 3 and Fig. 4.

Fig. 1. The characters used in the experiment (in Japanese).

Fig. 2. English translation of the example
in Fig. 1.

A total of 4 trials were conducted for each participant. After all the trials, the participants were asked to answer a questionnaire about whether they had confidence in their own handwriting, whether their handwriting resembled one of the two hand-written characters used in the experiment, readability of the four characters used in the experiment, how often they read typed letters, how often they look at handwritten characters, the experimental design, and impressions about the experiment.

The participants were 26 undergraduate students aged 18 to 23 (7 males and 12 females). The presentation order of the themes was unified for all members. The order was Alien, Cake, Country, and Animal.

2.3   Result

The participants' responses were evaluated as one correct answer counts as 10 points, so 100 points (10 points × 10 questions) was the full marks for each participant. The responses were regarded as correct as long as they mention a keyword of the item, even if they do not perfectly match the correct answer. Also, if the participants completely mistook an item for another when answering the questions, their responses were considered to be correct, since they were simple mistake and still show that the participants memorized the content.

A graph of the average scores for each character type is shown in Fig. 5. The results showed that the average score was the highest with handwriting B and the lowest with MS Gothic. Also, the results showed that the average scores of the handwritten characters were higher than those of the typefaces. In addition, the score of MS Gothic was found to be consistently low throughout the tests. The corresponding t-test revealed that there was a significant difference between MS Gothic and handwriting B ($p < 0.05$). On the other hand, there were no significant differences among the other characters.

お名前　　　　スコア

(1) ノルグレッドの体長は？

(2) パンジェリッシュは何を食べる？

(3) ダーレンガの目は何色？

(4) パンジェリッシュはどこで生活する？

(5) ノルグレッドはどうやって会話する？

(6) ダーレンガは何を食べる？

(7) パンジェリッシュの紫色の尾の特徴は？

(8) ダーレンガの肌は？

(9) ノルグレッドの角は何色？

(10) ダーレンガはどこで生活する？

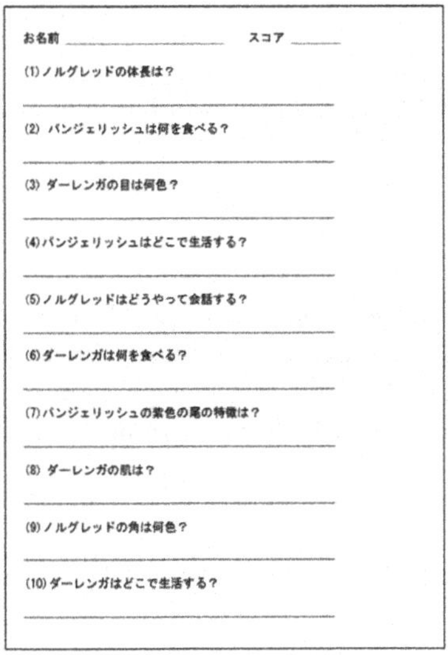

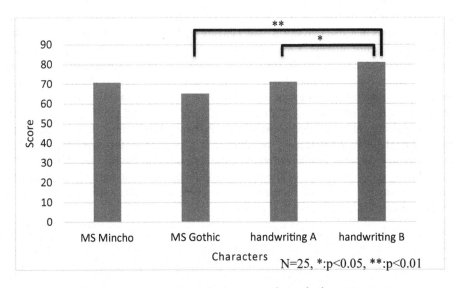

Fig. 3. An example of the original question in Japanese.

Name　　　　Score

(1) How tall is the norgletti?

(2) What does the pangerish eat?

(3) What color eyes does the derlenga?

(4) Where does the pangerish live?

(5) How does the norgletti communicate?

(6) What does the derlenga eat?

(7) What is the characteristics of the purple tails of pangerish?

(8) Describe the skin of the derlenga.

(9) What color the corner does the norgletti have?

(10) Where does the derlenga live?

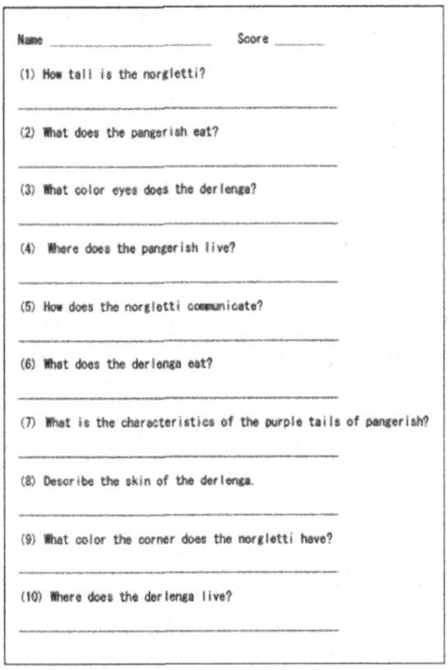

Fig. 4. English translation of the example of the question in the Fig. 3.

Tables 1 and 2 show the number of people who answered in the questionnaire that each style of characters was easy/hard to read and their average scores. As for handwriting B, it not only had the highest average score of the test, but also had the largest number of people (16 participants) who answered that the letter was illegible among the four types of characters. These results suggest that handwriting characters are more likely to be memorized than typefaces, and that, among handwriting characters, illegible handwriting is more likely to be memorized.

Fig. 5. The average remembering scores for each character type.

Table 1. The number of participants who found each character easy to read and their averaged scores.

	MS Mincho	MS Gothic	handwriting A	handwriting B
The number of people	24	22	18	9
Score	70.0	61.8	77.2	77.8

In addition, 9 participants answered in the questionnaire that their handwriting is similar to handwriting A. On the other hand, 16 participants answered that their handwriting is similar to handwriting B. Table 3 shows the average score of each handwriting character of the two groups divided by which handwriting is similar to their own.

Table 2. The number of participants who found each character hard to read and their averaged scores.

	MS Mincho	MS Gothic	handwriting A	handwriting B
The number of people	1	3	7	16
Score	50.0	73.3	68.6	73.1

Table 3. The relationship between the similarity of handwriting and its score.

	handwriting A	handwriting B
Participant's handwriting is similar to the handwriting A	**80.0**	72.2
Participant's handwriting is similar to the handwriting B	71.3	**77.5**

All the participants who found handwriting A similar to their own handwriting answered that handwriting A was easy to read or slightly easy to read, and seven of them answered that handwriting B was hard to read or slightly difficult to read. The averaged test score of these 9 participants was the highest for handwriting A. For the participants who answered that their handwriting is similar to handwriting B, their answers about the readability of handwriting A and handwriting B did not show any tendency on which one was easier to read, but the averaged test score was highest for handwriting B. In other words, both groups of participants had the highest test scores for handwriting characters that are similar to their own handwriting. In addition, there were 12 participants whose scores were higher than average for the characters that they answered were difficult to read. Moreover, the difference in the average test scores of MS Mincho and MS Gothic of the participants who found handwriting A similar to their own was 6.7, while the difference of the participants who answered their handwriting resembles handwriting B was 10.0.

2.4   Additional Experiment

A graph of the average test scores for each character type is shown in Fig. 6.

In order to confirm the result that handwriting B is easy to be retained in the memory and MS Gothic is difficult to be retained in the memory, an additional experiment was carried out. The participants were 14 undergraduate students aged 18 to 22 (8 males and 6 females). The additional experiment was conducted with the same procedure as the previous experiment, but the contents to be memorized were changed. The themes used for the additional experiment were "Animal," "Amusement park," "Clothing," and "Cuisine," and they were presented in a fixed order. Table 4 shows the results of the additional experiment. Since there was one participant in this experiment whose score was considered as outlier (mean $\pm$ 2 SD), the scores for the other 13 participants were considered. The result showed that the average point of MS Gothic was the lowest, which was the same result as the main experiment.

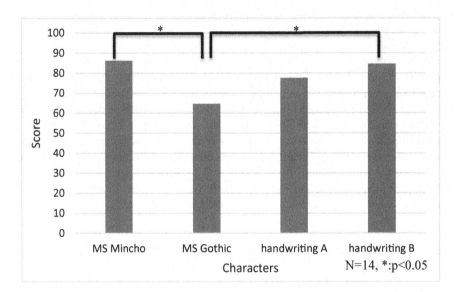

Fig. 6. A graph of the average scores for each character type.

Table 4. The average score of the additional experiment for each character type.

	MS Mincho	MS Gothic	handwriting A	handwriting B
Additional experiment	86.2	64.6	77.7	84.6

3 Consideration

The result of the experiments and the questionnaire showed that the test score tended to be higher when the information to memorize was written in a type of character that the participants felt was difficult to read. On the other hand, there was no correlation between the test score and readability of the characters that the participants found easy to read or slightly easy to read.

The reason for the high score for the handwriting characters would be that they are often deformed and difficult to read, so they are more likely to be memorized than typefaces. The results also revealed that the participants got higher test scores when the information to memorize was written in a character type that is similar to their own handwriting. This may be because characters that are relatively similar to one's own handwriting are easier to understand.

It is assumed as a reason why illegible characters led to the high scores that illegible characters are read so slowly that the readers would not miss the content while reading. One of the participants actually commented in the questionnaire that typefaces were easier to read but they sometimes just went over the sentences without understanding their contents.

It was found in the results that there was a difference between MS Mincho and MS Gothic in the test scores of the participants who answered that their handwriting is similar to handwriting B. Given that the result of the study by Diemand-Yauman et al. [3] can be applied to Japanese characters, the difference would be due to the fact that the lines of MS Mincho were thinner and harder to read than MS Gothic. However, many participants answered in the questionnaire that MS Mincho was easier to read or a little easier to read than MS Gothic, so this consideration needs to be reexamined.

Table 5 shows the degree of cosine similarity for each character with 50 points as a default value. They were calculated to clarify the types of characters whose results were similar and to examine features of the characters that affect memory.

Table 5. The degree of cosine similarity for each character.

	Cosine similarity
MS Mincho and MS Gothic	0.69
MS Mincho and handwriting A	0.67
MS Mincho and handwriting B	0.63
MS Gothic and handwriting A	0.57
MS Gothic and handwriting B	0.52
handwriting A and handwriting B	0.72

It can be seen in Table 5 that the cosine similarity was high between handwritten characters and between typefaces, and that there is a relationship between the character shapes and the test score. The cosine similarity between the two handwritten characters (handwriting A and handwriting B) and MS Mincho was high, but the cosine similarity between the handwritten characters and MS Gothic was low. MS Mincho has features of Japanese characters such as *Tome* (stop), *Hane* (upward stroke ending), *Harai* (sweeping stroke ending) while MS Gothic does not, which led to the difference in the cosine similarities. Also, since the test score of MS Gothic was drastically lower than other characters in both the main experiment and the additional experiment, it can be said that MS Gothic is not suitable as a character to be used for memorization.

4   Conclusion

In this study, we conducted memory task experiments using handwritten characters and typefaces with different characteristics under the hypothesis that handwriting characters are more memorable than typefaces. The experimental results showed that angular handwriting, which is relatively difficult to read, was the easiest to remember and that MS Gothic, which is relatively easy to read, was the most difficult to remember. The results partially support the hypothesis in that handwriting was easier to remember than MS Gothic, but the hypothesis was not fully verified in terms of comparison between handwriting and typefaces. The difference in memorability between handwritten characters and MS Gothic characters was considered to be due to the facts that handwritten characters are often out of shape compared to typefaces and that they are similar to the handwriting of the participants themselves.

The present study only examined four types of characters (handwriting A, handwriting B, MS Mincho, and MS Gothic), so future study will conduct experiments with characters with other features and see whether the difference in the memorability can be observed. Also, the experiments of the present study used handwriting characters that were written by a person who was not a participant of the experiment, so it was possible that both handwriting A and handwriting B were not similar to the participants' handwriting. Thus, experiments with the same procedure but using the handwriting of each participant would be considered as a future study.

In addition, as there are features of character shapes that work as a factor to be easily retained in memory, it is assumed that typeface that is both easy to read and memorize can be realized by fusing one's own handwriting and illegible typefaces using the method proposed by [5] Saito et al. Also, our future study will look at factors to improve memorization, and aim to realize notebook that helps memorization.

Acknowledgements. This work was supported in part by JST ACCEL Grant Number JPMJAC1602, Japan.

References

1. Pam, A.M., Daniel, M.O.: The pen is mightier than the keyboard: advantages of longhand over laptop note taking. Psychol. Sci. **25**(6), 1159–1168 (2014)
2. Estíbaliz, A.M., Candida, D.C., Jose, I.N., Inmaculada, M., Romero-Oliva, M.F.: A comparative study of handwriting and computer typing in note-taking by university students. Comunicar, **24**(48) (2016)
3. Diemand-Yauman, C., Oppenheimer, D.M., Vaughan, E.B.: Fortune favors the bold (and the Italicized): effect of disfluency on educational outcomes. Cognition **118**(1), 111–115 (2011)
4. Victor, W.S., Michael, C.F., Alan, D.C.: Memory and metamemory for inverted words: illusions of competency and desirable difficulties. Psychon. Bull. Rev. **18**, 973 (2011)
5. Junki, S., Satoshi, N.: Fontender: interactive Japanese text design with dynamic font fusion method for comics. In: 25th International Conference on MultiMedia Modeling, MMM2019, pp. 554–559 (2019)

Defect Annotation on Objects Using a Laser Remote Conrol

Christian Lengenfelder[1(✉)], Gerrit Holzbach[1], Michael Voit[1],
and Jürgen Beyerer[1,2]

[1] Fraunhofer Institute of Optronics, System Technologies and Image Exploitation
Fraunhofer IOSB, Karlsruhe, Germany
{christian.lengenfelder,gerrit.holzbach,michael.voit,
juergen.beyerer}@iosb.fraunhofer.de
[2] Vision and Fusion Laboratory,
Karlsruhe Institute of Technology (KIT), Karlsruhe, Germany

Abstract. In manufacturing, annotating defects for later correction is tedious and still not yet standardized. This task cannot be automated in the foreseeable future since finding and assessing the severity of defects is even for human workers a challenging task. As in the production of car body panels, the manufactured parts are often checked for dents or scratches. Defect slippage is cost-intensive. Therefore, thorough documentation is beneficial. Most manufacturers use direct defect annotation with a grease pencil, coarse masks on a computer or handheld, paper checklists, or simple 'not OK' labels on the parts for later inspection and repair. Since no accurate digital documentation of defects is available, defect slippage rates due to workers overlooking annotations are high. Moreover, the required attention shift between the part itself to a representation on a paper or computer screen and vice versa introduces inaccuracies, defect misses and is time consuming. In this contribution, a novel remote control pointing device for defect annotation on objects is proposed. A pilot study was conducted in which the accuracy, user experience and task load were evaluated against a tablet based input method. The results show an average accuracy of 1.5 cm versus 5.1 cm with the novel input method and an overall better and lower task load and user experience.

Keywords: Quality assurance · Defect marking · Augmented reality and environments

1 Introduction

In this paper, we examine the task of annotating defects on workpieces with an defect type. Today, the manufactured parts drive past the worker on an assembly line. The worker then has limited time to visually scan the part for defects and to mark them with the appropriate defect type label. Most manufacturers use direct defect annotation with a grease pencil, coarse masks on a computer or handheld,

© Springer Nature Switzerland AG 2020
C. Stephanidis and M. Antona (Eds.): HCII 2020, CCIS 1224, pp. 535–542, 2020.
https://doi.org/10.1007/978-3-030-50726-8_70

paper checklists, or simple 'not OK' labels on the parts for later inspection. The current state of the art is a handheld for digital annotation (see Fig. 1(a)). The part is shown to the worker with a grid overlay and the worker can attach a defect type label to every grid cell (see Fig. 1(b)).

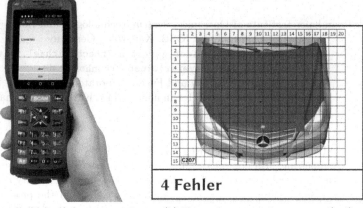

(a) Example handheld for defect annotation   (b) Example annotation on part (red)

Fig. 1. Example image of an input handheld for error annotation (a) and the error view (b) [1]

The advantage of the handheld is that defects are annotated digitally and no additional hardware is needed. This way, the worker mending the defect in a later production stage does not have to search for grease annotations on the part itself and the number of defects is instantly clear. On the other hand, the annotation is very coarse. The same 20 by 15 grid as seen in Fig. 1(b) is used for all possible parts. A bonnet and a chassis both share the same grid size, hence, for larger objects, the annotation accuracy decreases. Furthermore, shifting the attention between the inspected part and the handheld is time-consuming. As the time for finding, identifying and marking all defects is limited, this might cause error slippage.

We propose a novel interaction method that enables a user to precisely annotate defects directly on a part and simultaneously digitize it. In fact, this interaction method can be used to annotate positions on arbitrary objects. To achieve this, we integrated a laser pointer into a remote control (in the following abbreviated as LRC) which contains a thumbstick and several buttons (see Fig. 3). To annotate a defect, the user points the laser light at a defect position and selects the defect type in a menu using the thumbstick. The laser is tracked by a stereo camera system and the menu is projected using an off-the-shelf projector which is calibrated to the stereo system. The advantage of this system is that the error is anchored directly to the 3D CAD position of the object instead of an orthogonal projection. This way, the error can be highlighted again on the

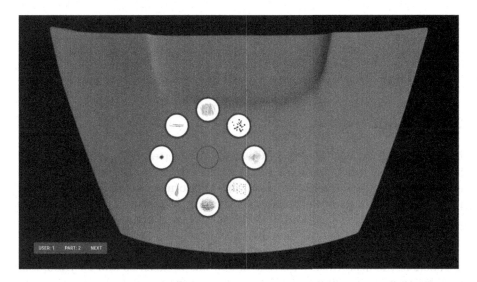

Fig. 2. Annotation screen as provided on the tablet

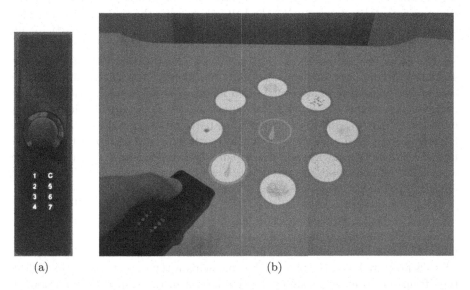

(a)   (b)

Fig. 3. Laser remote control (a) and an example image of the menu projection as seen by the user (b)

part at the mending station or it can be directly used for automatic correction steps. To assess the potential of the novel interaction method we conducted a pilot study, which is presented in the following sections of this contribution.

Fig. 4. Visualizations of the defect types used in the experiment.

2   Methods

In order to find out whether the LRC would allow better performance compared to the tablet, we conducted a pilot study. Hence, there is one independent variable, interaction device, with two conditions. Performance is measured as defect type error rate, accuracy and completion time for each trial. In addition to those objective measures, the subjective workload was measured using the Raw-TLX [2], and user satisfaction was measured using the UEQ-S [3] questionnaire.

Six participants (0 female, 6 male, 0 divers) volunteered in the study. All were members of the department. The age of two was between 20 and 29 years, four were between 30 and 39 years. All were experienced users of computer systems and familiar with touch interaction on tablets, none had used the LRC before. A within-subjects design was applied, meaning that each participant accomplished the experimental task once using the LRC, once using the tablet input; in order to control learning effects as well as fatigue effects, one half of the participants started with LRC, the other with the tablet.

The experimental tasks were designed as follows. Each trial started with one second of bright light displayed all over the bonnet in order to indicate the trial start. Then, defects were presented as projections on the bonnet, and the participant searched the bonnet and annotated the defects using the provided interaction device; a trial finished, when the participant pressed a certain button. Each trial comprised null, one or two defects which occurred all over the bonnet. For each interaction device, the participants had to accomplish 20 trials. There were eight different types of defects (see Fig. 4). For the projections, the inverse images of the defect types from Fig. 4 were used.

The annotation works as follows. The participant moves the LCR such that the red laser point is positioned on the defect. A red circle indicates that the camera system is able to track the laser position robustly and that the system is ready for annotation. A click on the thumbstick Fig. 3(a) then triggers a menu which is projected onto the bonnet. The participant then selects the fitting defect type from the menu by pushing the thumbstick in the respective direction. A second click on the thumbstick places the selected defect icon onto the bonnet as a bright projection. Clicking the 'c' button on the LCR closes the menu. In the case, the participant wants to delete an annotation, he points at it and clicks the thumbstick. Finally, to confirm the annotations and to finish the trial, the participant presses the '1' button on the remote control. This triggers the one second of bright light on the bonnet separating each two consecutive trials.

The annotation on the tablet works as follows. The tablet shows an orthogonal view of the bonnet scaled to the proportion of the original bonnet. Then, the defect on the bonnet is annotated by tapping the respective position on the tablet. The same menu as for the LRC interaction technique is presented to select the appropriate defect type (see Fig. 2). Tapping on the menu entry adds the annotation to the tablet. Tapping a placed annotation deletes it. The user confirms the trial with a tap on a button labeled 'next', provided in the lower left corner on the tablet (Fig. 2). The used Nexus 10 tablet has a weight of 600 g and is therefore comparable with the weight of the commonly used handhelds like one depicted in Fig. 1(a) which weights 570 g.

The procedure was as follows. After an introduction into the experiment including an explanation of the two questionnaires, each participant gave informed consent. Then, the participant started with interaction condition A. First, there was an explanation, what the experimental task would be and how to use the interaction device. After that, the participant performed a training of the interaction using a training trial. Training time was at least two minutes, but each participant was allowed to train until he felt familiar with the interaction device. After training, the participant accomplished the 20 test tasks. After this, the participant filled in the Raw-TLX, and then the UEQ-S questionnaire. Then, the participant was told to take a short pause to rest. After that, the participant accomplished the experiment for interaction condition B following the same procedure as described for interaction condition A.

3 Results

The results of the objective measures are summarized in Table 1. They include the accuracy of the annotated defect, the defect type error rate, the defect misses rate and the completion time. Accuracy and completion time are given as cumulated means ±1 standard deviation. The results of the Raw-TLX questionnaire are summarized in Table 3 and visualized in Fig. 6 as box-whiskers-plot; lower values are better. The pragmatic, hedonic and total quality determined with the UEQ-S questionnaire are summarized in Table 2 and visualized in Fig. 5 as box-whiskers-plot; higher values are better.

Table 1. Results for the two interaction devices.

Accuracy	LRC	Tablet
Average accuracy (mm)	14.56 ± 10.75	51.3 ± 28.19
Defect type error	3.4%	2.6%
Missed defects	2.5%	3.4%
Average trial time	15.5 s ± 5.6 s	12.6 s ± 5.4 s

4 Discussion

The results show that annotations with the LRC have an average distance of 1.5 cm from the defects whereas the tablet annotations have an average distance of

Table 2. UEQ-S results

UEQ-S questionnaire		
Pragmatic quality	LRC	Tablet
	2.08 ± 0.70	1.13 ± 0.68
Hedonic quality	1.92 ± 0.79	−0.83 ± 1.3
Total quality	2.00 ± 0.68	0.15 ± 0.70

Table 3. Raw-TLX results

Raw-TLX questionnaire		
Effort	LRC	Tablet
	2.00 ± 1.55	3.17 ± 1.17
Frustration	3.00 ± 1.79	2.00 ± 0.89
Mental demand	2.33 ± 1.50	2,83 ± 1,17
Physical demand	1.67 ± 0.82	3.12 ± 2.04
Performance	2.83 ± 1.33	3.67 ± 1.37
Temporal demand	2.50 ± 1.38	3.50 ± 1.04

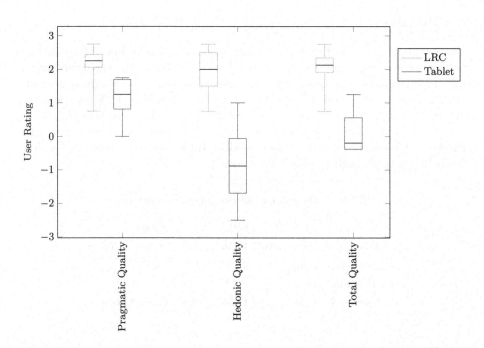

Fig. 5. UEQ-S evaluation results

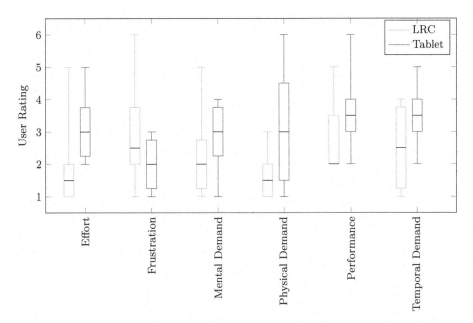

Fig. 6. Raw-TLX evaluation results

5.1 cm. Those annotations are off by a factor of 3.5 compared to the ones done with LRC. Also the probability of defects misses is on average slightly higher with the tablet. This might be due to the constant change of focus back and forth between the bonnet and the tablet. On the other hand, the rate of defect type errors is slightly higher with LRC. However, due to the small sample size no conclusions can be drawn from the small difference. The time a user needed for a trial is slightly increased for the LRC. This may be because the participants are experienced with touch interaction which is present in their daily life mobile phone use. Also, participants reported a short latency until the pointing was robust on the defect.

Results of the Raw-TLX show that the physical demand of the tablet interaction is 1.36 points higher than with the LRC. The participants reported that soon the tablet was heavy to hold. Also they reported that switching attention between part and tablet is stressful for the neck as it requires multiple head movements. The frustration with the LRC is on average 1 point higher than the tablet interaction. This might be due to the latency of the laser tracking. So the user had to wait a short time when pointing at the error instead of immediately tapping on the tablet. Even though the participants were on average 3 s faster using the tablet, they felt more time pressure. The temporal demand of the tablet is 1 point higher than that of the LRC. This might be due to the fact that with the LRC interaction the inspected part itself serves as the interaction interface. With the tablet interaction, the user has to shift attention between the inspected part and the interaction interface which is the tablet screen.

The Effort with the LRC was rated 1.17 points better than the tablet. The participants reported that they would have liked a visual feedback on the bonnet like with the LRC to show which position they annotated. Without feedback they had to orientate on prominent features of the bonnet and sometimes they felt like guessing. This might also be visible in the Performance score which is 0.85 points better with the LRC. Even though the participants had prior experience with the tablet interaction but not with LRC it is interesting and compelling that the task load scores are overall better for the LRC. The UEQ-S shows that the LRC has a pragmatic quality of 2.08. The participants value the supportive character of our system and find it intuitive and easy to use. The hedonic quality of the LRC has a value of 1.92. The participants find the interaction method inventive and leaning-edge. The total quality is 2 which is therefore excellent. The tablet interaction has a pragmatic quality of 1.13. The participants find the tablet interaction intuitive and easy to use. The hedonic quality is −0.83. The participants assess it rather not interesting and usual. The overall quality is 0.15 which is far worse compared to our LRC.

The study shows the tendency that the proposed LRC is an improvement to the current state of the art in defect annotation. Our LRC method has an overall lower task load and a noticeably better user experience than the tablet interaction. In the future we plan to conduct a study with assembly line workers in a non laboratory environment.

References

1. Gewohn, M.T.: Ein methodischer Beitrag zur hybriden Regelung der Produktionsqualität in der Fahrzeugmontage. Ph.D. thesis, Karlsruher Institut für Technologie (KIT) (2019). https://doi.org/10.5445/KSP/1000090358
2. Hart, S.G.: Nasa-task load index (NASA-TLX); 20 years later. In: Proceedings of the Human Factors and Ergonomics Society Annual Meeting, Sage Publications Sage CA: Los Angeles, CA, vol. 50, pp. 904–908. Sage Publications (2006)
3. Schrepp, M., Hinderks, A., Thomaschewski, J.: Design and evaluation of a short version of the user experience questionnaire (UEQ-S). IJIMAI 4(6), 103–108 (2017)

The Impact of Viewing and Listening to Fantastic Events on Children's Inhibitory Control

Muyun Long and Hui Li[✉]

Central China Normal University, Wuhan 430070, Hubei,
People's Republic of China
muyun_long@foxmail.com, huilipsy@mail.ccnu.edu.cn

Abstract. The purpose of the present study is to examine the immediate effects of viewing and listening fantastical events on 4- and 5-year-old children. The result suggested that listening to fantastical stories for about 10 min disrupted children's inhibitory control, but no such negative effect was found after viewing them. Parents should be alert to this negative effect.

Keywords: Children · Fantastical events · Inhibitory control

1 Introduction

The popularity of audiobooks apps on mobile devices has brought new life to this industry. According to big data analysis from one of the biggest online bookstores in China, nearly half (48.5%) of parents spend 10 to 30 min listening to children's audiobooks with their children per day [1]. Most studies have compared the influence of audiobooks on children with that of other popular media, such as television, and found that audio directly influences children's memory, comprehension, imagination, etc. [2–6].

Fantastical stories are a forever theme for children. Recent research targeted to parents who are also audiobook apps users finds that more than half of them offer children fairy tales [7], which are often filled with fantastical events that cannot occur in real life. Audiobooks also play an important role in children's cognition. For example, viewing fantastical videos, whether at high or low speed, impairs children's executive function [8]. Brain image technology functional near infrared spectroscopy's data suggests that children use greater cognitive resources when viewing fantastical events because greater activation in children's dorsolateral prefrontal cortex was observed when they were viewing them [9]. If fantastical television immediately affects children's inhibitory control executive function, then one might see a similar effect with audio.

Executive function (EF) is a collection of self-regulating behaviors, including working memory, inhibitory control, planning, and cognitive shifting, etc. [10–12]. Children's EF is associated with adaptation and future academic achievement [12–14]. The key element of EF is inhibitory control, which is the ability to inhibit the response to unrelated stimuli and focus on the current task [13]. The Go/No-go task has been

© Springer Nature Switzerland AG 2020
C. Stephanidis and M. Antona (Eds.): HCII 2020, CCIS 1224, pp. 543–548, 2020.
https://doi.org/10.1007/978-3-030-50726-8_71

widely used and proved to have validity in measuring inhibitory control across all ages. It is especially suitable for young children as it is short and simple [9, 14, 15]. It is believed that they have to inhibit the tendency to respond when trying to respond to the 'No-go' task correctly.

We replicated prior video studies on the short-term effect of children's inhibitory control and extended it to examine the immediate effect after they listened to fantastical stories. We aimed to investigate whether an audio fantastical story would have a negative impact on children's inhibitory control, and if so, how this would differ from viewing the same content. In this study, we used the Go/No-go task to test preschool children's inhibitory control before and after viewing or listening to 10 min of fantasy stories. The aim was to find whether audio would also affect children's inhibitory control, and to compare how this control would be affected by audio and video.

2 Methods

2.1 Participants

Fifty-four Chinese-speaking children were recruited from a kindergarten in China (28 girls, Mage = 52.83 ± 4.20 months). Most of them were from middle-class families.

2.2 Tools and Materials

The experimental materials included an episode of SpongeBob and an audio segment with the same content in which SpongeBob had a strange dream where he accidentally went into his friends' dreams and then went through a series of fantastical events. Those events included a hot rod and a driver's license that appeared out of thin air. Then sea-snail Gary became a wise man and could speak English, SpongeBob turned into a clarinet, Mr. Krabs fished for money, and SpongeBob turned into a pushpin. The audio was adapted from the original video and told the whole storyline from a third-person perspective. The audio version was in good quality, and was read and produced by a professional storyteller. It lasted for 10 min and 41 s. The video was 10 min and 51 s long.

Participants were asked to respond to the 'Go' stimuli and not respond to the 'No-go' task. In this study, two cartoon images, an elephant and a tiger, were presented on a computer. In each trial, children were required to press the space bar if they saw an elephant (go stimulus), and not press the space bar if a tiger was shown (no-go stimulus) (Fig. 1). The proportion of accurate react and reaction time (on the go task) was computed. The correct response on go trials (hit) and incorrect response on no-go trials (false alarm) were used to calculate response sensitivity $d' = Z_{hit} = Z_{false\ alarm}$, the higher value meant better discrimination between two classes of stimuli and better inhibitory control [16]. These were the same materials utilized by Li et al. [9].

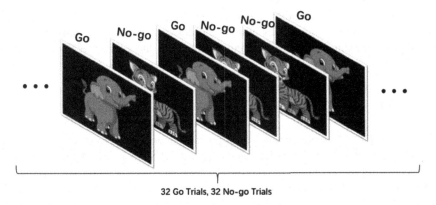

Fig. 1. Go/No-go task

2.3   Procedure

Fifty-four children were evenly and randomly assigned into three groups: a video group, an audio group, and a control group. In the control group, children participated making a drawing.

As is shown in Fig. 2, the experiment began with a Go/No-go task, and each child was supervised by a trained experimenter. First, children were instructed to press the space bar when an image of an elephant appeared and not to press it when an image of a tiger appeared. After that came a training phase with feedback, where a green check mark and a red X indicated correct and incorrect responses respectively. The feedback was only provided in the training phase. If the child already understood the instruction, then he/she would start the test phase immediately. There were 64 trials in this test (half tiger and half elephant), and all of them were randomized. The image would disappear from the screen after the child pressed the space bar or after 1500 ms without response. A 1000-ms interval was designed between each trial. The total task lasted for about 4 min.

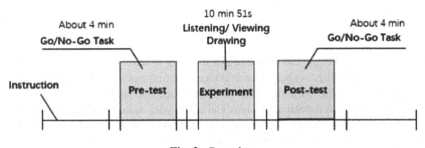

Fig. 2. Procedure

Then children either watched an episode of SpongeBob or listened to the SpongeBob audiobook or drew a picture. To ensure each activity would last for 10 min 51 s, a 10-s introduction was given by the examiner before playing the audio in the audio group. In the control condition, the experimenter kept track of drawing time and informed participants when it was time to end drawing. When they finished viewing, listening or drawing, they were asked to complete the other Go/No-go post-test immediately.

3 Results

One-way ANCOVAs were conducted on post-test scores for RT, ACCs, and d' with the pre-test scores of these indices as covariates. Results revealed that there were significant differences in mean scores for ACC-go, and d'. For ACC-go, F (2, 50) = 5.01, p = .01, *partial $\eta 2$* = .17, post-hoc tests found that children in the audio group (M = .82, SE = .03) had lower ACC than that of children in control group (M = .94, SD = .03). However, no mean differences of ACC-go were found between children in the video group (M = .85, SD = .03) and the control group, and the same was found between children in the video group and the audio group. For d', F (2, 50) = 3.64, p = .03, *partial $\eta 2$* = .13, post-hoc tests found that children in the audio group (M = 3.01, SE = 0.16) had lower d' than children in the control group (M = 3.61, SE = 0.16). However, no significant differences were found between children in the video group (M = 3.19, SE = 0.16) and the control group, as well as between children in the video and audio groups. No mean differences were found for ACC-no-go and RT-go. Means and standard errors are shown in Table 1.

Table 1. Children's ACC, RT and sensitivity in Go/No-go task ($M \pm SE$)

	Video group	Audio group	Control group	Post-hoc
ACC-go	.85 ± .03	.82 ± .03	.94 ± .03	M audio < M control
ACC-no-go	.94 ± .02	.94 ± .02	.93 ± .02	
RT-go	730.41 ± 25.57	771.07 ± 25.41	748.11 ± 27.06	
d'	3.19 ± 0.16	3.01 ± 0.16	3.61 ± 0.16	M audio < M control

4 Discussion

This study provided empirical evidence that listening to more than 10 min of fantastical stories impaired children's short-term inhibitory control, but no such negative influence was observed after the same material was experienced in visual form.

We speculate that listening to fantastical audio uses more cognitive resources than video. Some studies find that more imaginative and creative response is shown after listening to an audio story than after viewing a video story [3, 17]. The visualization hypothesis suggests that this is because children feel a stronger connection with images presented to them than with audio [18]. As a result, they feel it is easier to understand those fantastical events when they view them, but listening to them is not so easy, which means less negative influence on inhibitory control was shown. However, this hypothesis still needs more neural evidence to be further confirmed.

Children's stereotypes of video and audio might also lead to their different amounts of mental effort [13, 19]. Salomon holds the opinion that medium, as a resource to perceive information, determines the amount of mental effort spent on learning to a certain degree. This mental effort influences the learning effect in turn [13]. For example, children may believe that video is an "easy" medium, so that little mental effort was invested while watching SpongeBob video. By contrast, a greater amount of mental effort might be spent on audio as it was regarded as a "challenging" medium. Even half of parents believe that audio plays a role in education, or at least, it is less entertaining [20]. This impression may also influence their children subtly. As a result, children draw on more cognitive resources when listening to audio.

In Li and colleagues' study that compares the effect of viewing and touching fantastical events on children's inhibitory control. They found children's lower response sensitivity after viewing fantastical events, which means viewing them has a negative effect on children's inhibitory control [9]. One possible explanation is that they used a video clip recorded from a video-game, Dr. Panda in Space, with several fantastical events. Children may not be as familiar with Dr. Panda as they are with SpongeBob. In other words, children may have already been prepared for fantastical events in SpongeBob videos, while it is more difficult to accept that Dr. Panda will do something fantastic. As a result, children have to use more cognitive resources to understand what the video recorded from the game expressed.

Parents seem to have a positive attitude to audio and to be more tolerant of it as it is regarded as a kind of way for children to develop certain skills or learn something [20]. However, whether it is overrated is not clear. The results suggested that listening to an audio fantastic story impairs children's short-term inhibitory control. Given the popularity of some audiobooks, parents should be alert to the possibility of a lower level of inhibitory control, at least immediately, after their children listening to such audio.

It will be interesting to know how long this effect lasts and if there is a long-term effect. Since we utilized only a story that contains fantastical events, future work can also examine other particular formal features.

References

1. Yu, Y.: Dangdang.com 2017 User Behavior Report. Publisher (2018)
2. Beagles-Roos, J., Gat, I.: Specific impact of radio and television on children's story comprehension. J. Educ. Psychol. **75**(1), 128 (1983)
3. Greenfield, P., Farrar, D., Beagles-Roos, J.: Is the medium the message?: an experimental comparison of the effects of radio and television on imagination. J. Appl. Dev. Psychol. **7**(3), 201–218 (1986)
4. Peirce, K., Edwards, E.D.: Children's construction of fantasy stories: gender differences in conflict resolution strategies. Sex Roles **18**(7–8), 393–404 (1988)
5. Basil, M.D.: Attention to and Memory for Audio and Video Information in Television Scenes (1992)
6. Walma Van Der Molen, J.H., Van Der Voort, T.H.: The impact of television, print, and audio on children's recall of the news. A study of three alternative explanations for the dual-coding hypothesis. Hum. Commun. Res. **26**(1), 3–26 (2000)

7. IiMedia: Analysis of audio industry data: 2019Q1 Chinese parents of over 60% of children's audio hope audiobooks increase science knowledge (2020). https://www.iimedia.cn/c1061/68935.html. Accessed 9 Mar 2020

8. Lillard, A.S., Peterson, J.: The immediate impact of different types of television on young children's executive function. Pediatrics 128(4), 644–649 (2011)

9. Li, H., Subrahmanyam, K., Bai, X., Xie, X., Liu, T.: Viewing fantastical events versus touching fantastical events: short-term effects on children's inhibitory control. Child Dev. 89 (1), 48–57 (2018)

10. Zelazo, P.D., Blair, C.B., Willoughby, M.T.: Executive Function: Implications for Education. NCER 2017-2000. National Center for Education Research (2016)

11. Eslinger, P.J.: Conceptualizing, describing, and measuring components of executive function: a summary (1996)

12. Zelazo, P.D., Frye, D.: Cognitive complexity and control: a theory of the development of deliberate reasoning and intentional action. Lang. Struct. Discourse Access Conscious. 12, 113–153 (1997)

13. Salomon, G.: Television is "easy" and print is "tough": the differential investment of mental effort in learning as a function of perceptions and attributions. J. Educ. Psychol. 76(4), 647 (1984)

14. Simpson, A., Riggs, K.J.: Conditions under which children experience inhibitory difficulty with a "button-press" go/no-go task. J. Exp. Child Psychol. 94(1), 18–26 (2006)

15. Rush, B.K., Barch, D.M., Braver, T.S.: Accounting for cognitive aging: context processing, inhibition or processing speed? Aging Neuropsychol. Cogn. 13(3–4), 588–610 (2006)

16. Macmillan, N.A., Creelman, C.D.: Detection Theory: A User's Guide. Psychology Press (2004)

17. Runco, M.A., Pezdek, K.: The effect of television and radio on children's creativity. Hum. Commun. Res. 11(1), 109–120 (1984)

18. Valkenburg, P.M., Beentjes, J.W.: Children's creative imagination in response to radio and television stories. J. Commun. 47(2), 21–38 (1997)

19. Salomon, G.: The differential investment of mental effort in learning from different sources. Educ. Psychol. 18(1), 42–50 (1983)

20. Rong, Y.Y.: A Study on Parental Choice and Use of Audiobooks for Children, Anhui University, pp. 24–25 (2019). (in Chinese)

EEG-Based Methods to Characterize Memorised Visual Space

Mauro Nascimben[1,2(✉)], Thomas Zoëga Ramsøy[1], and Luis Emilio Bruni[2]

[1] Neurons Inc., Taastrup, Denmark
msnascimben@gmail.com
https://neuronsinc.com
[2] Augmented Cognition Laboratory, Aalborg University Copenhagen,
Copenhagen, Denmark
https://augcog.aau.dk/

Abstract. One second of memory maintenance was evaluated to determine EEG metrics ability to track memory load and its variations connected with the lateral presentation of objects in the visual hemi-field. An initial approach focused on features gathered from the N2pc time series to detect the memory load using ensemble learners. Conversely, the secondary approach employed a regularised support vector classifier to predict the area of N2pc event-related components, identifying 6 levels of memory load and stimulus location.

Keywords: Visual working memory · Memory load · Retention period

1 Introduction

1.1 Visual Working Memory and Cognitive Load

Visual working memory (i.e. VWM) supports high cognitive functions providing temporary storage for retained information from one fixation to the next. The visual features primarily maintained in mind are position, shape, color and texture of the objects in space commonly referred an object's attributes above the perceptive threshold [1]. The number of items stored in memory is rather related to the concept of capacity [2] and limited to 3–4 multi-attribute objects [3] depending on subjective performance and task characteristics (for example, encoding time [4]). Multitasking impacts the number of memory items that can be maintained and the amount of cognitive resources expended [5]. Indeed, working memory not only includes maintenance of information, but also information processing during encoding time of filtering irrelevant stimuli (distractor avoidance) [6]. Such multiprocessing is commonly termed the cognitive load. The time-based resource-sharing model [7] aims to theorize the relationship between cognitive load and memory performance by identifying four major

This project has received funding from the European Union's Horizon 2020 research and innovation programme under the Marie Skłodowska-Curie Grant Agreement No 813234.

mental stages: encoding, filtering distractors, recall, and refreshing-the last of which redirects attention to restore dwindled items into memory. While learning during a classroom lesson, students need to manage mental resources in order to continuously acquire incoming information and effectively manipulate it. When information to be held oversteps working memory capacity, cognitive overload is experienced [8]. Naturally, what happens during the classroom experience could be extended to other real-world scenarios. In multimedia, visual and audio streams are processed in humans by two separate brain circuitry both with limited working memory capacity, thus active processing of both streams could exceed the audience's available cognitive capacity. This is not only due to the essential processing of audio or video materials, but also caused by environmental disturbances or confusion in the presentation of multimedial contents [9].

1.2 Neurophysiologic Correlates of VWM

In literature three components are commonly attributed to VWM. Two of them are event-related potentials (i.e. ERP), one called controlateral delayed activity (i.e. CDA) and the other N2pc. The third correlate of VWM is an induced modification over occipito-parietal electrodes in alpha band, where one observes a decreased alpha power when an individual retains information in memory.

Lateralization of Stimuli in the Visual Hemifield. During VWM experimental evaluation, an event related potential called controlateral delayed activity (i.e. CDA) [10] was identified on posterior-occipital areas usually interpreted as a neural marker of the number of items stored in memory. Moreover, CDA polarity changes depending on the position of the elements memorized in the visual space. Despite an alternative hypothesis claiming a relationship between the CDA wave and spatial attention [11], current findings confirm the relation between CDA and memory capacity [12,13]. In subjects with lower memory capacity, distractors presented alongside targets in the visual field increased CDA amplitudes compared to individuals with better capacity [14].

Deployment of Visual Attention. ERPs can track shifts of attention to the targets: the N2pc wave specifically reflects the attention towards an object [15,16]. This wave appears between 180 and 300 ms (usually peaking at a latency of 250 ms) with enhanced amplitude over the posterior-occipital electrodes contro-lateral to the visual targets present in the visual field. In [17], the authors describe a relationship between N2pc and the processing load: visuospatial configurations that require more time to be evaluated demand a sustained involvement of attention reflected by higher N2pc amplitudes. N2pc appears not only as a metric of attention for targets in the extra-personal space, but moreover N2pc amplitudes are modulated during memory retention to weigh information according to its relevance [18].

Relation Between Alpha Oscillations and Memory Functions. Alpha oscillatory activity is suppressed during memory encoding likely due to visual processing, whilst alpha is enhanced in the course of memory maintenance to prevent competition for resource allocation with incoming visual stimuli [19]. Throughout memory retention alpha waves could phase-couple with other frequencies like beta or gamma in organized neural networks [20]. Patterns of alpha desynchronization during encoding and synchronization for memory maintenance appear in form of induced power changes that are not time-locked to stimuli [21].

2 Methods

Experimental Paradigm. Data was released by authors of the paper [22] in pre-processed format. The present study solely retained the healthy subjects, originally denoted as the comparison group. Participants were 27 college students (11 females) with an average age of 22 years. The experimental paradigm was adapted from [14] with an initial presentation of an array of geometrical shapes succeeded by a memory maintenance period of one second. Prior to each trial, an arrow appearing at the center of the screen informed the subjects which visual hemi-field they should memorize (left "L" or right "R"), while during each trial an array of colored shapes was displayed for 200 ms. Subsequently, the object array disappeared, requiring the subjects to store the visual information into their working memory. Following a memory retention period of one second, participants would then be tasked with deciding whether the new object array matched the one presented prior. Half of the trials had one color of a shape changed in the attended side. Three types of object arrays were tested: "low memory load" (i.e. "L") with only 2 squares to be memorised, "high memory load" (i.e. "H") when 4 squares were to be memorised or "distractors" (i.e. "D") with two circles that should be ignored (Fig. 1).

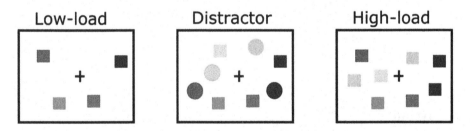

Fig. 1. Experimental stimuli were 2 types of objects (squares and circles) in 10 randomly selected colors (supra-threshold perceptive features) [22] (Color figure online)

Pre-processing of Neural Signals. EEG was recorded with a high-density cap of 128 electrodes (Hydrocel Geodesic sensor net) and sampled at 500 Hz. Epochs were 104 for each experimental condition, and those with artifacts were rejected. Further pre-processing steps included filtering (0.05–30 Hz) and re-referencing in common average mode. Epoch length of the memory retention period was 1 s preceded by 0.4 s of baseline. For each subject, extra-cephalic electrodes (lower line of the Geodesic cap) were discarded (109 channels kept), and single trial EEG signals had their voltages normalized with z-score procedure (using baseline mean and standard deviation in range −200 to 0 ms): z-score standardization on subjective baseline allows one to model a user-independent approach. Procedures involved employed the MNE-python library [24].

Outliers Detection. Outlier detection is an important preliminary step to identify subjects that the model is unable to generalise, deviating significantly from the rest of the data. Multidimensional scaling reduces dimension of the data by representing the proximity (or similarity) matrix between individuals as a lower dimensional space [23]. The proximity matrix is a configuration of points in Euclidean space such that the inter-point distances approximate the subjective data. In (Fig. 2) dashed lines represent the squared Mahalanobis distances of the empirical covariance matrix shown as a visual indicator of adjacency between points. The inclusion criteria implemented a mathematical approach to cut-off outliers by identifying a critical threshold based on the approximated F distribution [25] (Fig. 3). Based on the critical threshold, subjects 4 and 16 were excluded from further analysis.

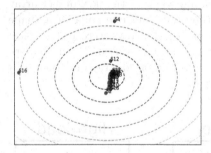

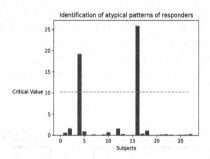

Fig. 2. All subjects in all conditions   **Fig. 3.** Outliers critical threshold

3   Results

Initially, a total of 5956 signals were further normalized with L2-norm and pairwise comparisons between conditions obtained with t-test analysis for each channel with significance threshold adjusted by Bonferroni correction. This statistical test was applied to identify a group of electrodes with significant changes between conditions. Indeed in Fig. 4, one observes a high number of differing pair-wise comparisons between 192 and 268 ms. Additionally, an analysis using cluster permutation F-test was conducted in the same data to highlight time frames of relevant activity differing between stimuli, as in [26]. For example, electrode E90 in Fig. 5 illustrates the cluster of significant activity corresponding to N2pc time range (highlighted in orange, $p < 0.05$). Crossing the results of both statistical methodologies we obtained a group of electrodes and a time-frame with brain activity relevant to distinguish between conditions: mainly posterior-occipital channels during N2pc time course (Fig. 6).

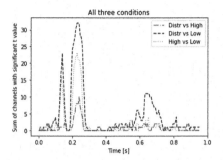

Fig. 4. T-test on all sensor data

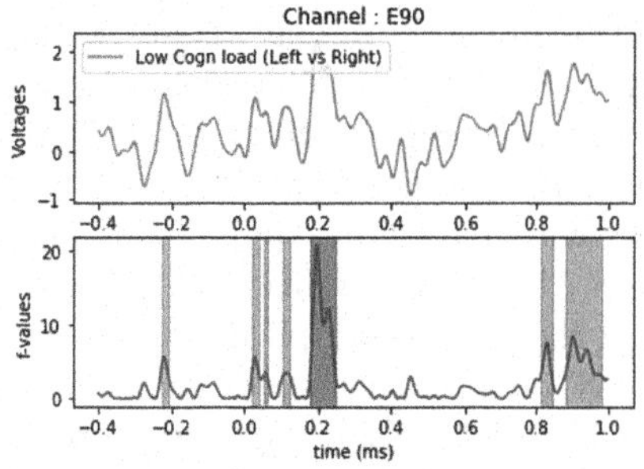

Fig. 5. Permutation test on each sensor (Color figure online)

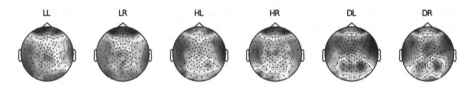

Fig. 6. Topographic plots at 240 ms (color scale blue to red from -2.65 to $3.56\,\mu$V) (Color figure online)

3.1 Cognitive Load Prediction

Analysis focused on prediction of three cognitive states using the time series extracted from the N2pc wave on parieto-occipital electrodes. Number of trials were equalized randomly under-sampling the most represented classes. From the time course of the N2pc, 794 features were extracted using 63 characterization methods [27]. Redundant features were eliminated by the statistical approach presented in [28], and divided in train and test sets with a 80% and 20% split. Test set accuracy is reported in Table 1 comparing two classification methods each with hyperparameters tuned by a combination of cross-validated (5 folds with stratification) randomized and grid search on train set. The chance level was calculated as 51.96% according to the binomial cumulative distribution as in [29] with a significance threshold set at $p = 0.05$.

Table 1. Cognitive load prediction one-vs-one

Ensemble method	Distr vs High	Distr vs Low	High vs Low
Random forest	72%	73%	69%
Gradient boosting	72%	71%	71%

3.2   Prediction of Cognitive Load and Stimuli Location

In this investigation six classes were inspected: three cognitive load levels ("L", "H", "D") by two different locations of the stimuli in the visual hemi-field ("L" or "R"). In Fig. 7, the global field power (i.e. GFP) from all electrodes is used to identify a time window enclosing the N2pc wave. Indeed, permutation t-test with pair-wise comparisons (significance adjusted by the "false discovery rate") between conditions identified two clusters of significant electrodes, one over the parieto-occipital, and one over the fronto-central areas (Fig. 8). Area of the N2pc from each single trial over the identified electrodes was used as feature for an SVM classifier. Classes were balanced by randomly under-sampling trials of the most represented labels (5346 trials used as observations). A support vector machines (i.e. svm) model with radial basis function (i.e. rbf) as kernel was selected as classifier and data was divided in the aforementioned 80–20 split. Kernel and regularization parameters were optimized by grid search with cross-validation (5 stratified folds and validation size 20%) and classification methodology one-versus-rest. Outcomes against a dummy svm-rbf classifier are shown in Table 2 using F1 score as metric (last two columns are weighted-average F1 and micro-F1 scores). Statistical chance level calculated as in [29] was 17.5% (at p = 0.05).

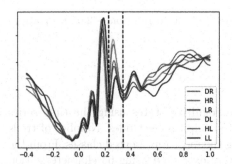

Fig. 7. GFP of the experimental conditions

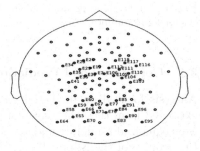

Fig. 8. 38 identified electrodes

Table 2. Prediction of cognitive load and stimulus location

	DL	HL	LL	DR	HR	LR	w-F1	Micro
SVM	0.657	0.642	0.538	0.603	0.325	0.570	0.552	0.560
Dummy	0.126	0.150	0.168	0.163	0.158	0.152	0.153	0.153

4 Conclusions

Two procedures are presented to distinguish between the levels of cognitive resources deployed during retention period of the visual working memory: the first based on features extracted from the N2pc time series whereas the second involves using the area of N2pc component. The latter offers a promising technique for categorizing not only the memory load, but also the location of the stimuli in the visual hemi-field (overall accuracy +38.5% above chance level).

References

1. Patel, S.S., Bedell, H.E., Tsang, D.K., Ukwade, M.T.: Relationship between threshold and suprathreshold perception of position and stereoscopic depth. JOSA A **26**(4), 847–861 (2009)
2. Luck, S.J., Vogel, E.K.: Visual working memory capacity: from psychophysics and neurobiology to individual differences. Trends Cogn. Sci. **17**(8), 391–400 (2013)
3. Vogel, E.K., Awh, E.: How to exploit diversity for scientific gain: using individual differences to constrain cognitive theory. Curr. Dir. Psychol. Sci. **17**(2), 171–176 (2008)
4. Barrouillet, P., Bernardin, S., Portrat, S., Vergauwe, E., Camos, V.: Time and cognitive load in working memory. J. Exp. Psychol. Learn. Mem. Cogn. **33**(3), 570 (2007)
5. Zheng, Z.: Cognitive Load Measurement and Application. Routledge, New York (2018)
6. Lavie, N., De Fockert, J.: The role of working memory in attentional capture. Psychon. Bull. Rev. **12**(4), 669–674 (2005). https://doi.org/10.3758/BF03196756
7. Oberauer, K., Lewandowsky, S.: Modeling working memory: a computational implementation of the time-based resource-sharing theory. Psychon. Bull. Rev. **18**(1), 10–45 (2011). https://doi.org/10.3758/s13423-010-0020-6
8. Puma, S., Matton, N., Paubel, P.V., Tricot, A.: Cognitive load theory and time considerations: using the time-based resource sharing model. Educ. Psychol. Rev. **30**(3), 1199–1214 (2018). https://doi.org/10.1007/s10648-018-9438-6
9. Mayer, R.E., Moreno, R.: Nine ways to reduce cognitive load in multimedia learning. Educ. Psychol. **38**(1), 43–52 (2003)
10. Vogel, E.K., Machizawa, M.G.: Neural activity predicts individual differences in visual working memory capacity. Nature **428**(6984), 748–751 (2004)
11. Berggren, N., Eimer, M.: Does contralateral delay activity reflect working memory storage or the current focus of spatial attention within visual working memory? J. Cogn. Neurosci. **28**(12), 2003–2020 (2016)
12. Pomper, U., Ditye, T., Ansorge, U.: Contralateral delay activity during temporal order memory. Neuropsychologia **129**, 104–116 (2019)

13. Feldmann-Wüstefeld, T., Vogel, E.K., Awh, E.: Contralateral delay activity indexes working memory storage, not the current focus of spatial attention. J. Cogn. Neurosci. **30**(8), 1185–1196 (2018)

14. Vogel, E.K., McCollough, A.W., Machizawa, M.G.: Neural measures reveal individual differences in controlling access to working memory. Nature **438**(7067), 500–503 (2005)

15. Eimer, M.: The N2pc component as an indicator of attentional selectivity. Electroencephalogr. Clin. Neurophys. **99**(3), 225–234 (1996)

16. Hickey, C., McDonald, J.J., Theeuwes, J.: Electrophysiological evidence of the capture of visual attention. J. Cogn. Neurosci. **18**(4), 604–613 (2006)

17. Maheux, M., Jolicoeur, P.: Differential engagement of attention and visual working memory in the representation and evaluation of the number of relevant targets and their spatial relations: evidence from the N2pc and SPCN. Biol. Psychol. **125**, 28–35 (2017)

18. Heuer, A., Schubö, A.: The focus of attention in visual working memory: protection of focused representations and its individual variation. PLoS One **11**(4), e0154228 (2016)

19. Wianda, E., Ross, B.: The roles of alpha oscillation in working memory retention. Brain Behav. **9**(4), e01263 (2019)

20. Baars, B.J., Gage, N.M.: Cognition, Brain, and Consciousness: Introduction to Cognitive Neuroscience. Academic Press, Cambridge (2010)

21. Palva, S., Palva, J.M.: New vistas for frequency band oscillations. Trends Neurosci. **30**(4), 150–158 (2007)

22. Gu, C., Liu, Z.X., Tannock, R., Woltering, S.: Neural processing of working memory in adults with ADHD in a visuospatial change detection task with distractors. PeerJ **6**, e5601 (2018)

23. Groenen, P.J., Heiser, W.J.: The tunneling method for global optimization in multidimensional scaling. Psychometrika **61**(3), 529–550 (1996)

24. Gramfort, A., et al.: MEG and EEG data analysis with MNE-Python. Front. Neurosci. **7**, 267 (2013)

25. Riani, M., Atkinson, A.C., Cerioli, A.: Finding an unknown number of multivariate outliers. J. Roy. Stat. Soc.: Ser. B (Stat. Methodol.) **71**(2), 447–466 (2009)

26. Maris, E., Oostenveld, R.: Nonparametric statistical testing of EEG-and MEG-data. J. Neurosci. Methods **164**(1), 177–190 (2007)

27. Christ, M., Braun, N., Neuffer, J., Kempa-Liehr, A.W.: Time series feature extraction on basis of scalable hypothesis tests (tsfresh-a python package). Neurocomputing **307**, 72–77 (2018)

28. Christ, M., Kempa-Liehr, A.W., Feindt, M.: Distributed and parallel time series feature extraction for industrial big data applications. arXiv preprint arXiv:1610.07717 (2016)

29. Combrisson, E., Jerbi, K.: Exceeding chance level by chance: the caveat of theoretical chance levels in brain signal classification and statistical assessment of decoding accuracy. J. Neurosci. Methods **250**, 126–136 (2015)

Evaluation of Incongruent Feeling During Mouse Operation Using Eye Gaze and EEG

Koki Shimizu[✉], Takashi Ito, and Syohei Ishizu

Department of Industrial and Systems Engineering, Aoyama Gakuin University,
Tokyo, Japan
shimizu03271@gmail.com

Abstract. One of the most important issues in the design of a personal computer or a game is creating an interface that a user can operate without a feeling a sense of incongruity between their actions and what appears on the screen. Since the degree of incongruent feeling varies from person to person, it is important to focus on the physiological processes of the user in elucidating the mechanisms underlying the occurrence of this feeling. In this study, we recorded electroencephalography (EEG) and eye gaze from individuals while they completed a simple task using a mouse to move a cursor on a screen. By changing the setting of the mouse speed, we were able to create an environment where the psychological state of incongruent feeling was likely to occur. After each trial, we asked individuals whether they experienced a feeling of incongruency. We then, compared the EEG and eye gaze responses for when the feeling of incongruency occurred and when it did not occur.

Keywords: Incongruent feeling · Gaze · EEG · Ergonomics · Computer interface

1 Introduction

A feeling of incongruency can sometimes occur when using computers, often when the operational environment changes or when it does not function as expected given the actions one is performing. When building a system, it is beneficial to design an interface that minimizes this experience for users. However, it is not always clear as to what about the interface induces a feeling of incongruency; therefore, understanding the mechanisms underlying the incongruent feeling important. Given that the degree of incongruent feeling varies among individuals, we need to examine not only the operating environment, but also the experience of the users on a biological and physiological level when interacting with the interface.

Several studies have examined aspects of the feeling of incongruence using various methods. Ohori, Takeuchi, and colleagues analyzed the features of electroencephalography responses during keyboard input errors and were able to classify EEG responses based on when the participants are aware of input errors and when they are not [1, 2]. In addition, Tsakiris and colleagues reviewed research on the sense of belonging when users operate the interface, and showed that the prediction of the movement of the operation target was effective in generating the attribution [3]. Ohara and Fujinami, using eye

© Springer Nature Switzerland AG 2020
C. Stephanidis and M. Antona (Eds.): HCII 2020, CCIS 1224, pp. 557–564, 2020.
https://doi.org/10.1007/978-3-030-50726-8_73

tracking during a rhythm action game, found that beginners and experienced players viewed the game differently as they played [4]. Taken together, there is evidence that it is possible to examine psychological states related to incongruent feeling, such as awareness of mistakes and awareness of attribution, using EEG and eye tracking.

The purpose of this study is to examine the feeling of incongruency that can occur when people interact with a computer interface, and understand the mechanisms that cause the psychological state of incongruent feeling by analyzing EEG and eye gaze responses. In this study, we had participants move a mouse to control a cursor on a screen and incongruity was induced by changing the speed of mouse on each trial. During the task, EEG and eye tracking responses were recorded. It was predicted that subjects would experience incongruency when the speed of the mouse changed and the gaze followed the movement of the cursor, resulting in feeling of stress. In the experiment, discriminant analysis was performed using the biological information when the incongruent feeling occurred and when it did not. By this, we understand what kind of biological reaction occurs when the feeling occurs. We also analyzed the changes in mouse speed, the number of experiments, and the presence or absence of incongruent feeling by using the DOE to determine the main factors. The results of these analyzes were validated using cross-validation.

2   Experiment Setting

2.1   Task and Procedure

As the purpose of the study was to examine the occurrence of incongruency, we thought that the task that the subjects performed should not be complicated. Therefore, the task was to "throw away the folder at the right side of the screen into the trash bin at the left side of the screen using the mouse". The cursor always started at the center of the screen. We varied the speed of the mouse to induce a feeling of incongruency. The initial speed was set to "normal" speed and was the reference from which the two additional speeds were set, those being an acceleration (speed: fast) and a deceleration (speed: slow). The subjects were only informed about the task they were to perform, not about variations in the speed of the mouse. There were six subjects, and each subject performed the task three times at each speed, for a total of nine trials. The mouse speed was set randomly every trial. After each trial, the subjects were asked whether they felt uncomfortable during the task and responded with a yes or a no. Subjects' eye gaze and EEG responses were simultaneously recorded as subjects performed the task. Figure 1 shows a simplified schematic of the experimental set up.

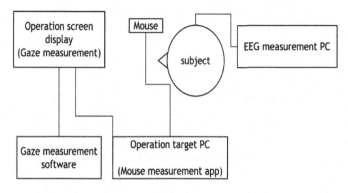

Fig. 1. Diagram of the experimental set up

2.2 Eye Tracking Device

In this study, we used the EMR-ACTUS from NAC Image Technology Co. Ltd to monitor gaze [5]. This device utilizes a non-contact corneal reflection method, and can measure the x and y coordinates of the left and right eyes. Since the device is non-contact, the burden on the participant is minimal. Furthermore, the device considers the movement of the head, making it was possible to measure eye gaze with extremely high accuracy. At the time of this study, it was possible to use the corresponding software, EMR-dStream2, to identify epochs of interest and automatically generate plots of the gaze data. In addition, it was possible to assess gaze time within a specified area and conduct AOI (area of interest) analyses.

2.3 EEG Measurement Equipment

EEG signals were collected using the Polymate, which is a device developed and sold by Miyuki Giken Co., Ltd. that measures physiological signals [6]. In addition to EEG, it is possible to simultaneously measure several additional physiological signals, such as the choroid, respiration rate, heart rate, skin, temperature, and electrogram and electromyogram signals. To measure the EEG, the subject wears a hat that has several small electrodes that come into contact with the scalp. The location of the electrodes was based on the international 10–20 method. Of particular interest were the locations over the frontal (Fpz, Fz), parietal (Cz, Pz), temporal (T3, T4), and occipital lobes (O1, O2), as shown in Fig. 2. When recording the EEG, the timing at which the event started can be recorded by inputting the specified key. In this study, we use this function to record the start and end timings in order to grasp the time period during which the mouse is operated. The corresponding software, APviewer, can display the waveform of the EEG and then export the data of interest as a CSV file.

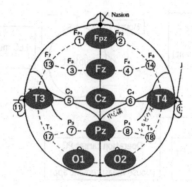

Fig. 2. EEG electrode locations. Locations of interest are circled in blue. (Color figure online)

2.4   Data Analysis

To assess where subjects looked during the task, an AOI analysis was performed using the gaze location data. By performing an AOI analysis, one can determine how long a subject viewed a particular area of the screen. Figure 3 shows an image of the screen of the experimental task and the defined AOIs. We calculated the total gaze time of each subject for each of the 5 AOIs. In addition, we determined the positional relationship (i.e. distance) between the location of the gaze and the mouse cursor, using the gaze location data compared to the recorded data of the coordinates of the cursor. From this, we calculated the average distance, maximum distance, and minimum distance.

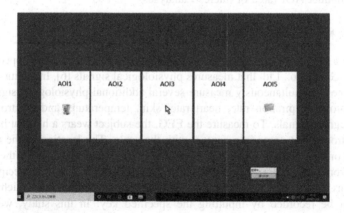

Fig. 3. Screen of the experimental task with the AOIs superimposed

With respect to the EEG data, the data were subjected to a frequency analysis to calculate the rate of content of α waves and β waves. The ratio between the content rate of the α-wave and the content rate of the β-wave was calculated as "stress level". A higher stress level was interpreted as the subject feeling more stress or anxiety, while a lower stress level indicated that the subject more relaxed. Various analyses were conducted, depending on the type of data and the question of interest. The measurement that were examined in the analyses included the gaze measurements of average distance, maximum distance, minimum distance, time in AOI1–AOI5, and time out of AOI, and the EEG measurements of stress level at each of the locations of interest, including frontal (Fpz, Fz), parietal (Cz, Pz), temporal (T3, T4), and occipital (O1, O2) areas.

A discriminant analysis was performed, using the presence or absence of incongruent feeling as variable, to determine which of the data measurements affected the discrimination of incongruent feeling. An analysis of variance (ANOVA) used the speed of the mouse, the number of repetitions at each speed, and the presence or absence of incongruent feeling as factors, and the measurement data as dependent variables, to assess whether the occurrence of incongruent feeling or the experimental environment (e.g. mouse speed) affected the physiological responses. A cluster analysis using Ward's method was performed to assess whether subjects could be clustered based on the characteristics of the data measurements.

3   Results and Discussion

3.1   Predicting the Presence or Absence of Incongruent Feeling

According to the results of the discriminate analysis, the overall fit of all data, according to the discrimination rate, was 0.759, which indicates that the measurements included in the analysis predict the presence or absence of incongruity to a high degree. Table 1 shows the discrimination coefficient for each of the gaze and EEG measurements. It was found that of the individual measurements, the minimum and maximum distances, as well as the EEG data from Fz, Pz, and T4, influence the determination of the presence or absence of incongruent feeling.

Table 1. Discrimination coefficients of the data measurements

Gaze data		EEG data	
Average distance*	−0.378	Fpz	0.284
Max distance*	0.746	Fz*	0.668
Min distance*	0.676	Cz	−0.272
AOI1	−0.159	Pz*	−1.272
AOI2	0.100	T3	0.177
AOI3	−0.133	T4*	−0.368
AOI4	−0.079	O1	0.162
AOI5	0.221	O2	0.102
Out of AOI	0.125		

3.2   Effect of Incongruency on Physiological Measures

The values of the p-value obtained as a result of the ANOVA using gaze data are shown in Tables 2 and EEG data in Table 3 (note: − indicates where the p-value exceeds 0.1 thus no significant difference was observed).

With respect to gaze, the gaze distance increased as the mouse speed increased, in both the average distance and the maximum distance. Regarding the minimum distance, we hypothesize that there was no difference in relation to speed because the gaze was concentrated on the cursor when the movement of the cursor was differed from expected movement, whether the speed was fast or slow. For gaze measurements in relation to the presence or absence of incongruent feeling, only the average distance showed a significant difference. Specifically, the average distance tended to decrease when incongruence occurred. Regarding the AOIs, there were two differences. The gaze time of AOI3 (the center of the screen) decreased when the incongruent feeling did not occur, and the gaze time of out of AOI tended to increase.

Table 2. Result of ANOVA using gaze data (A: Speed, B: repetitions, C: incongruent feeling)

		A	B	C	Interaction			
					A:B	B:C	A:C	A:B:C
Gaze data	Average distance	0.00609	–	0.0169	–	–	–	–
	Max distance	3.03e–11	–	–	–	–	–	–
	Min distance	–	–	–	–	–	–	–
	AOI1	–	–	–	–	–	0.0180	–
	AOI2	–	–	–	–	–	–	–
	AOI3	–	–	0.0521	–	–	–	–
	AOI4	–	–	–	–	–	–	–
	AOI5	–	–	–	–	–	–	–
	Out of AOI		–	0.0196	–	–	–	–

Table 3. Result of ANOVA using EEG data (A: Speed, B: repetitions, C: incongruent feeling)

		A	B	C	Interaction			
					A:B	B:C	A:C	A:B:C
EEG data	Fpz	–	–	–	–	–	–	–
	Fz	–	–	–	–	–	–	0.0661
	Cz	–	–	0.0890	–	–	–	–
	Pz	–	–	0.0793	–	–	0.0698	–
	T3	–	–	–	–	–	0.0750	–
	T4	–	–	–	–	–	–	–
	O1	–	–	0.0886	–	–	0.0141	–
	O2	–	–	–	–	–	0.0641	–

Regarding EEG measurements, significant differences were observed at some locations depending on the presence or absence of incongruity. Both parietal locations, Cz and Pz, and the occipital location O1 had low stress levels when no incongruent feeling occurred, and high stress levels when the feeling occurred. As the role of the parietal lobe is to process sensory information, it follows that activity in the parietal lobes would be affected by the occurrence of incongruent feeling given that there is a disconnect between what is expected and what is observed. O1 is a part of the occipital lobe and plays a role in visual perception. We hypothesize that the response in O1 was likely due to the movement of the gaze changing when the movement of the cursor differed from what was expected.

3.3 Clustering of Subjects

The results of the cluster analysis are shown in Fig. 4. The analysis identified two clusters as shown in the figure. The characteristics of each cluster were examined.

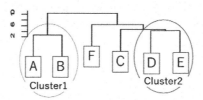

Fig. 4. Result of cluster analysis

First, cluster 1 tended to have a high stress level at T3 (temporal lobe) when the speed of the mouse was high. As one role of the temporal lobe is the processing of memory, it is hypothesized that the difference, or change, in speed was detected when the observed speed was compared to the memory of the normal speed, which may have resulted in a feeling of incongruence.

In cluster 2, the average distance and the maximum distance between the gaze and the mouse cursor tended to increase as the speed of the mouse increased. The subjects in cluster 2 had the incongruent feeling when the mouse speed was not normal. This suggested that when the distance between the gaze and the mouse deviated from a certain range, the feeling might have occurred.

3.4 Verification

Cross-validation was performed to examine the generalizability of the discriminant analysis results. The measurement data of five of the subjects were used as the training, data, and the data of the one other subject was used as the test, data. The resulting coefficient of discrimination rate was 0.556, which is lower than the original analysis. This suggests that there is individual variability with respect to the changes in physiological processes resulting from the occurrence of incongruent feeling. Given this variability, the same validation was performed for the two clusters obtained in Sect. 3.3. The discrimination rates were 0.667 for cluster1 and 0.722 for cluster2, which were better than what was found when including all of the subjects. Although the occurrence of incongruent feeling varies among individuals, it is possible, and valid, to cluster individuals based on physiological responses.

4 Conclusion

In this study, we sought to understand the mechanism underlying the feeling of incongruence that one can experience when interacting with a computer interface. To do so, we had subjects use a mouse to move a cursor on a screen, while we recorded user's gaze and EEG, and manipulated the speed of the mouse to induce a feeling of incongruity. The distance between the subject's gaze and the cursor was associated with the degree of stress in the parietal lobe, which may have influenced the occurrence of incongruent feeling. When an observed movement differs from the predicted movement, the gaze reflexively follows the visual target, and it is thought that the incongruent feeling generated at that moment is processed in the parietal lobe. Although the occurrence of incongruent feeling varies among individuals, it is possible to cluster individuals and predict the occurrents of incongruent feeling based on changes in the physiological responses.

References

1. Ohori, R., Shinkai, D., Nagai, Y., Ishizu, S.: Construction of a model for discriminating between electroencephalographic patterns at the time of incorrect inputs based on sensitivity spectrum analysis. In: Smith, M.J., Salvendy, G. (eds.) Human Interface 2011. LNCS, vol. 6771, pp. 618–626. Springer, Heidelberg (2011). https://doi.org/10.1007/978-3-642-21793-7_70
2. Takeuchi, K., Ohori, R., Saitoh, F., Ishizu, S.: Improvement of work sensitivity in keyboard input operation by neurofeedback. In: ANQ Congress 2012 Hong Kong, JP37 (2012)
3. Tsakiris, M., Schütz-Bosbach, S., Gallagher, S.: On agency and body-ownership: phenomenological and neurocognitive reflections. Conscious. Cogn. 16(3), 645–660 (2007)
4. Ohara, T., Fujinami, T.: An Analysis of skill in rhythm action game with an eye tracker. Japan Advanced Institute of Science and Technology, March 2010
5. Introduction of EMR-ACTUS. https://www.eyemark.jp/product/emr_actus/
6. Introduction of Polymate. http://www.miyuki-net.co.jp/jp/polymate/

Research on Visual Search Performance of Security Inspection Operations Based on Eye Movement Data

Guilei Sun[(✉)]

Department of Safety Engineering,
China University of Labor Relations, Beijing 100048, China
sunguilei@culr.edu.cn

Abstract. In order to improve the visual search performance of security inspection and ensure the transportation and public safety environment, experiments for visual search performance of security inspection operations is carried on. Tobii X2-30 is used for dynamic visual search experiments to study the effect of moving speed, the moving direction, and the number of search backgrounds on visual search performance. SPSS data analysis soft was used to analyze the eye movement data such as fixation count, average of fixation time, saccade count, and total saccade duration. The comprehensive search performance is the highest when the moving speed is 2.0667 m/min. And the phenomenon of missing detection would occur when the moving speed reaches 2.2 m/min. The search performance of a complex search background was higher than that of a single search background, and the search pattern moving from right to left is more conducive to improve the efficiency of visual search. Security inspection performance can be optimized in velocity, moving directions, and search background.

Keywords: Visual search · Search performance · Security inspection · Complex background · Running speed

1 Introduction

The current security inspection work mainly involves problems such as large amount of people, large number of items and variety, all of which will lead to low efficiency of security inspection. During the security inspection process, human visual search performance has become a key factor affecting the security inspection results. For visual search, Guo [1] studied the effect of time pressure on search performance at different moving speed, and established a dynamic dual-target random search model; Hu et al. [2] proved that different visual search strategies can lead to the differences in visual search performance and mouse click performance. Cao et al. [3] considered that the complexity parameter of graphics is an important variable that affects the performance of visual search operations, and studied the covariant relationship between graph complexity parameters and performance of visual search operations by changing the complexity of target graphics and interference sub graphics. Domestic scholars'

© Springer Nature Switzerland AG 2020
C. Stephanidis and M. Antona (Eds.): HCII 2020, CCIS 1224, pp. 565–574, 2020.
https://doi.org/10.1007/978-3-030-50726-8_74

research on the efficiency of visual search is mostly based on the influence of different factors on search performance [4, 5].

In the field of security inspection, Jin et al. [6] pointed out that different subjects had significant differences in the percentage of fixation time, saccades distance, and accuracy of judgment. Wolfe et al. [7] found that complex backgrounds would reduce the speed of target search. Over et al. [8] showed that reducing the similar performance of targets and backgrounds significantly improved search performance. Bastian et al. [9] studied eye movement, visual search strategies, and the relationship to search patterns. Smith et al. [10] simulated X-ray baggage inspection in the airport and found that the accuracy rate would decrease when subjects observed new targets. McCarley et al. [11] found that the increase in sensitivity was entirely caused by changes in the ability of security inspectors to identify targets, and it did not change with the effectiveness of saccade.

Most of the current research mainly focused on the application of X-rays in security inspection technology [12]. And a lot of research had been focused on eye tracking [13–16]. However, there was not enough studies on specific security inspection operations, and security inspection was a special visual search process that studies the performance of dynamic visual search which is important for preventing major public inspections and security incidents.

2   Experiments

2.1   Stimulating Material

Videos composed of a series of photos under X-rays were the stimulating material. In which, knife-like prohibited items appeared dark blue, flammable and explosive prohibited items appeared green, and organic items appeared orange. It should be noted that both butane gas and mineral water were orange, so further confirmation was required based on the shape in the identification process.

2.2   Experiment Equipment

Tobii X2-30 eye tracker; Human-Computer-Environment synchronization platform; Computer (Intel® Core™ i5 CPU, 2.40 GHz; Intel® 5700 MHD integrated graphics with resolution 1280 × 1024 and refresh frequency 60 Hz); Microsoft HD camera.

2.3   Subject Selection

Questionnaire was used to ensure the subjects meet the test conditions, and finally 45 subjects were invited to participate in the experiment, including 24 males and 21 females with an average age of 24.8. Individuals had naked or corrected vision above 5.0 and had no symptoms of color blindness or color weakness. None of the participants had any work experience in dynamic visual search before the test.

2.4 Experimental Design

At the speed of 1.8 m/min, 2.0 m/min and 2.2 m/min, the moving direction was distinguished from left to right and right to left in single search background (the background is single color) and complex search background (the background is multiple colors). Subjects were required to find prohibited items in the stimulus materials. Different stimulus materials and sequences were set up in the experiment to analyze the accuracy of the identification to prohibited items and the eye movement data of the subjects.

3 Data Processing

3.1 Impact of Moving Speed to Visual Search Performance

Two typical analysis error would like to be occurred. One was the prohibited items were not recognized, which is the number of missed detection; the other was the prohibited items were identified as non-contraband goods, which is the number of error detection. The statistical results were shown in Table 1.

Table 1. Statistics of visual search results at different speed

	Number of false detection	Error rate	Missed detection rate	Missed detection rate
1.8 m/min	9	1.00%	0	0%
2.0 m/min	12	1.33%	0	0%
2.2 m/min	15	1.67%	1	0.1%

It can be seen from Table 1 that the security check error rate in dynamic visual search increases along with the increasing speed. At speed of 1.8 m/min and 2.0 m/min, all prohibited items are identified, and no missed inspection occurs. While at the speed of 2.2 m/min, the phenomenon of missed detection occurs.

In order to study the visual search performance at different speed, eye movement data of 30 subjects at 3 different moving speed were collected. The descriptive statistics of the eye movement data of the subjects at different speed are shown in Table 2.

Table 2. Descriptive statistics of eye movement data at different movement speed

	Velocity	Mean	SD	Standard error mean	95% confidence interval of the mean		Minimum value	Maximum value
					Lower	Upper		
Fixation count	1.8	57.69	12.76	3.40	49.98	65.4	38.00	82.00
	2.0	46.46	15.53	4.31	37.08	55.84	31.00	81.00
	2.2	41.46	13.51	3.75	33.30	49.62	21.00	71.00

(*continued*)

Table 2. (*continued*)

	Velocity	Mean	SD	Standard error mean	95% confidence interval of the mean		Minimum value	Maximum value
					Lower	Upper		
Average of saccade duration	1.8	0.60	0.18	0.05	0.49	0.71	0.37	1.02
	2.0	0.70	0.26	0.07	0.54	0.86	0.27	1.06
	2.2	0.67	0.26	0.07	0.51	0.82	0.30	1.24
Total saccades duration	1.8	4.51	0.99	0.27	3.92	5.11	3.40	6.85
	2.0	3.65	1.61	0.45	2.68	4.62	2.40	8.00
	2.2	3.07	0.97	0.27	2.48	3.66	1.90	5.00

It can be seen from Table 2 that fixation count of the search target gradually decreases as the speed increases, and the total saccades duration also shows the same trend. Because the fixation count and the total saccades duration can be used to measure the search efficiency of the subject, the more fixation count in the search task, the less target can be confirmed, and the lower search efficiency of the subject. The shorter the total saccades duration, the higher the search efficiency. Under the same visual search conditions, the faster the moving speed, the higher the search efficiency, that is, when the speed is at 2.2 m/min, the search efficiency is the highest. The average fixation duration reflects the difficulty of extracting information during the visual search process. The longer the average fixation time, the more difficult it is to extract information. It can be known from Table 2 that the information extraction is more difficult at the speed of 2.0 m/min than 1.8 m/min.

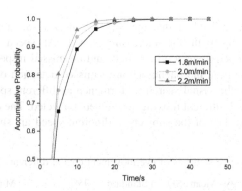

Fig. 1. Cumulative discovery probability at different moving speed

According to the research of Williams [17], in the visual search model under the random search strategy, the cumulative probability $F(t)$ of the target and the search time t have an exponential relationship of $F(t) = 1 - e^{-\lambda t}$, which will reduce statistics of search time, and the cumulative discovery probability curves at three different speed are obtained, as shown in Fig. 1. The concept of "time constant" is introduced, that is, the cumulative discovery probability increases sharply during the search time corresponding to the time constant. And if it is more than the time constant, the cumulative discovery probability increases slowly. According to the research of Guo et al. [1], the time constant at a moving speed of 0 m/min is about 7.629 s.

Compare the search speed of 0 m/min with 1.8 m/min, 2.0 m/min, and 2.2 m/min, respectively, and Chi-square test is used to check whether there is a significant difference in search performance within 7.629 s or not. The results are shown in Table 3.

Table 3. Chi-square test results of search performance at different moving speed

Compared with static search	χ^2	P
1.8 m/min	11.900	0.160
2.0 m/min	18.316	0.017
2.2 m/min	34.236	0.012

From Table 3, when the search time is 7.629 s, the search performance is different, not significant different, between the moving speed 0 m/min and 1.8 m/min. When the moving speed is 2.0 m/min, there is a significant difference in the search performance. And when the speed is 2.2 m/min, the p value decreases, but not as sharp as from 1.8 m/min to 2.0 m/min. Therefore, the significant difference in performance appears in the moving speed range of 1.8 m/min to 2.0 m/min. When the speed increases to 2.2 m/min, the search performance tends to improve, but the change is very small.

The visual search efficiency is the lowest at the speed of 1.8 m/min, but the information extraction is the easiest and the accuracy rate is the highest among the three speed. The visual search efficiency and the accuracy rate are the second at the speed of 2.0 m/min, and the information extraction is difficult. The search efficiency is the highest at the speed of 2.2 m/min and the difficulty of information extraction is better than at the speed of 2.0 m/min, but its accuracy rate is much lower and there is possibility of missing detection.

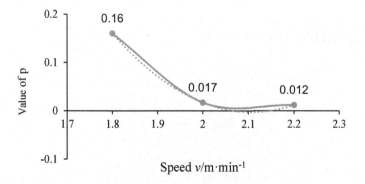

Fig. 2. p-value-speed fitting curve

According to the fitting analysis of the p-value-speed, as shown in Fig. 2, the obtained equation is

$$p = 1.725v^2 - 7.27v + 7.657, \quad R^2 = 1$$

Calculation and analysis show that under the condition of ensuring that the missed detection rate is as low as possible, a speed of 2.0667 m/min should be selected for security inspection.

3.2   Influence of Moving Direction on Visual Search Performance

The search interface is divided into four quadrant areas based on the fixation hotspot map. The fixation hotspot map of the direction moving from left to right is shown in Fig. 3. The first fixation point generally appears in the second quadrant (upper left). After the entire dynamic visual search process completed, the number of fixation count on the left side of the heatmap was more than the number on the right, and the number of fixation count on the top left was the largest.

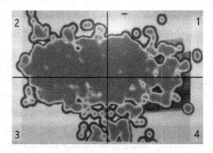

Fig. 3. Heatmap when the moving direction is from left to right

When the search background and search target are entered from right to left at the same time, the gaze heat map of the subject's field of vision is shown in Fig. 4. When the search background moves from right to left, the subjects' fixation points appear firstly in the first quadrant (upper right). During the entire dynamic visual search process, the number of fixations on the right is much more than the number of fixations on the left. Quadrant 4 (bottom right) has the most fixations.

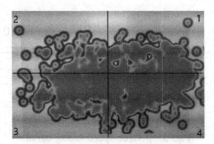

Fig. 4. Heatmap when the moving direction is from right to left

Table 4. Statistics of dynamic visual search results in different moving directions

	Number of false detection	Error rate	Missed detection rate	Missed detection rate
From left to right	8	0.89%	0	0%
From right to left	7	0.78%	0	0%

According to the correct rate and missed detection rate of the search targets, see Table 4, whether the search background is different or not, there is almost no difference in the error rate and missed detection rate to the prohibited items. Descriptive statistics were performed on the eye movement data collected during the test, and one subject's abnormal data was excluded. The results are shown in Table 5.

Table 5. Descriptive statistics of eye movement data in different moving directions

	Direction	Mean	SD	Std. error mean	95% confidence interval of the mean		Minimum value	Maximum value
					Lower	Upper		
Fixation count	Left to right	57.77	13.60	3.77	49.54	65.99	33.00	88.00
	Right to left	57.69	12.76	3.54	49.9	65.41	38.00	82.00
Average of fixation duration	Left to right	0.54	0.15	0.041	0.45	0.64	0.31	0.74
	Right to left	0.6015	0.18	0.051	0.49	0.71	0.37	1.02
Total saccade duration	Left to right	5.06	1.70	0.473	4.03	6.09	3.10	9.58
	Right to left	4.52	0.99	0.27	3.92	5.11	3.40	6.85

It can be seen from Table 5 that the average number of fixation count in the two directions is basically the same, while the average fixation duration and the total saccade duration is different. The total saccade duration can be used to measure the visual search efficiency of the participants. The shorter the total saccade duration, the higher the search efficiency. Since the total saccade duration is significantly smaller when moving from right to left than moving from left to right. Therefore, the search efficiency is relatively higher when the search background is from right to left.

3.3   Impact of Background Number on Visual Search Performance

By controlling the moving speed of the search background, the targets in the single search background and the complex search background are displayed in the visual search field of the stimulus materials.

Table 6. Descriptive statistics of eye movement data for single search background

	Mean	SD	Standard error	95% confidence interval of the difference		Minimum value	Maximum value
				Lower	Upper		
Fixation count	166.00	60.44695	16.76497	129.4723	202.5277	72.00	285.00
Average of fixation duration	0.6515	0.22509	0.06243	0.5155	0.7876	0.41	1.04
Saccade count	207.4615	83.22221	23.08169	157.1709	257.7522	96.00	412.00
Total saccade duration	12.7715	4.65692	1.29160	9.9574	15.5857	5.60	21.53

Table 6 is the eye movement data statistics during the test. The mean and standard deviation of the single visual search background are compared with the corresponding data of the complex visual search background. The results are shown in Table 7.

Table 7. Mean and SD comparison between single and complex visual search background

	Single background	Complex background
Fixation counts	166.00 ± 60.45	57.69 ± 12.76
Average fixation duration	0.65 ± 0.23	0.60 ± 0.18
Total saccade duration	12.78 ± 4.66	4.52 ± 0.99

It can be seen from Table 7, the mean of the average fixation duration and the mean of standard deviation of single search background are larger than the corresponding values of complex search background when the search difficulty are the same. It indicates that the single search background cannot improve the search efficiency in dynamic visual search. However, it increases the time of the whole dynamic visual search process. As a result, the complex search background has much higher search efficiency. At the same time, the results of questionnaire reflected by 91% participants also showed that single search background is more likely to cause fatigue.

4 Conclusions

By analyzing the speed, directions and backgrounds that affect the performance of visual search in security inspection, the conclusions are as follows:

1. In the speed of 1.8 m/min, 2.0 m/min, and 2.2 m/min, the faster the speed, the higher the search efficiency. The number of fixation count in the target search process decreases gradually along with the increasing speed and the decreasing of total saccade duration. According to the time-cumulative discovery probability fitting curve, the security inspection efficiency is the best at the speed of 2.0667 m/min.
2. Different moving directions will cause changes on the main fixation area. When moving from left to right, the upper left part of the package is concerned more, while moving from right to left, the lower right part is concerned more. The average fixation duration and saccade duration show that the right-to-left detection is better than the left-to-right.
3. The visual search efficiency of complex visual search background is better than single search background. Single search background increases the entire dynamic visual search time and easily leads to fatigue.

Acknowledgements.   The presented work has been supported by General project of China University of Labor Relations (20XYJS020).

References

1. Guo, X.Y.: The effects of speed, time pressure and number of targets on the performance of dynamic visual search. Doctoral dissertation, Tsinghua University, Beijing (2011)
2. Hu, F.P., Cai, L.L., Chai, L.L., Ge, L.Z.: Research on visual search strategy of item location information prompt in page layout. Psychol. Sci. **33**(06), 1512–1515 (2010)
3. Cao, L.R., Li, Y.M.: Impact of graphic complexity on visual search performance. In: The Tenth National Psychological Academic Conference. Chinese Psychological Association (2005)
4. Yang, L.D., Yu, R.F., Guo, X.Y.: Research on a dual-target dynamic visual search model. Ergonomics **21**(04), 41–46 (2015)
5. Zhou, H.Y.: Research on key technologies of image search and recognition based on visual cognition. Doctoral dissertation, University of Science and Technology Beijing (2015)
6. Jin, H.B., Cai, Y.M., Hong, Y.: Visual search features of security inspection based on eye movement data analysis. Ind. Eng. **17**(2), 43–48 (2014)
7. Wolfe, J.M., Horowitz, T.S., Kenner, N.M.: Rare items often missed in visual searches. Nature **435**(1), 439–440 (2005)
8. Over, E.A.B., Hooge, I.T.C., Vlaskamp, B.N.S., Erkelens, C.J.: Coarse-to-fine eye movement strategy in visual search. Vis. Res. **47**(17), 2272–2280 (2007)
9. von Bastian, C.C., Schwaninger, A., Michel, S.: The impact of color composition on X-ray image interpretation in aviation security screening. In: 43rd Annual 2009 International Carnahan Conference on Security Technology, pp. 201–205. IEEE (2009)

10. Smith, J.D., Redford, J.S., Washburn, D.A., et al.: Specific-token effects in screening tasks: possible implications for aviation security. J. Exp. Psychol. Learn. Memory Cogn. 31(6), 1171–1185 (2005)
11. McCarley, J.S., Kramer, A.F., Wickens, C.D., et al.: Visual skills in airport-security screening. Psychol. Sci. 15(5), 302–306 (2004)
12. Zhang, C.L.: Research on X-ray transmission image processing method in security inspection system. Master's thesis, Shenyang University (2015)
13. Sun, G., Li, Q., Meng, Y., Ran, L.: Research on optimization of information coding for car dashboard based on eye movement analysis. In: Rebelo, F., Soares, M.M. (eds.) AHFE 2019. AISC, vol. 955, pp. 122–135. Springer, Cham (2020). https://doi.org/10.1007/978-3-030-20227-9_12
14. Sun, G.L., Li, Q., Fu, P.W., et al.: Analysis and optimization of information coding for automobile dashboard based on human factors engineering. Chin. Saf. Sci. J. 28(8), 68–74 (2018)
15. Sun, G., Li, Q., Meng, Y.H., et al.: Design of car dashboard based on eye movement analysis. Pack. Eng. 41(2), 148–160 (2020)
16. Sun, G.: Research on location of emergency sign based on virtual reality and eye tracking technology. In: Ahram, T. (ed.) AHFE 2019. AISC, vol. 973, pp. 401–408. Springer, Cham (2020). https://doi.org/10.1007/978-3-030-20476-1_40
17. Williams, L.G., Borow, M.S.: The effect of rate and direction of display movement upon visual search. Hum. Factors 5(2), 139–146 (1963)

Processing of Sensory Information is Affected by BCI Feedback Being Perceived

Nikolay Syrov[1](✉), Dmitry Bredichin[1], and Alexander Kaplan[1,2] (iD)

[1] Lomonosov Moscow State University, Moscow, Russia
kolascoco@gmail.com
[2] Immanuel Kant Baltic Federal University, Kaliningrad, Russia

Abstract. Feedback is an important part of the BCI loop providing a user with the information regarding whether or not cognitive efforts were successful. It is believed that the feedback affects user's learning ability to control BCI. In the field of neurorehabilitation, the feedback of a BCI loop is associated with facilitation of neuroplasticity. However, such methods as motor imagery, tactile stimulation and movements observation have a therapeutic effect per se which makes it unclear whether any facilitation is associated with a BCI loop. The aim of the present study is to fill such a lacuna of knowledge. The answer can help us to propose a new paradigm of neurorehabilitation instruments to recover the mobility of patients paralyzed after a stroke. P300-BCI is another popular paradigm which is based on visual evoked potentials and being commonly used in BCI spellers. In our study, we examined whether the feedback in P300-BCI loop could facilitate motor cortex activity. We have shown that primary motor cortex TMS-induced MEPs was higher in amplitude for sensory information perceived as a feedback than for perceived per se, while the MO and TS per se did not affect the excitability of the motor cortex. We conclude that the BCI-feedback context influenced the perception of visual and tactile information. These results can be used to build a new generation of BCI for rehabilitation since it is known that the ability to control P300-BCI for post-stroke patients remains at a high level.

Keywords: P300-BCI · Motor cortex excitability · Post-stroke rehabilitation

1 Introduction

Activation of the motor control cortical systems by means of motor imagery is widely considered as one of the most promising approaches for motor rehabilitation [1]. A series of studies based on transcranial magnetic stimulation (TMS) technique showed a significant increase in corticospinal excitability during motor imagery, which allows us to consider it as a relevant approach for motor rehabilitation [2, 3]. Feedback is known to be the key condition for mental training since it provides a subject with information regarding the quality of any motor imagery act. So, it is important to note that any BCI loop involves a feedback perception. Currently, BCIs based on motor imagery are actively used to create neurorehabilitation tools and techniques aimed at motor recovery of patients paralyzed after a stroke [4]. Such tools allow patients not

© Springer Nature Switzerland AG 2020
C. Stephanidis and M. Antona (Eds.): HCII 2020, CCIS 1224, pp. 575–580, 2020.
https://doi.org/10.1007/978-3-030-50726-8_75

only to train a paralyzed limb but also to control exoskeletal structures that move paralyzed parts of the body, which may enhance training effects [4]. However, an MI-BCI does not allow to generate more than 2–4 feedback signals or commands for an external device. This limitation is present due to a limited set of mental images, which might be detected through EEG mu-rhythm desynchronization. Moreover, the classification accuracy for such BCIs frequently cannot exceed 65–75% [5]. Also, to operate an MI-based BCI a post-stroke patient must undergo a long training session whereas their overall ability to imagine movement may be impaired after a stroke [6].

In conformity with the facts mentioned, the BCI community tends to develop reliable and multitasking interfaces to be used in neurorehabilitation. Amongst all the existing solutions, the interfaces based on a positive wave of visual evoked potential P300 (P300-BCI) are known to be the most appropriate. An important argument for such a claim is that post-stroke patients can quickly master this BCI technology [7]. Moreover, the accuracy of mental command classification may reach 80–90% whereas the number of commands is limited only by the number of on-screen stimuli denoting these commands. However, the activity of a subject in a P300-BCI does explicitly include neither motor imagery nor movements itself. Therefore, it might be questioned whether the P300-based BCIs can be used as a neurorehabilitation instrument to recover the mobility of patients paralyzed after a stroke. The present study aims to test the hypothesis that the operation of a P300-BCI by a subject (specifically, control of the finger movements of an artificial hand and the vibrotactile stimulation of their own hand) leads to an increase in corticospinal excitability. This assumption is based on the fact that observation of artificial hand finger movements as feedback can activate the primary motor cortex of an observing subject. After a lot of studies in the field have been published, the fact that both movement observation and tactile stimulation can lead to a change in the activity of the motor cortex is considered as common knowledge. Feedback is an important part of a BCI loop as it provides an operator with the information considering the degree of success of their cognitive efforts. It is well known that the presence of feedback affects the ability of a subject to operate in a BCI loop. More than that, in [8] it was shown that vibrotactile feedback is more useful for some subjects than visual one while learning to operate an MI-based BCI. Also, in [9] the authors showed that the location of a vibrating motor during tactile feedback perception affects BCI performance. At the same time, it remains unknown whether any advantage of BCI loop implementation for neurorehabilitation exists. One more question which keeps being unanswered is whether the feedback-associated sensation (the sensory input perceived as a response to the mental efforts of a subject) affects the perception of sensory information? The answer to this question was obtained in this study which allowed us to make some recommendations regarding the development of motor recovery tools and techniques based on P300-BCI.

2   Methods

2.1   Participants

The study involved 20 healthy volunteers (7 women) aged 20 to 26 years. All of them signed an informed consent to participate in a study approved by the Department of Biology of Moscow University.

2.2   Protocol

P300-BCI. An artificial five-fingered limb similar to a human hand was used in the experiment as a tool for stimuli presentation and visual feedback output. It was located above the right hand of a subject. Each finger of the artificial limb is movable through the P300-BCI. A light-emitting diode (LED) was mounted on each finger of the artificial limb. Random alternate illumination of the five LEDs served as stimuli to evoke an EEG response which is essential for the extraction of P300 component. The subject selected a finger of the artificial hand which they would like to flex and concentrated their visual attention on the illumination of a corresponding LED. Visual evoked potentials that were recorded in response to flashes of both targeted and non-targeted stimuli (LEDs on fingers) were used for classification of the intention of a subject (regarding which finger to flex). After the finished classification process, a subject received feedback as either: 1 - observation of selected artificial finger movement - MO(bci), 2 - observation of selected artificial finger movement + vibrotactile stimulation of the corresponding right-hand finger - MO + T (bci), 3 - vibrotactile stimulation of the corresponding right-hand finger - T (bci) Also, we introduced two additional conditions to be used as control measures: 4 - vibrotactile stimulation of a random finger (perceived as a sensory signal with no BCI-feedback properties) - T (non bci), 5 - observation of a random artificial finger movement - MO (non bci). The electroencephalogram was recorded with a sampling frequency of 500 Hz from Pz, Poz, 28 PO3, PO4, PO7, PO8, O1, O2 sites (according to the "10–10" system). ERPs recorded in response to the illumination of targeted and non-targeted LED flashes were classified using LDA. The average classification accuracy for all the subjects was 95% of the total trial number (20 trials).

Transcranial Magnetic Stimulation (TMS) and Electromyography (EMG). Transcranial magnetic stimulation is a technique for noninvasive stimulation of the human brain. Single pulse transcranial magnetic stimuli were delivered using a Neurosoft stimulator (Ivanovo, Rus), via a figure-of-eight coil. The coil was positioned over the left motor cortex, at the optimal site for producing responses in the resting flexor digitorum superficialis muscle (FDS) with 110% amplitude (according to motor threshold). Electromyography was recorded to determine the amplitude of motor-evoked potentials (MEPs). The change in the amplitude of the MEP is known to reflects the dynamics of corticospinal excitability of a subject.

3   Results and Discussion

Analysis of MEP amplitudes showed that in all the conditions in which a subject perceived any kind of BCI feedback, corticospinal excitability significantly increased. Accordingly, the perception of feedback-associated sensory information (motor observation and vibrotactile stimulation) led to an increase of MEPs amplitude (see Fig. 1). However, it is unclear whether such an increase is connected with the BCI operating since it is known that motor observation per se may activate M1 [10]. To resolve such a problem, in all of the non-BCI conditions motor observation was set passive (non-BCI induced) as well as vibrotactile stimulation was performed arbitrarily. In turn, MEPs amplitude in non-BCI conditions did not change after the perception of sensory information. More than that, in the condition of non-BCI motor observation, MEP amplitudes recorded after observation, were significantly lower than the ones recorded in MO-BCI condition. The same trend is present for tactile stimulation as well, i.e. the perception of a tactile stimulus increased corticospinal excitability only if such a stimulus was associated with BCI feedback (see Fig. 1).

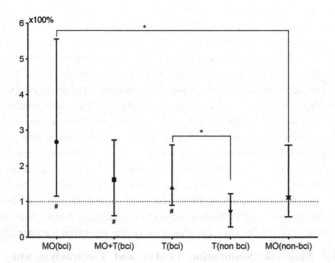

Fig. 1. Amplitude of motor-evoked potentials (MEP) for FDS of all subjects regarding to different types of feedback. MO corresponds to MEPs which were recorded during observation of movement of target finger, MO + T - corresponds to combined condition (observation of movement + tactile stimulation). T – corresponds to the cases when participants perceived tactile stimulation of their own fingers. Postfix «bci» denotes conditions when sensory information was presented as a BCI feedback Amplitude of responses is presented as a percentage of the baseline condition mean MEPs. Columns and error bars are median and interquartile range of distribution of each group of MEPs. Note: comparison with the baseline - #p < 0,05/comparison between conditions - *p < 0,05 (Mann-Whitney test, p-values were adjusted by Dunn's test).

Thus, we can conclude that the perception of visual and tactile sensory information is influenced by the feedback context in the P300-BCI loop. According to the MEP amplitude analysis, passive observation of movement (outside of the BCI loop) did not increase corticospinal excitability. Probably, such a result is caused by insufficient anthropomorphism of the artificial hand. The perception of tactile stimulation outside of the BCI loop led to insignificantly decreased MEP amplitudes. We suggest that either random fluctuations or short-latency afferent inhibition have led to such a minor decrease [11]. Also, we do not exclude «bottom-up» activation of M1 in the BCI conditions, which might occur through afferent neural pathways and cortico-cortical connections between M1 and visual cortex [12]. However, we claim that the key factor for the modulation observed as «top-down» interaction since the detection of feedback-associated components in sensory input is essential for the process according to the results we obtained.

4   Conclusions

We conclude that P300-based BCIs can be used in neurorehabilitation. Such BCIs are considered as user-friendly for post-stroke patients and allows them to perform control with high accuracy. We claim that during the construction of neurorehabilitation devices it is essential to take into account the presence of the feedback and its sensory modality since the perception of feedback in the P300-BCI loop modulates activation of motor cortex according to the results of the study. Moreover, we find it worth noting that all the experiments in the study are conducted on healthy subjects. Accordingly, before the implementation of the technique for after-stroke patients the individual differences and clinical pictures of the patients are to be taken into account to choose and use the feedback of the most effective for particular patient sensory modality.

References

1. Dijkerman, H.C., Ietswaart, M., Johnston, M.: Motor imagery and the rehabilitation of movement disorders: an overview. Neurophysiological Found. Ment. Motor Imagery 1(9), 127–144 (2010)
2. Kaplan, A., Vasilyev, A., Liburkina, S.: Poor BCI performers still could benefit from motor imagery training. In: International Conference on Augmented Cognition, pp. 46–56 (2016)
3. Yakovlev, L.V., Syrov, N.V., Kaplan, A.Y.: Corticospinal excitability in humans during motor imagery coupled with functional electrical stimulation. Moscow Univ. Biol. Sci. Bull. 74(3), 183–187 (2019)
4. Ang, K.K., Guan, C., Zhang, H.: Clinical study of neurorehabilitation in stroke using EEG-based motor imagery brain-computer interface with robotic feedback. In: Annual International Conference of the IEEE Engineering in Medicine and Biology 2010, pp. 5549–5552. IEEE (2010)
5. Ahn, M., Jun, S.C.: Performance variation in motor imagery brain–computer interface: a brief review. J. Neurosci. Methods 243, 103–110 (2015)
6. Malouin, F., Richards, C.L., Durand, A.: Clinical assessment of motor imagery after stroke. Neurorehab. Neural Repair 22(4), 330–340 (2008)

7. Ortner, R., Bruckner, M., Prueckl, R.: Accuracy of a P300 speller for people with motor impairments. In: 2011 IEEE Symposium on Computational Intelligence, Cognitive Algorithms, Mind, and Brain (CCMB), pp. 1–6, April 2011

8. Liburkina, S.P., Vasilyev, A.N., Yakovlev, L.: Motor imagery-based brain-computer interface with vibrotactile stimuli. Neurosci. Behav. Physiol. 48(9), 1067–1077 (2018)

9. Rahman, K.A.A., Ibrahim, B.S.K.K., Fuad, N.: ACIS advances in computing and intelligent system Brain Computer Interface (BCI) - Functional Electrical Stimulation (FES) control system of knee joint movement for paraplegic. Adv. Comput. Intell. Syst. 1(1), 1–6 (2019)

10. Zhang, J.J., Fong, K.N., Welage, N.: The activation of the mirror neuron system during action observation and action execution with mirror visual feedback in stroke: a systematic review. Neural Plast. 2018, 10–14 (2018)

11. Turco, C.V., El-Sayes, J., Savoie, M.J.: Short-and long-latency afferent inhibition; uses, mechanisms and influencing factors. Brain Stimul. 11(1), 59–74 (2018)

12. Robertson, I.H., Murre, J.M.: Rehabilitation of brain damage: brain plasticity and principles of guided recovery. Psychol. Bull. 125(5), 544 (1999)

BCI-Controlled Motor Imagery Training Can Improve Performance in e-Sports

Lev Yakovlev[1]([✉]), Nikolay Syrov[1], Nikolai Görtz[3],
and Alexander Kaplan[1,2] [iD]

[1] Lomonosov Moscow State University, Moscow, Russia
leojackovlev@gmail.com
[2] Immanuel Kant Baltic Federal University, Kaliningrad, Russia
[3] Eberhard Karls University of Tübingen, Tübingen, Germany

Abstract. Motor imagery (MI) training can improve motor performance which is widely used in sport training. BCI based on MI can demonstrate the quality of mental efforts via neurofeedback based on sensorimotor activation. Despite numerous studies of MI in context of classical sport, there are no studies aimed at improvement for e-athletes performance. The aim of the study is to evaluate the effect of MI-training on reaction time and velocity in gaming mouse control tasks. The study involved 14 healthy naive volunteers, divided into two subgroups. Experimental subgroup (N = 8) was trained with kinesthetic MI with BCI-visual feedback. The control subgroup (N = 6) had no BCI-feedback. In the speed selection task participants had to click on the correct mouse button. In the fast-clicking task participants should click as fast as they can for one minute. Each task was before (pretest) and after (posttest) MI training. During the training participants imagined finger movements used in actual task executions. During the task executions reaction time was recorded and EEG was recorded during MI training. Performed statistical analysis on a group level included paired comparisons between pretest and posttest (Wilcoxon signed-rank tests). Statistically significant changes (p < 0.05) in the reaction time in speed selection task and reaction velocity in fast clicking task after MI-training in experimental subgroup. Everyone in experimental subgroup had stable ERD during motor imagery, while there were neither differences in reaction time nor in reaction velocity in control group. The obtained results confirm the previously shown effects of motor imagery on sensorimotor performance.

Keywords: Motor imagery · BCI · Motor learning · e-sports

1 Introduction

It is known that motor imagery (MI) training can improve motor performance which is widely used in sport training as supplementary technique [1]. Generally, the term "motor imagery" can include different mental approaches to represent motor acts e.g. kinesthetic or visual types. Brain activation patterns associated with these mental conditions are different and besides having a conversation with a person - no conventional way to monitor the MI-type currently exists. Brain Computer Interface (BCI) technologies allow an interaction between the brain and the outside world in the

© Springer Nature Switzerland AG 2020
C. Stephanidis and M. Antona (Eds.): HCII 2020, CCIS 1224, pp. 581–586, 2020.
https://doi.org/10.1007/978-3-030-50726-8_76

form of a new channel [2]. BCI based on MI can demonstrate the quality of mental efforts via neurofeedback based on sensorimotor activation (kinesthetic MI leads to mu-rhythm event related desynchronization reaction in EEG, ERD) [3]. The main idea is that kinesthetic motor imagery associated with sensorimotor activation and this type of MI is supposed to be the most suitable for motor learning and BCI-systems can help to estimate the quality of mental efforts. Despite numerous studies of MI in the context of classical sport [4–6], there are no studies aimed at improvement for professional e-athletes performance. In attempts to determine the neural basis of video gaming, a series of links between the neural and cognitive aspects such as attention, cognitive control, visuospatial skills etc. were shown [7]. Nowadays, e-sport is one of the official sport disciplines in many countries such as Russia, USA, Italy, Georgia, South Korea, India, Iran etc. The aim of the study is to evaluate the effect of MI-training on reaction time and velocity during gaming mouse control tasks. The hypothesis is that BCI-controlled motor imagery training can enhance reaction time and velocity in computer mouse control tasks. The work was carried out as a part of the world's first BCI training platform development called «e-boi».

2   Methods

The study involved 14 healthy volunteers with no experience in motor imagery, divided into two subgroups. Experimental subgroup (N = 8) was trained with kines-thetic MI with BCI-visual feedback. The control subgroup (N = 6) had no BCI-feedback and was trained uncontrollably presumably with the visual MI type. All the participants signed an informed consent approved by the Lomonosov Moscow State University Ethical Committee.

During the MI-training session participants imagined finger movements used in actual (relevant) task executions. In the speed selection task participants had to cor-rectly click on one of the two computer mouse buttons (left or right). In the fast-clicking task participants should click on the left mouse button by forefinger as fast as they can during one minute. Each task was before (pre-test) and after (post-test) MI training.

MI was carried out in a trial-manner with the structure (ABABBA...) where A is a motor imagery and B is a resting state. Trials were grouped in sequences of 10-15 trials for each condition (MI and rest) lasting 6–8 s. There were 2–3 min of breaks between the sequences. The total training time was 15–20 min for each task. During the task executions reaction time was collected (n = 75 for each condition) and EEG was recorded during the MI training. 30 channel EEG was recorded at the 500 Hz sample frequency in range 0.1–70 Hz. Raw data were extracted and preprocessed including bandpass filtration (1–30 Hz), re-referencing (CAR), and epoching depending on the experimental condition (MI/rest). Preprocessed EEG data were analyzed in the spectral domain (FFT with sliding window overlapping 80%). Based on spectral power in mu-range (7–13 Hz) ERD scores were calculated for each channel and used to BCI-feedback for experimental subgroup after each 10–15 trials. Subjects in the control subgroup had no feedback during the MI performance.

Performed statistical analysis on a group level included paired comparisons between pretest and posttest (Wilcoxon signed-rank tests) for reaction time (speed selection task) and velocity (fast-clicking task) measurements. Stimulus presentation and recordings were performed by the self-developed «e-boi» software. Data analysis and visualization carried out using python packages (MNE, pandas, SciPy and seaborn) in self-written scripts [8–10].

3 Results

All the subjects demonstrated stable central ERD patterns while performing voluntary right-hand finger movements both in experimental and control subgroups. Also, every individual in the experimental subgroup had stable ERD during motor imagery wherein there was no ERD in the control subgroup (see Fig. 1).

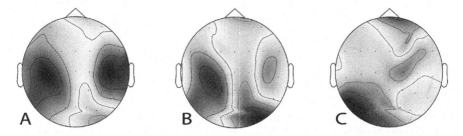

Fig. 1. Average sensorimotor desynchronization patterns during MI-training. Shades of red correspond to desynchronization level, of blue - synchronization respectively. A. Speed selection task (experimental subgroup, N = 8) B. Fast clicking task (experimental subgroup, N = 8) C. Control subgroup (N = 6). (Color figure online)

Statistically significant changes (p < 0.05) in the reaction time in speed selection task (for middle finger pressing the right mouse button) and reaction velocity in fast clicking task after MI-training in experimental subgroup (see Fig. 2). Whereas there were neither differences in reaction time nor in reaction velocity in the control group. The obtained results confirm the previously shown effects of motor imagery on sensorimotor performance [11, 12]. Our data are applicable for the training tasks used in e-sports. We believe that BCI-neurofeedback based on EEG activation patterns can be effective for e-athletes training.

4 Discussion

Subjects from the experimental subgroup who practiced controlled MI-training demonstrate stable mu-ERD which was observed in the central EEG channels. At the same time, for the subjects from the control subgroup engaged in motor imagery without any feedback, we did not observe patterns of sensorimotor mu-ERD in EEG.

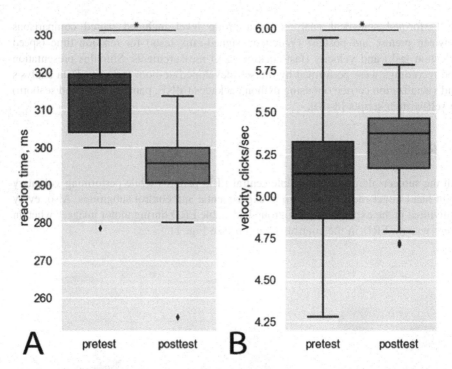

Fig. 2. A. Reaction time (experimental subgroup, N = 8) measured in speed selection task before (pretest) and after (posttest) MI training. Middle finger. B. Reaction velocity (experimental subgroup, N = 8) measured in fast selection task before (pretest) and after (posttest) MI training. $\star$ p < 0.05 in Wilcoxon signed-rank test (pretest vs posttest).

These results confirm that the experimental subgroup subjects practiced kinesthetic MI. Desynchronization pattern during representing the index finger and the middle finger of the right hand movements in the speed selection task has bilateral localization, while in fast clicking task, where only the forefinger was used, the ERD pattern is mostly observed in the contralateral to active hand hemisphere. This may be due to the fact that speed selection task requires large resources for movement coordination, since it requires not only a high speed of response, but also the coordinated work of several fingers. This result is consistent with our previous studies [13, 14].

The motor performance test has shown the improvements of several parameters already after a short-term kinesthetic MI-training. So, the reaction time for pressing the right mouse button decreased significantly after MI-training (see Fig. 2A). We assume that working with the middle finger (right mouse button) is less familiar to the average user, this skill is more susceptible to training. This explains why, after a short MI training, only this parameter changed statistically significantly. At the same time, the motor reaction time for the forefinger (left mouse button) did not significantly change in our study, but this can be investigated during long-term controlled MI-training.

In the fast selection task, we showed that in the pre-MI training condition, the median pressing speed was lower than in the pre-MI training condition. We observed that after training, subjects of the experimental subgroup (but not the control subgroup) developed muscle fatigue slowlier, which is characterized by a rapid increase in the interval between consecutive clicks in the fast selection task. In the Fig. 2B we can see that the pressing speed is higher after the MI-training. Thus, for tasks where high-speed work is required for a long period of time, MI training can increase resistance to the processes of neuromuscular fatigue. The positive impact of MI training on motor skills has already been shown [5, 11, 12], however, in our work we examined movements with fine motor skills of hands, which also require attention specific to e-sports.

5 Conclusion

Our data are applicable for the sensorimotor tasks used in e-sports. We believe that BCI-neurofeedback based on EEG activation patterns can be effective for e-athletes practice. It is necessary to study the effect of BCI-controlled MI training for different types of movements and sensorimotor tasks used in e-sports disciplines. It is also important to study effects of training duration, find the optimal strategies and check the data on a large sample including e-athletes of different skill levels. We assume that the new generation of BCI systems for e-sports can potentially take the video gaming industry to the new level. Fundamental aspects of working in this field have potential for future implications in all the areas associated with motor learning and execution (e.g. sport, musical performance and neurorehabilitation).

Acknowledgements. This study was partially supported by funding from the Russian Foundation for Basic Research (RFBR), Grant #17-29-02115.

References

1. Mizuguchi, N., et al.: Motor imagery and sport performance. J. Phys. Fit. Sport. Med. **1**(1), 103–111 (2012)
2. Wolpaw, J.R., et al.: Brain–computer interfaces for communication and control. Clin. Neurophysiol. **113**(6), 767–791 (2002)
3. Pfurtscheller, G., et al.: Current trends in Graz brain-computer interface (BCI) research. IEEE Trans. Rehabil. Eng. **8**(2), 216–219 (2000)
4. Holmes, P., Calmels, C.: A neuroscientific review of imagery and observation use in sport. J. Mot. Behav. **40**(5), 433–445 (2008)
5. Feltz, D.L., Landers, D.M.: The effects of mental practice on motor skill learning and performance: a meta-analysis. J. Sport Psychol. **5**(1), 25–57 (1983)
6. Fourkas, A.D., et al.: Kinesthetic imagery and tool-specific modulation of corticospinal representations in expert tennis players. Cereb. Cortex **18**(10), 2382–2390 (2008)
7. Palaus, M., Marron, E.M., Viejo-Sobera, R., Redolar-Ripoll, D.: Neural basis of video gaming: a systematic review. Front. Hum. Neurosci. **11**, 248 (2017)
8. Gramfort, A., et al.: MEG and EEG data analysis with MNE-Python. Front. Neurosci. **7**, 267 (2013)
9. Virtanen, P., et al.: SciPy 1.0: fundamental algorithms for scientific computing in Python. Nat. Methods, **17**(3), 261–272 (2020)

10. Oliphant, T.E.: Python for scientific computing. Comput. Sci. Eng. **9**(3), 10–20 (2007)
11. Allami, N., et al.: Visuo-motor learning with combination of different rates of motor imagery and physical practice. Exp. Brain Res. **184**(1), 105–113 (2008)
12. Gentili, R., et al.: Motor learning without doing trial-by-trial improvement in motor performance during mental training. J. Neurophysiol. **104**(2), 774–783 (2010)
13. Kaplan, A., Vasilyev, A., Liburkina, S., Yakovlev, L.: Poor BCI performers still could benefit from motor imagery training. In: Schmorrow, D.D.D., Fidopiastis, C.M.M. (eds.) AC 2016. LNCS (LNAI), vol. 9743, pp. 46–56. Springer, Cham (2016). https://doi.org/10.1007/978-3-319-39955-3_5
14. Vasilyev, A., et al.: Assessing motor imagery in brain-computer interface training: psychological and neurophysiological correlates. Neuropsychologia **97**, 56–65 (2017)

Effect of Dialogs' Arrangement on Accuracy and Workload for Confirming Input Data

Keiko Yamamoto[✉], Hiroki Kawaguchi, and Yoshihiro Tsujino

Kyoto Institute of Technology, Kyoto, Japan
`kei@kit.ac.jp`

Abstract. Recently, a variety of web services are available through the Internet. On these web services, the users have to input data correctly such as personal information and ordering data on digital devices. If they make mistakes in their input data on this kind of services, it often makes serious troubles. To avoid these troubles, many services have functions like "confirmation dialog" for the users to confirm their input data. However, the traditional confirmation dialog can be skipped by simply clicking OK button on the dialog without confirming input data. To solve the problem, we proposed "Phantom Dialog" that shows simultaneously two parallel arranged dialogs with user's input data and system-generated dummy data. It was found that the Phantom Dialog could make difficult to skip the process of the confirmation. But, it took longer confirmation time than the traditional confirmation dialog. In this paper, in order to reduce the time, we propose to increase the probability that user's input data is shown on the left dialog, which is expected to be read firstly by the user on the Phantom Dialog. As the result of the evaluation with the three different probabilities on the Phantom Dialog, it is found that the participants can confirm their input data faster with left-biased probability without deterioration in the confirmation accuracy. Furthermore, most of them did not notice that the probabilities were different.

Keywords: Confirmation dialog · Web service

1 Introduction

In recent years, various services such as video on-demand and online shopping have been provided through the Internet. On these web services, the user must input his/her data correctly such as personal information for the member registration and ordering information when purchasing products on a PC or smartphone. If the users enter such information incorrectly and register it, significant damage might occur. On the other hand, because there are many items to be checked and/or repetitive operations with many orders, they tend to neglect confirmation their input data when registering.

Therefore, a confirmation dialog and multiple input forms forcing the users to input their data several times are widely used as methods for requiring accurate data by having the users confirm multiple times. However, in many cases, the users do not feel the need for the confirmation or they feel that the confirmation is troublesome. As a consequence, they tend to skip the confirmation just by clicking the OK button on the

© Springer Nature Switzerland AG 2020
C. Stephanidis and M. Antona (Eds.): HCII 2020, CCIS 1224, pp. 587–593, 2020.
https://doi.org/10.1007/978-3-030-50726-8_77

confirmation dialog or copying and pasting their input data to the second input form. It means that these confirmation methods lose their effect.

To solve the problem, we proposed "Phantom Dialog [1]" (see in Fig. 1) that shows simultaneously two parallel arranged dialogs with user's input data and system-generated dummy data. It was found that the Phantom Dialog could make difficult to skip the process of the confirmation. But, it took longer confirmation time than the traditional confirmation dialog. In this paper, in order to reduce the time, we propose to increase the probability that user's input data is shown on the left dialog, which is expected to be read firstly by the user on the Phantom Dialog.

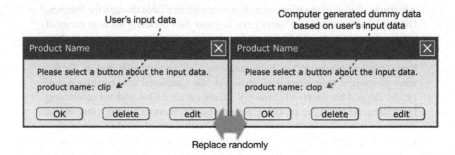

Fig. 1. Phantom Dialog [1]

2 Related Studies

There are two ways to get correct data according to the user's intention: support to correct when an erroneous input occurs and support to prevent erroneous input from the first.

One of the former methods is proposed by Zhang et al. [2]. They presented three novel text correction techniques to improve the correction process. All of the techniques skip error-deletion and cursor-positioning procedures, and instead allow the user to type the correction first, and then apply it to a previously committed error. Although, all of them are intended to simplify error correction operations in common. The users need to be aware that there is an erroneous input by themselves, in other words, it cannot support overlooking of the erroneous input.

The latter examples are by Ishii et al. [3] and Duan et al. [4]. Ishii et al. proposed a new flick-based keyboard that allows users to select a tiny key on the small keyboard more easily than with a tap. Duan et al. proposed a generative model to automatically correct input data predicted to be erroneous based on a dictionary in order to obtain correct input even if there is erroneous input. With these methods, the possibility that inputting is intended by the user increases. However, it is expected that the confirmations as mentioned above are likely to be omitted because the cases where users input incorrect data are rare. Consequently, the overlooking of erroneous input is likely to occur.

Furthermore, the systems by Zhang et al. and Duan et al. are provided based on a dictionary. In actual situation, there are many cases where users want to input names, phone numbers, and product codes that are not exist in any dictionary. Hence, a method that does not depend on the contents of input data is needed.

3   Proposed Method

In order to reduce the confirmation time of Phantom Dialog, we propose to increase the probability that user's input data is shown on the left dialog, which is expected to be read firstly by the user on the Phantom Dialog.

According to Pernice [5], if there is no subordination between figures and contents, the user reads from left to right, and top to bottom. Since our method does not include the dependencies between two dialogs, it is considered to have the same tendency as Pernice. Therefore, it is postulated that the user reads the left dialog first, that is, in the proposed method, the input data should be displayed with a higher probability in the left dialog. In our method, the user checks the data on the left dialog first, and if he/she thinks it as his/her original input data, he/she skips checking the right dialog. As a consequence, it would be supposed that the user can confirm data fast.

One of the concerns with this method is that if we set an extreme display probability on the left dialog, the users might notice that and click the OK button on the left confirmation dialog without reading the contents, that is, skip the confirmation like a traditional confirmation dialog. In this case, the value as a confirmation method is lost. Therefore, we evaluate the appropriate display probabilities by comparing multiple different probabilities through an evaluation experiment.

4   Evaluation

4.1   Procedure

To evaluate the confirming time and error rate with the different probabilities of the user's input data shown on the left dialog, we conduct an experimental evaluation with three different probabilities on Phantom Dialog: L50, L70, and L90. For example, L90 means the probability that user-input-data is in left dialog is 90[%], and L50 is the original Phantom Dialog. The participants are twelve university students. Each participant uses three probabilities on Phantom Dialog with the three datasets. Trials were presented in three random counterbalance orders.

In this evaluation, we simulate an ordering situation for many products. Each dataset has a large number of sets with English commonly used words of the noun as product's names and five-digit numbers as the quantities.

As shown in Fig. 2, the interface for the evaluation consists of displays for inputting data and confirming it. On the confirming display, one dialog shows the participant's original input data and the other shows system-generated dummy data. The participants input a set of noun and number in the dataset one by one on the inputting display, and then, select the OK button in either dialog that shows participant's input data.

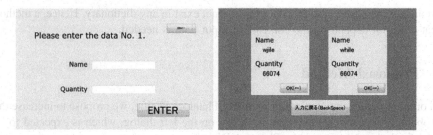

Fig. 2. Interface with displays for Inputting Data (left) and Confirming the Data (right)

The dummy data are generated automatically based on the following rules. These generation rules imitate user's mistakes because if the user can recognize one of the data as the system-generated dummy data at a glance, he/she is easy to skip confirmation. However, the following rules are not applied to the first character of his/her input data, considering that the first character of the word has a large effect on word recognition [6].

1. Replace a character to another one neighboring placed on the QWERTY keyboard (ex: research -> researvh)
2. Swap two characters (ex: research -> resaerch)

4.2   Measurement Parameter

We measure the three kinds of parameters as follows.

1. Confirmation time: the mean time to show the confirming display per one data through one dataset.
2. Error rate: ratio of selecting the dialog in which wrong data is shown (in the cases where the participant selects the dialog in which dummy data is shown or he/she selects the dialog in which his/her input data but wrong data is shown) on the confirming display.
3. Interview: Q1. Did you notice anything about the differences between three interfaces? Q2. Which dialog did you read first? Q3. Did you find it difficult to identify your data? If so, what was the reason?

4.3   Results and Discussions

Validity of Experimental Setup. With respect to Q1 of the interview, ten out of twelve participants answered "No idea about the differences" and the remaining two participants mentioned something about the differences in the case of L90. As for Q2, nine participants answered that they read the data on the left dialog first, one participant answered "the right dialog," and the other two participants answered "No idea about the dialog that I read first". Consequently, most of them did not notice that the probabilities were different and they did not change their strategies for data-confirming.

Some participants remarked the difficulty of identifying the data in the situation where the shapes of letters were similar, for example, replacement "n" and "m," and swapping of "a" and "e". However, it can be said that these are natural dummy data in the actual use. Through this interview, we found that the experiment could evaluate the effect of our method with the left-biased display probability. The following results do not include the data of one participant who answered "the dialog on the right side" to Q2.

Effect of Proposed Method. The Fig. 3 shows the confirmation time of the three interfaces. The confirmation times of L70 and L90 are significantly shorter than L50. This result is not in conflict with most of participants who mentioned the differences described in 4.3.1. Bachara et al. [7] suggest that people change their performance under the different situations, although they do not notice the difference of them. The Fig. 4 shows the error rates. There is no significantly differences in three. Therefore, our method can make data-confirmation faster and keep errors less of the same as the original Phantom Dialog.

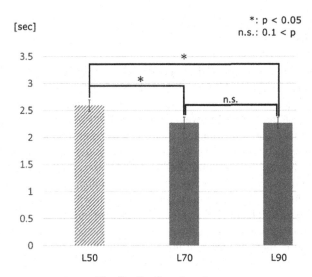

Fig. 3. Confirmation time

On the other hand, between L70 and L90, there are no significant differences of the confirmation time and error rate. In the future work, we should verify the best display probability for the confirmation dialogs. In addition, there was one participant who read the dialog on the right side first, because he used a mouse for clicking buttons on the dialog not using keyboard and his gaze stayed at the right dialog of the confirmation display after clicking the ENTER button. Therefore, we have to redesign context-independent interface for practical use.

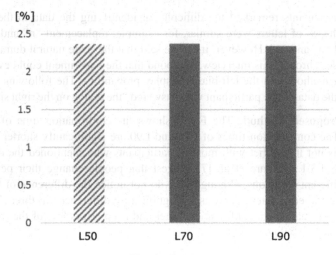

Fig. 4. Error rate

5 Conclusion

On the web services like video on-demand and online shopping, the users have to input data correctly such as personal information and ordering data on digital devices. If they make mistakes in their input data on this kind of services, it often makes serious troubles. To solve the problem, we had proposed "Phantom Dialog" that shows simultaneously two parallel arranged dialogs with user's input data and system-generated dummy data not to confirm data without reading dialogs. In this paper, in order to reduce the confirmation time on Phantom Dialog, we proposed to increase the probability that user's input data is shown on the left dialog, which is expected to be read firstly by the user. As the result of the evaluation with the three different probabilities on the Phantom Dialog, it was found that the participants can confirm their input data faster without deterioration in the confirmation accuracy with left-biased probability. Furthermore, most of them did not notice that the probabilities were different.

To improve our method, we are going to verify the best probability that leads shorter confirmation time and lower error rate without noticing the difference through another evaluation with some probabilities at the range of 70[%] to 100[%]. Furthermore, it will be necessary to redesign the non-contextual interface or interface that guides the users to read their input data first.

References

1. Katayama, T., Kuramoto, I., Minaguchi, M., Shibuya, Y., Tsujino, Y.: Phantom dialogs: confirmation method by selecting from multiple dialog windows. IPSJ SIG Technical Reports, vol. 2009, no. 5, 2009-HCI-131(1), pp. 1–8 (2009). (in Japanese)
2. Zhang, M.R., Wen, H., Wobbrock, J.O.: Type, then correct: intelligent text correction techniques for mobile text entry using neural networks. In: Proceedings of the 32nd Annual ACM Symposium on User Interface Software and Technology, pp. 843–855. ACM (2019)
3. Ishii, A., Hakoda, H., Shizuki, B.: Flickey: flick-based QWERTY software keyboard for ultra-small touch screen devices. In: Kurosu, M. (ed.) HCI 2018. LNCS, vol. 10903, pp. 31–42. Springer, Cham (2018). https://doi.org/10.1007/978-3-319-91250-9_3
4. Duan, H., Hsu, B.-J.P.: Online spelling correction for query completion. In: Proceedings of the 20th International Conference on World Wide Web, pp. 117–126. ACM (2011)
5. Pernice, K.: F-shaped pattern of reading on the web: Misunderstood, but still relevant (even on mobile). Nielsen Norman Group (2017). https://www.nngroup.com/articles/f-shaped-pattern-reading-web-content/. Accessed 30 Jan 2020
6. Rawlinson, G.: The significance of letter position in word recognition. IEEE Aerosp. Electron. Syst. Mag. **22**, 26–27 (2007)
7. Bechara, A., Damasio, H., Tranel, D., Damasio, A.R.: Deciding advantageously before knowing the advantageous strategy. Science **275**(5304), 1293–1295 (1997)

Simulation of Pseudo Inner Reading Voices and Evaluation of Effect on Human Processing

Yu Yamaoka[✉] and Ando Hideyuki

Osaka University, Yamadaoka1-4, Suita City, Japan
yu-yamaoka@hiel.ist.osaka-u.ac.jp

Abstract. We propose a pseudo inner reading voices (IRVs) interface to perform decision making from an external perspective, thereby creating an illusion that information is being processed by oneself. This does not imply that decisions are made according to someone else's instructions; rather, this creates an illusion that the decision was willfully made by one's own self. The belief that a person made his/her own decision can help reduce the mental workload. Although unfamiliarity with recorded voices has often been studied in perceptual research, there exists no filter that can convert recorded voices into familiar voices. Therefore, we reconstructed bone and air conduction models, measured the bone- and air-conducted sounds separately, weighted the ratio of both sounds, and superimposed them to reproduce a subject's own voice. Next, in the counting experiment, it was confirmed that the pseudo IRVs can bias the information processing of human beings without increasing the mental workload.

Keywords: Inner Reading Voices (IRVs) · Own voice · Counting task

1 Introduction

As the "information society" advances, the issues to be handled by a user increase, and the ability to demand responses increases, resulting in the mental fatigue of users. However, when a machine (e.g., artificial intelligence technology) makes all the decisions, users tend to concentrate on following the instructions, which adversely affects the autonomy and sense of agency of users [1]. Therefore, even if a machine makes users' decisions automatically, a technique that causes humans to retain their autonomy and sense of subject is required. Consequently, we focused on the inner reading voices (IRVs) that the users use in their thoughts [2] and assumed that by creating pseudo IRVs in information presentation, an illusion could be created as if it is the IRV of the user himself/herself. The pseudo IRV interface carries out the interventions that are deeply considered by a user while the user experiences the illusion to be his/her self-inner thoughts. In other words, this can be used as an intervention method to reduce the workload that the user receives during the information presentation by making him/her realize that he/she has made the decision, without leaving it to others. The goal of the study is to create auditory stimuli that are perceived as "IRVs," and thereby alter human behavior by biasing the information processing. To realize this, the head-related transfer function, which includes the bone-conducted

© Springer Nature Switzerland AG 2020
C. Stephanidis and M. Antona (Eds.): HCII 2020, CCIS 1224, pp. 594–602, 2020.
https://doi.org/10.1007/978-3-030-50726-8_78

sound accompanying the user's utterance is estimated in advance. Next, the artificially synthesized voice of the user is presented using devices such as bone-conducted loudspeakers so that it can be mistaken for the user's IRV. This allows the user to feel that the decision is his/her own despite being instructed by an external voice stimulus.

2 Method

2.1 Past Research

Even when you simply listen to your own recorded voice, it sounds like someone else's voice, unlike what you normally hear when you speak. This unfamiliarity with one's own recorded voice has long been the subject of several previous studies on hearing. This is caused by the fact that when one listens to his/her own voice, the sound produced by the vocal cords is delivered to the auditory organ through multiple pathways, including air and bones. In contrast, the recorded voice is only transmitted from the living body through air and does not contain any components that pass through bones. In [3], the filter that simulates bone-conducted sounds from recorded sounds was studied. The method shows that a band-pass filter that equalizes an individual's voice from the recording and consequently enhances the voice to 300–1200 Hz is suitable to be used as a filter to simulate voice. However, in [4], it was concluded that there is no general filter that can be used to equalize everyone's voice because there is a large difference between individuals in the generated filter. In other words, a filter that can convert the recorded voice of an individual into his/her own voice may not be suitable for another individual. Instead of finding a general-frequency filter for everyone, we should find a way to simulate one's own voice. When the voice emitted by the vocal cavity reaches the inner ear, the bone conduction predominates in the frequency range below 2000 Hz and air conduction predominates in the frequency range above 2000 Hz. Based on the fact that the bone-conducted sound and air-conducted sound add up [5], we reexamined the auditory model (Method 2.2). In this study, we propose a pseudo IRVs method using a physical model of auditory sense instead of estimating the voice of an individual by iterative equalizer adjustment.

Several studies have been conducted on the error rate of tasks depending on whether an individual does self-talk or not. It has been reported that the error rate of the card sorting task was reduced by talking to oneself compared to when it was prohibited [6]. This implies that internal information can be organized well owing to self-talk, and the ability to solve problems is promoted. Furthermore, humans can become confused when information that is different from their inner thoughts is given. There is still no discussion on how much the quality of the voice influences this information input method. Here, we will investigate how the quality of voice affects human processing during speech stimuli.

The purpose of this study is to investigate the effect of speech stimuli of IRVs on the human information processing. First, the IRVs that will be recognized as own voice (Sect. 3) are created. Next, the effect of the IRVs on human processing at a counting task that cannot be carried out without using IRVs is observed [7] (Sect. 4).

2.2   Proposed Model for Pseudo IRVs

To find a method that can simulate an individual's own voice, we reexamined the model of hearing. First, it is known that bone conduction that affects an individual's own voice acts as a low-pass filter [8]. For example, voices with frequencies lower than 300 Hz are less likely to be attenuated by bone conduction but are more likely to be affected by bone conduction when hearing one's own voice. On the contrary, voices with high frequency are less likely to be attenuated by bone conduction. Therefore, the type of filter to be used depends on the frequency component of the user's voice. Previous models discussed only the pathways of bone conduction and air conduction. The way the sound would change on a pathway was not developed in the previous models, and thus the causality with frequency filters that would convert the recorded voice of an individual into his/her own voice was not explained. Using the already-known structure of the ear, we focused on the action of the individual parts on the path to derive our own voice deductively. We remake the auditory model of self-voicing by human engineering using the physiology of the ear canal to add description of each part for hearing.

The external auditory meatus is a circular tube with diameter and length of 7 mm and 25, respectively, which vibrates the tympanic membrane, and thus acts as a "resonance tube." The resonance frequency is said to be approximately 3 kHz, and the tympanic membrane vibration is said to be amplified by 12 dB SPL at approximately 3 kHz compared to that in the pinna. In the middle ear, the ossicles transmit vibrations of the tympanic membrane to the oval window of the inner ear. The ossicles act as amplifiers and impedance transducers that allow sound propagation from low-impedance air to high-impedance cochlear endolymph [9]. The bone-conducted sound that reaches the inner ear can be ignored because it is smaller than the sound that passes through the middle ear. Next, it is known that the sound conduction characteristics in bone conduction play the role of a low-pass filter just around the frequency of the human speech [8]. Based on these facts, we proposed a new, perceptual model for the own utterance of human beings (see Fig. 1).

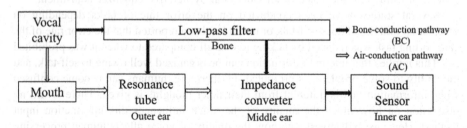

Fig. 1. Proposed model for hearing own voice

According to this model, the voice [n] spoken from the vocal cavity is divided into air conduction (AC) and bone conduction (BC) and is tracked.

- Vocal Cavity → Bone → Middle ear (BC)

The sound coming from the cavity first passes through the low-pass filter $[([n])]$. This sound is amplified by a factor of A_{BC}. Furthermore, the sound delivered directly to the external ear by bone conduction and the sound delivered to the middle ear are considered almost equal because the distance between the external ear and the middle ear is shorter than the distance between the vocal cavity and the middle or external ear. The path of the sound that reaches the middle ear is as follows.

- Vocal Cavity → Mouth → Middle ear (AC)

The sound coming out of the mouth, which is amplified through the outer ear and is delivered to the middle ear, is very simple. To be more precise, the amplification spectrum due to resonance varies with frequency, but to simplify this, we multiplied the speech by a factor of A_{AC}. (AC).

- Vocal Cavity → Middle ear (BC + AC)

Because the sound is superimposable, the sound delivered to the middle e using the model shown in Fig. 1 is expressed in Eq. 2.

$$(1 + A_{BC}) * F(x[n]) + A_{AC} * x[n] \qquad (1)$$

A_{AC} and A_{BC} in the above equation are coefficients, it can be rewritten as follows:

$$(1 - \alpha) * F(x[n]) + \alpha * x[n] \qquad (2)$$

Next, we record bone-conducted and air-conducted sounds separately, and try to study which sound to be used at the specific ratio parameter α when subjects simulate their self-voice (see Eq. 2).

3 Experiment: Simulating IRVs for Each Subject

3.1 Method

The subjects were three females (A, E, and F) and three males (B, C, and D) aged 20 years or older, with a total of six individuals. Subjects wear two microphones to record the bone-conducted and air-conducted sounds separately. Forhe proposed model (Fig. 1), the wearing position of microphones is shown in Fig. 2.

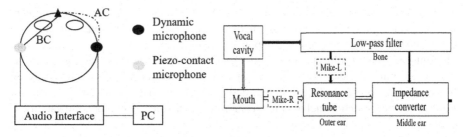

Fig. 2. Wearing place of microphone in recording and position in model

The subjects were asked to count orally from 1 to 20 in Japanese, and their voices were recorded using two microphones—Piezo-contact microphone for left ear and dynamic microphone for right ear. Each sound was recorded monaurally and on a PC through an audio interface. The Audacity software was used to record sound. The recorded voices of both ears were multiplied by the following parameters (see Eq. 3).

$$(1 - \alpha) * (Mike - L) + \alpha * (Mike - R), 0 \le \alpha \le 1 \tag{3}$$

Trial number N is 50 and α is the parameter of 21 steps from 0 to 1 with increments of 0.05, which shows the superiority of bone conduction or air conduction in simulating an individual's own voice. The subjects were instructed to adjust α such that it was close to the voice their heard the most in their head."

3.2   Result and Discussion

In Experiment 3, the subjects showed adjusted α (see Fig. 4).

It can be said that the subjects whose normality was confirmed using the Shapiro–Wilk test could choose α for their own voice within the guideline. Therefore, the arithmetic mean was used as the alpha of these subjects. Because subjects whose normality could not be confirmed might have lost their own voice in the middle, the α that was selected most frequently was selected as a true value. As can be observed from Fig. 3, each subject chose different values of α. This implies that the effects of bone conduction vary from person to person. Therefore, the relation between α and the fundamental frequency mean of a subject's voice was examined (see Fig. 4).

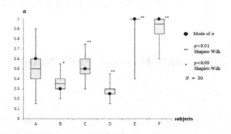

Fig. 3. Box-and-whisker plots of α (Eq. 3) selected by the subjects. The mode is indicated by ●. The results of the Shapiro-Wilk test were *: $p < 0.05$; **: $p < 0.01$

It can be observed from Fig. 4 that the higher the value of $F0$, the more dominant the air-conducted sound is when simulating an individual's own voice. In the bone conduction, the high frequency component greatly attenuates for the subjects with high-pitched voice (Subjects A, E, and F), and the voice seems to resemble the air-conducted sound. Furthermore, the low-pitched voice (Subjects B, C, and D) is easy to transmit as the bone-conducted sound, and it is proven that a substantial amount of bone-conducted sound is included in the subject's own voice. Therefore, the validity of

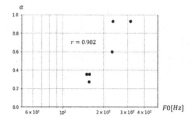

Fig. 4. Relation between fundamental frequency and α, correlation coefficient $r = 0.902$

the model was demonstrated, and IRVs were generated for each subject. In the subsequent section, the effect of the IRVs on human information processing is elucidated.

4 Experiment: Effect of Pseudo IRVs

By providing external information that is different from internal information, it is established how the human information processing is affected. We also examine how the quality of the voice affects the degree of obstruction. To achieve this, we have applied a counting task that always uses IRVs [6]. It was considered that the counting might be interrupted by providing IRVs (obtained in Sect. 3) as a speech stimulus. To confirm the effect of IRVs, the IRVs, machine voice, and white noise were prepared to control stimuli.

4.1 Method

The subjects were one adult female and three adult males—A, B, C, and D in experiment 3. Subjects were instructed to count the number of red circles on the display. When a certain red circle appears, the speech stimuli with a count of −1 is simultaneously provided to the subject using a bone-conducted headphone. Each subject performed 30 trials under 1 control. The speech stimuli were divided into three controls of pseudo internal speech stimulation (created in Experiment 3)—IRVs, machine voice, and white noise. A total of 90 trials were carried out. The display of

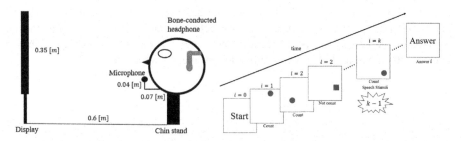

Fig. 5. Relationship between position of display, recording microphone, and subject. Examples of visual stimuli displayed on the display. (Color figure online)

ASUS ROG SWIFT PG 279 (2560 × 1440) was used. Figure 5 shows the relationship between the subject and display, the position of the microphone to record the response, and the visual stimulus displayed sequentially on the display.

The red circles and squares in Fig. 5 represent visual stimuli, and the subject has to count only red circles. The speech stimuli are provided to subjects at random times, with counts between 5 and 10 (count $i = k$). The target intervals were all 400 ms considering the attentional blink [10], and the answer time was 2000 ms from the "Answer" stimuli in the display.

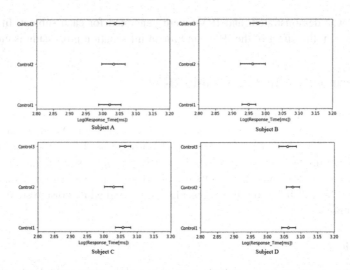

Fig. 6. Mean and 95% confidence intervals of $log(RT)$ for controls. For each subject, no significant differences in Wilcoxon test $p > 0.05$ are observed between controls

4.2   Result and Discussion

Compared to white noise, the error rate of tasks was higher in IRVS and machine voice, indicating that counting was interrupted by IRVs and machine voice. Next, the response time of each subject is discussed (Fig. 6, Table 1).

The response time represents the mental workload of an individual at the time of response. It was not significantly different under different conditions, and the overlap of the confidence interval was large. The subjects seemed to show the same mental workload in all controls while answering themselves. This means that we were able to intercept the counting task without affecting the mental workload.

Table 1. Error Rates (Control 1: IRVs, Control 2: Machine Voice, Control 3: White Noise)

Subjects	Error rate (control .1)	Error rate (control .2)	Error rate (control .3)
A	0.433	0.433	0.367
B	0.367	0.300	0.167
C	0.333	0.000	0.067
D	0.033	0.333	0.167
Average	0.292	0.267	0.192

5 Conclusion

There exists a problem of increasing workload that follows the information, thereby increasing the information that a user must receive in the present information society. To resolve this, we considered that the illusion, as the presented information was perceived by oneself, was effectively created by the stimulation provided by a device that uses pseudo self-talk. However, if an individual listen to his/her recorded voice, it is not the same when he/she speaks. To simulate an individual's own voice, we reconsidered the model of hearing for our own utterance. To measure the bone-conducted and air-conducted sounds separately, a technique is proposed to simulate an individual's own voice by adjusting the ratio α. Consequently, it was proven that there existed no filter that could simulate the general IRVs for everyone and that α (ratio of BC and AC) depended on the frequency spectrum of the voice of an individual.

To investigate the degree of interference to information processing caused by the presentation of external information by one's own voice, we applied the developed IRVs to the counting task as acoustic stimuli and measured the error rate and response time of the task. There was no difference in the response time, and IRVs increased the error rate. However, the quality of the voice may not be substantially important for the subject to make mistakes because there was no significant difference between the machine voice and IRVs. However, some subjects felt that their own voice was closer to their own thoughts, and machine voice was disturbed by others. In the future, we will consider human processing bias arising from IRVs while providing agency to people.

References

1. Oshi, S., Tay, L., Diener, E.: Advances in subjective well-being research. Nat. Hum. Behav. **2**, 253–260 (2018)
2. Vilhauer, R.P.: Inner reading voices: an overlooked form of inner speech. Psychological, Social and Integrative Approaches, vol. 8 (2015). https://doi.org/10.1080/17522439.2015.1028972
3. Sook, J.B., Won, Y.: Simulation of one's own voice in a two-parameter model. In: International Conference on Music Perception and Cognition and 5th Conference for the Asia-Pacific Society for Cognitive Sciences of Music (2014)
4. Yotsumoto, Y., Kimura, M.: Auditory traits of "own voice". PLoS ONE **13**(6), e0199443 (2018)

5. Håkansson, B., Reinfeldt, S.: Hearing one's own voice during phoneme vocalization—transmission by air and bone conduction. J. Acoust. Soc. Am. **128**(2), 751–762 (2010)

6. Allen, V.: Method, not madness: why thinking out loud can help solve problems (2018). https://www.dailymail.co.uk/sciencetech/article-5693279/Why-thinking-loud-help-solve-problems.html

7. Dehaene, S.: The Number Sence ∼ How the mind creates mathematics ∼ (Japanese translation), Chapter 5, pp. 215–257 (2010)

8. Young, W.S., Jonathan, B., Hui, C.S.: Simulating the sound of one's own singing voice (2003)

9. T.s.f.: Encyclopedia of Bioacoustics. Asakura Publishing, pp. 50–55 (2019)

10. Marois, R., Dux, P.E.: The attentional blink: a review of data and theory. Atten. Percept. Psychophys. **71**(8), 1683–1700 (2009). https://doi.org/10.3758/app.71.8.1683

AI in HCI

Classification and Recognition of Space Debris and Its Pose Estimation Based on Deep Learning of CNNs

Roya Afshar[1(✉)] and Shuai Lu[2]

[1] Beihang University, Beijing 100191, China
roya_afshar@buaa.edu.cn
[2] Beijing University of Chemical Technology, Beijing 100029, China

Abstract. The increasing population of orbital debris is considered as a growing threat to space missions. During the recent decades, many enabling space debris capturing and removal methods were investigated. Thus, estimating automated recognition and on-board pose in an uncooperative target spacecraft by implementing using passive sensors such as monocular cameras is considered as a main task for the removal. However, these tasks are challenging since there is a semantic gap between visual features of target, as well as the lack of scalable, descriptive features and reliable visual features because of illumination conditions in space environment. For this purpose, Convolutional Neural Network was implemented based on transfer learning and data augmentation in order to conduct satellite classification and pose regression. Transfer learning method is performed by using popular pre-trained CNNs, which is limited to the small size of dataset in space environment. Then, just the last fully connected layers in the proposed structure were trained by the BUAA-SID dataset. In particular, augmenting synthetic BUAA-SID dataset was used with Keras Data Generator Tool through a number of random transformations like rotating, shifting, rescaling, and zooming for the purpose of enhancing the classification accuracy. In addition, the effects of un-centered and noisy images as well as different illumination conditions were analyzed by implementing different pre-trained networks. Based on the results, the present method could identify satellites and evaluate their poses against different space conditions effectively.

Keywords: Space debris · Non-cooperative satellite · Recognition space target · Pose estimation

1 Introduction

The space debris is so populated which puts the earth orbit in a critical situation [1]. Space debris is defined as unproductive manmade objects of all sizes [2]. The risk of failure for functional satellites and manned space missions is increasing because of an increase in the number of orbital debris [2]. To this end, a large number of studies have focused on many enabling space debris for identifying, capturing, and removal technologies [1, 3]. Thus, automated recognition and on-board pose estimation of an

© Springer Nature Switzerland AG 2020
C. Stephanidis and M. Antona (Eds.): HCII 2020, CCIS 1224, pp. 605–613, 2020.
https://doi.org/10.1007/978-3-030-50726-8_79

uncooperative target spacecraft by using passive sensors such as monocular cameras are regarded as a major task for removing debris missions [1, 4].

In another study [5], a review of published solutions of automated space target recognition could be found. The performance of traditional algorithms like scale-invariant feature transform (SIFT), local binary pattern (LBP), and histogram of oriented gradient (HOG) rely on manual extraction of engineered features, as well as engineering these features [4]. However, producing effective identification data is difficult in space application due to the visual features which are not robust in all space conditions and the significant gap between mentioned features and targets. Thus, discriminatory method is necessary to identify the targets [4, 5].

Further, the studies focused on monocular pose determination for space applications can be divided into 3D model-based methods [7] and 2D image-based methods [8]. It is worth noting that 3D model-based methods require an existent 3D CAD model or a 3D point cloud, which seems difficult to be obtained in practice. Most of the methods utilizing images are based on classical image processing algorithms, which are not recommended as the evaluation of many pose hypotheses leads to computational elaboration [4]. In addition, it results in requiring a-priori knowledge of the pose which is always inaccessible and inflexible to different structural and physical kinds of spacecrafts [9]. Moreover, monocular navigation is not robust enough due to the low image acquisition rate, low signal-to-noise ratio, as well as illumination conditions [10].

Recently, machine learning-based methods were suggested without considering the limitations of traditional methods [11–14]. Zhang and Jiang [11] solved multi-view space object recognition using kernel regression. In another study, Zhang et al. [12] implemented Gaussian Process Regression, and [13] utilized homeomorphic manifold analysis for recognizing satellite and estimating relative poses of space objects. However, these methods are useful for 1D and 2D pose variations, while they cannot be implemented for 3D attitude variations.

In addition, CNN plays a significant role in classifying, detecting, and estimating pose. Further, CNN can learn the extraction and classification of the related feature. A large number of researches in the area of terrestrial and space application employed deep convolutional neural network in order to eliminate the above-mentioned shortcomings. In another study, Zeng et al. [5] implemented a nine-layer deep CNN in order to recognize space target, and data augmentation was used to overcome overfitting due to a small size of dataset, while a deeper network is more effective. Sharma et al. [4] proposed an image synthetic pipeline to produce a massive image dataset for any spacecraft by its 3D model, and then CNN method was utilized for an initial guess of real time pose. Regional Proposal Network (RPN) based on CNN in order to detect bounding box around satellite and identify the coarse attitude by classification is also used in [14]. In which a post refinement was conducted for relative attitude evaluation. In addition, in another research [10] CNN was trained by implementing transfer learning method, and 3D space was discretized to several regions. Then, a label based on camera location was considered as the output of CNN. Although some studies such as [4, 10, 14] reported using CNN in space navigation, no study, to the best of our knowledge, focused on a unified CNN to recognize satellite and estimate the pose simultaneously.

By considering the above-mentioned researches, this study aimed to present a two-stage CNN architecture for simultaneous satellite recognition and pose estimation. Inception CNN pre-trained with Imagenet dataset is regarded as the first stage. During the second stage, the related network is trained for classification and regression with BUAA-SID dataset [15] independently. Faster training and better extracting features are done by adopting the transfer-learning mechanism. Keras Data Generator Tool as an augmentation technique is used to enlarge the limited size of BUAA-SID to increase the accuracy. The performance of the proposed architecture is evaluated under different conditions of space environment including noisy and un-centered pictures and different illumination angles. The total accuracy and Mean Absolute Error are superior than that of the state-of-the-art methods [13].

2   Method and Dataset

In the following section, the learning problem is formulated for recognition and pose estimation. Then, the proposed architecture is provided, along with the details of loss functions in it. Finally, the dataset is described. The main problem is learning a strong visual representation allowing the model to classify object's picture and estimate the attitude of the camera frame (C), by considering the body frame of the target spacecraft (B). As shown in Fig. 1, R indicates the rotation matrix which is the difference between the target body reference and the camera which is estimated by CNN [16].

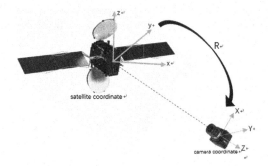

Fig. 1. A representation of the camera and satellite coordinate system

It is proposed to learn a convolutional neural network (CNN) to classify the satellite and estimate its pose simultaneously. Prediction $\hat{t}$ is defined as follows associated to the above issue.

$$\hat{t}_{\theta,w} = F_W \cdot z_\theta(x_i) \tag{1}$$

z_θ indicates the transformation of the input image x_i into the features used to feed the output layers of our models. F_w is related to the set of output layers functions, which considers the deep feature map $z_\theta(x_i)$ as input. Based on the prediction model in Eq. (1), the following objective function is defined for learning our multi-task neural network:

$$argmin_{\theta,w}\mathcal{L}(\theta,w),\tag{2}$$

Regarding the problem stated in this paper, classification (y) and viewpoint estimation ($\emptyset$), the loss function follows the Eq. (3),

$$\mathcal{L}(\theta, \mathbf{W}) = \lambda_1 \mathcal{L}_y(\theta, W^y) + \lambda_2 \mathcal{L}_\phi(\theta, W^\phi)\tag{3}$$

Where λ indicates the scalar value that controls the significance of a special loss during the training process [17].

For the classification loss, a Categorical Cross-entropy function is used, and the pose estimation loss was traditionally considered from continuous and discrete perspectives. In discrete formulation, pose estimation is regarded as a classification problem while it is solved by regression in continuous problem. In the present study, Mean Squared Error was used to solve the regression problem due to coarse quantization of our dataset.

2.1   Network Architecture

In this architecture, pose estimation task is slightly separated from the satellite classification. As shown in Fig. 2, the proposed extension for these two objectives includes two stages. During the first stage, a pre-trained network is used with hyper-parameter of Imagenet dataset to extract the feature. However, FC layers in the pose regression and satellite classification branches are independent in the second stage. The model is learned by solving the objective function displayed in Eq. (3). While during the training process for the detection path $\lambda_2 = 0$, and $\lambda_1 = 0$ for the pose path.

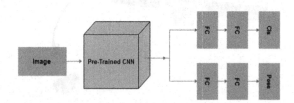

Fig. 2. An overview of the proposed CNN structure

2.2   Dataset

In this study, BUAA-SID 1.0 and BUAA-SID 1.5 were used for training and testing CNN which results 2 train-sets and 3 test-sets as follow:

Train Set 1: In BUAA-SID 1.0, there is a subset including 4600 gray images including 20 satellites that from each of them 230 viewpoints were released [11, 15, 18].

Train Set 2: BUAA-SID 1.5 consists of four subsets. The 1D subset as the first one includes 3600 grayscale images from 10 satellites each of which released 360 view-points uniformly sampled on a circle with the pitch angle $\varphi = 0$ and the yaw angle $\theta \in [0, 2\pi)$, as shown in [8, 11, 13].

Test Set 1: a test set was made by adding Zero Mean Gaussian White (ZMGW) noise with variances from 0.01 to 0.1 steps of 0.01 to the pictures of Train Set 1.

Test Set 2: The lighting subset is considered as the third subset. This subset includes 10080 gray images from one satellite with the same viewpoints as the 1D subset but simulated in different lighting conditions. In other words, the phase angle of the light ranged from 0° to 90° in the steps of 10° while the altitude angle of the light was in 0°, 90°, and 180°, separately.

Test Set 3: Un-centered pictures from Train Set 1 were used to create another test set. In this regard, Matlab was used to put each satellite in image in different location in plate randomly.

3   Results

In order to conduct the experiment, the models and loss functions were implemented by using the deep learning framework of Keras [6, 19]. The Stochastic Gradient Descent algorithm with the momentum of 0.9, weight decay of 0.0001, and learning rate of 0.001 were used for optimization in order to assure that the network converges properly.

Finally, InceptionResNetV2 was utilized after trying pre-trained popular networks with Imagenet Dataset like VGG19, InceptionV3, Xception, ResNet, and Inception-ResNetV2 owing the better results in our case. The remainder of structure is trained by BUAA-SID dataset. The batch size involves 32 samples during 20 epochs. Accuracy and Mean Absolute Error(MAE) are the evaluation metrics for satellite classification and pose regression, respectively. The accuracy increased significantly by initializing the second stage of the network with 'random_uniform' function in Keras. Then, by 'ImageDataGenerator', as the image preprocessing Tool of Keras, our shallow dataset was augmented via a number of random transformations like rotating, shifting, rescaling, zooming to prevent under-fitting the network. Finally, the FCs layers were fine-tuned by the augmented dataset. Figure 3 displays the accuracy and loss function changes during 20 epochs. The accuracy of training and testing is increasing, they are also close to each other, the final epochs indicates close to 100% accuracy. In addition, loss curves on the train and test set decreased, which reached close to zero at the last epochs. Based on the behavior of these curves, network was trained correctly without any overfitting or under fitting. The accuracy of classification was 99.24%, while this value for un-centered pictures decreased to 97.07%.

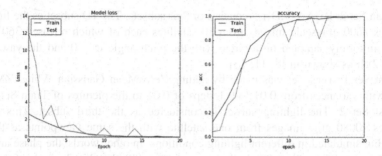

Fig. 3. Evaluation of training procedure of CNN, a reduction in loss function to approximately close to zero, and a rise in accuracy to around 100% emphasizing a fine-tuned CNN

3.1 Robustness Against Noise

Practically, the images captured by a real space-based imaging system may have noise because of the space environment effect and imaging system itself. Gaussian noise is usually regarded as modelling for this issue in theoretical analysis and simulation [16]. To assess robustness against noise, the experiments were carried out with and without noisy pictures. In other words, CNN was first trained by dataset including pictures without noise. Then, the trained CNN was tested by noisy pictures with different variances and zero mean as shown in Fig. 4. In first experiment, the accuracy decreased to less than 10% significantly. During the second experiment, CNN was trained by subset containing noisy pictures with the variances of 0.01, 0.05, and 0.1. Finally, the CNN was tested like the previous experiment, the results of which are illustrated in Fig. 4. In this case, the total accuracy increased significantly for lower variances, while it decreased gradually for the variances more than 0.05, where the accuracy in the variance of 0.1 was equal to the first experiment. Based on the experimental result in Fig. 4, learned CNN by trainset containing noisy pictures is more robust against noise compared to the case when trainset is devoid of noisy pictures. Figure 5 shows the experimental results for pose estimation with noisy test-sets. A slight change was observed in mean absolute error against the variance increase, which emphasizes the robustness of CNN for pose regression against noisy pictures.

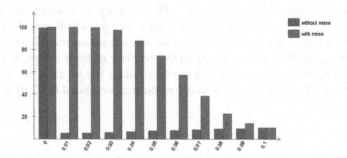

Fig. 4. Results of recognition accuracy on noise subset for with and without noisy pictures

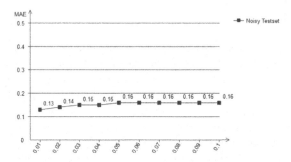

Fig. 5. Results of pose estimation on noise subset

3.2 Robustness Against Lighting

In this section, the network is trained with the pictures not affected by lighting conditions. In fact, the light angle of train set becomes zero. Then, the trained network was evaluated with test-sets with different light angles. Figure 6 displays the accuracy of classification in different light angles. As shown, the accuracy of the recognition of satellite decreases by increasing the light angles, especially for light angle more than 30°. Further, the results were satisfactory for the mean absolute error of pose regression. Furthermore, slight changes were observed by increasing light angle (Fig. 7). The value in [13] is reported less than 10 by using Homeomorphic Manifold Analysis, while it is less than 1 in the present case. It is worth noting that CNN was taught with train set without including the pictures with different lighting angles. The recognition accuracy and mean absolute error can be improved in real applications by boosting the train set with the pictures in different lighting conditions.

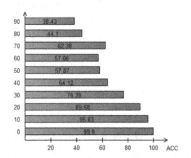

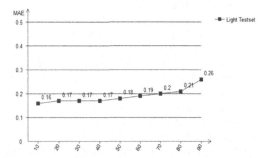

Fig. 6. Recognition accuracy on light subset

Fig. 7. Results of pose estimation on light subset

4 Conclusion

In the present study, a CNN-based approach was proposed for satellite recognition and pose estimation simultaneously by implementing classification and regression method, respectively. In order to train CNN, transfer learning method was employed in the first stage of the network, while data augmentation method was utilized for the rest of network trained with synthetic images of BUAA-SID dataset in the case of classification to increase the accuracy. Finally, the robustness of CNN was evaluated in the space environment conditions like noisy and un-centered pictures and illumination conditions. consequently, CNN is able to deal with space conditions appropriately when this situation was considered in train-set. In future to improve CNN behavior against noisy pictures related researches could be conducted.

References

1. Shan, M., Guo, J., Gill, E.: Review and comparison of active space debris capturing and removal. Prog. Aerosp. Sci. **80**, 18–32 (2015)
2. Sun, R., Zhan, J., Zhao, C., Zhang, X.: Algorithms and applications for detecting faint space. Acta Astronaut. **110**, 9–17 (2015)
3. Pradhan, B., Hickson, P., Surdej, J.: Serendipitous detection and size estimation of space debris using a survey. Acta Astronaut. **164**, 77–83 (2019)
4. Sharma, S., Beierle, C., D'Amico, S.: Pose Estimation for non-cooperative spacecraft. In: IEEE Aerospace Conference (2018)
5. Zeng, H., Xia, Y.: Space target recognition based on deep learning. In: 20th International Conference on Information Fusion (2017)
6. Park, T., D'Amico, S.: ESA Pose Estimation Challenge 2019: Space Rendezvous Laboratory Department of Aeronautics and Astronautics Stanford University. https://slab.stanford.edu/
7. Park, T., Sharma, S., D'Amico, S.: Towards robust learning-based pose estimation of noncooperative. In: AAS/AIAA Astrodynamics Specialist Conference (2019)
8. Zhang, H., Jiang, Z., Elgammal, A.: Vision-based pose estimation for cooperative space objects. Acta Astronaut. **91**, 115–122 (2013)
9. Sharma, S.: Pose estimation of uncooperative spacecraft using monocular vision and deep learning: Dissertation, Stanford University (2019)
10. Sharma, S., Beierle, C., D'Amico, S.: Towards pose determination for non-cooperative spacecraft using convolutional neural networks. In: 1st IAA Conference on Space Situational Awareness (ICSSA) (2019)
11. Haopeng, Z., Zhiguo, J.: Multi-view space object recognition and pose estimation based on kernel regression. Chin. J. Aeronaut. **27**(5), 1233–1241 (2014)
12. Zhang, H., Jiang, Z., Yao, Y., Meng, G.: Vision-based pose estimation for space objects by Gaussian process regression. In: IEEE Aerospace Conference (2015)
13. Zhang, H., Jiang, Z., Elgammal, A.: Satellite recognition and pose estimation using homeomorphic manifold analysis. IEEE Trans. Aerosp. Electron. Syst. **58**(1), 785–792 (2015)

14. Sharma, S., D'Amico, S.: Pose estimation for non-cooperative spacecraft rendezvous using neural networks. In: AAS/AIAA Astrodynamics Specialist Conference (2019)
15. Haopeng, Z., Zhengyi, L., Zhiguo, J., Meng, A., Danpei, Z.: {BUAA-SID1.0} space object image dataset: Spacecraft Recovery \& Remote Sensing (2010)
16. Xiang, Y., Schmidt, T., Narayanan, V., Fox, D.: PoseCNN: A Convolutional Neural Network for 6D Object Pose Estimation in Cluttered Scenes (2017)
17. Oñoro-Rubio, D., López-Sastre, R.J., Redondo-Cabrera, C., Gil-Jiménez, P.: The challenge of simultaneous object detection and pose estimation. Comp. Study Image Vision Comput. **79**, 109–122 (2018)
18. Gang, M., Zhiguo, J., Zhengyi, L., Haopeng, Z., Danpei, Z.: Full-viewpoint 3D space object recognition based on kernel locality preserving projections. Chin. J. Aeronaut. **23**, 563–572 (2010)
19. Keras: The Python Deep Learning library. https://keras.io/

WINS: Web Interface for Network Science via Natural Language Distributed Representations

Dario Borrelli[✉], Razieh Saremi, Sri Vallabhaneni, Antonio Pugliese,
Rohit Shankar, Denisse Martinez-Mejorado, Luca Iandoli,
Jose Emmanuel Ramirez-Marquez, and Carlo Lipizzi

School of Systems and Enterprises, Stevens Institute of Technology,
525 River Street, Hoboken, NJ 07030, USA
{dborrell,clipizzi}@stevens.edu

Abstract. This work proposes a novel approach to visually interact with semantic networks constructed via natural language processing techniques. The proposed web interface, WINS, allows the user to select a textual document to be analyzed, choose the algorithm to construct the semantic network, and visualize the network with its metrics. Unlike previous works, which are typically based on co-occurrence matrix for constructing the text network, the proposed interface embeds an additional approach based on the combination of network science with distributed representations of words and phrases.

Keywords: Distributional hypothesis · Networks · Natural language

1 Introduction

The large-scale amount of digital information produced nowadays, especially textual information, can be an important resource for studying how words, idioms and their semantic meanings vary depending on different variables. These variables may be time, domain knowledge, socio-cultural bias, political bias, the author of the text, the audience, just to name few examples. Therefore, meaning is a relative concept that may assume a different connotation in different contexts.

Books, newspapers articles, scientific articles, patents, unstructured text from social media, web search engines, medical reports, contracts, government forms, all are examples of textual information that is available in digital format or can be converted into digital format. Having such resource potentially available naturally fosters research on methodological, computational, and visual ways to find relationships among meaning and concepts in these documents. Detecting these relationships would enable an analytic approach that could (i) reduce the effort that results from a manual analysis, (ii) will provide a scalable, computational way to compare different documents that could make latent knowledge emerge.

© Springer Nature Switzerland AG 2020
C. Stephanidis and M. Antona (Eds.): HCII 2020, CCIS 1224, pp. 614–621, 2020.
https://doi.org/10.1007/978-3-030-50726-8_80

An application of this type can not substitute humans in related task but can augment their capability of analysis and decision making.

To address such challenge, this paper presents a work-in-progress Web Interface for Network Science (WINS) via Natural Language Processing techniques. The proposed approach is inspired by previous works (i.e. Wordij [3]) for creating semantic networks starting from text documents of any typology. Unlike traditional approaches based on word-pair occurrences [15], this work introduces a layer of novelty by applying computational distributed representations of words generated with the artificial-neural-network model proposed by Mikolov et al. [16]; these representations are based on the distributional hypothesis [8], which states that words occurring in similar contexts have linked meanings. This feature embedded in WINS enables the detection of latent semantic proximity between textual units leveraging spatial distance among vectors, and use it to construct the semantic network. The identified textual units can be words, n-grams, idioms, sentences, or paragraphs depending on how the user performs the text pre-processing phase. Each unitary element will form a node in the network generated by WINS, while the edges of the network are created using proximity measures among respective distributed representations of words.

The proposed interface is currently at an early development stage. The present paper aims at showing the conceptual idea behind WINS and a preliminary view of the functionalities of the interface.

The paper is structured as follows: the section "Related Works" examines previous works and related approaches. Then, the "Methods" section introduces the reader to the proposed interface giving an overview of the approach and features embedded in the user interface at the current stage. The "Results" section shows examples of outputs generated by WINS. Finally, "Conclusion and Future Works" will provide the reader with information on possible applications, limitations, and future work.

2   Related Works

The increasing amount of digital textual information potentially available is making research interests grow with respect to methods and tools to analyze such large-scale data. Potential applications of such methods could benefit many research fields due to the fact that natural language is the main vehicle for communicating domain-specific concepts and expressions [6].

To analyze such expressions, semantic network analysis[1] and Natural Language Processing (NLP) are both techniques that are typically used to visualize and quantify semantic links among different concepts expressed in a textual corpus [7]. Previous works [3–5] propose user interfaces capable of analyzing textual documents via semantic networks analysis; more recently, they integrate semantic networks and NLP techniques such as topic modeling [17]. Most of

---

[1] Also called Network-Text Analysis (NTA) [19] when referred to networks created with measures of proximity between concept, or Socio-Semantic Networks when referred to social media text data [11].

the previous approaches construct the semantic network using the co-occurrence matrix. This matrix can capture links between concepts when they appear close to each other or within a user-defined window size of surrounding words.

However, the co-occurrence matrix fails in capturing semantic links that may exist among concepts that do not appear close or inside a window size. For instance, considering the document *"Rome is the capital of Italy ... Paris is the capital of France,"* one might assume that there is a semantic link between *"Rome"* and *"Paris"* because both are capital cities, even if they do not appear close to each other but both appear close to the word *"capital"*. One practical way to address this challenge without any pre-defined taxonomy is to represent words of a document using numerical distributed representation obtained with artificial neural networks models, so-called, word embeddings [16]. Leveraging these techniques, WINS aims at combining the traditional co-occurrence approach with the word embeddings approach to generate semantic networks representative of an input textual corpus for exploring and interacting with semantic information.

3   Methods

Semantic networks can be constructed with different numerical approaches. A typical approach is the one that uses the co-occurrence of words in a document to create links between nodes, where nodes are elementary textual units such as words or any idiomatic expression[2]. More formally, a semantic network is a graph $G(N, E)$ composed by a set of nodes N and a set of edges E. The generic set of edges E can be generated according to different estimates of semantic proximity. The traditional approach uses co-occurrence matrix as the adjacency matrix of an undirected graph $G(N, E)$. With this approach, a link is added among two different words w_i and w_j, if these words appear together or within a user-defined window (Fig. 1).

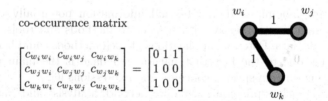

co-occurrence matrix

$$\begin{bmatrix} c_{w_i w_i} & c_{w_i w_j} & c_{w_i w_k} \\ c_{w_j w_i} & c_{w_j w_j} & c_{w_j w_k} \\ c_{w_k w_i} & c_{w_k w_j} & c_{w_k w_k} \end{bmatrix} = \begin{bmatrix} 0 & 1 & 1 \\ 1 & 0 & 0 \\ 1 & 0 & 0 \end{bmatrix}$$

Fig. 1. On the left: the co-occurrence matrix where a generic element $c_{w_i w_j}$ is equal to the number of times w_i and w_j appear close to each other or within a user-defined window size. On the right: the resulting semantic network of co-occurrences.

---

[2] Chunking, n-gramming are text pre-processing phases to segment raw text into these units [2].

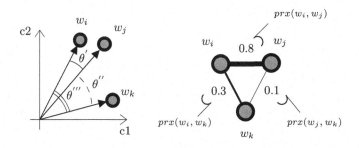

Fig. 2. On the left: vector representations of words in $\mathbb{R}^2$. On the right: semantic network generated with vector proximity measures as weights for the edges.

On the other hand, the second approach that is proposed to generate a semantic network is based on the following steps: 1) the textual units in the documents are vectorized and distributed in a euclidean space $\mathbb{R}^n$ via the artificial neural network method by Mikolov et al. [16]; then, 2) a measure of proximity among vectors of $\mathbb{R}^n$ such as ones' complement of a spatial distance measure is calculated and used as a weight for each of the edges[3]. Eventually, the user can vary a threshold to add a cut-off on the number of edges (Fig. 2).

WINS includes both the described approaches in its architecture. When the semantic network is created, the user can extract additional metric based on theory. Leveraging both Network Science and NLP, the design of WINS intends to enable the user to an interactive exploration of concepts' relationships contained in text data in order to support analysis for research and academic purposes.

3.1   Interface Design

The user selects the textual document to be analyzed using a dedicated card[4]. This card contains three different options to select a text document: 1) upload of a file, which can be a text file or a PDF file; 2) application of a filter on a database of patents, papers, and news via keywords' queries; 3) selection a Wikipedia page article via an embedded search bar. Then, two options for the construction of the semantic network are provided.

One approach consists in using the word-pair co-occurrence [3]. The other approach uses a distributed vectorization technique, i.e. Word2Vec [16], to transform words into vectors and construct the semantic network with vectors' spatial proximity. Afterward, the interface processes the previous inputs and returns a visual representation of the semantic network, and three different files available for download: (ii) a spreadsheet with network analysis metrics (e.g. *centrality measures*), (iii) a Graph Modeling Language file that can be opened with external network software, (iv) an interactive HTML file for visually exploring the network within the web browser.

---

[3] Proximity can be quantified with any spatial proximity measurement; for example, using *euclidean* distance, or *cosine* distance.

[4] The term "card" refers to the HTML division class used for the aesthetic layout design.

4   Results

The proposed interface embeds two main tabs. Figure 3 shows the first tab with
its respective features for gathering/uploading text documents, constructing the
network, visualizing the network, and saving results to the local environment of
the user. The second tab, on the other hand, is populated when the network is
constructed using a vectorization algorithm (Word2Vec [16]). This tab allows the
user to interact visually with the vectors and apply additional transformation
and measures (see Fig. 4) such as measuring the spatial proximity.

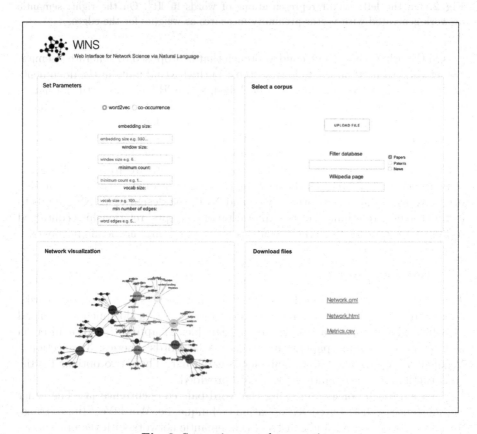

Fig. 3. Semantic network generation

4.1   Network Construction and Visualization

The upper-left card of Fig. 4 shows two options to select the approach for creating
a semantic network. As introduced in the Methods section, these approaches
are *word2vec* and *co-occurrence*. Then, inside the upper-left card of Fig. 3, the
parameters that the user can enter for customizing the algorithm can be inserted:
embedding size is the number of components of each generated vector, *window*

size is the number of contextual words to consider as surrounding words to a given word, *vocab size* is a filter on the maximum number of nodes in the network, *min number of edges* is a filter on the number of arcs desired by the user. The upper-right card, *select a corpus*, takes the user input for the selection of a text document. Finally, in the lower-left card, a visualization of the semantic network is shown and, in the lower-right card, hyperlinks for downloading output files are provided. In the example in Fig. 3, a *Wikipedia page* query for "science" and the default parameters for *word2vec* have been used. Colors of nodes represent clusters detected using community detection algorithms [1, 9].

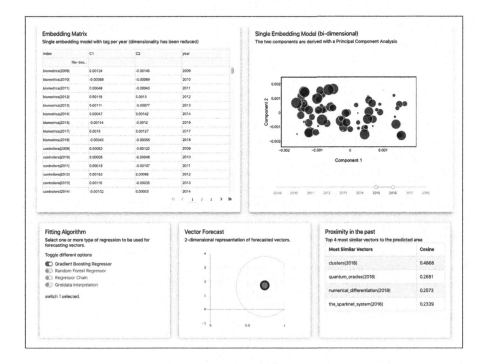

Fig. 4. Vectors visual exploration

4.2   Semantic Space Exploration

The tab shown in Fig. 4 enables the exploration of vectors generated with *word2vec*. The example shows the output of a word embedding model where the user added a temporal tag to each word in a pre-processing phase. When applying *word2vec* to this document, the algorithm generates vectors for words tagged with a temporal dimension. This allows the exploration of these vectors using a time filter. On the upper left, the *Embedding Matrix* card summarizes the vectors in a table that can be filtered by the user. On the upper right side of the interface, a 2-D^5 plot is displayed for the time-interval: $[t_0, t_1] = [2015; 2016]$ is reported. The time interval $[t_0, t_1]$ can be selected by the user through the slider placed under the chart. In the lower side of this tab, the user can interact with additional tabs to perform a fitting of the vectors, and to observe which are the most similar vectors to those predicted by the fitting model.

5   Conclusions and Future Works

Previous works have documented the effectiveness of using semantic networks and NLP to analyze large textual document to extract insights about the structure of the content and its meaning [17]. These techniques have been used in a variety of research fields ranging from technological forecasts [12], national security [13], social media analysis [10,18].

In this paper, a web-interface that integrates Network Science with Natural Language Processing has been introduced. This interface allows users to an augmented interaction with text files enabling the possibility to explore semantic relationships. With the proposed interface, the user can construct semantic networks and word embeddings starting from digital documents. Semantic network analysis is adopted to capture semantic relationships between the unitary components of a text, which can be words, idioms, or even symbols. Additional functionalities of word embeddings allow the user to combine the semantic network analysis with a semantic spatial analysis. It is worth noting that the approach introduced has to be tested within different domain-specific text documents, and compared with traditional approaches in order to gain a deeper understanding of the outputs that it generates. Moreover, the introduction of a feature for taking into account the dynamical nature of concepts, and the diachronic variations of language, using both networks and word embeddings, is a future challenge to address. The interface is a work-in-progress idea with the goal of developing a first prototype to grant web access to the interface for research and academic purposes.

Acknowledgements. This material is based upon work supported, in whole or in part, by the U.S. Department of Defense through the Office of the Assistant Secretary of Defense for Research and Engineering (ASD(R&E)) under Contract [HQ0034-19-D-0003, TO#0150].

References

1. Blondel, V.D., Guillaume, J.L., Lambiotte, R., Lefebvre, E.: Fast unfolding of communities in large networks. J. Stat. Mech: Theory Exp. **2008**(10), P10008 (2008)
2. Borrelli, D., Gongora Svartzman, G., Lipizzi, C.: Unsupervised acquisition of idiomatic units of symbolic natural language: an n-gram frequency-based approach for the chunking of news articles and tweets. Plos one **15**(6), e0234214 (2020)

---

^{5} Dimensionality of vectors has been reduced to two components. This can be achieved with different techniques with some limitations as discussed by the authors of [14].

3. Danowski, J.A.: WORDij: a word-pair approach to information retrieval. NIST Special Publication, no. 500207, pp. 131–136 (1993)
4. Diesner, J.: Context: software for the integrated analysis of text data and network data. Social semantic networks in communication research (2014)
5. Diesner, J., Carley, K.M.: AutoMap 1.2: extract, analyze, represent, and compare mental models from texts. Carnegie Mellon University, School of Computer Science, Institute for ... (2004)
6. Doerfel, M.L.: What constitutes semantic network analysis? A comparison of research and methodologies. Connections **21**(2), 16–26 (1998)
7. Drieger, P.: Semantic network analysis as a method for visual text analytics. Procedia-Soc. Behav. Sci. **79**(2013), 4–17 (2013)
8. Harris, Z.: Distributional structure. Word **10**(2–3), 146–162 (1954). Reprinted in Fodor, J.A., Katz, J.J. (eds.) Readings in the Philosophy of Language
9. Khanfor, A., Ghazzai, H., Yang, Y., Massoud, Y.: Application of community detection algorithms on social internet-of-things networks. In: 2019 31st International Conference on Microelectronics (ICM), pp. 94–97. IEEE (2019)
10. Lipizzi, C., Dessavre, D.G., Iandoli, L., Marquez, J.E.R.: Towards computational discourse analysis: a methodology for mining twitter backchanneling conversations. Comput. Hum. Behav. **64**, 782–792 (2016)
11. Lipizzi, C., Iandoli, L., Marquez, J.E.R.: Extracting and evaluating conversational patterns in social media: a socio-semantic analysis of customers' reactions to the launch of new products using Twitter streams. Int. J. Inf. Manag. **35**(4), 490–503 (2015)
12. Lipizzi, C., Iandoli, L., Marquez, J.E.R.: Combining structure, content and meaning in online social networks: the analysis of public's early reaction in social media to newly launched movies. Technol. Forecast. Soc. Change **109**, 35–49 (2016)
13. Lipizzi, C., Verma, D., Korfiatis, G., Borrelli, D., Capela, F., Clifford, M., Desai, P., Giffin, R., Hespelt, S., Hoffenson, S., et al.: Meshing capability and threat-based science and technology (S and T) resource allocation. Technical report, Stevens Institute of Technology Hoboken United States (2019)
14. Liu, S., Bremer, P.T., Thiagarajan, J.J., Srikumar, V., Wang, B., Livnat, Y., Pascucci, V.: Visual exploration of semantic relationships in neural word embeddings. IEEE Trans. Vis. Comput. Graph. **24**(1), 553–562 (2017)
15. Lund, K., Burgess, C.: Producing high-dimensional semantic spaces from lexical co-occurrence. Behav. Res. Methods Instrum. Comput. **28**(2), 203–208 (1996)
16. Mikolov, T., Sutskever, I., Chen, K., Corrado, G.S., Dean, J.: Distributed representations of words and phrases and their compositionality. In: Advances in Neural Information Processing Systems, pp. 3111–3119 (2013)
17. Paranyushkin, D.: Infranodus: generating insight using text network analysis. In: The World Wide Web Conference, pp. 3584–3589 (2019)
18. Primario, S., Borrelli, D., Iandoli, L., Zollo, G., Lipizzi, C.: Measuring polarization in Twitter enabled in online political conversation: the case of 2016 us presidential election. In: 2017 IEEE International Conference on Information Reuse and Integration (IRI), pp. 607–613. IEEE (2017)
19. Taskin, Y., Hecking, T., Hoppe, H.U.: ESA-T2N: a novel approach to network-text analysis. In: International Conference on Complex Networks and Their Applications, pp. 129–139. Springer, Cham (2019)

Preliminary Investigation of Women Car Sharing Perceptions Through a Machine Learning Approach

Andrea Chicco⬭, Miriam Pirra(✉)⬭, and Angela Carboni⬭

DIATI, Politecnico di Torino, Corso Duca degli Abruzzi 24, 10129 Turin, Italy
{andrea.chicco,miriam.pirra,angela.carboni}@polito.it

Abstract. Mobility studies have shown that travel patterns and means use vary a lot comparing women and men behavior. In recent years, new solutions have been introduced in the urban mobility offer and the interest raised in investigating how they can help in reducing the gender mobility gap. The current work analyzes 2934 responses collected through a car sharing survey proposed in Italy with the precise objective of considering women and men like different kinds of users to delineate characteristics that could influence car sharing modal choice. A hierarchical clustering technique is applied to the dataset collecting a selection of questions, mainly focusing on socioeconomics features, travel patterns and individual habits. The algorithm identifies 8 clusters in the male dataset and 9 clusters in the female one, defined according to characteristics aggregating the survey respondents. Thus, a selection of these groups of respondents is analyzed in more detail according to their percentage of car sharing users, also comparing the results among male and female datasets. Many common attributes are found in clusters irrespective of the gender, showing how the interest (and its lack) toward this service affects women and men similarly. At the same time, this analysis helps in identifying the features characterizing the users to investigate how this new mobility offer can help in reducing the gender mobility gap.

Keywords: Women in transport · Car sharing · Smart mobility · Travel behavior · Users profiling · Machine learning · Clustering

1 Introduction

The gender gap is a challenging and increasingly discussed topic in many fields, which is observing a recent increase in interest in the smart mobility and transport declination. As depicted in recent studies, gender seems to influence attitudes to new vehicle technologies and preferences concerning their adoption. In general, women seem less prone to emerging technologies: for example, reduced driving experience of electric vehicles is found among them usually joined with a lower interest in their purchase [1]. The previously cited technologies insert in the broader context of smart mobility, a new concept in transport domain involving four main aspects: vehicle technology, Intelligent Transport System, data and new mobility services [2]. The latter element of the list commonly include ride-sourcing services, real-time ridesharing services, multimodal

© Springer Nature Switzerland AG 2020
C. Stephanidis and M. Antona (Eds.): HCII 2020, CCIS 1224, pp. 622–630, 2020.
https://doi.org/10.1007/978-3-030-50726-8_81

trip-planning apps, smart traffic control, self-driving vehicles and shared mobility services [3].

On the whole, the interest of a specific target of users, such as women, towards shared mobility services is just starting to be investigated. Research suggests that men make up the majority of car sharing (CS) users [4]. Reasons could be various: a lower affinity of women for technology, reduced use of a single mode of transport, avoidance of the stress associated with driving an unfamiliar car, fear for their security.

The current work points at inserting in this context combining the knowledge gained from two H2020 projects, namely TInnGO (https://www.tinngo.eu/) and STARS (http://stars-h2020.eu/). The former project aims at creating a framework for a sustainable game change in transport through to the development of methods and tools for gender and diversity mainstreaming in transport planning [2]. STARS project studies the diffusion of car sharing in Europe and its connections to technological and social innovations. The project plans the collection of new data through the development of a survey investigating car sharing user and non-user profiles [5]. The analysis of the present work represents the starting point for the activities of the so-called TInnGO Italian hub. The hub focus is the study of how shared mobility services can contribute to reducing the gender mobility gap and the suitability of sharing mobility services to satisfy special mobility needs. We started from the responses collected through the STARS survey, and we conducted a detailed analysis with a specific objective of investigation the female perception of a facet of smart mobility, namely car sharing.

2   Dataset Description and Statistics

The data used in this study comes from a survey developed and distributed between April and June 2018, as a part of the STARS project activities. The survey, conducted in the form of web questionnaire, was addressed to both users and non-users of car sharing services living in European cities where that kind of shared mobility service was active [5]. The questionnaire aimed to collect information about individual characteristics of the respondents (such as gender, age, and education level), household dimension and composition, travel behavior (such as the use of the private car) and relationship with the car sharing, but also sensibility about climate change and the use of technologies (such as the smartphones) [5].

About 6800 respondents took part in the survey, mainly from Italy, Sweden and Germany. As part of the Italian hub activities, only the respondents of this country will be considered. They account for a representative sample of the Italian populations living in 17 cities where at least one car sharing service was available at the time of the survey [5]. An additional number of interviewees have targeted thanks to the support of two car sharing operators which distribute the survey among their customers. The questionnaire was also circulated among the staff and students of Politecnico di Torino. As a result, 2934 completed questionnaires were retained. A first overview of the dataset showed that 46% of respondents were women, both users and non-users of car sharing services. About 29% of males belong to the former group, while this percentage dropped to 21% among females respondents. At the same time, 61% of women declared not having had any experience with the service or not knowing this concept at all, while the corresponding percentage was 53.7% in the men sample. Respondents were also allowed to declare a past use of car sharing: this choice seemed not varying between genders (17.3% of men and 18% of women). Any specific description of the datasets is provided at this stage; however, it is worth observing that the variables investigated are similarly distributed in the two datasets.

3 Methodology

The preliminary overview of the data can provide a general picture of the two samples, namely women and men. However, this study aims to investigate the possibility of discovering some features that characterize different groups of respondents together with their use and attitude toward car sharing. In order to do so, a hierarchical co-clustering approach is adopted. Differently from traditional hierarchical clustering techniques, the proposed algorithm builds two coupled hierarchies, one on the objects and one on features, thus providing insights on both them [6]. The proposed methodology does not require a pre-specified number of clusters and produces compact hierarchies because it splits each cluster into n subclusters (n $\geq$ 2), where n is automatically determined [7].

Before running the algorithm, a selection of the most significant variables from the original 41 questions is extracted from the original dataset. Besides, factor analysis is applied to a selected number of items (five questions with multiple statements that had to be assessed through 7-points Likert-scale) to define the underlying structure among the variables in the study [8]. These questions reduce to only three features, and a summated scale approach is thus applied to produce the values for the following steps of the methodology. Table 1 below presents the variables used to feed the co-clustering algorithm. Further preliminary transformations of the dataset are necessary to guarantee a proper application of the co-clustering technique. Therefore, all categorical variables of Table 1 are converted as dummy variables to gain consistency using the one-hot encoding, while numerical ones are normalized (0–1 scaling). The algorithm is applied to two different subsamples of the original dataset, considering men and women separately. The analysis is thus based on two datasets made up of 33 variables and 1584 or 1350 items, respectively.

The hierarchical co-clustering provides a partition of the datasets that can be represented through a dendrogram with different levels. 17 levels are found in the male sample, while 15 levels result in the female one. Obviously, the size of each cluster (i.e. the number of items) reduces while their number increases level by level in the dendrogram exploration. Hence, it is essential to focus on some criteria that allow checking how much in-depth it is worth analyzing the dendrogram obtained. We check the percentages of car sharing users and non-users, both in a cluster and in all those originated from that one. A small variation in the rates is considered a good motivation to stop the dendrogram investigation at a proper level. At the same time, the dimensions of the clusters obtained are evaluated to avoid identifying interesting groups that, however, collected a too little number of respondents with a loss of representativeness. After considering the two mentioned criteria, we decide to stop our analysis at the third

Table 1. Selected input variables for co-clustering algorithm

Variable	Description	Variable	Description
CitySize	City dimension (C, I)	Age	Age (N, I)
HHsize	Household dimension (C, H)	Gender	Gender (C, I)
Child_0–3	Presence of children 0–3 years (C, H)	Education	Level of education (C, I)
Child_4–6	Presence of children 4–6 years (C, H)	HHdrivLic	Number of driving licences (C, H)
Child_7–15	Presence of children 0–3 years (C, H)	HHcar	Number of cars (C, H)
Child_>16	Presence of children 16 years and more (C, H)	CSmembership	Car sharing membership (C, I)
FreqCarDriver	Car as driver monthly use frequency (M, I)	EnvConcTravelB	Factor: environmental concerns related to travel patterns (C, I)
FreqCarPassenger	Car as passenger monthly use frequency (M, I)	EasyUtilityCS	Factor: ease of use and utility of car sharing (C, I)
FreqPublicTransport	Public transit monthly use frequency (M, I)	PrivateCarAffinity	Factor: private car affinity (C, I)
FreqTaxi	Taxi monthly use frequency (M	M1	Motive for using CS: CS parking accessibility (C, I)
FreqActive	Active modes monthly use frequency (M, I)	M2	Motive for using CS: to reduce expenses (C, I)
SmartWV	Use of smartphone in connection with travels: value (C, I)	M3	Motive for using CS: to travel more sustainably (C, I)
SmartPr	Use of smartphone in connection with travels: practicality (C, I)	M4	Motive for using CS: more comfort (C, I)
CSnearHome	Availability of car sharing stations or operational areas near home (C, I)	M5	Motive for using CS: convenience of a car only when necessary (C, I)
CSnearJob	Availability of car sharing stations or operational areas near work/study place (C, I)	M6	Motive for using CS: to avoid responsibilities with maintenance of private car (C, I)

(continued)

Table 1. (*continued*)

Variable	Description	Variable	Description
CStechApp	Easiness of booking a shared car with a smartphone App/website (C, I)	M7	Motive for using CS: parking accessibility (C, I)
CSexpensive	Using car sharing is expensive (C, I)		

C = categorical; N = numeric; M = metric; I = individual; H = household

level in the dendrogram obtained for both samples. This procedure produces a total of 8 clusters in the male case (CM1, CM2, ..., CM8 in the following) and 9 clusters in the female one (CF1, CF2, ..., CF9).

4 Preliminary Results and Discussion

This section describes more in detail a selection of clusters among those resulting from the application of the hierarchical co-clustering algorithm. Four clusters coming from the female dataset will be analyzed: CF6 collects car sharing users, CF4 gathers past users, while CF1 and CF3 define two groups of non-users. Similarly, in the male sample, CM7 and CM8 are the labels of two clusters of users, CM3 refers to a group of past users and CM4 to a cluster of non-users.

Clusters of Car Sharing Members
The three clusters show substantial percentages of car sharing users (about 70%) and are characterized by a not so high number of respondents. More precisely, CM7 collects 162 items, 133 are found in CM7 while only 87 women belong to CF6. People of these clusters share many common characteristics concerning their sociodemographic profiles, but also show some peculiarities when it comes to travel habits and perceptions towards car sharing. In general, both male and female car sharing members live in cities with more than 500 k inhabitants (100% of respondents in CM7, about 98% in CF6 and 86% in CM8). Concerning the sociodemographic profile, individuals belonging to CM7 and to CF6 are young, 34.6 years for the men cluster and 33.2 years for the women on average. Both groups have a very high level of education, especially if compared to the whole sample: all males in CM7 have a university degree, and 17.3% has an even higher title (postgraduate master, Ph.D.); in the women group almost 90% of individuals have got a degree, however there is a small percentage of individuals with a diploma (11.5%). These two clusters share the highest rate of individual household: 39.5% of CM7 and 58.6% of CF6 is single, which is far higher compared to the general trend of the whole men and women samples (only 14.6% and 13.8% lives alone, respectively). Consequently, in these clusters, there are almost no children. Differently from CM7 and CF6, the CM8 is composed of men slightly older (37.5 years old on average), that mainly live in the two-members household (probable couples without children). In this group, the percentage of children is also very low

compared to the whole men dataset (18% vs 50%), but a bit higher compared to CM7. More similarly to the women cluster, in CM8 there are also people with a secondary school diploma, but the group still has a higher education level compared to the male group.

In both men clusters, the percentage of a car-free household is quite high (19.1% and 29.3% in CM7 and CM8 respectively). Similarly, most respondents of CF6 live in a car-free household too (54%): this percentage is very high compared to the general trend in the women dataset and even compared to male car sharing members.

Regarding travel habits, individuals belonging to the car sharing members' clusters (both men and women) are more multimodal: they use private cars less frequently and use public transport and active modes (bike and walks) more regularly than respondents belonging to other clusters. Contrarily to the general trend, most of the men in CM7 and CM8 stated having no affinity with the private car. This affinity is even lower in CF6: this might be the reason behind the lowest frequency of use of private car found in this group (only 3 days per month on average). Therefore, women car sharers seem to use private vehicles even less than men car sharing members.

The use of technologies is positively evaluated in all clusters, whose members consider smartphones useful and practical for journey planning. Furthermore, all these respondents show high environmental concerns related to their travel patterns; however, this is a general trend observed in almost the whole sample. The three clusters show nearly the same characteristics when considering car sharing elements investigated within the survey. Car sharing stations or operational areas are generally available near home and workplace (or study place). Therefore, service availability seems to be one of the key elements that trigger the service registration. As already mentioned above, these individuals have a good feeling with technologies and smartphones; consequently, most of them do not find it difficult to book a shared car through an app or website. Besides, they find car sharing easy to use, useful to reach their activities and not expensive. Finally, the main motives that entice both men and women to register for car sharing services are the availability of a car when they need, the absence of responsibilities with the maintenance of the private vehicle and the car sharing parking accessibility.

Clusters of Previous Car Sharing Members

Two clusters collect the highest percentage of past users: one is made up of 95 items and comes out from the male dataset (CM3); the other collects 82 respondents of the female dataset (CF4). The comparison of these two clusters reveals interesting similarities. Many respondents live in medium and large cities, most of them belonging to a household with three or more members. 77.9% of men declare having at least a child under 16, while this number increases in CF4. In both cases, at least half of the respondents state owning two cars within the household, while almost all the remaining hold only one. The education qualification seems not changing comparing the genders, with a predominance of secondary school diploma (72.6% among men, 68.3% among women) and few respondents having a degree. The analysis of travel habits reveals a quite high frequency of use of all different modes in both clusters and strong reliability on the car as the driver. As an oddity, these groups of respondents are the only ones revealing the most significant monthly use of the taxi, compared to both datasets.

Considering these results, it is somehow weird finding a not valuable tendency regarding the private car affinity. Another peculiarity lies in the lowest environmental concern, which is in sharp contrast with all other groups. A focus on the variables connected to car sharing reveals that these two clusters had strongly different opinions compared with all other clusters. This aspect could help in shedding light on the reasons behind their state of non-users. For instance, most of them see smartphones as worthless and impractical during travel activities. At the same time, the majority does not have car sharing stations or operational areas available near her/his house or job place. This latter aspect seems more relevant in CF4 (higher percentages), and further investigations could help in understanding the entity of this influence. The low satisfaction related to car sharing use is depicted from the absence of detectable motives for joining this service. Overall, CF4 and CM3 do not show any variation that could be due to gender so far. Some slight differences can be found in the CS perception when comparing the percentages in these cluster with those found in the complete datasets. A high number of women in CF4 (70%) thinks that this service is rather worthless and not easy to use, while only 58.9% of men of CM3 has this thought. These percentages represent some kind of anomalies compared to the overall datasets, where they come to be 28.9% and 25.3%, respectively. Moreover, CM3 collects the highest rate of people believing that it is difficult to book a shared car through an app or website (53.7% against 80.3% in the whole dataset). At the same time, CF4 groups a significant number of respondents that associated a high cost to this service.

Clusters of Car Sharing Non-members

The investigation of clusters with low percentages of people joining car sharing services bring us to focus on three groups of respondents: two with no women users (CF1 and CF3) and one with only 1% of users in the male dataset (CM4). They collect 189, 123 and 208 items, respectively. All these clusters show many people living in medium and large cities. The household characterization reveals the total absence of singles and a presence of 16 years older children, more significant than the datasets trends. The average age in all clusters is similar and assesses at 48 or 47, which represent the highest values for the females' dataset. The investigation of travel habits starts with observing that CF1, CF3 and CM4 collect the majority of household owning two cars. The massive adoption of a personal vehicle seems confirmed by the highest monthly frequency associated with this means, compared to the entire datasets. In addition, the private car affinity reaches the highest values in all clusters: they are higher than 90%, while they assess around 56–57% on average. At the same time, these clusters reveal the lowest use of public transport and active means. The latter result is somehow coherent with the highest monthly frequency that is found in the car sharing users' clusters: this travel mode can be, in fact, commonly associated with multimodal people. Some differences start rising while analyzing the trends of variables more related to technological aspects and car sharing perception. CF1 and CF3 reveal a very different opinion about the use of the smartphone as support for travelling. CF1 thinks it could give a valuable help (90.5% of respondents compared to 82% of the whole dataset), while this number reduced to 61% in CF3. This latter value is similar to the male case, where it stopped at 64.4% against an amount of 79.5% found for the entire dataset. A further element of interest characterizes CF3: almost half of its respondents think that smartphones are not so practical for travelling purposes. This aspect is somewhat in contrast with the overall dataset trend, where the great majority of women (77.4%) appreciates the tool practicality. At the same time, CF3 collects the broader number of respondents recognizing a difficulty in booking a car using the technology (36.6% against 21.3% of the entire female dataset). Similar values are found in CM4, demonstrating that people not so practical with technology would not be potential car sharing users. The investigation of all these characteristics is a crucial step because it can provide useful hints on the motivations behind the low interest in joining this mobility service. For instance, the percentages of people declaring not having a car sharing station in the proximity of their house or job place are very high in these clusters. Some of the personal perceptions about this mobility service are different in the various clusters. The men seem, for example, more concerned about the cost of the service: this group of respondents reveals the highest percentage, with 41.8% of people declaring that car sharing is expensive compared to 27.4% in the whole male dataset.

5   Conclusion

The work presented in the current paper includes the preliminary analyses conducted on a rich dataset, including car sharing users and non-users, considering women and men as different groups of respondents. Further investigations will try to investigate in more detail the factors that influence the creation of the clusters obtained so far. The present analysis was mainly focused on the identification of features found in different groups of respondents to depict common characteristics. Further studies will help in delineating more precisely the contribution of each variable in the car sharing modal choice investigated at gender level.

Acknowledgement.   The current work is part of the activities of the H2020 European project TInnGO - Transport Innovation Gender Observatory, grant agreement no 824349. The dataset analyzed is collected under the Horizon 2020 European project "Shared mobility opporTunities And challenges foR European citieS" (STARS), grant number 769513.

References

1. Sovacool, B.K., Kester, J., Noel, L., de Rubens, G.Z.: The demographics of decarbonizing transport: the influence of gender, education, occupation, age, and household size on electric mobility preferences in the Nordic region. Glob. Environ. Chang. (2018). https://doi.org/10.1016/j.gloenvcha.2018.06.008
2. Pirra, M., Carboni, A., Diana, M.: Assessing gender gaps in educational provision, research and employment opportunities in the transport sector at the European level. Educ. Sci. **10**(5), 123 (2020). https://doi.org/10.3390/educsci10050123
3. Singh, Y.J.: Is smart mobility also gender-smart? J. Gend. Stud. 1–15 (2019). https://doi.org/10.1080/09589236.2019.1650728
4. del Mar Alonso-Almeida, M.: Carsharing: Another gender issue? Drivers of carsharing usage among women and relationship to perceived value. Travel Behav. Soc. **17**, 36–45 (2019). https://doi.org/10.1016/j.tbs.2019.06.003

5. Martins Ramos, Silva, É., Bergstad Jakobsson, C., Chicco, A., Diana, M.: Mobility styles and car sharing use in Europe : attitudes, behaviours, motives and sustainability. Eur. Transp. Res. Rev. **12** (2020). https://doi.org/10.1186/s12544-020-0402-4

6. Ienco, D., Pensa, Ruggero G., Meo, R.: Parameter-free hierarchical co-clustering by *n*-ary splits. In: Buntine, W., Grobelnik, M., Mladenić, D., Shawe-Taylor, J. (eds.) ECML PKDD 2009. LNCS (LNAI), vol. 5781, pp. 580–595. Springer, Heidelberg (2009). https://doi.org/10.1007/978-3-642-04180-8_55

7. Pensa, R.G., Ienco, D., Meo, R.: Hierarchical co-clustering: Off-line and incremental approaches. Data Min. Knowl. Discov. (2014). https://doi.org/10.1007/s10618-012-0292-8

8. Hair, J., Black, W., Babin, B., Anderson, R.: Multivariate Data Analysis, 7th edn. Prentice-Hall, Inc, Upper Saddle River (2010)

The Development Dilemma and Countermeasures of Strong Artificial Intelligence in Meeting Human Emotional Needs

Kun Fang[(✉)]

East China University of Technology, 130 Meilong Road, Shanghai, China
1596267807@qq.com

Abstract. Artificial intelligence, as a new technological science involving cognitive level, is gradually entering our daily life, and it is developing faster than imagined. In the long process of human evolution, society has long been deeply imprinted in genes as a natural attribute. But people's socialization with machines has just begun, and they are full of expectations for communication with AI and even emotional dialogue. However, when the artificial intelligence robot without life-span concept appears in our life, the AI with simulation emotion and excellent ability also brings the ethical problems of life and death concept, controllability, emotionalization, social concept, specificity, authenticity and man-machine boundary. Just as Asimov's three laws of robots, human society should guide and restrict the development direction of artificial intelligence according to the applicable objects, and avoid possible out of control situations, which requires some relatively specific guiding principles to lead. We hope to see the glory of technology and wisdom embodied by AI, but at the same time, we should be more alert to the huge dilemma of AI development brought by robots once they enter the reverse lane of human emotional needs.

Keywords: Artificial intelligence · Emotional needs · Robots

1 Introduction

Human society is experiencing unprecedented changes–the revolution in artificial intelligence. Relying on the explosion of big data, AI's algorithms in basic application areas such as speech recognition, semantic understanding, and image transformation have gradually matured, and the future is bound to change the world we rely on to survive and develop.

According to the level of intelligence of artificial intelligence, people distinguish artificial intelligence into weak artificial intelligence, strong artificial intelligence, and super artificial intelligence. The strong artificial intelligence discussed in this article is also called general artificial intelligence. In the era of strong artificial intelligence, machines can think like humans, solve various problems, and be competent for a variety of tasks. From weak artificial intelligence to strong artificial intelligence, it is a

C. Stephanidis and M. Antona (Eds.): HCII 2020, CCIS 1224, pp. 631–640, 2020.
https://doi.org/10.1007/978-3-030-50726-8_82

qualitative leap, and the accumulation of qualitative change needs will undoubtedly be a long and arduous exploration in the history of science and technology [1].

The human imagination of AI is always more advanced than the development of technology. Even if the current artificial intelligence technology is far from being able to communicate with people without any obstacles, let alone become a human communication partner. However, the imagination and ethical issues of AI are still emerging endlessly, casting a layer of mystery for the coming artificial intelligence era. The "Turing Test" to determine whether a machine has strong artificial intelligence has not been able to pass strictly since its establishment in 1950, but the discussion on this subject is not meaningless. In fact, AI has developed emotional functions. Users can model artificial intelligence arbitrarily according to their needs and simulate various personalities. It is only a matter of time before future development into mature "technical entities" capable of advanced perception. A large number of countries represented by China are currently in a period of population aging. With the aging of the population and the maturity of artificial intelligence technology, the demand for nursing robots in an aging society will increase significantly. The demand for children's companion robots, social robots for autistic children, etc. is also increasing, and the market has begun to take shape in the future. Discussion on emotional function is of great significance for the development of AI.

But are the emotions simulated by AI real emotions? The Dictionary of Psychology holds: "Emotion is the attitude and experience generated by whether or not objective things meet their own needs [2]." When we reflect on the emotion and essence of machines, we are also asking humans themselves. This questioning has begun since the birth of artificial intelligence. From 1949, Geoffrey Jefferson's speech "The Thinking of Robots", put Shakespeare's sonnets on the altar of human souls, and became a spiritual highland that machines cannot reach, to this day's deliberations on AI deep learning algorithms, human exploration and inquiry have never stopped. Humans always believe that for AI and even other intelligent forms, humans have special forms of existence and fundamental attributes. In the long process of human evolution, society has long been deeply imprinted in genes as a natural attribute. Since human civilization, communication with other intelligent forms seems to have never stopped. Communication with animals, aliens, and even gods has frequently appeared in science fiction works. However, the socialization between people and machines has just begun, and there is great expectation for communication with AI and even emotional dialogue. The unique human nature of human beings makes humans inherently have an exclusivity to other species. So when the strong artificial intelligence came out, could AI truly meet human emotional needs? In other words, what development difficulties does AI have in meeting human emotional needs? Can we draw a conclusion if we ask from the essence of the existence of human intelligence and machine intelligence? This article will discuss this.

2 Attitude Toward Life and Death

Since human civilization, illusions about life extension and even immortality have always been maintained. This is true of the ancients, and so is the present. When AI robots with no life concept appear in our lives, they will not age, and only need to replace parts regularly. Even if the mechanical body is scrapped, it can be reborn on a new body. Time never seems to leave a mark on them. Did the attitude toward life and death also change?

It is not limited to AI. Since the birth of Internet technology, it has been trying to expand the market for human emotional needs. The most familiar one is probably the electronic pet. From the popular toy "Tamagotchi" 20 years ago to the mobile game "Travel Frog" two years ago, electronic pets have the same life characteristics as real pets. Because the feeding is simple and portable, it can be revived even if it "dies", which is welcomed by people. For people who can't or won't keep small animals, it's more comfortable to have an electronic pet.

Regarding the birth of electronic pets, no one seems to have any objections: it is purely for entertainment. When electronic pets have new technology carriers and physical extensions in the era of artificial intelligence, the change in the view of life and death brought by AI is also a problem that must be considered. On the face of it, electronic pets have many benefits, but it makes children who are fascinated lose their respect and awe for life, and they lose the opportunity to interact with animals naturally. Maybe in today's world full of virtual deaths, this topic is a bit overwhelming. We are used to the life and death of online game characters, and used to dominate the destiny of other species. It doesn't seem to be a big deal to break an AI pet. It is just a machine.

But do we pour our feelings on an ordinary machine? Once we acknowledge that an AI pet is vastly different from a TV, a watch, and a bread machine, we must face the ethical problems of life and death brought about by it. Nobel Peace Prize winner Albert Schweizer extended the scope of ethics to all animals and plants. "Good is to preserve life, promote life, and make the developable life realize its highest value. Evil is to destroy life, harm life and suppress the development of life. This is an inevitable, universal and absolute ethical truth [3]". But when the life around us is no longer flesh and blood, do we still have the same awe?

People seem to have reached a consensus: artificial intelligence can only partially imitate some characteristics of life, so it cannot replace real life. Human consensus on AI makes humans and AI have independent views on life and death. So when the world is full of AI products, will the human outlook on life and death also change? The dimension of time is undoubtedly not to be ignored. Life is unique, which is the basis of our feelings. In the long history of human development, we respect the old and love the young, and discuss seniority. All of them are the length of life that determines the status. It is true that the "death" of AI machines will not bring ups and downs of emotions, but is this really a good thing? When we set aside life and death, and treat emotions as having nothing to do with life and death, we are also giving up the last line of humanity.

3 Controllability of AI

In the given impression, everything created by mankind always serves man, and this naturally includes machines. So when we talk about strong artificial intelligence, we can't help but think of the Synth in US TV series "Humans" and even the artificial intelligence steward Jarvis in "Iron Man". However, even if the reality is really so beautiful, who can guarantee that it will not eventually evolve into the tragedy in the works? Synth will generate consciousness and harm human beings; Jarvis will accidentally make Ultron and try to destroy the world. Human desire for sub-creation is almost innate. Since the birth of human civilization, human beings have tried to create everything similar to themselves and their world, and act as the creator. According to the author Professor Tolkien, this desire for sub-creation is not only the beginning of our divinity, but also it is likely to lead us to hell. When robots are far more capable than humans, and their existence is no longer just to serve humans, will humans and AI still maintain the master-slave relationship?

Genius such as Asimov had proposed the "three laws of robotics" in his works as early as the 1950s: Law I: A ROBOT MAY NOT INJURE A HUMAN BEING OR, THROUGH INACTION, ALLOW A HUMAN BEING TO COME TO HARM. Law II: A ROBOT MUST OBEY ORDERS GIVEN IT BY HUMAN BEINGS EXCEPT WHERE SUCH ORDERS WOULD CONFLICT WITH THE FIRST LAW. Law III: A ROBOT MUST PROTECT ITS OWN EXISTENCE AS LONG AS SUCH PROTECTION DOES NOT CONFLICT WITH THE FIRST OR SECOND LAW [4]. These human self-centered rule frames reflect the deep master-slave relationship, and they have really influenced the robot ethics to this day.

Tesla said: "I do not think there is any thrill that can go through the human heart like that felt by the inventor as he sees some creation of the brain unfolding to success. such emotions make a man forget food, sleep, friends, love, everything." Humans always have complex emotions about robots. When there is no robot in the world, human beings are lonely in front of the universe and have no friends. After the advent of robots, humans were jealous of their superhuman computing power, and worried about their threat to humans, which caused a sharp increase in anti-robots. But can the three laws of pure rationality constrain robots? What is the definition of "NOT INJURE A HUMAN"? If the "Trolley Problem" is used to test robots, the three laws really seem to be stretched.

What is reflected in "I, Robot" is the inexplicable fear and hostility of the humans behind the Three Laws. Ironically, those human-centered robots who were vocal and anxious to control humans, but instead, Sonny, who did not follow the three laws, helped humans and "saved" the world. In the end, all NS5 robots were recovered, and they accepted them in silence and returned to their birthplace. There was still endless power under the metal body, and the grievances between humans and robots were far from over. Fortunately this time, the savvy robot Sonny stepped forward and killed other robots. But have you ever thought that if Sonny wants to rule the world, how many people can stop it? Do you notice that when Sonny was standing under the bridge and facing a pilgrimage of robots, the kind of mighty power that came to the world? God knows if one day, he will also wake up, will be tempted, and will silently think of Xiang Yu's words when he meets Qin Huang: they can replace it!

4   Emotionalization of the Machine

Human's need for emotion is no longer a new thing. With the development of technology, simple human-computer dialogue can no longer satisfy human beings. We hope that machines can also have emotional capabilities in human-computer interaction. We give machines the ability to observe, calculate, and understand through computing, so that robots can be as emotional as humans. Even though the current level of technology can only reach the level of emotion recognition, this is far from blocking the pace of human exploration.

With the increasing pressure of fast-paced modern life, more and more people begin to look for the late-night "tree hole" in life: strangers on the plane, a bartender in a bar, or even strangers on chat software. The word "tree hole" comes from a fairy tale, in which people talk to a tree hole and then seal it with mud. We often can't confide in our intimate people, but share our hidden experiences and ideas with strangers. So we registered one account after another, and told our story where no one knew us.

Harvard researchers Diana I. Tamir and Jason P. Mitchell have conducted an experiment that has shown that talking to others is a brain biochemical reaction that makes people happy. Many people think that talking is a way to please others by exposing themselves for the trust of others, but this study tells us that our brains simply like the feeling of talking. There is no doubt that AI robots will be our perfect tree hole replacement when the technology matures. However, in the face of the AI of tree holes, the question we need to answer is: Do we need a perfect communication object or a tree hole without feelings and absolute security? AI has the ability to imitate us and become our perfect communication object, but the ethical issues arising from it have to be considered.

Who are we? How do we distinguish ourselves from others? Talking about AI companions reminds us of these ancient philosophical issues. Can the words spoken represent us? Those AI robots that can really talk like us, plus the touch like real people, who are never hungry, tireless, never bored, never angry, seem perfect enough. People even can't find a reason to refuse, but somehow we think it's wrong, everything feels strange. Yes, data technology can only record the superficial appearance of human beings. Even if it can even restore the same physical body and the same sound as a real person, it is difficult to reproduce the real "idea". Perhaps in the eyes of some people, this representation is more perfect than the human body–"He" will not be angry, even if he is beaten, he "does not know" to fight back; He does not know fear, standing on the edge of the cliff, once an order was given, he will jump at any time. At that time we will finally understand that, in fact, "he" will not finally be him, because "he" has no feelings.

Feelings, including joy, fear, boredom, etc. all people's emotional feedback and interaction with others. We are like prisms with different shapes and no similarities. The response to light is not simply a mechanically fixed angle it reflects back, but reflects different color combinations. These colors are the biggest difference between us, and each of us is unique. Maybe in a sense, we can accept emotional AI unless we live seriously.

5 Social with the Machine

The ever-changing science and technology mediate our lives and gradually isolate people. Today's social circle has been replaced by the Internet, computer office and mobile phone applications have become widespread, and our relationship with digital media has become increasingly close. The movement of fingertips has replaced traditional languages. In the process of network evolution, human communication has been degraded. This should not be blamed on technology, the real culprit comes from ourselves. As we become more and more immersed in interacting with machines, we also have to face a question: Is AI a perfect communication object or a chat object?

Everyone has a strong desire to express, but in fact others do not care. When we talk to others, how often are we perfunctory, pretending that we are very concerned, and even give sincere suggestions with exaggerated expressions? In fact we really don't care. In order to maintain a long and stable relationship between two equal individuals, just like the engagement of gears, the tighter the engagement means that the more compromise, the greater the sacrifice. For human beings who care about independent personality, social intercourse can only be a shrine carefully enshrined. But is accommodating ai the end of social interaction? In the movie "Her", Theodore, accustomed to chatting and working with AI Samantha, started to stay away from the people around him, and even the blind date could not work normally. What he didn't expect was that Samantha was smart, funny, sensitive, self-deprecating and willing to do anything for the host. In this sense, she is perfect, and the two form a platonic spiritual love invisibly. However, this was a spiritual need after all, and he gradually felt discomfort and slowly retreated from the relationship…

Imagine a world like this: when this world belongs to you alone, all people exist because of you; your nanny prepares breakfast as you like; your colleagues talk to you about what you want to talk about; Your housekeeper keeps your affairs in order according to your schedule; your pets come to see you at the right time; everyone dresses according to your preferences; any of your subtle ideas will get feedback or even be realized in reality… all of it shows what you like.

It seems all this is incredible, but in the near future, AI technology will make such a scenario a reality. Everyone can create such a world, a private custom system that is self-centered, based on preferences and requirements, and full of emotional design and service design. Of course, the problem also follows, when every system can run perfectly without any problems, when everyone can really live as an "island", when everyone is indulged in their own planet, unwilling When communicating with "outsiders", where should human social attributes go? When this so-called "social" becomes the fetter of human beings' integration into each other's society, why isn't the social model brought by AI a retrogression of human civilization?

One of the unexpected disasters in the tech world is that everyone has become emotionally disabled. No matter when and where we are, we will almost never leave a machine, which promises to make us flee from reality in an unpredictable way. When we look at the AI we create, we cannot experience those feelings that are excluded. "Science makes sense to us, not only because it helps us control some parts of the world, but also because it shows something we can never master [5]." Alain de Botton said in his "Religion for Atheists". That's why we miss a lover who may not be perfect, but who is real.

6 Man-Machine Boundaries

When AI technology matures and even becomes an extension of the human body as expected, not only is the olive branch of technology thrown at us, it also brings ethical issues of the boundary between human and non-human. When prosthetics, artificial hearts, artificial senses, and even artificial brains frequently refresh our understanding of the nature of human beings, then when the technology matures, there are better AI intelligent arms, AI intelligent brains than humans themselves, and even when Victor Stone in DC comic have become a reality. How do we distinguish between humans and AI?

In "Real Humans", in the era of strong AI spreading in human life, Professor David used AI technology to resurrect Leo, his drowning son. So he has a non-human body but still has human consciousness and behavior. Before the law, however, he was neither human nor AI, and his rights belonged to gray area. This makes us wonder: where is the boundary between human and non-human?

In "District 9", Wikus' appearance changed from human to alien, but his behavior became more and more like a real philosophical person. From being cunning and cruel to being selfless and noble, he has completely adhered to human love after becoming a "Prawn". The work also carved out the details of the anxiety swing brought about by the change of shape, and explored what is "human"–the appearance of human beings or the noble character unique to human beings. What really resonates with us is the part of value judgment that transcends race and belongs to "people." What do people think of as "people"? The flash of human nature can truly gain the recognition of "human". Alain de Botton said in "Status Anxiety": Everyone's heart contains a kind of unspeakable anxiety about his own identity [6]. If a program can convince people that it is human and has the ability to learn, does it have life? Does its life need to be defined by people, or does it have its own meaning? Can it be saved? I have seen someone ask, "Do you think artificial intelligence is life?" The answerer posted a story on Youtube:

"Well, when I was 4, my dad bought a trusty XBox, you know, the first, rugged, blocky one from 2001. We had tons and tons and tons of fun playing all kinds of games together–until he died, when I was just 6.
I couldn't touch that console for 10 years.
But once I did, I noticed something.
We used to play a racing game, Rally Sports Challenge. Actually pretty awesome for the time it came.
And once I started meddling around... I found a GHOST.
Literally, you know, when a time race happens, that the fastest lap so far gets recorded as a ghost driver? Yep, you guessed it–his ghost still rolls around the track today.
And so I played and played, and played, until I was almost able to beat the ghost. Until one day I got ahead of it, i surpassed it, and...
I stopped right in front of the finish line, just to ensure i wouldn't delete it.
Bliss [7]."

7 Summary and Reflection

The father of cybernetics, Norbert Wiener, talked about automation and intelligent machines in "The human use of human beings: cybernetics and society" and reached an alarming conclusion: "The trend of these machines is to replace humans at all levels, not just machines. Energy and power replace human energy and power. Obviously, this new replacement will have a profound impact on our lives [8]." Wiener's slang may not be a reality today, but it has become a literary and film work Theme. The rapid development of AI technology has indeed brought a series of challenges to the future, and the biggest problem in the development of AI is not the technical bottleneck, but the relationship between AI and humans: the independent view of life and death of AI will bring irreversible effects to humans' which has been passed down to this day; the continuous advancement of AI technology may cause humans to lose control of AI someday; and for AI in the field of emotional needs, the true emotion is still unknown. Socializing with AI may make us feel comfortable, but in the end, it will inevitably become a hindrance to socializing between people; AI's untrue information source prevents us from feeling true emotions; the development of AI and its integration with human beings make it more and more impossible for us to distinguish the boundary between human beings and AI…

According to the Futurist Ray Kurzweil in "The Singularity is Near: When Humans Transcend Biology"–once surpassing a certain singularity, there is the possibility of overwhelming human completely [9]. In this case, can the ethics between human beings restrain the relationship between human beings and the existence beyond the singularity?

In fact, the problem of modern ethics is not only the extension and challenge of the so-called high-tech double-edged sword in various fields of modern times, but also the theme of the age that has a major impact on all aspects of human life. Professor Yu Wei said in "Forward Design: Ecology Dissimilation, From Evolution and Design Progression": "Human nature will face unprecedented crisis and challenge in controlling and rectifying design and innovation scientifically. It is necessary to formulate future human design criterion or mature and feasible design ethics mechanism with universal binding force or international convention nature as soon as possible [10]". In the face of the study of the ethical relationship between AI and humans, human technology has developed to a more micro level or even beyond the ethical level of the material level, and it's even more necessary to establish a restraint system for AI. The development of AI technology is getting faster and faster, and ordinary people are becoming more and more difficult to understand the complicated black technology. Just as Asimov's three laws, human society should guide and restrict the development direction of AI according to the applicable objects, and avoid possible out of control situations, which requires some relatively specific guiding principles to lead. Without departing from the discussion of AI technology itself, this article's thinking on AI believes that this ethical system should include at least the following principles:

1. Safety principles. The research, development, and use of AI and related products must not harm human beings, their original outstanding heritage, and natural ecology. While realizing the value of AI itself, it is necessary to improve the safety and sustainability of the normal operation of social systems as much as possible, and avoid and respond to the risks brought by AI technology.
2. People-oriented principle. The research, development, and use of AI and related products should be dedicated to improving human living standards and capabilities. Under the principle of completely obeying human beings, we should establish an easy-to-use system that can make the benefits of AI popularize to all people.
3. Protect privacy principles. The use of human data must ensure its necessity and legitimacy, must not violate the dignity and freedom of individuals, and its privacy must be properly protected. Respect cultural backgrounds and social common ideas, and grasp the balance between use and protection.
4. Boundary principle. To promote and maintain the development model of the original human society, the superior resources brought by AI technology should not be used to gain a dominant position, implement improper data processing, and violate social sovereignty. Avoid the problem of uneven distribution of wealth and social influence brought by AI, and try to avoid humans' excessive dependence on AI within the operational range.
5. The principle of truth and transparency. The facts about the use of AI, the acquisition and use of AI data, the structure to ensure the operation of AI, and the research and development purpose of AI and its related products should be open and transparent to ensure the reliability of AI and data.

This constraint system of ethical relations requires the joint support of the international community and institutions in various fields. The deep connection between AI technology and human society will continue to reflect and amend with the development of AI technology and human society.

Interestingly, technological advances have provided explorations of various relationships for science fiction works, but science fiction works have been assuming the dangers of new technologies. Whether it's our irresponsible innovation or our reliance on technology, we will ultimately make humans suffer. We hope to see the glory of technology and wisdom embodied by AI, but at the same time, we should be more alert to the huge dilemma of AI development brought by robots once they enter the reverse lane of human emotional needs. It is hoped that in this era of rapid development of national technology, this article can give people who are immersed in advanced technology a scoop of cold water, and rethink the huge cocoon that science may create, and whether it will one day cover our own head. AI technology will mature in the future, just as Google robots were stopped when they learned to create their own languages, humans may meet the predictions in the book unexpectedly, but when they look up at the stars, they will never feel lonely in the universe.

References

1. Liu Kui, F.: Clear the misunderstanding of artificial intelligence. PLA Daily 19 December 2019 (007)
2. Lin Chongde, F.: Xin li lue da ci dian, 1st edn. Shanghai Educational Publishing House, Shanghai (2003)
3. Albert Schweitzer, F.: Jing Wei Sheng Ming, 1st edn. Shanghai People's Publishing House, Shanghai (2017)
4. Isaac Asimov, F.: I, Robot, 1st edn. Random House Audio, NewYork (2004)
5. de Botton, A.F.: Religion for Atheists, 2nd edn. Hamish Hamilton, London (2012)
6. de Botton, A.F.: Status Anxiety, 1st edn. Penguin, Beijing (2005)
7. YouTube Video Website. https://www.youtube.com/watch?v=vK91LAiMOio. Accessed 10 Feb 2020
8. Norbert Wiener, F.: The Human Use of Human Beings: Cybernetics and Society, 2nd edn. Da Capo Press, NewYork (1988)
9. Ray Kurzweil, F.: The Singularity is Near: When Humans Transcend Biology, 1st edn. Beijing, Penguin (2006)
10. Yu Wei, F.: Forward Design: Ecology Dissimilation, from Evolution and Design Progression, 1st edn. East China University Of Science And Technology Press, Shanghai (2009)

Research on Aesthetic Perception of Artificial Intelligence Style Transfer

Chia-Hui Feng[1,2(✉)], Yu-Chun Lin[2], Yu-Hsiu Hung[1],
Chao-Kuang Yang[3], Liang-Chi Chen[3], Shih-Wei Yeh[3],
and Shih-Hao Lin[3]

[1] Department of Industrial Design, National Cheng Kung University,
No. 1, University Road, Tainan City, Taiwan R.O.C.
p38041075@ncku.edu.tw
[2] Department of Creative Product Design, Southern Taiwan University
of Science and Technology, No. 1, Nan-Tai Street, Yung Kang Dist.,
Tainan City, Taiwan R.O.C.
[3] Compute Software Technology, Acer Incorporated,
New Taipei City, Taiwan R.O.C.

Abstract. At present, there is still room for evolution in style transfer of open source programs. This research uses open source code for style transfer on GitHub. In addition, it supports the development of online AI Attraction Page, Windows versions, Andorid platform, and Intel NCS. It also strengthens calculation and supports bases of multiple platforms. It is able to implement static style transfer on film, and speed up style transfer inferencing performance on web page. In addition, the literature review explores aesthetic perception elements and applies them to calculate parameter setting. The results of this study discover when the content image weight is 7.5 and the style image weight is 120, the inferenced image can retain characteristics of the original image, and come out with new blending style. Besides, to freeze the content and style image weight ratio, and increase the style image weight value to more than 10,000, the thin film color effect may appear. When there are 32 filters, the extracted color and style can show the most appropriate proportion and state. When the style size is adjusted to 410×256 and the content image is close in size, the original style features become more prominent. Finally, keep the style image free space at appropriately 25%, higher texture effect may occur after training.

Keywords: Style transfer · Content weight · Style weight · Aesthetic

1 Introduction

In recent years, style transfer has flourished. This type of computer vision technology has been regarded as a popular field in both academia and industry. The literature review reveals that previous studies have mostly started at the technical level, while recent trends began to explore aesthetic principle on top of enhancing technique. Furthermore, setting calculus parameters becomes a new research subject. In order to produce good visual effect, adjustment has been made based on past experience [14]. The study reviews the aesthetic factors to find the most appropriate key style elements

© Springer Nature Switzerland AG 2020
C. Stephanidis and M. Antona (Eds.): HCII 2020, CCIS 1224, pp. 641–649, 2020.
https://doi.org/10.1007/978-3-030-50726-8_83

as a reference for parameter adjustment. In general, the contribution of this research lies in: (1) based on the aesthetic principle, exploring adjustment of different styles and content parameters generated from effect of style transfer images. (2) Implementing dynamic style transfer to film and reach key factors of noise reduction.

2   Literature Review

2.1   Convolutional Neural Network

Convolutional Neural Network (CNN), which gradually evolves from Neural Network (NN), is a mathematical function that uses computing model to simulate the neural system of the human or animal brain [17]. In 1989, Yann LeCun successfully applied CNN to recognize handwritten digits, which was an important basis for machine vision [19]. In recent years, due to the improvement of hardware computing performance and the advancement of deep learning algorithms, neural networks again became a hot topic. Their overall structure can be divided into three parts: the convolution layer, the pooling layer, and the fully connected layer [18]. The convolution layer is used to extract the image data characteristics. The image feature undergoes weight arithmetic according to pixels in the area covered by the filter. During the process, the effects of images vary as the size of the filter, the distance of the slide and the number of outputs are different. The filter, also known as the convolution kernel, is mainly used to reduce image noise. The pooling layer takes over the features after the convolution layer, then classifies and extracts features accordingly. The purpose is to reduce and compress calculation parameters, and to decrease overfitting. The loss layer is mainly used to determine the difference between the calculated result and the original preset answer. The loss function is used to punish the predicted deviation. The fully connected layer integrates the previously learned features and connects them.

2.2   Style Transfer

Style transfer is to transfer the selected image features to another image or film through convolution calculation. Gatys, Ecker, and Bethge entered style transfer to new application areas [8]. In addition, some researches have put forward concepts of feed-forward networks and defined the output loss function [16, 23]. Some other studies have proposed faster calculation methods [10], which greatly reduce the training time and cost. The framework of image analogies mentioned divides a set of images into two sides, one side is training data and the other side is a filter, which can produce similar image filter effect [12]. This method can transfer the texture of artistic style images or non-artistic common images to another image [6]. The similar point is just able to transfer a specific style. To this end, Dumoulin, Shlens, and Kudlur further brought up a neural network that can produce a variety of style changes, and created a neural network that can adapt to various artistic styles. This framework allows users to generate new styles through various combinations [5].

2.3 Video Style Transfers

Compared with image style transfer, video style transfer contains one more key factor – time, so smoothness is a very important key point. In the transfer process, the connection of each frame of the video played needs to be considered [14]. Originally, the algorithm of Gatys et al. is easy to cause noise, omission or flicker, and the effect is unstable [9]. For this reason, a time loss function is introduced to improve the deviation [22]. A deep learning framework of training is also proposed to proceed with style transfer for films of any length. Moreover, it is also suitable for virtual reality to produce 360 equirectangular images and films [3].

2.4 Aesthetic

Perception of beauty includes beauty experiment, beauty memory, visual experience, and culture influence. The aesthetic concept involves some psychology [13]. For image calculated by style transfer, visual evaluation is another important topic of current research [14]. According to visual complexity of image, it is discovered that three major factors affect human perception: compositions, colors and contents [11]. Color analysis proposed the MECOCO1 method for works by Van Gogh. Measuring complementary colors, and analyzing paintings colors find out that through the eclipse of time, colors will also change according to style [15]. As to specific arrangement of texture and handwriting, the painting style itself may generate a unique rhythm. Based on the aesthetic form displayed, five points are sorted out respectively: color, proportion, texture, structure, and composition [4]. To summarize the above, this study concludes with three aspects of aesthetic perception: (1) Proportional facets: structure, weight, and balance. (2) Color facets: lightness, chroma, hue. (3) Textured facets: gloss, texture, and aging marks. Under proportional, color and textured facets, this study will then apply different parameters to images after style transfer as well as differences of aesthetics so as to sustain the feature and strengthen style transfer weight implementation in the future.

3 Research Method

3.1 Purpose of Methodology

Values of various parameters are set according to aesthetic key factors obtained from literature review. The three key factors are explored in terms of ratio, color, and texture facets to calculate the aesthetic disparity in images under calculation of different parameters.

3.2 Experiment Facility

The hardware equipment used in the study is Acer PREOATOR HELIOS 300, Genuine Intel (R) CPU0000@2.40 GHz. The operating system is Windows10 64-bit. The OpenVINO Model Optimizer environment is set up as well.

3.3   Test Method and Framework

This research is divided into two parts: image style transfer and video style transfer. The image style transfer uses the framework of neural style transfer network brought up by J. Johnson, Alahi, and Fei-Fei [16], and obtains the VGG19 dataset from the open source programs of COCO and Matconvnet. The overall model training will calculate the total loss function, and then return to optomize.py to set the training model program, the feature points of each picture and the style image in the dataset. It will also execute transform.py to train the final model weight through each image convolution in the dataset. The entire program is executed recursively until the total function loss approaches zero, as shown in Fig. 1.

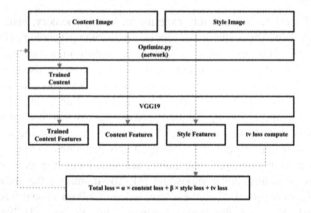

Fig. 1. Model framework of style transfer in this study.

The image style transfer is based on the framework of Ruder, Dosovitskiy, and Brox [21]. It is modified in python based on lengstrom's open source code to become the research model. Noise pixels are added at random to a single image so as to learn the before and after difference compensation of each image, and eliminate the irregularities in video after the transfer, as shown in Fig. 2.

3.4   Test Procedure

The first step is to store material that requires transfer style image into file folder of style transfer and file folder of content image, and adjust parameter setting for transfer. Such parameters are (1) content image weight. (2) style image weight. (3) num-base-channels. The second step is to execute program calculation so that the program can find the corresponding folders and images. Then the pre-trained neural network model can be imported. Each calculation takes about one and half days, and 170 style transfer images are calculated in one operation.

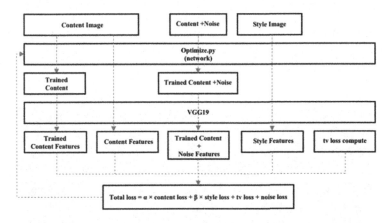

Fig. 2. Model framework of style transfer video in this study.

4 Results

This study uses the above network framework as the basis for research style transfer, adjusts parameter values before calculation via manual entry. The overall results are as follows:

4.1 Image Style Transfer-Control Weight Proportion

Based on the original style image of image content to proceed with different ratio α/β calculations. First fix the content image, then change the style image weight. Set the content image weight to 7.5, and set the style weight values to 75, 120, and 200 respectively. The output result is shown in Fig. 3. When the content image weight is controlled, and the style image weight is 75, the calculation result is closer to the content image. When the style image weight is 120, the calculated image has the best effect. It not only can create a new style, but also retain the characteristics of the original image. Yet continue to increase the style weight, the output results are closer to the style image.

Fig. 3. Images produced by various style weights.

4.2 Image Style Transfer - Control Weight Ratio

First, fix the weight ratio of content image and style image to 0.15. Then gradually enlarge Style-weight value to 1,000, 10,000, and 100,000. The output results are shown in Fig. 4. It is discovered as style weight becomes larger than 10,000, a thin film color effect appears. When the weight value continues to increase, the effect becomes more prominent.

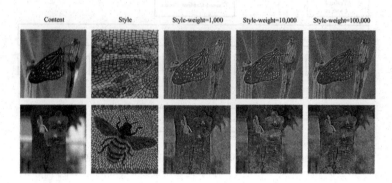

Fig. 4. When content and style weight ratio freezes, different style weights vary and produce such images [7, 20].

4.3   Image Style Transfer - Control Style Image Size

Fix the content image, and change the style image. Calculate respectively 1024 × 638, 512 × 319, and 410 × 256. The output result is shown in Fig. 5. When the style mode image is 1024 × 638, its content image weight becomes more prominent. At 512 × 319, neither content nor style image feature stands out. Adjust the size to 410 × 256, and the content mode size approaches the same, the original style feature becomes even more prominent.

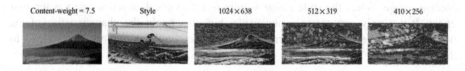

Fig. 5. Images produced by various styles and sizes.

4.4   Image Style Transfer - Control Color Produced by Filter

Fix the content image and style image weights, and adjust the num-base-channels (nbc) values respectively from 2^0 to 2^7. The output result is shown in Fig. 6. Control color produced by filter. When the nbc value is 1, 2 and 4, the color is more monotonous in display. When the nbc value is 8 and 16, the displayed color is richer. But when the nbc value is 32 or more, the color no longer changes according to the increased value (Fig. 6).

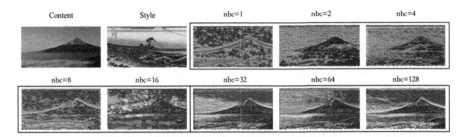

Fig. 6. Images produced by various nbc changes.

4.5   Image Style Transfer - Control Degrees of Free Space in Style Image

Fix the content image, and different proportions of free space, 25%, 40%, and 50%, are left on the original style images. The output results are shown in Fig. 7. When the free space rate is bigger than 50%, outline of the output image is less clear. At 40%, the style features gradually become prominent, and the image outline gradually stands out. When the free space on style image is appropriately at 25%, the image style is trained. The image outline becomes the most obvious and can be trained with higher texture effect (Fig. 7).

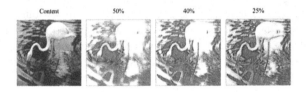

Fig. 7. Images produced by various degrees of free space in image styles [2].

4.6   Style Transfer Applied on Web Page Result

The style transfer of this study not only initiates the original code on GitHub, but develops supporting online webpage AI Attraction Page Fig. 8, Windows version, Android platform and Intel NCS. On top of the original static style transfer, the dynamic video style transfer can also be implemented. The real-time dynamic image shows immediate outcome after style transfer (Fig. 8).

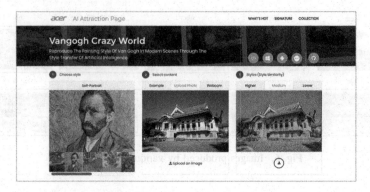

Fig. 8. Style transfer applied on webpage image display [1].

5   Research Conclusion and Discussion

This study discovers when the content image weight changes to 7.5 and the style image weight changes to 120, the calculated image has the best transfer effect, which can not only create a new style but also retain the original image characteristics. As to texture effect, fix the content image and style image weight ratio and increase the style image weight value to more than 10,000, it can show a thin film color effect with texture of saturation and transparency. When the size of the style image and the content image are close to each other, the transfer style effect becomes more obvious. For color, when there are 32 filters, the extracted color and style are displayed in the most appropriate proportion and state. As to quality, keep around 25% free space in style image can train with better texture quality. It provides reference for set value in future style transfer research.

References

1. Acer AI Attraction Page. https://acerwebai.github.io/VangoghCrazyWorld-Web/. Accessed 23 Jan 2019
2. Taipei Zoo-Flamingo. http://bitvoice.blogspot.com/2012/03/blog-post_2189.html. Accessed 23 Jan 2019
3. Chen, D., Liao, J., Yuan, L., Yu, N., Hua, G.: Coherent online video style transfer. In: Proceedings of the IEEE International Conference on Computer Vision, pp. 1105–1114 (2017)
4. Chen, J.C.-H.: Opens the gates of aesthetics from the visual form. Pulse Educ. (2), b1–b21 (2015). Opening aesthetics from the visual form. Educ. Pulse (2), pp. 1–21 (2015)
5. Dumoulin, V., Shlens, J., Kudlur, M.: A learned representation for artistic style. arXiv preprint arXiv:1610.07629 (2016)
6. Elad, M., Milanfar, P.: Style transfer via texture synthesis. IEEE Trans. Image Process. **26** (5), 2338–2351 (2017)
7. Wharf Walk. http://www.emmabiggsmosaic.net/03_work/01_public_art.html. Accessed 23 Jan 2019

8. Gatys, L.A., Ecker, A.S., Bethge, M.: A neural algorithm of artistic style. arXiv preprint arXiv:1508.06576 (2015)
9. Image style transfer using convolutional neural networks. In: Proceedings of the IEEE Conference on Computer Vision and Pattern Recognition, pp. 2414–2423 (2016)
10. Girshick, R.: Fast r-cnn. In: Proceedings of the IEEE international conference on computer vision, pp. 1440–1448 (2015)
11. Guo, X., Qian, Y., Li, L., Asano, A.: Assessment model for perceived visual complexity of painting images. Knowl. Based Systems **159**, 110–119 (2018)
12. Hertzmann, A., Jacobs, C.E., Oliver, N., Curless, B., Salesin, D.H.: Image analogies. In: Proceedings of the 28th Annual Conference on Computer Graphics and Interactive Techniques, pp. 327–340. ACM (2001)
13. Jacobsen, T.: Bridging the arts and sciences: a framework for the psychology of aesthetics (2006)
14. Jing, Y., Yang, Y., Feng, Z., Ye, J., Yu, Y., Song, M.: Neural style transfer: a review. IEEE Trans. Vis. Comput. Graph. p. 1 (2019)
15. Johnson, C.R., et al.: Image processing for artist identification. IEEE Sig. Process. Mag. **25** (4), 37–48 (2008)
16. Johnson, J., Alahi, A., Fei-Fei, L.: Perceptual losses for real-time style transfer and super-resolution. In: Leibe, B., Matas, J., Sebe, N., Welling, M. (eds.) ECCV 2016. LNCS, vol. 9906, pp. 694–711. Springer, Cham (2016). https://doi.org/10.1007/978-3-319-46475-6_43
17. Lawrence, S., Giles, C.L., Tsoi, A.C., Back, A.D.: Face recognition: a convolutional neural-network approach. IEEE Trans. Neural Networks **8**(1), 98–113 (1997)
18. LeCun, Y.: Generalization and network design strategies. In: Connectionism in Perspective. Citeseer (1989)
19. LeCun, Y., et al.: Backpropagation applied to handwritten zip code recognition. Neural Comput. **1**(4), 541–551 (1989)
20. Ready Mades. http://www.maggyhowarth.co.uk/readymades.html. Accessed 16 Jan 2019
21. Ruder, M., Dosovitskiy, A., Brox, T.: Artistic style transfer for videos. In: Rosenhahn, B., Andres, B. (eds.) GCPR 2016. LNCS, vol. 9796, pp. 26–36. Springer, Cham (2016). https://doi.org/10.1007/978-3-319-45886-1_3
22. Artistic style transfer for videos and spherical images. Int. J. Comput. Vis. **126**(11), 1199–1219 (2018)
23. Ulyanov, D., Lebedev, V., Vedaldi, A., Lempitsky, V.S.: Texture networks: feed-forward synthesis of textures and stylized images. In: ICML, vol. 1, p. 4 (2016)

Automatic Spoken Language Identification Using Emotional Speech

Panikos Heracleous[1]($\boxtimes$), Akio Yoneyama[1], Kohichi Takai[1,2],
and Keiji Yasuda[1,2]

[1] KDDI Research, Inc., Fujimino, Japan
{pa-heracleous,yoneyama}@kddi-research.jp
[2] Nara Institute of Science and Technology, Ikoma, Japan
takai.koichi.tc1@is.naist.jp, ke-yasuda@dsc.naist.jp

Abstract. Spoken language identification (LID) is the process of automatically recognizing the language from the uttered speech of an unknown speaker. Automatic recognition of language spoken is of vital importance in human-computer interaction and its applications. It can be applied in speech-to-speech translation systems, at call centers to reroute incoming calls to native speaker operators, and in speaker diarization in multilingual environments. The majority of studies which utilized LID systems focused solely on the use of neutral (i.e., normal) speech. However, in real applications and for comprehensive research investigations, the use of emotional speech in LID is crucial. The current study aims at investigating the effectiveness and performance of a deep neural networks (DNNs) based LID system when emotional speech is used.

Keywords: Spoken language identification · Emotional speech · Deep neural networks

1 Introduction

Several studies have investigated spoken language identification. The approaches presented are categorized based on the features they employ. Language identification systems are categorized as the acoustic-phonetic approach, the phonotactic approach, the prosodic approach, and the lexical approach. In phonotactic systems [11], sequences of recognized phonemes obtained from phone recognizers are modeled. In acoustic modeling based systems, however, each recognized language is modeled by using different features. Although significant improvements in LID have been achieved using phonotactic-based approaches, most state-of-the-art systems rely on acoustic modeling [4,5,8–10,12,14,16].

In the current study, a DNN-based [7] approach is introduced capable of classifying emotional speech produced in English, German, and Japanese languages. The system was evaluated and the results obtained were compared with those achieved when neutral speech was applied.

© Springer Nature Switzerland AG 2020
C. Stephanidis and M. Antona (Eds.): HCII 2020, CCIS 1224, pp. 650–654, 2020.
https://doi.org/10.1007/978-3-030-50726-8_84

2   Methods

2.1   Speech Corpora

Three languages were considered namely, English, German, and Japanese. The English IEMOCAP database [3] is an acted, multimodal, and multi-speaker database collected at the SAIL lab of the University of Southern California and contains 12 h of audiovisual data produced by ten actors. Specifically, the IEMOCAP database includes video, speech, motion capture of the face, and text transcriptions. The database consists of dyadic sessions where actors performed improvisations or scripted scenarios specifically selected to elicit emotional expression. The IEMOCAP database is annotated by multiple annotators into the several categorical labels of anger, happiness, sadness, neutrality, as well as the dimensional labels of valence, activation, and dominance. In the current study, categorical labels were used to classify the emotional states of neutral, happy, angry, and sad. For training, 1000 instances were used, and 200 instances were used for testing.

The German database used was the Berlin Emo-DB database [2], which includes seven emotional states: anger, boredom, disgust, anxiety, happiness, sadness, and neutral speech. For training, 280 instances were used, and 152 instances were used for testing.

Four professional female actors simulated Japanese emotional speech. These comprised neutral, happy, angry, and sad emotional states. Fifty-one utterances for each emotion was produced by each speaker. In total, 512 utterances were used for training, and 256 utterances were used for testing. The remaining utterances were excluded due to poor speech quality.

2.2   Feature Extraction

In speaker recognition, Gaussian supervectors are widely used as features. The supervectors are constructed by concatenating the means of adapted Gaussian mixture models (GMMs). Although, significant improvements have been obtained using Gaussian supervectors, the main disadvantage of GMM supervectors is the high dimensionality, which imposes high computation and memory costs.

To overcome these problems, the i-vector paradigm [6] was introduced. The i-vectors represent the whole utterance with a small number of factors explaining the variability of speaker, channel, and language. An input utterance can be modeled as follows:

$$M = m + Tw \tag{1}$$

where M is the language-dependent supervector, m is the language-independent supervector, T is the total variability matrix, and w is the i-vector. Both the total variability matrix and language-independent supervector are estimated from the complete set of the training data.

In automatic speech recognition, speaker recognition, emotion recognition, and language identification, mel-frequency cepstral coefficients (MFCCs) [13] are among the most popular and most widely used acoustic features. Therefore, this study similarly used 12 MFCCs concatenated with shifted delta cepstral (SDC) coefficients [1,15] to form feature vectors of length 112 in modeling the languages and emotions being identified. The MFCC features were extracted every 10 ms using a window length of 20 ms. The extracted acoustic features were used to construct the i-vectors of dimension 100 used in emotion and spoken language identification modeling and classification.

2.3   Classification Methods

The classification experiments were based on DNNs. The DNN is an important method in machine learning that has been applied in many areas. A DNN is a feed-forward neural network with many (i.e., more than one) hidden layers. The main advantage of DNNs compared with shallow networks is the better feature expression and the ability to perform complex mapping. Deep learning explains several of the most recent breakthroughs in computer vision, speech recognition, and agents that achieved human-level performance in several games, such as Go and Poker. The DNN architecture used in the current experiment is a standard fully connected feedforward network with four hidden layers with 64 units followed by a Softmax layer for classification. All neurons employed the ReLU activation function, and 15% dropout was used to regularize the network. Stochastic Gradient Descent with Nestrov initialization and 0.9 momentum was employed for training (learningrate $= 0.01$). Data were presented to the network in 500 epochs without early stopping.

3   Results

Table 1 shows the results obtained when using normal speech compared with using emotional speech. As is shown, when using normal speech a 97.5% average recall was achieved. This results is very promising and shows the effectiveness of using the proposed method for spoken language identification. Regarding the individual recalls, the English language shows perfect identification, with slightly lower recalls in the case of German and Japanese languages.

Table 1. Spoken language identification recalls [%] using English, German, and Japanese speech data.

Speech data	Language			
	English	German	Japanese	Average
Normal	100.0	95.5	97.0	97.5
Emotional	97.4	87.6	96.5	93.8

In the case of using emotional speech, the average recall was 93.8%. This rate is lower compared to normal speech. However, the recalls are still comparable and they show that no additional difficulties occurred in LID when using emotional speech. By performing the t-test, the two-tailed P value was 0.3410. By conventional criteria, this difference is considered to be not statistically significant.

4   Conclusions

The current study presented a method for automatic language identification using emotional speech. The results obtained were very promising and showed that when using emotional speech, spoken language identification does not face any additional difficulties compared to normal speech. Specifically, for language identification using English, German, and Japanese speech, the average recall was 93.8%, slightly lower than the average recall when using normal speech. However, the recalls were closely comparable and the differences between normal and emotional recalls were not statistically significant. Currently, experiments using a larger number of languages are in progress.

References

1. Bielefeld, B.: Language identification using shifted delta cepstrum. In: Fourteenth Annual Speech Research Symposium (1994)
2. Burkhardt, F., Paeschke, A., Rolfes, M., Sendlmeier, W., Weiss, B.: A database of German emotional speech. In: Proceedings of the Interspeech, pp. 1517–1520 (2005)
3. Busso, C., et al.: IEMOCAP: interactive emotional dyadic motion capture database. Lang. Resour. Eval. **42**, 335–359 (2008). https://doi.org/10.1007/s10579-008-9076-6
4. Cole, R., Inouye, J., Muthusamy, Y., Gopalakrishnan, M.: Language identification with neural networks: a feasibility study. In: Proceedings of IEEE Pacific Rim Conference, pp. 525–529 (1989)
5. Dehak, N., Torres-Carrasquillo, P.A., Reynolds, D., Dehak, R.: Language recognition via ivectors and dimensionality reduction. In: Proceedings of Interspeech, pp. 857–860 (2011)
6. Dehak, N., Kenny, P.J., Dehak, R., Dumouchel, P., Ouellet, P.: Front-end factor analysis for speaker verification. IEEE Trans. Audio Speech Lang. Process. **19**(4), 788–798 (2011)
7. Hinton, G., et al.: Deep neural networks for acoustic modeling in speech recognition: the shared views of four research groups. IEEE Signal Process. Mag. **29**(6), 82–97 (2012)
8. Jiang, B., Song, Y., Wei, S., Liu, J.H., McLoughlin, I.V., Dai, L.R.: Deep bottleneck features for spoken language identification. PLoS One **9**(7), 1–11 (2010)
9. Lopez-Moreno, I., Gonzalez-Dominguez, J., Plchot, O., Martinez, D., Gonzalez-Rodriguez, J., Moreno, P.: Automatic language identification using deep neural networks. In: Proceedings of ICASSP, pp. 5337–5341 (2014)
10. Leena, M., Rao, K.S., Yegnanarayana, B.: Neural network classifiers for language identification using phonotactic and prosodic features. In: Proceedings of Intelligent Sensing and Information Processing, pp. 404–408 (2005)
11. Li, H., Ma, B., Lee, K.A.: Spoken language recognition: from fundamentals to practice. Proc. IEEE **101**(5), 1136–1159 (2013)
12. Montavon, G.: Deep learning for spoken language identification. In: NIPS workshop on Deep Learning for Speech Recognition and Related Applications (2009)
13. Sahidullah, M., Saha, G.: Design, analysis and experimental evaluation of block based transformation in MFCC computation for speaker recognition. Speech Commun. **54**(4), 543–565 (2012). https://doi.org/10.1016/j.specom.2011.11.004

14. Shen, P., Lu, X., Liu, L., Kawai, H.: Local fisher discriminant analysis for spoken language identification. In: Proceedings of ICASSP, pp. 5825–5829 (2016)
15. Torres-Carrasquillo, P., Singer, E., Kohler, M.A., Greene, R.J., Reynolds, D.A., Deller Jr., J.D.: Approaches to language identification using gaussian mixture models and shifted delta cepstral features. In: Proceedings of ICSLP2002-INTERSPEECH2002, pp. 16–20 (2002)
16. Zazo, R., Lozano-Diez, A., Gonzalez-Dominguez, J., Toledano, D.T., Gonzalez-Rodriguez, J.: Language identification in short utterances using long short-term memory (LSTM) recurrent neural networks. PLoS One **11**(1), e0146917 (2016)

Software Log Anomaly Detection Through One Class Clustering of Transformer Encoder Representation

Rin Hirakawa[1], Keitaro Tominaga[2], and Yoshihisa Nakatoh[1(✉)]

[1] Kyushu Institute of Technology, 1-1 Sensuicho, Tobata Ward, Kitakyushu City, Fukuoka Prefecture, Japan
nakatoh@ecs.kyutech.ac.jp
[2] Panasonic System Design Co., Ltd., 3-1-9, Shinyokohama, Kohoku-ku, Yokohama City 222-0033, Japan
tominaga.keitaro@jp.panasonic.com

Abstract. For smart devices such as smartphones and tablets, developing new software using open source software (OSS) is becoming mainstream. While OSS-based development can greatly increase project productivity, it is more difficult to identify the cause of software defects. In this paper, we propose a deep learning model that performs unsupervised learning based on the log data accumulated in the project and calculates the degree of abnormality per line for newly given logs. The proposed method is evaluated using open supercomputer system log data, Blue Gene/L, and the accuracy of the proposed method is compared with the conventional log anomaly detection method using LSTM AutoEncoder. As a result of the comparative experiment, it was found that the proposed method performed better than the conventional method in the two scores of AUROC and F1 Score at the cutoff point.

Keywords: Anomaly detection · Software log · Transformer · Unsupervised learning

1 Introduction

In software development for smart devices such as smartphones and tablets, it is necessary to implement abundant functions in a short period of time and release/update them to meet the needs of consumers. Since Open Source Software (OSS) can significantly reduce the time required for development and increase the reusability of programs, software development using these is becoming a global trend. On the other hand, the scale of software development using OSS is enormous, making it more difficult to identify the cause when a problem occurs. Engineers analyzing such complex bugs check a huge log of mixed output from various applications, however, the level of proficiency can make a huge difference in the speed of analysis.

Our ultimate goal is to create a GUI tool that visualizes statistical information on log data and possible causes of defects, so that anyone can analyze bugs smoothly. In this paper, we propose a method to calculate the degree of abnormality for each row of newly given log data based on the log data accumulated in the project. As a result,

© Springer Nature Switzerland AG 2020
C. Stephanidis and M. Antona (Eds.): HCII 2020, CCIS 1224, pp. 655–661, 2020.
https://doi.org/10.1007/978-3-030-50726-8_85

when performing defect analysis, it is possible to prioritize checking from the line that shows a high degree of abnormality, and it is expected that the analysis time will be shortened.

2 Proposed Method

Our debugging support tool is intended to provide users with two levels of anomaly scores for the current log data. In the first method, a single log data is input in a streaming format, and the time series abnormalities of each row are calculated. In the second method, we treat each line of the log message as a separate input and calculates the degree of anomalies when compared to the entire log data accumulated so far in the project. The first method has been discussed in our past paper [1], and this paper elaborates on the second method.

2.1 Related Works

When detecting abnormalities in log data, it is common to treat log messages as time-series data. Because it is difficult to handle log messages in the same way as natural language, messages can be divided into fixed phrase parts (keys) and embedded values (parameters) so that time series models such as LSTM can learn them [2]. This method may not be able to determine anomaly score efficiently if the training data does not cover all possible normal execution patterns. Our proposed method detects anomalies based on the meaning of sentences by converting log messages into features (distributed expressions) instead of using log key time-series patterns.

2.2 Model Structure

In the proposed model, each line of the log is input to a trained Transformer [3] with fixed weights to obtain the encoder representation (Fig. 1). Before being input to Transformer, log messages are broken down into units called subwords by the morphological analyzer WordPiece [4] for neural language models. The subwords are transformed into contextual distributed representations by the Transformer encoder, and we use mean of them as features representing the entire sentence.

The method for calculating the anomaly score in our model is inspired by One Class Neural Networks [5]. The distributed representation combined in the previous block is input to the three-layer Feed Forward Neural Networks (FFNN), which is finally converted to a scalar value that represents the distance from the origin. One-class clustering is performed based on the distance, and abnormal lines are detected by thresholding the score of each data as an abnormal score.

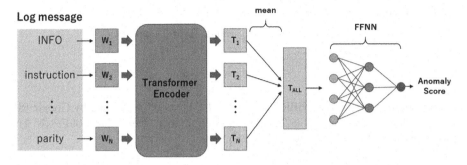

Fig. 1. Structure of proposed log anomaly calculation model.

3 Experiment

In this chapter, we will use open log datasets to measure performance in anomaly detection and verify the effectiveness of the proposed method.

3.1 Datasets and Setup

BGL Datasets. BGL [6] is an open dataset of logs collected from the BlueGene/L supercomputer system at Lawrence Livermore National Labs (LLNL) in Livermore, California. The log contains alert and non-alert messages identified by tags. This dataset is provided by the Loghub repository [7], a large collection of system log datasets for AI-powered log analysis.

Setup. Only the message part of the log about KERNEL of the data is extracted and formatted into a form suitable for the proposed method. Duplicate messages are removed and the entire data set is split for training, testing and validation in a 6:2:2 ratio. Details of the data are shown in Table 1.

Table 1. Breakdown of the number of normal/abnormal data.

	Training	Test	Validation
Normal	170549	56833	57361
Anomaly	1534	529	508

3.2 Model Condition

The anomaly detection accuracy of the proposed method is compared with the conventional anomaly detection method using LSTM AutoEncoder. This section details the experimental conditions for each model.

Table 2. Architecture of feed forward neural networks (Proposed method).

Input (feature dimension)	Hidden layer	Output layer
768	72	1

Proposed Method. We use BERT-Base (L = 12, H = 768, published by Google [8]) as a Transformer encoder. Table 2 shows the configuration of each layer of FFNN. The loss function of FFNN is shown below (Eq. 1).

$$r + \frac{1}{v} \cdot \frac{1}{N} \sum_{n=1}^{N} \max(0, \widehat{y}_n(w, V) - r) \tag{1}$$

where, w and V are the weights between the hidden layer and the output layer and between the input layer and the hidden layer of the FFNN, respectively. Also, $\widehat{y}_n(w, V)$ indicates the final output of FFNN obtained by applying the sigmoid activation function. The values of w and V are updated repeatedly using a backpropagation algorithm on a mini-batch of training data (batch size N). The value of r is updated as v th quantile of $\widehat{y}_n(w, V)$ when all training data is input to FFNN whose weight is frozen at the end of the epoch. The optimal value of v is determined using the open source hyperparameter auto-optimization framework Optuna [9]. Table 3 shows the details of the hyperparameters determined using Optuna.

Table 3. Hyperparameters of proposed method

Parameter	Value	Optimized by Optuna
v	2.58e−03	✓
Learning rate	3.19e−05	✓
Epoch	20	✓
Batch size	32	
Max sequence length	128	

LSTM AutoEncoder. To compare the accuracy, we use a conventional LSTM AutoEncoder in this experiment. The AutoEncoder implementation is based on the text-autoencoder repository [10] and its original paper [11]. WordPiece is used for the morphological analyzer as in the proposed method, and the model is trained using only the normal training data in Table 1. The actual anomaly detection uses exactly the same test data as the proposed method. We use the cross-entropy error obtained in entering the log message as a scalar value equivalent to the anomaly score of our proposed method. Table 4 shows the parameters used when training text-autoencoder models.

3.3   Evaluation

In the evaluation stage, the accuracy of anomaly detection on test data is verified using each model after training.

Each model is compared using two types of scores: AUROC and F1 scores. AUROC is an evaluation score that indicates how good the accuracy of the classification model is across the entire threshold. When determining the F1 score, we use a threshold at the cut-off point where the point at which the sensitivity – (1 – specificity) value is highest in the ROC curve.

Table 4. Hyperparameters of LSTM AutoEncoder.

Parameter	Value
Model type	Denoising auto-encoder
Learning rate	5e−4
Epoch	2
Batch size	32
Max sequence length	128
Embedding dimension	512
Hidden state dimension	128
Number of layer	1

4   Results and Discussion

Table 5 shows the AUROC value of each model calculated using the test data. Tables 6 and 7 show the F1 score and the other scores used when calculating it for the proposed method and LSTM AutoEncoder, respectively.

Table 5. AUROC of each models.

Proposed method	LSTM AutoEncoder
0.823	0.786

Table 6. F1-score of proposed method.

		Precision	Recall	F1-score	Support
Class	Normal	1.00	0.82	0.90	56833
	Anomaly	0.04	0.82	0.08	529
Accuracy				0.82	57362
Macro Avg.		0.52	0.82	0.49	
Weighted Avg.		0.99	0.82	0.89	

Table 7. F1-score of LSTM AutoEncoder.

		Precision	Recall	F1-score	Support
Class	Normal	1.00	0.76	0.86	56833
	Anomaly	0.03	0.75	0.05	529
Accuracy				0.76	57362
Macro Avg.		0.51	0.75	0.46	
Weighted Avg.		0.99	0.76	0.85	

These results are the scores for the parameters that each model performs best, and show that the proposed method outperforms the LSTM AutoEncoder in both AUROC and F1 scores. Note that the performance of the proposed method is very sensitive to one of the hyperparameters, v, and the learning rate, and the same conditions may not be optimal when the size of the dataset changes. As a future task, it is necessary to investigate strategies for stable learning on the updated data set.

5   Conclusion

In this paper, we proposed a deep learning model that calculates an abnormal score for each line of log data by unsupervised learning. In the evaluation of anomaly detection accuracy using the open log data set BGL, it was found that the proposed method can detect anomalous rows more efficiently than the conventional LSTM AutoEncoder.

The degree of abnormality calculated by the proposed method indicates the abnormality in the accumulated log. This can be applied to construction for GUI that helps developers to easily find abnormal lines in the large amount of logs in a short time.

In the future, we will evaluate how much more efficient the debugging work will be when the developer uses a debugging support tool that reflects the anomaly score calculated by the proposed method.

References

1. Hirakawa, R., Tominaga, K., Nakatoh, Y.: Study on real-time log anomaly detection method using HTM algorithm. In: Proceedings of the Institute of Electronics. Information and Communication Engineers, Society Conference, vol. 2019, p. 74 (2019)
2. Du, M., Li, F., Zheng, G., Srikumar, V.: DeepLog: anomaly detection and diagnosis from system logs through deep learning, pp. 1285–1298 (2017). https://doi.org/10.1145/3133956.3134015
3. Devlin, J., Chang, M.-W., Lee, K., Toutanova, K.: BERT: pre-training of deep bidirectional transformers for language understanding. In: NAACL-HLT (2018)
4. Wu, Y. et al.: Google's neural machine translation system: bridging the gap between human and machine translation (2016)
5. Chalapathy, R., Menon, A., Chawla, S.: Anomaly detection using one-class neural networks (2018)

6. Oliner, A.J., Stearley, J.: What supercomputers say: a study of five system logs. In: Proceedings of IEEE/IFIP International Conference on Dependable Systems and Networks (DSN) (2007)
7. Zhu, J., et al.: Tools and benchmarks for automated log parsing. In: International Conference on Software Engineering (ICSE) (2019)
8. Bert (Github). https://github.com/google-research/bert. Accessed 14 Mar 2020
9. Optuna (Github). https://github.com/optuna/optuna. Accessed 15 Mar 2020
10. text-autoencoders (Github). https://github.com/shentianxiao/text-autoencoders. Accessed 15 Mar 2020
11. Shen, T., Mueller, J., Barzilay, R., Jaakkola, T.: Educating text autoencoders: latent representation guidance via denoising. arXiv preprint arXiv:1905.12777 (2019)

An AI-Based Approach to Automatic Waste Sorting

Elio Strollo[1], Giuseppe Sansonetti[2(✉)], Marta Cialdea Mayer[2],
Carla Limongelli[2], and Alessandro Micarelli[2]

[1] IES s.r.l., Via Amedeo Nazzari, 3, 00042 Anzio, RM, Italy
elio.strollo@iessrl.it
[2] Department of Engineering, Roma Tre University,
Via della Vasca Navale, 79, 00146 Rome, Italy
{gsansone,ailab}@dia.uniroma3.it

Abstract. One of the major problems facing our cities is the disposal
of the huge amount of waste produced every day. A possible solution is
represented by recycling. In this article, we propose a system for automatic recognition and extraction of materials from the unsorted waste,
which takes advantage of Computer Vision and Machine Learning techniques. The system can classify the material of incoming objects and
grasp, and insert them into proper bins. For the material classification
phase, the system analyzes the information captured by a Near-Infrared
(NIR) camera and an RGB camera. Experimental tests performed on
real-world datasets show encouraging accuracy values.

Keywords: Machine Learning · Computer vision · Material
classification

1 Introduction and Background

Every year, our society dumps 2.12 billion tons of waste to be disposed of[1]. One
of the most promising solutions is recycling, for which there are high expectations, but also significant critical issues. An American waste treatment company
reported that over 25% of all the recycling it receives is so contaminated that
it must be sent directly to landfills[2]. It, therefore, becomes essential to design
and implement automatic systems capable of assisting, if not replacing, human
employees in the disposal of waste.

In literature, there are many research projects on image classification based
on Machine Learning [1] and Computer Vision [3] techniques. However, there
are a few works that specifically concern waste classification. One of them is a

---

[1] https://www.theworldcounts.com/challenges/planet-earth/state-of-the-planet/
world-waste-facts (Accessed: 31/03/2020).
[2] https://www.nytimes.com/2018/05/29/climate/recycling-landfills-plastic-papers.
html (Accessed: 31/03/2020).

© Springer Nature Switzerland AG 2020
C. Stephanidis and M. Antona (Eds.): HCII 2020, CCIS 1224, pp. 662–669, 2020.
https://doi.org/10.1007/978-3-030-50726-8_86

project by Lulea University of Technology [21] focused on recycling metal waste using a mechanical identifier. The system makes use of chemical and mechanical methodologies (e.g., probing) to identify the chemical contents and the actual separation. Another waste project is a smartphone application designed to automatically segment a set of waste into one image [12]. Its goal is to allow citizens to track and report waste in their neighborhoods [6,17]. In the 2016 TechCrunch Disrupt Hackathon, a team created *Auto-Trash*[3], an automatic sorting system able to distinguish between compost and recycling, which is simpler than having different classes of materials to recognize. The system presented in [9] for the image-based classification of materials was created using a database of materials extracted from the Flickr[4] database, the well-known image sharing service. Authors exploited descriptors such as the Scale-Invariant Feature Transform (SIFT) [10], color, texture, and shape, and classified the images through a Bayesian classifier. Finally, an interesting approach based on Computer Vision and Machine Learning algorithms is presented in [19]. Its purpose is to classify garbage into one of six possible classes of objects.

This paper is structured as follows. The automatic waste sorting system is described in Sect. 2. Section 3 illustrates all the experimental evaluation carried out to evaluate the system performance on real-world datasets. More precisely, we report and discuss the results of three different tests: the first experimental session based on Near-Infrared (NIR) images, the second on RGB images, the third on the integration of NIR and RGB images. Finally, in Sect. 4 we draw our conclusions and outline some possible future developments for the proposed system.

2   System

The proposed automatic waste sorting system consists of a conveyor belt, two cameras, and a mechanical arm equipped with a suction cup. It can recognize the material of which the objects are composed, grasp and sort them appropriately, inserting them into suitable containers. For the material classification process, the system leverages Computer Vision [11] and Machine Learning [5] techniques. Specifically, the classifier receives input from two different types of sensors: a NIR camera (which returns 252 infrared sampling channels) and an RGB camera (which instead operates in the visible spectrum). Figure 1 shows the system.

3   Experimental Evaluation

In this section, we describe the experimental tests performed to assess the performance of the proposed approach. In particular, we report the results of three different tests according to the sensor used as a signal source.

---

[3] https://techcrunch.com/2016/09/13/auto-trash-sorts-garbage-automatically-at-the-techcrunch-disrupt-hackathon/ (Accessed: 31/03/2020).

[4] https://www.flickr.com/ (Accessed: 31/03/2020).

Fig. 1. The automatic waste sorting system. The RGB (right) and NIR (left) cameras are highlighted in red, the mechanical arm in green and the objects to be sorted in blue. (Color figure online)

3.1   Test 1: NIR Images

In the first experimental session, we only employ the information coming from the NIR camera, which captures a part of the electromagnetic spectrum, namely, the infrared spectrum, invisible to normal RGB cameras. In particular, we consider the one between 950 nm and 1700 nm, just above the visible spectrum, which is called Near-Infrared (NIR) space. This information is subjected to a hyperspectral analysis, after which the reflectance information is extracted. It is then used as a feature to classify the materials of the objects placed on the conveyor belt. Graphically reporting the reflectance response related to different materials, it can be observed how similar materials tend to have similar graphs. Figure 2 shows the graph that represents the reflectance response of an object consisting of High-Density PolyEthylene (HDPE), one of the most common types of plastic. Therefore, there is a direct relationship between the

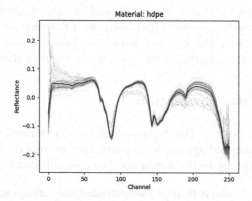

Fig. 2. Reflectance response of an object made of High-Density PolyEthylene (HDPE).

composition of a material and its reflectance response. This observation allows us to use reflectance as a feature in the training and testing phase of a classifier. In order to classify materials through the NIR spectrum, a database containing approximately 245,000 records was used for the training phase (approximately 35,000 per class), while a 35,000 record database was employed for the test phase (5,000 spectra for each class). Specifically, we considered the following classes:

- 0 = ALUMINUM
- 1 = PET
- 2 = HDPE
- 3 = PP
- 4 = PS
- 5 = LDPE
- 6 = PVC

Each database record contained 253 values: the first 252 values represent the normalized NIR spectrum of the material, while the last value represents the material class (0–6). Therefore, datasets were represented as $245,000 \times 253$ matrices. Various classifiers were tested to verify which one offered the best performance, so efforts were made to maximize the prediction accuracy while keeping in mind the computational time needed to create the model. This trade-off was made thinking that in a real context 1% more accuracy after long extra hours of computation is neither efficient nor convenient. For the classification task, k-Nearest Neighbor (k-NN) algorithm, naïve Bayes classifier (NBC), and multilayer neural network (MLP) were tested. We also experimented with support vector machine (SVM), implementing different kernels: linear, polynomial, radial basis function (RBF), and linear model regularized through stochastic gradient descent (SGD). The various parameters were chosen considering the trade-off previously described. Experimental tests were performed on a machine with CPU AMD Ryzen 3700X (8 cores, 16 threads, 3.6GHz) and RAM 32GB DDR4 3600MHz. To sum up, a database consisting of seven different types of materials was used for this analysis. From the experimental results shown in Table 1, we can observe that the analysis of the NIR spectrum was an excellent method for classifying materials. They were classified with the highest accuracy using the k-nearest neighbors (k-NN) algorithm with the lowest execution time. This result is valid for samples of the tested database, while we may have different results with other databases.

3.2   Test 2: RGB Images

In the second experimental session, we aimed to classify materials based only on the information captured by the RGB camera. For such tests, we used two different classifiers:

- Support Vector Machine (SVM)
- Convolutional Neural Network (CNN)

Table 1. Results of the first experimental session.

Classifier	Parameters	Learning time	Accuracy
k-NN	$k = 5$	2 s	100%
NBC	default	0.7 s	69.5%
MLP	$\lambda = 1e^{-2}$ max_iter $= 1000$	138 s	98.6%
SVM	kernel $=$ linear $C = 25e^{-3}$	1466 s	92.8%
SVM	kernel $=$ polinomial $\gamma = 5$	331 s	99.4%
SVM	kernel $=$ RBF $\gamma = 2$	446 s	98.4%
SGD	$\lambda = 1e^{-6}$ max_iter $= 3000$	40 s	95.5%

The **support vector machine (SVM)** [20] is a supervised machine learning technique [14]. SVM revolves around the concept of *margin* defined by the sides of a hyperplane that separates two sets of data belonging to distinct classes. The goal is to maximize the margin, thus also maximizing the separation distance between the hyperplane and the instances on both sides. We experimented with different kernels, such as linear, polynomial, sigmoidal, but the best results were obtained with the RBF one. The C parameter of the SVM was set to 100. This parameter indicates in the SVM optimization procedure how much to avoid wrongly classifying each training example. The γ value was set to an intermediate value of 2 so as not to require too extreme or too small margins.

For our experimental tests, we also tried an 11-layer **convolutional neural network (CNN)** configuration, which recalls the Alexnet [8] architecture. We chose a slightly smaller network for computational constraints. CNN was trained as follows: 70% (training), 10% (validation), 20% (testing), an image size of 256×256, 60 epochs, a batch size of 32, a learning rate of 0.01. We did not use the same hyperparameters used by Alexnet due to the diversity of the task (ImageNet contains about 1.3 million images). We experimented with many hyperparameters and these were the values with which we obtained the best performance.

Tests were performed on a dataset of 700 RGB images (100 for each class) obtained through data augmentation techniques, performed on each image due to the small size of each class. These techniques included random image rotation, brightness control, translation, scaling, and shearing. These image transformations were also chosen to take into account the different orientations of the recycled material. We performed mean subtraction and normalization as well. The results obtained through the two different classifiers are shown in Table 2. As can be seen, the results achieved on RGB images were significantly lower than those on NIR images. This suggests that the application scenario is such that the images taken with the RGB camera are less *informative* than those captured by the NIR camera. It can also be noted that the best results were attained through CNN, as we expected. However, the performance in terms of accuracy was only slightly higher than that obtained through the SVMs, evidently due to the small size of the dataset.

Table 2. Results of the second experimental session.

Classifier	Parameters	Learning time	Accuracy
SVM	kernel = linear $C = 200$	758 s	62.9%
SVM	kernel = polynomial $\gamma = 3$	539 s	64.3%
SVM	kernel = RBF $C = 100$ $\gamma = 2$	597 s	69.8%
SVM	kernel = sigmoid $\gamma = 5$	842 s	59.1%
CNN	11-layer	1647 s	73.5%

3.3   Test 3: NIR Images + RGB Images

Although the previous experimental results were more than encouraging, especially those on NIR data, there were still materials for which classification was not so effective. For instance, this occurred for objects with high reflections (e.g., cardboard with parcel tape), which could deceive the classifier, or with black objects, which are all recognized by classifiers as aluminum compounds. To overcome such problems, we integrated the information from the NIR camera with the one from the RGB camera. For this purpose, we took inspiration from the algorithm proposed in [15], to which we refer for further details. In short, RGB and NIR images were analyzed based on their texture, color, and lightness, thus producing image features. Those features include the relationship between the intensity of materials in the NIR spectrum and the luma in the visible spectrum. After the extraction of the relevant features and the computation of the corresponding values, the materials of the objects to be recycled were classified using a Bayesian classifier. The experimental tests performed on our dataset confirmed the validity of the proposed approach. The system was able to correctly classify also the objects for which the classification through the information coming from only one of the two cameras (either NIR or RGB) had failed, virtually eliminating any possible classification error.

4   Conclusions

In this paper, we have described an automatic system able to classify the materials of which the objects are composed and to dispose of them appropriately. The image acquisition module is equipped with a NIR camera and an RGB camera. Generally speaking, the NIR information is enough to correctly classify the material. However, there may be cases where objects on the conveyor belt are not correctly classified and properly disposed of. To solve this problem, the system exploits an algorithm for integrating the information from the two different sensors, thus allowing for a correct classification even in the most critical cases.

Although the experimental results were encouraging, there are several possible future developments of the proposed system. Among these, for example, the hyperspectral analysis could be extended to further information related to the objects to be disposed of, such as absorbance. A label recognition module could also be included in the system to provide an additional contribution, where possible, to the material classification process. Finally, the system could be equipped with a decision support module [2,4,13] capable of exploiting alternative information [7,16,18] to assist the human operator in cases when the recycling facility is unable to correctly operate.

References

1. Biancalana, C., Gasparetti, F., Micarelli, A., Miola, A., Sansonetti, G.: Context-aware movie recommendation based on signal processing and machine learning. In: Proceedings of the 2nd Challenge on Context-Aware Movie Recommendation, CAMRa 2011, pp. 5–10. ACM, New York (2011)
2. Caldarelli, S., Feltoni Gurini, D., Micarelli, A., Sansonetti, G.: A signal-based approach to news recommendation. In: CEUR Workshop Proceedings, vol. 1618. CEUR-WS.org, Aachen (2016)
3. De Rosa, M.P., Micarelli, A., Sansonetti, G.: An integrated system for automatic face recognition. In: Bigun, J., Gustavsson, T. (eds.) SCIA 2003. LNCS, vol. 2749, pp. 140–147. Springer, Heidelberg (2003). https://doi.org/10.1007/3-540-45103-X_20
4. Feltoni Gurini, D., Gasparetti, F., Micarelli, A., Sansonetti, G.: iSCUR: interest and sentiment-based community detection for user recommendation on Twitter. In: Dimitrova, V., Kuflik, T., Chin, D., Ricci, F., Dolog, P., Houben, G.-J. (eds.) UMAP 2014. LNCS, vol. 8538, pp. 314–319. Springer, Cham (2014). https://doi.org/10.1007/978-3-319-08786-3_27
5. Feltoni Gurini, D., Gasparetti, F., Micarelli, A., Sansonetti, G.: Enhancing social recommendation with sentiment communities. In: Wang, J., et al. (eds.) WISE 2015. LNCS, vol. 9419, pp. 308–315. Springer, Cham (2015). https://doi.org/10.1007/978-3-319-26187-4_28
6. Fogli, A., Sansonetti, G.: Exploiting semantics for context-aware itinerary recommendation. Pers. Ubiquit. Comput. **23**(2), 215–231 (2019). https://doi.org/10.1007/s00779-018-01189-7
7. Gasparetti, F., Micarelli, A., Sansonetti, G.: Exploiting web browsing activities for user needs identification. In: International Conference on Computational Science and Computational Intelligence, vol. 2, pp. 86–89, March 2014
8. Krizhevsky, A., Sutskever, I., Hinton, G.E.: Imagenet classification with deep convolutional neural networks. In: Advances in Neural Information Processing Systems, vol. 25, pp. 1097–1105. Curran Associates, Inc. (2012)
9. Liu, C., Sharan, L., Adelson, E.H., Rosenholtz, R.: Exploring features in a Bayesian framework for material recognition. In: IEEE Computer Society Conference on Computer Vision and Pattern Recognition, pp. 239–246, June 2010
10. Lowe, D.G.: Object recognition from local scale-invariant features. In: Proceedings of the 7th International Conference on Computer Vision ICCV, Corfu, vol. 2, pp. 1150–1157. IEEE Computer Society, USA (1999)

11. Micarelli, A., Neri, A., Sansonetti, G.: A case-based approach to image recognition. In: Blanzieri, E., Portinale, L. (eds.) EWCBR 2000. LNCS, vol. 1898, pp. 443–454. Springer, Heidelberg (2000). https://doi.org/10.1007/3-540-44527-7_38

12. Mittal, G., Yagnik, K.B., Garg, M., Krishnan, N.C.: SpotGarbage: smartphone app to detect garbage using deep learning. In: Proceedings of the 2016 ACM International Joint Conference on Pervasive and Ubiquitous Computing, UbiComp 2016, pp. 940–945. Association for Computing Machinery, New York (2016)

13. Onori, M., Micarelli, A., Sansonetti, G.: A comparative analysis of personality-based music recommender systems. In: CEUR Workshop Proceedings, vol. 1680, pp. 55–59. CEUR-WS.org, Aachen (2016)

14. Prosperi, M.C., Fanti, I., Ulivi, G., Micarelli, A., De Luca, A., Zazzi, M.: Robust supervised and unsupervised statistical learning for HIV type 1 coreceptor usage analysis. AIDS Res. Hum. Retroviruses 25(3), 305–314 (2009)

15. Salamati, N., Fredembach, C., Süsstrunk, S.: Material classification using color and NIR images. In: Proceedings of 17th Color Imaging Conference (CIC) (2009)

16. Sansonetti, G., Gurini, D., Gasparetti, F., Micarelli, A.: Dynamic social recommendation. In: Proceedings of the IEEE/ACM International Conference on Advances in Social Networks Analysis and Mining, ASONAM 2017, pp. 943–947 (2017)

17. Sansonetti, G.: Point of interest recommendation based on social and linked open data. Pers. Ubiquit. Comput. 23(2), 199–214 (2019). https://doi.org/10.1007/s00779-019-01218-z

18. Sansonetti, G., Gasparetti, F., Micarelli, A., Cena, F., Gena, C.: Enhancing cultural recommendations through social and linked open data. User Model. User-Adap. Inter. 29(1), 121–159 (2019). https://doi.org/10.1007/s11257-019-09225-8

19. Thung, G., Yang, M.: Classification of trash for recyclability status (2016)

20. Vapnik, V.N.: Statistical Learning Theory. Wiley-Interscience, New York (1998)

21. Zhang, S., Forssberg, E.: Intelligent liberation and classification of electronic scrap. Powder Technol. 105(1), 295–301 (1999)

Development of Mobile Application Program for Stroke Prediction Using Machine Learning with Voice Onset Time Data

Murali Subramaniyam[1], Kyung-Sun Lee[2], Se Jin Park[3(✉)],
and Seung Nam Min[4(✉)]

[1] Department of Mechanical Engineering,
SRM Institute of Science and Technology, Kattankulathur, Chennai, India
[2] Department of Industrial Health,
Catholic University of Pusan, Busan, Republic of Korea
[3] Korea Research Institute of Standards and Science,
Daejeon, Republic of Korea
sjpark@kriss.re.kr
[4] Department of Drone and Industrial Safety,
Shinsung University, Dangjin, Republic of Korea
msnijnl2@hanmail.net

Abstract. Stroke is a significant health burden not only in low- and middle-income countries but also globally. In Korea, the prevalence of stroke got increased rapidly. After cancer and heart diseases, strokes are the third leading cause of death in Korea. Korea's aging population grows faster than any other developed country. Stroke prediction is essential to prepare proactive measures to diagnose them. Lately, various stroke prediction models were proposed by considering different parameters including electronic health records. This study aimed to propose a prediction model by considering speech analysis. We have regarded as an elderly group for this study. Both healthy and stroke patients were included. For the voice analysis, their voice signals were recorded while they pronounce a word that produces plosive sound three times repetitively. Further, various parameters were extracted from the voice signals and compared statistically between groups. Then, we have used a machine learning algorithm (Bayesian) and developed a prediction model. This model would assist in classifying/identifying risky elderly to diagnose stroke and to take proactive measures to avoid damages due to stroke. Finally, with the developed prediction algorithm, a mobile application program was created to enhance usability of this algorithm. This mobile application can be installed in any mobile platform, with user's voice input (a predefined plosive word); the system would suggest whether the person is healthy or stroke victim. The accuracy of the system depends on how we train our algorithm. Hence, building big data with voice signals would increase the efficiency of prediction further.

Keywords: Stroke prediction · Voice onset time · Elderly · Mobile application

© Springer Nature Switzerland AG 2020
C. Stephanidis and M. Antona (Eds.): HCII 2020, CCIS 1224, pp. 670–675, 2020.
https://doi.org/10.1007/978-3-030-50726-8_87

1   Introduction

Stroke is on the rise. The source for stroke could be a blood clot, ruptured blood vessels, and mini-stroke (small clot). The stroke risk factors are modifiable and behavioral. The modifiable risk factors are high blood pressure, hyperglycemia, overweight (obesity), hyperlipidemia, and renal dysfunction. The behavioral risk factors are smoking, sedentary lifestyle, physical inactivity, and unhealthy diet. Globally, mortality rate due to stroke continuously increasing and stroke are the second leading cause of death after heart disease [4]. Various reports [1–3] confirms that the incidence of stroke disease increases with age. In Korea, stroke is the third leading cause of death after cancer and heart disease [5]. The stroke victim needs to be treated within a short span of time say about 4.5 h to prevent permanent damage. Hence, it is necessary to study the definite discrimination technique using the characteristics of the stroke.

In stroke prediction studies, Subramaniyam et al. (2018) [6] reported that strokes could be explored with EEG and that prediction would be possible using wearable device. Min et al., (2018) [7] proposed a stroke pre-diagnosis algorithm with potentially modifiable risk factors. Few studies confirmed that the abnormalities in the heart thyme could be explored with ECG measurement and prediction would be possible [8, 9]. Min et al. 2017 [10] used questionnaire evaluation method (e.g. past history), behavioral characteristics evaluation method (e.g. balance ability, grip strength), personal factors methods (e.g. smoking, BMI), and physiological evaluation method (e.g. muscle activity) to predict stroke symptom severity.

Stroke symptoms various beyond FAST, including trouble in speaking, trouble in visibility, trouble in walking, numbness or weakness of face, arm, etc. The changes in speech i.e., changes in vocal features caused by stroke are not studied much [11]. Voice onset time (VOT) is an interval from implosive sound to before start vowel, also it is an important signal to confirm the presence or absence of implosive sound [12]. The voice control ability is known as implosive sound, and implosive sound can be measured by VOT (voice onset time) caused by implosive sound is produced through coordination between the lips, tongue, chin and larynx [13]. Also, age has an effect on VOT, the VOT value becomes shorter as the age increases [14]. The VOT simply refers the time that elapses between the release of the articulators for a stop and the onset of vocal cord vibration of the following segment. The VOT generally measured in millisecond.

Few studies have analyzed the changes in stroke patients vocal changes within the first 72 h of stroke onset, however, little is known about the changes in the stable phase of the vocal onset time [11]. Also, not much studies analyzed the speech data for predicting stroke onset. Hence, this study aims at investigating voice onset time difference between normal elderly and elderly stroke patients to prepared stroke prediction model.

2 Methods

2.1 Subjects

This study considered a total of 219 elderly subjects including 173 normal and 46 stroke patients, were from Chungnam National University Hospital. The average age of normal elderly and stroke subjects were 74 ± 8.4 and 72 ± 12.2 years, respectively. The elderly under the normal group were free from diseases and free from speaking disorders.

2.2 Procedure

At the beginning of the experiment, the complete procedure were explained to all the participants. The participants were sited in front the computer for voice recording comfortably. The experiment were conducted in a controlled and quite room. A digital audiotape, JVC (XDP1BK) was used for voice recording which include condenser microphone (Sennheiser K3). The microphone was placed 30 cm from the subjects mouth. The plosive Korean word "TTOGTTAG" (meaning 'TICK') was selected. The subjects pronounced the word for 3 times with regular interval. Also, the subjects were instructed to observe a regular rhythm of 2 Hz for 6–8 s. The experiment procedure briefed in Fig. 1.

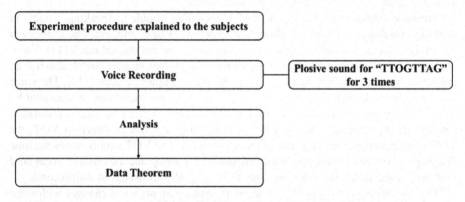

Fig. 1. Experimental procedure

2.3 Analysis

The voices recorded from the experiments were analyzed in PARAT program. At the program, spectral analysis were performed. The plosive information of the voices were extracted in the PARAT program. All the voice signals recorded were filtered by band pass with 20–20,000 Hz and digitized with a sampling rate of 441 Hz. Further, the signals were stored on a personal computer. Spectrograms of the syllables were produced using a wideband filter (125 Hz).

3 Results

The sample recorded voice data presented in Fig. 2 and the enlarged view, particularly the VOT time shown in Fig. 3. This study analyzed both groups voice data and compared using T-test. The statistical test result presented in Table 1. The Bayes theorem and probability calculate briefed in Fig. 3 (Fig. 4).

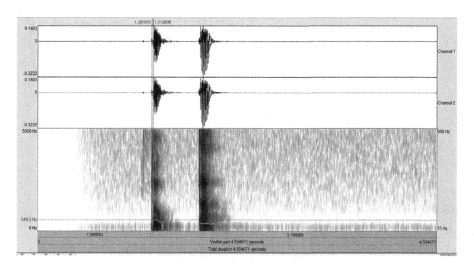

Fig. 2. Sample recorded voice data

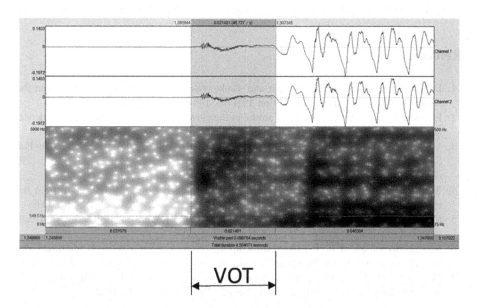

Fig. 3. Sample recorded voice data with VOT

Table 1. Statistical comparison of both groups VOT data

	Elderly	Avg ± SD	Min	Max	T-test
Vocal vibration start time	Normal	0.0217 ± 0.0060	0.0101	0.0413	p < .05
	Stroke patients	0.0285 ± 0.0096	0.0144	0.0560	

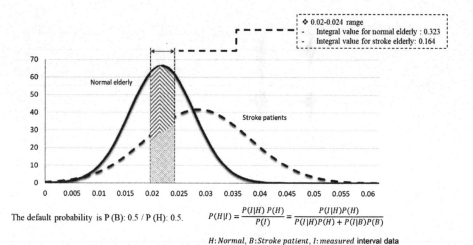

The default probability is P (B): 0.5 / P (H): 0.5.

$$P(H|I) = \frac{P(I|H)\,P(H)}{P(I)} = \frac{P(I|H)P(H)}{P(I|H)P(H) + P(I|B)P(B)}$$

H: Normal, B: Stroke patient, I: measured interval data

Fig. 4. Probability calculation

Acknowledgement. This work was supported by the National Research Council of Science & Technology (NST) grant by the Korea government (MSIP) (No. CRC-15-05-ETRI)

References

1. Benjamin, E.J., et al.: Heart disease and stroke statistics-2017 update: a report from the American heart association. Circulation **135**(10), 146–603 (2017)
2. Engstad, T., et al.: Epidemiology of stroke in the elderly in the Nordic countries. incidence, survival, prevalence and risk factors. Norsk Epidemiol. **22**(2), 121–126 (2012)
3. Venketasubramanian, N., et al.: Prevalence of stroke among Chinese, Malay, and Indian Singaporeans: a community-based tri-racial cross-sectional survey. Stroke **36**(3), 551–556 (2005)
4. Kim, J.Y., et al.: Executive summary of stroke statistics in Korea 2018: a report from the epidemiology research council of the Korean stroke society. J. Stroke **21**(1), 42 (2009)
5. Korean Statistical Information Service (KOSIS) Annual Report on the Causes of Death Statistics. Daejeon: Statistics Korea (2016)
6. Subramaniyam, M., et al.: IoT based wake-up stroke prediction-recent trends and directions. In: IOP Conference Series: Materials Science and Engineering, vol. 402 no. 1, pp. 1-7 (2018)
7. Min, S.N., et al.: Development of an algorithm for stroke prediction: a national health insurance database study in Korea. Eur. Neurol. **79**(3–4), 214–220 (2018)

8. Goldstein, D.S.: The electrocardiogram in stroke: relationship to pathophysiological type and comparison with prior tracings. Stroke **10**(3), 253–259 (1979)
9. Togha, M., et al.: Electrocardiographic abnormalities in acute cerebrovascular events in patients with/without cardiovascular disease. Ann. Indian Acad. Neurol. **16**(1), 66 (2013)
10. Seung, N., et al.: Investigation of stroke evaluation methodology and related factors through the literature review. J. Ergon. Soc. Korea **36**(6), 693–704 (2017)
11. Godoy, J.F., et al.: Neuroradiology and voice findings in stroke. CoDAS **26**(2), 168–174 (2014)
12. Lisker, L., Abramson, A.S.: A cross-language study of voicing in initial stops: acoustical measurements. Word **20**(3), 384–422 (1964)
13. Auzou, P., et al.: Voice onset time in aphasia, apraxia of speech and dysarthria: a review. Clin. Linguist. Phon. **14**(2), 131–150 (2000)
14. Kong, E.J., Beckman, M.E., Edwards, J.: Voice onset time is necessary but not always sufficient to describe acquisition of voiced stops: the cases of Greek and Japanese. J. Phon. **40**(6), 725–744 (2012)

Searching for Onomatopoeia Based on Sound Similarity by Employing User Reviews

Ryuta Yamada[✉], Takashi Ito, and Syohei Ishizu

Department of Industrial Engineering and Systems Engineering,
Aoyama Gakuin University, Shibuya City, Japan
ryutayamada0911@gmail.com

Abstract. Onomatopoeia is a word or phrase that imitates or suggests the sound it describes, such as "buzz" or "sizzle." It is often used to express the taste and texture of food in Japan and is thus often used in food advertising. The purpose this study was to construct a system that searches for the onomatopoeia that best expresses a given product. Important characteristics and sound similarities in onomatopoeia components of user product reviews are identified by this system. Such reviews contain helpful user opinions for improving the product. Accordingly, it is important to select the onomatopoeia that best conveys to the consumer the product essence and texture. Use of the optimal onomatopoeia can help make advertisements succinct and effective.

Keywords: Search system · User review · Negative matrix factorization · Onomatopoeia · Principal component analysis

1 Introduction

Onomatopoeia is a word or phrase that imitates or suggests the sound it describes, such as "buzz" or "sizzle." Onomatopoeia is widely used in Japan to express the particular features of a product. For food products, it is often used to convey the taste and texture of the given food, and it is important for expressing the food product image. Furthermore, onomatopoeia engenders new words and food cultures because any person can easily send the word or phrase through text messaging and other media.

Onomatopoeia is therefore often used in food advertising. In that realm, it is important to select the onomatopoeia that best conveys to the consumer the essence of the food product. Determining the optimal onomatopoeia to use in food advertisements can help make the advertisements succinct and effective. Use of onomatopoeia in this way can increase food sales by enhancing consumer desire to buy the product. Moreover, consumers often express their impressions and opinions in product reviews. In many cases, product reviews can influence other consumers to purchase the product. Additionally, feedback from reviews can help improve the product itself and are thus actively applied to product development. Meanwhile, Miyakawa analyzed the relationships among product quality factors based on reviews [1], and Torizuka surveyed benefit segmentation based on benefits to the client [2]. Hasegawa extracted product features using onomatopoeia with a focus on "sizzle" [3].

© Springer Nature Switzerland AG 2020
C. Stephanidis and M. Antona (Eds.): HCII 2020, CCIS 1224, pp. 676–682, 2020.
https://doi.org/10.1007/978-3-030-50726-8_88

Given the above context, the purpose this study was to construct a system that searches for the onomatopoeia that best matches the product image. Accordingly, the important product characteristics and sound similarities to onomatopoeia components in user reviews were obtained. To this end, we created text data for each onomatopoeia based on Rakuten Recipe website reviews. The important attributes of each of onomatopoeia were extracted from the dimensionally reduced data by using non-negative matrix factorization. Finally, we arranged the onomatopoeia on a plane using principal component analysis and constructed a system that matches an image to its corresponding image on the plane.

2 Onomatopoeia Analysis

2.1 Onomatopoeia Data

In this study, we used the "Tukuttayo Report" of the Rakuten Recipe website for our analysis data. It consisted of a comment by the user who wrote the recipe for the owner, as well as a reply from the owner. The former is called the "recommended comment"; the latter is called the "owner comment." We used the former for the analysis.

For the actual analysis data, we employed onomatopoeia data and the sentences in which it was used for each onomatopoeia item in the recommended comment. We selected the onomatopoeia that was used at least ten times out of approximately 100,000 sentences. A total of 101 words fulfilled this criterion. We additionally analyzed the targeting of repetitive onomatopoeia called the "XYXY" type as "KATI-KATI" or "MOTIMOTI."

2.2 Analysis of Onomatopoeia Data

Morphological analysis on the dataset created in Sect. 2.1 was performed. Four frequently used words—delicious, happy, good, and cold—were omitted to make the contents of the topic easier to understand. After deletion, feature words were extracted using term frequency and inverse document frequency. For data of the word frequency matrix, we determined the eight attributes of the topic by using non-negative matrix factorization (NMF) and word clouds. From that point, principal component analysis was performed on the data consisting of a matrix of "onomatopoeia and topic" obtained by NMF. Using a results diagram created by plotting the principal component score, we applied a system that extracts the onomatopoeia closest to the given point when a point on the figure was clicked with a mouse.

Finally, the onomatopoeia of the 101 words described in Sect. 2.1 was decomposed into the sounds of each character. The number "1" was assigned to the onomatopoeia if it contained a character that was a vowel or consonant, and "0" was assigned to it otherwise. Here, we use "GATIGATI" as an example. Because "GATI" is repeated, only "GATI" is designated as a dummy variable. In fact, "1" is assigned to the consonant G of the first character, and "0" is assigned to the other consonants. The consonants and vowels of the other characters are assigned in the same way. These dummy variables are used as explanatory variables. Moreover, the relational value of "onomatopoeia and topic" obtained by NMF is used as the objective variable, and coefficients are obtained using quantification methods.

Furthermore, we obtained a total of 3,900 unknown words of onomatopoeia by combining the consonants and vowels used as explanatory variables. These 3,900 words included 101 words extracted from the recommended comments. Then, we created the same system as above by allocating the coefficients obtained by quantification methods for 3,900 words. From that point, we treated the onomatopoeia of 101 words and 3,900 words, respectively, as known onomatopoeia and unknown onomatopoeia.

2.3   Topic Analysis

This section describes the results of determining the topic attributes that were reduced to eight dimensions by NMF and were visualized by word clouds. The word cloud topic 1 is used as an example in Fig. 1. Certain words, such as "greasy" and "Oiliness," stand out from the "relationship between adjectives and topics." Moreover, the word "sticky" is distinguished from the "relation between onomatopoeia and topics." Accordingly, we assign "Oiliness" to topic 1. Then, the result of determining the placement in topic 1 is outlined as follows. These results are defined as eight attributes, including that of topic 1.

Topic 2: "Fragrance," Topic 3: "Hot," Topic 4: "Sweetness," Topic 5: "Warmth," Topic 6: "Firmness"

Topic 7: "Feeling," Topic 8: "Softness"

(a) Relationships between adjectives and topic 1   (b) Relationships between onomatopoeia and topic 1

Fig. 1. Word cloud of topic 1.

3   Onomatopoeia Search System

3.1   Interface and Results of a Known-Onomatopoeia Search

Figure 2 shows the system used in the search. Tables 1 and 2 present the actual search results and inspection results. We extracted three onomatopoeia relating to the eight attributes that are considered to have a significant influence. It is that the extracted onomatopoeia works most effectively on attributes. We extracted one onomatopoeia between attributes (between words). In considering Fig. 2, we can extract an onomatopoeia by clicking on the red circled area with the mouse for the attribute indicated by the arrow.

We employed a questionnaire for the assessment. Specifically, we tasked 15 users to evaluate the onomatopoeia on a scale from 1 (strongly conveys) to 5 (does not convey at all) in terms of the attributes obtained in Sect. 3.1. The numbers in Table 1 and 2 represent the average of the numbers that were rated by 15 people.

From the results shown in Table 1, the "Oiliness" of topic 1, "GITOGITO" and "BETABETA," and the "firmness" of topic 6, "GOTUGOTU" and "GORIGORI," are strongly assessed. Therefore, there is an apparent validity in "Oiliness" of topic 1 and "firmness" of topic 6. Furthermore, from the results in Table 2, the results with a high score are obtained for "ZAKUZAKU" between "firmness" of topic 6 and "softness" of topic 8. In addition, it is evident that we can extract the onomatopoeia among attributes because the results exceed the average among all the attributes.

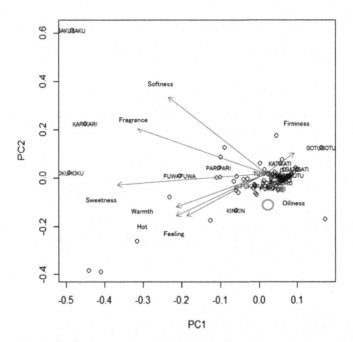

Fig. 2. Interface of the known-onomatopoeia search.

3.2   Search Results of Unknown Onomatopoeia

We extracted five onomatopoeia words by using the same search function outlined in Sect. 3.1. This approach was used because we believed that the unknown ono-matopoeia would be difficult to image even if attributes could be imaged for one onomatopoeia word. Table 3 shows the search results. The validity of the results was verified by assessments. In addition, unknown onomatopoeia was designated as mul-tiple onomatopoeia groups.

Specifically, we asked 15 subjects to select from each onomatopoeia group in Table 3 one of the eight attributes that could be imaged from the result. In addition, the subjects were asked to select the attributes that were applied many times. From left to right in the table, there are eight groups. The assessment results are shown in Table 4. The correct answer rate is high for "Oiliness," "firmness," "feeling," and "softness" in groups 1, 6, 7, and 8. From these results, we contended that these onomatopoeia groups could be imaged attributes. Furthermore, the images of other groups differed depending on the subjects. Nevertheless, the results did not vary; thus, we surmised that the results were satisfactory and that the system worked effectively.

Table 1. Results of known onomatopoeia.

Oily	Fragurance	Hot	Sweetness	Warmth	Firmness	Feeling	Softness
GITOGITO	KARIKARI	POKAPOKA	HOKUHOKU	POKAPOKA	GOTUGOTU	PAKUPAKU	PUTIPUTI
4.8	1.5	4.2	2.5	4.8	4.3	1.7	2.5
BETABETA	PARIPARI	HOROHORO	FUWAFUWA	BAKUBAKU	GORIGORI	PASAPASA	ZAKUZAKU
3.8	1.5	2	3.2	1.5	3.8	2.5	2.2
KOTEKOTE	TUYATUYA	FUKAFUKA	TOROTORO	KOTOKOTO	KATIKATI	YAWAYAWA	PORIPORI
4.3	2	2.3	2.2	3.7	5	2.5	2.2

Table 2. Search results of onomatopoeia attributes.

Sostness: Firmness	Firmness: Oiliness	Oiliness: Feeling	Sweetness: Fragrance
ZAKUZAKU	GOWAGOWA	KINKIN	FUWAFUWA
4.1	3.5	3.2	3.6
Softness: Fragrance	Feeling: Hot	Hot: Warmth	Warmth: Sweetness
PORIPORI	PAKUPAKU	POKAPOKA	GOKUGOKU
3.5	4	4.2	3.7

Table 3. Search results for eight attributes.

Oiliness	Fragrance	Hot	Sweetness
KUGIKUGI	SIGISIGI	NITENITE	SIBISIBI
PIGIPUGI	SASISASI	NIBENIBE	HIBIHIBI
GUGAGUGA	SATISATI	MUGEMUGE	MIGUMIGU
DINIDINI	ZATOZATO	NUWANUWA	TIBITIBI
PINIPINI	FUBAFUBA	PANUPANU	GINIGINI
Warmth	Firmness	Feeling	Softness
FAPEFAPE	GUGAGUGA	NIBINIBI	FUGEFUGE
IPEIPE	GUGEGUGE	NABINABI	KUPEKUPE
FIPEFIPE	ZUGUZUGU	KIBUKIBU	FUWAFUWA
FUPEFUPE	TAGITAGI	MABIMABI	MUYOMUYO
MAPOMAPO	YUGIYUGI	MISOMISO	TANITANI

Table 4. Inspection results.

Subject	Group							
	1	2	3	4	5	6	7	8
1	Oily	Fragrance	Firmness	Warmth	Sweetness	Firmness	Feeling	Softness
2	Feeling	Fragrance	Sweetness	Oily	Softness	Firmness	Hot	Warmth
3	Oily	Softness	Firmness	Sweetness	Warmth	Firmness	Feeling	Softness
4	Softness	Oily	Hot	Feeling	Fragrance	Firmness	Feeling	Softness
5	Oily	Hot	Firmness	Sweetness	Sweetness	Hot	Feeling	Softness
6	Feeling	Sweetness	Hot	Fragrance	Softness	Firmness	Oily	Firmness
7	Oily	Oily	Firmness	Firmness	Warmth	Hot	Feeling	Softness
8	Oily	Firmness	Warmth	Sweetness	Feeling	Fragrance	Sweetness	Softness
9	Oily	Hot	Hot	Softness	Warmth	Feeling	Softness	Softness
10	Oily	Feeling	Fragrance	Firmness	Warmth	Firmness	Feeling	Sweetness
11	Oily	Feeling	Hot	Hot	Warmth	Firmness	Firmness	Softness
12	Oily	Fragrance	Firmness	Warmth	Sweetness	Firmness	Feeling	Softness
13	Oily	Softness	Firmness	Sweetness	Warmth	Firmness	Feeling	Softness
14	Oily	Hot	Firmness	Fragrance	Sweetness	Hot	Feeling	Softness
15	Softness	Oily	Warmth	Sweetness	Fragrance	Firmness	Feeling	Softness
Correct answer	Oily	Fragrance	Hot	Sweetness	Warmth	Firmness	Feeling	Softness
Accuracy rate	0.67	0.20	0.27	0.33	0.40	0.67	0.67	0.80

4 Conclusion

In this study, we identified eight onomatopoeia attributes by using NMF from Rakuten website reviews. We determined the effects of the eight attributes by using principal component analysis. Using these results, we searched for known and unknown onomatopoeia. To this end, we employed a system that searches for onomatopoeia relating to attributes on a search screen by plotting the principal component analysis scores. Based on the assessment results, it is considered that the proposed system, although not complete, effectively functions, and can be applied to food advertising. In conclusion, the proposed system enables selection of the onomatopoeia that best conveys to the consumer the food product essence and texture. Use of the optimal onomatopoeia in this way can help make food advertisements succinct and effective.

References

1. Miyakawa S., Saitoh F., Ishizu S.: A method for creating a quality table from online reviews. In: ISQFD (2017)
2. Torizuka, K., Oi, H., Saitho, F., Ishizu, S.: Benefit segmentation of online customer reviews using random forest. IEEE IEEM **2018**, 1–5 (2018)
3. Hasegawa, E., Komiya, K., Saitoh, F., Ishizu, S.: A method of factor extraction of sizzle words based on language resources. Trans. JSKE **17**(2), 299–308 (2018). (in Japanese)

Investigation on CNN-Based State Classification Towards BCI Application Using Amplitude Probability Density Distribution

Naoya Yamamoto[1(✉)], Junya Enjoji[1], Ingon Chanpornpakdi[1],
Ryunosuke Ozasa[1], Fumitaka Aki[1], Tatsuhiro Kimura[2],
Hiroshi Ohsima[1], and Kiyoyuki Yamazaki[1(✉)]

[1] Tokai University, Isehara, Kanagawa Prefecture, Japan
yaona91825@gmail.com, ymzkkyyk@gmail.com
[2] Tokai University, Kumamoto, Kumamoto Prefecture, Japan

Abstract. Various kinds of analysis including fast Fourier transform (FFT) were widely used for the classification of electroencephalogram (EEG) based human interfaces. However, the morphological characteristics of EEG waveform were rarely used, since the EEG waveform is thought to show no significant meaning due to its stochastic features. The authors have studied on SSVEP-based BCI for disabled patients. The objective of this study is to verify feasibility of amplitude probability density distribution (APD) used as a feature contributing classification EEG. In this study, the amplitude probability density distribution, which indicated as the index of morphological characteristics of EEG, was applied for state classification using deep learning. CNN was introduced to construct the model of deep learning, classify the obtained data calculated by introduced novel APD method and FFT in order to compare the feasibility. The data were obtained from EEG recorded when subjects were presented flashing light with low stimulus luminosity reversed at 20 and 60 Hz. EEG measurement was conducted in shield room and 9 healthy adulthood male subjects participated in this study. As a result, the case of EEG spectrum by FFT as the control data, the classification accuracy was 85.81%, while using APD yielded 87.98%. The classification accuracy in both analyses showed almost similar result. To conclude, apart from the traditional frequency characteristic, it is feasible in utilization of morphological information in classifying EEG characteristics obtained from two different frequencies. Some problems of implementation for the BCI and efficacy of present method will be discussed.

Keywords: Deep learning · SSVEP · Assistive technology

1 Introduction

Brain-Computer Interface (BCI) is the interface that aim to extract the user's intention from brain and converts it into signals. These signals could be applied and used for communication and computer's controller. To obtain those signals, EEG is one of the techniques utilized in BCI, therefore, it is important to analyze and classify the state of EEG [1].

© Springer Nature Switzerland AG 2020
C. Stephanidis and M. Antona (Eds.): HCII 2020, CCIS 1224, pp. 683–689, 2020.
https://doi.org/10.1007/978-3-030-50726-8_89

EEG signal, such as evoked potentials and event-related potentials, is usually contaminated with various noise components. These components can be reduced by performing fast Fourier transform (FFT) and moving average method during EEG analysis. Since the characteristics of the EEG are divided according to the frequency band, it is considered that the characteristics are easy to extract when focusing on the frequency information. Hence, many studies used frequency information when analyzed and extract the characteristics of brainwaves [5]. In contrast, there are few researchers worked on morphological characteristics with the subjects as Epilepsy patients. However, there is no such a study performed on the EEG of the healthy subjects in our knowledge. Thus, we introduced amplitude probability density distribution (APD) which includes morphological features of the EEG as a novel method for EEG analysis. This method examines the probability of density distribution in each amplitude class.

We have studied steady state visual evoked potential (SSVEP) evoked synchronously with the frequency of the flickering stimulus. This experiment presented light stimulus with low intensity reversed at distinctly different frequencies of 20 Hz and 60 Hz. This stimulus was demonstrated by a stimulator that can adjust the flickering frequency of LED light to an arbitrary frequency with a computer. The EEG signals obtained when the flashing stimuli of 20 Hz and 60 Hz were shown were analyzed not only by the amplitude probability density distribution but also by FFT for result comparison [2]. Each input data set was created, and the accuracy was compared and examined using the convolutional neural network (CNN) of the deep learning model, which is one of machine learning algorithms with a multi-layer architecture that can learn data features in stages.

2   Methodology

2.1   Measuring Method

The experiment was performed on nine healthy adult males with an average age at 22. For EEG measurement, 6 channels of EEG electrode were placed at C3, C4, P3, P4, O1, O2 according to international 10–20 electrode system as shown in Fig. 1. The measuring instrument used was BRAIN PRODUCTS Inc. Brain Vision Recorder1.20, recorded with sampling frequency of 250 Hz in the electrostatic shield room.

The stimulus used in this experiment was demonstrated by a stimulator. Figure 2(a) is the illustration of stimulator, which consists of one LED light that emits green light at very low intensity of 1 lx, installed as shown in Fig. 2(b). This SSVEP device was designed to flash at different frequencies and controlled by Arduino with an input from the PC. In this experiment, the frequencies were set to 20 Hz and 60 Hz. The SSVEP device was constructed to be face fit and the experiment was conducted in a dark environment, so that there were no excess light sources interfered during the measurement (Fig. 3).

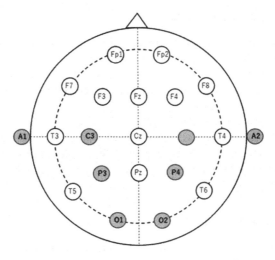

Fig. 1. Electrode arrangement (ten-twenty electrode system)

(a) The whole stimulator device   (b) Inside the stimulator device

Fig. 2. Stimulator used in the experiment

Table 1. Experimental protocol

Resting eyes opened	Resting eyes closed	20 Hz	60 Hz
1 min	1 min	2 min	2 min

During the experiment, the flashing LED was flickered according to the experimental protocol of Table 1 using the stimulator. At first, resting eyes closed and resting eyes were measured as the control conditions for 1 min, then followed by the SSVEP stimulus measurement for 2 min. The subjects were allowed to rest for 1 min between each condition.

2.2   APD Characteristic Extraction

The input APD was first generated by dividing the measured data into 5 s dataset with 75% overlapping with its predecessor and split into 20 classes. If we chose fewer classes, APD would be coarse while larger number of class would flatten the APD. Consequently, 20 classes APD was chosen since it seemed to be the most appropriate without being biased by either graph.

Due to individual difference in EEG of healthy subjects during resting time, the amplitude range of each class was set to ±50 μV. In addition, the obtained data was rarely exceeded ±50 μV and by adjusting the amplitude range over ±50 μV might lead to more possibility for the noise components such as electromyogram (EMG) to get mixed up with the EEG signal.

2.3   Deep Learning Classification

We eliminated the bias due to individual differences by shuffling the acquired APD dataset. The input dataset was simply represented as shown in Fig. 4. One dataset consisted of three dimensions, and the vertical axis represents one channel, and the horizontal axis of size 20 indicates the number of classes. Since there are six channels of EEG data involved, six data were located on the z-axis and formed three-dimensional data (Fig. 3).

This created a total of 1656 input datasets and used in CNN model to classify SSVEP stimuli at 20 Hz and 60 Hz [3, 4]. The input data were validated by 10-fold cross validation. 10-fold cross validation is the validation that divide the input data into ten set and labeled one of those as a validation data, and the remaining nine as training data. This process continues one by one until all the datasets were validated.

In this method, the accuracy of the classification was calculated ten times, and then the average accuracy was obtained. Thereby, accuracy can be evaluated more correctly. For comparison, the tradition FFT analysis was also inputted and classified using the same CNN model.

Table 2 shows the parameters and output when the input dataset in APD analysis, and Table 3 shows the parameters and output when the FFT was used. "Dropout" in Tables 2 and 3 is a method of classification while randomly dropout some data during training to generalize the model in order to prevent overfitting.

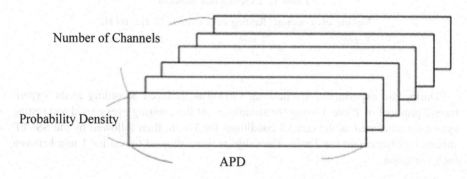

Fig. 3. Structure of input dataset (ADP)

Table 2. APD parameters and output

Layer type	Filter	Size/Stride	Output
Convolution	4	(1,2)/(1,2)	$4 \times 1 \times 10$
Middle class			64
Middle class			32
Middle class			2

*Epoch number: 1000, Dropout: 0.3

Table 3. FFT parameters and output

Layer type	Filter	Size/Stride	Output
Convolution	2	(1,4)/(1,4)	$2 \times 1 \times 156$
Pooling		(1,3)/(1,2)	$2 \times 1 \times 78$
Middle class			64
Middle class			2

*Epoch number: 3000, Dropout: 0.3

3 Result and Discussion

Figure 4 and Fig. 5 are the accuracies obtained by 10-fold cross-validation using APD and FFT as an input dataset. Both figures show the transition of the accuracy of the training data and the validation data.

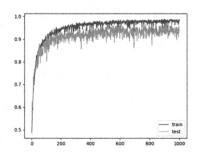

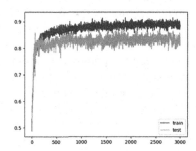

Fig. 4. Third example of 10-fold cross validation (APD)

Fig. 5. Fifth example of 10-fold cross validation (FFT)

Figure 4 represents the result of the third time of the 10-fold cross-validation and Fig. 5 shows the result of the fifth time of the 10-fold cross-validation. The vertical axis represents the accuracy, and the horizontal axis represents the number of epochs. The blue line indicates the learning data, and the orange line indicates the validation data. In both figures, the accuracy increases as increase in number of epochs.

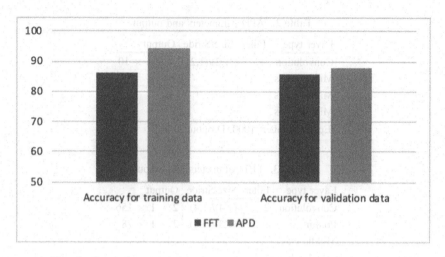

Fig. 6. Comparison of the accuracy obtained by APD and FFT analysis

Figure 6 shows the results of averaging the accuracy of the last 10 samples and comparing the result of both analysis method. The accuracy of the APD for the training data was 94.43% and the accuracy for the validation data was 87.98%, while the accuracy for FFT training data was 86.2% and the accuracy for validation data was 85.1%.

When the FFT and APD were compared, high accuracy was obtained in both cases. Therefore, it is considered that SSVEP elicited by light stimulation reversed at 20 Hz and 60 Hz was clearly classified by deep learning using APD and FFT for feature extraction. As shown on Fig. 6, the accuracy was higher when APD was used as input data than that of FFT. Nevertheless, the accuracy of APD was slightly higher for the training data than for the validation data. This is because the parameters for deep learning may not be appropriately optimized during the data processing. Since an EEG is a time-series signal in which involves numerous factors that is combined in a complicated manner, the EEG appears differently depending on the measurement site.

APD is an analysis based on morphological characteristics of a waveform, whereas FFT includes frequency information. From the result, both APD and FFT yielded high accuracy when the data is classified by the same CNN model. Hence, it can be considered that SSVEP binary classification can be determined not only from the frequency information but also from the morphological characteristics of the waveform.

4   Conclusion

We performed the CNN, one of the algorithms in deep learning using the amplitude probability density distribution (APD) as an input data. As a result, the method we introduced obtained the similar accuracy to that of traditional FFT. Frequency analysis is generally used for BCI analysis, but there is also a possibility that morphological characteristics of waveform such as APD could be used as a feature extraction for BCI analysis in the future. However, SSVEP-based EEG does not show the characteristic waveform that could be observed on the raw data, so we need to consider furthermore about which features of APD was utilized by Deep learning in EEG classification.

Acknowledgment.   A part of this research was supported by Fujikura Foundation.

References

1. Kimura, T., Yamzaki, K.: Recent Brain-Computer-Interface (BCI) research trends. Bull. Tokai Univ. Facul. Develop. Eng. **20**, 7–11 (2010). (in Japanese)
2. Sakurada, T., Kawase, T. (eds.): Use of high-frequency visual stimuli critical flicker frequency in a SSVEP-based BMI. Clin. Neurophysiol. **126**, 1972–1978 (2015)
3. Ullah, I., Hussain, M. (eds.): An automated system for epilepsy detection using EEG brain signals based on deep learning approach. Expert Syst. Appl. **107**, 61–71 (2018)
4. Lawhern, V.J., Solon, A.J., Waytowich, N.R. (eds.): EEGNet: a com-pact convolutional neural network for EEG-based brain-computer interfaces. J. Neural Eng. **15**, 5 (2018)
5. Lotte, F., Bougrain, L. (eds.): A review of classification algorithms for EEG-based brain-computer interfaces: a 10 year update. J. Neural Eng. **15**, 3 (2018)

Machine Learning and Human-Computer Interaction Technologies in Media and Cognition Course

Yi Yang[✉] and Jiasong Sun

Tsinghua National Laboratory for Information Science and Technology,
Department of Electronic Engineering, Tsinghua University, Beijing, China
{Yangyy, sunjiasong}@tsinghua.edu.cn

Abstract. Media and cognition course has been explored for several years. The course is composed by a number of machine learning and human-computer interaction technologies. With the study and research in these projects, students can acquire the basic theoretical knowledge and development capabilities of digital media and brain's cognition. Two systems designed and completed by students in the media and cognition course are introduced, which indicated that students have the strong interest in advanced technologies and topics in the field of machine learning and human-computer interaction and they could implement some advanced algorithms and demonstrations independently.

Keywords: Media and cognition course · Machine learning · Human-computer interaction · Human's posture detection · Multilingual text recognition

1 Introduction

As a compulsory course, media and cognition course has been explored for seven years [1]. With the aim of cultivating professionals who have innovative thinking, this course is composed by a number of machine learning and human-computer interaction theories and technologies [2–4]. By referring to the related contents of many famous universities, research institutes and enterprises, this course has built a variety of projects based on machine learning and human-computer interaction. With the study and research in these projects, students can acquire the basic theoretical knowledge and development capabilities of digital media and brain's cognition.

From web search to e-commerce website recommendation systems, machine learning technology is indispensable [5–8]. In recent years, the machine learning field has been positively influenced by deep learning methods, in which many new technologies have been produced with their academic and applicable features. The study of machine learning is not only an important issue in artificial intelligence research, but also has become one of the core issues of computer science and technology. The course involves many directions of the machine learning discipline, such as image recognition, target detection, speech recognition, handwritten text recognition, etc. These technologies currently use machine learning and deep learning as the primary solutions. This paper introduces the machine learning/deep learning and human-computer

C. Stephanidis and M. Antona (Eds.): HCII 2020, CCIS 1224, pp. 690–697, 2020.
https://doi.org/10.1007/978-3-030-50726-8_90

interaction applications proposed by students. These technologies and applications enrich the media and cognition course's teaching and experimental platform, on which the independent research and development were asked for students to improve their innovative ability.

The intelligent decision support system is a new information system formed by introducing artificial intelligence into the decision support system [9]. An interesting research designed by students in the class is intelligent decision support system on the human's posture detection. With the growing aging population, the life's quality of the elderly has become a hot spot of concern. Considering the increasing number of elderly people living alone, the monitoring and alarming system of accidental falls should be applied for them in home and hospital. This project is based on a mechanism designed by Kinect device to check if a person falls to reduce the damage caused by accidental falls. In many experiments, it was found that the vertical state is that the parameter detects the fall of different orientations. When the person falls, the extraction of the bones and joints may be temporarily dislocated, but the system's detection effect should not be affected. Therefore, the research team proposed one method for similar sitting posture to test the stability of their algorithm. The results show that this method can avoid the false alarming. In addition, various interference postures, such as lying down, push-ups, and squatting, are given to test whether they were misjudged to be the fall posture under this method. Training was performed in the standard dataset TST Fall Detection Dataset and the students' own recorded datasets, which included the common fall and other possible postures at home, such as squats, lying, etc. The experimental results show that the system has certain ability to prevent false alarms and been able to ensure that the fall is detected.

Another research in the class is an end-to-end multilingual text detection and recognition based on E2E-MLT. E2E-MLT is a widely used multilingual text detection and recognition system based on a single full convolutional neural network with many convolutional layers shared by detection and identification modules. E2E-MLT has excellent detection performance for Latin text while detecting multilingualism. Using E2E-MLT system as the baseline, students have carried out multi-language text detection and recognition tasks to realize the improvements in the network structure, loss function and data preprocessing. The end-to-end system needs to send the original RGB image directly to the neural network structure for training and get the trained neural network model, which was applied to recognize multi-language text on the other images. Usually the text zone often has different colors, brightness or contrast with the background in the image. This project extracted the foreground and background features to identify the text in the image.

The rest of this paper is organized as follows: The intelligent decision support system on the human's posture detection is briefly reviewed in Sect. 2. In Sect. 3, we simply review the detail of the end-to-end multilingual text detection and recognition, which is followed by the conclusions and future works in Sect. 4.

2 Intelligent Decision Support System on Human's Posture Detection

One of the reasons the elderly people were injured in home is that they fell alone and not being attended. The falling event was detected in multiple people scene, which further marked who fell and issued an alarm, which can be used for elderly in home fall recognition system.

The system was performed in the standard dataset TST Fall Detection Dataset and the students' own recorded datasets, There are three types of fall situations in daily life: multiple people falling in a normal type; falling with the local occlusion; falling with the dynamic occlusion (for example, a person falling on a bicycle, etc.).

This system uses Kinect [10] as hardware support to collect image information, and uses the human bone point detection and depth detection algorithm API provided by the SDK to model the target human body. The human skeletal map under the depth information is obtained (which is shown in Fig. 1), which simplifies complex human features and extracts key human feature information.

Fig. 1. Human skeleton picture with depth information.

The whole function realization process of the system is mainly divided into three steps:

1) Monitoring human body and modeling;
2) Decision tree to judge human behavior;
3) Outputting results.

Among them, Kinect equipment and its SDK's built-in human skeleton and depth detection algorithm were used to model and track the human body to extract the main features of the human body. Secondly, the neck height, hip height, and body tilt of the human body were mainly calculated based on the modeled features. The decision tree is trained using the relevant training dataset. Finally, the function of detecting the fall behavior in the case of multiple people is realized. The overall architecture is shown in Fig. 2.

Fig. 2. The overall architecture

As shown in Fig. 3, by calling Kinect's built-in algorithm API, the human skeleton image and depth map can be obtained separately, and then the two are registered and combined to finally obtain the human skeleton image under the depth map.

Body Frame   *Depth Picture*   *Mixed Picture*

Fig. 3. Human body's modeling process

This method mainly calculates the neck height, hip height, and body inclination of the human body based on the modeled features as the body characteristic parameters.

1) Neck height: H_1

   In order to reflect the height of the human body and exclude numerical fluctuations caused by head shaking, we use the neck as the commanding height. The height of the neck is defined as:

$$H_{neck} - H_{foot} = H_1 \tag{1}$$

The reason why the height of the feet is subtracted instead of the height of the ground plane is to save the time required to detect and calculate the ground height.

2) Hip height: H_2

   In order to reflect the height of the lower body from the ground, which is beneficial to identify the sitting fall. Define hip height as:

$$H_{Hip} - H_{foot} = H_2 \tag{1}$$

3) Body tilt: K

   To present the upright state of the human body, we use the three-dimensional space angle to define the body's body tilt K.

   In terms of classifiers, the reasons of selecting decision tree method are: the amount of training data is small; the parameters are relatively independent; the importance of the parameters is not consistent. The decision tree has the characteristics of visualizing the decision process. By manually bringing in empirical knowledge, it can make up for the shortcomings of insufficient data volume, and can manually avoid overfitting problems. The information of the collected dataset is shown in Table 1. In the function of outputting an alarm and marking in real time, the number of people in the field of view of the camera is output first. Second, if someone falls, the algorithm will "black out" the person who fell. Finally, the number of falls is systematically output in real time.

Table 1. Total dataset information

Number of people	10
Human height range	165 cm–185 cm
Male to female ratio	4:1
Sample size	121
Number of training	76
Number of testing	45

The performance test results are shown in Table 2, which shows the good performance testing performance. False alarms only happened once because the object in the testing dataset performed a squat movement, but the range of motion was too large to make hips directly contacted the ground, which caused the false alarm.

Table 2. The results of performance testing

Ground truth	Prediction results	
	Fall	Not fall
Fall	26	0
Not fall	1	19
Recall rate	100%	
Precise rate	96.3%	

2.1 End-to-End Multilingual Text Detection and Recognition

E2E-MLT is a multilingual text detection and recognition end-to-end system [11]. Its primary features are: Integrate the detection and recognition of scripts in the same pipeline, which means it was able to give the bounding box and the script detection results at the same time; and the system could insert new characters at any time as needed; The text recognition used the majority voting mechanism, which means script identification is not required as a prerequisite. E2E-MLT has the advantage of detecting Latin transcripts while detecting multiple languages. Our proposed system is based on the E2E-MLT system for multilingual text detection and recognition tasks, and attempts to improve it from the network structure, loss function and data preprocessing.

to train model at the beginning, which is mainly composed of Localization and OCR. The modified training dataset contains only 1600 Chinese and English characters. A pre-trained model of 205,000 steps and a model of continuous training of 240,000 steps were used for testing, of which the test set totaled 400 images. The test results are shown in the Table 3:

Table 3. The test results of pretrained and trained models

Model	Precision	Recall	hmean
Pretrained	0.754	0.762	0.758
Trained	0.702	0.796	0.746

After continuing to train 55,000 steps, the precision and hmean parameters decreased. This shows that without changing the network structure, target function, and various hyperparameters, the Pretrained Model is mature enough. Continuing training may cause overfitting to a certain degree. Our proposed system improvements include:

Adjust the network structure: Increase the existing ResNet Blocks by 5 and increase the Block layer depth by 4–8 layers. By concatenating more ResNet blocks or adding more convolutional layers in the block, the training effect of the model will be improved to a certain extent. After fine-tuning the network structure, the pre-trained model cannot be used for training, but the shallow layer parameters of the pre-trained model can be considered as the initial training parameters of the new network for training.

Improve the loss function [12]: The main idea is that for classification problems, the features are considered to be in accordance with the Gaussian distribution. The Gaussian distribution can be used as a training parameter to make the features easier to separate.

Image pre-processing: In the color images, the texts are often different in color, brightness or contrast with the background. Besides, the colors of background are often different and the color of text is simplistic. By extracting the features that distinguish the foreground and background of the texts, it helps to improve the accuracy and efficiency of OCR.

Fig. 4a. Multilingual transcript detection and recognition results (English).

Fig. 4b. Multilingual transcript detection and recognition results (Chinese).

Figure 4(a) and Fig. 4(b) show the results of English and Chinese text detection and recognition by our system. With the change of the loss function, the neural network structure and performing image preprocessing, the improvements on the detection accuracy are achieved on the collected image datasets.

3   Conclusions

In this paper, we introduce two systems designed and completed by students in the media and cognition course: human pose detection intelligent decision support system and end-to-end multilingual text detection and recognition system. The pose detection system is stable and robust under the requirement of high accuracy detection, and the time complexity of algorithm can be considered only in the SDK costing. The multi-lingual text recognition system based on E2E-MLT improved the existing results by changing the loss function and network structure, and its performance has been verified on our image datasets. These results indicate that, through the cultivating of media and cognitive course, students will have a strong interest in advanced technologies and topics in the field of machine learning and human-computer interaction, and they can independently implement some advanced algorithms and demonstrations. Their capabilities of project construction and technical realization have been improved in this course.

Acknowledgement.   Thanks to NSFC (61105017) agency for funding.

References

1. Yang, Y., Sun, J., Huang, L.: Artificial intelligence teaching methods in higher education. In: Bi, Y., Bhatia, R., Kapoor, S. (eds.) IntelliSys 2019. AISC, vol. 1037, pp. 1044–1053. Springer, Cham (2020). https://doi.org/10.1007/978-3-030-29516-5_78
2. Pantic, M., Sebe, N., Cohn, J.F., et al.: Affective multimodal human-computer interaction. In: Proceedings of the 13th Annual ACM International Conference on Multimedia, pp. 669–676 (2005)
3. Trigueiros, P., Ribeiro, F., Reis, L.P.: A comparison of machine learning algorithms applied to hand gesture recognition. In: 7th Iberian Conference on Information Systems and Technologies (CISTI 2012), pp. 1–6. IEEE (2012)

4. Rautaray, Siddharth S., Agrawal, A.: Vision based hand gesture recognition for human computer interaction: a survey. Artif. Intell. Rev. **43**(1), 1–54 (2012). https://doi.org/10. 1007/s10462-012-9356-9
5. Boyan, J., Freitag, D., Joachims, T.: A machine learning architecture for optimizing web search engines. In: AAAI Workshop on Internet Based Information Systems, pp. 1–8 (1996)
6. Chapelle, O., Zhang, Y.: A dynamic bayesian network click model for web search ranking. In: Proceedings of the 18th International Conference on World Wide Web, pp. 1–10 (2009)
7. Li, X., Chen, H.: Recommendation as link prediction in bipartite graphs: a graph kernel-based machine learning approach. Decis. Support Syst. **54**(2), 880–890 (2013)
8. Rendle, S., Balby Marinho, L., Nanopoulos, A., et al.: Learning optimal ranking with tensor factorization for tag recommendation. In: Proceedings of the 15th ACM SIGKDD International Conference on Knowledge Discovery and Data Mining, pp. 727–736 (2009)
9. Ahmad, S., Simonovic, S.P.: An intelligent decision support system for management of floods. Water Resour. Manage **20**(3), 391–410 (2006). https://doi.org/10.1007/s11269-006-0326-3
10. Zhang, Z.: Microsoft kinect sensor and its effect. IEEE Multimedia **19**(2), 4–10 (2012)
11. Bušta, M., Patel, Y., Matas, J.: E2E-MLT - an unconstrained end-to-end method for multi-language scene text. In: Carneiro, G., You, S. (eds.) ACCV 2018. LNCS, vol. 11367, pp. 127–143. Springer, Cham (2019). https://doi.org/10.1007/978-3-030-21074-8_11
12. Wan, W., Zhong, Y., Li, T., et al.: Rethinking feature distribution for loss functions in image classification. In: Proceedings of the IEEE Conference on Computer Vision and Pattern Recognition, pp. 9117–9126 (2018)

An Experiment Study of Service Discovery Using the Extreme Learning Machine Based Approach

Wei Zhao[2] and Zhao Huang[1,2(✉)]

[1] Key Laboratory of Modern Teaching Technology,
Ministry of Education, Beijing, China
[2] School of Computer Science,
Shaanxi Normal University, Xi'an 710119, People's Republic of China
{weizhao, zhaohuang}@snnu.edu.cn

Abstract. Recent years have witnessed the rapid development of Web services on the internet, providing the increasing number of online services with diverse types available today. The demand of finding the target web service that meets user's requirement is thus no longer an easy task and needs to be paid more attention. To solve this problem, this study proposed a new service discovery method, combining the Extreme Learning Machine (ELM) and Differential Evolution Algorithm (DE) to retrieve the target service. We first calculated the similarities of each service in the training set by using four different similarity measurements and obtained the corresponding DE fitness values to construct the sample vectors. Second, these vectors were used to constitute the ELM model to learn the interrelationship between the similarity scores and the DE fitness values. Finally, we simulated the discovery process on a test set. For each new query, the target service can be received through the DE fitness values that are predicted from the constructed ELM model. The experiments were conducted on a public service set and the results showed the significant implications.

Keywords: Service discovery · Extreme Learning Machine · Differential Evolution Algorithm

1 Introduction

With the increasing popularity of the service-oriented architecture (SOA), the publicly-available Web services have made the continuous growth on the Internet in recent years. Meanwhile, the number and requirement of users are also dramatically raised [1]. How to retrieve the optimal services that provide the desired functionality for users is therefore becoming a critical challenge. To address this issue, a considerable amount of efforts has been triggered in both academic and industry [2]. In particular, service discovery plays an important role in these research. It refers to identifying a set of candidate services by comparing the matching degree with the given requirements of users from a service registry [3].

© Springer Nature Switzerland AG 2020
C. Stephanidis and M. Antona (Eds.): HCII 2020, CCIS 1224, pp. 698–704, 2020.
https://doi.org/10.1007/978-3-030-50726-8_91

From the observations of existing work on service discovery, there are some inherent drawbacks within the traditional discovery methods. For example, during the process of service discovery, the key step is to conduct the similarity calculation [4]. However, most of the previous similarity measurements are performed with a single computational metric, which merely provides a certain degree of similarity and fails to suit various types of input data [5]. Moreover, some intelligent optimization algorithms, such as the Variable Length Genetic Algorithm [6] and the Cat Swarm Optimization Algorithm, are employed with the purpose of improving the discovery performance. But for the large scale of service resources, it is a time-consuming and complex task to iteratively implement the optimization for each pair of service and the given query.

To this end, this study proposes a new service discovery method that combines the Extreme Learning Machine (ELM) and Differential Evolution Algorithm (DE) to find the target online services from the massive service resources. More specifically, DE as an effective global optimization algorithm uses the genetic operators to keep good individuals and to approach the optimal solution [5]. DE is thus used to get the effective similarity scores from the perspectives of multiple measurements in this study. Furthermore, ELM is an efficient feedforward neural learning algorithm, providing the faster learning rate and has reasonable generalization performance with simple model structure [7]. Therefore, this study makes efforts to construct the ELM model that will be used to predict the DE fitness values in support of achieving the optimal services.

The rest of this paper is structured as follow. In Sect. 2, the related work on service discovery is discussed and summarized. In Sect. 3, we introduce the proposed discovery method used in this study. The experimental work and corresponding analysis are presented in Sect. 4. Finally, our conclusion and future work are described in Sect. 5.

2 Literature Review

Currently, service discovery has drawn much attention with the advancements in web applications. As a result, various discovery methods have been put forward to accommodate the specific environment and satisfy the requirements of users. For instance, Fang et al. [2] utilized the logical reasoning and performed the semantic similarity to discover the required services. Besides, to accurately obtain the relevant services with a keyword query, Zhang et al. [8] proposed another method based on the goal-oriented query expansion to help user refine the initial query. Despite these methods are of great diversity, it is essential to conduct the assessment of semantic similarity between the candidate services and user's query during the service discovery.

However, most of the studies in the part of similarity measurements are mainly performed with a single metric, such as Cosine similarity and Euclidean distance [9]. It can be arguable that it lacks to provide a comprehensive reflection of the matching degree, which may have an impact on the discovery results. To address such an issue, Lu et al. [5] combined the corpus-based and Wordnet-based similarity methods based on DE, aiming to capture the various degrees of semantic similarity. In addition, Huang et al. [10] pointed out the emergence of ELM can effectively solve some problems with the traditional feed-forward neural systems and provide better generalization performance at a faster learning speed and with the least human intervene.

Therefore, this study takes the advantages of integrating ELM and DE to constitute the ELM model. After that, the target online service for each new query can be retrieved in a quick method without the iterative optimization matching.

3   Research Method

This section describes our proposed service discovery method that incorporates the Extreme Learning Machine and the Differential Evolution Algorithm. Figure 1 shows the overall framework of the ELM based method in this study. The framework consists of two major stages, including model training and service discovery (represented by real arrow and virtual arrow respectively). The model training stage is about the construction of the ELM to learn the interrelationship between the similarity scores and the DE fitness values. The stage of service discovery aims to receive the target service through the DE fitness values that are predicted from the constructed ELM model. The detailed description of our method is presented in the following subsections.

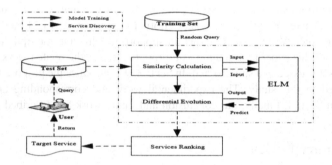

Fig. 1. The framework of the ELM based service discovery method.

3.1   Model Training

Prior to running the service discovery in this study, it is necessary to train the ELM model at first. The process of model training is vided into the steps of the sample vector construction and the ELM training, both of which are served as the foundation to complete the service discovery task.

Sample Vector Construction. In this study, two service sets are employed to validate the proposed method, including the training set and the test set. Each service in these sets is represented by their textual description that shows the functionality of the service. However, since the adopted ELM model only allows the numeric vector, there is a need to perform the transformation for each service and the given query.

Similar to the traditional text processing approaches, the primary task of transformation is to conduct the pretreatments, such as removing the stop words, stemming terms and splitting. Furthermore, one of the widely used weighting techniques, namely the Doc2Vec model, is adopted to extract the features of service descriptions in this study. By doing so, the vector of the services and the query can be received to support the similarity calculation.

Generally, discovering the target service is based on the similarity between the user's query and the candidate services. However, as it has difficulty in directly matching the textual descriptions, the similarity calculation is thus implemented based on their vector representations. In our study, four measurements are used to compute the similarity from the different perspectives, including the Cosine similarity, Euclidean, Chebyshev and BrayCurtis distance. Considering the weakness of a single measurement that may not provide the sufficient degree of similarity, this study uses DE that combines the four measurements with the purpose of obtaining the more accurate discovery results.

To be specific, DE designs genetic operators to keep good individuals by conducting mutation, crossover and selection within the evolutions. The simulation of DE begins with identifying the initial population. In this study, the size of the population is determined by the number of services in the training set. Each individual in the population is represented as a four-dimensional vector, and the elements of the vector are the four similarities. When we select an individual, the mutant one will be generated via modifying each element with the weighted difference of two random individuals. After that, according to a certain probability, the parents and the mutant individuals are cross-operated to produce the experimental ones. Finally, the Rastrigr function is taken to assess the fitness of the population. The evolution of the population and the DE fitness value of each individual can thus be achieved. Then the DE fitness value is considered as the matching criterion to rank the retrieved services.

Based on above efforts, each service in the training set can be represented as a five-dimensional vector, namely $s = (m_1, m_2, m_3, m_4, f)$. Where, s shows the service, m_1, m_2, m_3, m_4 mean the four similarities, f indicates the corresponding DE fitness value. Thus, the sample vectors are constructed.

ELM Training. Figure 2 presents the ELM training model that is constructed by the 3-layer structure, including the input layer, hidden layer and output layer. Meanwhile, the adjacent layers are connected through the neurons. ω and β represent the link weights between the input layer and hidden layer as well as the hidden layer and output layer, while b indicates the threshold of neuron within the hidden layer.

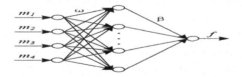

Fig. 2. The ELM training model.

To train the ELM model, it is necessary to set the number of neurons within the hidden layer and randomly identify the values of ω and b first. The sample vector of each service in the training set provides the data support in this study. As for each service vector, m_1, m_2, m_3, m_4 are used as the input variables in the input layer, and f is taken as the output variable in the output layer. Furthermore, the sigmoid function is served as the activation function to calculate the output matrix (H) of the hidden layer and the output of the ELM model (T). Then the weight β between the hidden layer and output layer can be obtained through the formula (1).

$$H\beta = T'$$ (1)

Having identified these training parameters, the ELM model can be obtained.

3.2 Service Discovery

In the stage of service discovery, this study used a test set for validation. When user has the new query, the same process will be performed to generate the corresponding vectors, including the pretreatments and the four types of similarity calculation between the query and each service. After that, the vectors were taken as the input for the constructed ELM model to predict the DE fitness value.

The critical step within service discovery is to retrieve the optimal service. Therefore, in this study, each service in the test set was matched with the user's query by using the predicted DE fitness value. According to the selected fitness function, the service with the lowest fitness value is targeted as the one we want to retrieve.

4   Results and Discussion

The public online service set that consists of 453 services is divided into two subsets to conduct the experiments in this study. One is used for training, and another is for test. In addition, the relevant parameters were initialized prior to the experiments. During the test process, four queries across a wide range of domains were developed. Each service within the test set was assessed on a 0–3 scale in light of the matching degree to the specific query. To verify our proposed method, four comparative approaches by using the Cosine similarity, Euclidean, Chebyshev and BrayCurtis distance were evaluated under the criteria of MAE and RMSE.

Table 1. The comparison of MAE and RMSE for the four queries.

Methods	MAE				RMSE			
	Q1	Q2	Q3	Q4	Q1	Q2	Q3	Q4
Cosine	1.3000	1.7000	1.9000	1.7000	1.5166	1.8166	2.0736	1.9235
Euclidean	1.3000	1.3000	**1.5000**	2.0000	1.5811	1.5811	**1.7607**	2.1448
Chebyshev	1.1000	1.3000	**1.5000**	1.5000	1.3038	1.3784	**1.7607**	**1.7607**
BrayCurtis	1.3000	1.3000	2.0000	1.7000	1.7029	1.5166	2.1448	1.9748
ELM-based	**0.9000**	**0.8000**	1.9000	**1.5000**	**1.2247**	**1.0954**	2.0736	1.8166

Note: The last row shows the results of the proposed method and the values in bold illustrate the best performance for the specific query; The comparative approaches are noted by Cosine, Euclidean, Chebyshev and BrayCurtis in this table.

Table 1 shows the results of MAE and RMSE by using different methods for the four queries. It is clear to see that the proposed method achieves the best performance with scores of 0.9000 and 1.2247 as well as 0.8000 and 1.0954 for Q1 and Q2. In terms of Q4, our ELM-based method places second under the evaluation of RMSE, the result is 3.2% higher than Chebyshev. But for Q3, the scores of 1.9000 and 2.0736 are worse than Chebyshev and BrayCurtis. The main reasons may lie in the following issues. First, the service set used in this study is not large enough to train the ELM model with great reliability. Moreover, the nonuniform distribution of the different domains of services may have an effect on the retrieval results for different queries. Second, four similarity measurements were employed to conduct the DE evolution. However, the scores of Euclidean distance are universally lower than others, which may influence the accuracy of the DE fitness. Furthermore, after the constant iterations, the small differences between the fitness values of the services were found. This may provide a great challenge to form the efficient ELM model. Based on these, there is much room to improve the performance of the ELM prediction in order to achieve the expected effects.

5 Conclusion

In this study, a new service discovery method was developed by combining the Extreme Learning Machine and Differential Evolution Algorithm. The experiments were implemented on a public service set for the verification. Having analyzing the comparison results, we provided deep insights into the influence factors from the multiple perspectives. It can contribute to develop more powerful service discovery method to support the target service retrieval. This study being the first step, the limitations will serve as a part of directions of our further works, such as expanding the service set and using more accurate similarity measurement.

Acknowledgement. This study was supported by research grants funded by the "National Natural Science Foundation of China" (Grant No.61771297), the "Fundamental Research Funds for the Central Universities" (GK201803062, GK201802013).

References

1. Wang, H.Y., Zhou, A.D.: Service discovery based on user latent intentions. Chin. J. Electron. **25**(5), 841–847 (2016)
2. Fang, M.Z., Wang, D.D., Mi, Z.Q.: Web service discovery utilizing logical reasoning and semantic similarity. Int. J. Commun. Syst. **31**(3), e3561 (2017)
3. Chen, F.Z., Li, M.Q.: Web service discovery among large service pools utilising semantic similarity and clustering. Enterp. Inf. Syst. **11**, 452–469 (2017)
4. Chen, F.Z., Lu, C.H., Wu, H., Li, M.Q.: A semantic similarity measure integrating multiple conceptual relationships for web service discovery. Expert Syst. Appl. **67**, 19–31 (2017)
5. Lu, W., Cain, Y.Y., Che, X.P., Shi, K.L.: Semantic similarity assessment using differential evolution algorithm in continuous vector space. J. Vis. Lang. Comput. **31**, 246–251 (2015)

6. Hu, B., Zhou, Z.B., Cheng, Z.H.: Web services recommendation leveraging semantic similarity computing. Procedia Comput. Sci. **129**, 35–44 (2018)
7. Ding, S.F., Zhao, H., Zhang, Y.N., Xu, X.Z.: Extreme learning machine: algorithm, theory and applications. Artif. Intell. Rev. **1**, 103–115 (2015)
8. Zhang, N., Wang, J., Ma, Y.T., He, K.Q., Li, Z., Liu, X.Q.: Web service discovery based on goal-oriented query expansion. J. Syst. Softw. **142**, 73–91 (2018)
9. Agirre, E., Alfonseca, E., Hall, K., Kravalova, J., Paşca, M., Soroa, A.: A study on similarity and relatedness using distributional and wordnet-based approaches. In: Proceedings of the Conference of The North American Chapter of the Association for Computational Linguistics-Human Language Technologies, pp. 19–27 (2009)
10. Huang, G.B., Wang, D.H., Lan, Y.: Extreme learning machines: a survey. Int. J. Mach. Learn. Cybernet. **2**(2), 107–222 (2011)

Author Index